THE MIGHT
OF NATIONS
WITHDRAWN **WORLD POLITICS IN OUR TIME**

THE MIGHT OF NATIONS

WORLD POLITICS IN OUR TIME

NINTH EDITION

John G. Stoessinger

Trinity University
San Antonio, Texas

McGRAW-HILL PUBLISHING COMPANY

New York St. Louis San Francisco Auckland Bogotá Caracas
Hamburg Lisbon London Madrid Mexico Milan Montreal New Delhi
Oklahoma City Paris San Juan São Paulo Singapore Sydney Tokyo Toronto

To My Mother
and the Memory
of My Father

This book was set in Times Roman by the College Composition Unit
in cooperation with General Graphic Services, Inc.
The editors were Bert Lummus and Sheila H. Gillams;
the production supervisor was Leroy A. Young.
The cover was designed by Robert Anthony.
R. R. Donnelley & Sons Company was printer and binder.

THE MIGHT OF NATIONS
World Politics in Our Time

1 2 3 4 5 6 7 8 9 0   DOC   DOC   8 9 4 3 2 1 0 9

ISBN   0-07-540919-4

Library of Congress Cataloging-in-Publication Data

Stoessinger, John George
     The might of nations: world politics in our time/John G. Stoessinger.—9th ed.
          p.   cm.
     Includes bibliographical references.
     ISBN 0-07-540919-4
     1. World politics—(date).   I. Title.
D843.S826   1990
327′.09′04—dc20   89-13219

ABOUT THE AUTHOR

On the eve of World War II, John G. Stoessinger fled from Nazi-occupied Austria to Czechoslovakia. Three years later, he fled again, via Siberia, to China, where he lived for seven years. In Shanghai, he served with the International Refugee Organization.

Dr. Stoessinger came to the United States in 1947, received his B.A. degree from Grinnell College in 1950, and then went to Harvard where he earned his Ph.D. degree in 1954. He entered the teaching field immediately and has taught at Harvard, MIT, Columbia, Princeton, and the City University of New York. In 1969, he led the International Seminar on International Relations at Harvard University, and in 1970 he received an Honorary Degree of Doctor of Laws from Grinnell College, Iowa, and from the American College of Switzerland. He is now a Distinguished Professor of International Affairs at Trinity University in San Antonio, Texas.

Dr. Stoessinger is the author of ten leading books in international relations: *The Might of Nations: World Politics in Our Time,* which was awarded the Bancroft Prize by Columbia University in 1963 as the best book in international relations published in 1962. The book has gone through nine editions (1962, 1965, 1969, 1973, 1975, 1979, 1982, 1986, 1990). He also has authored *The Refugee and the World Community* (1956); *Financing the United Nations System* (1964); *Power and Order* (1964); *The United Nations and the Superpowers* (1965, 1970, 1973, 1977); *Nations in Darkness: China, Russia, and America* (1971, 1975, 1978, 1986, 1990); *Why Nations Go to War* (1974, 1978, 1982, 1985, 1990); and *Henry Kissinger: The Anguish of Power* (1976). Dr. Stoessinger also served as Chief Book Review Editor of *Foreign Affairs* for five years and is a member of the Council on Foreign Relations.

From 1967 to 1974, Dr. Stoessinger served as Acting Director of the Political Affairs Division at the United Nations.

Dr. Stoessinger's autobiography, *Night Journey,* was published in 1978. His latest book, *Crusaders and Pragmatists: Movers of Modern American Foreign Policy,* was published by W. W. Norton in 1979, 1985, and 1990.

CONTENTS

PREFACE

Almost thirty years have passed since the first edition of this book appeared. Since then the international system has changed before our very eyes, almost as if a kaleidoscope had been shaken vigorously and the pieces had formed new patterns. A new generation is in the process of redefining its international relationships. The year 2000 is now only a decade away.

I wrote the first edition of this book to make some sense out of the chaos of international relations and to transmit this understanding to my students. I have continued to try, over the years, to present my ideas in clear and simple language, without doing violence to the complexity of the subject matter.

The book deals essentially with international relations since World War II. Although events are described in chronological order, they are also organized conceptually around two basic themes: the struggles for power and for order in world politics.

Revising a book always involves soul-searching. Authors must submit their work to the test of time, which is a writer's way of saying that he must face himself. To work on this edition was a joy as well as labor, since my conviction that the basic conception of the book is sound has deepened with the passing years.

In a very basic sense, this book represents a common quest. Over the years, I have had a multitude of letters about it from teachers and students all over the world. Many of these contained suggestions for improvement and have found their way into the present edition. For all of these, and for the reviews of the manuscript, I am sincerely grateful to: Richard Hirtzel, Western Illinois University; Stephen Markovich, University of North Dakota; and George Rice, University of West Virginia. No teacher could be more fortunate.

Of all the revisions this book has undergone, the present one is probably the most extensive. The world has changed quite dramatically during the past three years. To bring the book completely up to date, I have incorporated the following major topics into the ninth edition:

United States–Soviet–China relations during the Gorbachev era
A new case study on South Africa and apartheid
A comparative analysis of major wars in our time
A case study of the Palestinian uprising and its consequences
An analysis of the economic competition between the United States and Japan
The Iran-Contra affair
A new case study of the Nuclear Disarmament Treaty of 1987
An analysis of the recent resurgence of the United Nations
Recent developments in the European Common Market
Reflections on the coming global environmental crisis
Updating of the bibliographical suggestions following each chapter

It gives me great happiness to know that this book continues to live. The response of a generation of students gives me the courage to go on searching and growing as a teacher despite the harshness of the times. A dear friend of mine, a poet, has expressed this feeling very poignantly in a fable of our times, which I should like to share with my readers:

One day a teacher came to Sodom. Night and day he walked the streets speaking out against evil and indifference. In the beginning, people listened and smiled ironically. Then they stopped listening; he no longer even amused them. The killers went on killing just the same.

One day a young student, moved to compassion for the unfortunate teacher, approached him with these words: "Poor stranger, you shout, you expend yourself body and soul: don't you see that it is hopeless?"

"Yes, I see," answered the teacher.

"Then why do you go on?"

"I will tell you why. In the beginning, I thought I could change man. Today, I know that I cannot. If I still shout today, if I still scream, it is to prevent man from ultimately changing me."*

John G. Stoessinger

---

*Adapted from Elie Wiesel, *One Generation After*. New York: Random House, 1965, p. 72.

THE MIGHT OF NATIONS

WORLD POLITICS IN OUR TIME

PART ONE

THE NATURE OF INTERNATIONAL RELATIONS

CHAPTER **1**

INTRODUCTION

The struggle itself toward the heights is enough to fill a man's heart. One must imagine Sisyphus happy.

Albert Camus, *The Myth of Sisyphus*

Sisyphus, according to Homeric legend, had been condemned by the gods forever to exert his entire being toward accomplishing nothing. He was to roll a rock to the top of a mountain only to see it fall back each time into the depths. The crime that had won him this dreadful penalty was hubris—presumptuous ambition. His crime was greater even than that of Prometheus, who had attempted to steal the eternal fires. Sisyphus had a passion for life and refused to heed the call from the underworld when his time had come. By decree of the gods, Mercury had to come and snatch him from his joys. Upon arrival in the infernal darkness, Sisyphus managed to trick Death and put her in chains. For a time Hades was deserted and silent. Then Pluto, god of the underworld, dispatched the god of war to liberate Death. The wrath of the gods now descended on the man whose love of life and hatred of death had made him challenge the eternal laws. His rock was waiting for him.

Countless generations have breathed life into this myth. Its underscoring of our impotence in an indifferent and often hostile universe has seemed relevant to people everywhere. In ancient and medieval times, the ever-present threat to humanity's existence lay chiefly in the vast and inscrutable forces of nature. Today, these physical conditions of our survival are for the most part understood and, in the Western world at least, controlled. Yet the menace to the

3

species has, if anything, become more ominous than ever before. And, tragically, it is no longer anything preordained or mysterious that now confronts us with the possibility of our doom. It is the instruments of destruction that we have fashioned ourselves.

Nowhere would we have better reason for abandoning ourselves to a sense of hopelessness about the fate of modern man than when we contemplate the state of relations among today's nations, the great collective actors in whose hands the decisions as to whether we survive or perish ultimately rest. Who of us, in witnessing the frantic preparations for yet another world war during the darkest days of the cold war, when the first edition of this book appeared, did not at times despair and conclude that the entire spectacle was a manifestation of organized insanity? Who of us did not have moments in which he or she was tempted to dismiss the efforts of those working for peace as a futile Sisyphean labor?

Yet it is from this very myth of Sisyphus, as the great French writer Albert Camus has told us, that humanity can take heart. For, according to Camus, the important part of the story is not really Sisyphus' ascent up the mountain. It is during his return to the plain that the hero is most inspiring. "That hour," as Camus sees it, "like a breathing-space which returns as surely as his suffering, that is the hour of consciousness. At each of those moments when he leaves the heights and gradually sinks toward the lairs of the gods, he is superior to his fate. He is stronger than his rock."[1]

In Camus' view, therefore, Sisyphus' fate does not teach us a lesson of acceptance and resignation. Rather, it serves as a symbol of that higher courage that revolts against our fate and raises rocks even with the knowledge that this revolt may be in vain. It shows us that so long as the rock is still rolling, the struggle is not futile. Man says Yes and his effort must be unceasing.

The relevance of this interpretation of the Sisyphean myth to modern world politics is clear. In many respects, modern man has descended to unprecedented depths, yet in others he has soared to greater heights than ever before. He has not only built concentration camps and perfected weapons of mass destruction; he has also learned to control hunger and disease and has created the United Nations. Nations still make intensive preparations to destroy each other. But at no previous time has humankind striven more desperately to avert such destruction. After a generation of unrelenting arms race, the two superpowers *did* agree to sign a treaty eliminating an entire class of nuclear weapons and to do so with on-site inspection provisions. Thus, our generation is involved in the fiercest struggles for power in history. Yet it also has the privilege of participating in the most determined struggle for order ever waged. If, therefore, we have cause for shame and despair, we also have grounds for pride and hope. We may never solve the problems of our human condition—in international relations or in anything else—completely and permanently. But what remains crucial for us, as it was for Sisyphus, is that we do not permit our rock to crush us.

It is the purpose of this book to contribute in whatever small measure it can to this effort. While it hopes to offer more than a mere description of our crisis-ridden international situation, it does not pretend to advance any full-scale theory of international relations. It is my judgment that until the discipline of international relations becomes more developed, a much more useful task is to review and analyze its vast and complex subject matter in terms of certain major organizing concepts.

The treatment of international relations here presented is focused in terms of three such broad conceptual principles. The first of these is the ever-present *tension between the struggle for power and the struggle for order*. Throughout the book, care is taken to emphasize that these two processes of international intercourse are always closely interrelated, that every form of relationship, even war itself, includes elements of cooperation, while every form of order, even the most tranquil condition of peace, bears within it seeds of conflict. The second and related organizing concept here employed is that of the *divergence between the images that nations entertain of world affairs and of each other and the international realities as they actually are*. This divergence between what is and what is taken to be often exacerbates the international struggle for power and slows the international struggle for order. Finally, the book is focused upon what the author believes are the two truly dominant events of our time: *the struggle of East versus West,* and *the struggle of North versus South—the rich and the poor*. It is chiefly with reference to the latter two struggles—and the linkages between them—that the data and analyses offered are topically organized.

The book is divided into four sections. Part I examines the nation-state system and the nature of power. Part II deals with the international struggle for power—including both the East-West conflict and the North-South struggle, as well as the many linkages between them. Part III undertakes a similar analysis of the political, military, and economic dimensions of the international struggle for order. And Part IV attempts a fuller development of the three key concepts, in terms of which the empirical materials presented in the body of the book are analyzed and interpreted.

The general approach to the subject is an interdisciplinary one. Nothing less will do in a field that requires both breadth and depth. I am painfully aware of serious shortcomings in my command of both these dimensions. Yet, taking my inspiration from Camus' version of the myth of Sisyphus, I feel that the struggle to make international relations into a coherent discipline must continue. The pages which follow constitute an effort in that direction.

REFERENCE

1 Albert Camus, *The Myth of Sisyphus and Other Essays*. New York: Knopf, 1955, p. 121.

2

THE NATION-STATE SYSTEM AND THE NATURE OF POWER

Some are born great; some achieve greatness; And some have greatness thrust upon 'em.

Shakespeare, *Twelfth Night*, II, 5

THE ANATOMY OF THE NATION-STATE

Our world is made up of over one hundred sixty political units called nation-states. There is hardly a place on this planet that is not claimed by a nation-state. Only a century ago the world still abounded with frontiers and lands that remained unpreempted. But in our time, one can no longer escape from the nation-state system—unless one migrates to the frozen polar zones or to the stars. The nation-state has become ubiquitous. And everywhere it is the highest secular authority. It may decree that a person dies; and, with no less effort, it may offer the protection that enables a person to live. When no state wants him—when man is naked in his humanity and nothing but a man—he thereby loses the very first precondition for his fellows even to be able to acknowledge his existence. Whether it be to be born, to live, or to die, no one can do without official recognition—the recognition of a nation-state.

This modern-day fact of life is astounding when one considers that the nations that possess this inescapable power of life and death are in many ways only abstractions, figments of the human imagination. For though the power that is brought to bear to implement a nation's will is ultimately physical, the will itself is chiefly the result of human images, images of what a nation is and about why and how its will should be expressed and obeyed.

There are two principal aspects of this universal political image. In the first place, humans have endowed the nation-state with a quality that it shares with no other human association—the attribute of *sovereignty*. It is indeed no coincidence that the theory of sovereignty was first formulated in the sixteenth century, at a time when the nation-state system was in the process of emerging from the universalism of the medieval world. Its first systematic presentation was contained in the writings of the French political thinker Jean Bodin. Bodin's definition of sovereignty as "the state's supreme authority over citizens and subjects," set forth in his *De La République* in 1576, is still largely valid today. The nation remains the final arbiter over the lives of its citizens, leaving them recourse to no higher law. And while this is true in peacetime, it is even more totally and dramatically the case in times of war. For in the latter eventuality, the sovereign state has the right to send its citizens to their death and, through its sanction, to transform even the most brutal forms of killing into acts of patriotic heroism.

It is frequently asserted that the concept of sovereignty is about to become obsolete. We are undergoing a "systemic revolution." Just as the Greek and Roman city-states and the medieval church-state were destined to pass, so the nation-state system is in turn bound to yield to a different form of political organization. As one thinker has pointed out, the very core of sovereignty, the "impermeability and impenetrability" of nation-states, has been brought to an abrupt end by the advent of the atomic age:

> In a symbolic way (in addition to their possible practical use for hostile purposes) satellites circling the globe and penetrating the space above any territory of the globe, regardless of "sovereign" rights over air spaces and duties of "nonintervention," serve to emphasize the new openness and penetrability of everything to everybody.[1]

There is much to be said for the argument that the first atomic weapon "blew the roof off the sovereign nation-state." It is probably true that in case of nuclear war, little sovereign invulnerability would remain. But it is equally true that in the absence of violent conflict, and especially in what the state continues to be able to demand of its citizens, sovereignty remains very much intact.

The truth is that in our time sovereignty is being both strengthened and weakened. This apparent contradiction is resolved if we survey the different parts of the globe. The Atlantic Community, especially Western Europe, seems to be slowly relaxing the grip of sovereignty. In that part of the world, sovereign states are moving toward larger units of political integration such as the European Common Market. But if sovereignty is "obsolete" in Western Europe, it is just coming into its own in Asia, the Middle East, and Africa. While the Atlantic Community is moving toward cohesion, these other areas are veering toward fragmentation. In fact, more sovereign states have been born in our generation than in the preceding three-hundred-year history of the nation-state system. As a result of the triumph of sovereignty among the non-white peoples of the earth, the membership of the United Nations has, since

1945, more than tripled. Hence, we would seem to be living in one of those rare and fascinating transitional periods in history in which the human race is at the same time looking both forward and backward. When we consider the Western world and see sovereignty beginning to be replaced by various new forms of regionalism, we see signs of the future. When we turn to the new nationalism in Asia, the Middle East, and Africa, we witness what is in effect a rekindling of the past. Until, therefore, the world has internationally evolved somewhat further, sovereignty is bound to remain an integral part of our lives.

Despite the fact that sovereignty is omnipresent in the nation-state system, it is very difficult, if not impossible, to discover where and in whom this sovereignty is actually vested. The reason for this is that the concept is essentially an abstraction that defies precise and concrete location. The problem was much simpler as long as states in international relations were identified with their absolute rulers. Louis XIV's alleged claim ''*L'Etat, c'est moi*,'' left little doubt about the locus of sovereignty. But the advent of modern forms of government, both democratic and totalitarian, complicated the task enormously. Who, precisely, is the ''sovereign'' United States in international relations? Is it the President, the Congress, or the Supreme Court? The American separation of powers and the principle of ''checks and balances'' prevent the concentration of sovereignty in any one center. Yet the very essence of sovereignty, according to Bodin, is its absoluteness and indivisibility. The Soviet Union, too, claims absolute sovereignty in international relations. But does it reside in the person of the premier? Or in the Presidium of the Communist party? Or, as Soviet dialecticians maintain, in the multinational Soviet people? No easy or precise answer is possible.

Despite all its contradictions, however, sovereignty remains an essential characteristic of the nation-state system. Even if the term itself should disappear, the substance of sovereignty—the absolute authority of states in international relations—will probably survive as long as the nation-state system itself. It is sovereignty, more than any other single factor, that is responsible for the anarchic condition of international relations. Bodin conceived of sovereignty as essentially an *internal* phenomenon, ''the state's supreme authority over citizens and subjects.'' While the advent of democratic government has rendered this power far less than absolute, no government, democratic or totalitarian, has been willing to yield major portions of its sovereignty in its relations with *other* nation-states. Hence, it would seem that sovereignty in our time is fundamentally a phenomenon of *international* relations, a fact of life in political intercourse among nations. Over three hundred years ago the image of Leviathan was created. In some parts of the world Leviathan is humanity's servant; in others, he remains the master. But no Leviathan yields to another except by its own consent. Sovereignty, originally no more than a political construct defining man's relationship to the state, has taken on a life of its own on the international scene. In the internal affairs of states, sovereignty has often created political order and stability. In international relations it has led to anarchy.

The second key component that has come into the making of nations has been the phenomenon of *nationalism*. In the broadest terms nationalism may be defined as a people's sense of collective destiny through a common past and the vision of a common future. (For an analysis of the anatomy of the new nationalism of Asia, the Middle East, and Africa, see Chapter 4.) In a very real sense, a nation's "personality" is its common past, or history. Empirically, a nation is merely a group of people occupying geographic space. But nations exist much more in time than in space. The history of common triumphs and suffering evokes powerful bonds of solidarity for nations large and small. Common suffering seems to be more important in this respect than are victories. The Civil War was probably the most tragic—and continues to be the most written-about—experience of the American nation. Yet both North and South have come to regard this grim American tragedy as a period of glory. The case of Israel affords an even clearer illustration. Ethnically and culturally, the Jews of Israel are certainly anything but homogeneous. Even in their religion they range from strict orthodoxy to frank agnosticism. Yet what gives Israel its national identity in spite of these differences is the common history of suffering experienced by its people in the Diaspora. Since a similar logic characterizes nationalism everywhere, it is clear that this image of a common past exercises a most crucial function. It enables the citizens of the state to share vicariously in collective greatness and to merge their own identity, often colorless and insecure, into the larger identity of the nation. It is significant that Ernest Renan's definition of a nation, advanced in 1882 at the Sorbonne, has become a classic: "What constitutes a nation," he said, "is not speaking the same tongue or belonging to the same ethnic group, but having accomplished great things in common in the past and the wish to accomplish them in the future."

The vision of a common future constitutes the second ingredient of nationalism. Here, too, an individual's aspirations are often projected onto the larger stage of politics and international relations. The unconscious realization that one's personal future may be bleak and devoid of larger meaning is often unbearable. Hence, as Erich Fromm has brilliantly demonstrated in his *Escape from Freedom,* people may seek compensation for their lack of a personal future in the reflected glory of the nation's collective future.[2] This form of identification may manifest itself in socially constructive ways; it may also lend itself to nationalism of a more destructive kind, as it did, for example, in Nazi Germany. The process whereby the identification is generated takes place largely in the "illogical, irrational, and fantastic world of the unconscious."[3] Hence, the insights of social psychology and psychoanalysis may have a profound bearing on the study of international relations. A case study of the development of one such image of the future, that of Nazi Germany, will serve to illustrate the point.

Many scholars now believe that the Nazi image of the ultimate enthronement of the "Aryan" superman had its roots in the authoritarian structure of the German family.[4] Erik Erikson paints a convincing portrait of the German father whose frequent remoteness and tyranny over his children made the maturation process excessively difficult:

> When the father comes home from work, even the walls seem to pull themselves together. The children hold their breath, for the father does not approve of "nonsense"—that is, neither of the mother's feminine moods nor of the children's playfulness. . . . Later when the boy comes to observe the father in company, when he notices his father's subservience to superiors, and when he observes his excessive sentimentality when he drinks and sings with his equals, the boy acquires the first ingredient of *Weltschmerz:* a deep doubt of the dignity of man—or at any rate of the "old man." . . . The average German father's dominance and harshness was not blended with the tenderness and dignity which comes from participation in an integrating cause. Rather, the average father, either habitually or in decisive moments, came to represent the habits and ethics of the German top sergeant and petty official who—"dress'd in a little brief authority"—would never be more but was in constant danger of becoming less; and who had sold the birthright of a free man for an official title or a life pension.[5]

This kind of father, of course, creates for the son an unusually difficult adolescence, a period of "storm and stress," in Goethe's words, which becomes a strange mixture of open rebellion and submissive obedience, of romanticism and despondency. For each act of rebellion the boy suffers profound pangs of guilt, but for each act of submission he is punished by self-disgust. Hence the search for identify frequently ends in stunned exhaustion, with the boy's "reverting to type" and, despite everything, identifying with his father. The excessively severe *superego* implanted by the father in his son during childhood has entrenched itself like a garrison in a conquered city. The boy now becomes a "bourgeois" after all, but with an eternal sense of shame for having succumbed.

   The catalytic agent that during the 1930s offered the possibility of escape from this vicious circle was Adolf Hitler. In the Fuehrer's world the adolescent could feel emancipated. "Youth shapes its own destiny"—the motto of the Hitler Youth—was profoundly appealing to a youth whose psychological quest for identity was often thwarted. Erikson points out that Hitler did not fill the role of the father image. Had he done so, he would have elicited great ambivalence in the German youth. Rather, he became the symbol of a glorified older brother, a rebel whose will could never be crushed, an unbroken adolescent who could lead others into self-sufficiency—in short, a leader. Since he had become their conscience, he made it possible for the young to rebel against authority without incurring guilt. Hermann Goering echoed the sentiments of the Hitler Youth when he stated categorically that his conscience was Adolf Hitler. Parents were to be silenced if their views conflicted with the official doctrines of the Third Reich: "All those who from the perspective of their experience and from that alone combat our method of letting youth lead youth, must be silenced."[6] The young Nazi was taught that he was destined by Providence to bring a new order to the world, *das tausendjahrige Reich,* the Aryan millennium of the superman. Young Nazi women, too, felt a surge of pride when they were told that childbirth, legitimate or illegitimate, was a meaningful act because "German women must give children to the Fuehrer." This writer recalls how, on numerous occasions, large groups of young women would march the streets chanting in chorus: "We want to beget children for our Fuehrer." National Socialism made it possible for the young to rid themselves of their profound personal insecurities by merging their identity into the image of a superior and glorious German nation. This image of a common future was well expressed in the famous Nazi marching song: "Let everything go to pieces, we shall march on. For today Germany is ours; tomorrow the whole world."

The dynamics and forms of expression that characterized the imagery of Nazi nationalism are not, of course, typical. Indeed, the precise nature of the relationship between family structure and national and international imagery varies with each nation and is in all cases difficult to ascertain empirically. Yet subtle and complex or not, its role in the genesis of nationalism is always crucial.

It would, of course, be a mistake to claim that the psychological phenomenon of nationalism and the legal institution of sovereignty are the sole foundations of a nation. There are also a number of more "objective" ingredients that play an essential part. Most prominent among these are territorial and economic ties and the presence of common language, culture, and religion.

Clearly, the very first requirement of a nation would seem that it possess a *geographical base,* a territory of its own. Yet, as the struggle of the Palestinians for a homeland indicates, a people may consider itself a nation even though it still has no sovereign territory to call its own. However, it is not necessarily true that attachment to the soil of a homeland primarily explains the fact of national unity. The insights of social psychology would seem to indicate that individuals may remain attached to a much more specific and limited location, such as their place of birth or the countryside where they were raised. In fact, people may feel more "at home" in a spot in a foreign land that reminds them of their youth than in an unfamiliar locale in their own country. Moreover, powerful emotional ties to specific locales may even divide a nation. When this is the case, the nation in question tends to be vulnerable to serious disunity and, frequently, internecine strife. Yet even when strong local attachments are not present, a really active attachment to the national territory as a whole usually results only from powerful nationalistic propaganda.

Another major contributing factor to the existence and unity of a nation lies in its common and interdependent *economic patterns.* Especially has this come to be the case since the advent of modern technology and mass production, with their need for vast national markets. Yet this same economic logic has also tended to undermine the nation-state system. For why limit production and distribution to nationally protected markets? And significantly, the only genuinely "supranational" organizations in existence in our time are of a primarily economic character. (For a full analysis of these organizations, see Chapter 13.) It is therefore incorrect to assert that economic ties reinforce the nation exclusively. Modern technology and the enlargement of markets work equally for the development of economic patterns that reach far beyond national boundaries.

It is similarly difficult to generalize about the part that is played in the making of a nation by the presence of a *common language*. In many countries, as for example the United States, a common tongue is an important integrative factor. In other nations, the fact that the same common language may be spoken in many different versions definitely constitutes a divisive influence. This is very notably the case with the Chinese language, for instance, which consists of hundreds of dialects. Thus, if a native of Shanghai wants to communicate with a Cantonese, he or she can do so only by falling back on written Chinese or by resorting to some third language that both may know. Switzerland, on the other hand, with its three different major languages, has achieved a very high degree of national unity. Still other nations have hoped to increase national cohesion by resurrecting a dead language. The revitalization of the Hebrew language in Israel is a case in point. (But it is safe to assume that language is a relatively minor factor in Israeli unity.) At times the quest for a national language has caused endless internal friction. The attempt to make Urdu the national language of Pakistan met with bitter resistance from that part of the Pakistani population which spoke Bengali. And India, after independence, had to accept English, a "foreign" language, as its temporary *lingua franca*. Hence the role of language in the life of nations is clearly a rather ambiguous one.

Surely one of the most perplexing concepts is that of *"national character."* Few social scientists would deny that certain cultural patterns occur more frequently and are more highly valued in one nation than in another. But it is almost impossible to find agreement among scholars on precisely what these common patterns are. In other words, we are faced with the paradox that national character seems to be an indisputable factor but that no one knows exactly what it is. This confusion probably stems from the fact that cultural patterns continue to live as stereotypes. For example, the stereotypes of the "volatile Frenchman" and of the "materialistic American" are strictly time-bound. Only a century ago almost opposite images were current. Moreover, patterns may differ from region to region in the same country. And it is never difficult to find exceptions to the prevailing images. On the whole, it would therefore appear that though national character patterns are a fact, their uniqueness and their significance in supporting national unity vary from nation to nation. Perhaps the concept "national character" is itself obsolete and it would be more accurate to speak of a "political culture."

The role of *religion*, finally, is equally two-edged. In the United States, religion has neither substantially contributed to nor detracted from national unity. In other countries, Israel for example, religion has proved a very significant factor in making for unity in national terms. Yet in certain other cases religion has played a key part in preventing national unity. Thus it was chiefly the religious friction between Moslems and Hindus that in 1947 made necessary the partition of the Indian subcontinent into two separate nations—India and Pakistan. Religions have probably tended as much to keep nations divided as to aid their unity.

In summary, then, what constitutes a nation-state in our time may be characterized as follows. First and foremost, it is a sovereign political unit. Second, it is a population that in being committed to a particular collective identity through a common image of past and future shares a greater or lesser degree of nationalism. And finally, it is a population inhabiting a definite territory, acknowledging a common government, and usually—though not always—exhibiting common linguistic and cultural patterns.

Having examined the structure of the nation-state, we can now focus our attention on the heart of our subject matter—the behavior *among* nations. As a first step in this larger analysis, we must devote some attention to that most crucial of all the concepts in the study of international relations, the concept of *power*.

THE NATURE OF POWER

The nature of a nation's power vis-à-vis other nations is one of the most elusive aspects of international relations. It is frequently suggested that a nation's *power* is simply the sum total of its *capabilities*. Yet such a definition fails to do the concept of power full justice. For though power always involves capabilities, it concerns other dimensions as well. Most importantly, while capabilities are objectively measurable, power must in every case be evaluated in more subtle psychological and relational terms.

The psychological aspect of power is crucial, since a nation's power may depend in considerable measure on what other nations think it is or even on what it thinks other nations think it is. The relational aspect of power can be illustrated as follows. Let us assume that two nations, for example the United States and the Soviet Union, are approximately balanced in their capabilities. To the extent that this condition prevails, the power of either nation vis-à-vis the other is almost nil, even though their capabilities might suffice to wipe each other from the face of the earth. Hence, because power is a relational thing, whereas capabilities are not, there may upon occasion be no correlation whatsoever between the two. Indeed, when capabilities are equal, as in a stalemate, power tends to disappear altogether. To put it crassly, when everybody is somebody, nobody may be anybody.[7] By the same token, of course, even a small increase in the capabilities of one of the two nations might mean a really major advantage in terms of its power.

Under certain circumstances there may even turn out to be an inverse correlation between power and capabilities. Just as an experienced driver would probably give a car marked ''Auto School'' a wide berth, a leading nation might be doubly careful not to provoke the volatile leader of some smaller nation. The United States, for example, might be more inclined to appease a small state armed with atomic missiles than it would a major nuclear power like the Soviet Union. Paradoxically, a weakness in capabilities—instability of leadership—might actually enhance such a small state's relative power. Indeed, as a scholar of the role of small states in international relations has pointed out, the East-West struggle has resulted in giving greater power and freedom of maneuver to small nations at the very time that their inferiority in military capabilities has vastly increased.[8]

In the above illustration of the experienced driver, of course, there is little doubt that the person in question would make it a general rule also to accord the right of way to a large truck. Similarly, a small nation is likely to do its utmost not to provoke one of the superpowers. Yet, as the Iranian hostage crisis has made clear, there may be striking exceptions to this rule. Fanaticism and the willingness to die for a cause may contribute greatly to a nation's power. The psychological and relational aspects of power must, therefore, be recognized as hardly less significant than the objectively measurable capabilities themselves.

Coming now to the analysis of the anatomy of power as a whole, including its tangible capability aspects, we find it frequently asserted that "the most stable factor upon which the power of a nation depends is geography."[9] In the words of Hans J. Morgenthau:

> The fact that the continental territory of the United States is separated from other continents by bodies of water three thousand miles wide to the east and more than six thousand miles wide to the west is a permanent factor that determines the position of the United States in the world.[10]

In the opinion of other scholars, however, the advent of the atomic age and the development of intercontinental ballistic missiles have brought about the obsolescence of "territoriality." As John H. Herz has put it, "now that power can destroy power from center to center, everything is different."[11]

It would be difficult to agree with Morgenthau that *geography* is always and necessarily a crucial factor in the power of nations. No doubt the enormous land mass of the Soviet Union prevented that country from being conquered by three different invaders in three succeeding centuries. Yet there may also be circumstances in which geographical considerations are much less relevant. Thus, the same Russia whose vast expanses proved the undoing of Charles XII of Sweden, Napoleon, and Hitler, was in 1904 brought low in a naval battle by tiny Japan. It would be misleading, however, to go all the way with Professor Herz and suggest that the role of geography has drastically declined. Even the coming of nuclear weapons and intercontinental missiles may be less significant in this regard than is often claimed. As many military strategists have pointed out, mutual nuclear deterrence on the part of the superpowers may result in the wars of the future being "limited" to weapons and strategies not much different from those that have been used in the past. And to the extent that this might be the case, facts of national geography, location, and topography would continue to retain very considerable importance in the balancing of international power.

Nevertheless, it would seem that, all in all, the significance of geography as a factor in the power of nations has been decreasing. Only a generation ago it was still possible for scholars to regard the influence of geography on international relations as decisive and to elevate its study into an entirely separate discipline, the "science of geopolitics." The Scottish geographer and strategist Sir Halford Mackinder, for example, in 1904 advanced the geopolitical formula that "he who rules Eastern Europe commands the Heartland of Eurasia; who rules the Heartland, commands the World Island of Europe, Asia and Africa; and who rules the World Island commands the World."[12] The determinism of Mackinder's heartland theory was matched by that of Alfred T. Mahan, an American geopolitician of the late nineteenth century who believed in the decisive importance of sea power.[13] Even during World War II, power calculations of nations were still influenced by geopolitical thinking. A German geographer, Dr. Karl Haushofer, deeply impressed by Mackinder's heartland theory, argued for a German-Russian-Japanese axis. He predicted a German defeat if Hitler were to attempt an invasion of the Soviet Union. Hitler not only ignored his advice but sent Haushofer to a concentration camp. Today such geographical determinism would not find the wide audience it did in the 1920s and 1930s. With the coming of the atomic age, the "science" of geopolitics has largely disappeared from the scene.

A second major element in a nation's international power is usually considered to be its possession of *natural resources*. Yet though this factor is always significant it, too, is in itself by no means decisive. For it is not primarily the possession of raw materials that makes a nation powerful; it is above all the *use* that nation is able to make of the resources it has available. So long as the Arab states of the Middle East were unable to coordinate their oil policies toward the Western world, even their huge oil deposits did not make them into powerful nations. But when in 1973 they managed to agree on a common oil embargo policy vis-à-vis the West, and to establish an oil price cartel, they suddenly acquired formidable power on the world stage. The result was a serious "energy crisis" that threatened the economic bases of some of the richest and most powerful nations on earth.

What use a nation is able to make of the raw materials it possesses depends primarily on the extent of its economic and industrial development. To develop a powerful military establishment, nations today must first command an advanced technological base. How vital this requirement may be can be seen from the examples of Germany, Italy, and Japan in World War II. In the possession of strategic raw materials, all three of these countries are relatively poor. Yet because of their highly developed industry and technology, they proved able to build military machines that almost succeeded in bringing about an Axis victory. That the power of the Allies triumphed in the end is largely attributable to the fact that the latter possessed *both* an abundance of essential raw materials *and* the advanced industrial apparatus.

Since World War II a strong industrial economy has become even more important as a factor in the power of nations. This may be seen in the degree to which both the United States and the Soviet Union are admired and envied by the smaller and economically less developed countries. The two superpowers have been fully aware of this and have capitalized on it by using foreign aid and technical assistance to influence the nations in question. Though the "lesser developed" states concerned have often felt ambivalent about the superpowers themselves, they have done their best to conduct themselves so as to induce the superpowers to give them the greatest possible amount of such aid and assistance.

It is possible that the gradual dispersion of atomic energy among most of the world's nations will diminish the importance of industrialization as a power factor. The two superpowers have used atomic energy as an object of competition in the East-West struggle and have made it easier for some of their respective allies to produce nuclear weapons on their own. As a result, some nations are in the incongruous position of controlling the most sophisticated product of an advanced technology without having the supporting base of an industrial economy. A small nation equipped with atomic weapons might, through atomic blackmail, prove as powerful as one of the superpowers. Yet its advantage would be military only, and would be operative only in terms of a one-shot nuclear war. It is probable that as conventional sources of energy are increasingly replaced by the harnessed energy of the atom, the economic and hence general power of nations with large uranium deposits will somewhat increase. But unless such nations also possess the advanced technology necessary to turn uranium into actual atomic energy, their initiative in the power struggle is likely to remain limited.

The same point that has been noted in regard to geography and natural resources is also true of a third major element of national power, *population*. Once again, though a nation's population is certain always to be important as a factor in its power, the actual extent of its significance depends on many other considerations as well. Though both very populous, neither China nor India was in the past considered very powerful. Indeed, as the case of China illustrates, population is primarily *potential* power. As a result, it has been possible for nations with large populations to be weak, but impossible for nations without large populations to be powerful. Though the advent of atomic weapons may diminish the importance of manpower in warfare, the Vietnamese war would seem to have shown that the foot soldier has by no means been superseded. In the future as in the past, large populations are likely to remain an important military advantage. Hitler found it necessary to import slave labor from Eastern Europe to make up for labor shortages in Germany. An armed conflict with a nation as populous as China would prove a struggle of the most overwhelming proportions. Even though it at the time had little else but its vast population, China was at the end of World War II accorded great-power status in the United Nations.

Population becomes most important of all as a power factor when it is combined with industrialization. It is common knowledge that those countries now going through the process of industrialization are also the ones that are growing most rapidly in population. This fact, known as the "demographic transition," significantly affects a nation's power. Industrialization leads to an increase in population, which in turn may make possible further industrialization. As the case of China demonstrates once again, the potential power of population is actualized only when it is *used*, most profitably in the development of a modern industrial base which in turn makes possible a first-rate military establishment. In the view of many observers, once China succeeds in harnessing its immense population, it may in time become the most powerful nation on earth.

On the other hand, it is well to remember that population is not in itself any guarantee of power. The *will* to commit the population in battle must be present. Hence, once again the impact of a national image may be decisive. India has great population resources; yet, judging by the image of itself that it projects upon the world, India has been fairly reluctant, until recently, to mobilize its population for military combat. Fascist Italy, on the other hand, with a relatively small population, was whipped into a fighting frenzy by Mussolini. On balance, even in the atomic age there is still a partial truth in the nineteenth-century dictum that "God is on the side of the biggest battalions"—provided a nation has the will and resources to mobilize them.

A fourth element of national power whose effects it is difficult to assess concerns the nature of a country's *government*. It is tempting to assume that a democratic form of government provides greater national strength than a dictatorship. Yet though the historical record does not invalidate this assumption, it certainly places it in question. The victory of Sparta over Athens is only one of many instances in which a dictatorship emerged triumphant. But any analysis of this issue must remain inconclusive. There are simply too many imponderables involved to permit any easy conclusion.

It is generally assumed that a dictatorial government has its greatest advantages for national power in time of war, when centralized control, secrecy, and swiftness of execution are most important. Actually, the record does not support this conclusion. In wartime, most democracies have managed to fashion temporary "constitutional dictatorships," which quickly balanced the initial advantages of the aggressive dictator. Britain's wartime cabinet and America's reaction to Pearl Harbor are cases in point. Centralized control and self-discipline have usually been an effective counterpoise to secrecy and regimentation.

Many observers point out that democracy has a great advantage because it rests on the consent and voluntary support of the governed, where dictatorship requires coercion. While there is much truth in this oft-repeated assertion, it has been overdone. Modern totalitarianism has developed highly effective means of psychological indoctrination. Nazi Germany, Fascist Italy, the Soviet Union, and China each developed a highly organized youth movement for this express purpose. In addition, "brainwashing"—a kind of psychoanalysis in reverse—was widely applied to "reactionary elements" in China during the Cultural Revolution. These techniques, when coupled with the fact that modern totalitarianism deprives a population of standards of comparison in both time and space, have made possible the emergence of a new type of government: "totalitarianism with the consent of the governed." At times, totalitarian governments do not have to create popular support through these methods. The Nazi dictatorship, for example, enjoyed the fanatical support of most of the German population before 1941. Hence, a broad base of popular support as a source of power is not a monopoly of the democracies.

A dictatorship seems to have an advantage in the development of its industrial resources. Forced collectivization and industrialization of the Soviet and Chinese varieties would be unthinkable in a democratic framework. In both countries there resulted a great increase in power status, albeit at the cost of millions of human lives. But the democracies have been more generously endowed with prosperous economies and this has been a balancing factor. It is probably not an accident that most modern dictatorships have tended to be "have-not" nations. A totalitarian nation with a wealthy economy might indeed have a decisive advantage.

The total record is inconclusive. Perhaps the only democratic source of power which is denied to dictatorship is the fact that most people *think* that a democracy is inherently more powerful. Even the Soviet Union and China have found it necessary to camouflage totalitarian reality behind the democratic facade of a "people's democracy." The Soviet Constitution of 1936 was hailed by Stalin as "the most democratic in the world." In a world in which most of the nations of Africa, the Middle East, and Southeast Asia are uncommitted in the struggle between democracy and dictatorship, the image of democracy's greater power might be decisive. In short, democracy exerts a magnetism and possesses a kind of mystique which dictatorship cannot muster. Yet we must remember that very few of these uncommitted nations have any tradition in democratic government. If, despite this handicap, the new nations should embrace democracy, such an act might in large measure depend upon their conviction that democracy is compatible with the dictates of power.

It appears from the above that the objective or "capability" attributes of a nation's power depend, above all, on the *use* which its government makes of such physical factors as geography, population, and natural wealth. In the hands of a resourceful government, democratic or totalitarian, geography is turned to strategic advantage, and population and natural resources become twin pillars of power—military preparedness and industrialization. But as we have stated at the outset, despite their great importance these objective bases of national power are by no means the whole story. Of no less importance for a nation's power arsenal are its image of itself and, perhaps most crucial of all, the way it is viewed by other nations. To understand the latter dimension of power we must consider chiefly the factors of national character and morale, ideology, and national leadership.

We have seen earlier that the concept of *national character*, or "political culture," is highly elusive, and that it refers to something that is constantly

changing. Its relevance to power does not lie so much in its objective existence, which is still disputed by many scholars, but in the persistence of stereotypes that are imputed by one nation to another. The instability of these
stereotypes themselves denies the permanence of national character. Yet that
they vitally affect a nation's power nevertheless can be seen from the following situation. Before the United States had established any physical contact
with Japan, the American image of the Japanese was that of a quaint, roman-
tic, and picturesque society, almost rococo in its fragility. Hence when the
Americans decided to ''open'' Japan to the West in the mid-nineteenth century, they simply sent Commodore Perry and a few warships to force the door.
Actually, the Japan of 1850 was a rigidly stratified society that had been ruled
for over two hundred years by an authoritarian military clan, the Tokugawa.
Under the Western impact, Japan modernized with astounding rapidity.

For centuries, the Japanese image of China had been that of a great master.
Japan's written language, its art and literature—even its political institutions—
had been copied from China, though they often had to be foisted onto the
Japanese scene artificially. But between 1850 and 1900 the Japanese image of
China swung to the other extreme, with the West now assuming the role of
teacher and master. By 1915 Japan had only contempt for China and presented
its former idol with the ''Twenty-One Demands,'' which would have turned
China into a Japanese colony had the West not interceded. When in 1931 Japan
invaded China, most Japanese militarists were convinced that China would
crumble in a matter of weeks. By this time many Japanese regarded the
Chinese as less than human.

Americans' image of Japan had also changed rapidly. The ''sweet and doll-
like'' Japanese of Perry's day had become ''leering, bespectacled sadists''
who raped and murdered innocent women and children. By the late 1930s, the
Japanese image of the West, especially of the United States, became that of a
decadent, corrupt, and spineless society which would disintegrate in the wake
of a determined military attack. This distorted perception of America was
matched by a Japanese self-image of absolute superiority and invincibility. In
other words, a high *national morale* now became a major power factor. If the
Japanese in 1941 had perceived themselves and the United States as they really were, there would have been no Pearl Harbor. It would have been obvious
that Japan could not possibly win a war against the United States, that, in
short, the objective fact of vastly superior capabilities was bound to over-
whelm it. It was the power of an image that precipitated the Japanese attack.
The incredible feats of little Japan during World War II cannot be explained in
terms of its meager objective resources, but must be attributed above all to the
existence of a self-image that was translated into superior national morale.
This national morale became an immense storehouse of power. A well-known
student of Japan, Ruth Benedict, provides a fascinating illustration of this morale factor in her report of a Japanese radio broadcast describing the behavior
of a Japanese pilot during the war:

> After the air battles were over, the Japanese planes returned to their base in small formations of three or four. A Captain was in one of the first planes to return. After alighting from his plane, he stood on the ground and gazed into the sky through binoculars. As his men returned, he counted. He looked rather pale, but he was quite steady. After the last plane returned he made out a report and proceeded to Headquarters. At Headquarters he made his report to the Commanding Officer. As soon as he had finished his report, however, he suddenly dropped to the ground. The officers on the spot rushed to give assistance but alas! he was dead. On examining his body it was found that it was already cold, and he had a bullet wound in his chest, which had proved fatal. It is impossible for the body of a newly-dead person to be cold. Nevertheless the body of the dead Captain was as cold as ice. The Captain must have been dead long before, and it was his spirit that made the report. Such a miraculous feat must have been achieved by the strict sense of responsibility that the dead Captain possessed.[14]

To a non-Japanese, this story might seem like an outrageous yarn. But this writer himself heard the particular broadcast and was able to observe the reaction of Japanese military personnel in occupied Shanghai. The story was believed almost without exception. It was common knowledge that a disciplined spirit was master of the body, that indeed "a composed spirit could last a thousand years."[15] Why should it not be possible that the spirit of a man could outlive his body by a few hours if that man had made duty and responsibility to the Emperor the central tenets of his life?

Iran, under the leadership of the Ayatollah Khomeini, may be another case in point. Shi'ite Moslems believe that if they die in a holy war, they go directly to paradise. Perhaps American reluctance to take forceful military action against Iran during the hostage crisis was motivated not only by fear for the lives of the captives, but also by the despairing realization that the Iranian people might virtually welcome death as martyrdom in a sacred revolutionary cause. In other words, the intensity of Iran's religious fanaticism significantly enhanced its national morale and power. This was true not only during Iran's lengthy showdown with the United States, but also in its war with neighboring Iraq. There, too, Iran held out surprisingly well. "They fought like fanatics," a surprised Iraqi general exclaimed after a particularly bloody battle in which the Iranians had held out to the last man.

The roots of national character and national morale as sources of power are probably to be found in the culture, historical experience, and social and religious structure of nations. Once again, the insights of the social psychologist and sociologist have relevance to the study of international relations. Empirical research has not advanced sufficiently to permit definite conclusions in this vital area of study, but it has provided some important clues. And certainly the phenomena to be explained are remarkable indeed. The German social scene, for example, changed significantly between the two world wars. Is there any connection between these changes and the fact that Germany capitulated with relative ease in 1918 but fought on fanatically in 1945? If so, what is that connection? What explains the Germans' conviction in 1941 that they would dictate peace terms to Stalin in a matter of weeks? And what, on the other hand, accounted for the tremendous staying power of the Red Army? What made British morale during World War II the object of almost universal admiration, whereas France collapsed within a few weeks? What made the United States gather its resources after Pearl Harbor in an iron determination to force the enemy into unconditional surrender? The answers to these questions must await further insights into the nature of political culture. What is clear is that political culture and morale provide tremendous reservoirs of power.

We saw earlier that the very essence of nationalism is a nation's image of a common past and a common future. Hence, it goes without saying that nationalism vitally affects a nation's power. Under certain conditions, moreover, the vision of a common future may become an *ideology*. This occurs when a nation's image of the future includes *the notion of a dynamic evolution toward some universal utopia*. Ideology has largely become the monopoly of totalitarian nations. Napoleon's vision of universal empire was rationalized by the ideology of the French "*mission civilisatrice.*" The ultimate vision of Nazi Germany was the enthronement of the "Aryan race." To accomplish this end, it became necessary for Germany to expand into ever wider areas of *Lebensraum,* or "living space." The Japanese "Co-Prosperity Sphere" was based on similar assumptions. The Communists, in turn, have their own blueprint for the world, which predicts the growing influence of the Soviet Union and China. In all these cases, the nation is seen as the dynamic instrument for world-wide dominion.

It would be too simple to assert, as does Morgenthau, that ideology is simply "a flattering unction" for the concealment of imperialist expansion:

> It is a characteristic aspect of all politics, domestic as well as international, that frequently its basic manifestations do not appear as what they actually are—manifestations of a struggle for power. Rather, the element of power as the immediate goal of the policy pursued is explained and justified in ethical, legal, or biological terms. That is to say: the true nature of the policy is concealed by ideological justifications and rationalizations....
>
> Politicians have an ineradicable tendency to deceive themselves about what they are doing by referring to their policies not in terms of power but in terms of either ethical and legal principles or biological necessities. In other words, while all politics is necessarily pursuit of power, ideologies render involvement in that contest for power psychologically and morally acceptable to the actors and their audience.[16]

Not only is it an exaggeration to claim that *all* politics is a pursuit of power, but the relationship between power and ideology is a much more complex and multifaceted one. In the first place, a widespread belief in the "truth" of an ideology may hasten its realization and thus become a power factor. For example, the ideological conviction of many Communists that the victory of communism is ordained by history has added immensely to the power of the Soviet Union. This faith in a metaphysical determinism has tended to inspire communism with a self-image of invincibility. Second, ideology may assume an authority all its own, precisely because its adherents are convinced of its metaphysical validity. Power, in the last analysis, must rest on the capacity of physical force. Authority, on the other hand, may attain similar compliance because it is accepted as legitimate or "true." Ideology serves the peculiar function of "justifying power and transforming it into authority, thus diminishing the amount of power which must be applied to achieve compliance or to produce the desired effect."[17] Moreover, the image of an ideology's ultimate universal ideal takes on a life of its own, which even all-powerful dictators ignore only at their own peril. This inner dynamic has been well stated by one student of ideology:

> Since an important ingredient of the movement's power is the element of explicit and proclaimed purpose which furthers its seizure of political power, the fulfillment of major portions of the ideologically stated objectives becomes a necessity dictated by power, by the inner dynamic of the movement itself. It is therefore doubtful that Hitler could have survived without gradually increasing the scope of the National-Socialist revolution in Germany, or that Stalin and his regime could have maintained the New Economic Policy without ultimately losing power....
>
> A skeptical leader would run a serious risk of undermining his power if he were to allow himself to question the ideology. It is very doubtful that even Stalin could have done it.[18]

The relationship between power and ideology seems, up to a point, to be one of mutual reinforcement. Commitment to an ideology creates an image of the future which is based on the confident expectation of victory. This confidence is a source of tremendous long-range power. The enhancement of power in turn necessitates the further development and refinement of ideology along ever more ambitious lines. Theoretically, this mutual enhancement of ideology and power would end only in world domination. But if the reality lags too far behind the longed-for utopia, if the dichotomy between image and reality is too sharp, ideology begins to erode and lose its authority. It is for this reason that each Soviet Five-Year Plan has been "the final great effort" which would make entrance into the promised utopia a reality. As long as confrontation with reality does not uncover too great discrepancies, as long as image and reality tend to converge, ideology remains a vast fountainhead of power. But the point of diminishing returns is usually reached when no further victories can be won and expansion is brought to a standstill.

In former times, the peculiar character of ideology with its claims of expansion toward universal power was limited to religious movements. Modern ideology has become the psychological counterpart of messianic religion. Although its ultimate goals are secular rather than supernatural, it has been able to command as much power as the most fanatical of religious movements. The implications for international relations of the presence of competing ideologies have been well stated by Hans Morgenthau:

> The claim to universality which inspires the moral code of one particular group is incompatible with the identical claim of another group; the world has room for only one, and the other must yield or be destroyed. Thus, carrying their idols before them, the nationalistic masses of our time meet in the international arena, each

group convinced that it executes the mandate of history, that it does for humanity what is seems to do for itself, and that it fulfills a sacred mission ordained by Providence, however defined.[19]

Ideology as a source of power is largely a monopoly of totalitarianism. A democracy may have goals or ideals but not an ideology. Since the very essence of a democracy is the principle of the right of disagreement on substantive goals, such a nation lacks the fanaticism and uniformity that lend an ideology its coherence and drive. The citizens of the United States may disagree on America's "national purpose." A totalitarian society, on the other hand, has only one official ideology. This does not mean, of course, that democracy has no resources to marshal against the aspirations of a universal ideology. As we have seen, it has other great sources of power. Besides, ideology is not *only* a source of power. It is the great overreacher of international relations. By definition, its goals are boundless and its horizons of conquest unlimited. The time must come, as it always has, when the image of a universal ideology is thwarted by an unyielding reality—when power encounters concerted counterpower. Hence each ideology carries within itself the seed of its own destruction, the hubristic assumption that power can expand without limit.

Finally, the quality of a nation's *leadership* and the image which it projects upon the world are important sources of power. If leadership is defective, all other resources may be to no avail. No amount of manpower or industrial and military potential will make a nation powerful unless its leadership *uses* the resources with maximum effect on the international scene. If the tangible resources are the body of power, and the national character its soul, leadership is its brains. It alone can decide how to apply its nation's resources. For example, the United States before World War II possessed virtually every single attribute of a powerful nation. But it played a relatively minor role in international relations because its leadership was committed to a policy of isolation. Hence, as far as American power was concerned, the advantages of geography, natural resources, industrial and military potential, and size and quality of population might as well not have existed at all, for though they did in fact exist, American leadership proceeded as if they did not.[20]

Leadership may build and save nations; it may also destroy them. The former capacity is symbolized in Winston Churchill's immortal challenge to the Nazis: "We shall fight on the beaches, we shall fight on the landing grounds, we shall fight in the fields and in the streets, we shall fight in the hills; we shall never surrender." It would be difficult to understand the power of the young American republic without reference to the outstanding leadership of its early statesmen. What would Britain have been without Castlereagh, Disraeli, and Canning? France without Talleyrand? Czechoslovakia without Masaryk? Or, for that matter, could one explain the far-reaching reforms in the Soviet Union today without the leadership of Mikhail Gorbachev? On the other hand, leadership may provide the power for national extinction. The early triumphs of Nazi Germany were the product of Hitler's mind. But the utter nihilism of the Third Reich and its final act of national suicide also grew out of Hitler's leadership. As historians have demonstrated, Hitler cast an almost hypnotic spell over Germany long after the war was considered lost by most of his entourage. His will alone resulted in the prolongation of the war at the cost of millions of lives. The German image of the Fuehrer invested him with the power of life and death.

In concluding our analysis of power, we must take note of two striking paradoxes: While the power gap between big and small states has never been greater, never have big states been less able to impose their will upon lesser countries. The conflicts between the United States and North Vietnam, France and Algeria, the Soviet Union and Afghanistan, and the United States and Iran and Lebanon are cases in point. Part of the reason for this is, of course, the fact that whenever one superpower is engaged against a lesser state, the other superpower tends to be arrayed on the other side. Yet the French experience in Algeria, the French and American experiences in Indochina as well as the American confrontation with Iran demonstrate that power also has a great deal to do with a nation's will and readiness to accept punishment. American policy in Southeast Asia failed because the threshold of suffering for North Vietnam and the Vietcong was much higher than Washington had assumed, while the American threshold was considerably lower. The United States dropped more bombs on North Vietnam than it dropped on the Axis powers during the entire period of World War II. Yet that little nation virtually fought the United States to a standstill and finally won the war. It seems that, with the coming of the atomic age, the power of big states has diminished while the power of small states has increased. At any rate, power can no longer be calculated simply by adding up a nation's physical capabilities. Psychology and will must be given as much weight as resources and hardware.

Finally, it must be noted that any up-to-date analysis of power must include nonstate entities as well. The rise in recent years of various national liberation groups in different parts of the world suggests that power may no longer be limited to national states alone. It is now also beginning to reside in the cracks of the state system. The Palestine Liberation Organization (PLO) is a case in point. The fact that some of these liberation groups resort to terror and blackmail to enforce their territorial demands only underlines this point. Even though some states have begun to take measures against international terrorism, it is the very randomness and irrationality of the terrorists that give them a measure of power. The helplessness of the American government during the Iranian hostage crisis in 1980 and again several years later, when it was unable to secure the release of American hostages held captive in Lebanon, demonstrated the destructive power of a small but disciplined group of terrorists. And we must also not forget that, in our anarchic world, one person's terrorist may be another's patriot or hero.

Now that we have analyzed the anatomy of power, we may propose the following definition: *Power in international relations is the capacity of a nation to use its tangible and intangible resources in such a way as to affect the behavior of other nations.*

THE BALANCE OF POWER

Perhaps the most enduring "law" of international relations has been the principle of the balance of power. It is generally agreed to have been operative for over three hundred years, since the emergence of the multistate system. In its simplest form, the principle operated as follows: In the anarchic world of nation-states, each protagonist sought to maximize its safety through the enhancement of its power. In this competition, the quest for safety expressed itself chiefly in a search for allies. The safety of all was assured only if no one nation or group of nations was permitted to achieve a preponderance of power—if, in other words, a rough balance was achieved. Whenever the system threatened to break down, a "balancer" would ally itself with the weaker group of nations and thus restore the unstable equilibrium known as the "balance of power." This role was traditionally played by Great Britain. The Pax Britannica, when seen in terms of the balance of power principle, was therefore in essence guaranteed by Britain's capacity to tip the scales by allying itself with the weaker nations against whatever state or combination of states threatened to become predominant.

In order to analyze the concept of its applicability meaningfully and unambiguously, it is necessary to make our definitions as precise as possible. In his *Power and International Relations,* Inis L. Claude, Jr., has pointed out that students of international relations have used the balance of power concept in four different ways.[21] First, and most commonly, it has been used to connote a *system* for the operation of international politics in a world of multiple states. This system can be seen as working automatically, like a physical law; semiautomatically, since Britain seemed exempt from this law in its traditional role as balancer; or manually, with every actor manipulating the system through its own contrivance. Second, writers have referred to the balance of power concept as a *situation,* either of equilibrium or preponderance, between two states. Third, it has been used to describe a *policy* of equilibrium or preponderance. And finally, it has often served as a *symbol* of concern with the problem of power without substantive content. Throughout this book, the term *balance of power* will be used to describe a system of either the semiautomatic or manually operated type. The term *bipolarity,* or *balance of terror,* will connote the rough equilibrium of mutual atomic deterrence between East and West; and *multipolarity* will be used to describe a system of international relations in which a large number of protagonists engage in the balancing process without any one single nation playing the role of balancer.

Essentially, the balance of power system was a process of checking power with counterpower. The favorite technique used to accomplish this end was the formation of alliances and counteralliances. These unions were not perma-

nent; those partner to them frequently switched sides whenever the maintenance of equilibrium seemed to require it. One classic example of the rapidity
of such realignments was the Austro-British alliance against France and
Prussia in 1740, which only a few years later changed to an Anglo-Prussian
alliance against France and Austria. One of the chief alleged benefits of the
balance of power system, when it operated successfully, was to guarantee the
independence of small nations who were protected by the "balancer" from being devoured by the large ones. And perhaps most important, of course, the
system was supposed to ensure peace in an anarchic world.

A careful scrutiny of this theory of the balance of power as almost a kind of
"natural law" of classic international relations leaves one with many doubts
about its actual validity. First, while the theory assumed that every nation
would strive to enhance its power, it curiously viewed at least one nation—the
balancer—as somehow exempt from this apparently universal rule. This balancer was seen as motivated not by national egotism but by international al-
truism. Since it was the British who traditionally played this balancing role,
Great Britain was perceived as a sort of Olympian arbiter, allegedly above and
exempt from the rules of international intercourse that governed the actions of
other nations. As A. F. K. Organski has pointed out,

> The English modestly and the rest of the world credulously assigned this role to
> England. England has been the balancer because Englishmen believed that she was,
> said that she was, and the rest of the world believed them. The specifications for the
> role of balancer have been written with England in mind: the balancer must be a big
> power slightly removed from the center of controversy, preferably an island and
> mistress of the seas. Later, the fact that England met these specifications was used
> as added proof that England was the balancer.
>
> Just why England's motives should differ so from those of other nations is never
> explained. Why a preponderance of power in England's hands should be a balancing
> factor is not explained, either, nor can it be, for it is not true.[22]

Actually, of course, Great Britain's balance strategy was as motivated by national interest as were the strategies of all the other European nations. It was
grounded, above all, in two circumstances. One was the fact that as an island
and the predominant naval power, Britain was likely to prove invulnerable to
conquest save possibly by a state that had gained control over the whole
European continent. The other was that in view of its size, population, and
resources, Britain could not—as France did under Napoleon and Germany did
under Hitler—reasonably aspire to win and maintain hegemony over Europe
on its own. Hence Britain's optimum strategy was to settle for the compromise
policy of playing the European balancer—preventing anyone else from developing control over all of Europe by always siding against whichever happened
to be the ascendant power, in alliance with the state or states that potentially,
along with Great Britain, seemed at the moment most seriously threatened.

The further assumption that nations participating in the balance of power
were free to switch partners at will, like the dancers in a quadrille, also seems
open to question. Could international combinations really be formed that me-

chanically? To be sure, alliances changed their membership in an almost ka-leidoscopic fashion, but just as often the bonds of tradition and friendship made rapid shifts difficult and well nigh impossible. This has not, admittedly, been the case in countries whose governments have been authoritarian or to-talitarian. Though Hitler and Stalin, for example, had denounced each other for a decade as mortal enemies, in 1939 they proved able to make a complete turnabout and, acknowledging what appeared to them to be the dictates of their respective national interests, overnight became close, if temporary, al-lies. However, in countries where government, including foreign policy, is di-rectly responsible and responsive to the electorate, such a rapid shift of sides would be impossible. Any major realignment would require a lengthy period of popular rethinking and reconditioning—as the United States' difficulty in fac-ing up to the sudden post-World War II challenges of its former ally, the Soviet Union, amply illustrates. And for the United States to go so far as to throw its weight against such long-standing friends, partners, and allies as Britain and France—even if the maintenance of the balance of power would seem to de-mand it—is rare indeed.

The most fundamental criticism of the theory concerns the assumption that a rough equilibrium among nations generally ushered in periods of peace. It is well known that the Pax Romana was one of the longest periods of relatively undisturbed peace in the history of Western civilization. This peace was guar-anteed not by a balance, but by the absolute predominance of Rome. This ex-ample may be dismissed as invalid because it preceded the emergence of the nation-state system; however, it would be difficult to disregard the century of relative stability and peace that was ushered in by the Congress of Vienna in 1815. This peace was guaranteed by the preponderant power of the combined forces of the Concert of Powers: Britain, Austria, Prussia, and Russia. Indeed, the peace was broken only when, once again, a condition of relative balance emerged at the beginning of the twentieth century. Organski goes so far as to state that "the relationship between peace and the balance of power appears to be exactly the opposite of what has been claimed. The periods of balance, real or imagined, are periods of warfare, while the periods of known preponder-ance are periods of peace."[23] This view, however, falls into the opposite error. Rather, the evidence seems to point to the fact that the long-alleged causal re-lationship between equilibrium and the attainment of peace simply does not exist.

Whatever success in maintaining peace the balance of power may or may not once have had, its effectiveness definitely ended with the emergence of bipolarity. It might be objected, of course, that bipolarity was merely another form of balance, simple rather than multiple. And it is undoubtedly true that each side has attempted to enhance its position vis-à-vis the other. But who has been the balancer? Britain, allegedly the traditional holder of the balance, has long since lost the independence that the role would require today—as the Suez crisis of 1956 dramatically showed. Moreover, the development of a rough equilibrium between the two superpowers may actually have increased the danger of war. Indeed, so long as the West possessed an atomic monopoly and thus a preponderance of power, there was little danger of a major war.

As we have seen earlier, bipolarity as a type of international power configuration has ample precedent. In such cases, as Organski has pointed out, wars have been most likely to occur when there was an approaching balance between the dominant nation and a major challenger.[24] Peace, on the other hand, has been most likely when one bloc has enjoyed a decided preponderance over the others. Thus, the "bipolar" wars between Sparta and Athens and between Rome and Carthage occurred at a time when the antagonists were in a condition of approaching equilibrium. The balance of terror of our time differed from traditional bipolarity in the fact that it was at the same time a nuclear bipolarity. While the equilibrium between the two military blocs of East and West increased the chances of war, the condition of mutual deterrence acted as a counterweight.

Recent developments indicate, however, that the bipolar international system has been superseded by a multipolar one. A war between the two major superpowers, though possible, is not probable. The ascendancy of China, Japan, and Western Europe has irrevocably changed the power equation. In addition, the widening gulf between rich and poor nations in the "Third World" has decentralized the world's power balance even further. There is, moreover, the constant danger of further nuclear dispersion and even of nuclear theft. The rise of international terrorism conjures up horrendous scenarios if nuclear weapons should ever fall into irresponsible hands in the international community. A "nuclear Sarajevo" triggered by a state such as Libya, for example, has become an almost universal nightmare. Thus, nuclear war, though "unthinkable," still remains a possibility. In view of this fact, the foreign policies of nations are absolutely crucial. Domestic policy can hurt, but foreign policy can kill.

Two final observations must be made about the balance of power. First, most states do not strive for balances with others; they strive for superiority *over* others. Yet, that striving for superiority calls forth similar efforts by other states, thus resulting in balances as unintended by-products of the striving for superiority. Today's rough balance between the superpowers is a case in point. Second, as Kenneth Waltz brilliantly illustrates in his book *Theory of International Politics,* powerful states that have achieved such an unintended balance at times decide to impose a measure of order on an anarchic system if for no other reason than to preserve their own favored positions. Thus, the United States and the Soviet Union have engaged in a decades-long struggle for power, but they have also collaborated in important ways to make the world a less disorderly place: to slow down the spread of nuclear weapons, to control the size of nuclear arsenals, to prevent the stationing of nuclear weapons in outer space, and to preserve Antarctica from the territorial claims of other states. Thus, a semblance of order can be created by checking each other's ambitions and the ambitions of others. And, paradoxically, the quest for power in world politics can therefore lead to a measure of balance and of order.

THE NATURE OF FOREIGN POLICY

We have now examined the nation as the unit of action in international relations. We have seen that it consists of both imagery and objective attributes. We have also seen that power—the nation's ability to affect the behavior of others—is more than the sum total of its attributes. It, too, consists of both image and reality. We have yet to see toward what *goals* this power is applied—in brief, the ends toward which a nation's foreign policy is conducted.

A nation's foreign policy is the expression of its national interest vis-à-vis other nations. To define foreign policy in this manner is, in a sense, to beg the question: What *is* the national interest? And merely to state that each nation provides its own definition is to underline the obvious. Yet might it nevertheless be possible to discover some universal guiding principle that governs the foreign policies of *all* nations? In brief, is there any one goal that is shared universally in the nation-state system?

One of the most challenging theories of international relations is that advanced by Morgenthau, who considers the central and universal goal of foreign policy to be power. Accordingly, it is always in terms of power that he views the national interest:

> The main signpost that helps political realism to find its way through the landscape of international politics is the concept of interest defined in terms of power....We assume that statesmen think and act in terms of interest defined as power, and the evidence of history bears that assumption out....[25]

In short, Morgenthau postulates that nations will tend to use their power in the quest for further power. Moreover, he rejects as unrealistic the proposition that the national interest may be defined in terms of abstract moral principle. Rather, in his view, the national interest becomes virtually identical with national security. Excessive preoccupation with questions of morality and law is condemned as "moralism" and "legalism." These are out of place in the making of foreign policy:

> Intellectually, the political realist maintains the autonomy of the political sphere, as the economist, the lawyer, the moralist maintains theirs. He thinks in terms of interest defined as power, as the economist thinks in terms of interest defined as wealth; the lawyer, of the conformity of action with legal rules; the moralist, of the conformity of action with moral principles.[26]

Morgenthau's is a brilliant exposition of a single-factor analysis. But like all such efforts, it is a tour de force which simply does not stand up under critical scrutiny. In the first place, we have seen that the essence of power is relational, that it depends upon comparison to be meaningful. To define the national interest in terms of the maximization of power is to assume that the goals of *all* nations are *competitive*. This is incorrect on two counts. First, many nations are interested in enhancing the power and welfare of others, rather than in competing with them. And, more important, the goals of some nations are not competitive but are *absolute*, not being defined in relation to other states at all. It is true that most of the powerful nations are competitive and seek even greater power. But can this be said with equal validity of small nations like Switzerland or Sri Lanka? Neither of these can be said to define its national interest primarily in terms of power. Moreover, competitive goals may change into absolute ones in the same nation. Sweden, for example, was once a powerful nation with fiercely competitive goals. But in our time Sweden's goals are absolute and in essence unrelated to those of other nations. Hence, the maximization of power is a major ingredient of the national interest, but not the only one. Nations have and always have had both competitive and absolute goals.

The statement that power is a vital goal of most of the world's powerful nations does not solve our problem. We have seen that the anatomy of power is highly complex. It also is an oversimplification to assert, as Morgenthau does, that a nation's foreign policy must be based either on national interest or on moral principle and should be based on the former. The two considerations are seldom if ever mutually exclusive. As W.T.R. Fox has aptly pointed out:

> Moral principle necessarily enters into any valid formulation of national interest which must itself reconcile the desirable and the possible. Against the view that there can be no compromise, I assert that there can be no escape from compromise. This is what makes politics a vocation only for the mature, for the responsible, for the man who does not despair when he discovers incommensurate values placed in such a juxtaposition that one or another has to be sacrificed.[27]

Indeed, power and moral principle might be considered as two concentric circles. At times power is the larger and includes morality. This is true when a nation is powerful and can "afford" to act morally. But at other times, and this is equally important, morality may include power; that is, greater power may accrue to a nation from moral behavior. Or, conversely, a nation may lose a measure of its power through immoral behavior. For example, suppose the United States should break a promise to one of its allies in NATO, hence acting "immorally." The ally might leave NATO and become neutralist. The United States would thereby lose a measure of power by ignoring moral principle. (The relationship between power and morality is discussed more fully in Chapter 8.)

We see, therefore, that it is misleading to define the national interest in terms of any one concept. In fact, our definition of foreign policy as the formulation of the national interest is purely *formal*. To say, "Always follow the national interest!" is to devise a kind of categorical imperative. But, like Kant's famous dictum "Always treat man as an end, never as a means," the formula of the national interest is ambiguous and frequently not at all helpful when applied to a concrete situation. Simply to assert that it is identical with power is equally imprecise. Perhaps we can bring the concept of national interest into clearer focus by ascertaining the *types* of goals as well as the goals themselves which nations tend to pursue in international relations.

We have seen above a useful distinction between *competitive* and *absolute* goals. The pursuit of power, by definition, is a competitive goal. The pursuit of peace or order, on the other hand, may be defined as an absolute goal. Another useful distinction may be made between goals that are *clearly defined* and those that are *diffuse*. A clearly defined goal is shared by an entire nation or, at least, an overwhelming majority in that nation. Nazi Germany's aim to annex Austria was such a case. But most of the time it is exceedingly difficult to abstract a national goal which is common to most members of a nation. For example, does the United States have a national interest which can be objectively determined? Is the guideline of its foreign policy the maximization of power, the consolidation of economic prosperity, or the pursuit of peace? Or is it a combination of the three? Moreover, as one scholar has demonstrated, the foreign policy views of most Americans tend to fluctuate greatly and depend primarily on mood.[28] Sometimes diffuse goals may change in the direction of a more clearly defined policy. The foreign policy of France under the Fourth Republic was an example of extreme diffusion, but with the ascendancy of General de Gaulle to the presidency, national goals were set forth with far greater clarity. A third distinction may be drawn between a nation's *declaratory* policy and its *action* policy. Often a nation's stated goals are very different from its real intentions. The Soviet slogan of "peaceful coexistence" during the Khrushchev era was a good example of declaratory policy. But it was quite possible that the Soviet leader conceived of peaceful coexistence as merely a phase in the struggle for world domination. However, there is mounting evidence that Mikhail Gorbachev's *perestroika,* or restructuring of Soviet society, has begun to move from declaratory to action policy. Finally, a foreign policy may be either *static* or *dynamic*. Some nations are interested in the preservation of the status quo in international relations, while others are equally eager for change.

We may now attempt to make some general observations about the national interest. The goals of nations are subject to constant change. There is no single concept that explains the national interest. It is true that many nations use their power for the pursuit of greater power. This is especially true in the case of nations which are already powerful. But it is equally true that nations may employ their power in the pursuit of cooperation and international order. National goals may be competitive or absolute, clear or diffuse, overt or covert, static or dynamic. Beyond this it would be hazardous to generalize.

THE STUDY OF WORLD POLITICS

In a sense, the study of world politics is a study of the interplay of the foreign policies or of the national interests of nations. But while architects of foreign policy tend to regard the world from the vantage point of their own nations, students of world politics must look at the world in the round. It is appropriate, therefore, before concluding this chapter, to describe briefly the various schools of thought in the field of international relations and to locate the place of this book in the mainstream of recent thought about the subject.

World politics—or international relations—as a separate discipline was developed primarily by European scholars in American universities after World War II. Before that time, it was the province of historians, international lawyers, and philosophers. War and conflict were then still regarded as departures from "normal" peaceful relations. World War I, after all, had been "the war to end all wars." Scholars during the interwar period, therefore, tended to be idealists advancing theories of federation, collective security, and even world government. The rise of Nazi and fascist totalitarianism, however, and the death of forty million people during World War II challenged the basic assumptions of the idealists. Their hopes and aspirations lay shattered in the wake of Auschwitz and Hiroshima.

The founder of the new "realist" school of international relations was, not surprisingly, a European refugee from the Nazi holocaust: Hans J. Morgenthau. His belief that power was the most reliable signpost on the landscape of world politics was first advanced in his *Politics Among Nations*. This book, deeply pessimistic about human nature and strongly influenced by Machiavelli's *Prince,* was rejected by several American publishers before it appeared in its first edition in 1948. Thereafter, it went through five editions and gradually attained the status of a classic. Students and practitioners of foreign policy openly acknowledged their intellectual debt. When Morgenthau died in 1980 at the age of seventy-six, the main eulogy was delivered by Henry Kissinger. The former secretary of state opened his remarks by declaring simply: "Hans Morgenthau was my teacher."

During the 1950s and 1960s, a new school of thought emerged that was critical of both the "idealist" and "realist" approaches. These scholars, aiming to give international relations greater scientific content, tended to think in terms of "models," "systems," and "behavioral" approaches, relegating "idealists" and "realists" alike to an outdated traditionalism. In their aim to inject greater precision into the study of world politics, they tended to borrow concepts from the more exact sciences. To name only a few examples from the vast body of "scientific" or "behavioral" literature: Morton Kaplan's *System and Process in International Politics,* which is indebted to physics and talks about "fields of force"; J. David Singer's *Quantitative International Politics,* which explores the possibilities of injecting greater mathematical precision into the field; Karl Deutsch's *The Nerves of Government*, heavily influenced by communications theory; Richard Snyder's *Foreign Policy Decision Making,* which attempts to analyze individual policy decisions under a microscope; Ole Holsti's *The Belief System and National Images: A Case Study,* which seeks to reconstruct a statesman's political beliefs through a content analysis of his books and speeches; Herbert Kelman's *International Behavior,* heavily influenced by behavioral psychology; Thomas Schelling's *Strategy of Conflict,* indebted to games theory; and Richard Sterling's *Macropolitics,* which benefits from the field of economics.

In essence, international relations as a field of study has been dominated ever since the 1960s by a dialogue between the "scientific" and "traditional" approaches. The "scientific" scholars have tended to accuse "traditionalists" of fuzziness and imprecision. They assert, for example, that the "balance of power," a favorite concept of the "realists," is little more than a vague metaphor since no balance in world politics is ever exact or subject to quantitative measurement. The "traditionalists," in turn, challenge the behavioral scholars by asking, for example, how genius in leadership or self-destructive leadership, for that matter, could be quantified, or even subject to scientific analysis. The study of world politics or of foreign policy, they contend, can never be free of values or subjective judgments. In short, it can never be a science, but is destined to remain an art.

This book, while in essence traditionalist, is not limited to Morgenthau's assumptions about the primacy of power. Half of the book analyzes the struggles for power in the world, but the other half examines the struggles for a better world order. If I have borrowed from other disciplines, it has primarily been history. World politics, without history, in my judgment, has no roots, just as history without application to the present may bear no fruits. I was also shocked to read that 60 percent of the freshman class in a leading American university in 1980 did not know the difference between World War I and World War II.[29] The price of such ignorance comes high in blood and treasure.

Most important, however, this book focuses on the human element in world politics. In our time, we have been led to think of states almost as living actors on the world scene. How often do we hear a phrase such as "The United States decided" or "The United States agreed"? To speak of "actors," "powers," or of "systems" merely beclouds the basic truth that human beings, made of flesh and blood, make these decisions on behalf of collectivities called states. States have no existences apart from the lives of men and women. They are creatures of the human will. Hence, I tend to give considerable weight to the personalities of leading figures and their impact on the world—for better or for worse. It makes a difference, in my judgment, *who* is there at a given moment. In summary, I do not believe in the division of human knowledge into neat and separate compartments. World politics, perhaps more than any other field of study, requires a unified renaissance approach. Nothing less will do if we are to begin to understand the tragedy of our human condition.

THE ULTIMATE QUESTION: WHO WILL RISE AND WHO WILL DECLINE?

As we look toward the year 2000, it may be useful to speculate about the relative future power of those nations that are the most powerful today. In 1988, a British historian, Paul Kennedy, published an excellent book, *The Rise and Fall of the Great Powers,* which addressed this theme. His basic argument was that, over the last 500 years, one great nation after another declined after its military obligations and foreign commitments extended beyond its economic capacities. The author termed this condition one of "imperial overstretch," an imbalance which, if left uncorrected, leads a nation into the twilight of decline. Portugal, Spain, and England all suffered this fate. Even though England won World War II, her economic base had become much too weak to support her global empire. Hence, Britain gradually lost her great-power status over the next few decades.

Paul Kennedy's predictions about the United States are also sobering. At the end of World War II, the United States' share of world industrial production crested to close to 50 percent. But then, as the United States built up her former enemies, Germany and Japan, and paid for a vast network of military alliances all over the world, her relative power declined as her economic base began to shrink. The Vietnam War was an important turning point in this respect. Now, half a century after the outbreak of World War II, the United States still carries enormous military obligations but has become the world's leading debtor country. This classic condition of "imperial overstretch," in Kennedy's view, does not bode well for the future of US power.

A similar trend seems to be at work in the Soviet Union. An expensive network of military allies in Eastern Europe as well as client states in Cuba, Nicaragua, and Angola have sapped Soviet energies over the years. A Vietnam-type war in Afghanistan accelerated this process. Perhaps here we can look for a major reason for Mikhail Gorbachev's push for nuclear disarmament treaties with the United States: to cut down on Soviet "imperial overstretch" and to re-energize a flabby unproductive economy. Be that as it may, in Kennedy's view, *both* the United States and the Soviet Union may be in decline by the year 2000.

Two "Asian tigers," however, are rapidly rising: Japan and China. Japan's military commitments are minimal. In fact, the United States still shoulders a large share of Japan's defense expenditures. Yet, under this US umbrella, Japan has become the world's leading creditor country and has bought up large chunks of US real estate. In 1941, Japan bombed Hawaii; today, Japanese investors own huge properties in the Hawaiian Islands. The Americans, with a low savings rate, go into debt. The Japanese, who love to save, invest their savings in the United States.

China, too, has only modest military commitments, yet her economic base is broadening and is potentially colossal. She, too, is using US technology as a guide to modernization. With a population of one billion people, her potential productivity is formidable. And her leadership seems determined to leave orthodox communism behind in favor of a mixed economy. I recall a Chinese teacher of mine in Shanghai who said to me in 1941: "The twentieth century is most unusual; it is the first century in more than 2000 years in which China does not perceive herself to be at the center of the world; but in the next century, things will be back to normal again."

Kennedy wisely rejects the notion of inevitability. Yet, as one surveys the historical scene, the precedents are disturbing. Whether in ancient Rome, in Philip IV's Spain, or in Edwardian Britain, the pattern was more or less the same. When each empire passed its crest, its leaders were seized by anxiety and summoned advisers to point the way back to global hegemony. The wise people obligingly laid out their recommendations, yet in each case, after much fanfare, the leadership did nothing. As Kennedy himself puts it, "I always check myself when I'm asked if any nation sliding downhill has reversed itself, without tremendous violence or dislocation. I can't think of any, but then again, we do have history, and we can learn from that."[30]

No event in history, I submit, is inevitable, unless enough men and women *believe* it to be so and then, looking back upon it, say that it *was* in fact inevitable. In that sense, prophecies are not decreed by destiny but are self-fulfilling through the strengths and weaknesses of mortal men and women. Scholars and historians such as Paul Kennedy serve as warnings or as inspirations. Perhaps blindness in the past can sharpen *our* sight today. And perhaps past wisdom can give *us* courage for tomorrow. The year 2000 will not be shaped by "destiny"; it will be shaped by us and our children.

REFERENCES

1 John H. Herz, *International Politics in the Atomic Age*. New York: Columbia University Press, 1959, p. 22.
2 Erich Fromm, *Escape from Freedom*. New York: Rinehart, 1941, *passim*.
3 Louis L. Snyder, *The Meaning of Nationalism*. New Brunswick, N.J.: Rutgers University Press, 1954, p. 89.
4 See the provocative analysis by Erik Erikson in *Childhood and Society*. New York: Norton, 1950, pp. 284–315.
5 *Ibid.*, p. 289.
6 *Ibid.*, p. 300.
7 Charles P. Kindleberger, "International Political Theory from Outside," in William T. R. Fox, ed., *Theoretical Aspects of International Relations*. South Bend, Ind.: University of Notre Dame Press, 1959.
8 Annette Baker Fox, *The Power of Small States*. Chicago: University of Chicago Press, 1959, p. 186.
9 Hans J. Morgenthau, *Politics Among Nations*, 4th ed. New York: Knopf, 1967, p. 106.
10 *Ibid.*
11 Herz, *op. cit.*, p. 108.
12 Sir Halford Mackinder, *Democratic Ideals and Reality*. New York: Holt, 1919, p. 150.
13 Alfred T. Mahan, *The Influence of Sea Power upon History*. Boston: Little, Brown, 1890, *passim*.
14 Ruth Benedict, *The Chrysanthemum and the Sword*. Boston: Houghton Mifflin, 1946, p. 25.
15 *Ibid.*, p. 26.
16 Morgenthau, *op. cit.*, pp. 83–84.
17 Zbigniew K. Brzezinski, *The Soviet Bloc: Unity and Conflict*. Cambridge, Mass.: Harvard University Press, 1960, pp. 386–387.
18 *Ibid.*, pp. 387–389.
19 Morgenthau, *op. cit.*, p. 249.
20 *Ibid.*, p. 136.

21 Inis L. Claude, Jr., *Power and International Relations*. New York: Random House, 1962, pp. 11–39.
22 A. F. K. Organski, *World Politics*. New York: Knopf, 1958, p. 286.
23 *Ibid.,* p. 292.
24 *Ibid.,* p. 338.
25 Morgenthau, *op. cit.,* p. 5.
26 *Ibid.,* p. 11.
27 William T. R. Fox, "The Reconciliation of the Desirable and the Possible," *The American Scholar,* Spring 1949.
28 Gabriel A. Almond, *The American People and Foreign Policy*. New York: Praeger, 1960, *passim.*
29 Cindy Ris, "Why Johnny Doesn't Know His History," *The Wall Street Journal,* October 29, 1980.
30 Peter Schmeisser, "Is America in Decline?", *The New York Times Magazine,* April 17, 1988. p. 96.

SELECTED BIBLIOGRAPHY

Arendt, Hannah. *The Origins of Totalitarianism*. New York: Harcourt, Brace, 1951. A definitive classic on the subject, with emphasis on Nazi Germany and Soviet Russia.

Isaacson, Walter, and Evan Thomas. *The Wise Men*. New York: Simon & Schuster, 1986. A brilliant portrait of the friendship of six extraordinary men—Averell Harriman, Dean Acheson, Charles Bohlen, George Kennan, John McCloy, and Robert Lovett—who helped shape the destiny of the postwar world.

Kennedy, Paul. *The Rise and Fall of the Great Powers*. New York: Random House, 1987. If a nation's military commitments greatly exceed its economic base, such a nation's power is likely to diminish relative to other nations, the author contends in this carefully documented and cogently argued book. The United States has apparently embarked on that slippery slope.

Morgenthau, Hans J., rev. by Kenneth W. Thompson. *Politics among Nations: The Struggle for Power and Peace*. 6th ed. New York: Knopf, 1985. A revision of a leading classic of the realist school of thought in international relations, first published in 1948.

Stoessinger, John G. *Crusaders and Pragmatists: Movers of Modern American Foreign Policy*. 2d ed. New York: Norton, 1985. An analysis of US foreign policy from Woodrow Wilson to Ronald Reagan in terms of two basic personality types.

Waltz, Kenneth W. *Theory of International Politics*. Reading, Mass.: Addison-Wesley, 1979. A highly sophisticated analysis of the balance of power, for the advanced reader.

PART TWO

THE INTERNATIONAL
STRUGGLE FOR POWER

THE EAST-WEST STRUGGLE

There are at the present time two great nations in the world, which started from different points, but seem to tend toward the same end. I allude to the Russians and the Americans....Their starting point is different and their courses are not the same; yet each of them seems marked out by the will of Heaven to sway the destinies of half the globe.

Alexis de Tocqueville, *Democracy in America,* 1835

THE ROOTS OF THE COLD WAR

"No, I am not a Marxist," Karl Marx was supposed to have said shortly before his death in 1883. Today, a century later, it is even more important to separate the man from the myth. Who was the founder of communism and how did his doctrine get to Russia?

Marx was a German philosopher who was deeply disturbed by the conditions of the workers in mid-nineteenth-century Europe. There were reasons for his outrage. Sweatshops, child labor, and starvation wages were the order of the day. Unions did not exist nor did profit-sharing plans. Together with his collaborator, Friedrich Engels, Marx published the *Communist Manifesto* in 1848. Its clarion call, "workers of the world unite, you have nothing to lose but your chains," has echoed down to our time. Marx believed that workers had no homeland since nations were simply the representatives of capitalists whose only goal was to accumulate ever more wealth. Workers, therefore, would engage in a global "class struggle," and the time would come when, in a spontaneous revolution, they would throw off the capitalist yoke and establish a socialist state. In such a state, the workers would own the means of production. In his famous book, *Capital,* published in 1867, Marx asserted that these developments would have to happen, that they were indeed inevitable. History moved forward through a process of challenge and response, and its great turning points came about through economic forces. This "dialectical materialism" would ultimately usher in the victory of communism in which struggle would cease and men and women would live harmoniously in a "classless society."

Marx believed that the revolution would strike first in the most highly industrialized countries where the misery of the working classes was the greatest: Germany and England. This was not to be, however. In Russia, at the turn of the century, a young seminarian named V. I. Lenin was scarred for life when his brother was executed by the secret police for plotting to assassinate the Tsar. Lenin embraced the ideas of Karl Marx, but with a crucial difference. He did not believe that a workers' revolution would ever happen spontaneously. It would have to be organized by a "dictatorship of the proletariat" made up of professional revolutionaries who dedicated their lives to the cause. There would have to be iron discipline and strict obedience to authority. Lenin soon became the spokesman for these men and women and had to go into exile with a price upon his head. During World War I, he found himself in Germany working for the revolution. The German High Command, however, fighting the British and French in the West and the Russians in the East, proposed a deal to Lenin instead. It would smuggle him into Finland in a sealed train and help him finance the Russian revolution if Lenin would promise to take Russia out of the war with Germany. Lenin agreed and was dropped into Russia like a time bomb in the spring of 1917. By that time, the Tsar had abdicated and a provisional government under Alexander Kerensky had assumed control. Lenin agitated against Kerensky, promising "land to the peasants, factories to the workers, and an end to the war." Not surprisingly, he was successful and in October, in a determined coup, his men toppled the Kerensky government and took over the reins of power. Thus, it came about that a German philosopher inspired a Russian student for the priesthood to spark the Bolshevik Revolution. The world has not been the same since that event.

For more than forty years, the East-West struggle hovered over us all like a "brooding omnipresence in the sky." It became so much a part of our daily lives that we virtually came to accept it as an axiom of international relations. While its presence and fearful implications were obvious to all, its causes were far from simple. It is to these that we must first address ourselves.

It is tempting to explain the genesis of the East-West struggle purely in terms of the expansionary zeal of Communist ideology. Indeed, a fairly good case can be made for such a position. Marxism, with its prediction that the "expropriated" would expropriate the "expropriators" on an international scale, envisaged world revolution as its ultimate goal. Leninism fashioned a network of Communist parties—the Comintern—to "give history a push" and hasten the day of Communist victory. This inherent aggressiveness of the

Communist ideology, emanating from the Soviet Union as its citadel and directing center, elicited protective countermeasures in the West. These, in turn, generated suspicions of "capitalist encirclement" in the Soviet Union. Suspicion begot countersuspicion, gradually drawing East and West into a vicious circle. And thus the East-West struggle was launched.

A moment's reflection shows that this description of the "cold war," though tempting, is all too simple. It does not explain the fact that the Soviet Union on many occasions pushed forward its frontiers for reasons other than ideology. For example, it could hardly be said that the absorption of part of Poland and of the Baltic states in the wake of the Nazi-Soviet Pact of 1939 was the result of Communist ideology. Nor could it be assumed without question that the extension of American influence in Europe and Asia during World War II was purely a countermove to Communist expansion. Even a cursory inspection suggests that the East-West struggle may have some of its roots in geographic, historical, or cultural factors. This is not to say that ideology is not important. But the first and crucial question which we must ask is *how much* of the East-West struggle is rooted in the expansionary zeal of Communist ideology?

As one careful scholar of Soviet foreign policy has pointed out, it is a striking fact that Russian expansion can often be explained without reference to Marxist-Leninist ideological factors. For example.

> In the Second World War the Soviets could scarcely have permitted their Anglo-American partners to extend Western influence into all sections of the power vacuum created by the Axis defeat. American expansion in both Europe and Asia has often been hesitant and reluctant. Nevertheless, the war ended with an American general in Berlin and another in Tokyo. This the Soviets could hardly afford to neglect.[1]

It is, of course, impossible to determine the exact contribution of Communist ideology to Soviet expansion. But a perusal of Soviet foreign policy suggests that ideology alone did not prompt the Soviet Union to join or to break any alliance that it would not have joined or broken on the grounds of national interest. There are indications, however, that ideology in some cases retarded the shift or speeded up the change. Certainly, Marxism compounded the difficulties besetting the Grand Alliance during World War II and contributed to its disintegration. Lenin's strategy of Communist party infiltration, put to work so effectively in Eastern Europe following World War II, no doubt hastened the coming of the cold war. This "residual" quality of ideology has had one very important result:

> ...the Marxist-Leninist tradition has made it very difficult to reach a *modus vivendi* with the Soviets, which the Americans have been genuinely anxious to do. A belief in the inherently aggressive tendencies of modern capitalism obviously excludes any agreement except an armed truce of undetermined duration. Likewise, the acceptance of the Leninist theory makes it almost impossible to believe in the friendly intentions of American leaders.[2]

Hence, the Soviet perception of the West is to some degree, at least, colored by the lenses of ideology. And to the extent that this has been the case, the Soviet Union has, in effect, been struggling not so much with the West itself as with its ideologically conditioned image of the West.

More broadly, ideology has lent a Jekyll-and-Hyde quality to Soviet behavior vis-à-vis the West. In one sense, the Soviet Union has de-emphasized ideology and has acted as a nation among nations: it has made and broken alliances with Western nations; it has used diplomacy as an instrument of its national policy; and it has participated in the League of Nations and the United Nations. But on another level, the Soviet Union has always considered itself as the citadel of a revolutionary ideology destined ultimately to dominate the world. Thus, while ideology cannot be considered *the* cause of Soviet expansion and, hence, of the East-West struggle, it is clearly one very important cause.

There are other possible explanations for Soviet expansion that deserve analysis. First, it is often asserted that authoritarian states, by the very nature of their being, have need of an external enemy in order to deflect the frustrations of the population from the government to an external scapegoat. While there is some psychological truth in this claim, it cannot be carried too far. Authoritarian Sparta, for example, had no more expansionary zeal than its ''democratic'' counterpart, Athens. Nor did authoritarian Japan attack the United States in the nineteenth century; it was democratic America that forced open the door of Japan. We cannot demonstrate empirically that authoritarian regimes are by necessity more aggressive than democracies. Nor can the oft-asserted claim be validated that a good part of Soviet expansion is due to a power drive in the personalities of the Soviet leadership. Another explanation is sometimes sought in historical and geographic factors. Thus, some scholars maintain that Soviet expansion is merely a continuation of Tsarist aggrandizement and that certain Soviet territorial claims have their roots in the historical Russian strategic interest in warm-water ports. While it may well be that Soviet leadership derives some of its inspiration from the expansionist dreams of Tsarism, it is important to bear in mind that though history can teach by analogy, it never repeats itself exactly. The roots of Soviet expansionism must therefore equally be sought in what the men in the Kremlin believe to be the needs and opportunities of their country's contemporary situation. There is no doubt, for example, that economic factors enter into the picture. The Soviet absorption of most of Eastern Europe in the wake of World War II is generally agreed to have been dictated in some measure at least by very conscious economic considerations.

In sum, then, Soviet expansion cannot be explained in terms of any single-factor analysis. Its roots must be seen in a syndrome of forces among which are ideological and economic considerations, as well as factors of historical and geographic continuity. It is quite possible, although this cannot be demonstrated, that ideology constitutes the most important single element in this syndrome.

The temptation to explain American world strategy during and after World War II purely in terms of countermoves to Soviet expansionism is almost as great as the temptation to explain the latter exclusively in terms of Marxist-Leninist ideology. Yet here again we must beware of the pitfall of the single-factor analysis. No doubt there is much truth in such an interpretation of American policies, but it explains only part of the picture. Over a century before the cold war developed, the great De Tocqueville predicted its coming. Indeed, as one scholar has pointed out:

> Well before 1945 the map of the world suggested the primacy of America and of Russia. Already by 1850 the United States formed one of the greatest land empires of the globe, stretching from the Atlantic to the Pacific and from the Canadian frontier to the Gulf of Mexico and the Caribbean Sea; already by 1800 the Russian Empire, stretching from Manchuria to Warsaw, covered over one-sixth of the entire land of our globe. Already by 1850 there were as many Russians as there were Frenchmen and Englishmen and Germans; already by 1890 there were more Americans than Frenchmen and Englishmen together; already by 1900 the United States produced more steel than any other country in the world; already during the First World War the financial wealth of the world shifted to America. Well before 1945 the United States and Russia were becoming the two largest Empires in the history of mankind.[3]

It is true that the United States had liquidated many of its possessions by the end of World War II. By 1946 the Philippines were given their independence and the remaining American possessions were being steadily prepared for self-government or statehood. On the other hand, it is quite clear that World War II had broadened the United States' perception of its strategic interests. Soon after hostilities had ended in Europe, the entire North Atlantic, from the Azores to Iceland and Greenland, had come within the sphere of American influence. And as a result of the occupation of Japan, the Pacific was transformed into what was virtually an American strategic lake. Indeed, World War II had created several power vacuums which the United States had decided to fill long before the cold war actually crystallized.

A number of "revisionist" scholars have gone even further and have actually blamed the United States for the outbreak of the cold war. Gar Alperowitz, in his *Atomic Diplomacy,* for example, argued that the United States, using its atomic monopoly, tried to push the Soviet Union out of Europe, and Gabriel Kolko, in his *Politics of War,* advanced the thesis that American capitalist society was, by its very nature, expansionistic. One does not have to be a Marxist, however, to appreciate the fact that the United States was not entirely blameless. The Soviet Union lost more than twenty million men during World War II. Yet Franklin D. Roosevelt twice postponed the creation of a second front against the Nazis in Europe, thus forcing the Russians to take the brunt of the German assault. Little wonder that Stalin was highly suspicious of American postwar intentions and tried to place as much territory as possible between Germany and Russia by the creation of Communist governments in Eastern Europe. It is thus not unreasonable to claim that *both* the United States and the Soviet Union share the responsibility for the origins of the cold war.

Perhaps the most intelligent comment on the roots of the cold war came from Mikhail Gorbachev. "Let historians argue who is more and who is less to blame for it," he declared at the United Nations in December 1988.[4] We might let the matter rest there and turn to the more productive task of analyzing the actual dynamics of the superpower struggle in our time.

THE DYNAMICS OF THE UNITED STATES-SOVIET-CHINA STRUGGLE

Phase One: The Comintern and the West, 1917–1949

When the Soviet Union emerged from the Bolshevik Revolution of 1917 it was largely guided in its relations with the West by the tenets of Marxism-Leninism. Indeed, Lenin proclaimed a complete divorce from the past. The new Soviet Union was to be a revolutionary society that would spread the Communist idea to other lands, beginning with the highly industrialized nations of the West. The first three years of the new state's existence, known as the period of War Communism, were a time of great ferment. Though engaged in a murderous civil war, the Soviet Union embarked on a program of ambitious experimentation in virtually every field of human endeavor. The Communist party assumed complete control of all political activity; the Komsomol (Soviet Youth Movement) was organized; industry was nationalized; atheism became official dogma; marriage was regarded as unnecessary; and education was completely reoriented. In its relations with the Western powers, the new Soviet government repudiated most of the debts contracted by its predecessor. It announced that within a short time the revolutionary tidal wave of communism would engulf the West as well. According to the Soviet leaders, there were omens and portents to justify this prediction: some of the Western nations, especially England and Germany, had reached the point of "capitalist concentration," a reliable signal of impending doom. Moreover, Lenin was confident that the struggle of these nations for colonies in World War I was a final and desperate maneuver to prevent their imminent collapse. To hasten this process, Lenin instructed the Comintern, which over a period of fifteen years had been built into a formidable revolutionary instrument, to concentrate its activity on Germany and England. This network of Communist parties was controlled unequivocally though clandestinely by the Communist party of the Soviet Union. Lenin's tenet of unquestioning obedience to the leadership of the Soviet Union was its governing organizational principle.

The West's reaction was a mixture of awe and terror. Many Western intellectuals were sincerely attracted by the bold new Soviet experiment. But the vast majority among the peoples of Western Europe and the United States recoiled from the "Red Terror." In the United States stringent security measures were taken; under Attorney General A. Mitchell Palmer thousands of arrests and deportations for alleged Communist subversion were made. The

Western nations broke off all diplomatic relations with the new Soviet government and intervened in the civil war on the side of the Tsarist generals. In 1918, the Soviet Union stood alone, fighting a battle for survival at home and treated as a pariah abroad.

By 1920 the Soviet government faced imminent catastrophe. Not only had the Comintern failed in its international revolutionary efforts—save for brief Communist interludes in Bavaria and Hungary—but the Soviet Union itself was in desperate straits. Nationalization did not prove to be a magic formula for a country whose resources had been sapped by a destructive civil war, nor was a thorough knowledge of Marxism a substitute for technical competence in the factory and on the farm. The withdrawal of foreign investments and credits left the Soviet Union economically ostracized and on the verge of bankruptcy. Lenin was faced with a difficult dilemma: To continue the pursuit of world revolution would almost certainly lead to the destruction of the Soviet Union itself; on the other hand, to save the Soviet Union from the specter of bankruptcy would mean the betrayal of the revolutionary ideal. Lenin, shrewd pragmatist that he was, took a middle course. He announced the formula of "One step backward in order to take two steps forward." The answer was to be found in the postponement of world revolution, not its abandonment. The struggle against the West would simply be pursued by other means. Lenin announced the New Economic Policy. Under this directive the Soviet government made an about-face in both domestic and foreign affairs. Almost all industry was denationalized, *Pravda* celebrated Soviet millionaires, social mores were tightened once again, and foreign investors were reinvited to the Soviet Union. Lenin instructed the Comintern to camouflage its tactics and adopt a policy of United Front with other leftist political parties in national parliaments. The Soviet Union concluded its first treaty in 1922—with Germany at Rapallo—and expressed interest in entering nonaggression pacts with France and Czechoslovakia. It seemed as if the Soviet Union had taken its place among the nations of the world community.

The Western world greeted the New Economic Policy with tremendous relief. Most Western observers concluded that the storm and stress period was over and that the Soviet Union had come of age. It now seemed that the "Red Terror" had been but a passing phase and that the Soviet Union had abandoned its struggle against the West. This impression was strengthened when Lenin died in 1924 and a bitter struggle for the succession left the Politburo little time or energy for the business of world revolution. Besides, both the Soviet Union and the West became increasingly apprehensive about the new threat of a remilitarized and aggressive Germany that loomed ever larger as the 1920s passed. The German Communist party, one of the most powerful in the Comintern network, found itself without effective leadership at a time when it was embattled with the National Socialist party for the control of Germany. The German population, harassed by the aftermath of a lost war and tormented by a galloping inflation, was ready to vote for political extremism of either Left or Right. The Nazi party attacked the Communists as agents of a foreign power and pointed to itself as the party of true patriots. The Communist tactic of the United Front proved unavailing and in 1933 the Nazi party assumed complete control of Germany.

The United Front technique proved equally unsuccessful in England—the second Western nation on the revolutionary timetable—when the British Communist party attempted to use a depression in the coal industry to bring England into the Communist orbit. Instead, a Liberal-Labour coalition took power. Thus, ten years after the foundation of the Soviet Union, neither the direct subversion of the early years nor the United Front of the 1920s was able to demonstrate any territorial gains for the cause of world revolution.

Stalin's accession to power in 1928 ushered in a period of complete transformation in Soviet domestic affairs. The New Economic Policy was abruptly terminated. In its place, a rigorous Five-Year Plan was announced, mobilizing the industrial and agricultural resources of the nation in order to build "socialism in one country." Stalin saw no inconsistency between this present emphasis on national power and the future goal of world revolution. The more powerful the Soviet Union was as a national state, he maintained, the better equipped it would be to export its revolutionary ideology later. But to accomplish "socialism in one country" during the 1930s, the complexion of the Soviet state underwent profound changes. Industry was nationalized once again and agriculture was forcibly collectivized in a ruthless campaign. The Communist party changed from a group of ideologues to a group of production experts; ability to overfulfill the Plan rather than a knowledge of Marxism-Leninism became the criterion of party membership. The party itself became an elite. Equality of pay was denounced as a "bourgeois superstition"; "Stakhanovites," or shock workers, were given higher wages and bonuses. In short, Stalin used Western capitalist methods to overcome the West. The goal was clear:

> To slacken the tempo of industrial growth in the Soviet Union would mean to fall behind. And those who fall behind get beaten. But we refuse to be beaten! One feature of the history of old Russia was the continual beatings she suffered for falling behind, for her backwardness. She was beaten by the Mongol khans. She was beaten by the Turkish beys. She was beaten by the Polish gentry. She was beaten by the British and French capitalists. All beat her—for her backwardness. Lenin said during the October Revolution: "Either perish—or overtake and outstrip the capitalist countries; either we do it—or they crush us."[5]

In foreign affairs, Stalin continued the policy of the United Front. A growing fear of Nazi Germany prompted him to de-emphasize Communist subversion of the Western countries. In 1936 he promulgated the so-called Stalin Constitution, which he proclaimed as the world's most democratic. The Soviet Union joined the League of Nations and its representative, Maxim Litvinov, proclaimed the USSR's adherence to the principles of collective security. The early 1930s was a fairly inactive period for the Comintern. One attempt at revolutionary coup—in France—was foiled by the French government. The growing fear of Nazism coupled with the opportunity of at last delivering one country into the orbit of the Soviet Union prompted Soviet intervention in the Spanish Civil War during the late 1930s. When Nazi intervention on the side of General Franco seemed to assure the latter's victory, Stalin decided to aid the Loyalists to redress the balance. But, in the midst of the Spanish war, the Great Purges took place in the Soviet Union. These cost the lives of many of the country's top military leaders. The Comintern, like every other Soviet power structure, was deeply affected by this gigantic bloodletting. It took its toll also in Spain and, coupled with the neutrality of the Western powers in the Spanish Civil War, gave victory to Franco by default. The Comintern had failed once again.

By 1938 Stalin felt increasingly insecure in his temporary alliance with the West. He may even have suspected that the West aimed at encouraging Hitler to strike to the East to promote a death struggle between the Soviet Union and Germany. At any rate, the Western fiasco at Munich confirmed the Soviet leader in his suspicion that an alliance with Hitler, who had just absorbed Austria and was rapidly gaining strength, would yield greater advantages. Stalin calculated that a pact with Hitler would safeguard the Nazi dictator's Eastern flank and thus give him the green light to launch an offensive against the West. Since, in Stalin's view, Nazi Germany and the West were approximately equal in strength, a mutually exhausting war would ensue that would give the Soviet Union an opportunity to grow stronger in peace and ultimately to absorb both adversaries. Besides, Stalin reasoned, a pact with Hitler would buy time and since the Great Purges had seriously weakened the Soviet military machine, time was most necessary. Moreover, the Soviet Union would at last be able to make some territorial gains: part of Poland and the three Baltic states of Latvia, Lithuania, and Estonia. Thus, in 1939, a strange alliance took shape between two incompatible dictators, and Marxism-Leninism was sacrificed on the altar of Machiavelli. As it turned out, Stalin's hopes were premised on a great miscalculation: It took Hitler not years but weeks to conquer most of Western Europe. By 1940, therefore, Stalin was dismayed to see himself confronted with a Nazi colossus preparing to break an alliance that had outlived its usefulness. Moreover, the ill-fated pact with Hitler had cost the Comintern many loyal followers who had been unable to accept the new dictum that the Nazis were to be the allies of the Soviet Union.

On June 22, 1941, Nazi troops crossed the Soviet border. Hitler vowed to dictate peace terms from the Kremlin within six weeks. As the Nazi forces advanced deep into Soviet territory, Soviet foreign policy became one desperate cry to the Western powers for help. The Allies responded with lend-lease supplies in late 1941, but refused to open an immediate second front in Europe. As a condition for further help, they insisted on the dissolution of the Comintern, since they thought it illogical to buoy up a government whose policy it was to subvert them. Accordingly, in 1943, the Comintern was dissolved.

Perhaps the greatest paradox of this phase of the East-West struggle is the fact that the Comintern was most successful at a time when the Soviet Union had reached its lowest ebb. The Communists, who had been suspect in the United Fronts of the 1920s and 1930s, were now welcomed. Their ruthless methods, which were formerly so feared, now proved a valuable asset in the common resistance against the Nazis. Communist party membership swelled again all over Western Europe. As the Red Army pursued the retreating *Wehrmacht* after the victory at Stalingrad, plans were laid for the absorption of liberated territories into the Soviet orbit. During the last two years of the war, preparations were worked out for the absorption of eight Eastern European countries. In carrying out this objective, the Soviet Union generally operated in three stages: first, a genuine anti-Nazi resistance coalition was to be formed with existing socialist and peasant parties; second, the Communist party would attempt to split the opposition parties by exploiting regional and ethnic jealousies, thereby transforming the coalition into a bogus alliance controlled by the Communist party; and finally, a coup d'état would establish complete Soviet control.

While the Soviet Union was thus preparing to take over most of Eastern Europe, American and Russian armies met in the heart of Europe, near the German town of Torgau, in April 1945. This event was the prelude to the division of Germany and most of Europe into American and Russian spheres of influence. Soon after, the first open misunderstanding arose and the "cold war" began to take shape. While the West had lowered its guard, the Soviet Union established control over seven Eastern European countries whose absorption had been prepared during the last years of the war: Albania, Bulgaria, Hungary, Poland, East Germany, Yugoslavia, and Rumania. In March 1946 Winston Churchill visited the United States and delivered his famous "Iron Curtain" speech in which he warned the West of Soviet intentions. During the following year, the United States took two specific steps to counter the Soviet challenge. In March 1947, through the Truman Doctrine, the United States took over from Britain the responsibility of protecting Greece and Turkey from communism. In June 1947 General George Marshall proposed the outline of a vast European Recovery Program at a commencement address at Harvard University. The aim of the Marshall Plan was the ultimate restoration of the economies of Europe through American aid. This aid was also offered to Eastern Europe and the Soviet Union, but Stalin refused to accept it. Relations between the Soviet Union and the United States now deteriorated rapidly. The four-power negotiations over a German peace settlement bogged down and a tougher American policy was adumbrated by George Kennan writing under the pseudonym "Mr. X" in the journal *Foreign Affairs*. Indeed, this policy of "containment" was soon to become the official American posture. In February 1948 the Soviet Union electrified the West by absorbing the eighth Eastern European country, Czechoslovakia, into the Communist orbit. In this case, all three Soviet techniques of subversion described above were employed successfully.

In the United States and Western Europe, the Communist coup in Czechoslovakia came as a most painful shock. Under its two great leaders

Thomas G. Masaryk and Eduard Beneš, Czechoslovakia had during the 1920s and 1930s become the only really well-established and sophisticated democracy in Eastern Europe. Moreover, the country had been woven into the Western political community through defense alliances with Britain and France and had received a guarantee from the Soviet Union for help against the Nazi threat provided that Britain and France would fulfill their obligations. From the Czechoslovak point of view, however, the Munich Conference of 1938, resulting in the subsequent absorption of the country by Nazi Germany, signified a complete betrayal by the Western powers of their treaty obligations. This ''Munich hangover'' played an important role in the Soviet success. The eastward orientation of Czechoslovakia was given further impetus by the fact that the Red Army liberated most of Czechoslovakia, including the capital, Prague, in 1945. Communist party membership at the conclusion of World War II was substantial. The party was instructed to exploit the regional jealousies between the Bohemians and the Slovaks. Capitalizing on its anti-Nazi record, the Communist party now claimed control of the Ministry of the Interior. By 1947 the vote for the Communist party exceeded 40 percent of the population and the Red Army surrounded four-fifths of the Republic. At this juncture, the United States offered economic aid to Czechoslovakia under the Marshall Plan, which President Beneš was eager to accept. Stalin informed the Czechoslovak government that he would take a grave view of Czech acceptance of American aid. When, after an agonizing debate, the Czechoslovak government decided to decline the American offer, the Soviet Union knew that the Czech ship of state was foundering and was no longer an independent entity. In February 1948 Soviet Deputy Foreign Minister Valerian Zorin arrived in Prague, ostensibly to supervise the delivery of Soviet wheat. During the next few days the Communists completed the take-over through a coup d'état.

The success of the Communist coup in Czechoslovakia galvanized the West into action. Twelve nations, under the leadership of the United States, formed the North Atlantic Treaty Organization (NATO), a regional defense alliance for the purpose of containing Soviet expansion. For the United States, membership in a peacetime alliance was a drastic reversal of foreign policy. The fear of the Soviet Union and its newly acquired allies now dominated political thinking in all of the Western nations. The fact that the Comintern was reconstituted by 1947 in Warsaw—although under the innocuous-sounding title of Communist Information Bureau, or Cominform—was widely interpreted in the West as a sign pointing to renewed Soviet emphasis on the goal of world revolution. The West now determined to stand fast.

The showdown came in Germany. In Berlin, the former capital, the cold war reached a point of rigidification. It will be remembered that, in 1945, Germany had been occupied by the four major victorious powers, the United States, Britain, France, and the Soviet Union. The Yalta and Potsdam Agreements of 1945 had divided Germany into four zones, three Western and one Soviet. Berlin, the former capital, was situated in the Soviet zone but was itself divided into four sectors. Under the agreements, none of the Occupation powers was to have the right to change the status quo without the consent of the others. In 1948, however, shortly after the absorption of Czechoslovakia, Stalin began to put pressure on the Western garrisons in Berlin. The Soviet administration suspended all communications between West Berlin and the Western zones of Germany. The object of this blockade was to turn West Berlin into an island and to starve it into submission. The American response was the famous Berlin Air Lift, which effectively countered the Soviet move by supplying the population of West Berlin from the air. In May 1949 the blockade was lifted.

By this time, the division of Germany as a whole had begun to be accepted as a long-time condition. Both superpowers attempted to absorb their zones of occupation into their respective orbits. The three Western zones emerged as the Federal Republic of Germany, with its capital at Bonn, and the Eastern zone was turned into a Soviet dependency. The vast majority of the German people, however, desired the reunification of their country.

The Western condition of German reunification was, in essence, a free election to be held in all of Germany. This was unacceptable to the Soviet Union because both East Berlin and West Berlin would probably opt for the West and thus remove the city from Soviet influence. Moreover, the population of all of Germany would probably prefer the West. Such a development would bring Germany within the Western orbit and extend Western influence to the Czech and Polish borders, thereby threatening Soviet control in Eastern Europe. The Soviet demand in return for granting German reunification was the neutralization of Germany and Western withdrawal from Berlin. These conditions seemed unacceptable to most Western statesmen. It was felt that the East German Communist government would then be in a position to absorb West Berlin through a process of strangulation. Moreover, the United States alleged that German neutrality would play into the hands of the Soviet Union, since American troops would withdraw across the Atlantic while the Red Army could be based in Eastern Europe and thus return at any moment to fill the power vacuum. Perhaps most important, the West feared that meeting the Soviet conditions would convince the Eastern European nations that they had been abandoned by the West and, hence, cause them to settle in the Soviet orbit for good.

The deadlock over Germany ended the first phase of the East-West struggle, which till then had still been characterized by large areas of maneuverability. It ushered in a period of increasing rigidity, in which each superpower stipulated conditions that were unacceptable to the other. This sort of relationship—mutually exclusive positions short of actual physical conflict—was to characterize the East-West struggle from then on.

At the very time that the Soviet Union encountered stiffened Western resistance in Berlin, the Soviet orbit also began to undergo internal changes with great significance for the East-West struggle. Indeed, the Czech coup was the last major Communist action in which Moscow was the absolute master of communism. For thirty years Moscow's orders had been executed without question by Communist parties everywhere. This relationship was now subjected to profound changes. In 1948, for the first time in Communist history, another Communist party defied Moscow's authority: the Yugoslav party under the leadership of Tito. Tito had always been a loyal Communist; he and his fellow partisans had distinguished themselves in guerrilla warfare against the Nazis, whom they had fought bravely and relentlessly. Stalin, however, let it be known that the Soviet Army had driven the Germans from Yugoslavia while the partisans had just engaged in mopping-up operations. Though Tito took a dim view of this version of events in Yugoslavia, the episode no doubt would have passed without major repercussions if Stalin had permitted the fulfillment of Tito's fond dream of organizing a Balkan Federation. It was Tito's desire to form an empire within an empire, with Yugoslavia exercising its rule over Albania and Bulgaria. Stalin not only scotched this ambition but proceeded to rebuke Tito for the slow advance toward collectivization in Yugoslavia. When Tito defended himself by pointing out the difficult conditions he had to face in coping with the local peasantry, Stalin threatened to send to Yugoslavia Soviet Communist inspectors who were to be paid out of Yugoslav funds. Tito interpreted this as an attack upon his control of the Yugoslav Communist party and refused to follow orders. Stalin thereupon expelled Tito from the Cominform.[6] By this act of excommunication Stalin fully expected to end Tito's political revolt—and probably his life as well. But there was to be no walk to Canossa. Instead, the West immediately offered assistance to Tito's government and Stalin decided not to crush the defector by force. Tito, though continuing to identify himself as a Communist, thenceforth refused to submit to Cominform authority. He remained suspended precariously between East and West.

Later during the same year, the Chinese Communist party came to power on the mainland of China. As we shall see in Chapter 5, this party had been ruggedly independent of Moscow's control from its very beginnings. With its formula for the organization of communism on a peasant, rather than an urban, industrial basis, it had come to power to the surprise of both the West and the Soviet Union. Though describing himself as a Communist, Mao Tse-tung, the political leader of the new China, had, in effect, developed an ideology sharply at variance with the orthodox, Moscow-directed Communist creed. What this of course meant for Stalin was that shortly after the Yugoslav fiasco, he found himself confronted with a second and similar dilemma: should he insist on the ideological conformity of Mao Tse-tung and thereby risk the defection of China from the Communist orbit? Or should he recognize the ideological deviation of the Chinese leader and thereby encourage the development of Peking as an independent Communist power center? Stalin chose the latter course and in late 1949 the Soviet Union extended recognition to the new Communist government in China.

The Yugoslav defection and the developments in China ended Moscow's unquestioned authority within the Communist orbit. By 1949 there were three centers of communism: Moscow, Belgrade, and Peking. In communism's struggle against the West, this internal transformation signified both a strength and a weakness. It portended a greater threat to the West because increased ideological flexibility could be expected to inject new life into a credo threatened by petrification. On the other hand, after 1949 the Cominform was no longer able to count on the blind obedience of its membership, which had guaranteed it such swiftness of political action in the past.

In evaluating this first phase of the East-West struggle, we can come up with at least two interesting observations. The first concerns the striking number of blunders committed by the Comintern during the 1920s and 1930s. Indeed, it did not achieve its first successes until during and immediately after World War II. Nevertheless, the Western view of the Comintern during the interwar decades for the most part remained that of an implacable foe, a kind of consummate chess master impervious to the mistakes of ordinary people. Many acts of the Comintern were seen in the West as carefully worked out and long-planned stratagems and many of its errors were interpreted as strategic retreats according to plan.

What were the reasons for this collective "inferiority complex" on the part of the West? In part, it no doubt stemmed from fear of the "built-in" expansionism of Communist ideology. But the Nazis were equally imperialistic and, moreover, were locked with the West in an all-out military conflict, which communism never was. Yet the West was more afraid of Communist than of Nazi ideology. This may be attributable to the facts that communism attacked private property and was a highly sophisticated ideology that offered something to almost everyone: an ultimate vision of humanitarianism and equality to the democrat; revolution to the revolutionary; a better life for the worker; and a sophisticated dialectic to the intellectual. Most important, it offered a coherent secular religion:

> The dictator becomes God, the only God for that matter; and the Party becomes the church. As a variant, collective leadership becomes a sort of Trinity. The central committee and the local leaders take care of polytheistic needs. The parallels could be pressed further. The point is that all the essential mundane elements of religion except the Virgin Mother are represented.[7]

One group of students even went so far as to state that communism by 1946 had become a "father image the like of which the world had never seen—harsh, revengeful, jealous, and unpredictable."[8] Something like this was implied by John Foster Dulles when he made the following statement in 1946:

> Few men in political life anywhere act without first thinking whether they will please or displease the leaders of the Soviet Union. Never in history have a few men in a single country achieved world-wide influence.[9]

Yet as we have seen, this "superman" image by no means squares with the record. The history of the Comintern until 1949 presents a mixture of failures and successes, of rational and irrational acts, and of much gross distortion of the facts of international life.

The second observation that deserves to be noted about this early phase of the East-West struggle concerns the difficulty of sorting out its "causes." The great importance of Communist ideology is clearly apparent; but it is equally clear that the cold war also grew out of the meeting between Russians and Americans in the heart of Europe at the close of World War II. Indeed, the entire pattern suggests the validity of Barrington Moore's point that it is futile to argue about the primal causes of the struggle since each move by one superpower elicited a countermove from the other. What is important is that the East-West struggle had rigidified in Europe by 1949. There was virtually no maneuverability left as power confronted concerted counterpower. Thus, it was no accident that the major arena of the East-West struggle during the next decade shifted away from Europe. And the rise of China as an independent power center in the Communist orbit helped move this arena to East Asia.

Phase Two: The Rise of China

Napoleon was once reported to have said, "Let China sleep; when she awakens, the world will be sorry." These were prophetic words. During the last century the impact of the colonial West first awakened China from its traditional past. That awakening has resulted in the modern Communist regime of Peking today. The events in this development excellently illustrate how closely the two great political conflicts of our time are connected.

It is a significant fact, frequently not realized in the West, that ours is the first century in over four thousand years in which China does not consider itself to be at the center of the universe. The Chinese Empire was also known as the Middle Kingdom. For over four millennia it conceived of itself as the hub of civilization, the great school of the world—much as Athens had once considered itself to be the school of the ancient Mediterranean world. Although dynasties came and went, the political structure of the empire remained essentially static. The emperor, aided by a small intellectual elite, controlled the government. Insofar as the large mass of the population was concerned, this government was an amorphous force, inscrutable and unpredictable. The emperor ruled by the Mandate of Heaven, and his edicts had the authority of the philosopher-king. The Socratic dictum "virtue is knowledge" could have been the motto of the Confucian scholars, or "mandarins," whose major qualification for government office was a knowledge of the great literary classics of the empire. Admission to government posts was not decided by imperial fiat or arbitrary violence, but through the institution of a highly formalized system of civil service examinations held in the capital. These examinations, open to all, were the first of their kind in history.

The world beyond the Great Wall of China did not hold much interest since, in the eyes of the Chinese, it was populated by barbarians. Hence, the foreign relations of the empire were in essence tributary relationships: long caravans laden with gifts for the emperor would weave their way across the land to the Imperial Court at Peking; the envoy would kowtow before the Son of Heaven, present the tribute, and hope for the favor of being permitted to trade with the great empire. The arts of war and the use of violence were not held in high esteem in the Confucian ethos. The Chinese believed that since it was perfectly evident that their empire was a superior civilization, it would be in the interest of all barbarians to learn from it rather than destroy it. The military preparedness of the empire was therefore limited to defense against intermittent incursions by barbarians into China's territory.

This self-sufficient and almost static society had virtually no contact whatsoever with the West. The travels of Marco Polo in the twelfth century and the Jesuit mission of Father Matthew Ricci in the sixteenth were of too brief duration to create a lasting impression. The first massive Western impact occurred in the eighteenth century, when the British in their quest for more lucrative trade became intent upon establishing trade relations with the empire. The Chinese, significantly enough, attempted to fit these British overtures into their traditional tributary framework. When, in 1793, a British trade mission led by Lord Macartney arrived at Peking, it was labeled as a tributary mission from the King of England. In exchange for the privilege of presenting his gifts, Lord Macartney was expected to kowtow, that is, to perform three kneelings and nine prostrations before the emperor. When the British Lord objected to this procedure, he was politely requested to go home, although his tribute was graciously accepted. Shortly thereafter the emperor sent an Imperial Edict to the King of England. This document is so significant that parts of it deserve to be quoted:

> You, O King, are so inclined toward our civilization that you have sent a special envoy across the seas to bring to our Court your memorial of congratulations on the occasion of my birthday and to present your native products as an expression of your thoughtfulness. On perusing your memorial, so simply worded and sincerely conceived, I am impressed by your genuine respectfulness and friendliness and greatly pleased.
>
> The Celestial Court has pacified and possessed the territory within the four seas. Its sole aim is to do its utmost to achieve good government and to manage political affairs, attaching no value to strange jewels and precious objects. The various articles presented by you O King, this time are accepted by my special order to the office in charge of such functions in consideration of the offerings having come from a long distance with sincere good wishes. As a matter of fact, the virtue and prestige of the Celestial Dynasty having spread far and wide, the kings of the myriad nations come by land and sea with all sorts of precious things. Consequently there is nothing we lack, as your principal envoy and others have themselves observed. We have never set much store on strange or ingenious objects, nor do we need any more of your country's manufactures.... [10]

There was one commodity, however, for which the British did find a market in China, and a lucrative one indeed: opium. Large quantities of opium were brought into China by traders of the British East India Company and in the early nineteenth century over one million Chinese became addicted to the poison. The emperor became increasingly perturbed and authorized one of his mandarins to appeal to the conscience of the British ruler to discontinue the smuggling of opium into China. One of his officials, Commissioner Lin, sent a poignant note of protest to Queen Victoria in 1839, at a time when the use of the drug threatened to undermine the health of the entire population. This protest is an historic document:

> We find that your country is sixty or seventy thousand li [three li make one mile, ordinarily] from China. Yet there are barbarian ships that strive to come here for trade for the purpose of making a profit. The wealth of China is used to profit the barbarians. That is to say, the great profit made by barbarians is all taken from the rightful share of China. By what right do they then in return use the poisonous drug to injure the Chinese people? Even though the barbarians may not necessarily intend to do us harm, yet in coveting profit to an extreme, they have no regard for injuring others. Let us ask, where is your conscience? I have heard that the smoking of opium is very strictly forbidden by your country; that is because the harm caused by opium is clearly understood. Since it is not permitted to do harm to your own country, then even less should you let it be passed on to the harm of foreign countries—how much less to China! Of all that China exports to foreign countries, there is not a single thing which is not beneficial to people; they are of benefit when eaten, or of benefit when used, or of benefit when resold; all are beneficial. Is there a single article from China which has done any harm to foreign countries? Take tea and rhubarb, for example; the foreign countries cannot get along for a single day without them. If China cuts off these benefits with no sympathy for those who are to suffer, then what can the barbarians rely upon to keep themselves alive?[11]

The request went unheeded and finally Commissioner Lin decided to take strong action. He issued orders to blockade British merchants at Canton and to destroy their opium. The British interpreted this seizure as an interference with freedom of trade and as an act of aggression. Instead of ending the smuggling of opium, Commissioner Lin precipitated the Opium war. This war was little more than a skirmish, settled by the Treaty of Nanking in 1842. The war itself, which signified the first violent contact between China and the West, showed how distorted were the perceptions that the two sides held of each other. The British, surprised by the weak show of resistance exhibited by the Chinese, interpreted this weakness as a surrender and proceeded to advance up the coast to occupy all the major coastal ports of China. The Chinese, on the other hand, with a few exceptions like Commissioner Lin himself, firmly believed that the British, like other barbarians before them, would recognize the self-evident superiority of Chinese civilization and behave accordingly. The Treaty of Nanking, marking the beginning of Western imperialism in China, was thus a surprise to both sides: to the Chinese because they found themselves unable to eject the "barbarians" by moral persuasion; to the British because they encountered almost no effective military resistance.

   The first massive Western influence on China, therefore, was one of violent intrusion. It now remained for the West to consolidate its position in the empire. This was accomplished through a series of arrangements known as the "unequal treaties," which gradually divested the Chinese Empire of its territorial integrity. The British were quickly followed by other Western nations, who were lured to China by the British example: French, Portuguese, and German colonizers attempted to negotiate similarly advantageous treaties with the empire. The empire had little choice but to grant the foreigners extensive concessions, with the result that by the mid-1840s China's sovereignty was little more than a fiction. The ominous and omnipresent threat of Western gunboats and superior military techniques were simply more than the old China could effectively resist.

The treaties which carved up China among the Western powers all had certain elements in common. First, there was the legal device of extraterritoriality. Under this system, foreigners in China were not subject to Chinese law but remained under the jurisdiction of their own governments. Many desirable sites on Chinese soil, including most residential areas in the large Chinese cities, were made inaccessible to the Chinese. Thus the Chinese suddenly found themselves in the incredible position of not being permitted to enter the choicest buildings and parks in their own cities unless permitted by a "barbarian" to do so. China's foreign trade and its customs and tariff policy were placed under the control of an Englishman, Inspector General Sir Robert Hart. One of the most anomalous consequences of this one-sided treaty system was the influx of Christianity into China. The picture of Christian missionaries attempting to repair the ravages of opium addiction caused by their conationals became a source of additional confusion.

The most important single feature of the unequal treaty system was the so-called "most-favored nations clause." Professor John K. Fairbank, a leading American authority on China, has called this "the neatest diplomatic device of the nineteenth century." The clause simply meant that all Western nations would participate in whatever any one of them could obtain. For example, if Germany was able to persuade China to give it a ninety-nine-year lease on an important port, all of the other Western powers had the automatic right to similarly favorable leaseholds. This rule of the "highest common denominator" made it a foregone conclusion that by mid-nineteenth century the entire coastal area of China, including its most important cities, were virtually in the hands of the West.

The rise of Chinese nationalism, including its culmination in the Communist Revolution, must be understood in terms of this initial Western impact. During the past century, China has undergone five major convulsions: the Great Peasant Rebellion, the Boxer Rebellion, the Self-Strengthening Movement, the Nationalist Revolution, and the Communist Revolution. Each of these has been in essence a desperate attempt to regain national status, and each has its roots in the Western policy of imperialism mounted against China a little over a century ago. We shall now analyze each of these five nationalist movements.

The Great Peasant Rebellion of 1851 was one of the great social upheavals of modern times. It marked the first time in the history of the empire that the Chinese population was politically activated en masse. An estimated twenty million people lost their lives in the course of this fifteen-year rebellion. Its leader, Hung, was a disappointed office-seeker. He claimed to have experienced a vision in which a venerable sage exhorted him to save humanity. Hung began to play on the population's fear of the "foreign devils" and its impatience and disgust with the tottering empire which seemed to be at the mercy of the "barbarians." Hung vowed to unseat the bankrupt Manchu government and ultimately to eject the foreigners. He began to describe himself as "the younger brother of Jesus" and developed a philosophy incorporating tenets of Christianity and an ambitious program of agrarian reform. Millions of peasants supported his cause. Many believed that Hung had the Mandate of Heaven for a new dynasty that would displace the weak and discredited Manchus. Many peasants were also deeply fearful of the foreigners. For example, the foreigners built railroads and suspended wires in the air; when it rained, these wires would rust and reddish drops would fall onto the ground; the Chinese peasants believed that these reddish drops were the blood of the good spirits which had impaled themselves on the wires cunningly placed there by the foreign devils. A terrible famine gave the rebellion its final impetus. Millions of peasants began to advance rapidly toward Peking, led by Hung, who vowed to establish his strange theocracy. By the mid-1850s, the rebels were in control of half of China. The Manchu government as well as the Western powers on the coast became increasingly terrified. In desperation the Manchus formed an alliance with the foreigners in order to present a united front against the rebels. The battle seesawed back and forth for an entire decade. Finally, the imperial forces, buttressed by modern arms and aided by foreign military leaders, were able to stem the rebellion. Hung committed suicide in 1864 and his death marked the defeat of the Great Peasant Rebellion.

This first reaction to the impact of Western imperialism is interesting for several reasons. The rebellion was the first example of popular nationalism in China and proved so powerful that only an alliance between the Manchu government and its worst enemy was able to crush it. It was in effect the first mass movement in China's history and, in historical perspective, was clearly a forerunner of the Communist Revolution.

China's second attempt to rid herself of the West was the pathetic and ill-fated Boxer Rebellion of 1900. The Manchu dynasty, which had received a new lease on life, decided on a show of force. The Boxers, fanatical members of anti-Western secret societies who believed themselves to be invulnerable, decided to besiege the foreign community in its own legations in Peking. For two months in the summer of 1900 most foreign officials were the prisoners of the Boxers. The suicidal futility of this venture became apparent when reinforcements arrived and the Western plenipotentiaries and their families were liberated. Retribution was swift: the leaders of the rebellion were executed and a heavy indemnity was exacted from the Chinese treasury. This second attempt at nationalist revolt was an utter and dismal failure.

During the second half of the nineteenth century it became increasingly clear to many Chinese intellectuals that their entire way of life was being undermined by the firepower of foreign arms and by superior Western technology. The Peasant and Boxer rebellions, though very different, had proven equally futile because of China's backward state of military development. As a typical example of this state of affairs, in Fairbank's words, "the British had used on the coast of China a shallow bottomed paddle-wheel iron steamer called the *Nemesis*. It carried swivel cannon fore and aft and was capable of moving into the wind and against the tide in a manner disastrous to China's fortunes."[12] The realization of China's inadequacy vis-à-vis the West led to the development of the so-called Self-Strengthening Movement, which spanned the latter half of the nineteenth century. The premise of the movement was a simple one: "Chinese learning as the fundamental structure, Western learning for practical use."[13] Its leaders felt that the only way of restoring the national status of China was for the Chinese themselves to utilize Western science and military techniques. In short, some of the ways of the foreigner would have to be copied in order to get rid of him. Accordingly, shipyards, arsenals, and science academies began to flourish. The Self-Strengtheners emphasized, over and over again, that this Western technology must be used to preserve Chinese values, not to destroy them. Thus, for example, Chinese students were sent to the West but were always accompanied by Confucian chaperones who made sure that these future leaders of China would not be infected by Western ideas. The fallacy of the Self-Strengthening Movement lay in its assumption that knowledge and life could be neatly compartmentalized, that one could adopt the tools of the West but totally ignore its values, that one could leap into the modern world only halfway. Inevitably, "one Western borrowing led to another, from machinery to technology, from science to all learning, from acceptance of new ideas to change of institutions, eventually from constitutional reform to republican revolution."[14] In the last analysis, the principal net effect of the Self-Strengthening Movement was to prepare the ground for the Nationalist Revolution of 1911.

One of the outstanding leaders of the Self-Strengthening Movement was Dr. Sun Yat-sen, destined to become the leader of the Nationalist Revolution. The life of Dr. Sun affords a fascinating case study of a revolutionary. He was born in Portuguese Macao, received his education in an English school, and was converted to Christianity early in life. He decided to study medicine in Hong Kong, where he came under the influence of a British missionary doctor, Sir James Cantlie. Cantlie acquainted the young Sun Yat-sen with Western ways ranging from the study of physics to the playing of cricket. Sun received his medical degree and hoped to set up practice as a surgeon in Macao. The Portuguese, however, debarred him from practice in his own country. Subsequently Dr. Sun abandoned his new profession and embarked on a revolutionary career. Between 1894 and 1911 he organized revolutionary sentiment against both the tottering Manchu dynasty and the Western powers. Like Lenin, he lived in exile with a price upon his head and relentlessly worked for the cause of revolution. At one point, in 1896, during a stay in London, he was abducted and imprisoned in the Chinese legation for shipment back to China and certain death. He managed to inform Sir James Cantlie, who lived nearby, of his plight. Cantlie mobilized Scotland Yard and Sun was saved through British intervention. From this time onward, Sun was recognized as the undisputed leader of the Nationalist Revolutionary Movement.

It was during this incubation period of the revolution that Dr. Sun developed his philosophy of the "Three Principles of the People": Nationalism, Democracy, and the People's Livelihood. This concept went beyond the philosophy of the Self-Strengthening Movement; Sun insisted that in order to become free, China would have to borrow not only science but ideas as well. Sun's first principle of Nationalism simply meant "China for the Chinese." Democracy, as conceived by him, was to be an amalgam of American, British, and Swiss constitutional principles. And the People's Livelihood stood for a gradualist program of socialism patterned after the example of the Fabians in Britain. Armed with this synthesis of Western political thought, Dr. Sun Yat-sen engineered ten revolutionary attempts against the Manchu government, all of which failed. Finally, in October of 1911, Sun went to the United States to raise funds for his cause. During his campaign he received a coded cable which he was unable to decipher because he had shipped his code book ahead. As it turned out, the cable contained news of yet another plot. This time the plot was successful. A few days later, on October 10, 1911, Sun Yat-sen read in the newspapers that a Nationalist Revolution had broken out in China and that he was to be the first president of the new Republic.

It now remained for Sun to consolidate the Nationalist Revolution. This was by no means an easy task. With the collapse of imperial authority, China was now controlled by numerous warlords who were unwilling to yield to Sun Yat-sen's demand for unification under the Nationalist banner. The revolution seemed abortive. The warlords were not receptive to Sun's new ideas of parliamentary democracy, for these were wholly alien to the authoritarian tradition in which the empire had been ruled for centuries. Moreover, they refused to reconcile their parochial interests with the national programs of the revolution. In 1912, as a result, Sun resigned as president and it seemed that the Nationalist Revolution had foundered on the rock of warlordism. Yet Sun continued to work for his ideal and, in desperation, approached the Western powers, pleading with them for aid in his struggle for national unification. The response, however, was negative, partly because a divided China was preferred by the West and partly because the energies of the great powers were primarily engaged in Europe, which was drifting toward the brink of war.

Western indifference to Sun Yat-sen during this period helped to direct the course of Chinese nationalism toward authoritarianism. Sun turned away from the West in disappointment and became increasingly disillusioned with parliamentary democracy as a way toward unification. It was no accident that when, at this critical moment in the fortunes of Chinese nationalism, another vast revolution took place—that in Russia in 1917—Sun looked toward the newly formed Soviet Union. To his amazement he saw that the Bolsheviks were able to subdue a country larger than China in a relatively short space of time, whereas China, a decade after the revolution, still lay prostrate at the mercy of the warlords. It was at this moment that Chinese nationalism began to look to communism for inspiration. Sun Yat-sen had found Lenin.

Both Lenin and Sun Yat-sen were professional revolutionaries, yet no two men could have differed more. Sun Yat-sen was a Christian and by temperament inclined toward parliamentarianism rather than the use of violence; Lenin was a tough, shrewd revolutionary strategist who firmly believed that only a tightly organized, blindly obedient party could accomplish the goals of revolution.

The Bolshevik success induced Sun Yat-sen to accept Lenin's advice and organize a Nationalist party, the Kuomintang, patterned on authoritarian principles. Soviet advisors, most prominent among whom was the Comintern agent Michael Borodin, helped in the organization of the new Nationalist party at Nanking. By 1924 the Nationalist party apparatus was sufficiently permeated with Communists that China could have been absorbed into the Communist orbit without much difficulty. But in that year Lenin died and during the remainder of the 1920s the energies of Soviet leaders were absorbed in a brutal struggle for succession.[15] As a result, though China seemed to lie within their grasp, none of the Soviet leaders gave it much attention. As Stalin put it, when the time came, the Soviet Union would "squeeze the Chinese Nationalists like a lemon."

In 1925 Dr. Sun Yat-sen died. Unlike Lenin, who had not groomed a successor for his mantle, Sun had prepared one of his most brilliant disciples to follow in his footsteps. This man was Chiang Kai-shek, a young military leader who had been sent by Sun to the Soviet Union for study, to acquaint himself with Soviet political and military techniques. When Chiang Kai-shek took over the leadership of the Nationalist Revolution, he was quite aware of the Comintern's plans to absorb China. He decided to "squeeze the lemon" first. Using techniques that he had learned from the Communists, Chiang Kai-shek decided to stage a workers' strike. He then blamed this strike on the Communists in his own party and used it as an excuse to purge them ruthlessly from the Kuomintang, forcing them on the famous "Long March," which was to last seven years and was to take them to the other end of China.

By 1930 Chiang Kai-shek, having assumed the title of generalissimo, was at the zenith of his power. He had expelled the Communists and was now able to embark on his goal of unification of all of China, the first aim of the Nationalist Revolution. He announced that China was to be under the political tutelage of the Nationalist party until conditions became stable enough to make possible the transition to constitutional democracy.

Under the leadership of the generalissimo, the new Nationalist government made a determined effort to rid itself of the unequal treaties with the West. Chiang Kai-shek mapped out his program in his book, *China's Destiny,* in which he blamed most of the ills of China on Western imperialism. He announced a "Rights Recovery Movement" and a "New Life Movement." The former was a plan gradually to wipe out extraterritoriality, Western customs control, and the foreign concessions in the major Chinese cities. The latter was an attempt to restore the old Confucian virtues which had been displaced by the West. The Kuomintang was to serve as the instrument of the generalissimo's will.

Chiang Kai-shek's nationalism was in essence an attempt to revive the past and the tradition of the empire. It was a somewhat modernized version of the old imperial hope that government by Confucian precept and example would restore China to its rightful place of centrality in the comity of nations. The party ruled in an almost completely authoritarian manner, providing little opportunity for popular participation in government. The lesson of the Great Peasant Rebellion was forgotten; once more the peasant was virtually disfranchised and little attempt was made to ease his lot through land reform. The New Life Movement was symbolic of the Kuomintang approach: the anomalous picture of old greybeards preaching the restoration of Confucius to impatient university students brimming with the excitement of new ideas and yearning for a whole new way of life.

Moreover, Chiang Kai-shek's conservative nationalist program was never really tested in time of peace. In 1931 the country was attacked by Japan and after 1937 the Nationalist government had to bear the brunt of the full fury of the new Japanese imperialism. In the face of this deadly threat, Chiang Kai-shek was compelled to suspend his domestic programs and to employ almost his entire resources in the battle for national survival. Even so, the invaders succeeded in capturing the capital at Nanking and forcing Chiang Kai-shek to relocate the seat of his government in the mountains of the interior, at Chungking.

Meanwhile, the few thousand Chinese Communists who arrived exhausted in Yenan in 1934 appeared destined for oblivion. Chiang Kai-shek had turned his attention to the Japanese and the Comintern had written them off as hopeless. But during the Long March a new and tenacious leadership had emerged which was ultimately to bring the Communists to a complete national victory. Mao Tse-tung, surely one of the most complex figures of our time—a mixture of scholar, poet, party organizer, and military strategist—took command. The redoubtable leader Chu Teh became responsible for military operations; and Chou En-lai, the most cosmopolitan of the three, took charge of the Chinese Communists' foreign relations.

Yenan in the mid-1930s provided a privileged sanctuary to the Communists. The first American reporter to visit them there in 1936 described the startling contrast between the electric atmosphere of optimism prevailing in Yenan and the dank smell of defeat in Chiang Kai-shek's wartime capital.[16] It was during this period that Mao Tse-tung worked out the program whereby his Communist forces were to take over the leadership of Chinese nationalism. For one thing, the Chinese Communist party completely emancipated itself from control by Moscow and thereby became the only Communist party in the world that was independent of the Soviet Union from the very beginning of its rise to power. Mao Tse-tung embarked on an important ideological deviation by declaring that in China, communism would have to be built on an agrarian rather than an industrial base. "Just as fish cannot live without water," he said, "communism in China cannot survive without the support of the peasants."

The second significant aspect of Mao's program was his strategy of attempting to win the allegiance of the peasantry by capitalizing on the economic and social inadequacies of the Chiang Kai-shek government. Mao Tse-tung promised an extensive land reform program and pledged that no Communist soldier would be permitted to live off the land, that indeed the Communist soldier should be considered as the friend of the peasant. The Communists organized festivals and dances to woo the peasantry and gained thousands of recruits. Their great opportunity came in 1936. Chiang Kai-shek, badly pressed by the Japanese, was being beseeched by his officers to form a United Front with the Chinese Communists against the common enemy. When he refused, he was kidnapped by some of his own military leaders and forced to ask the Communists to join in the battle. As soon as he had reluctantly agreed, the Communists sallied forth from their sanctuary and swept across the countryside, picking up nearly a half million new recruits on the way. As Chiang Kai-shek had suspected, the United Front was for the Communists largely a project in self-aggrandizement. Given minimal help by the Communist Chinese Eighth Route Army, he had to fight the Japanese alone until the entrance of the Allies into the war.

This writer witnessed the liberation of Shanghai from the Japanese by Chiang Kai-shek's forces in 1945. Seldom was there a more Pyrrhic victory; the Nationalist soldiers entered the city tattered, exhausted, and demoralized, while the Communist forces stood poised only a few hundred miles away, fresh and ready for the decisive encounter. Hence the defeat of Japan did not bring peace to Chiang Kai-shek's government. Instead of being free to implement his long-postponed programs, he was compelled to mobilize his resources to attempt to block the steadily advancing armies of the Communists. In the ensuing four years of civil war, the generalissimo's fortunes steadily declined. Mediation attempts by the United States—first through Ambassador Patrick Hurley and then through General George C. Marshall—proved to be of no avail. Chiang Kai-shek refused to form a coalition government with the Communists because he feared their techniques of infiltration. Mao Tse-tung was equally unwilling to agree to a compromise because he was certain of ultimate victory. In addition to his program of economic and social reform, Mao Tse-tung now bitterly attacked the rampant corruption of the National government and proceeded to portray Chiang Kai-shek as a lackey of Western imperialism. The Nationalists, corroded by inflation, corruption, and defeat, finally had to quit the mainland in 1949 in a desperate scramble for refuge on the island of Formosa. The Mandate of Heaven passed from their hands. It was now the Communist party that assumed leadership of the new nationalism in China.

The course of these Chinese developments affords some interesting insights into the linkage of the East-West and the North-South struggles. It is clear that both the Nationalist and the Communist revolutions in China were in essence reactions against Western imperialism. The five upheavals in which this reaction became manifest were not isolated events but consecutive expressions of a continuing development. Indeed, so far as China is concerned, the East-West conflict was a direct outgrowth of the long struggle of Chinese nationalism against Western imperialism.

In the United States, which consistently supported Chiang Kai-shek, the struggle between the Nationalist government and the Chinese Communists has received much attention and aroused a great deal of emotion. It was widely believed that the two sides represented completely opposite motives and aspirations. Few Americans perceived the complex truth that the Nationalist and Communist revolutions were *both* in essence anti-Western movements and that the struggle between them was more a struggle for power between competing forms of authoritarian nationalism than a conflict between radically different ideologies. It was a measure of the extent to which Americans had failed to recognize this basic fact that during the 1950s so many people in the United States were prepared to accept the allegation that the United States had "lost" China as a result of the machinations of subversives in the American government. Though it is not within the purview of this case study to examine the problem of subversion, it must be noted that underlying this "explanation" of the recent course of Chinese history is the assumption that a handful of Americans actually had it in their power to determine the fate of the one billion people of China.

During the quarter century of nonrelations between the United States and China, most Americans regarded Chiang Kai-shek as a soldier-saint who could do no wrong. After all, he had fought the Japanese and the Communists and was a Christian. Mao Tse-tung, on the other hand, was perceived as the Communist devil in league with Stalin. This devil image of Mao Tse-tung, so prevalent in America, helps to explain why a détente between the two nations was so long in coming. When in 1954 Secretary of State John Foster Dulles refused to shake hands with Chou En-lai in Geneva, he expressed the feelings of most Americans at the time: one does not engage in commerce with the devil. Another eighteen years had to elapse before an American President shook hands with the Chinese premier, this time on Chinese soil. In truth, the similarities between Chiang Kai-shek and Mao Tse-tung over half a century had always been greater than the differences.

In conclusion, our case study demonstrates the continuity between the Nationalist and the Communist revolutions. The pattern is, in fact, a continuum: China's role in the East-West conflict actually grew out of the struggle between nationalism and Western imperialism. In this struggle for national self-assertion against the West, Communist China used the Soviet Union as an ally. There were, after all, striking elements of similarity between the old authoritarian nationalism of the Chinese Empire and the new authoritarian nationalism of the Russian Communists. Communism, like the empire, saw itself as occupying a central position in the world, almost messianic in character.

And communism, too, had its "barbarians"—the West—to be treated with contempt and derision. Communist ideology was the anti-Western cement that temporarily bound the two nations together. But once China had demonstrated its new prowess to the West, it turned against the East as well. The alliance with the Soviet Union had now outlived its usefulness. Remembering that Russia, too, had in the nineteenth century joined in the predatory policies of the Western powers, China now pressed territorial claims along the Sino-Soviet border. And by the 1980s, China had become so fearful of the Soviet Union that she forged a de facto alliance with the United States. America once more became the model and China's major hope against the Russian "barbarians." Things had come full circle.

It is perhaps well to remind ourselves again that ours has been the only century in the past four thousand years in which China has not seen itself as the center of the universe. Is it possible that communism may turn out to be the instrument that the new nationalism in China has forged for itself to restore China to the central place that she considers to be rightfully hers by the verdict of history? This may yet be the ultimate bearing that the two great power struggles of our time have on the fate of China.

Phase Three: American Détente with Russia and China

The Cuban missile crisis of 1962 represented a great turning point in Soviet-American relations. Both superpowers had gone to the edge of the nuclear abyss and turned back just in time. The narrow escape from atomic holocaust left its mark on the Soviet and American leadership alike. Slowly, the frozen hostility of cold war thawed and gave way to a less abrasive relationship characterized by greater realism and a more businesslike approach. Shopworn slogans and polemics were replaced by more objective assessments of each other's character, intent, and power. An atmosphere of confrontation slowly yielded to an attitude conducive to productive negotiations.

The first concrete result was the partial nuclear test-ban treaty, concluded in Moscow in 1963. President John F. Kennedy had called for such a ban in a major address at American University in June 1963. During the remainder of the decade, despite the rapid escalation of the Vietnamese war, Soviet-American relations gradually improved. Agreements were hammered out to prevent the spread of nuclear weapons and to insulate outer space and the ocean floors from the atomic arms race. But it was not until 1969 that the new policy was openly articulated. President Richard Nixon, newly elected, declared that an "era of negotiation" would begin and the Soviet leadership, with a wary eye on China, decided to cooperate with its great capitalist adversary. The process of gradual détente that followed marked the end of the cold war and the beginning of a new pattern of "adversary-partnership." This fundamental change in superpower relations deserves careful and systematic scrutiny.

At first, the new policy was applied selectively, primarily in two fields in which an interest in reaching agreement had been previously defined and where viable options could be identified: Berlin and arms control. The United States and the Soviet Union began talks on the status of Berlin in March 1970. While little visible progress was made during that year, the talks signaled a shift in policy toward the recognition of the status quo in Europe, a necessary prerequisite to further negotiations in this crucial arena of contention. During 1970 two rounds of Strategic Arms Limitation Talks (SALT) were convened in Vienna and in Helsinki, firmly emphasizing the interest of the two superpowers in negotiating bilateral agreements on weapons control. In November 1970 the United States also received private assurances from the Soviet Union that it would not introduce offensive weapons into the Western Hemisphere or establish bases there, a conciliatory gesture on a point of special American concern. The United States, together with other NATO members, also invited "all interested states" to hold exploratory talks on a mutual and balanced reduction of NATO and Warsaw Pact forces. The Warsaw Pact countries suggested a limited discussion on the reduction of foreign armed forces on the territory of European states, but indicated that such talks should follow a conference on general European security. The NATO countries agreed that such a conference was desirable, but suggested that it be held after the successful conclusion of the negotiations over Berlin.

During 1971 the negotiations on both Berlin and SALT continued. The first phase of the quadripartite negotiations on Berlin was completed, leading to subsequent negotiations between the German authorities themselves. These were successfully concluded in December 1971. Despite the increased level of fighting in Southeast Asia, the SALT talks resumed in March 1971. In April the Soviet interest in détente was articulated and legitimized by the Twenty-fourth Communist Party Congress and Secretary Brezhnev's call for eased world tensions and improved relations between the United States and the Soviet Union. In May a new area of cooperation became manifest when Soviet officials made it known that they were interested in negotiating trade agreements with the United States.

From the Soviet perspective the pressure for improved Soviet-American relations took on a new urgency with the announcement in July 1971 that President Nixon would visit the People's Republic of China the following spring. In August, President Nixon stated that his trip to China would be followed by a summit conference in Moscow.

By November 1971 it had become evident that the Soviet Union had yet another rationale for quickening the momentum of détente. Not only had American overtures to China made Soviet-American rapprochement a necessary counterweight to an increasing Chinese role, but shortages in vital sectors of the Soviet economy had made a rapid trade expansion with the United States most advantageous. Arrangements were made for the sale of three million tons of feed grain to the Soviet Union to cover the short-fall resulting from a poor harvest. In November, Secretary of Commerce Maurice Stans visited Moscow and announced that the United States might buy oil and natural gas from the Soviet Union. From the Soviet viewpoint, the remaining barriers to an even faster acceleration of bilateral trade between the two countries were the absence of most-favored-nation status, the lack of export credits, and the extensive list of strategic goods blocked for sale to Communist countries. On the American side, the question of Soviet Jewry and the outstanding World War II lend-lease debt served as inhibiting factors. Nevertheless, limited trade continued when contracts were signed for the sale of $65 million of American mining and oil drilling equipment and for the purchase of $60 million of nonferrous metals from the Soviet Union.

The year 1972 represented a high-water mark in Soviet-American détente. During that year more agreements were concluded than at any time since diplomatic relations had begun in 1933.[17] In February the Soviet Union informed the United States that it was willing to reopen negotiations, suspended for twelve years, on the repayment of the outstanding Soviet World War II lend-lease debt. The talks opened in Washington in April. At the same time, a series of arms-control negotiations took place, ranging from measures to prevent incidents at sea to the SALT talks. Moreover, the loss of much of Russia's winter grain crop made imminent the prospect of substantial Soviet purchases of American grain.

Despite Soviet displeasure with President Nixon's trip to China and American dissatisfaction with Moscow's role in the massive North Vietnamese offensive, it was announced in April that the Soviet Union was ready to approve plans for a joint earth-orbiting mission by Soviet and American astronauts. In May President Nixon visited Moscow, highlighting the progress reached thus far. The trip raised cooperation between the two countries to the highest level since the wartime alliance of the 1940s. The summit was indicative of the "momentum of achievement" on which both leaderships were banking. The commitment of each side to détente was symbolized by the signing of a declaration embodying twelve basic principles of relations between the United States and the Soviet Union. Recognizing the necessity of coexisting, the two nuclear powers undertook to prevent the development of situations capable of dangerous exacerbation and agreed to do their utmost to avoid military confrontations. Both pledged to exercise restraint in their mutual relations, to recognize the sovereign equality of all countries, and to promote conditions in which no country would be subject to outside interference in its internal affairs.

The 1972 summit also resulted in a number of specific agreements. Foremost among these was a treaty on the limitation of Antiballistic Missile Systems and an Interim Agreement with Respect to the Limitation of Strategic Offensive Arms, which effectively terminated phase one of SALT. These agreements, for the first time, placed limits on the growth of American and Soviet strategic nuclear arsenals. A ceiling of two hundred launchers was established for each side's defensive missile system and both countries committed themselves not to build nationwide systems of antimissile defenses. The interim accord on offensive systems froze land-based and submarine-based intercontinental missiles at the level then in operation or under construction, though it placed no limitations on qualitative improvements, on the number of warheads each missile could carry, or on the number of strategic bombers. Agreements were also signed on environmental cooperation, on joint medical research, and on the formation of a joint commission to devise a comprehensive trade agreement. In late June 1974, a few weeks before his resignation, President Nixon visited the Soviet Union for yet another summit meeting.

President Gerald Ford and Soviet Party Chairman Leonid Brezhnev met for the first time in November 1974 in Vladivostok. On that occasion the two leaders reached tentative agreement on an overall ceiling of about twenty-four hundred nuclear missiles and bombers for each side. About thirteen hundred of these on each side would be missiles with multiple atomic warheads (MIRVs). The ceilings, however, were quantitative, rather than qualitative. No restrictions were set on missile flight tests to increase accuracy, nor on the development of land-mobile and air-mobile intercontinental ballistic missiles, nor on cruise missiles launched from submarines.

Even though the ceilings were high, Secretary Kissinger expressed the hope that the accord would "put a cap on the arms race" for ten years between 1975 and 1985.[18] In that sense, the Vladivostok meeting signified a modest new impulse to the momentum of détente and showed that a minimum of trust had been attained at last in the tensely guarded realm of arms control: both sides considered it more important to agree on a broad formula of strategic parity than to press for specific numerical advantages. On balance, the "cap on the arms race" meant a quantitative limitation on further arms development, not a reduction of existing stockpiles. In that sense, the agreement reached at Vladivostok was a meaningful, though not historic one.

President Jimmy Carter, despite a new emphasis on human rights, continued to pursue détente and the limitation of strategic arms. In a far-ranging speech on foreign policy, delivered at the United Nations two months after his inauguration in January 1977, the new President called for sweeping reductions in nuclear arms and for a freeze on new kinds of weapons. In the same speech, however, President Carter placed great importance on human rights and asserted that "no member of the United Nations [could] claim that mistreatment of its citizens [was] solely its own business."

This new accent on human rights, which included statements of support on behalf of Russian dissidents, irritated the Soviet leaders, who accused the United States of hypocrisy and "selective morality." The President, the Soviet leaders claimed, ignored violations of human rights in fascist dictatorships, such as South Korea, Chile, and Iran, which the United States considered to be of vital strategic value. The United States declared that SALT II would not be made contingent upon internal changes in the Soviet Union. Evidently, the Carter administration was convinced that it could pursue *both* détente and human rights in its relations with the Soviet Union. The Russian response was skeptical. The United States, the Soviet leadership declared, had no right to play the role of moral world police. Party Chairman Brezhnev stated that it was "unthinkable" that Soviet-American relations could develop normally on such a basis. When Secretary of State Cyrus Vance visited Moscow in March 1977 in order to pursue SALT II, the Soviet leadership flatly rejected two American plans to limit strategic weapons, without offering any new proposals of its own. Thereafter, President Carter became less vocal on human rights and Soviet dissidents and, in a surprise move in July 1977, announced that he had decided not to authorize the construction of the B-1 bomber. Protracted negotiations on SALT II resumed soon afterward, and even when, in July 1978, the Soviet government sentenced several of its leading dissidents to long prison terms, these negotiations were not interrupted. Nor did the Soviet offensive in the Horn of Africa affect this policy in any substantial way, although the rhetoric on both sides became somewhat more strident. The President was both Lion and Beaver. The Lion roared but the Beaver continued to work toward SALT II. Thus, while President Carter had denounced the policy of the "lone ranger," Henry Kissinger, it seemed that, despite the new initiatives on human rights, Secretary Kissinger's détente policy was continued, essentially unchanged. Morality in foreign policy, it seemed, would have to be balanced against strategic interests. This meant that human rights would have to be pursued more quietly. Ethics in international affairs, in other words, were subordinate to power.

On balance, it was clear that despite periodic setbacks, the Carter administration did not desire a return to the confrontation policies of the predétente era. Even when, in 1978, the Soviet Union, using Cuban proxy troops, infiltrated the Horn of Africa, Ethiopia, and Zaire and a pro-Soviet coup toppled the government of Afghanistan, the American public did not become overly excited. When one considers the fact that less than two decades earlier, Soviet Russia and the United States almost went to war against each other over missiles in Cuba, the détente achievement was enormous. War between the superpowers seemed a remote possibility in the 1970s, but had not been at all unlikely in the 1950s and 1960s. Objective changes in the global power constellation, in particular the rise of China, had provided the initial impetus to détente. But it was equally important that the leading personalities on both sides had the intelligence to seize the opportunity. Such moments are rare indeed in history. They seldom offer themselves a second time. And in their recognition lies the secret of historic statesmanship.

For an entire generation, Chinese and Americans had perceived each other through dark screens that often produced caricatures out of realities. They had fashioned images of one another that were based on their deepest fears and terrors. Political accommodation was quite impossible under such circumstances. They had met on fields of battle in Korea and had narrowly averted a catastrophic encounter in Vietnam. And then, at last, after more than twenty years of estrangement, a great desire to become reacquainted developed on both sides. Chinese and Americans once more decided to establish direct contacts and to move toward reality.

The roots of détente on the American side rested in the decision of President Nixon, upon entering the White House in 1969, to order a reexamination of America's China policy and to "Vietnamize" the war in Indochina. The new administration realized the sterility of past China policy and saw the need to deal with China on the basis of present facts, rather than old fears. Moreover, the reestablishment of relations with China would thrust the United States into the role of balancer between China and the Soviet Union as long as the hostility between the two great Communist powers continued to exist. On the Chinese side, the conviction gradually crystallized that the United States was a less formidable threat than the Soviet Union. After all, Americans were withdrawing from Asian soil while Soviet troops were massing on the Chinese border. Détente with the United States would eliminate the danger of a two-front cold war. Thus, to the Chinese leadership, détente with the United States became a matter of national security.

The American withdrawal from Vietnam took almost four years to complete. The first troop cut was announced in July 1969 and the Paris Accords were signed in January 1973. During that time China and the United States took a number of concrete steps toward rapprochement. The most important of these are well worth examining against the background of the gradually deescalating war in Indochina.

The first initiative was taken on the American side in February 1969 when Secretary of State William Rogers announced that the United States government wished to encourage scientific and cultural exchanges. In July 1969, when the peak figure of 541,500 American troops in Vietnam was reduced by a first cut of 25,000 men, American citizens were also permitted to bring into the country up to $100 worth of Chinese goods. This constituted the first loosening of a twenty-year-old embargo against goods from mainland China. In addition, the President announced the Nixon Doctrine, declaring that, in the future, the United States would avoid entanglements like Vietnam by limiting its support to economic and military aid rather than active combat participation. Peace negotiations began in earnest in Paris and a protest held in Washington against the war drew huge crowds demanding a rapid withdrawal of American troops. In January 1970, however, under the euphemism of "protective reaction" to cover air reconnaissance missions over North Vietnam, the United States renewed the bombing of North Vietnam.

In February 1970, in his message to Congress, President Nixon formally announced his objective of improving relations with Peking. Two months later, by executive order, the President authorized the selective licensing for export to China of goods produced by American subsidiaries abroad. A jarring note was struck on April 30, 1970, however, when President Nixon, in a nationally televised address, announced an American-led South Vietnamese "incursion" into Cambodia in order to eliminate Vietcong supply depots and sanctuaries and to demonstrate that the United States was "no pitiful, helpless giant."

In November 1970 a simple majority of the membership of the United Nations supported the seating of mainland China. While insufficient for action, the vote was significant because of its psychological importance. One month later, on December 18, in an interview with Edgar Snow, Mao Tse-tung declared that he was ready to receive President Nixon in Peking. The President responded to this invitation in his message to Congress on February 25, 1971, by affirming his intention to establish a dialogue with the Peking government without, however, breaking off relations with Taiwan. Restrictions on the travel of American citizens to mainland China were lifted in March and, one month later, in the first concrete response to these American moves, the United States table tennis team was invited to China.

The United States government immediately responded to this Chinese gesture in four specific moves. In the first place, it conveyed to American oil companies the objections of the Chinese government to their search for petroleum deposits off the China coast. Second, President Nixon announced the termination of a twenty-one-year ban on direct trade with China. Third, the Lodge Commission Report supported a system of dual Chinese representation in the United Nations. Finally, Mr. Nixon declared that he would be happy to visit China.

In July 1971 it was revealed that Dr. Henry Kissinger, the President's Special Assistant for National Security Affairs, was in Peking. On this historic occasion, Dr. Kissinger held lengthy consultations with Premier Chou En-lai and the two men developed an excellent rapport. Dr. Kissinger stated that Chou En-lai was one of the greatest statesmen of the time and the Chinese premier returned the compliment by declaring that his American visitor had a "Chinese mind." Shortly after the meeting, it was announced that President Nixon would visit China in early 1972. In August, Secretary of State Rogers declared that the United States would fight for a system of representation in the United Nations under which both Chinas would be in the organization. This plan did not succeed. On October 25, 1971, on the last day of Dr. Kissinger's second visit to China, the General Assembly voted for the seating of mainland China and the exclusion of Taiwan. On November 30, Dr. Kissinger stated that the problem of Taiwan should be resolved by direct contact between Peking and Taiwan. The road was now clear for a summit meeting between the top leadership of China and the United States.

President Nixon's visit to Peking in February 1972 was the occasion of the first substantive bilateral agreements between the two countries in more than twenty years. In the Shanghai Communiqué of February 24, it was agreed to facilitate bilateral trade and cultural exchanges. Senior United States representatives would be sent to China from time to time to further the normalization of relations. In March the Chinese table tennis team visited the United States, and in April the first American businessmen were invited to visit the Canton spring trade fair.

Détente underwent a serious test in mid-1972 when President Nixon decided to mine the port of Haiphong in North Vietnam ten days before he was scheduled to visit Moscow. However, Moscow and Peking apparently placed a higher priority on their relationship with the United States than on their alliance with North Vietnam. The Nixon visit took place on schedule. Hanoi now realized that it could not depend too much upon Soviet and Chinese support.

The United States, in turn, found itself in the anomalous position of having reached détente with one billion Communists—800 million Chinese and 200 million Russians—and yet pursuing a relentless war against a small Communist peasant country which it accused of aggression against its neighbors. Thus, so far as the United States was concerned, the Vietnam war now increasingly seemed like an anachronism. History had simply passed it by. On January 23, 1973, a cease-fire was reached in Paris which extricated the United States from combat participation in the Vietnam war.

On February 15, less than a month after the Paris agreement, Dr. Kissinger once again visited Peking. This time, the United States and China agreed to open liaison offices in Washington and Peking. At the same time, China agreed to release two captured American pilots and to review the sentence of John Downey, a CIA agent held prisoner in China since the Korean war. It was also decided to negotiate the settlement of American claims against China and of Chinese assets "blocked" in the United States since Korea.

In March 1973 David Bruce was appointed to head the United States liaison office in Peking, and Huang Chen, China's former ambassador to France, was named to fill the Washington post. The liaison offices were formally opened in May 1973.

Under the impact of political détente, trade between the two countries expanded considerably, despite the fact that China was not granted most-favored-nation status. A National Council for U.S.-China Trade was established and a delegation was sent to Peking for the first formal meeting between an American business group and Chinese trade authorities in almost twenty-five years.

In November 1973, Dr. Kissinger once again visited China. At that meeting, it was agreed to expand the functions of the liaison offices. Premier Chou En-lai stated that the full normalization of relations between China and the United States could be realized only on the basis of confirming the principle of one China. But each side decided to remain ambiguous on just how this goal of a single China was to be attained. It seemed clear, however, that a solution by force was ruled out by both sides. Thus, the delicate issue of Taiwan was neatly transformed from a problem to be solved immediately into a process to be managed over a longer period of time.

The trade pattern followed an erratic course. Two-way Chinese-American trade approached the $1 billion mark in 1974. During that year, the United States became China's second-most-important trading partner. In 1975, however, the figure was slashed in half and the Chinese abruptly canceled a large order for American wheat and corn. Taiwan's trade with the United States in 1975 was almost ten times as large, and Hong Kong's was four times as large. The evidence suggests that the Taiwan issue inhibited a more rapid expansion of commercial contacts. Financing problems, the American refusal to grant China most-favored-nation status, and the lack of a formal trade agreement could all be traced back to the absence of full diplomatic relations. Thus, Kissinger's liaison-office solution did not resolve the Taiwan problem, but merely circumvented it. By 1975 rapprochement between China and America had reached a fairly stable plateau. There was little, if any, forward movement. Even a trip to Peking by Secretary Kissinger and President Gerald Ford in the fall of 1975 did not restore the old momentum.

After the deaths of Mao Tse-tung and Chou En-lai in 1976, a power struggle erupted in China over the succession to the legendary chairman. Chiang Ching, Mao's widow, led a radical group that believed the United States was a greater threat to China than was the Soviet Union. She lost the fight to Deng Hsiao-ping and a more moderate faction that believed the Soviet Union posed a greater danger to China than did the United States. Chiang Ching was purged from the Chinese leadership, and the successors of Chou En-lai took over the reins of power.

In the United States, the administration of President Jimmy Carter and Secretary of State Cyrus Vance decided not to deviate in any significant way from the China policy of their predecessors. In 1977, Secretary Vance visited China to underline this continuity and, in 1978, Zbigniew Brzezinski, Jimmy Carter's National Security Adviser, during a visit to Peking, emphasized the cordial relations that existed between China and the United States. The fact that this statement was made at a time of Soviet-Cuban initiatives in the Horn of Africa was not lost upon the Soviet government. It was clear that Henry Kissinger's triangular policy was still in operation. This trend was the result of objective changes in the global power constellation. America's withdrawal from Vietnam, the Soviet presence on the Chinese border, and the American decision to balance its relations with China and the Soviet Union but to remain equidistant from them both were primarily responsible for this great turning. Yet it was also true that both China and America had been fortunate to have as diplomatic leaders men of the caliber of Henry Kissinger and Chou En-lai, both equipped with realistic perceptions of themselves and of each other, a rare knowledge of history, and an even rarer gift for empathy. This personal dimension no doubt accelerated the movement away from fantasy and fiction toward reality and rapprochement. Henry Kissinger and Chou En-lai had recognized the objective conditions necessary for a turn for the better in the relations between China and America. They had seized the crucial moment at one of history's great junctions and helped to make it happen.

One other common element in the personalities of the four main architects of Sino-American détente seems significant. Each of these men was a survivor. Mao Tse-tung and Chou En-lai had survived decades of adversity. Kissinger had been a refugee from the Nazi holocaust, and Nixon had made several comebacks from political defeat. Perhaps this common theme helped to fashion a rapport among these men and helped them turn away from hatred toward a measure of acceptance.

During the opening days of 1980 the Soviet Union did something it had never done before: it used its own troops to invade a neutral country.

As close to a hundred thousand troops smashed into Afghanistan, President Carter announced that his "opinion of the Russians [had] changed more drastically in the last week than in the previous two and a half years.'' Describing the invasion as a ''quantum jump in the nature of Soviet behavior,'' and the most serious crisis since World War II, the President announced an embargo on grain and high-technology products against the Soviet Union. In his State of the Union address in January 1980, he declared that the United States would use armed force, if necessary, to repel any Soviet assault on the Persian Gulf region. This new ''Carter Doctrine'' thus extended the NATO alliance concept to the Middle East. Containment now included all regions of vital strategic or economic interest to the United States. The SALT II negotiations were suspended and, by year's end, had become a casualty. Suddenly, all the détente efforts of the 1970s seemed in jeopardy. Nineteen eighty seemed more like 1950. What was behind these shattering events?

The evidence suggests that the Soviet leadership made its move based partly on objective considerations of strategy and power balance, but also partly on its perceptions of what the United States might or might not do.

The ''objective'' factors apparently were the following: Moscow's primary purpose was probably to tighten its control over a rebellious border state. The tide of Islamic fervor which had already shaken Iran was now threatening Afghanistan. Unless it was checked quickly, it might spread across the border into Soviet Central Asia and stir unrest among the Soviet Union's fifty million Moslems. Second, the invasion was probably part of a long-range strategy to gain influence over Pakistan, Iran, and other Persian Gulf nations. It might ultimately place the Soviet Union in the strategic position of controlling Western oil supplies. Finally, Moscow probably intended to send a message to Peking that it was prepared to resort to force if its border interests were threatened.

Perceptions of American intent probably also played a role. In the first place, the Soviet leadership had apparently concluded that SALT II had little chance of winning approval during an election year. Moreover, since NATO had decided in December 1979 to deploy in Western Europe, by the mid-1980s, new atomic-tipped missiles capable of striking targets in the Soviet Union, SALT was simply not all that important any longer. Second, Moscow may have reached the conclusion that the United States was so distracted by Iran that it would not act strongly on Afghanistan. After all, at that point the fifty-two American hostages held captive in Teheran by Iranian militants had dominated America's attention for two months. And finally, one might venture the following speculation: When the United States, during the 1960s and early 1970s, had more than half a million combat troops fighting in Vietnam, and had mined Haiphong and bombed Hanoi, the Soviet Union had not canceled SALT I. In fact, ten days after the mining of Haiphong harbor in May 1972, Richard Nixon and Henry Kissinger arrived in Moscow to meet with Leonid Brezhnev in a summit meeting to sign the first strategic arms limitation treaty between the superpowers. Why, then, should the United States overreact if the Soviet Union took advantage of an opportunity that came its way in 1980? It is entirely possible that the Soviet leadership underestimated the American response to Afghanistan in a manner similar to the way in which Nikita Khrushchev underestimated the U.S. response to Soviet missiles in Cuba in 1962.

So far as Afghanistan itself was concerned, it was not subjugated easily. Insurgency seems to come naturally to the Afghan people. Their character is well illustrated by an episode in 1841 when an occupying army was reduced to a single survivor—a disaster without equal in British history.

In the years of British colonialism, Afghanistan was an independent buffer state between India and Tsarist Russia. In 1839, British fears about Russian influence in Kabul prompted an Afghan war. With little resistance, the British marched into Afghanistan and installed a puppet king. This British envoy was soon pleased to report from Kabul: "All things considered, the perfect tranquillity of the country is to my mind perfectly miraculous. Already our presence has been infinitely beneficial."[19]

The occupiers were unprepared for the riot that followed. Kabul's British resident was hacked to pieces. The Afghan king whom the British had deposed led an uprising. Prudently, the British commander accepted Afghan terms for a supposedly safe exodus to the Khyber Pass, ninety miles away over difficult terrain. But his entire army was destroyed. In the first week, twelve thousand were killed; by the eighth day, only twenty officers and forty-five foot soldiers remained; a day later, only a sole survivor was alive. He was Surgeon Bryden of the Army Medical Corps. When he reached the Indian frontier, a waiting British colonel, anxious for news of the Kabul army, sighed in relief: "Here comes the messenger!"

One may wonder whether the Russian occupiers had read their history.

A dispassionate Olympian view of Soviet-American relations during the 1960s and 1970s might conclude that when it comes to testing détente through intervention, the superpower score is very close to even. The United States intervened in Vietnam, Cambodia, and the Dominican Republic, and the Soviet Union intervened in Hungary, Czechoslovakia, and Afghanistan. It is true that Afghanistan was a neutral country, but Cambodia was, too. Unfortunately, however, when passions are inflamed, such Olympian views enjoy little popularity. Empathy gives way to an "us-and-them" psychology. The lessons of the Cuban missile crisis are forgotten and the arms race gathers momentum once again.

Phase IV: Reagan I—Back into Cold War

Under the first term of Ronald Reagan's presidency, the Soviet-American relationship deteriorated to a level not seen since the days of the Cuban missile crisis. During the détente years of the 1970s, there was little talk of nuclear war. Instead, the two nations pursued a pragmatic, businesslike relationship. Ten years later, however, in 1983, a television version of nuclear holocaust was watched by one hundred million frightened Americans. In my university classes in New York City more than half of the students expected to perish in a nuclear war before the year 2000. The unthinkable had become possible once again. What had happened? And who was to blame?

In the first place, President Reagan brought to the presidency an extremely negative view of the Soviet Union. Of all American presidents, his perception was probably the darkest and his rhetoric the harshest. A few examples will serve to make the point. In his first press conference in 1981, President Reagan called the USSR a nation ruled by men who "reserve unto themselves the right to commit any crime, to lie, to cheat." A few months later, he told an audience of West Point cadets that the Soviet Union was an "evil force." And in March 1983, in an address to a conference of Christian fundamentalists in Orlando, Florida, the President referred to the USSR as the "focus of evil in the modern world...an evil empire."[20]

Not only did he label the Soviet Union evil, but he predicted it would not last much longer. "The West won't contain Communism, it will transcend Communism," the President told the graduating class of the University of Notre Dame in 1981. "Communism is a bizarre chapter in human history whose last pages are even now being written." And in June 1982 President Reagan declared before the British Parliament that "the march of freedom and democracy [would] leave Marxism-Leninism on the ash heap of history." The Soviet experiment was in the process of full decay.

Ronald Reagan seemed more interested in seeing the USSR in the dustbin of history than seeing it for himself. When Leonid Brezhnev died in 1982, after eighteen years of rule, the President did not see fit to attend his funeral. And when his successor, Yuri Andropov, died in 1984, once again Ronald Reagan chose not to put in an appearance in Moscow. At age 74 he had yet to visit the Soviet Union for the first time in his life.

Not only did the American President perceive the Soviet Union as an "evil empire," but he tended to regard leftist movements in the Third World as tentacles of the USSR. Guerrillas in El Salvador and the Sandinistas who ruled Nicaragua were both seen as direct extensions of Soviet ambition. Poverty and social inequality were seen as far less important causes than Soviet revolutionary subversion. Hence, in El Salvador, President Reagan supported the government against guerrillas, and in Nicaragua he supported guerrillas against the government. The President's perceptions of communism did not allow for nuances and shadings. It was "us against them," good against evil. In Ronald Reagan's universe, Joseph Stalin had never died.

The Soviet leadership probably hoped at first that Ronald Reagan would turn out to be another Nixon: tough in his rhetoric but pragmatic in his actions. Brezhnev, in his final year, was quickly disabused of this notion. Hence, fearful that the United States might try to detach Poland from the Soviet orbit in a "rollback policy" reminiscent of John Foster Dulles, Brezhnev used a Soviet-trained Polish general to declare martial law in Poland and to outlaw the Solidarity Union.

On September 1, 1983, a dreadful tragedy occurred that no doubt confirmed the perceptions of the American President. The Soviets shot down a Korean airliner on a night flight to Seoul with a loss of 269 civilian passengers. Even though the plane had overflown Soviet air space for more than an hour, and the decision to destroy it had apparently been taken by a regional Soviet commander without Politburo authorization, the barbarism of this act poisoned Soviet-American relations even further. Self-righteous "explanations" about "American spy planes" and "sanctity of Soviet air space" only increased American wrath. Name-calling reached a peak after this catastrophe. President Reagan and Secretary of State George Shultz both described the USSR as an international outlaw. Andrei Gromyko, a senior Soviet diplomat, not only failed to apologize for this example of mass murder but announced that the Soviet Union would do it again if its air space were violated. Thus, the American leader's devil image and the Soviet leadership's wooden-headedness combined to drag the relationship to its lowest ebb since the bleakest days of the cold war.

Three weeks after the Korean disaster, Yuri Andropov, the former KGB boss who now ruled the Soviet Union, delivered a major policy statement. In this document Andropov in effect accused Reagan of killing détente. "Even if someone had any illusions about the possible evolution for the better in the policy of the present U.S. Administration," Andropov declared, "the latest developments have actually dispelled them."[21] A few weeks later, Soviet diplomats and "Americanologists" such as Georgi Arbatov began to compare Ronald Reagan to Adolf Hitler. The door-slamming and bridge-burning rhetoric continued on both sides, almost to the time of Andropov's death in February 1984.

Beginning in early 1984 the President, apparently for domestic and political reasons, adopted a somewhat more conciliatory tone. In his State of the Union address in January 1984 he "reached out" to the Soviet Union. Yet, he made a gross historical error. "Our two countries have never fought each other," he declared. Apparently he had never heard of the American intervention in 1918, designed to bring down the new Soviet regime of V.I. Lenin. And again in May, in a speech before the Irish Parliament, he appealed to Moscow to reduce tensions.

Yet a great deal of damage had been done. Neither side had found the courage to say "I am wrong" on a single issue. It was as if two nasty cross-eyed men, both armed to the teeth, were continuing to bump into one another, the first one shouting at the second, "Why don't you look where you are going?" and the second one shouting back "Why don't you go where you are looking?" Worst of all, both sides were to blame for endangering the future of the planet and of generations yet unborn, for this breakdown in diplomacy had spilled over into the vital area of arms control.

When two countries despise and distrust each other as thoroughly as the United States and the Soviet Union did in the early 1980s, diplomacy itself becomes militarized. Arms control then becomes not a genuine search for reductions, but a competitive jockeying to gain an advantage over the adversary. Every proposal contains a "joker" which makes the package unacceptable to the other side. The result is not reduction, but mutual escalation.

The Soviet Union's greatest fear during the early 1980s was that the United States would implement a 1979 NATO decision to place more than five hundred Pershing and Cruise missiles into Western Europe in order to balance Soviet SS-20 missiles which were aimed at Western European targets. In late 1981 President Reagan proposed the so-called "zero option," offering not to deploy the American missiles if the Soviets dismantled theirs. After two years of intensive bargaining, the Soviets rejected the "zero option," claiming that it would still leave French and British nuclear missiles aimed at the Soviet Union and thus give NATO a net advantage. Even a much publicized "walk in the woods" near Geneva in late 1982, by Paul Nitze and Yuli Kvitsinsky—the two main arms negotiators—was not able to break the impasse.

In early 1984 the United States began to deploy the Pershings and Cruises in several European countries. President Reagan declared that the United States had to have something to bargain with, apparently expecting the Soviets to negotiate more intensively at the table. Instead, the Soviet team simply walked out and broke off all negotiations.

In the matter of strategic intercontinental missiles, the President regarded the SALT II treaty as "fatally flawed." Instead, he proposed his own START program, which stalled almost immediately. Reagan pushed vigorously for two new initiatives: first, the MX missile, which he named the "peacekeeper." The MX was an intercontinental missile equipped with ten warheads, each of which carried several hundred times the explosive power of the Hiroshima bomb and each of which could be released in flight at different times and at different targets. It was difficult for the Soviets not to perceive the MX as a first-strike weapon. Second, in early 1983, the President gave an address, quickly dubbed the "Star Wars" speech, in which he advocated laser beam stations in space designed as shields to abort a possible Soviet missile attack. Reagan described this "Strategic Defense Initiative" as purely defensive. His hope was that it would ultimately render nuclear weapons obsolete. Scientists were divided over whether the SDI was technologically feasible. The concept was immediately attacked by the Soviet leadership, which perceived the "shield" as a thinly disguised American plot to hit the USSR first without suffering a retaliatory strike. Yet another Reagan plan to "build down" nuclear arms by trading in two obsolete weapons for each new one was rejected by the Soviet Union as a design to modernize the American arsenal, not to reduce it.

By 1984 there were no negotiations between the two superpowers on virtually anything, including arms control. Konstantin Chernenko, Andropov's successor, apparently remembering the American boycott of the Moscow Olympics in 1980, decided to boycott the American Olympics in Los Angeles in 1984. The atmosphere was as icy and dangerous as it had been in the darkest days of the cold war.

Neither side had reason to be proud of its record in the early 1980s. The American President was a crusader who shunned the pragmatism and more businesslike approach of most of his predecessors. All three Soviet leaders—Brezhnev, Andropov, and Chernenko—responded with a good deal of sanctimonious wooden-headedness. Neither side was able to say the liberating phase: "You have been wrong, but I too have made mistakes," or to echo the words of President John F. Kennedy of a quarter century before: "Let us begin."

Phase Five: Reagan II and the Gorbachev Era—
End of Cold War?

The opening of Ronald Reagan's second term in 1985 coincided with the ascendancy to power in Soviet Russia of a new kind of chief of state: Mikhail Gorbachev, who at fifty-four years of age was the first leader younger than the Soviet Union itself.

The relationship between these two men ushered in a new détente between the superpowers that went far beyond that of the Nixon-Brezhnev years. It led to five summits, in Geneva, Reykjavik, Washington, Moscow, and New York; the first arms reduction treaty in history; a Soviet pullout from Afghanistan; and a pronounced turn for the better in Soviet-US relations.

The reasons for these remarkable developments were complex: on Reagan's side, a growing concern for his historical legacy and a first exposure to a pragmatic, reasonable, and even likable Soviet leader; on Gorbachev's, an overriding need to modernize a backward economy and thus to divert money and brainpower from a top-heavy military sector. The results of this fortunate conjunction of personalities and objective factors were far-reaching, holding out the promise of an end to the cold war by the year 2000.

For decades, Americans had perceived Soviet leaders as aging men waving feebly from the Kremlin walls or scowling at the United States while saying "nyet." During Ronald Reagan's first term, Comrade Death became a growing embarrassment to the Soviet Union. As Brezhnev, Andropov, and Chernenko died in rapid succession, Red Square began to resemble a giant funeral parlor. But when, at last, in March 1985, Andrei Gromyko nominated "that man with the nice smile who has iron teeth" to the most powerful post in the Soviet Union, that of general secretary of the Communist party, a spring thaw began to melt the glacial ice of decades. A child of the post-Stalin generation was now at the helm of the Soviet Union: Mikhail Gorbachev, who, with a beautiful outspoken wife by his side, was to become a kind of communist John F. Kennedy.

Born in 1931, young Mikhail did not have an easy childhood. As a youngster, he lived through several years of Nazi occupation and worked as a combine driver on a state farm. When Stalin's reign of terror came to an end in 1953, Gorbachev was a law student at Moscow University. As a young party *apparatchik,* he attracted Nikita Khrushchev's attention through his competence and efficiency in the Stavropol region. After Khrushchev's demise, Gorbachev was promoted by Leonid Brezhnev; Gorbachev moved to Moscow and soon became a member of the Central Committee of the Communist party. After Brezhnev's death, Yuri Andropov coopted him as a special protégé, as did Konstantin Chernenko a year later. After the latter's death in March 1985, the remaining members of the old guard in the Kremlin decided not to bet against the actuarial tables any longer and took a chance on young Gorbachev.

The new Soviet leader moved quickly to consolidate his personal power. His principal rival for the top job, Leningrad party boss Giorgi Romanov, went into sudden retirement. By mid-1985, Gorbachev had embarked on his double-track policy: economic modernization and reform at home and arms reduction with the United States abroad. On November 21, 1985, Reagan and Gorbachev met for the first time face-to-face in Geneva. The meeting was cordial, and the two men agreed that a nuclear war could never be won and must never be fought. At the same time Gorbachev announced his plans for a dramatic re-structuring of Soviet society, or *perestroika,* in an atmosphere of greater po-litical openness, or *glasnost.* These two Russian words were to become sym-bols of a new Gorbachev era.

The most important element of Gorbachev's *perestroika* was to be eco-nomic modernization. The USSR, the new Soviet leader said, must become a *real* superpower. Implicit in that phrase was an amazing confession: Take away the Soviet Union's missiles and men under arms, and it would be a Third World country. And indeed, this was true. The Soviet economy was a dino-saur of inefficiency. In early 1986, for example, it was reported that the Soviet Union had exported 30,000 automobiles to Romania. A Romanian inspector, however, discovered to his chagrin, that every key of each Soviet automobile fitted every ignition. Needless to say, the cars had be to be shipped back to Russia. Stories of this kind convinced Gorbachev that, unless the bloated So-viet bureaucracy was streamlined and the economy modernized, the only country in the world that would continue to regard the Soviet Union with ad-miration might be Albania. But the price of economic reform at home was arms control abroad. A breathing spell was needed from all-out military com-petition with the West. Hence, when the two leaders met for their second sum-mit in Reykjavik, Iceland, in late 1986, Gorbachev decided to try a high-risk gamble. When alone with the US president, he pulled four typed pages from his briefcase which contained a sweeping proposal: The Soviet Union was pre-pared to destroy 50 percent of its strategic missiles if the United States would do the same and limit the testing of the Strategic Defense Initiative (SDI) to the laboratory. Reagan, who had expected a modest Soviet initiative limited to missiles in Europe, responded by rejecting the proposal, since, in his view, it would kill the SDI. Suddenly, almost overnight, the initiative in arms control had passed to the Soviet Union. For decades the Americans had said yes and the Russians *nyet;* now, for all the world to see, a Soviet leader came up with creative arms control proposals, and the Americans were rejecting them. One leading scholar offers a good analysis of this reversal:

> Americans used to come to the table as if arms control were poker, with the U.S. as the dealer while the Soviet Union played it as plodding defensive chess. Gorbachev changed all that. In terms of poker, he shuffled the deck, dealt himself new cards,

upped the ante, bluffed and called. In terms of chess, he played with the aggressive, unorthodox, intuitive style of the new Soviet champion, Gary Kasparov.[22]

The collapse of the Reykjavik summit did not stop Gorbachev. Believing that the SDI might ultimately be killed by the US Congress anyway, for technological and financial reasons, he now began to concentrate on a more modest objective: the signing of an intermediate-range nuclear forces (INF) treaty with the United States.

Actually, this "zero option" had originally been President Reagan's idea. As early as 1981, he had proposed the elimination of an entire class of Soviet missiles in exchange for the withdrawal and destruction of the US missiles then deployed in Europe. Brezhnev had rejected the idea, but now, by 1987, it became the centerpiece of a third superpower summit to be held in Washington. To Gorbachev, the zero option made sense. It had long been an objective of Soviet policy to prevent NATO from surrounding the Soviet Union with nuclear missiles. Brezhnev had permitted this to happen. Gorbachev would get the missiles out.

Gorbachev's visit to Washington in December 1987 was an historic turning point for the better in the forty-year struggle between the two superpowers. The two men signed the first Soviet-American disarmament treaty in history: 1600 Soviet missiles and 400 US missiles, all stationed in Europe, were consigned to the scrap heap under rigorous on-site verification procedures that made cheating next to impossible. Gorbachev agreed to this asymmetry in order to compensate for the vast superiority of Soviet conventional forces in Europe. Even though the total number of missiles to be destroyed (2000) added up to only 4 percent of their combined arsenals of approximately 50,000, both men described the INF treaty as an auspicious beginning. When it was all over, President Reagan declared that the meeting had "lit the sky with hope for all people of good will." Cold war rhetoric was giving way to frank discourse and personal rapport. Neither man forgot the vast ideological differences that separated them, but both staked out common ground on which to build for the future. The person who knew Ronald Reagan best—his wife Nancy—probably described this evolving relationship better than anyone:

> There is good chemistry between the two men. They can talk candidly now and they do. They enjoy the one-on-one. I know Ronnie likes it, and Chairman Gorbachev likes it. They both understand there are big differences like Afghanistan and human rights. But they know where that point is beyond which they do not press each other. When they get there, they cool it.[23]

Ronald Reagan himself admitted to a change of heart before Gorbachev left Washington. In a television interview, he recalled the Marxist goal of a one-world communist state. But then he added: "All right, we now have a leader who is apparently willing to say that he is prepared to live with other philosophies in other countries."[24]

Rapprochement with the United States was not the only foreign policy task Gorbachev had set for himself. The other was rapprochement with his Eastern

European allies, most of whom still remembered Khrushchev's invasion of Hungary, Brezhnev's invasion of Czechoslovakia, and the crushing of the Solidarity Union in Poland. Gorbachev travelled extensively in these countries, promoting *perestroika, glasnost,* and pronouncing Stalin a criminal. His efforts enjoyed a moderate success in these countries, and new jokes began to surface. In Poland, for example, the story made the rounds that the Soviet government had issued a commemorative stamp of Joseph Stalin. There was a problem with the stamp, however: It did not stick too well because people kept spitting on the wrong side. In Czechoslovakia, someone asked the question: "What is the definition of a string quartet?" Answer: "The Leningrad Symphony Orchestra after a tour of the United States."

In East Germany, on the other hand, Stalinism was still so deeply rooted that Gorbachev's new book *Perestroika* was not translated into German. The authorities feared that Gorbachev's recommendations for reform were so far-reaching that they might threaten the stability of the entrenched communist regime in East Germany.

Ronald Reagan, for his part, had begun to realize that the Soviet Union was a real place with real people, not an abstraction from the memory of a movie actor who had grown up during the times of Lenin and Stalin. Impressed by yet another Gorbachev concession—a military pull-out from Afghanistan—Reagan decided, for the first time in his life, to see Soviet Russia for himself. In May 1988, the seventy-eight-year-old President and his wife visited Moscow. During this fourth summit, the emphasis was not on arms control but on human rights. The US President spoke about freedom of speech, religion, and emigration and met with prominent dissidents. His hosts were not thrilled at being lectured to in their own country, and Georgi Arbatov, the Kremlin's leading Americanologist, wondered out loud how President Reagan would respond if Chairman Gorbachev were to set up a field kitchen in New York City and ladle out soup to New York's homeless. Yet, even though the two leaders struck sparks off one another, the cordiality of their relationship remained unimpaired.

There was a bit of progress on arms control as well. The US Senate ratified the INF Treaty on the eve of the Moscow summit by an overwhelming vote of ninety-three to five. This strengthened the hand of both leaders even though little headway was made on the main objective: to cut Soviet and US strategic arsenals in half. Verification obstacles, such as permitting Soviet inspectors access to missiles stationed on US submarines, prevented a breakthrough on a Strategic Arms Reduction (START) Treaty.

Nonetheless, both leaders agreed that progress had been made. Gorbachev announced that "the age of disarmament ha(d) begun." And President Reagan retracted his statement made five years earlier that the Soviet Union was an "evil empire." When queried by reporters why he had changed his mind, the President responded that the "evil empire" belonged to "another time, another era," and that Gorbachev was "a serious man committed to serious change."

On balance, perhaps the most important result of the first four summits between the two leaders was this: Both men declared at the first summit in 1985 that nuclear war was no longer a viable option for the superpowers. By the time of their fourth meeting in Moscow three years later, they meant it.

Mikhail Gorbachev's farewell visit to Ronald Reagan in New York in December 1988 was no doubt his most dramatic. In an eloquent and audacious speech before the United Nations, the Soviet leader offered a sweeping vision of a "new world order" for the twenty-first century, including specific initiatives on a variety of Western concerns such as Afghanistan, emigration, and human rights. Most compelling was a unilateral decision to reduce, within two years, the total Soviet armed forces by 10 percent; to withdraw 50,000 troops from Eastern Europe; and to cut in half the number of Soviet tanks in East Germany, Hungary, and Czechoslovakia. What was memorable about Gorbachev's address was not only the package of specific proposals but also his departure from the shopworn slogans and ideological dogmas that had driven Soviet foreign policy for more than half a century. "Today the preservation of any kind of closed society is hardly possible," he declared.

This statement was put to the test the very day after Gorbachev uttered it, when a powerful earthquake hit Soviet Armenia, destroying several cities and killing more than 50,000 people. The Soviet leader immediately returned to his homeland to lead the rescue effort. Significantly, however, with *glasnost* well entrenched, the magnitude of the disaster and its consequences were relayed promptly to the West, and Moscow accepted help from abroad—even from the United States—which had not been done since the days of World War II. This reaction stood in sharp contrast to Moscow response to the Chernobyl nuclear disaster of March 1986, when the Soviet Union had shrouded itself in its traditional secrecy. Not surprisingly, the US response to the catastrophe in Soviet Armenia was open-hearted and generous. In 1986, the world was suspicious and angry; in 1988, it shared in the grief and helped as best it could.

As US leaders were quick to point out after they studied Gorbachev's speech, troop and tank reduction proposals still left the Soviet Union with a sizable margin of superiority in conventional military strength over the NATO countries. But what was perhaps more important than these numbers was the growing conviction in the United States that Gorbachev was seeking not just a breathing space but a fundamental change in the Soviet system. The big question in the West about the Soviet leader was no longer "Is he sincere?" but "Can he last?"

And, indeed, the philosophical base of Mikhail Gorbachev's speech made one wonder whether a Soviet leader could indeed have spoken those words. The following statements from his UN address could easily have been made by US President. Here are some that are worth quoting:

> The use or threat of force no longer can or must be an instrument of foreign policy.... All of us, and primarily the stronger of us, must exercise self-restraint and totally rule out any outward-oriented use of force.... It is now quite clear that build-

ing up military power makes no country omnipotent. What is more, one-sided reliance on military power ultimately weakens other components of national security.

It is also quite clear to us that the principle of freedom of choice is mandatory. Its nonrecognition is fraught with extremely grave consequences for world peace. Denying that right to the peoples under whatever pretext or rhetorical guise means jeopardizing even the fragile balance that has been attained. Freedom of choice is a universal principle that should allow for no exceptions....As the world asserts its diversity, attempts to look down on others and to teach them one's own brand of democracy become totally improper, to say nothing of the fact that democratic values intended for export often very quickly lose their worth.

What we are talking about, therefore, is unity in diversity....We are not abandoning our convictions, our philosophy or traditions, nor do we urge anyone to abandon theirs. But neither do we have any intention to be hemmed in by our values. That would result in intellectual impoverishment, for it would mean rejecting a powerful source of development—the exchange of everything original that each nation has independently created.

We are, of course, far from claiming to be in possession of the ultimate truth.[25]

Not only did President Reagan and President-elect George Bush warm up to Gorbachev, but so did the American people. According to a Gallup poll, 65 percent of the respondents believed that the Soviet Union was undergoing major rather than cosmetic changes, and 76 percent believed that Moscow was now more likely to live in peace with its neighbors.[26] Perhaps most important, Americans began to perceive the Soviet leader as a real human being, not a cardboard figure waving feebly from the Kremlin Wall. As a New Yorker put it, "To me, he is more like a human being than the other people who have held power there. He showed more of a human side when he went home where he belonged to deal with the Armenian earthquake. He didn't go with politics."[27]

Roy Medvedev, the dissident Soviet historian, observed that Gorbachev's speech was the best of any world leader since John F. Kennedy. And indeed, there were parallels: the wit, the crowd appeal, and a latent dread that this man was risking too much and might be pushing his luck.

For forty years, the United States had proposed initiatives and successive Soviet leaders had scowled and said *nyet.* Now, Mikhail Gorbachev was proposing sweeping initiatives and the United States, delighted but taken aback, was saying maybe. By the time Ronald Reagan left office and the new President was sworn in, the entire choreography had changed: 1988 had clearly become a transition year from the cold war to something better and more humane.

* * *

Under the administration of President Ronald Reagan, Sino-American perceptions warmed to the point of friendship. The United States redefined China as a "friendly nonaligned country," and the President visited it in 1984. China, in turn, instituted English as the official second language to be taught in all Chinese schools. The reason for this increasing closeness was not only the obvious negative bond forged by the iciness that prevailed in U.S.-Soviet relations during President Reagan's first term but the equally important positive bond created by China's decision to modernize and to move toward a mixed economy. For this modernization program, China needed America's help.

The China that Ronald Reagan saw was no longer a Maoist country. Deng Hsiao-ping, the eighty-year-old leader and survivor of the Long March, had dismantled some Maoist institutions. Most important, the new leadership had virtually decollectivized agriculture. While it was still illegal to buy or sell land, peasants now signed long-term contracts with the government. These obligated them to meet certain production quotas. Beyond these quotas, however, peasants disposed of surpluses in any way they saw fit. Many began to amass considerable wealth by working above and beyond the demands of the state quotas. Deng commented approvingly that it was correct "to make some people rich first so as to lead all the people to wealth."[28] The "supply-side" flavor of this economic philosophy may have appealed to Ronald Reagan. In addition, private plots on rural communes were expanded and prices of produce from these plots were determined by supply and demand. As a result of this increase in "free enterprise," agricultural output in China rose dramatically during the 1980s. "It doesn't matter what color the cat is," Deng said, "so long as it catches mice." While, under Mao, probably one hundred million peasants did not have enough food to eat, under his successors, starvation became virtually a thing of the past.

The increase in disposable income sparked a consumer revolution in China. A growing middle class indulged itself in television sets, refrigerators, and washing machines. In towns and cities, individuals could open restaurants and motels. Wealthy families were even permitted to hire cooks and nannies.

One scholar, in a perceptive essay, has compared this Chinese modernization to the Soviet system in the 1920s under Lenin's New Economic Policy.[29] While this may be correct, it must not be forgotten that the NEP period in Russia was eclipsed by Joseph Stalin. It is most unlikely that a Chinese Stalin will succeed Deng Hsiao-ping. Far too many of his reforms have become irreversible.

Tens of thousands of Chinese students were studying abroad during the 1980s. In the United States alone, there were more than ten thousand. These are almost certain, over time, to constitute a group committed to keep China's door open to the outside world. Dozens of new universities sprang up all over China. In Shanghai alone, there were over fifty institutions of higher learning.[30] In 1984 the Chinese Ministry of Education purchased $4 million worth of scientific books from the United States in order to help China overcome the "dark age" of the Cultural Revolution. Christian churches and Buddhist temples were reopened. Foreign trade with the United States went up from $1 billion in 1978 to $5 billion in 1984. In that year alone, over a thousand contracts were signed to import advanced Western technology and equipment.[31]

The political system, too, was liberalized slightly. While there were no free elections and no civil liberties in the American sense, political controls were loosened and people were less afraid to voice their opinions. Economic decision making was decentralized, and it became possible for provinces and municipalities to sign contracts with foreign governments without having to get Peking's approval. Tourist trips to Hong Kong were organized and visits to the United States were no longer an impossible dream.

President Reagan's visit to China in April 1984 was very successful. Even though the Chinese deleted some passages about God, capitalism, and freedom from the President's speeches, the encounter between the two leaders was warm and cordial. A number of agreements were signed, including one pertaining to the development of nuclear reactors in China. Even the Taiwan issue no longer appeared as an insurmountable problem. President Reagan left with good feelings about his first trip in a Communist country, albeit one in which Russians were no longer popular and where millions of little children were busily studying English.

During Ronald Reagan's second term as President, US rapprochement with China continued to accelerate, probably as a result of the Chinese leaders' decision to modernize their country and to move away from orthodox communism to something resembling a mixed economy. In Deng Hsiao-ping's own inimitable phrase, China now had to "improve Communism through Capitalism."

During those years a stock exchange was established in Shanghai, and the touchy issue of Hong Kong was defused, at least temporarily, by considerable Chinese flexibility in negotiations with the British over the future status of the crown colony.

As the leadership of the Communist party in 1987 passed from the aging Deng Hsiao-ping to Zhao Ziyang, the economic reforms began to gather increasing momentum. Not only did Communist party slogans begin to disappear and signs proclaiming "Time is money" make an appearance, but at Beijing University, the country's most prestigious institution of higher learning, a towering statue of Mao Tse-tung was hauled down in the middle of the night. Many members of the faculty interpreted this event as a symbol of the decline of rigid communist ideology. Mao in China seemed to be suffering the same posthumous fate under his successors as Stalin did under Gorbachev in Russia. Yet, there remained one major difference between the Soviet and Chinese reforms: Gorbachev placed political reforms ahead of economic ones, whereas Deng's priorities were the reverse. Hence, in China, the economy improved but the political dictatorship remained, but in Russia signs of democracy emerged but the economy continued to languish.

Not everything went smoothly, of course, for China's economy. During 1988, China's growth under the new mixed economy became so rapid that unmistakable signs of overheating, including inflation, began to surface. The cities grew at a faster pace than the countryside, and a good deal of corruption and panic buying of staple commodities finally convinced the leadership that the rate of growth had to be slowed. "We have been bold enough," declared Deng Hsiao-ping, "now we need to take our steps in a more cautious way." As a result, the central government reined in the free markets in some localities and reimposed central controls. Hotels, restaurants, tour companies, taxi fleets, and commodity trading companies were investigated, and, in cases of flagrant corruption and profiteering, severe punishments were meted out. It was not likely, however, that these developments signaled a return to orthodox Marxism. Much more likely, they signified the inevitable birth pains of a new economic system, or perhaps more accurate, a partial return to a more traditional, uniquely Chinese, economic way of life.

What is the explanation for China's amazing about-face under Mao's successors?

One clue may be found in the fact that Mao's widow remained in prison under a commuted death sentence. She continued to symbolize the horrors of the Cultural Revolution that almost tore China apart in the 1960s and 1970s. During those years, probably close to a million people were killed or driven to suicide. Millions of others were sent to labor camps or remote rural areas. Universities were closed, intellectuals were harassed, and science and technology were set back by at least two decades. The Chinese people, embittered and exhausted, began to question the very legitimacy of Communist party rule. Respect for the socialist system was at an all-time low.

Mao's successors realized that only drastic changes could ensure their political survival. They had no desire to return to the repression of the Mao era, and began to regard the "Great Helmsman" with the kind of ambivalence with which the Russians regarded Joseph Stalin. Gradually, the Soviet model became associated in Chinese perceptions with the horrors of the Cultural Revolution. The Americans, on the other hand, did not trigger too many bitter memories. The Korean war, after all, was a generation removed by now. Besides, the Americans, too, mistrusted the Soviet Union's domestic repression and imperialist foreign policy. Hence, Mao's Cultural Revolution served as the catalyst which triggered China's modernization program and the friendship with the United States. The founder of Chinese Communism also became the architect of its ultimate undoing. History is a great teacher of irony.

Thus, two nations that had lived in enmity for a generation were gradually drawn together by perceptions of a common danger and of a common opportunity. Afghanistan was probably the watershed event that moved the United States from a position of dead center between Russia and China clearly to the side of China. And the decision to modernize China, taken by Mao's successors, accelerated this trend. Once again, as in bygone days, Chinese students came to the United States to acquire science and technology. Once again, they wanted to capture the "foreign fire" for themselves. But this time China was determined to use the American "barbarians" against the Russian "barbarians." After all, since 1949 China had managed to throw out all barbarians except the Russians. What could be more logical than using the American "fire" against the only other Western nation that refused to leave territories that China considered to be its own? And what, from the American perspective, could be more logical than using China in its new hard-line policy against the Soviet Union?

And then came Mikhail Gorbachev, the catalyst of a new era in superpower relations. Ronald Reagan, the man who ended détente with the "evil empire" in 1983, resumed it with Gorbachev's Russia five years later. Similarly, China's new leaders repudiated many of the teachings of Mao Tse-tung and began to enjoy détente with both the United States and the Soviet Union.

Glasnost and *perestroika* also had their day in domestic Soviet politics. A few weeks after the fourth superpower summit, Mikhail Gorbachev presided over a memorable Communist party conference in Moscow. In an atmosphere of free debate not seen in Russia since the early years of Lenin, more than 4000 delegates debated the major issues of political and economic reform.

In a stormy session on July 2, 1988, the delegates approved plans for the establishment of a new a powerful post of president, who would oversee both domestic and foreign policy. The position was to be filled by the Party leader, Mikhail Gorbachev, and would be limited to two 5-year terms. In addition, the conference approved a partial transfer of power from the party to popularly elected legislatures and an end to party interference in the day-to-day management of almost every aspect of Soviet life. The "old guard" came in for scathing criticism. One delegate even demanded the resignation of Andrei Gromyko from his largely ceremonial post of president, and Gromyko did indeed resign. As a gesture of atonement for the crimes of Joseph Stalin, the delegates voted to build a monument to the victims of his twenty-five years of tyrannical rule.

So far as economic reforms were concerned, the delegates were highly critical. Despite *glasnost* and *perestroika,* most complained, store shelves were still empty and consumer goods rare. Some suggested that a badly needed overhaul of the sluggish Soviet economy should be given priority over political reforms. In the view of many, the Chinese approach of putting economic reforms first made sense in the Soviet Union as well.

Although the long-range effects of this historic conference cannot as yet be fully evaluated, one conclusion is already clear. Mikhail Gorbachev was deadly serious in his determination to engage in a major restructuring of the Soviet system. A man of extraordinary charisma and self-confidence, he declared that "if the Soviet Union (did) not reform its political system, all our initiatives, the whole massive task we have set for ourselves, will grind to a halt."

As George Bush embarked upon his presidency in 1989, the Soviet Union was convulsed by even more dramatic changes. In April, the first contested elections in more than seventy years gave an overwhelming mandate to Gorbachev's reform program and in May the new 2,250-member Congress of People's Deputies elected the Soviet reformer to the post of President for a five-year term with a limit of two terms in office. As one of the new deputies put it: "This is our first lesson in the first grade of the school of democracy."

Eastern Europe, too, was changing beyond recognition. A free election took place in Poland; the barbed wire between Hungary and Austria came down; and Lithuania, Latvia, and Estonia demanded independence from the Soviet Union. The Yugoslav government announced flatly that communism did not work. "What is communism today?" one Belgrade resident was supposed to have asked another. "Communism," the other man replied, "is the longest and most painful road from capitalism back to capitalism." There was little doubt that by 1990 the Soviet grip on Eastern Europe had loosened considerably. Nationalism and democracy simply proved to be more enduring forces than Marxist ideology.

In historical perspective, it is striking to note that, by current Soviet standards, most of the nation's leaders in the past were either criminals like Stalin or incompetents like Brezhnev. Neither had the integrity or vision to do justice to the Russian people. Perhaps Mikhail Gorbachev, at long last, after decades of darkness and brutality, would let in the sunlight. If this be so, then the Soviet elections of 1989 may rank among the most significant political events since World War II.

Interestingly, and not without a note of irony, Mikhail Gorbachev's political reforms ignited a bonfire in Beijing, China. The Soviet leader had scheduled a visit to the Chinese capital in May 1989, in order to mend a thirty-year rift between China and the Soviet Union. He and Deng Hsiao-ping had planned worldwide publicity for this first visit in thirty years by a Soviet leader to Beijing. History, however, takes no reservations.

Tens of thousands of Chinese students, yearning for freedom and democracy, saw Gorbachev's visit as a catalyst for pressing their demands. The Sino-Soviet summit was almost totally eclipsed by a million protesters crowded into the one-hundred-acre Tiananmen Square in Beijing. The students were joined by workers, peasants, teachers, soldiers, and ordinary citizens from all over China. "Give us democracy or give us death," thousands of banners screamed, paraphrasing Patrick Henry. "We have rice, but we have no laws," one student exclaimed. "The Russians have Gorbachev, but whom do we have?" asked another. Three thousand students went on a hunger strike to emphasize their determination. Deng Hsiao-ping and his conservative Premier, Li Peng, called out the army to quell the uprising, but the trucks were stopped by the students and, at first, the troops refused to shoot at them. On May 30, 1989, the Chinese students placed a replica of the Statue of Liberty in Tiananmen Square, directly across from the portrait of Mao Tse-tung. Thus, China's youth had planted their own version of freedom's most powerful beacon in the middle of the nation's capital.

Three days later, with sudden ferocity, everything changed. On direct orders from the aging Deng Hsiao-ping, the Chinese army forced its way into Tiananmen Square and crushed the uprising with fierce brutality. More than 3,000 students were killed and tens of thousands wounded in a Saturday night massacre on June 3, 1989, as the People's Army turned its guns on its own people. On Sunday morning, the square was occupied by the army and the "goddess of democracy" was crushed by a tank. With one stroke, Deng Hsiao-ping, the economic reformer, had become the butcher of Beijing. China's first popular uprising since the communist victory of 1949 was drowned in blood.

The old men who ruled China now wasted no time to reassert their power. Zhao Ziyang, who had been sympathetic to the students, was stripped of all his posts and replaced by men loyal to Deng. A Stalinist purge descended on China. Chinese citizens accused of "counter-revolutionary activity" were paraded through the streets, tried publicly, and executed by a pistol shot in the head. Foreigners were told that the student uprising had never happened. Indeed, the government declared, students had shot and killed over 300 innocent soldiers. It was George Orwell's *Nineteen Eighty-Four* all over again, complete with the "Ministry of Truth" telling a pack of lies. For American students, there was a profound lesson in the Beijing uprising and its tragic climax. Students their age were prepared to lay down their lives in order to gain a fraction of the freedom that Americans sometimes take for granted.

It is often said that freedom, once out of the bottle, cannot be stuffed back in again; it is bound to reassert itself. This may be true; but often it takes a very long time to reappear. In 1956, after a few heady days of freedom, Soviet tanks crushed it in Hungary. More than thirty years had to pass before Imre Nagy, Hungary's hero of freedom, was reburied in Budapest to the accompaniment of church bells. In 1968, after a few months of "socialism with a human face, " Brezhnev's tanks invaded Czechoslovakia and crushed freedom there for an entire generation. In China, however, the old leaders lost all claim to legitimacy by turning on their own people. Leaders who shoot at their own future do not have much of a future. For that reason, the next convulsion in China may come sooner rather than later. And somewhere in China, awaiting his turn after the old men have died, may be a Chinese Gorbachev.

In the longer view, it is virtually certain that the uprising of 1989 will stand as a major historical event. It proved that economic reform must inevitably lead to demands for political reform. As Alexis de Tocqueville observed in his study of the French Revolution, people tend to revolt not when things are at their worst, but when they are getting better.

The spring of 1989 clearly was historic, both in Russia and China. Real elections were held in the former and demanded by millions in the latter. Communism was in convulsions everywhere. The Chinese purge of 1989 may be the last gasp of a dying beast called Maoism. Democracy seemed to be the wave of the future. Since the last edition of this book appeared, yet another historic change has taken place. Five years ago, nuclear war still seemed a real possibility. Today it is remote. After half a century of brandishing the nuclear sword, the leaders of the superpowers have come to realize at last that the only way to win the nuclear war game is not to play the game at all.

REFERENCES

1 Barrington Moore, Jr., *Soviet Politics—The Dilemma of Power*. Cambridge, Mass.: Harvard University Press, 1950, p. 392.
2 *Ibid.*

3 John Lukacs, *A History of the Cold War*. New York: Doubleday, 1961, pp. 18–19.

4 *Time,* December 19, 1988, p. 18.

5 Merle Fainsod, *How Russia Is Ruled*. Cambridge, Mass.: Harvard University Press, 1953, p. 285.

6 For a perceptive analysis of the Soviet-Yugoslav dispute, see Adam B. Ulam, *Titoism and the Cominform*. Cambridge, Mass.: Harvard University Press, 1952.

7 Robert Strausz-Hupé, et al., *Protracted Conflict*. New York: Harper, 1959, p. 188.

8 *Ibid*.

9 John Foster Dulles, "Thoughts on Soviet Foreign Policy," *Life,* June 3, 1946, p. 124.

10 John K. Fairbank and Ssu-yu Teng, *China's Response to the West*. Cambridge, Mass.: Harvard University Press, 1954, p. 19.

11 *Ibid.,* p. 25.

12 John K. Fairbank, *The United States and China*. Cambridge, Mass.: Harvard University Press, 1958, p. 142.

13 *Ibid.,* p. 143.

14 *Ibid*.

15 For an excellent description and perceptive analysis of this period, see Conrad Brandt, *Stalin's Failure in China*. Cambridge, Mass.: Harvard University Press, 1958.

16 Edgar Snow, *Red Star over China*. New York: Random House, 1938, passim.

17 "The Danger of Détente," *The New Leader,* October 1, 1973.

18 *The New York Times,* November 25, 1974.

19 Quoted in *The New York Times,* December 27, 1960.

20 Strobe Talbott, *The Russians and Reagan*. New York: Vintage Books, 1984, p. 32.

21 Foreign Policy Statement by Yuri Andropov, September 28, 1983.

22 Strobe Talbott et al., *Mikhail S. Gorbachev: An Intimate Biography*. New York: Signet, 1988, pp. 10–11.

23 *Ibid.,* p. 234.

24 *The New York Times,* May 29, 1988.

25 *Time,* December 19, 1988, p. 18.

26 *The New York Times,* December 12, 1988.

27 *Ibid*.

28 Donald S. Zagoria, "China's Quiet Revolution," Foreign Affairs, Spring 1984, p. 883.

29 *Ibid.,* p. 880.

30 *The New York Times,* July 1, 1984.

31 Zagoria, *op. cit.,* p. 889.

SELECTED BIBLIOGRAPHY

Bialer, Seweryn and Michael Mandelbaum. *The Global Rivals*. New York: Knopf, 1988. A persuasive case that Mikhail Gorbachev, for good reasons of his own, is trying hard to establish new relationships with the United States, China, Europe, and the Third World.

Fairbank, John K. *The United States and China*. 4th ed., Cambridge (Mass.): Harvard University Press, 1978. The definitive work on the subject, by the dean of US China scholars.

Gorbachev, Mikhail. *Perestroika: New Thinking for Our Country and the World*. New York: Harper & Row, 1987. The blueprint for Soviet society, and foreign policy, from the general secretary's own pen.

Hewett, Ed A. *Reforming the Soviet Economy*. Washington, D.C.: Brookings, 1988. A thorough history of the Russian economy since Khrushchev, with emphasis on the Gorbachev reforms.

Hough, Jerry. *Russia and the West: Gorbachev and the Politics of Reform*. New York: Simon & Schuster, 1988. A lively and stimulating reinterpretation of Russian history with some challenging insights about the Gorbachev phenomenon and the US response.

Stoessinger, John G. *Nations in Darkness: China, Russia, and America*. 4th ed., New York: Random House, 1986. An analysis, through case studies, of Sino-Soviet-American relations.

Talbott, Strobe, and Editors of *Time*. *Mikhail S. Gorbachev: An Intimate Biography*. New York: Time, 1988. An excellent, perceptive, and well-written biography of the Soviet leader, for the general reader.

4

THE NORTH-SOUTH STRUGGLE

The day of small nations has passed away; the day of empires has come.

Joseph Chamberlain, Birmingham, 1904

Empires have fallen on evil days and nations have risen to take their place.

Rupert Emerson, Cambridge, Massachusetts, 1960

THIRD WORLD NATIONALISM

During the lifetime of a person born at the midpoint of this century, more new nations were born than in the entire history of the nation-state system put together. Most of these nations have emerged in the Third World—Asia, the Middle East, and Africa. Almost all of them rose from the ashes of dying European empires upon which the sun finally set after centuries of colonial rule. This new Third World nationalism has altered the world map more profoundly than any other phenomenon in this century.

A word of caution is in order before we begin our analysis. The term "Third World," though widely used, is an unfortunate cliché. It implies that there is a "first" and a "second" world, presumably the Western and Communist worlds respectively. The "Third World" concept, therefore, assumes an East-West division of the world and it is precisely this perspective that is *not* shared by most of the new nations. They see a world divided less between Communists and anti-Communists, and more between rich and poor, whites and nonwhites, people starving and people on a diet. They regard the phrase *Third World*—not entirely unjustly—as prejudicial and condescending.

We have tentatively defined nationalism as a people's vision of a common past and a common future. This definition of nationalism provides a general form, but is still lacking in content. We shall now attempt to build a more complete definition of nationalism in our time by analyzing those attributes that the new nations seem to hold in common. After examining the anatomy of the new nationalism in this manner, we shall subject its great adversary—colonialism— to a similar analysis. Only if we are clear about the nature of the two antagonists can we understand the pattern of their interaction.

The first striking fact about the new nationalism is its peculiar vision of a common past. Its birth took place in the crucible of the declining Western empires. In the words of Rupert Emerson, "empires have fallen on evil days and nations have risen to take their place."[1] The fight that these new nations waged against Western powers was their great formative experience. As the adult person is conditioned by the conscious and unconscious memories of his childhood and adolescence, the nation-state is also conditioned by its memories—in other words, its history. This explains the fact that the world view of the new nationalism is oriented toward anticolonialism rather than anticommunism.

This common colonial heritage of the new nations has resulted in their extreme ambivalence toward all things Western. Most of the new nationalist leaders harbor great admiration for many of the Western institutions and mores which they absorbed during the days of colonialism, but in their fight for national identity they are psychologically compelled to reject to close an identification with the West. It is not an accident that many of the leaders of independence movements were educated in Western universities as well as Western jails. Gandhi of India, Sukarno of Indonesia, and Nkrumah of Ghana are cases in point.

The psychological dependence on the colonial past sometimes reaches a point of fixation. A good example of this was Indonesia's insistence on annexing West New Guinea. The Indonesians had nothing in common with Guinea either ethnically or culturally. The only link that united them was the fact that both Indonesia and Guinea were parts of the Dutch empire. For this reason alone, it was felt, Guinea must belong to the new state of Indonesia. The hypnotic effect of the colonial past thus continues to play a vital role in the political policies of the new nationalism.

A final aspect of this psychological phenomenon is the paradoxical fact that in the very name of independence the new nationalism often tends to claim as its own many Western institutions that it absorbed during the colonial period. The following report from Nigeria shortly before independence will make this point clear:

> With Nigerian independence approaching, government officials are pleading with Africans to wear clothes. Abakaliki Province officials said it would not be dignified for nature-loving Nigerians to go naked in independence as they did under British colonialism. In other provinces the people have donned clothes. But in Abakaliki not even a fig leaf, much less loin cloth is worn. Provincial secretary J. W. Leach

said Abakaliki residents must get clothes in thirty days. Any person found naked or scantily clothed will be prosecuted, the secretary said.[2]

In sum, the colonial heritage has left a deep and lasting impression. Even though sovereign national status is in the process of superseding Western colonialism almost everywhere in our time, the distinctive psychology of the former colonies, especially their emotions of "independicitis," are certain to persist for a long time to come. When one considers the fact that virtually everything that shaped colonial peoples was determined by the white West, this prediction should surprise no one. Their god was an alien god, their language was foisted upon them, and even their territorial boundaries, as in Africa, were drawn arbitrarily by Western hands.

The "colonial hangover," therefore, echoes down from the past into the twentieth century. We can say many critical things about the Soviet Union, but we cannot say that Russians colonized Africa. The Western nations did, and hence Africans often fear Westerners more than they fear the Soviet Union or China. One cannot free oneself from the colonial past easily or without great pain.

Turning to the vision of a common future, a second important attribute of the new nationalism is the determined quest for racial equality. All the major colonial powers practiced the color bar with varying degrees of rigor. It was an inexpensive, rapid, and reliable instrument that enabled the white man to establish his political, economic, and psychological domination. There was a relative permanence in the racial line of demarcation that was absent from other lines of demarcation, such as economic status, occupation, language, or religion. It is probably not an exaggeration to maintain that the color bar, of all the attributes of colonial rule, was the one most fiercely resented. Until the end of World War II, the alleged inherent superiority of the white man was accepted almost as an axiom by the peoples under colonial dependency. This superiority, rationalized by various concepts, such as "the white man's burden" or *la mission civilisatrice,* was frequently impressed upon the African and Asian peoples by force. There is a poignant account in Gandhi's *Autobiography* of an episode in South Africa which left a lasting impression on the young man's life. The scene took place on a train to Pretoria. In Gandhi's words:

A passenger came next and looked me up and down. He saw that I was a "coloured" man. This disturbed him. Out he went and came in again with one or two officials. They all kept quiet, when another official came to me and said, "Come along, you must go to the van compartment."

"But I have a first class ticket," said I.

"That doesn't matter," rejoined the other. "I tell you, you must go to the van compartment."

"I tell you, I was permitted to travel in this compartment at Durban, and I insist on going on in it."

"No, you won't," said the official. "You must leave this compartment, or else I shall have to call a police constable to push you out."

"Yes, you may. I refuse to go out voluntarily." The constable came. He took me by the hand and pushed me out. My luggage was also taken out. I refused to go to the other compartment and the train steamed away.[3]

Once nonwhite peoples began to win battles, the myth of the white man's invincibility began to disintegrate. This writer witnessed the process of disintegration in Asia, at a time when the Japanese war machine swept the continent and forced the English from Burma, the French from Indochina, and the Dutch from the East Indies. Although the Japanese victory was short-lived, the lesson was clear: the white man could be beaten. And when the colonialists returned in 1945, they found to their bitter surprise that they could not go home again, that indeed a relentless demand for equality rang in their ears and would not be silenced. The Japanese invasion had served as a kind of catalyst, which demonstrated that the white man could be challenged successfully. In the case of the former British colonies, sovereignty was won with relatively little bloodshed: India, Pakistan, Burma, and Malaya gained their independence through legal transfers of power. Indonesia, however, emerged from Dutch colonialism only after four years of bloody conflict; and the French colony of Indochina was liquidated only after a decade of terrible jungle warfare culminating in the disastrous battle of Dienbienphu in 1954. This battle was a major landmark in the rise of the new nationalism: it signified the first great military encounter since the Russo-Japanese war of 1904 in which a nonwhite people was victorious over the white man and made its victory stick.

The importance attached to racial equality in the new nationalist countries may also be seen in their reactions to racial problems outside their own boundaries. Preoccupation with this problem frequently distorts their perception of conditions elsewhere. The view held of the United States, for example, was never more favorable than in 1954 when the United States Supreme Court in a unanimous decision declared segregation in public schools unconstitutional. But when this decision subsequently had to be enforced at Little Rock, the United States stood condemned in the eyes of the new nationalist world. Similarly, the passage of comprehensive civil rights legislation in the United States a decade later was widely hailed, but the simultaneous racial crises were seen by many Africans as virtually a civil war. Hence, the understandable though often single-minded quest for racial equality motivating the African and Asian peoples makes it difficult for them to arrive at an objective appraisal of political forces in those parts of the world where different conditions apply. It is clear that in the perspective of the new nationalist powers, racial equality is the most important single principle of their new-found sovereignty.

The quest for equal status with the Western powers is also expressed in the economic goals of the new nationalism. Almost all of the new nations have adopted programs of industrialization, their leadership being convinced that industrialization is an essential precondition for economic development in general. As a rule, this new "industrial revolution" works in favor of centralization in both government and economy. In fact, a case may be made that rapid industrialization leads to the development of elites inimical to the democratic process. Severe splits have arisen in African and Asian societies between those who favor industrialization and those who oppose it in the name of tradition. Indeed, since such circumstances as the overpopulation of urban centers, the breakdown of kinship systems, and the breakdown of traditional handicraft economies tend in many ways to conflict with the official goal of industrialization, there is generally a great deal of such opposition. And not infrequently, the new national leadership does not shrink from resorting to undemocratic means to eradicate those who oppose it. In this struggle, there often emerge one-party machines and various other arrangements of an authoritarian nature. Former Prime Minister Nkrumah of Ghana, for example, simply sent the opposition into exile when it challenged his authority, and President Sukarno of Indonesia frankly announced the institution of "guided democracy" shortly after he came to power.

It must, of course, be admitted that the end of political colonialism does not always necessarily mean the end of economic dependency upon the former colonial power. In many cases, a new nation's financial and trading patterns are still heavily influenced by the colonial past. Ghana's cocoa crop, for example, is still marketed primarily through London, and the price of cocoa is largely determined by the demand picture in Western countries. These vestiges of colonial dependency, described by the new nationalist leaders as "neo-colonialism," are likely to persist for a considerable time, even though it is the declared policy of most of the new nations to become self-sufficient as rapidly as possible.

A third and somewhat disturbing generalization concerns the political structures that seem to be evolving in the new nationalist countries. The trend is clearly not in the direction of democratic parliamentary regimes. Most of these new nations are leaning toward some kind of authoritarian political organization. One-party governments, weak legislative bodies, and military elites are common to most. This fact simply demonstrates that the fight for national self-determination is not necessarily synonymous with a struggle for democracy. It is a curious fact that the Western conception of the new nationalism has not sufficiently grasped this truth. Instead, many Westerners have continued to expect that, after a period of tutelage in the arts of self-government under one or another of the Western powers, the new nations of Asia and Africa would quickly develop into sound and sophisticated democracies. Yet in view of the fact that most of the new nations have a centuries-long heritage of tribalism, feudalism, or autocracy, the authoritarian trend of the new nationalism is entirely consistent with their historical tradition. One cannot expect that a single generation of political independence can quickly erase centuries of political domination.

A fourth characteristic of the new nationalism is its reluctance to ally itself with either of the two superpowers. Most of the new nations desire to stay aloof from the East-West struggle. That is the reason why Westerners have developed the habit of referring to the new non-Western nations as the Third

World. In Asia, India for many years considered itself the leader of this policy of nonalignment before Prime Minister Indira Gandhi in 1971 concluded a twenty-five-year treaty of friendship with the Soviet Union. The Indians' reasoning regarding this early stand was that since their own experience had been such a unique synthesis of Asia's past and the West's present, their country might be better suited than most others to act as a mediator in the East-West struggle. In Africa, Nigeria took the lead in the adoption of such a bridge-building policy before it was convulsed by civil war in the late 1960s.

We must remind ourselves here that the term "uncommitted," when applied to the new nationalism, refers only to the East-West struggle. In the other struggle, that against colonialism, the movement is very much committed. Even in the East-West conflict, the policy of nonalignment is applied, strictly speaking, only in the avoidance of military alliances. In their political sympathies most of the so-called uncommitted nations are much less scrupulously impartial, but tend, in fact, to lean in either one direction or the other. Liberia, for example, inclines toward the West, whereas Guinea, through its late leader, Sekou Touré, was deeply influenced by Marxism. Others of the new nations, such as Indonesia and Burma, have flirted with both sides in the course of their brief histories. Cambodia presents a particularly tragic case. After many years of nonalignment during which Cambodia enjoyed a relatively prosperous economy, the nation was pulled into the vortex of the war in Indochina and was virtually devastated as a result.

In its attempts to gain the allegiance of the new nationalism in the struggle with communism the West has consistently pointed out that Western colonialism is a phenomenon of the past that is today in rapid process of dissolution. The West maintains that a far more threatening and virulent form of colonialism than that of the dying Western empires is that posed by communism. The Soviet invasion of Afghanistan in 1980 is cited as a case in point. Yet, while most of the new nations were deeply disturbed by the events of Afghanistan, they find it difficult to forget the experiences of their own history, which is the history of Western domination. And the fact remains—historical accident though it undoubtedly was—that there were no Russian colonizers in Africa and in the Middle East. The absorption of Eastern Europe and Soviet military interventions in Hungary and Czechoslovakia have been geographically too far removed from most of the African and Asian nations to arouse the indignation and concern that they have in the West.

Fifth, many of the new nations want to go back to their religious roots: Islam. The Arab nations, of course, are Moslem, but so are many Asian and African states. Indonesia and Somalia are only two examples. Christianity was identified in many of these nations with colonial oppression and Islam with freedom and resurgence. When the Ayatollah Khomeini decreed in 1980 that Iran return to Moslem fundamentalism, he did not perceive this as a backward step. After all, Islam in the eighth century had been a flourishing civilization and Moslem warriors had conquered half of Europe. By the 1980s, Islam was the only one of the world's great religions that was growing rapidly. It was estimated that there were 750 million Moslems in the world and that by the year 2000, Islam would match the one billion adherents of the Christian faith.

Finally, most of the Third World nations, with the exception of the oil-rich Arab states, are poor, some desperately so. They see an oil cartel on one side and a food cartel on the other, and they generally have few resources left to purchase either oil or food. Most Third World countries also have far too many mouths to feed. And many now angrily demand their seat at the world's banquet table. Growing access to technology, particularly nuclear technology, has made these demands more strident and more dangerous. The West will have to learn to share its wealth, or else there may be more violence and random terrorism. It is not likely that nations that are starving will watch idly while others are so overfed that they must go on reducing diets. The world, to adapt Abraham Lincoln's telling phrase, cannot endure one-quarter glutted and three-quarters hungry.

The new nationalism, then, may be defined as a movement profoundly conditioned by a Western colonial past, leaning toward authoritarian political organization, and declaring as its goal political, economic, and social equality with the West—that is, sovereignty, racial equality, and a modern industrial economy.

We shall now turn to an analysis of the great antagonists of the new nationalism.

IMPERIALISM AND COLONIALISM

Among the nations of Africa and Asia, imperialism and colonialism are generally viewed as monopolies of the white man. This view has become so widespread that the terms *imperialism* and *colonialism* have assumed a pejorative connotation in the West itself. To call a nation imperialistic has come to be an indictment, and to describe a dependent territory as a colony is likely to be construed as an insult. In effect, the two concepts have in the Western world become the symbols of a kind of collective guilt complex. Yet as a noted historian has pointed out, the West's record in this regard is by no means as unqualifiedly deserving of condemnation as is often alleged or felt to be the case. For,

> Though the brief history of Western imperialism has witnessed many injustices and cruelties, which however were in no way worse than the normal happenings in Asia and Africa before the advent of the white man, it has been on the whole a period of which the West, and especially Britain, has not to be ashamed. It would be wrong to apply twentieth century standards and principles of international law to preceding centuries. By doing that—and it should not be forgotten that these new twentieth century standards were developed by the Western world—the West suffers a bad conscience.[4]

Actually, the terms *imperialism* and *colonialism* simply denote a power relationship of one political entity over another. Imperialism describes the process of establishing that power relationship, and colonialism has to do with the pattern of domination and rule once the relationship has been consolidated. Neither is a monopoly of the white man or an exclusively modern phenomenon. Yellow peoples have dominated each other for centuries; black peoples are known to have exercised power over one another many centuries before the white man set foot on the African continent; and the history of political evolution in the West is the story of white men dominating other white men.

Historical perspective shows that these two terms have not always been in disrepute. The imperialist or colonizer of the nineteenth century was a hero to his contemporaries. Today a very different view is taken of Cecil Rhodes, for example, in both the West and in the new nations, than was taken of him two or three generations ago. The concept of colonialism has undergone a radical transformation in both time and space. The truth is, of course, that as concepts the terms *imperialism* and *colonialism* are neutral. Whether the relationship of domination they refer to is good or bad depends entirely on the values of the beholder. Power always remains power, but the values regarding what constitutes desirable or undesirable power relationships are ever changing.

It is clear that, in our day, the new nationalism sees Western colonialism as its great antagonist and directs most of its energies toward destroying it. This tendency to place colonialism and the new nationalism at opposite poles may be somewhat misleading. Actually, when viewed in historical perspective, the relationship between imperialism and nationalism has not been one essentially of antagonism, but of dialectical interrelation. Frequently, as in the course of the French Revolution, imperialism has grown out of nationalism; and such imperialism, in turn, has spawned new nationalist movements, as witness the rise of nationalism against the Napoleonic Empire. Indeed, the germs of imperialism are already in evidence in the nationalism of some of the new countries. Former Premier Nkrumah's aim to create a Pan-African movement under the leadership of Ghana was a case in point. President Nasser's Pan-Arab ambitions were another, as was the Libyan invasion of neighboring Chad. And the war between Iraq and Iran in the 1980s, too, was fueled by nationalist passions. In the words of one thoughtful observer, "Nations have arisen from the ashes of empire. Must they follow the ruinous course of their cantankerous predecessors?"[5]

Imperialism and colonialism in our time cannot be understood without reference to their historical development. We shall therefore begin by examining the origins of Western imperial expansion and then compare the policies of the Western colonial nations in their respective empires.

Imperialism, like most things human, cannot be explained by a single factor, although the attempt is persistently made. The Soviet explanation of Western colonialism, for example, is based on an exclusively economic interpretation. Third World leaders, too, as a rule, fail to see the complexity of the truth.

Imperialism was, first of all, a function of the struggle for prestige and power among nations. During the nineteenth century the possession of colonies was a major criterion of national power. It is a remarkable fact that only a century ago over half the world's territory was ruled by European nations. Hence, when war broke out between two or more European powers, the hostilities held with them the seeds of world conflagration. The intense competition among Britain, France, and Germany for colonies in the nineteenth century was essentially the expression of a struggle for preponderance of power.

A second source of Western colonial expansion lay in the kind of secularized missionary zeal represented in Rudyard Kipling's concept of "the white man's burden." The stated purpose of this sense of mission was to bring the blessings of an allegedly more advanced civilization to the non-European areas of the world. And, frequently, genuine humanitarianism did indeed play a significant part. Yet nearly always there were important less altruistic motives. At times the Europeans' civilizing zeal largely expressed itself in a claim of self-styled superiority. On other occasions it served as a cover for what was chiefly a desire to export some particular religious cause. And not infrequently, as in the case of Cortes in Mexico, it stood simply for the universal human urge for adventure.

A further ingredient in "the white man's burden" attitude, as well as a factor of the greatest importance in itself as a contributor to the development of Western imperialism and colonialism, was the motive of economic self-interest. In its early form, this was usually referred to as "mercantilism." The primary reason for colonization by Spain, for example, was the mercantilist quest for gold—the quest for the riches of an overseas empire to strengthen the mother country's standing and power at home and among the other nations of Europe. As has already been pointed out, the Communist explanation of the genesis and dynamics of imperialism and colonialism limits itself to the various ramifications of this economic factor.

The principal Communist work on this subject is Lenin's *Imperialism, the Highest Stage of Capitalism.* This treatise, heavily influenced by J. A. Hobson's *Study of Imperialism,* published in 1902, still provides the official Soviet interpretation of Western imperialism and has gained wide currency in the newly emerged countries of Asia and Africa. It therefore deserves careful analysis. Lenin's thesis is based on the Marxist view that the economic struggle in the highly industrialized societies in Europe necessarily leads toward monopoly capitalism. As this state of affairs develops, there occurs a concentration of more and more wealth in the hands of fewer and fewer people, with an ever-growing group of dispossessed swelling the ranks of the proletariat. At the point of "capitalist concentration," the few remaining monopolists have no choice but to turn upon each other. When this stage in the struggle is reached, Lenin maintained, the capitalists discover a reprieve for themselves to stave off the inevitable doom that faces them at the hands of the masses of dispossessed. This reprieve is imperialism. The capitalists, instead of turning upon each other, now proceed to annex colonies overseas, which afford them vast new outlets for the export of capital, thus relieving their highly saturated markets and giving them a new lease on life. But this is a reprieve only, Lenin claimed, not an amnesty; imperialism is merely a last desperate maneuver by the capitalists to avert their inevitable collapse. All that this maneuver can accomplish is postponement of the inevitable. Hence, in Lenin's view, an imperialist policy pursued by a highly industrialized nation was a sure sign that capitalism in that nation had reached its final stage before decomposition.

Lenin's case is not to be dismissed lightly; it is the most important single weapon used by the Soviet Union to gain the adherence of the new Third World countries. In an objective appraisal, it is evident that there is much truth in Lenin's view. It is true, for example, that the quest for colonies was pursued largely by the highly industrialized powers: Britain, France, Belgium, Germany, and, to a lesser extent, the United States. On the other hand, it must be pointed out that the rule of one people over another is not the monopoly of capitalist countries. The United States granted the Philippines their freedom; some industrialized countries like Sweden never actively sought colonies. In our time, in fact, Lenin's thesis could be turned with some validity even against the major noncapitalist power, the Soviet Union.

Lenin's thesis, while a brilliant tour de force, points up the dangers inherent in any one-factor analysis. For the fact is that the causes of imperialism and colonialism must be seen in terms of a subtle interplay among many factors, of which the economic, albeit the most significant, is only one. Nevertheless, the view of Western colonialism most often held in the new nationalist countries still closely resembles the single-factor interpretation first created by Lenin. Moreover, it is applied almost indiscriminately to all the varied forms of the Western colonial experience in Africa and Asia. All Western colonialism is thus lumped together and roundly condemned. And yet, in actual fact, there have been wide divergencies among the different types of Western colonialism. Each of the major Western powers—Britain, France, Holland, Belgium, and Portugal—evolved its own special colonial techniques. If the subject of colonialism is to be done justice, these differing techniques, and the philosophies behind them, deserve careful comparative analysis.

To begin with, the differences between the colonial policies of the two greatest Western empires, those of Britain and France, have been striking indeed. The British, as a general rule, exercised a form of indirect control over their possessions. The government operated through the existing local administrative patterns and usually permitted some degree of local participation. A viceroy usually symbolized the might of the British Empire; but this viceroy, though resplendent in the pageantry of his office, made it a point not to interfere in local customs and mores unless these jeopardized the interest of the empire. This policy of indirect rule stood in sharp contrast to the French concept of direct rule from Paris, which in the early period of colonization permitted no local self-government whatever. Overseas colonies were considered as much a part of France as were Normandy or Brittany. As the British developed their concept of the Commonwealth, which in our time was gradually to supersede the empire, they began to prepare their dependencies for ultimate self-government. As happened most notably in India, for example, the ground was laid for the eventual peaceful transfer of power by absorbing into the colonial administration more and more indigenous talent. The ultimate goal of the French colonial government, on the other hand, was the exact opposite: assimilation to the French way of life, in other words, "Frenchification." While for the British the political advancement of their dependent territories qualified them for secession and independence, similar advancement in the French colonies meant closer integration into the French way of life and greater participation in the French government. In practice, only a small group of the indigenous elite were "Frenchified" under this system. The vast majority continued to live under their own customs, recognized by the French under a separate legal code, and, as a rule, very much underrepresented in the French government. The British tended to emphasize the color bar more strongly than the French; the French might be said to have observed a "culture bar" more than a color bar. Hence, the masses tended to fare better in the British colonies but the educated elite had greater opportunities under the French system.

After the battle of Dienbienphu in 1954, French colonial policy began to emulate the British. The French Community under General de Gaulle's Fifth Republic sought to pattern itself after the British Commonwealth as a voluntary grouping no longer postulating assimilation as a necessary goal but aiming at a more flexible association. In 1958 President de Gaulle in effect offered the possibility of secession to all French dependencies save Algeria, and only one colony—Guinea—elected to sever all its ties with France. Virtually all the others elected to become independent states within the French Community. Six of these—Chad, Gabon, Senegal, the Central African Republic, the Malagasy Republic, and the Congo Republic—have participated in the community, while the nine others have remained fairly inactive. Considering the community's late start, it has been a moderate success.

There was, as noted above, one exception to the new French policy: Algeria. Algeria's legal status was never that of a dependency; it was always considered an integral part of France. Moreover, almost one tenth of the ten million people of Algeria were Frenchmen, known as *colons,* with large holdings and vested interests in North Africa. For these reasons, Algeria could not be neatly fitted into the emerging pattern of the French Community. The majority of the *colons* persistently demanded continued integration with France, while the indigenous population fought with equal insistence for independence. The Fourth Republic of France fell as a result of this apparently insoluble dilemma. It continued to be a severe irritant to the Fifth Republic as well, since protracted warfare over the issue steadily drained the resources of the mother country. In a bold and dramatic move, President de Gaulle in 1959 attempted to break the impasse by offering three alternatives to Algeria: integration, eventual complete independence, or voluntary association in the French Community. A year later, in a popular referendum on the Algerian question, a large majority of the population of France and its overseas territories supported the President in his offer. Himself favoring a voluntarily associated Algeria with the French Community, De Gaulle consistently attempted to use his great prestige to bring about a compromise between the demands of the long-embattled French *colons* and the indigenous Algerian peoples. At first this policy achieved only slow and halting success. Extremism on both sides repeatedly stalled all progress. But in 1962 De Gaulle's solution prevailed and Algeria received its independence. Shortly thereafter, a mass exodus of *colons* from Algeria fundamentally changed the internal political complexion of that newly independent country.

The Netherlands, Belgium, Portugal, and Spain are known as the lesser colonial powers of the West. On the whole, their record is less enlightened than that of the major powers. For three hundred years the East Indies were one vast sugar plantation yielding enormous revenues for the Dutch government. The indigenous population was compelled to give up its land, volunteer its labor, and generally devote itself to the improvement of the economy on behalf of the Netherlands. Severe famines, a sharp population decline in the colony, and primitive labor conditions characterized the period from 1600 to 1900. Not until the twentieth century were somewhat more enlightened welfare and educational policies adopted and the rudiments of self-government introduced through advisory councils. But even this paternalism came too late. When the Japanese forced the Dutch from the Indies, they were welcomed in many parts as liberators. And even when it became clear that the Japanese form of imperialism was even harsher than that of the Netherlands, the Indies refused to join the Dutch in their struggle to get the colony back. A determined independence movement denounced both the Dutch and the Japanese with a "plague on both houses," and insisted on a sovereign state of Indonesia. This goal was realized in 1949 and motivated a major policy change on the part of the Netherlands in what remained of its colonial empire. The new concept, which evolved and was applied in Dutch island possessions in the Caribbean, was in essence the commonwealth concept: voluntary association with political autonomy in the local affairs of the dependencies. In effect, the Netherlands has emulated the British example.

The Belgian experience again is unique. From 1908 to 1960 the Congo was a major source of revenue. Until 1957 all authority over the Congo was in the hands of the Belgian government, which appointed a resident governor-general who had the power to rule by decree. The distinctive aspect of the Belgian colonial experience was its enlightened economic and social policy. Minimum wage laws, housing and medical provisions, and a relatively high standard of living—among the highest in Africa—combined to give the colonial subjects of Belgium many benefits. Yet in the realm of government, the Belgian authorities were much less liberal. They insisted, in fact, on a policy of complete and uncompromising political paternalism. In 1959 this policy began to be confronted with rapidly spreading demands for independence. The Belgians, reversing their former policy, were quick to grant the formation of elective municipal and territorial councils. But this proved not enough, for with each new concession the Belgians made, Congolese demands increased and widened. The tide of new nationalism could not be stemmed and in mid-1960 Belgium withdrew from its colonial position altogether. Their social and economic advantages notwithstanding, the Congolese—wisely or unwisely—had insisted on complete sovereignty.

One Western colonial empire continued to live on with relatively little disturbance for almost five hundred years—at least until recently. That last stronghold of colonialism was Portugal, the first of the European states to acquire overseas territories and the last one to give them up. Angola, Portuguese Guinea, and Mozambique were considered integral parts of the mother country and were tightly controlled from Lisbon. A small indigenous elite was considered "assimilated," but the vast majority remained illiterate. The Portuguese practiced conscription of labor and, for control purposes, maintained a strict system of internal passports. Their forced-labor prison colonies were notorious throughout Africa.[6] While it lasted, Portuguese Africa was without a doubt the most rigid Western colonial regime of our time. Finally, in early 1974, the lid blew off. A dissident general, Antonio de Spinola, assumed power in Lisbon through a military coup. Spinola had been profoundly critical of his country's colonial policy in Africa and promptly began to explore ways in which Angola, Portuguese Guinea, and Mozambique could be prepared for independence with the least amount of turbulence both in Lisbon and in the colonies. In view of Portugal's five-hundred-year rule over these territories, this was not an easy task. It was obvious, however, by the mid-seventies, that Portugal's long career as a colonial power was near an end, and that it would follow in the footsteps of Britain, France, Belgium, and Holland. In August 1974, Guinea-Bissau, formerly Portuguese Guinea, was admitted as a sovereign state to the United Nations, and one year later, Angola and Mozambique achieved their freedom. Western colonialism in Africa was rapidly passing into the pages of history.

In reviewing the Western colonial record, one is able to make several interesting generalizations. First, most of the Western empires have adopted the commonwealth concept of voluntary association and all have come to terms with the prospect that sooner or later their colonial holdings must be liquidated altogether.

Second, it is significant that at first the new nationalism was most vociferous and insistent in its demands in those dependencies, like the British, that had enjoyed the most liberal colonial regimes. The more the colonial administrators taught the colonial elite about democracy, the more the demand for democracy made itself heard. It is not an accident that the most repressive colonial regime, that of Portugal, was the last to be troubled by political unrest. In part this may be explained by the fact that Portugal, itself an authoritarian regime, managed so ruthlessly to insulate its African population and, hence, to deprive it of outside contacts and standards of comparison. This observation might lead a Machiavellian observer to the paradoxical conclusion that the virtues rather than the vices of the West led to the graveyard of Western colonialism. Yet this would be very shortsighted. For if, as seems the case, the disappearance of colonialism is sooner or later inevitable, there are far greater advantages—at least in the long run—in a policy of meeting the demands of colonial peoples gradually and while a spirit of mutual respect still remains. The Belgians, for example, by seeking to control and hold on to their colonial positions too uncompromisingly, in the end not only lost out completely in the Congo but reaped widespread international ill will as well. The British, in contrast, have been rewarded for their more liberal policies in India by the continuation of valuable political and economic bonds between the two countries as well as by deep admiration on the part of Western and non-Western peoples alike. The world's last colony may well be British: the crown colony of Hong Kong. But even that possession is scheduled to revert to China by 1997.

The third observation that can be noted about Western colonialism is that, though it is in fact in the process of liquidation, it continues to be denounced as the new nations' most mortal threat. Although, as we have seen, there have been very different types of Western colonialism, it tends to be represented and reacted to as one and the same reprehensible phenomenon. Communist expansion, on the other hand, has so far largely escaped this kind of wariness and opposition. Most of the representatives at the Bandung Conference, held in April 1955 by twenty-nine Asian and African nations in Bandung, Indonesia, had the West in mind when the Conference resolved that "colonialism in all its manifestations is an evil which should speedily be brought to an end." The suggestion by the delegate from Ceylon that the Soviet Union was practicing colonialism in Eastern Europe was rejected by Prime Minister Nehru of India—the major speaker at the conference—who declared that there was no such thing as Soviet colonialism. There has been some modification of this attitude since the Soviet invasion of Afghanistan, but Gorbachev's pull-out from that country in the late 1980s might exonerate the Soviet Union from the colonial stigma once again. The United Nations, too, has been a major arena for the colonial struggle. Relentlessly, the new nationalist powers, steadily growing in numbers and strength, have demanded the "speedy and complete end of Western colonialism" in all organs of the world organization. The United Nations was unwilling to stop India from annexing the Portuguese enclave of Goa and was actually used as the vehicle for effecting the transfer of West New Guinea from Holland to Indonesia. These precedents seem to indicate that the world organization is unlikely to interfere with the liquidation of colonialism even if that liquidation may at times be accompanied by a show of force.

We shall now undertake three case studies of interaction between nationalism and colonialism: first, the emergence of India and Pakistan from British colonial rule; second, the death of Southern Rhodesia and the birth of Zimbabwe; and finally, the tragedy of South Africa and apartheid.

NATIONALISM AND COLONIALISM: PATTERNS OF INTERACTION

Democratic and Authoritarian Nationalism: India and Pakistan

The unique character of modern Indian nationalism has its roots in the tremendous power of the religions that shaped the nature of ancient Indian society.

Any analysis of India nationalism must therefore begin with an examination of the three great religions of India: Hinduism, Buddhism, and Islam.

Ancient Hinduism was an austere doctrine subscribing to the view that the cause of all evil in the world was human desire. The path toward redemption, therefore, lay in man's capacity to extinguish desire within himself through an act of will, and thus reach a state of Nirvana. Hinduism conceived of life as a never-ending cycle, or karma. Death simply meant passage into another incarnation of life. The form this new incarnation would take depended on performance in the previous one. Hence, it was quite possible for a man to pass into a lower or a higher form of life. The standard of excellence toward which the Hindu was to aspire was the attainment of Nirvana, or renunciation of desire. Since men were by nature unequal, only a few could attain this goal. This concept of the inequality of men was expressed in the social structure of ancient India, the caste system. Society was divided into four rigidly separated castes: The Brahmins, or priests, who had come closest to the Hindu ideal; the warriors who were to defend the society; the merchants; and the laborers. Actually, the social system was even more complex, since each caste had numerous subdivisions. At the bottom of the social pyramid were the outcasts, or pariahs, also known as "untouchables."

The great inroads made by Buddhism in ancient India may be explained largely in terms of the austerity of the Hindu doctrine. While Buddhism, too, was directed toward the afterlife, its view of man was much more optimistic. Under its influence, the Nirvana concept gradually changed from a doctrine of extinction and renunciation to a goal not unlike the Christian paradise. The figure of the Bodhisattva entered Indian life—the priest who, though entitled to enter Nirvana, has decided to postpone his own entrance in order to show the way to others. Late Buddhism, in fact, steered away more and more from the austerity of the Hindu faith. Sometimes only a few invocations would suffice to gain entrance to Nirvana, and Bodhisattvas frequently became deities who played the role of "social workers," assisting their less fortunate brethren. Despite this radical transformation of Hinduism, it must be remembered that Buddhism was able to grow out of Hinduism because the latter lent itself to the absorption of new forms of faith quite readily.

The third major religion of ancient India—Islam—stands in striking contrast to the other two. It came to India around 1000 A.D. Unlike Buddhism, Islam was never absorbed by the Hindus. The only attribute that Islam shares with its predecessor is its accent on the hereafter; there the similarity ends. While the Hindu worships a pantheon of gods, Islam is strictly monotheistic. When the Moslems first came to India, they destroyed all the Hindu temples and sculptures they found because they considered them idolatrous. The Hindu made no effort to convert others to his faith; Islam, like medieval Christianity, tended to proselytize by the sword. Even the social customs differed sharply. The Hindu was forbidden to eat beef, the Moslem was enjoined from eating pork. Worship in Hindu temples was often accompanied by music, whereas the Moslem in his mosque insisted on strict silence. The two religions were virtually irreconcilable. After sections of India in the northeast and the north-west were conquered by Moslems, the Hindus tended to regard them as an-other caste to be kept rigidly separate. The religious conflict between Hinduism and Islam still exists and is at the root of the struggle between India and Pakistan. Thus, by the time the West arrived there, India was a society politically divided, a society in which two radically different ways of life com-peted for the allegiance of the population: Hinduism, which was tolerant of dissension and absorptive; and Islam, which was militant, exclusive, and dog-matic.

British rule in India was established in the early seventeenth century through the instrument of the East India Company. In their campaigns to gain control of the subcontinent, the British followed a strategy of "divide and rule." The many satraps were played against each other until, by the late eigh-teenth century, most of India was in British hands.

The administration of British India presents a story full of contradictory harmonies and conflicts. The coming of the British added yet another element to the already highly complex Indian society. Christianity was brought to India, and yet the materialism of the Christian colonizers stood in stark con-trast to the spiritualism of the Hindu. The individualism of the British differed sharply from the group-centered culture of India. The democratic ideal of equality seemed strange to the caste-conscious Hindu. The British tried very hard, on the whole, to harmonize these many conflicts, and generally suc-ceeded.

In the pattern of indirect rule initiated by the British, a viceroy was put in charge of colonial administration. Local customs were left intact so long as they did not present a direct threat to the British presence or radically offend the British social ethos. Thus, the British did not interfere much with the caste system, although they did insist on the abolition of the Hindu custom of suttee, the immolation of widows on the funeral pyres of their husbands. They also outlawed infanticide and "thuggee," the practice of sacrificing unsuspecting travelers in lonely mountain passes to the goddess Kali.

The British made every effort to teach the Indians about British democracy, thus shaping the thinking that later was to result in the Indians' demand for self-rule. Imported British law and contractual relationships were often super-imposed upon the Indian culture. Especially in the later colonial period, indig-enous talent was admitted into the civil service. On the other hand, the British often exhibited extreme insensitivity. For example, in 1857 a full-dress rebel-lion was started by the rumor that pig and cow fat were being used to grease cartridges in rifles to be employed by Hindu and Moslem recruits in the army. The Sepoy Rebellion of 1857 that was touched off by this incident was crushed by the British with extreme cruelty.

The economic side of the Indian colonial experience presents a similarly mixed record. The early profits made by the East India Company were enor-mous. The British flooded India with manufactured goods and in turn com-pelled the indigenous population to concentrate on the production of raw materials, thus causing an imbalance in the economy and a decline in Indian industry. On the other hand, the industrial development of India meant the development of modern roads, telegraphs, harbors, mails, and railroads. Some aspects of this industrialization did not conflict with traditional customs, but at times even helped to revive them. For example, a modern network of railroads made religious pilgrimages easier for many Hindus. Another important byproduct of British colonialism was the rise of a whole new class of bankers, traders, educators, and lawyers who were to play a major role in the rise of the new India.

It is impossible to say whether modern India has benefited or suffered more as a result of its experience with British colonialism. To be sure, colonialism had many unfortunate effects. It frequently meant the exploitation of indigenous labor in order to develop the natural resources of the colony. And it resulted in the dislocation of the economy by turning the colony into a raw-material-producing area—a condition of "economic colonialism" that was to last much longer than its political counterpart. On the other hand, the British also did much to prepare India for the modern world: they bestowed upon the country an enlightened health and education program; they provided at least the foundations for a higher standard of living; and they educated an elite of future leaders.

In sum, then, India's experience with Western colonialism was by no means entirely negative. In view of this fact, combined with the tolerant faith of the Hindu religion, it is not surprising that when the nationalist reaction in India came, it followed an essentially nonviolent and democratic path.

The Indian nationalist movement was marked by the overwhelmingly powerful personality of Mahatma Gandhi. Gandhi was the spiritual father of the Indian Congress, the nationalist resistance organization under the British, which, without his unifying influence, would have been destroyed by factionalism. Indeed, without the charismatic leadership of Gandhi, Indian nationalism might well have run a very different and far more violent course.

Gandhi's nationalism was rooted in the Hindu doctrine of *ahimsa,* or noninjury to any living being. This concept was translated into the political doctrine of passive resistance, or "civil disobedience," a technique of nationalist assertion that the British found very embarrassing. Gandhi, himself of humble origins, lived most unpretentiously. He used a spinning wheel to produce his few garments. He denied himself all comforts and often endured long fasts in order to find support for his causes. When, in 1930, the British imposed a heavy tax on salt, Gandhi walked 165 miles to the sea to make his own salt. His example of employing a spinning wheel led to a widespread boycott of foreign cloth. Rather than cooperate with the British, he exhorted the population to go to jail. He himself was frequently imprisoned. But always, he emphasized the nonviolent character of Indian nationalism. His rejection of bloodshed as a deplorable aberration was, indeed, the movement's most basic moral and political principle. The steady advance toward independence made by India between 1900 and 1947 was due in large measure to Gandhi's insistence on spiritual rather than physical power.

Despite his enormous influence, Gandhi was unable to forge Indian nationalism into a cohesive whole. The Congress was always viewed with suspicion by the Moslems of the colony who feared persecution at the hands of a Hindu majority once India became independent. Though he tried his utmost to do so, Gandhi never succeeded in composing the differences between the two faiths. In the end, in 1948, he was assassinated by a Hindu fanatic who found the Mahatma's dogged attempts at reconciliation unbearable.

The Moslems early developed their own nationalist organization, the Moslem League. Its leader, Mohammed Ali Jinnah, insisted on the creation of a separate state of Pakistan for the Moslem minority. The great chasm between Hinduism and Islam robbed the Indian nationalist movement of much of its effectiveness. Often the two antagonists feared each other more than they did the colonial rule of Britain. The depth of the conflict may be seen from the fact that not even the unparalleled prestige of Gandhi was able to persuade his Hindu followers to make common cause with Islam. Nor did the Moslems feel any less strongly. As their view was expressed by Jinnah:

> How can you even dream of Hindu-Moslem unity? Everything pulls us apart: We have no intermarriages. We have not the same calendar. The Moslems believe in a single God, and the Hindus are idolatrous. Like the Christians, the Moslems believe in an equalitarian society, whereas the Hindus maintain their iniquitous system of castes and leave heartlessly fifty million Untouchables to their tragic fate, at the bottom of the social ladder.[7]

It is quite possible that this intense communal strife would have enabled the British to maintain control over India for an indefinite period. But World War II forced the British to make their peace with the prospect of Indian sovereignty. As a condition of India's collaboration in the war, Gandhi demanded a promise of immediate independence. When the British hedged, the Indian leader stated caustically that he was unwilling to accept "a post-dated check on a bank that was obviously failing." Even a British guarantee of speedy independence did not prevent some Indian nationalist leaders, like Subhas Chandra Bose, from throwing in their lot with the Japanese. After the conclusion of the war, it fell to the British Labour government, which itself had always been severely critical of Conservative policy toward India, to honor Britain's pledge. But when, in 1947, Indian nationalism finally triumphed, it left the country a house divided. In spite of Gandhi's repeated fasts and prayer meetings against it, partition seemed the only practicable solution. Hence, India and Pakistan emerged from British colonial rule as two separate sovereign states.

The triumph of nationalism in India was thus severely marred by the tragedy of partition. Three staggering problems were the direct result of this tragedy. The first aftermath of partition was a gigantic population exchange, one of the most massive in history. Over seven million Hindus, fearful of persecution in Pakistan, frantically sought refuge in India, and a similar number of Moslems fled to safety from India to Pakistani soil. The integration of these millions of refugees presented an almost insurmountable problem to both of the new states.

The second problem was economic in nature. Colonial India had been an economic unit for centuries and now suddenly found itself divided into three parts: India, East Pakistan, and West Pakistan. East Pakistan, formerly East Bengal, was separated from West Pakistan by almost one thousand miles of Indian territory. These two Moslem enclaves, dating from the Moslem conquest, had in common their religion but almost nothing else—not even language. Regional jealousies and economic competition immediately rose to the surface between the two Pakistans. Worse, Pakistan and India almost at once began economic warfare. India devalued her rupee, but Pakistan refused to follow suit. Jute, an important raw material grown mostly in Bengal, now became prohibitively expensive in India. In short, the three parts of the Indian subcontinent, which for centuries had been operating as an economic entity, now found themselves in the throes of a destructive economic feud. Overshadowing all the other disputes between the two new nations was the struggle for contested territory, especially the princely state of Kashmir. India demanded Kashmir on the ground that its ruler had been a Hindu, but Pakistan claimed the state on the basis that over three fourths of the population of Kashmir was Moslem.

The political structures of Hindu and Moslem nationalism also diverged sharply after independence. India, under the leadership of Jawaharlal Nehru, Gandhi's successor, immediately embarked on the ambitious and unprecedented experiment of shaping an overwhelmingly illiterate country into an advanced democracy. The Indian national elections of 1951–1952 were indeed an impressive performance. The new Indian government spared no effort to make this election a truly democratic one, and, on the whole, succeeded admirably. The Congress party, now pursuing a policy of gradual socialism patterned after the example of the British Labour party, became the dominant political power, with Nehru as its undisputed leader. In foreign affairs, the new India began at once to pursue its policy of nonalignment in the conflict between East and West and continued its primary emphasis on the struggle against colonialism. Pakistan set out on a very different road. It followed the general pattern of the new nationalism by developing its political structure along authoritarian lines; yet it departed from that pattern in its foreign policy by almost immediately embracing the side of the West in the East-West struggle.

The death of Nehru in 1964, however, marked the end of the postcolonial era in India. In the elections of 1967, the Congress party, now no longer associated by the opposition with the independence movement but rather with a stagnant status quo, suffered severe setbacks. Pakistan, too, changed course. While technically remaining a member of two Western alliances, SEATO and CENTO, the policies of its president, Ayub Khan, tended to remove it from the Western orbit. Relations between the two countries remained bitterly hostile. In 1965 fighting broke out along the Kashmir cease-fire line, ending later that year with another UN cease-fire. In January 1966 Soviet Premier Kosygin, at a meeting in Tashkent, persuaded both Pakistani President Ayub Khan and Indian Prime Minister Lal Bahadur Shastri to withdraw to the pre-1965 cease-fire lines in Kashmir. In 1966, Indira Gandhi, Nehru's daughter, was elected Prime Minister of India in a democratic election, while in 1969, President Ayub Khan turned Pakistan over to General Yahya Khan who placed the country under martial law.

In 1970, conditions on the Indian subcontinent deteriorated dramatically when severe tensions between East and West Pakistan erupted into open conflict. The catalyst was the worst cyclone of the century, which swept through East Pakistan, killing almost half a million people. In the aftermath of the storm, the Bengalis of East Pakistan felt that West Pakistan did not respond adequately to the needs of the victims. This sentiment led to increasingly insistent demands by the Bengalis for regional autonomy, articulated by their leader, Sheik Mujibur Rahman. During 1971, the West Pakistan government resorted to extremely repressive measures to deal with Bengali demands for autonomy. Severe fighting broke out and massive waves of Bengali refugees fled for their lives into the territory of their former enemy, India. By late 1971 the number of refugees approached the ten million mark. This flood of homeless and dispossessed people imposed a severe strain on the Indian economy and pressure mounted on Mrs. Gandhi to move toward a showdown with Pakistan.

In August 1971 India signed a defense treaty with the Soviet Union and shortly thereafter its forces crossed into East Pakistan, now renamed Bangladesh by the Bengalis. India's objective was to sever Bangladesh from West Pakistan, stop the flow of refugees into India, and dismember its old enemy. Indian soldiers were welcomed as liberators by the Bengalis, Pakistan was divided in half, Sheik Mujibur Rahman returned to Dacca in triumph, and Bangladesh became a political reality. At the United Nations, the Security Council met, but repeated Soviet vetoes prevented a cease-fire until the Indian forces had attained their military objectives. China supported West Pakistan, but with little more than rhetoric. By 1972 the political complexion of the Indian subcontinent had fundamentally changed.

The above analysis suggests that independence is no unmixed blessing. The two nations that emerged from British colonialism never really managed to live in peace with one another. When, moreover, West Pakistan decided to persecute its Moslem brethren in the East, India used this event as a pretext for a war that ended in the dismemberment of Pakistan. The great powers were also drawn into the vortex of this confrontation in the Third World. The Soviet Union backed India and thus increased its influence on the subcontinent. China backed Pakistan, largely as a function of its split with the Soviet Union, and the United States "tilted" toward Pakistan, since President Nixon, on the eve of his visit to China, found it tactically advisable to do so. Neither India nor Pakistan, during its thirty years of independence, made any radical changes in its political structure. India's government, except for two years of an authoritarian rule by Indira Gandhi in the mid-1970s, remained a constitutional democracy while the two Pakistans preferred authoritarian rule. For both countries, nationalism had been a bulldozer that had pushed them into the twentieth century. They now enjoyed the blessings of self-determination, but also inherited all the travails and turbulence of the modern world.

Strife between Hindus and Moslems still erupts periodically. In 1984, for example, major riots took place in several Indian cities. In addition, the Sikhs, followers of a monotheistic blending of Hinduism and Islam that began about 1500, waged a campaign for self-determination against the Indian government. Prime Minister Gandhi ordered the military suppression of the Sikh insurrection. In November 1984 she was assassinated by Sikhs who resented her strong-arm methods. Her death, in turn, triggered new outbursts of violence against the Sikh community in India.

Indira Gandhi's son, Rajiv Gandhi, succeeded his mother as prime minister. During his first term in office, between 1984 and 1989, a considerable amount of the new prime minister's energies were taken up by continued efforts to crush uprisings by Sikh militants in the Punjab demanding self-determination. In one of history's more striking ironies, the nation that had fought so hard against colonialism now had to face a nationalist insurgency of its own.

When one surveys the histories of India and Pakistan since the end of British colonial rule, it is difficult to avoid the conclusion that, in terms of human suffering, a high price has been paid for independence.

Nationalism in Africa: From Rhodesia to Zimbabwe

The most dynamic arena of nationalism in our time is the continent of Africa. In the course of a single generation, the mounting discontent and will to independence of the peoples of Africa have resulted in the liquidation of several massive Western empires whose imperial rule had lasted for centuries. The pacemaker of the new African nationalism was the state of Ghana, formerly known as the British Gold Coast, the first African colony to receive its independence in the twentieth century. When Ghana became a sovereign state in 1957, the frenzied shouts of jubilation celebrating its triumph sounded the death knell of the Western empires in all of Africa. Thereafter, the birth of a new African nation became an annual—at times even monthly—event. In April 1980, the continent's last white-dominated colony, Southern Rhodesia, emerged as Zimbabwe, Africa's fifty-first independent state. The present case study will trace the painful, often violent, transition from Southern Rhodesia to Zimbabwe.

Cecil Rhodes, the founder of Southern Rhodesia, was a classical British empire builder of the nineteenth century. He had gone to Africa as a teenager and was immediately successful with claims in the newly discovered diamond fields in Kimberley. Before the age of thirty, he controlled most of the world's diamond production. Believing that the Anglo-Saxon race was the highest to be evolved in a divine plan and eager to secure its predominance, Rhodes assembled a "Pioneer Column" in 1890 which shattered numerous black tribes and established the British South Africa Company. Under Rhodes' philosophy, which was a mixture of Adam Smith's *laissez faire* and Charles Darwin's survival of the fittest, the conquered territory was quickly transformed into a white man's colony. Its diamond mines were taken over and blacks were regarded as children unfit to govern themselves. In 1897 Rhodes faced and defeated bloody rebellions by the blacks whose lands had been usurped. Still striving to annex yet more land and gain more wealth for himself and the British Empire, Rhodes died in 1902 with the words: "So little done, so much to do!" In 1923 Britain formally annexed the territory and granted internal self-rule to its white settlers. The blacks, who outnumbered the whites by a ratio of thirty to one, were given no voice in the shaping of their destiny.

Southern Rhodesia, with its capital at Salisbury, experienced relatively little unrest until the tide of liberation began to sweep across Africa in the 1960s. In 1961, when Britain approved a new constitution that completely disfranchised the blacks, an angry nationalism began to gather momentum. The following year, the United Nations General Assembly, in an increasingly anticolonial mood, demanded that Southern Rhodesia be placed under UN supervision and that the 1961 constitution be abrogated in favor of universal adult suffrage. Britain, which had granted independence to Ghana in 1957, began to counsel compromise to the whites in Salisbury. In 1965, however, Ian Smith, the leader of the ruling white minority, broke away from Britain in a defiant unilateral declaration of independence. The whites now were not only in revolt against their motherland, but also faced rising black guerrilla warfare and angry condemnations by the United Nations. In 1966, for the first time in UN history, the Security Council, in a vote of 11 to 0, imposed selective economic sanctions against the Smith regime. The following year, Secretary-General U Thant reported that, although ninety-two nations had complied with the resolution, the sanctions were not sufficient to bring down the Salisbury government. The United States, for example, continued to import chromium from Rhodesia. In 1968 the Security Council resolved to extend the sanctions to all imports and exports except for emergency food and medical supplies. Despite this growing hostility from abroad and increasing violence at home, the white minority government continued to stand fast.

In 1976 Secretary of State Henry Kissinger, alarmed by the emergence of a new, pro-Marxist government in Angola and convinced that the tide of black liberation in Africa had become irresistible, placed the prestige of the United States behind majority rule in Southern Rhodesia. He announced that the United States would give no further material or diplomatic support to the Smith regime in its conflict with black Africa. Together with Britain, Kissinger worked out a plan whereby Rhodesia's white minority would be compensated for acquiescing to black majority rule. Confronted with the stark choice of adapting to the inevitable or leaving the country, the whites tried to stall for

time. Yet it seemed a losing battle. Black guerrilla attacks intensified in ferocity and scope, and neighboring Mozambique—formerly a white ally—had now
become a nationalist staging center. In November 1977 Ian Smith finally
bowed to the inevitable and accepted the one-man-one-vote rule as a basis for
negotiations. However, pressures for immediate reform continued to rise because of the Soviet Union's increasing support for the black guerrillas. By
1978 the cost of fighting these guerrillas constituted more than half of
Rhodesia's national budget. Later that year, Ian Smith, in an effort to achieve
an interim solution, made an agreement in Salisbury with three black leaders.
In 1979 a moderate black leader, Bishop Abel Muzorewa, became prime minister, retaining Ian Smith in the cabinet as a minister without portfolio. Shortly
afterward, however, the heads of the governments of the British Commonwealth met in Lusaka, Zambia, and declared that the compromise settlement
was defective. Nothing short of free and universal elections would do. The
United States supported the Lusaka agreement and refused to lift the sanctions
against Rhodesia. After prolonged negotiations punctuated by increasing guerrilla violence, agreement was finally reached to hold elections in February
1980. As whites and blacks went to the polls that month, the nation held its
breath. Out in the bush, a white soldier said grimly: "Now I know what it's
like to be waiting for the end of the world."[8] The election results were stun-
ning: a landslide victory for the black guerrilla leader, Robert Mugabe. The
whites were horrified and talked bitterly of "gapping it"—their Rugby-derived
term for emigrating. The blacks, needless to say, were overjoyed. On April 18,
1980, the Union Jack was lowered for the last time in what had been Rhodesia
for ninety years. In its place rose the multistriped banner of newly born
Zimbabwe. In neighboring Tanzania, President Julius Nyerere, who had suspected that the election would be rigged in favor of the moderate, Bishop
Muzorewa, celebrated Mugabe's victory with a champagne toast. "This is not
the first time I have been proven wrong," Nyerere declared with a broad
smile, "and it is not the first time that I'm very pleased that I'm wrong."[9]

Mugabe's victory had been the climax of twenty years of struggle. The son
of a poor laborer, Mugabe had been educated in Roman Catholic mission
schools. After earning degrees from two South African universities, he had
embarked on a career as schoolteacher, but ultimately immersed himself in
Rhodesian nationalist politics during the 1960s. He was repeatedly arrested for
his political activities and spent more than ten years in jail. As a prisoner, he
completed three more university degrees by correspondence. Released in
1974, Mugabe went into exile in Mozambique. There, sheltered by Marxist
President Samora Machel and armed largely by Communist China, he organized his Zimbabwe African National Liberation Army and launched a full-
scale guerrilla war against the Smith regime. In 1976 Mugabe formed a Patriotic Front Alliance with Joshua Nkomo, another guerrilla fighter, whose
smaller, Soviet-armed Zimbabwe People's Revolutionary Army was operating
out of bases in Zambia. Based on Mugabe's history, therefore, whites and

blacks alike expected that this pro-Marxist guerrilla leader would carry his radical principles with him into independence. They were to be mistaken.

In a speech to the new nation shortly after an eternal flame commemorating 27,000 dead guerrillas had been lit, Prime Minister Mugabe vowed his commitment to a policy of peace and reconciliation. "Tomorrow we are born again," he said, "born collectively as a nation of Zimbabweans." Addressing the nation's 200,000 whites, he said: "If yesterday I fought you as my enemy, today you have become a friend and ally with the same national interest."[11]

The task of national conciliation was not an easy one and the scars of war were deep indeed. In December 1980 Edgar Tekere, Minister of Manpower, Planning, and Development in Mugabe's cabinet, was found guilty of murdering a white farm manager. However, the court accepted Tekere's claim that he had acted to suppress terrorism. Tekere was set free.

Ironically, the law that permitted such justice was not the product of the country's new black leadership. It had been enacted in 1975 as a protection for whites, under the leadership of Ian Smith, when the "terrorists" the whites had sought to suppress had included Edgar Tekere and Robert Mugabe. By 1980 the "terrorists" were whites.

The challenge was clear. A black-ruled Zimbabwe would have to be more than a white racist Rhodesia in reverse. If law is not to be blind, it must be color-blind.

Zimbabwe in 1980 was virtually bankrupt and in debt to white-ruled South Africa for $350 million. The war had turned 850,000 people into homeless refugees and another 70,000 remained in Mozambique and Zambia. Two hundred thousand people were dependent on Red Cross food shipments. Britain, the United States, and the United Nations provided disappointingly modest sums for refugee aid. Mugabe nonetheless pursued a policy of nonalignment and refused to depart from his moderate conciliatory course. One senior government official, angered by the small amounts of aid, commented ironically: "If we had turned to Moscow after the election, we would be drowning in dollars and pounds now."[11]

The birth of Mugabe's Zimbabwe increased anxiety in neighboring South Africa, the continent's last bastion of white minority rule. Prime Minister Botha issued a stern warning to Zimbabwe-style liberation fighters: "Anyone planning violence had better not try it. You will rue it." Tensions were particularly high in Namibia, formerly known as Southwest Africa. This large, uranium-rich territory was administered by a South African-backed minority regime in defiance of United Nations demands for black majority rule. There was little doubt, however, that in the long run, Namibia would follow Zimbabwe's example. The only question was whether the ultimate victory of the blacks would be attained through peaceful elections or by a bloody, possibly ruinous, struggle.

The birth of Zimbabwe suggests that nationalist revolutionaries, once in power, may often become moderates. Managing power may be more challenging than seizing it. Mugabe demonstrated considerable talent in both areas. After 1980 he worked hard at the impossible: to satisfy black aspirations, retain white confidence, and keep the peace. And he did well in reconciling opposites. Bernard Miller, the white editor of the monthly *Rhodesian Farmer,* declared: "We were all wrong about him. Everyone's got egg on his face."[12] Independence thus did not separate the people from their leader, nor the leader from the hope for moderate solutions. Sporadic violence, of course, continued. But as Joshua Nkomo, Mugabe's former guerrilla rival and new Home Affairs Minister, put it in late 1980: "What is happening is what takes place after a veld fire. You see small areas where the wood is still smoldering and burning off. That's what we have in Zimbabwe today. The smolderings are burning themselves out." Most Zimbabweans profoundly shared that hope.

The name "Zimbabwe," which now supplants Rhodesia as the name of the nation, derives from stone ruins in the southeastern part of the country believed to date from about the ninth century. Although the origin of the Zimbabwe ruins is in dispute, black nationalists see them as evidence of an advanced civilization in the region long before the domination of Cecil Rhodes and the white colonizers began.

Today, Zimbabwe stands both as a warning and as an inspiration. To the Afrikaner minority in South Africa, it is an abhorrent example to be avoided at all costs; but to most blacks in Africa, it constitutes proof that the transfer of power from white to black can be accomplished without the violence of revolution.

South Africa and Apartheid: Profiles in Black and White

Since the last edition of this book appeared, I have visited South Africa four times. I shall do my best to set down here the observations I made on three different crucial issues that are at the heart of the South African tragedy: first, the demographic composition of the country and the current status of race relations; second, South Africa's relations with the international community, including the arguments for and against economic sanctions; and finally, an analysis of the probabilities of evolutionary versus revolutionary change in the nation's future.

The first impression of the country is one of incredible natural beauty. As one travels across the great South African plain and marvels at its unique fauna and flora, one is tempted to think of the pristine beauty of Genesis in the clear light of creation. But then, as one visits the slums of Soweto where blacks live in misery and squalor, one is jarred back to a terrible reality: apartheid, or the separation of the races, as decreed by the laws of the land.

The racial dilemma of South Africa, in philosophical terms, is that of a clash between one right and another right: the competing claims of its white minority and its nonwhite, predominantly black, majority. The first whites who came to South Africa 300 years ago were Dutch; their descendants are today's Afrikaners. The British made their appearance 100 years later, and today the nation's whites comprise only 15 percent of its total population of 32 million; 60 percent of these whites speak Afrikans, and the remaining 40 percent are English-speaking. Since 1963, when South Africa seceded from the British Commonwealth, South Africa has had an Afrikaner parliament.

Seventy-three percent of the nation is black. Despite this overwhelming numerical majority, not a single black person has ever been permitted to cast a vote for the all-white national parliament of South Africa. The small minority of whites holds all political and most economic power including all gold and platinum mines and the nation's most fertile and productive lands. The whites do not regard themselves as intruders in South Africa, however. Quite the contrary, they consider themselves as an indigenous African tribe which, like the blacks, tilled the soil, wrested from it a difficult livelihood, and made a vital contribution to the country's economic wealth and power. In short, they believe that they are in South Africa to stay. Wedged in between blacks and whites are 9 percent "coloreds" of mixed racial descent and 3 percent Indians.

The three-fourths of the country that is black is divided into nine tribes or "nations" such as the Zulu, Chosa, and Tswana, as well as several million urban blacks who live in the ghetto-like conditions near the nation's largest cities. The Zulu tribe, for example, comprises six million people whose leader, Western-educated Prince Gatsha Buthelezi, is a descendant of a famous Zulu chief who fought the British army to a standstill in the nineteenth century. Today, the prince is the leader of a nonviolent Zulu resistance movement called *Inkatha*. The township of Soweto near Johannesburg is a community for urban blacks, many of whom serve white "masters" in the city during the day and return to their impoverished dwellings after nightfall.

To complicate the situation even further, whites clash with other whites and blacks with other blacks. The ruling political party today is the National party under its Afrikaner president, P. W. Botha and his successor F. W. de Klerk. In a recent national election held in May 1987, this party won a comfortable majority of 122 out of 166 seats in the all-white South African parliament. The National party, though predominantly Afrikaner, has done away with some of the most offensive aspects of apartheid, such as the Immorality Act, which forbade sexual relations between the races under penalty of imprisonment. In 1986 it also eliminated the Pass Laws under which blacks had to carry identity cards at all times and were restricted to travel in their own country. However, President Botha steadfastly refused to share real power with the blacks nor did he grant them voting rights. Instead, he approved a "Group Areas Act" under which blacks were encouraged to migrate to "homelands," which tended to resemble Indian reservations in the United States. Moreover, although the National party authorized the creation of a "colored" parliament for the coloreds and even an Indian Parliament for the nation's Indians (3 percent), the National party never bothered to create a black Parliament. The blacks therefore continue to live in a state of total disenfranchisement.

To make matters even grimmer, the National party's main political opposition now emanates from the political Right, not the Left. The Conservative party, under the leadership of a strict racial segregationist, Afrikaner Andries Treurnicht, captured twenty-seven seats of the Parliament in 1987. In its role as official opposition party to the Nationalists, it made further reforms very difficult. The English-speaking whites were represented by a Progressive Liberal party under the aegis of an ardent foe of apartheid, Helen Suzman, who retired in 1989. This party lost a considerable number of seats in the country's swing to the Right. Needless to say, conservatives and liberals are barely on speaking terms, with the Nationalists controlling the political center. President Botha liked to see himself as a reformer who was mistakenly perceived abroad as a reactionary. "If I move quickly on reforms to eliminate apartheid, the conservatives will wrest control from us," he told me in a conversation in Pretoria; "hence we must proceed slowly. Do not push us!" And indeed, since May 1987, reforms have come to a virtual standstill. Apartheid is still the law of the land; and in their treatment of the nation's blacks the Afrikaners continue to march backward into the future. In 1986, they declared a "state of emergency" throughout the nation which resembled a kind of martial law.

Blacks, too, are far from united. There are conservative blacks, such as Prince Buthelezi who opposes economic sanctions against South Africa. There is a Noble laureate, Bishop Desmond Tutu, who supports sanctions. And then, there is the African National Congress, whose leader, Nelson Mandela, has refused to abandon the use of force as a weapon in the struggle against apartheid.

On balance, South Africa is the only country in the entire world where a white minority continues to rule a nonwhite majority and insists that it can go on like this forever. It is this anachronism that explains much of the fury that has descended on South Africa from the outside world in recent years.

The most concrete manifestation of this attitude toward South Africa is the issue of punitive economic sanctions, a controversy that has been hotly debated in most countries that trade with South Africa. In the United States, for example, sanctions against South Africa have set the President against the Congress. Most members of the Congress have strongly advocated sanctions as a weapon to push the whites toward a sharing of power and to weaken their ability to suppress the blacks. Theirs has been a stand based on the moral position that apartheid is an evil system that must be eliminated as quickly as possible and one with which the United States should not do business. President Reagan chose to adopt a more strategic position of *Realpolitik,* arguing, among other things, that South Africa was a producer of 80 percent of the world's platinum, a precious metal which the United States needed for its industrial strength. "Constructive engagement," in his view, was preferable to sanctions. He vetoed a Congressional sanctions bill, the Congress overrode that veto, and, in 1986, the Comprehensive Anti-Apartheid Act came into being. Ever since then, the executive branch of the United States has been legally obliged to pursue a policy that it openly opposes.

In my visits to South Africa, I had the occasion to observe the effects of sanctions first-hand. My major observation was that while I found apartheid repulsive in the extreme, sanctions did not seem to be the answer. In the first place, sanctions hurt the black economy more than they hurt the white. I saw thousands of black fruit pickers and coal miners out of work because of sanctions against South African fruit and coal exports. I saw the consequences of leading US companies such as IBM leaving South Africa. Role models of integration were lost because in these US companies, blacks and whites worked together, ate together in the same cafeterias, and had their children play together in the same playgrounds. These Americans showed that racial integration was not the end of the world. When they sold out and left, South African whites made windfall profits and quickly restored the old apartheid practices. Perhaps most important, sanctions do not work unless everyone observes them. In South Africa in 1987, the Japanese replaced the United States as the nation's leading trading partner. They happily filled the vacuum left by the Americans and British and, in recognition for that service, were promoted by the South African government from "colored" to "honorary" white. Finally, I saw considerable evidence that the elections of May 1987 that pushed the country toward the Right were a backlash effect of the US santions, an angry response to what was perceived as US interference in the internal affairs of South Africa.

If sanctions will not end apartheid, then what will? I found it interesting, when I spoke with Helen Suzman, the white leader of the Progressive Liberal Party, and Gatsha Buthelezi, the black chief of the Zulus, that both these prominent personalities agreed on the futility of sanctions. "You cannot build democracy in an economic wasteland," Helen Suzman said. Chief Buthelezi agreed with that assessment. If black and white moderates like these would stand together against extremism of both black and white, violent revolution in South Africa might yet be averted.

I realized, when I was in South Africa, that the ruling Nationalist party would never consent to a one-person, one-vote solution, since this would lead to its own demise and a black majority government. Yet President Botha agreed that the total exclusion of blacks from the political process could not go on forever, either. When I pointed out the absurdity of the South African tricameral legislature, which was comprised of white, colored, and Indian chambers and yet omitted a black chamber, he stated that such a black chamber might not be out of the question in the future. He was less optimistic about two other suggestions I made: first, to admit the nine chiefs of the nine black ethnic tribes to the all-white parliament, thus augmenting that chamber from 166 to 175 seats, and second, to grant some kind of representation to the urban blacks from townships such as Soweto. If the Nationalist party consented to such changes, he declared, it would lose its mandate to the far more reactionary Conservative party. "In that case," I asked, "how will you ever share power with the blacks?" "It took you Americans 100 years to integrate your 10 percent blacks," he replied. "Why are you so impatient with us when you learn that almost three-quarters of our population is black? Why don't you help us instead of pushing us? We refuse to end up like Zimbabwe!"

I left South Africa with a sense of foreboding. The situation had all the ingredients of a Greek tragedy. When all was said and done, the white minority was determined to stop short of real power-sharing with its majority. And the black majority was equally determined to attain it. History teaches that this is the stuff that tragedy is made of.

There was one glimmer of light in the darkness. In December 1988, after years of negotiations, South Africa finally agreed to grant independence to Namibia in exchange for the withdrawal of all Cuban troops from neighboring Angola. The United Nations was to supervise the transition to Namibian freedom as well as the Cuban pullout from Angola.

In April 1989, a 4,650-member UN peacekeeping force moved into the field. Unfortunately, Namibia's transition to independence was stalled when South African police clashed with infiltrators from the Southwest Africa People's Organization (SWAPO). It was unlikely, however, that this incident was going to scuttle a process that had been painstakingly worked out in a succession of world capitals over a number of years. Namibia's independence was now only a matter of time.

Finally, there may be hope that F. W. de Klerk, P. W. Botha's successor to the South African presidency, may be more willing to scuttle apartheid than his predecessor. Even though he too was an Afrikaner, he declared that five million whites could no longer expect to dominate thirty million blacks. Richard Nixon long opposed negotiating with Communist China. Only a leader with impeccable conservative credentials could have changed course and have been credited with superlative diplomacy. Perhaps de Klerk, too, may possess authentic ingredients of such statesmanship in South Africa. It appears that the Afrikaners must ponder a historic choice between power-sharing with the black majority or Armageddon.

CONCLUSIONS

As diverse as the above three case studies of the interaction between nationalism and colonization are, they permit several general conclusions. First, it is clear that the patterns of colonial rule have varied widely, that the results for the colonies have been both beneficial and harmful, but that Third World nationalism continues to view the entire Western colonial experience as a monolithic and unmitigated evil. Second, race has been a pervasive theme that has deeply affected and in many cases poisoned relations between the new nations and their former colonial masters. Although in India and Zimbabwe power was transferred relatively bloodlessly from white to nonwhite, in South Africa, the white minority seems determined to keep the black majority in a state of political subjugation for as long as possible, even at the risk of revolution. Third, as white Western rule passes into the pages of history, with South Africa the white man's last stand, colonialism may well be seen in historical perspective as the vehicle that brought the non-European peoples into the modern world, for better or for worse. Herbert Lüthy has made this point well:

Europe's colonization of the world was neither a chain of crimes nor a chain of be-neficence; it was the birth of the modern world itself. Not one of the former colonial peoples remembers it with gratitude, for it was an alien rule, but none wishes to turn back the clock and this perhaps is colonialism's ultimate historical justification.[13]

Finally, in our time, the axis of the world's greatest power struggle is slowly shifting from East-West to North-South. Although the past generation was ob-sessed with the conflict between communism and democracy, our children might witness the end of the cold war era. Instead, they may have to confront yet another global tug of war: that between the rich and poor, the whites and nonwhites, the haves and have-nots of this earth.

REFERENCES

1 Rupert Emerson, *From Empire to Nation*. Cambridge, Mass.: Harvard University Press, 1960, p. 3.
2 *The New York Times,* July 4, 1960.
3 Mohandas K. Gandhi, *An Autobiography*. Boston: Beacon Press, 1971, p. 111.
4 Hans Kohn, *Is the Liberal West in Decline?* London: Pall Mall Press, 1957, pp. 69–70.
5 Emerson, *op. cit.,* p. 419.
6 For further reference, see the perceptive book by James Duffy, *Portuguese Africa*. Cambridge, Mass.: Harvard University Press, 1959.
7 Quoted in George McT. Kahin, *Major Governments of Asia*. Ithaca, N.Y.: Cornell University Press, 1958, p. 268, fn. 35.
8 "Mugabe Takes Charge," *Time,* March 17, 1980, p. 42.
9 *Ibid.*
10 "Festive Birth of a Nation," *Time,* April 28, 1980, p. 28.
11 *Ibid.,* p. 29.
12 *Ibid.*
13 Herbert Lüthy, "The Passing of the European Order," *Encounter,* November 1957, p. 12.

SELECTED BIBLIOGRAPHY

Emerson, Rupert. *From Empire to Nation*. Cambridge, Mass.: Harvard University Press, 1960. A prophetic, early classic on the politics of decolonization in Africa, Asia, and the Middle East, by a leading scholar.
Finnegan, William. *Crossing the Line: A Year in the Land of Apartheid*. New York: Harper & Row, 1986. The sensitive and articulate memoir of a young American who taught for a year at a school for "coloreds" outside Capetown and then hitchhiked around the country.
Mehta, Ved. *A Family Affair: India under Three Prime Ministers*. New York: Oxford University Press, 1982. A highly perceptive impressionistic portrait of modern India, by a leading Indian writer.
Minter, William. *King Solomon's Mines Revisited: Western Interests and the Burdened History of Southern Africa*. New York: Basic Books, 1986. The author shows in penetrating detail just how strong Western economic interests in South Africa are and how these have shaped policy. An extremely valuable study.

Treverton, Gregory F., ed., *Europe, America, and South Africa*. New York: Council on Foreign Relations, 1988. A number of distinguished Western politicians and scholars wrestle with the South African dilemma. Thoughtful observations, but no consensus.

Whitaker, Jennifer Seymour. *How Can Africa Survive?* A former Peace Corps teacher in Nigeria reflects on the human enigma and tragedy of the African continent. An elegant and thought-provoking book.

CHAPTER 5

THE STRUGGLE BETWEEN COMPETING NATIONALISMS IN THE MIDDLE EAST: THE ARAB-ISRAELI CONFLICT AND THE IRAN-IRAQ WAR

For something to be born, the parents have to meet at least once.　　　Abba Eban

The triumph of nationalism over Western colonial rule did not banish the specter of violence from the Third World. Quite on the contrary, many new nations chose to follow the paths of their cantankerous predecessors and began to engage in furious struggles of their own, usually over contested territory. The Middle East, more than any other part of the world, has been the scene of ferocious strife between competing forms of nationalism. We shall examine two case studies in which competing claims over land that both sides regarded as either sacred or indispensable led to protracted and relentless wars and the most terrible human suffering: the Arab-Israeli conflict and the war between Iraq and Iran in the Persian Gulf.

THE FORTY YEARS' WAR IN THE HOLY LAND: ISRAEL AND THE ARABS IN 1948, 1956, 1967, 1973, 1982, AND 1988

Historical tragedies do not arise from encounters in which right clashes with wrong. Rather, they occur when right clashes with right. This is the heart of the conflict between Israel and the Arab states in Palestine. A large number of Jews, responding to the horror of Hitler's systematic extermination of the Jews of Western Europe, attempted to save themselves by creating a state of their own. They established it in a land that had been occupied by Arabs for

123

centuries, at the precise moment when the Arab peoples were emerging from the crucible of Western colonialism and were rediscovering their own national destinies. Thus Jewish nationalism clashed head on with Arab nationalism in Palestine.

The six wars between Israel and her Arab neighbors have been the result of this collision. The modern Middle East has been the scene of both irreconcilable hopes and aspirations and bitter hatreds and violent passions. The wars were fought with the deepest emotion. Each contestant regarded his rights as self-evident and firmly based on the will of God, morality, reason, and law. As passions rose, irrationality become commonplace. Desperate deed was heaped on desperate deed until right and wrong, responsibility and guilt could no longer be distinguished. Each side had done things that the other could neither forgive nor forget.

This tragic clash between two valid claims and two appeals for justice has not abated much with time. Nor has it been possible to break the impasse through a lasting peace settlement.

Perhaps no solution to the Arab-Israeli problem exists outside the course of history. In the meantime, it is the scholar's duty to offer a diagnosis, even though it may not be possible to prescribe a cure for a "sickness unto death." The six Palestine wars were merely massive eruptions of an historical encounter that is nothing less than a protracted war spanning an entire generation. As such they offer us insight into, but not liberation from, some of the darkest recesses of the souls of nations and men.

The Palestine War of 1948

The Zionist movement was founded in 1897 with the publication of a book entitled *The Jewish State,* by Dr. Theodore Herzl, an Austrian journalist who urged the settlement of Jewish agriculturists and artisans in Palestine. These pioneers, Herzl hoped, would realize an ancient Jewish dream: the reestablishment of a Jewish homeland in the Promised Land and the gathering of the Jewish people from their Diaspora of 2000 years. Responding to Herzl's vision and reacting to anti-Semitic pogroms in Russian and Poland, 60,000 Jews emigrated to Palestine between 1881 and 1914. The land that was used for the Jewish settlements was purchased from absentee Arab landlords by wealthy philanthropists such as Baron de Rothschild of Paris or through funds collected by the Zionists abroad. By 1914 almost 100,000 acres of Palestinian land had been purchased by the Jews.

In 1917 Chaim Weizmann, a scientist of world renown and a fervent Zionist, persuaded British Foreign Minister Lord Arthur James Balfour to issue a proclamation that would convert Herzl's dream into a British pledge:

> His Majesty's Government views with favor the establishment in Palestine of a national home for the Jewish people, and will use their best endeavours to facilitate the achievement of this object, it being clearly understood that nothing shall be done which may prejudice the civil rights and political status enjoyed by Jews in any other country.

In 1922 Britain was given a League of Nations mandate over Palestine.

The Palestinian Arabs, understandably enough, objected to the Balfour declaration and became increasingly uneasy about the large influx of Jewish immigrants. During the 1930s, as Hitler's persecution of European Jews gathered momentum, Jewish immigration soared dramatically. By 1937 the Jews constituted almost one-third of the total population of Palestine. Between 1928 and 1937 their number had risen from 150,000 to 400,000. As the Zionist movement looked toward Palestine as the last refuge from the impending Nazi holocaust, Arab alarm grew accordingly. It was no longer a question of land purchased by individual settlers but the threat of an alien state in a land that had been inhabited by Arabs for over 1000 years. The British, caught in a vise between their pledge to the Jews on the one hand and to Arab oil and strategic interests on the other, tried to temporize but finally placated the Arabs by imposing a ceiling on Jewish immigration. The Jews, in their plight, tried to run the British blockade. In most cases, the British intercepted the immigrant vessels and shipped the passengers to internment camps in Cyprus. In the particularly tragic case of the immigrant ship *Exodus,* the British sent the helpless Jews back to Germany. As one survivor put it, "The Germans killed us, and the British don't let us live."[1]

Despite the British blockade, tens of thousands of Jewish immigrants landed in Palestine illegally. The Arabs became increasingly restive, and bitter fighting erupted. The British, caught in the lines of fire, were unable to restore the peace. In 1947, in total frustration, Britain announced her intention to relinquish the mandate over Palestine and decided to place the entire problem before the United Nations.

The undisputed leader of the more than half-million Jewish settlers in Palestine in 1947 was David Ben-Gurion. Ben-Gurion's commitment to the Zionist ideal was total and unswerving. He had come to Palestine in 1906, had been a leading delegate to the World Zionist Congress, and by 1935 had become chairman of the Jewish Agency, which represented the World Zionist Movement. No single leader represented the Arab cause, but most influential were Haj Amin el-Husseini, the grand mufti of Jerusalem; Azzam Pasha, the secretary-general of the Arab League; King Abdullah of Transjordan; and Glubb Pasha, the commander of the British-trained Arab Legion. The grand mufti had been in Germany during the war and had helped the Nazis plan their "final solution" to the Jewish problem. He had designs to rule all Palestine, and for this reason was distrusted by the other Arab leaders. Azzam Pasha was an Egyptian diplomat with relatively moderate views. King Abdullah of Transjordan, who had a reputation for compassion and humanity, met secretly once with Golda Meir to explore the possibility of an Arab-Jewish compromise. And Glubb Pasha's Arab Legion was the only Arab military force that was truly feared by the Zionists.

In early 1947 a specially constituted United Nations Committee on Palestine (UNSCOP) visited the area and examined the alternatives. After several months of highly charged debate, the committee finally recommended that Palestine, with its population of 1.2 million Arabs and 570,000 Jews, be partitioned into two states—one Arab and one Jewish—with Jerusalem held as trustee of the UN. The Jewish state would include 55 percent of the land and its population would be 58 percent Jewish, and the Arab state would encompass 45 percent of the land and have a 99 percent Arab population. This partition plan was eagerly welcomed by the Jews and denounced with equal fervor by the Arabs.

A number of meetings on the partition plan took place between Arab and Jewish leaders. In one such encounter, Abba Eban, then an official of the Jewish Agency, met with Azzam Pasha to discuss the possibility of a compromise. Eban stated that "the Jews [were] a fait accompli in the Middle East and that the Arabs [would] have to reconcile themselves to that fact."[2] He then went on to propose an economic program for joint development of the Middle East. Azzam Pasha conceded that the plan was "rational and logical" but added that "the fate of nations [was] not decided by rational logic." "We shall try to defeat you," he said. "I am not sure we will succeed, but we will try. We were able to drive out the Crusaders, but on the other hand, we lost Spain and Persia. It may be that we shall lose Palestine. But it is too late for peaceful solutions."[3] When Abba Eban interrupted by pointing out that this left no alternative but a test of strength through force of arms, Azzam Pasha replied:

> It is in the nature of people to aspire to expansion and to fight for what they think is vital. It is possible that I don't represent, in the full sense of the word, the new spirit which animates my people. My young son who yearns to fight, undoubtedly represents it better than I do. He no longer believes in the old generation. . . . The forces which motivate peoples are not subject to our control. They are objective forces. Nationalism, that is a greater force than any which drives us. We don't need economic development with your assistance. We have only one test, the test of strength.[4]

An eyewitness to this encounter detected no hatred in Azzam Pasha's tone. He referred to the Jews over and over as "cousins." Not once during the two-hour conversation did he express an unkind thought or use a hostile expression about the Jews. But he did confirm the character of the position of the Arab majority, a position based not on logic but "on a blind fatalism, ungovernable as the wind."[5] Sadly and without hatred the two leaders took their leave of one another.

The lobbying for and against the partition resolution was the most intense that the United Nations had experienced in its short history. A two-thirds majority was required for passage of the resolution by the General Assembly. To offset the votes of just the Arab and Moslem nations the Zionists needed twenty-two votes, and for each additional vote against partition they needed two in favor. Although the Zionists were by no means certain that they could muster a two-thirds majority, they were encouraged by the fact that the two main antagonists in the cold war, the United States and the Soviet Union, both supported them. In the United States President Truman was deeply sympathetic to the Jewish cause. Moreover, his political instincts told him that the

Jewish vote might well be crucial to the presidential election of 1948. Overruling the objections of leading State Department officials over the Soviet threat and the US access to military bases, Truman personally warned the US delegate to the United Nations, Herschel Johnson, to "damn well deliver the partition vote or there will be hell to pay."[6] From the Soviet point of view partition seemed the easiest way to oust Britain from the Middle East and to keep the United States at arm's length while playing the Arabs off against the Jews. Two days before the vote it became clear that the fate of Zionism was in the hands of a few small, remote nations, in particular Liberia, Haiti, the Philippines, and Ethiopia. The Zionists persuaded the United States to apply strong pressure on these countries. Nevertheless, on November 29, 1947, the outcome was very much in doubt. On one hand, Moshe Sharett, the Jewish Agency's "foreign minister," solemnly warned the assembly that the Jewish people would never submit to any attempt to subjugate them to an Arab majority. On the other hand, Jamal Husseini, the acting secretary-general of the Arab League, declared that if the assembly did vote for partition, the Arabs of Palestine would go to war against the Jews as soon as the British left: "the partition line will be drawn in fire and blood."[7]

Two eyewitnesses have left a poignant account of that fateful vote on November 29:

> An aide set a basket before Aranha (the President of the General Assembly). In it were fifty-six slips of paper, each bearing the name of one of the nations represented in the hall. Aranha extended his hand and slowly drew from the basket the name of the nation whose vote would begin the poll. He unfolded the piece of paper and stared an instant at the men ranged before him.
>
> "Guatemala," he announced. At his words, a terrible silence settled over the Assembly. Even the press gallery fell quiet. For an instant, the three hundred delegates, the spectators, the newsmen, seemed united in awe of the moment before them, in their awareness of the grave and solemn decision about to be taken.
>
> The delegate of Guatemala rose. As he did, suddenly, from the spectators' gallery, a piercing cry sundered the silence of the Assembly hall, a Hebrew cry as old as time and the suffering of men: "Ana Ad Hoshiya. O Lord, save us."[8]

With a vote of thirty-three votes in favor, thirteen against, and ten abstentions, the partition resolution was adopted. The Zionists were ecstatic, but the Arab delegates walked out of the General Assembly, declaring that their governments would not be bound by the UN decision.

Both Ben-Gurion, who had heard of the Zionist victory 6000 miles away from the United Nations, and the grand mufti of Jerusalem, who had followed every word of the Palestine debate in New York, knew that the vote was no guarantee that the Jewish state would actually come into being. Between the vote on that late November afternoon and the expiration of the British mandate in Palestine, scheduled for May of the following year, lay a span of time that might well be decisive. Both men immediately set out to strengthen their forces for the battle that loomed ahead. Violent Arab-Jewish clashes occurred in Jerusalem and other parts of the country the day after the UN vote. The

Jews were fearful that Arab resistance would deprive them of the fruits of the partition vote. The Arabs were enraged at a decision that, in their view, deprived them of their patrimony. On both sides, there seemed to be no time to lose.

The search for arms now dominated the minds of Arab and Jewish leaders alike. In this vital quest, the Zionists were at a disadvantage. The right to buy arms openly on the international arms market was the prerogative of sovereign states. Lebanon and Syria, which had won their independence in 1943 and 1946, respectively, were legally free to purchase arms for the Arab cause. Syria's defense minister, for example, was able to place an order for 10,000 rifles with a leading arms manufacturer in Czechoslovakia. The Jews, however, had to resort to clandestine means. The *Haganah,* the underground Zionist army, bought up US surplus arms and machine tools that were destined to be converted into scrap metal. To bypass the British arms embargo, most of the equipment was broken down into its component parts, classified by code, and then shipped to Palestine in random bits and pieces under official import permits for such items as textile machinery. Another technique used by Ben-Gurion's troops was to place an order on the stationery of a sovereign state. One such order, from "Ethiopia," reached the same Czechoslovak arms manufacturer who had served the Syrians. That order too was filled. Thus by late 1947 a jostling for territory between Arabs and Jews was threatening to erupt into organized warfare between two desperate peoples.

In December 1947 the seven members of the Arab League met in Cairo to discuss the threat of a Jewish state in their midst. The states that were represented at this historic meeting were Egypt, Iraq, Saudi Arabia, Syria, Yemen, Lebanon, and Transjordan. Together, their leaders ruled some forty-five million people and had at their command five regular armies. Azzam Pasha, the secretary-general of the Arab League, had labored patiently to reach a consensus among the seven Arab leaders, whose only common bond was their hostility to Zionism; they were otherwise deeply divided by historic rivalries and future ambitions. After protracted debate, the leaders resolved to "prevent the creation of a Jewish state in Palestine and to conserve Palestine as a united independent state."[9] To that end they pledged to furnish the league with 10,000 rifles, 3000 volunteers, and £1 million sterling to provide an immediate beginning for guerrilla operations against the Zionists in Palestine.

At the same time David Ben-Gurion summoned his *Haganah* leaders to an emergency meeting in Jerusalem. "It is time," he told all men before him, "to start planning for a war against five Arab armies."[10] Ben-Gurion perceived the threat of war with the Arabs as a terrible menace that could strangle the Jewish state before it was born. However, Ben-Gurion also thought that if the Arabs insisted on going to war, the frontiers of the Jewish state would not be the boundaries assigned to it by the United Nations but those that the Jews could seize and hold by force of arms. If the Arabs rejected the UN decision and went to war, Ben-Gurion thought, that would give his people "the right to get what we could.''[11] Thus, paradoxically, the Jewish leader turned the Arab cause into a handmaiden of Zionist aspirations.

As the two hostile armies engaged in strikes and counterstrikes that mounted in frequency and ferocity during the final months of the British mandate, events were taking place in Washington that once again placed the birth of the Jewish state in serious doubt. Shaken by the violence of Arab resistance and skeptical of Jewish military strength, President Truman was extremely reluctant to enforce the United Nations partition resolution with US troops even if such troops were part of a UN force. Moreover, the State Department continued to be deeply critical of a partition and considered it to be legally unenforceable. In December 1947 the department prevailed upon the President to declare an arms embargo to the Middle East. Since under various agreements Britain was still free to ship arms to the Arabs, this embargo amounted to a ban on arms to the Jews. Perhaps most damaging to the Zionist cause was the fact that President Truman had become resentful of certain Zionist leaders, particularly Rabbi Abba Hillel Silver, who, in the President's opinion, had exerted improper pressure to support the Jewish cause. Thus, the United States abandoned its support of the partition plan and now proposed an international trusteeship over Palestine. In desperation the Zionists appealed to the aging, almost blind, Chaim Weizmann, who had enjoyed a close relationship with the US President over many years. On February 10, 1948, Weizmann wrote Truman a letter asking ''for a few minutes of [his] precious time.''[12] The request was refused.

Sitting at Weizmann's bedside, Frank Goldman, president of B'nai B'rith, came up with a last-ditch plan to change Truman's mind. He offered to telephone Eddie Jacobson, who was once a partner with Harry Truman in a haberdashery store and who, Goldman thought, might persuade the President to receive Dr. Weizmann. Jacobson responded favorably and was granted an interview with the President on March 12. Truman at first was not receptive to the overtures of his former business partner, but Jacobson persisted. His appeal to the president made a crucial difference in Zionist fortunes:

> Chaim Weizmann is a very sick man, almost broken in health, but he travelled thousands and thousands of miles just to see you and plead the cause of my people. Now you refuse to see him because you were insulted by some of our American Jewish leaders, even though you know that Weizmann had absolutely nothing to do with these insults and would be the last man to be a party to them. It doesn't sound like you, Harry.[13]

According to the same account, President Truman, after a long silence, looked Jacobson straight in the eye and said: ''You win, you baldheaded son-of-a-bitch! I will see him.''[14] One week later Truman met with Weizmann and promised the Jewish leader that he would work for the establishment and recognition of a Jewish state.

The battle was not yet won by the Zionists, however. On March 19, US Ambassador Warren Austin announced in the Security Council that the United

States would propose the suspension of the partition plan and the establishment of a temporary trusteeship in Palestine in its place. When a shocked and
angry Truman wanted to know how such a thing could have happened, he discovered that Secretary of State George Marshall, who had not been privy to
the President's personal pledge to Dr. Weizmann, had directed Austin on
March 16 to make the trusteeship speech at the earliest appropriate moment.
The Zionists were in despair, the Arabs were jubilant, Secretary-General
Trygve Lie of the United Nations briefly considered resigning, and President
Truman, according to his counsel, Clark Clifford, was "boiling mad."[15] He
now had to go along with the trusteeship idea, at least for the time being, since
yet another reversal would have deprived the United States of all credibility.

As the British mandate drew rapidly to a close, the fighting in Palestine became increasingly desperate. In April 1948 Jewish extremists of the *Irgun* and
Stern groups massacred the inhabitants of Deir Yassin, a small village near
Jerusalem. Even though Ben-Gurion personally cabled his shock at the slaughter, and the Chief Rabbi of Jerusalem excommunicated the Jews who had participated in it, Deir Yassin became a stain on the conscience of the Jewish
state. Not only did it elicit demands for vengeance and retribution, but in the
years ahead it was to become a symbol of the homelessness of hundreds of
thousands of Arab refugees. The mass exodus of terrified Arabs from Jewish-
controlled areas began in earnest after this event. The Arab decision to encourage the refugees to leave and to broadcast the massacre in all its horror
contributed to the growing panic. Thus Deir Yassin marked the beginning of
the Palestinian problem that was to haunt the Middle East for decades to
come.

Several days after the carnage of Deir Yassin, Ben-Gurion sent Golda Meir
on a final peace mission. Disguised as an Arab woman, Meir traveled to
Amman for a secret meeting with King Abdullah of Transjordan to discuss the
possibility of preventing a collision. The king proposed that the proclamation
of the Jewish state be postponed and that Palestine be kept united with the
Jews autonomous in their areas. He also suggested a parliament composed
equally of Arab and Jewish deputies. He desired peace, he told his visitor, but
if his proposals were not accepted, war, he feared, would be inevitable. Meir
replied that the postponement of the birth of a Jewish state was unacceptable
and added that the Jews would fight as long as their strength lasted. Abdullah
said that he realized that the Jews would have to repel any attack and that it
was probably no longer in his power to act as mediator between his fellow
Arabs and the Zionists. "Deir Yassin has inflamed the Arab masses," he said.
"Before then I was alone. Now I am one of five and have discovered that I
cannot make any decisions alone."[16] Thus, this last effort to stave off the catastrophe ended in failure.

In May, with the days of the British mandate numbered, the Jews faced a
crucial dilemma. Should they proclaim the Jewish state immediately, or, in
light of the erosion of US support and the massing of Arab armies, should they
wait? On May 12 Ben-Gurion called a secret meeting of the provisional Na-

tional Council to make a decision. Opinion was sharply divided. Some council members felt that it would be wise to wait, since the United States would probably not come to the aid of a self-proclaimed state but might do so if the Arabs acted first and invaded a United Nations–declared state. Others felt that the Jewish state would have to stand alone under any conditions, and so statehood should be proclaimed without delay. Ben-Gurion was for immediate statehood, even though he gave the Jews only a fifty-fifty chance for survival. When the vote was taken, six of the eleven council members voted to go ahead. By a margin of one vote the council decided to proclaim the new state on May 14, a few hours before the British mandate was to expire.

At 4 P.M. on May 14, 1948, two hours before the termination of the British mandate, David Ben-Gurion announced the birth of Israel. The news triggered a frantic debate in the UN General Assembly in New York, but the world body was unable to reach a decision. A short time after Ben-Gurion's proclamation, Warren Austin, on the personal instruction of President Truman, announced that the United States had recognized the new state of Israel. Shortly thereafter, the Soviet delegate followed suit. "We have been duped," said Charles Malik of Lebanon in an assault of fury on the US and Soviet delegations. It was now 6:15 P.M., and the mandate had ended. Ben-Gurion broadcast a personal message of thanks from Tel Aviv to the American people. As he spoke, the building shook from the impact of an Arab bomb. "The explosions you can hear," he told his audience across the Atlantic, "are Arab planes bombing Tel Aviv."[17] The war for Palestine had broken out.

At dawn on May 15 Israel was simultaneously invaded by the Egyptian army from the south, the Transjordan Arab Legion from the east, and the forces of Syria and Lebanon from the north. The total strength of the invading Arab armies was approximately 23,500 men, equipped with tanks, airplanes, heavy artillery, spare parts, and ammunition. The Israelis had approximately 3000 regulars under arms plus 14,000 recruits. They also had 10,000 rifles, 3600 submachine guns, and 4 ancient cannons smuggled in from Mexico; they had no tanks. The United States and the Soviet Union both disapproved of the invasion. Andrei Gromyko, speaking for the Soviet Union in the Security Council on May 29, 1948, stated: "This is not the first time that the Arab states, which organized the invasion of Palestine, have ignored a decision of the Security Council or of the General Assembly."

At the end of several months' fierce fighting, interspersed by periods of truce, Israel was left in possession of the whole of Galilee, a section of central Palestine connecting the coastal area with Jerusalem, and the whole of the Negev. Jerusalem became a divided city. The entire area controlled by Israel in 1949 was somewhat larger than the area that had been allotted to the Zionists in the partition resolution of 1947. Thus the Arab invasion had played into the hands of the Jews. Almost one million Arabs were rendered homeless by the conflict and entered Syria, Transjordan, and the Egyptian-controlled Gaza Strip as refugees. From their midst would rise the *fedayeen* and the Palestinian resistance fighters who would hold Israel responsible for depriving them of their homeland. Thus the bloody birth of Israel set the stage for a mortal conflict between two nationalisms—one Arab, the other Jewish—equally desperate and determined to secure what to each was holy ground.

The Sinai Campaign and the Suez Crisis of 1956

Time did not appease feelings even after the armistice agreements were concluded in 1949. On the Arab side, the plight of almost one million refugees was a constant reminder of the alien Zionist presence. No matter how defensive or conciliatory Israel's policy would be, this massive displacement would make the Jewish state into a standing provocation in the eyes of the entire Arab world. The Jews, of course, were fearful of allowing the refugees to return to their former homes. How could 700,000 Jews permit nearly 1 million Arabs to return to their land without also risking the destruction of the Jewish state? And yet how could they refuse it without inflicting on innocent people the very injustice they had themselves suffered in the Diaspora? Thus the Jews took back a few and compensated some, but most continued to linger in refugee camps in Jordan, Lebanon, Syria, and Egyptian-controlled Gaza. At the same time large numbers of Jews were driven out of Iraq, Yemen, Egypt, and Morocco.

During the early 1950s Palestinian Arab *fedayeen* from the refugee population mounted raids on Israeli territory that steadily increased in ferocity and frequency. The Israelis in turn engaged in massive and powerful reprisals. Thus, despite the military armistice, a state of belligerency continued to exist.

In 1952 Gamal Abdel Nasser, who had distinguished himself in the Palestine war, became president of Egypt and was soon the unrivalled champion of Arab nationalism. He instituted a blockade on Israeli shipping through the Suez Canal and in 1953 extended this blockade to include all goods being shipped to Israel. This left the Israelis with only the port of Elath, at the head of the Gulf of Aqaba in the Straits of Tiran. In late 1953 Nasser began to restrict Israeli commerce through the straits by making its ships subject to inspection by Egyptian coastguards. In 1955 he broadened the blockade and imposed a ban on overflights by Israeli aircraft. In Israel Prime Minister Ben-Gurion, who considered the port of Elath vital to Israel's survival, wanted to strike at Egypt immediately but was restrained by his colleagues. By 1956 relations between Egypt and Israel had reached the boiling point.

At this juncture the Arab-Israeli conflict blended into a broader confrontation between Arab nationalism and the remnants of the Anglo-French postcolonial presence in the Arab world. This confrontation was brought to a head by two huge engineering structures, one long in existence and the other about to be constructed: the Suez Canal and the High Dam at Aswan. President Nasser viewed the former as a leftover from colonial times and the latter as a modern pyramid to be built as a symbol of a resurgent Arab nationalism.

The United States had initially agreed to help finance the Aswan High Dam through the World Bank, but Secretary of State John Foster Dulles was irked by President Nasser's decision to purchase arms from Czechoslovakia in 1955 and his recognition a year later of Communist China. As a result, the United States reneged on its pledge to finance the dam, ostensibly because the Egyptian economy was deemed unsound, and Nasser became incensed. In his rage, he declared that the United States "should drop dead of fury, but [it would] never be able to dictate to Egypt."[18] Two days later, in an emotional "declaration of independence from imperialism," he announced the nationalization of the Suez Canal, which was partially owned by British and French financial interests. Thus Britain and France were made to pay for Dulles' policy reversal, and, fatefully, the two Western European powers now perceived a common interest with Israel: the removal of Gamal Abdel Nasser from power.

The perceptions of the British and French leaders now began to play a crucial role in the gathering crisis. In Britain, Prime Minister Anthony Eden's memories of Hitler at Munich were still fresh, and he now compared Nasser's actions to those of the German dictator in the 1930s. In the words of one thoughtful student of British policy at the time, the prime minister "saw Egypt through a forest of Flanders poppies and gleaming jackboots."[19] French Premier Guy Mollet shared this perception. He had been an anti-Nazi resistance chief at Arras during World War II and now "saw Nasser as Hitler more plainly than anyone."[20] The two men became so obsessed with Nasser's action that "Lady Eden is believed to have complained that the Suez Canal was running through her drawing room."[21]

There was, of course, good reason for consternation in Britain and France. The International Convention of Constantinople of 1888 had provided that "The Suez Maritime Canal shall always be free and open, in time of war and in time of peace, to every vessel of commerce or of war without distinction of flag." Thus the two Western powers considered Nasser's action as a violation of their legal rights. Moreover, to Britain, control of the canal symbolized her status as an empire and as a world power. To the French, who blamed Egypt for supporting the Algerian rebellion against France, seizure of the canal served as a kind of last straw. For both, the issue at stake was not merely safeguarding the economic rights of their shareholders in the Suez Canal Company; far more important was their emotional reaction to the seemingly insolent and Hitler-like nationalism represented by the Egyptian leader.

To Nasser, however, the Suez Canal had become the symbol of a shameful colonial past. Its architect, Ferdinand de Lesseps, had become an Egyptian folk ogre. Under his brutal direction, as Nasser saw it, more than 100,000 Egyptian workers had died to build a canal that was to belong not to them or their country but to a foreign company that profited for its own enrichment and never for Egypt's benefit. "Instead of the Canal being dug for Egypt," Nasser declaimed, "Egypt became the property of the Canal and the Canal Company became a state within a state. But now the days of alien expoitation [were] over; the Canal and its revenues [would] belong entirely to Egypt. We shall build the High Dam and we shall gain our usurped rights."[22]

These sharply divergent perceptions set the stage for a violent encounter. During the weeks that followed Nasser's action the conflict broadened. Eden and Mollet privately sounded out US reactions to the situation. They were partially reassured by the fact that Secretary of State Dulles also appeared outraged by Egypt's action. In their conversations with Dulles the British and French leaders again compared Nasser's action to Hitler's behavior at Munich and stated in the strongest terms that this type of Western appeasement must not be allowed to occur again. Secretary Dulles replied that "force was the last method to be tried, but the United States did not exclude the use of force if all other methods failed."[23] From this statement, Eden and Mollet inferred that at best the United States would present a united front with Britain and France in a show of force against Nasser and at worst remain benevolently neutral.

Britain and France now prepared for military action. They hoped to mount a lightning attack against Egypt, occupy the canal, depose Nasser, and then negotiate with his successor from a position of strength. In the course of these preparations, highly secret meetings took place with Israeli leaders for the purpose of coordinating the attack. Prime Minister Ben-Gurion and his chief of staff, General Moshe Dayan, were intent on seizing Gaza, the main base of *fedayeen* activities, and Sharm-el-Sheik on the Tiran Straits, from where the Egyptians maintained their blockade of the Gulf of Aqaba against ships bound for the port of Elath. Mollet pledged that if the Israelis would thrust into Sinai, French forces would join them, and Israel could seize Sinai and end the Egyptian blockade. Ben-Gurion hesitated; he feared that Egyptian bombers might attack Tel Aviv while Israeli forces were advancing into Sinai.[24] But when Eden pledged to use British airpower to prevent Egyptian air attacks on Israel, Ben-Gurion agreed to move into Sinai.

The final plans worked out among the three prime ministers were the following: Israel was to launch her attack on October 29. As soon as Dayan's troops began their advance into Sinai, Britain and France were to issue an ultimatum to Israel and Egypt, requiring them to cease fire, to withdraw their forces 10 miles on either side of the canal, and to "accept the temporary occupation by Anglo-French forces of key positions at Port Said, Ismailia and Suez."[25] As soon as Israel had agreed to these terms and Egypt had rejected them, British bombers were to destroy the Egyptian air force and disrupt Egypt's communications and military capabilities in preparation for an Anglo-French invasion by paratroops from Cyprus and sea-borne forces from Malta. Then, when these forces had occupied the canal from Port Said to Suez, a further attack was contemplated, aimed at the occupation of Cairo, if necessary to depose Nasser. As these arrangements were being concluded, by a fateful coincidence in time, thousands of miles away, Russian tanks rolled into Budapest to crush the two-day-old Hungarian revolt against Soviet domination.

On the afternoon of October 29 Israel's army launched its four-pronged advance against Egypt. Two thrusts were aimed at the canal, and the third and fourth were to seal off the Gaza Strip and seize Sharm-el-Sheik. On the following day, while Israeli forces were advancing rapidly across the Sinai Peninsula, Britain and France issued their prearranged ultimatum, which in effect told the Egyptians to retreat and the Israelis to advance. Caught by complete surprise, Nasser rejected the ultimatum but was unable to put up much military resistance. He was convinced, however, that world opinion in the United Nations would come to his rescue.

On October 31 British and French bombers began air attacks against Egyptian targets, including Cairo. In retaliation, Nasser sank ships in order to block the canal. Within six days, Israel overran the greater part of the Sinai Peninsula and achieved its main military objective, the occupation of Sharm-el-Sheik.

The United Nations entered the picture on October 30. The US delegation called for a meeting of the Security Council and, to the consternation of Britain and France, introduced a resolution calling on Israel to leave Egypt without delay and asking all member states to "refrain from the use of force or threat of force."[26] The resolution was immediately vetoed by Britain and France. As the Security Council stood paralyzed and the Anglo-French-Israeli action continued, Soviet Premier Nikolai Bulganin, in a news conference in Moscow, warned of the possibility of a third world war and declared that Soviet "volunteers" were ready to aid the Egyptian forces. He proposed that the United States and the Soviet Union restore the peace through a joint show of force. This suggestion was rejected as "unthinkable" by President Eisenhower. The United States was eager to prevent the establishment of a Soviet presence in the Middle East.

On November 2, in an emergency session of the General Assembly, the United States took a leading role in calling for a cessation of the fighting and the immediate withdrawal of the Anglo-French-Israeli forces from Egypt. The United States found support for this action from a not particularly welcome source—the Soviet Union. Thus the United States found itself in the paradoxical position of being allied in the United Nations with its great antagonist in the cold war and at odds with its closest friends and allies, Britain and France.

By November 6 Britain had to yield. Confronted by UN resolutions charging her with aggression, dismayed by the action of the United States, and troubled by an increasingly hostile opposition at home, Prime Minister Eden terminated his abortive venture. As one critical British analyst summed it up: "The spectacle of over one hundred thousand men setting off for a war which lasted barely a day and then returning has few parallels in the long gallery of military imbecility."[27] France had no choice but to follow suit, but Israel still clutched tenaciously what her army had conquered in the six days of the war.

The role of the US leadership, of course, was crucial in the evolution of the crisis, and personalities played an important part. Both President Eisenhower and Secretary Dulles felt a sense of outrage because Eden and Mollet had not bothered to consult them on a matter as important as military action in the Middle East at a time when a national election was imminent in the United States. From a purely military standpoint, only the Israelis were attaining their objectives. The Anglo-French punitive expedition seemed to be foundering and thus could not be presented to the General Assembly as a fait accompli. The United States, by supporting the Anglo-French venture, or even by taking a neutral view of it, would have risked the ill will of a large majority of the UN membership and might have had to look on hopelessly while the military action failed or bogged down. Moreover, such a US response might have persuaded many neutralists that the United States, by countenancing aggression in the Middle East, differed little from the Soviet Union, which was aggressively crushing a rebellion in Hungary with military force. Most important, the United States feared the possibility of Soviet intervention in the Middle East through ''volunteers'' and the risk of sparking a major war through direct superpower confrontation in the contested area.

From the Soviet point of view, the Suez crisis was a windfall: The British and French appeared to be digging their own graves in the Middle East, and the United States seemed to be doing its best to help them. Thus, by appealing to the cause of Arab nationalism, the Soviet Union saw its opportunity to eject all Western influence from the Middle East and to gain a foothold of its own. The fact that Israel was allied with the two colonial powers also played into Soviet hands.

Britain and France were clearly the main losers in the Suez affair. In humiliation, they had to watch Nasser snatch a political victory from a military defeat. Abandoned by their closest and oldest ally, they had to admit that they could no longer act like great powers and that, in the last analysis, their initiative in world politics depended on the decisions of the United States. The very issue that they had set out to rectify by force of arms—the internationalization of the Suez Canal—now seemed beyond redemption. For all practical purposes, the Suez crisis terminated Anglo-French authority in the Middle East. Suez had become another Dienbienphu.

The greatest victory in the Suez crisis was won by Arab nationalism. Nasser was now clearly master of the Suez Canal. The two great superpowers had supported him. Not only did he triumph in the showdown with Britain and France, but his other great foe, Israel, now came under increasing pressure to withdraw. Dag Hammarskjold, secretary-general of the United Nations, had been successful in dispatching to the Middle East a special peace force, the UN Emergency Force (UNEF). Under strong US pressure Israel agreed to evacuate most of the territories it had conquered from Egypt, and beginning on November 15 the UNEF soldiers replaced the Israeli troops. Only an explicit US guarantee, however, that Israel's right to free and innocent passage in the Gulf of Aqaba would not be infringed upon persuaded the Israelis to evacuate the last fruits of their Sinai campaign: the Gaza Strip and the east coast of the Sinai Peninsula down to the Straits of Tiran. By March 1957 Israel had given up all the territories it had conquered, on the understanding that UNEF would prevent *fedayeen* raids from Jordan and the Gaza Strip. Hence, Israel emerged from the Sinai campaign with a marginal gain.

President Nasser was now at the zenith of his power. Among the Egyptian people he enjoyed the title of *rais,* or captain of the ship of state. With deep satisfaction he watched Eden and Mollet resign their posts. Thus encouraged, he now planned to turn on his archenemy, the Zionist state. In March 1957 he appointed an Egyptian civil governor of Gaza, a move that was viewed with indignation and misgivings in Israel. At the same time Radio Cairo declared that "the Gulf of Aqaba will be closed to Israeli ships and our commandos will continue to sow terror in Israel."[28] Thus the seeds of the next war, which was to erupt a decade later, were sown.

The Six-Day War of 1967

Once again, time did not heal but exacerbated the tensions between the Arab states and Israel. Within the Arab world, deep rifts had appeared on the over-riding question of policy vis-à-vis Israel. By early 1967 three basic positions had crystallized.

First, the Syrians, who were the most radical and whose country was a major base for border raids against Israel, had created an organization named *El Fatah*, or "conquest." Its commando units carried out attacks against Israel in the tradition of the earlier *fedayeen* raids. In addition, Syria's President Al Atassi demanded a war of liberation against Israel similar to the one being fought against the United States in Vietnam. Second, and at the other end of the spectrum, was King Faisal of Saudi Arabia, who was relatively friendly toward the West and who regarded the violent temper of the Syrians with considerable distrust. While the huge oil deposits of Saudi Arabia provided the king with a formidable economic weapon, they also made him dependent to some extent on the Western nations for his revenue. President Nasser of Egypt found himself caught between these two rival factions. Eager to maintain his role as the embodiment of Arab nationalism, his ear was more sensitive to the gravitational pull of the Arab radicals than to the more conservative and traditional Arab leaders such as King Faisal of Saudi Arabia and King Hussein of Jordan. This made him vulnerable to Syrian efforts to involve him in a larger war with Israel.

In April 1967, a major clash took place on the Israeli-Syrian border. Six Syrian Mig fighters were shot down by Israel in the course of the battle. *El Fatah* raids continued to mount in ferocity, and on May 14 Israeli Prime Minister Levi Eshkol declared that a serious confrontation with Syria would be inevitable if the attacks continued. The Syrians responded by declaring that Israel was concentrating huge armed forces on her border in preparation for an attack against Syria. Eshkol denied this charge and invited the Soviet ambassador to visit the areas in question. The Soviet diplomat refused. The pressure on President Nasser to help the Syrians was mounting rapidly. On May 16, Nasser proclaimed a state of emergency for the Egyptian armed forces and took measures to work out a joint Syrian-Egyptian defense agreement. The Syrian leadership, however, continued to taunt the Egyptian president by accusing him of "hiding behind the sheltering skirts of the United Nations Emergency Force."[29] A wave of emotion now spread throughout the Arab world from Casablanca to Baghdad. Demonstrations against Zionism took place in virtually every Arab country. On May 16, the Palestine Service of Radio Cairo declared:

> The menace and challenge of Israel have persisted far too long. The very existence of Israel in our usurped land has endured beyond all expectation. An end must be put to the challenge of Israel and to its very existence. Welcome to aggression by Israel which will send us into action to destroy it! Welcome to the battle for which we have long waited! The hour of battle is imminent. In fact, this is the hour of battle.[30]

President Nasser chose to ride the emotional tide of Arab nationalism rather than to resist it. This meant, however, that he had to take an active part in escalating the crisis, and so he decided to terminate the presence of the UN Emergency Force in Egypt and the Gaza Strip. On May 18 Foreign Minister Mahmoud Riad asked United Nations Secretary-General U Thant to withdraw UNEF "as soon as possible." He reminded the secretary-general that the force had been stationed on Egyptian soil at the invitation of the Egyptian government and that its continued presence depended on Egyptian approval.

The UN Emergency Force had patrolled the 100-mile Egyptian-Israeli frontier for ten years. It had been stationed on the Egyptian side of the border but not on the Israeli side. During the decade the force had been in effect, border eruptions had been kept to a minimum, and so the demand for its withdrawal caused considerable dismay at the United Nations. Although U Thant never questioned Egypt's legal right to demand the withdrawal of the force, he expressed "serious misgivings" about its termination. He immediately referred the matter to the UNEF Advisory Committee. The Indian and Yugoslav representatives made it clear that their contingents were likely to be withdrawn in any case. Since they made up almost half of the force of 3300, additional pressure for withdrawal was thus applied. Furthermore, UN forces were already being jostled out of their positions by Egyptian troops. So the secretary-general complied with the Egyptian demand, reasoning that UNEF could no longer remain in the area if the consent of the host government were withdrawn.

Few actions have been discussed more heatedly by governments, the world press, and public opinion than U Thant's withdrawal of the UN Emergency Force. Criticism was particularly sharp in the United States, the United Kingdom, Canada, and, of course, in Israel. The Israeli ambassador to the United Nations, Abba Eban, stated caustically that "the umbrella was removed at the precise moment it began to rain." U Thant answered these charges by stating that he had no alternative by law but to accede to a request that was rooted in Egypt's sovereign rights. He also reasoned that if he did not comply with the request of a sovereign government, then consent for the admission of a UN peace-keeping force in a future crisis might be infinitely more difficult to obtain. Given all these conflicting considerations, the secretary-general made his difficult and fateful choice.

The withdrawal of UNEF brought the crisis to a new and much graver stage. Israeli and Egyptian forces now confronted each other directly across the border. Israel ordered a limited mobilization of reserves to which Egypt, on May 21, responded in kind. Encouraged by the ease with which he had accomplished the removal of the United Nations buffer force, and spurred by the groundswell of emotions in the Arab world, President Nasser, on May 22, announced the decision that was to become the direct cause of the Six-Day War: closure of the Straits of Tiran at the entrance of the Gulf of Aqaba to Israeli shipping, thereby blockading once again the port of Elath. In an emotional speech at the Egyptian Air Force Headquarters in Sinai he declared:

> The armed forces yesterday occupied Sharm-el-Sheik. What does this mean? It is affirmation of our rights and our sovereignty over the Gulf of Aqaba which constitutes territorial waters. Under no circumstances will we allow the Israeli flag to pass through the Gulf of Aqaba. The Jews threaten war. We tell them you are welcome, we are ready for war, but under no circumstances will we abandon any of our rights. This water is ours.[31]

The imposition of the blockade catapulted the crisis into the international realm. Israel had withdrawn from the Straits of Tiran only after receiving explicit assurances that the Western powers would guarantee freedom of passage for its ships. On May 23 Prime Minister Eshkol reminded the Western powers of their obligations, and Abba Eban, Israel's foreign minister, was dispatched to Paris, London, and Washington to secure the necessary assurances.

The responses of the Western powers to Israel's appeal for help were sympathetic but did not amount to guarantees. President Lyndon Johnson described the blockade as ''illegal and potentially dangerous to peace.'' It was unlikely, however, that in the light of the US experience in Vietnam, the United States would be prepared to risk military intervention in the Middle East. In fact, President Johnson emphatically urged Israel not to take unilateral action. Little support came from anyone else. The British too were sympathetic but did not offer a definite commitment to keep the waterway open, and President de Gaulle of France, observing a glacial neutrality, stated: ''France is committed in no sense or on any subject to any of the states involved.''[32]

These responses were not reassuring to Israel. Prime Minister Eshkol was under increasing pressure to assume a more belligerent position. On May 24 the UN Security Council convened but was unable to take any action whatsoever to lift the blockade. The sense of foreboding in Israel increased. On May 26, when President Nasser asserted that the Gulf of Aqaba was only part of the major problem that was caused by Israel's aggression in simply existing, the response in Israel was electric. Pressure now became intense to appoint General Moshe Dayan, the hero of the 1956 Sinai campaign, to the ministry of defense. On the same day that Nasser delivered his belligerent address, his friend Mohammed Hasanein Haikal, the editor of the leading Egyptian newspaper *Al-Ahram,* wrote a remarkably frank and perceptive article:

The closure of the Gulf of Aqaba means, first and last, that the Arab nation, represented by the UAR, has succeeded for the first time vis-à-vis Israel in changing by force a fait accompli imposed on it by force. To Israel this is the most dangerous aspect of the current situation, not who can impose the accomplished fact and who possesses the power to safeguard it. Therefore, it is not a matter of the Gulf of Aqaba but of something bigger. It is the whole philosophy of Israeli security. Hence, I say that Israel must attack.[33]

This was a fair assessment of Israel's predicament. On June 1 it was announced that General Dayan was appointed minister of defense. This move was widely interpreted as a sign that Israel had decided that she could not depend on outside help and would therefore have to resort to a preemptive attack to break her hostile encirclement. On June 2, Ahmed Shukairy, leader of the Palestine Liberation Organization, called for a holy war for the liberation of Palestine. Addressing a large congregation in the Old City of Jerusalem, he declared that the Arabs wanted "fighters, not Beatles" and called on Arab women to don battle dress, adding that "this is no time for lipstick and miniskirts." Meanwhile, on June 3 General Dayan stated at a press conference that, although Israel welcomed all the help it could get on the diplomatic front, it wished to fight her own battles with its own troops. He added that he did "not want British or American boys to get killed" in the defense of Israel. Asked whether Israel had lost the military initiative, General Dayan replied: "If you mean to say we stand no chance in battle, then I cannot agree with you."[34] The brink was reached.

At 7:45 A.M. on Monday, June 5, the Six-Day War began. The Israeli air force attacked Egyptian airfields in a series of lightning strikes. By the end of the week, the armed forces of Israel occupied the Sinai Peninsula, the Gaza Strip, the whole West Bank of the Jordan, the entire city of Jerusalem, and the Golan Heights. The armies of Egypt, Jordan, and Syria had been completely routed. Israel had destroyed or captured 430 aircraft and 800 tanks and had inflicted 15,000 fatal casualties on Arab troops. It had taken 5500 officers and soldiers as prisoners. Its own losses were 40 aircraft and 676 dead.

A study made by the Institute for Strategic Studies in London by Michael Howard and Robert Hunter summarizes the campaign:

The third Arab-Israeli war is likely to be studied in Staff Colleges for many years to come. Like the campaigns of the younger Napoleon, the performance of the Israeli Defence Force provided a textbook illustration for all the classical principles of war: speed, surprise, concentration, security, information, the offensive—above all, training and morale. Airmen will note with professional approval how the Israeli air-force was employed first to gain command of the air by destruction of the enemy air-force, then to take part in the ground battle by interdiction of enemy communications, direct support of ground attacks and, finally, pursuit. The flexibility of the administrative and staff system will be examined and the attention of young officers drawn to the part played by leadership at all levels. Military radicals will observe how the Israelis attained this peak of excellence without the aid of drill sergeants and the barrack square. Tacticians will stress the importance they attached in this, as in previous campaigns, to being able to move and fight by night as effectively as they did by day. Above all, it will be seen how Israel observed a principle which appears in few military textbooks, but which armed forces neglect at their peril: the Clausewitzian principle of political context which the British ignored so disastrously in 1956. The Israeli High Command knew that it was not operating in a political vacuum. It worked on the assumption that it would have three days to complete its task before outside pressures compelled a cease-fire.[35]

On the deepest level, the secret of Israel's military success probably lay in the realization of every one of its citizens that losing would have meant the end of the nation's existence. In that light, the comparison, offered by the Soviet delegate to the UN Security Council, of Israel's offensive with Hitler's attack on the Soviet Union was hardly persuasive. In a sense, Israel's military system was the very opposite of that of nineteenth-century Prussia, which had resulted in the militarization of society. The Israeli approach led to the civilianization of the army; officers maintained their authority not by orthodox discipline but by personal example. Thus the Israelis got the utmost from their soldiers and their machines.

President Nasser was so shocked by the swiftness and efficiency of Israel's offensive that he believed, or purported to believe, that the United States and the United Kingdom had given assistance to the Zionists by maintaining an "air umbrella" over Israel. The truth was that in the Arab countries political fanaticism simply was no substitute for military expertise, and fantasies of victory could no longer mask the totality of the disaster.

Israel's leaders knew that they had to achieve their victory quickly to make it stick. They operated on the assumption that they had three days to defeat the Arabs before outside pressures compelled a cease-fire. In fact, they had four and needed five. The chorus of disapproval that arose even in the West when Israel ignored a United Nations cease-fire call and, on the fifth day of the war, opened its offensive against Syria showed how narrow was the time margin in which Israel had to work. Israel knew that there was a tacit agreement between the two superpowers not to permit the Arab-Israeli war to escalate into a larger conflict, provided that the war was quickly brought to an end. Once it had ended, the great powers were reluctant to risk a second conflict in order to undo the victory that had been achieved in the first. Thus a premium was placed on preemption and the lightning speed of Israeli arms.

An analysis of the changes in power constellations after the Six-Day War reveals some interesting comparisons and contrasts with the crisis of 1956. First, the Soviet Union had backed a loser this time, whereas she had been on the winning side a decade earlier. Most of the military hardware that the USSR had shipped to the Arab states was destroyed or captured by the Israelis. The United States, however, was on the winning side, and superficially her policy seemed successful. But on a deeper level it was clear that the swiftness of

Israel's victory had saved the United States from having to make some difficult decisions. Had the war gone badly for Israel or remained inconclusive, the United States might have been forced to intervene and risk a confrontation with the Soviet Union.

Israel, which had to withdraw in 1956, was determined this time not to yield its military gains except in exchange for an end to belligerency. Within six days Israel had exchanged its vulnerability for a position of unprecedented military domination in the Middle East. Within two brief decades, a fledgling Jewish state in Palestine had become a formidable power.

The October War of 1973

Israel's swift and decisive victory in 1967 had left a legacy of shame and bitterness on the Arab side. Diplomacy had not been able to dislodge the Israelis from the five territories that they had captured from three Arab countries in June 1967: Sinai and the Gaza Strip from Egypt; Old Jerusalem and the West Bank from Jordan; and the Golan Heights from Syria. The UN Security Council had been able to adopt only a single resolution on the Middle East over a period of six years. That resolution, which was passed on November 22, 1967, linked a promise of secure and recognized boundaries to Israel with a promise of withdrawal from occupied territories to the Arabs. But neither side was willing to take the first step, and so the entire situation remained frozen. No face-to-face negotiations between Arabs and Israelis ever took place. The Arabs gazed across the cease-fire line with increasing fury and frustration as Israel made plans to populate the territories with Jewish settlers. Israel seemed bent on de facto annexation, and the Arabs seemed equally determined to prevent it.

Anwar Sadat, who became Egypt's new president after Nasser's death in 1970, gradually and without much fanfare prepared the ground for an Arab counterattack. Unlike Nasser, the less flamboyant Sadat did not divide the Arab world but doggedly worked toward a consensus. The Soviet Union, though not prepared to give the Arabs offensive weapons for use against Israel, did replace the military hardware that had been captured or destroyed by Israel in 1967. The Soviets also trained Egyptian and Syrian commanders in Soviet military strategy and tactics in order to prevent a repetition of the debacle of the Six-Day War. By 1973 the Arabs were encouraged to believe that at least some of the lost territories could be regained by force of arms. Thus the stage was set for yet another violent encounter.

On Yom Kippur, the Jewish Day of Atonement, Syria and Egypt launched a well-coordinated surprise attack. In the north, Syria attacked the vital Golan Heights in an effort to regain the vantage point over Israeli settlements in the valley below. In the Sinai, Egypt threw a major military force across the Suez Canal, capturing Israeli positions on the eastern bank and sending Israel's defenders backward into the desert.

The Arab attack had not come as a complete surprise to the Israeli leadership. Defense Minister Moshe Dayan claimed several days later that he had had advance information that some sort of attack was imminent but had decided against a preemptive strike. The reason for this decision, according to Mr. Dayan, was to "have the political advantage of not having attacked first, even at the expense of the military advantage."[36] Israel's image abroad would thus be improved with resultant long-term political benefits.

The price that Israel paid for this apparent self-restraint was heavy. On the Suez front, the Egyptians swarmed across the canal in large numbers, laid down bridges, and landed hundreds of tanks and other war material. They managed to overrun the famous Israeli defense installation, the Bar-Lev line, with heavy air and artillery assaults. The lightly defended Israeli positions had to be abandoned. On the Golan Heights an enormous Syrian force equipped with 800 tanks plunged across the cease-fire line at four points. Commando units landed by helicopter on Mount Hermon and seized a major Israeli position. Overwhelmed by the force of the attack, Israeli defenders had to evacuate several outposts.

One explanation of these early Arab successes may be found in Israel's perception of its own military superiority and of the Arabs as notoriously poor, bumbling soldiers. The Israeli leadership had convinced itself of its own superiority to such an extent that it believed that any Arab attack would be suicidal. Israel, in short, was suffering from a case of military hubris.

By the end of the first week of war Israel had stemmed the Arab onslaught, but the myth of its invincibility had nevertheless been shattered. Egypt had managed to install almost 100,000 men on the East Bank of the Suez Canal, and the fiercest tank battles since World War II were raging in the Sinai desert and the Golan Heights. Casualties were heavy on both sides, and new Soviet ground-to-air missiles presented a grave threat to the Israeli air force. Buoyed by the successes of Syria and Egypt, other Arab countries joined in the battle. Iraq and Jordan supplied troops for the Syrian front, and Saudi Arabia and other oil-rich Arab sheikdoms applied increasing pressure on the United States to abandon its support of Israel.

As casualties mounted and both sides suffered staggering losses in war material, the superpowers entered the arena. The Soviet Union began to resupply the Arab states with ammunition and light weapons. When the United States decided to do the same for Israel, the Soviet Union escalated its supply operations to tanks and planes. This, too, was matched by the United States. Thus, by the end of the first week, the war had reached a new and dangerous plateau. Not only was the armor of both sides locked in a death struggle, but the fragile détente between the Soviet Union and the United States hung in the balance.

During the second week of war Israel gradually gained the upper hand on both the Syrian and Egyptian fronts. After fierce tank battles in the Golan Heights, the Israelis not only threw back the Syrians but embarked on the road to Damascus. In the words of General Dayan: "We have to show them (the Syrians) that the road leads not only from Damascus to Tel Aviv, but from Tel

Aviv to Damascus.''[37] The Israeli advance into Syria came to a standstill at the village of Sasa, 20 miles from the Syrian capital.

On the Egyptian front, Israeli troops, in a daring tactical maneuver, entered the West Bank of the Suez Canal on Egyptian territory. Their aim was to encircle the Egyptian troops on the East Bank in Sinai and to cut off their retreat across the canal back to Egypt. After massive air and tank battles, the Israeli objectives were attained. The Egyptian troops were trapped in two large pockets in Sinai, and the Third Army was at Israel's mercy for its supply of food and water. At this juncture, with the balance shifting rapidly in Israel's favor, the superpowers once more intervened.

On October 21, acting with great urgency to protect its Egyptian ally, the Soviet leadership agreed with Secretary of State Henry Kissinger on a formula for a cease-fire resolution. This resolution, which was rushed through the UN Security Council on the following morning under joint Soviet-American sponsorship, provided for a cease-fire in place and called on all parties to start immediate negotiations toward implementing the 1967 Security Council plan for peace in the Middle East. The cease-fire began shakily, with the Egyptian forces trapped behind Israeli lines trying to break out and Israel seeking to destroy the Egyptian forces once and for all. A second cease-fire call still did not end the fighting. As a result, the Soviet Union proposed that a joint Soviet-American peace force be dispatched to the Middle East. This proposal was rejected by the United States, which feared the possibility of a military confrontation in the area. The Soviet Union then declared that it would introduce its own troops into the area unilaterally. To this Soviet threat, President Nixon responded by placing the armed forces of the United States on military alert.

During the "alert" crisis, a compromise was worked out. The UN Security Council approved a third resolution sponsored by the nonaligned countries that authorized the secretary-general to send a UN buffer force to the area. This 7000-soldier emergency force would be patterned after the old UN Emergency Force that had been created by Dag Hammarskjold in 1956. It was to exclude the permanent members of the Security Council from active participation. To save face, however, the two superpowers insisted on sending a small number of observers into the cease-fire area. The first UN troops began to arrive from Cyprus on October 27. By then, all fronts were quiet. The precarious Soviet-American détente had held after all.

As the "October war" drew to a close after seventeen days of violent fighting, Israel had won another victory, but a costly one in blood and treasure. Although it had managed to roll back the initial Arab advance and had assumed a commanding military position on both fronts, the price paid in human lives for this achievement was far higher than the toll that had been taken in the war of 1967. The heavy losses made the victory somewhat joyless. Moreover, the immediate postwar Israeli attitude on the question of the occupied territories hardened. If an Arab surprise attack had been launched along the pre-1967 armistice lines, then Tel Aviv and Jerusalem—not the Golan Heights and the Bar-Lev line—would have had to absorb the initial shock. Thus, in the

Israeli view, tens of thousands of their people could be killed if such a surprise attack were only slightly more successful than the one launched in October 1973. In Abba Eban's words:

> If we had been mad enough to abandon the Golan Heights and Sharm el Sheikh and all the Sinai and the whole West Bank, would not the massive attack launched on October 6 have murdered thousands of our civilians, devastated our population centers and brought us to catastrophe? I tell you, a massacre more hideous than Auschwitz would have been a real prospect and Israel's survival would be in doubt. To suggest a restoration of the pre-1967 lines is sheer irresponsibility in the light of what has been revealed.[38]

Just as the setbacks of the first few days of war were deeply etched on Israeli minds, so the Arabs cherished and glorified their short-lived victory. Despite his ultimate defeat, President Sadat proclaimed that "Egyptian forces had performed a miracle by any military standard" and had thus "restored the honor of the nation." Egypt and Syria had been able to break out of the frustration and futility of unending diplomatic stalemate. They had placed Israel on notice that it could not hold on indefinitely to occupied territory unless it was prepared to accept the risk of yet another war with the odds against it. As Egypt's foreign minister, Mohamed El Zayyat, put it:

> The Israeli attitude had been to assume that they were invincible and that we were meek and weak. They pictured Egyptians as people who would never fight. The argument that this occupied territory serves as a protective buffer for Israel—that was the argument of Hitler. What we are asking for is very simple: that our territorial integrity and the rights of the Palestinians be respected. These two elements are the sine qua non conditions for peace in the Middle East.[39]

Thus the fourth round ended with positions hardened on both sides and passions unallayed. The Israelis were embittered by the Yom Kippur surprise attack and, in their bitterness, tended to forget that the attack was launched in order to regain lost territories. The Arabs were so intent on restoring their dignity and regaining lost ground that they believed that they had won even though actually they had lost. Neither side was able any longer to understand the fears of the other. All empathy was lost. For two weeks the superpowers had made the desert a proving ground for new destructive weapons. Kings played chess while pawns bled on the battlefield. Only when the kings were fearful that the battle might engulf them too did they stop the bloodshed. Once again the United Nations was used as a rescue operation at the edge of the abyss. Frantic cease-fire resolutions had to take the place of preventive diplomacy. And only a fragile superpower détente prevented yet another fateful escalation with dire consequences for humankind.

The October War of 1973 had one positive result. Under superpower pressure, Israelis and Arabs did agree to meet in a peace conference in Geneva in December 1973, their first face-to-face diplomatic encounter in a quarter of a century. As Abba Eban put it: "For something to be born, the parents have to meet at least once." Chastened by four wars, Arabs and Jews alike began to feel that unless wisdom and reason ultimately prevailed, the only alternative would be mutual annihilation.

The role of the United States during and after the October War was primarily defined by Secretary of State Henry Kissinger. For the next three years, the Middle Eastern scene was dominated by the tireless peace-making efforts of this extraordinary statesman.

Kissinger's role in the October War can be described as neither pro-Israeli nor pro-Arab but as essentially proequilibrium. Before the war erupted, Kissinger perceived Israel as the stronger side and thus warned the Jewish leaders "not to pre-empt." But when he turned out to have been mistaken and Syria and Egypt launched their coordinated surprise attack, Kissinger switched sides and provided US military aid to Israel in order to restore the military balance. And when the Israelis, with the US assistance, gained the upper hand, Kissinger switched sides again and insisted on the rescue of 100,000 trapped Egyptian soldiers. When a cease-fire was finally proclaimed by the United Nations, both sides were exhausted and roughly even—exactly what Kissinger had wanted. It had always been his firm belief that only a war without victory or defeat could contain the seeds of peace.

As Kissinger surveyed the ravages of the October War, he conceived his plan for peace in the Middle East. He decided to subdivide the problem into manageable segments instead of addressing it in its totality. He would approach it step by step, beginning with the least forbidding obstacle, and then, after having built a basis of trust between the rivals, he would try to negotiate the more formidable hurdles. A first tentative step had already been taken. Egypt had agreed to talk to Israel. If Kissinger could achieve a military disengagement between Israel and Egypt, a momentum toward peace might then be set in motion. It would perhaps then be possible to leap over yet another hurdle and effect a military disengagement between Syria and Israel. If such military interim agreements were possible, perhaps one might be able to move the rivals toward political accommodation. Once Egypt and Syria had entered into negotiations with Israel, Saudi Arabia might be persuaded to lift her oil embargo, and, if luck held, it might even be conceivable to think about a compromise between Israel and the Palestinians and a Jerusalem settlement. Such was Kissinger's train of thought. The peace-making process would be like a steeplechase, with each successive hurdle higher and more treacherous. But Kissinger believed that the step-by-step approach would yield at least some limited successes and should not be a total failure.

The objective that Kissinger had in mind, of course, was equilibrium. Israel would have to withdraw from some of the conquered territories, but in the context of its national security. The diplomatic reemergence of the Arabs would be encouraged, but in a context of realism and responsibility. An effort would be made to woo the Arabs away from the Soviet Union. They would come to the United States because, in Kissinger's judgment, "they could get weapons from the Russians, but territory only from the United States." Thus by delivering some real estate to the Arabs, Soviet power in the Middle East would be diminished and US influence strengthened. To achieve this objective, however, pressure would have to be applied on Israel. It would have to be encouraged to trade territory for security. And if Kissinger's reasoning was wrong, he would have to protect Israel by always being generous with arms.

Kissinger's step-by-step approach to peace was not greeted with universal acclaim. The Soviet Union was highly critical and pushed for a general peace conference to be held in Geneva. There was also criticism in the United States. Numerous Middle East experts asserted that Kissinger's approach was that of a doctor who planned to stitch up one wound while permitting the infection to rage unattended elsewhere.

According to these critics, Kissinger, by concentrating on Egypt, intended to woo the moderate Sadat away from the Arab camp. This would not only remove the most conciliatory voice from Arab councils, but it would postpone and ultimately make more difficult the moment of truth. The heart of the matter, Kissinger's critics declared, was neither Egypt nor Syria, but the problem of the Palestinians, which Kissinger had chosen to postpone indefinitely, in addition to Jerusalem, which he had chosen to ignore completely. Thus, as George Ball, one of Kissinger's most trenchant critics, put it, "the step-by-step approach was the work of a tactician when the times called for a strategist."

Kissinger was undaunted by these attacks. He believed that the aftermath of an inconclusive war was the best time for a concentrated peace effort. Shortly after the last shot had been fired, he decided to commit his skill, energy, and reputation to a highly personal diplomatic peace offensive in the Middle East. During the next few months he would visit virtually every Arab capital, shuttle between Aswan and Jerusalem, and later between Damascus and Jerusalem. Sadat would call him "brother"; Faisal would welcome him even though he was a Jew; Hussein would pilot him in the royal helicopter; even Assad would learn to like him; and Golda Meir would have endless conversations with him in her kitchen. The result of this extraordinary diplomatic tour de force was the successful negotiation of the first two hurdles. In January 1974 Kissinger was able to produce a military disengagement accord between Israel and Egypt, and four months later, after immense effort, he was able to achieve a similar accord between Israel and Syria.

The high point of Kissinger's "shuttle diplomacy" was the Sinai agreement between Israel and Egypt, signed in Geneva in September 1975. The Sinai agreement bore the imprimatur of a Kissinger settlement. Neither side was happy with it but neither side could offer a better alternative that was acceptable to both. The Israelis promised to return two mountain passes and an oil field. In exchange they received pledges from President Sadat to the effect that Egypt would refrain from the threat or use of force against the Jewish state. Sadat also agreed to continue negotiations toward a final peace agreement and to extend the mandate of the UN buffer force annually for at least three years.

What finally made it possible, however, for Israel to conclude the agreement was a specific US commitment that Kissinger had not made before.

Kissinger offered to station 200 American civilian technicians in the Sinai between the contending parties. They would serve as a kind of early warning system in case either side planned an attack on the other, and they would report
to both Israel and Egypt. In addition, Kissinger pledged to recommend a US
aid commitment of $2.3 billion to Israel. Israel, which did not trust the UN
buffer force, found the pledge of a small symbolic US presence reassuring.
The aid package too was attractive, and furthermore, Prime Minister Rabin
could tell the opposition that Israel still retained over 85 percent of the Sinai
and the entire Gaza Strip. Sadat received his coveted mountain passes and oil
fields plus a US commitment of $700 million needed for the impoverished
Egyptian economy. The 200 Americans were welcome, too, since their presence only underscored Sadat's growing independence from the Soviet Union.
Thus Egypt gained some territorial allowances, and Israel received political
concessions. What could not be bridged between the parties directly was
bridged by the US commitments. Some senators grumbled that the 200
Americans in the Sinai reminded them of the beginning of Vietnam, but
Kissinger was quick to point out that the Americans in the Sinai were civilians
who were to aid both sides in keeping the peace, not soldiers who were to help
one side to win a war.

On the whole, Kissinger was pleased with the second Sinai interim agreement. It was, after all, the first accord between Israel and an Arab nation that
was not the immediate consequence of war. He knew that it was far from a
genuine peace treaty, but he was convinced that his step-by-step approach was
still the best way to proceed. In his judgment, most Americans were still willing to take great risks to preserve the state of Israel but were not willing to
take such risks to preserve Israel's conquests.

During most of 1976 a *deus ex machina* postponed the moment of truth for
Israel: Syria and the Palestine Liberation Organization, Israel's two bitterest
adversaries, turned on each other in a murderous war in Lebanon. While it
lasted Israel was in no mood to make concessions. By 1977, however, when
Jimmy Carter assumed the presidency of the United States and Menachem Begin became prime minister of Israel, the Lebanese war had tapered off, and a
renewed Arab alliance confronted the Jewish state.

Thus by 1977 it had become clear that the step-by-step approach had
reached a dead end. The heart of the matter was now the problem of the
Palestinians. Israel was confronted with a dreadful choice. If it agreed to negotiate with the PLO and return some territories to be used for the creation of
a Palestinian state, such a state would clearly be a dagger pointed at the heart
of Israel. If, however, Israel refused to negotiate, it risked another war or another oil embargo, as well as slow economic strangulation and increasing isolation. Despite the risks involved, President Carter believed that ultimately
Israel would have to face the Palestinians as a reality that would not go away,
just as the United States after more than two decades had been forced to adjust to the reality of a China that was communist. There were now three million Israelis and three million Palestinians. Both were permanent realities, and

sooner or later a compromise solution would have to be discovered. The alternative was yet another war.

In November 1977 the world held its breath when, in a spectacular and unprecedented move, President Sadat visited the Jewish state and addressed the Israeli *Knesset*. Though neither Sadat nor Prime Minister Begin made any substantive concessions during that first face-to-face encounter in Jerusalem, both leaders made a solemn pledge never again to go to war with one another. Whereas peace, unlike war, did not break out, the Sadat mission was widely heralded as a major turning point in the thirty-year-old conflict between Arab and Jew. At last an Arab leader had openly recognized the Jewish state. Two old enemies had suddenly become friends.

In September 1978 President Carter, in an all-out effort to forge a peace settlement between Begin and Sadat, invited the two leaders to a summit meeting at Camp David. After two weeks of intense and secret deliberations, two important agreements were hammered out. First, Begin and Sadat agreed on a ''Framework for Peace between Egypt and Israel'' that provided for the phased withdrawal of Israeli forces from the Sinai and the signing of a fullfledged peace treaty. Second, the two leaders agreed on a broader ''Framework for Peace in the Middle East'' that was designed to enable the Palestinian issue and the West Bank problem to be resolved progressively over a five-year period.

But at the very moment these agreements were being made, the Shah of Iran was deposed and driven into exile by the fundamentalist Islamic forces loyal to the Ayatollah Ruhollah Khomeini. As Iranian oil exports plummeted, the United States became increasingly dependent on Saudi Arabian oil. Recognizing their advantage, the Saudis insisted on a linkage between the separate Egyptian-Israeli peace treaty and progress toward the far more difficult issues of the West Bank, the Palestinians, and the status of Jerusalem. Motivated by US energy needs, Carter in turn exerted pressure on Israel to be more flexible. Finally, in March 1979, Begin and Sadat, after yet another Carter visit to the Middle East, signed a separate peace treaty. The president's tenacity and faith had finally borne fruit. After thirty years of war the Middle East had taken a large step toward peace.

Many vexing issues remained unresolved, of course. The fate of Jewish settlements on the West Bank continued to torment the Israelis, who also worried about the very real possibility of the ultimate creation of a Palestinian state. In 1981, Israel, using US-made planes, destroyed an Iraqi nuclear reactor that had been constructed with French and Italian help. This preemptive strike precipitated a diplomatic crisis between the United States and Israel. On the Arab side, Jordan and Saudi Arabia were dubious about the Israeli-Egyptian treaty; Syria and the PLO were bitterly opposed and regarded Sadat as a traitor. And perhaps most important, all Arabs insisted that Israel withdraw from Jerusalem and renounce the city as its capital. Israel in turn declared in 1980 that Jerusalem would remain its capital for ''all eternity.'' In 1981, President Sadat was assassinated by Moslem fanatics. Under his successor, Hosni

Mubarak, Egypt's relations with Israel cooled considerably. Worst of all, Israel launched an invasion of Lebanon which not only raised levels of violence in the region to new ferocity but upset the entire balance of power in the Middle East.

The Lebanese Tragedy

There was a time when Lebanon was a peaceful, happy land, a kind of Middle Eastern Switzerland, with its graceful seaport capital, Beirut, a major tourist attraction. This tranquillity depended on a fine balance between the Moslem and Christian populations of the country. Without that balance, Lebanon gradually descended into an abyss of devastation. Jealous factions fighting for turf dismembered Lebanon piece by bloody piece until it became a country without an effective government. Unable to control its own destinies, Lebanon was drawn into the vortex of the major power struggles in world politics. It became a bitterly divided country, with Beirut a divided city.

After Israel occupied the West Bank in 1967, hundreds of thousands of Palestinians moved to Lebanon over the years, gradually upsetting the fragile balance between Moslems and Christians. In 1975 the country erupted in civil war, triggered by a round of local murders which were to become typical of the Lebanese scene. Beirut was devastated for the first time. Syria's President Assad, seeing an opportunity for expansion, sent a "peace-keeping" force into Lebanon which became the beginning of the Syrian occupation of central Lebanon. Israel's Premier Begin, apprehensive about Syrian intervention, carved out for Israel a "security strip" in southern Lebanon in 1978. Four years later, in June 1982, Israeli forces invaded Lebanon in full force, all the way to Beirut. Their goal was to drive the Palestinian guerrillas out of southern Lebanon and to counter Syria's growing influence in that war-torn country.

At this juncture, the United States, fearful that the apparent disintegration of Lebanon might play into Soviet hands, decided to become involved. The Reagan administration worked out an agreement with three of its allies—Britain, France, and Italy—to send about 5000 marines into Lebanon. The objective of this "multinational peace-keeping force" was to monitor the withdrawal of PLO forces from Lebanon and, it was hoped, to persuade Israel to pull out so that Syria, too, might withdraw. The United States hoped, in short, that it might be helpful in returning Lebanon to the Lebanese. Unfortunately, this was not to be.

As the Palestinians were evacuated and the Israelis returned West Beirut to President Amin Gemayel's forces, the mission of the four-power peacekeeping force became somewhat unclear. Gradually it was redefined as providing support for the Gemayel government. But the young president acted more like the head of the Christian faction than the leader of the entire country, and the force quickly became identified as pro-Christian and anti-Moslem. A new tragedy was in the making.

In October 1983, a Moslem fanatic drove a truck loaded with explosives, kamikaze-style, into the sleeping quarters of the US marines in Beirut. The vehicle exploded with such force that the structure collapsed in seconds, killing 241 American servicemen. Simultaneously, another suicide mission killed 58 French soldiers, also asleep in their compounds. For the United States, this was the highest death toll since Vietnam, for France the heaviest since the Algerian war.

When looked at in the cold light of political analysis, this dreadful tragedy had all the overtones of a neocolonial conflict. The Moslem fundamentalists who committed these murders probably perceived the American, British, French, and Italian soldiers not only as partial to the Christian cause in Lebanon but also as the vanguard of a new Western imperialism. After all, these were the very four nations that had engaged in colonial adventures not all that long ago. Lebanon had been a French colony, Libya had belonged to Italy, much of the Middle East to Britain, and the United States was, of course, the main instigator of this renewed colonial intrusion. Islam, especially Shi'ite Islam inspired by Iran, perceived itself as the main bulwark against Western aggression. The murderers were thus not really murderers. They were freedom fighters, and their reward would be immediate entry into paradise.

After this catastrophe, the days of the multinational peace-keeping force were numbered. Senator Ernest Hollings of South Carolina put it well when he called on President Reagan to withdraw the marines within sixty days: "If they've been put there to fight, then there are far too few," he said, "but if they've been put there to be killed, there are far too many."[40] Accordingly, after some fruitless shellings by the battleship *USS New Jersey,* the American soldiers were withdrawn from Lebanon in February 1984. Shortly thereafter, their French, British, and Italian counterparts too, were removed. Lebanon by now was a carcass, and a dismembered one at that. For all practical purposes, by mid-1984, Lebanon was a divided country. Within its divisions, there were further factions which made the country look like a crazy quilt or Chinese puzzle. Nevertheless, these factions tended to fall, either directly or indirectly, along East-West lines. On the Western side were the Israeli forces stationed in southern Lebanon, now left to fend for themselves after the US withdrawal. The Maronite Christians and, to a lesser extent, the Sunni Moslems, were not unfriendly to Israel and the Western cause. On the other side, Druze and Shi'ite Moslems supported the Syrian presence which, in turn, was backed by the Soviet Union. President Gemayel, virtually powerless after the pullout of the Western forces, had to accept the indefinite presence of the Syrians and even felt compelled to host a Soviet delegation in Beirut. When, in early 1985, Israel began a phased withdrawal of its troops from Lebanon, Gemayel's hold on power became even more precarious. In historical perspective, Israel's incursion into Lebanon seemed like an ominous portent: Israel had to withdraw after three years of war, with its mission unaccomplished. And worse was yet to come.

By the late 1980s, Lebanon had become a disaster area, a place of war of all against all. Not only were Moslems pitted against Christians once again, but several outside powers continued to aggravate the conflict: Syria, which had 25,000 troops stationed on 60 percent of Lebanon's territory; Iran, which wielded influence through Shi'ite Moslems and Revolutionary Guards in the east of the country; Israel, through the continued occupation of an enclave in southern Lebanon which it called its "security zone"; and 400,000 Palestinians including a guerrilla force of 10,000. Lebanon itself was virtually without a government with a regular army of only 37,000 soldiers with Moslems in the majority in the ranks but with Christians controlling the officer corps. The prime minister was a Sunni Moslem, the speaker of Parliament a Shi'ite, and the president, Amin Gemayel, a Christian.

It appeared that, with all these factions, military strength would continue to dictate who controlled the country, or more accurately, who would keep it out of someone else's hands. No end appeared in sight to the destructive civil war that had erupted in 1975. Lebanon remained a tragic and dismembered land.

The Palestinian Uprising

Israel celebrated its fortieth birthday in May 1988. It was marred, as Israel's birth had been, by the sound of gunfire. But this time, the violence did not emanate from invading armies but erupted instead in two areas conquered by Israel in the Six-Day War of 1967: the West Bank and Gaza. Two decades of Israeli occupation had finally inflamed the passions of almost two million Palestinians yearning for an independent state.

By 1988, more than half of the Palestinian population of Gaza and the West Bank had lived all their lives under Israeli rule. These younger Palestinians were among the best educated groups in the Middle East, yet had only limited opportunities to apply their skills. Most made a meager livelihood in teeming villages, towns, and refugee camps. The rage and frustration of these young people finally boiled over in demonstrations in Gaza which quickly spilled over into the West Bank. Thousands of young Palestinians began to throw rocks, iron bars, and an occasional Molotov cocktail at Israeli security forces and insisted on flying the colors—red, white, green, and black—of the banned Palestinian flag.

What began as occasional protests by groups of embittered youth quickly developed into an organized resistance movement with an underground leadership and a well-planned strategy. By spring of 1988, the movement had gone far beyond rock-throwing to economic boycott of many Israeli products, non-payment of taxes to Israel, mass resignations of Israeli-appointed Arab police and local government officials, and strikes that closed down trade, transport, education, and other essential public services. The movement also had a name: *Intifadeh,* the Palestinian uprising. It had grown into something quite new in the context of the Arab-Israeli conflict: a massive civil resistance movement, demanding self-determination and an end to military occupation. Israel suddenly faced an entirely new kind of challenge: war from within.

Israel's efforts to quell the uprising through thousands of arrests, imprisonments, and beatings brought no real respite. The larger the number of arrests, the wider the *Intifadeh*. Gradually, even though the Palestinians were no military match for the Israelis, they gained an important political advantage: The uprising raised Palestinian national consciousness and once again focused world attention on the Palestine problem. By the summer of 1988, much of the outside world regarded Israel as an occupation power and the Palestinians as the underdog. To the dismay of the Israeli authorities, some of the Western media even began to compare Israel's occupation policies to those of South Africa. Sympathies had begun to shift. In an age of national self-determination, it had become counterproductive for a country of three million people to keep two million under permanent subjugation.

The uprising further deepened the profound rifts within Israel over the occupied territories. The Likud party of Prime Minister Itzhak Shamir perceived the uprising as a conspiracy to end Israel's very existence. In the Likud's view, the Palestinians were not after a Palestinian state in Gaza and the West Bank; they were out to destroy Israel altogether. Hence, a tough policy was the only appropriate response. The Labour party under its leader, Shimon Peres, however, other hand, advocated a more flexible policy. Believing that ultimately the Jews would be outnumbered in their own country if Israel held on to the territories, the Labour party was in favor of negotiations. The peace initiative of U.S. Secretary George Shultz, for example, was welcomed by Labour but foundered on the rock of Likud's refusal to compromise.

In a sense, the uprising redivided Israel. Many Israeli civilians became reluctant to enter the territories, and Israel's 700,000 Arab citizens became increasingly ''Palestinianized.'' Even Jerusalem—enthusiastically described by its mayor, Teddy Kollek, as a united city of Arabs and Jews—became *de facto* divided once again. Very few Jews ventured into the increasingly hostile Arab sector of the city. Nor did many Palestinians cross over into the new predominantly Jewish sector. The clock had been turned back.

By late 1988, the Arab-Israeli conflict was at a complete impasse. The Palestinians demanded complete self-determination which the Israelis were totally unprepared to grant. The Palestinians asserted that the PLO was their only legitimate representative, a premise rejected by the Israelis. Efforts by the Americans to search for mediators such as King Hussein of Jordan also came to naught, when the Jordanian king, in August 1988, removed himself from the scene by relinquishing his claim to the West Bank to the PLO. A contest of wills had taken shape in which Israel remained militarily the stronger but was losing the political initiative to the Palestinians. The Arabs, after five unsuccessful wars, had at long last discovered a formula that worked.

Events now began to move more quickly. In November 1988, the PLO met in Algiers and a jubilant Yassir Arafat proclaimed national independence for a state of Palestine. He then applied for a visa to the United States to address the UN General Assembly. When the State Department denied the visa on the grounds that Arafat had been an accessory to terrorism, the United Nations opted to reconvene in Geneva, where it decided by overwhelming vote to recognize Palestinian independence and to place the Israeli-occupied West Bank and Gaza under UN supervision. Arafat, in a shrewd political move, also declared in Geneva that he recognized "the right of all parties in the Middle East conflict to exist in peace and security," implying the recognition of Israel. Moreover, he renounced "all forms of terrorism, including individual, group and state terrorism." Secretary Kissinger had declared in 1975 that if the PLO ever recognized Israel and gave up terrorism, the United States would be prepared to open a dialogue with the Palestinians. According to his successor, George Shultz, these conditions had now been fulfilled, and hence, the United States decided to hold its first meeting with PLO representatives in December 1988 in Tunisia. The Israeli government, in considerable dismay, reiterated that it would not negotiate with the PLO under any conditions. Arafat had succeeded in driving a large wedge between Israel and her US ally and, moreover, had won a considerable propaganda victory. He could now claim that the United Nations had created Israel by majority vote in 1947. In 1988, more than forty years later, the United Nations had passed an even more overwhelming vote on behalf of the Palestinian people. Hence, in Arafat's view, the time for the creation of a Palestinian state had clearly arrived.

What of the future? In this writer's view, Israel will let the Palestinians rise to their feet only if the Jewish state's survival is an absolute certainty. The memory of the Holocaust will not permit the Jews to place their state at risk. And deep in their bones, most Jews believe that the Palestinians want to do away with Israel. It will take a Palestinian Sadat to convince them otherwise. In the meantime, the Palestinians will not go away. On the contrary, they will grow politically stronger and ever more resourceful. Like the Jews, they will continue to insist on a sovereign state of their own. Israel's ambivalence over Gaza and the West Bank will probably continue too. Israel does not really want the territories yet is afraid to give them up. In that sense, Israel's greatest military victory in 1967 might have sown the seeds of a political disaster, a kind of Israeli Versailles.

David Ben-Gurion, Israel's first prime minister, believed that sooner or later, the territories would have to be traded for security. And indeed, Israel did make peace with Egypt for the price of Sinai. Sooner or later, similar compromises will have to be worked out, so that *both* Jews and Palestinians will enjoy their right to nationhood. That is the fundamental message of the Palestinian uprising.

Conclusions

When people of good will despair of finding a solution, they tend to take solace in time as the great healer of wounds. But the experience of the six wars between the Arab states and Israel has not inspired such confidence in the curative power of time. The shock inflicted on the Arab consciousness by the establishment of Israel and the resulting homelessness of a million native Palestinians grew more, rather than less, acute as Arab nationalism gathered momentum. This trauma was accentuated by the fact that Israel—four times its original size—was seen as an ever-growing menace by the Arab world. Many Arabs feared that if expansion continued at this rate, Israel would soon dominate the whole of Palestine.

On the Jewish side, time has turned Israel into virtually a garrison state. How strange it is to contemplate the fact that the Jews, who lived homeless in the Diaspora for two millennia, should within the span of only four decades create a state with such fearsome military capability. Who would have guessed that the Jews, to whom things military were anathema, should now make them their first priority? Yet this is exactly what time has done.

Four times the Arabs made fatal mistakes that the Zionists used to their advantage. In 1948 five Arab armies invaded a Jewish state whose modest boundaries had been assigned to it by the United Nations. The Jews repelled the invaders and engaged in some annexation of their own, managing to enlarge their territory. The Sinai campaign of 1956 demonstrated vividly what Israeli arms could do even though the territorial gains had to be given up. In 1967 Nasser's blunder, the blockade of Aqaba, led directly to his humiliation and to Israel's spectacular victory. In October 1973 the Israelis turned an initial setback into yet another costly victory. But in 1982, Israel's invasion of Lebanon involved the Jewish state in a long and divisive war. And the Palestinian uprising confronted the Jewish state with the real possibility of civil war. The question by the late 1980s was whether Israel and her Arab neighbors, involved in six wars in a generation, would finally settle for permanent coexistence without victory or defeat.

There is one ultimate and final paradox that emerges from Israel's victories. The six wars with the Arabs created a situation in which three million Jews came to control territories that contained nearly two million Arabs. It is difficult to see how Israel can keep the fruits of victory and yet remain a Zionist state.

Perhaps this is the form that destiny assumes on earth. For the Jews Zionism was a response to the threats to their national survival. In their own need and plight, they drove more than a million other human beings to despair. Of the two nationalisms that clashed in Palestine, the Jewish was militarily superior but not politically stronger. The vanquished are yearning for redress. Zionism, to endure, will have to find the courage not to inflict on others what had been inflicted on the Jews throughout history. This will take a generosity of spirit that had seldom been extended to the Jews in their Diaspora. According to their faith, they had been chosen to have a great capacity for suffering. Now, at long last, they are no longer chosen; they themselves must choose.

THE UNITED STATES, THE PERSIAN GULF, AND THE IRAN-IRAQ WAR: THE PRICE OF MARTYRDOM

On January 16, 1979, after thirty-seven years of autocratic rule, Muhammad Reza Pahlevi, the shah of Iran, left his country never to return. From exile he watched his mortal enemy, the Ayatollah Khomeini, establish an Islamic theocracy which demanded Pahlevi's execution, called Iran's old ally, the United States, the "Great Satan," and turned more than fifty US embassy personnel into hostages in their own embassy. The Shah's death in Egypt in July 1980 unleashed a frenzied orgy of jubilation in Teheran, capped by executions of "enemies of the Islamic Revolution." Khomeini, now leader of Iran "for life," predicted the destruction of "satanical" America. A tyrant friendly to the West had been replaced by a fanatical adversary. How did these shattering events come about?

The shah of Iran had been a complex man. Austere and remote in his demeanor, he had nonetheless been a man of vision. For thirty-seven years, he had pursued a grand design with single-minded zeal: under his tutelage, Iran was to become a powerful industrial state. This modern Persian renaissance was to be achieved through the shah's "White Revolution," a "shock program that would allow Iran to overcome in 25 years its centuries of suppression."[41] In the shah's own words, this march toward a "Great Civilization" would turn Iran into "one vast workshop in which all the elements indispensable to modernization would spring up: universities, school groups, professional institutes, hospitals, roads, railroads, dams, electric plants, pipelines for gas and oil, factories, industrial, cultural, artistic, and sports complexes, cooperatives, metropolitan areas, and new villages."[42] Within a single generation, Iran would wrest its oil resources from foreign ownership and use its new-found wealth in the service of modernity and power. In this quest, the shah had found a natural ally: the United States. For decades, US firms supplied the shah's Iran with the technology and weapons that were the instruments of his "White Revolution." And the shah, in return, supplied the United States with badly needed oil and an unconditional fidelity in the struggle against communism. Friendship and foreign policy thus went hand in hand.

Unfortunately, the shah exacted a high price for his modernization program. In the first place, he had created a secret police, *Savak,* to deal with enemies of the state. *Savak's* net was wide and its techniques ruthless. Torture and abuse were commonplace in *Savak* prisons. It is estimated that over a hundred thousand Iranians died in *Savak's* dungeons. Even the shah himself admitted that "there were people arrested and abused," and that his country "fell victim to excesses."[43] "To let saboteurs act freely," the shah explained, "would not have permitted the program's realization."[44] In other words, terror was essential for the attainment of the "Great Civilization." Who, then, were the saboteurs?

Khomeini and his Islamic fundamentalists considered the shah an archtraitor to his country. According to the Moslem Shi'ite clergy, the shah had sold Iran out to the West and stolen its resources, all for the sake of personal wealth and glory. Islam, in the fundamentalists' opinion, had to cut loose from the United States and return to its historical tradition. The shah's program had led only to sinfulness and atheism. Women would have to wear the veil again, as they did before the shah's emancipation program. Justice would be meted out according to the Koran, including the stoning of adulterous women. Secular government officials would be subject to "spiritual leadership" by members of the Shi'ite clergy. These "mullahs" were the shah's bitterest enemies and, together with victims of *Savak,* communists, and "student" militants, prepared the ground for the Iranian monarch's fall.

Until the advent of Jimmy Carter in 1977, the alliance between Iran and the United States had continued relatively undisturbed. The new US president, however, deeply committed to the cause of human rights, criticized the shah and pressed him to institute reforms. Political prisoners, the President demanded, should be given a fair trial and set free if found not guilty. Human rights abuses, President Carter declared in the United Nations, would no longer be the offending nation's exclusive domestic business. The United States would punish the offenders by cooling off relations. Iran was one of many nations that Amnesty International had described as "serious violators of human rights." The shah, shaken by these criticisms emanating from his ally, embarked on a program of liberalization. By November 1977 "the police-state atmosphere had altered drastically to a mood of vastly greater individual freedom and relaxation."[45] This very loosening of controls, however, emboldened the shah's enemies and prepared the ground for revolution.

The US President did not seem to be aware of the coming revolution in Iran. No one in Washington, including the Central Intelligence Agency, expected the shah to fall. It was generally assumed that the liberalization moves would save and strengthen the regime. Besides, Carter had begun to realize the shah's importance as an ally. Muhammad Reza Pahlevi had been an unconditional friend of the United States for thirty-seven years. He had sold the Americans oil during the Arab embargo of 1973; he had even sold Israel oil; he had provided the United States a listening post on the Soviet border; he had refueled the US fleet without question; he had bought aircraft and technology from the US firms and paid cash; and he had been a staunch anticommunist. Accordingly, Jimmy Carter, on New Year's Eve 1978, visited the shah in Teheran and made the following statement: "Iran, because of the great leadership of the Shah, is an island of stability in a turbulent sea."[46] He also spoke effusively about the "love and admiration" which the Iranian people apparently gave to their leader. A week later, on January 7, 1978, the first riots erupted that, one year later, were to seal the doom of the Pahlevi dynasty.

During most of 1978, the year of the shah's slide to oblivion, Jimmy Carter temporized. Had he remained consistent and continued to press on for human rights, the new revolutionary government might have been more friendly when it came to power. Alternatively, a show of force by the United States including military aid might just possibly have saved the shah. As it turned out, Carter's policy of vacillation got him the worst of both worlds. It did not save the shah nor did it save his victims while he ruled Iran. Henry Kissinger, in early 1979, added the final touch: "A foreign policy that makes human rights its corner-stone, invites revolution." Jimmy Carter did not have an answer. The Iranian tragedy, more starkly perhaps than any other case, showed up the dilemma of human rights and naked power. By year's end, desperate emotions had swept events beyond the possibility of compromise.

On November 4, 1979, with the shah mortally ill in a New York hospital, the United States endured one of the worst humiliations in its history. Iranian mil-itants seized the US embassy in Teheran and held ninety-eight persons hos-tage, demanding that the United States return the deposed Shah and make res-titution on the wealth that he had "stolen" from Iran. The seizure of embassy personnel in their own compound had few precedents in the annals of diplo-macy and was in clear violation of all established norms of international law. As anti-American fervor rose to a fever pitch in Teheran, with President Carter burnt in effigy as the "Great Satan," the Ayatollah Khomeini gave his blessing to the seizure of the hostages. Under the new Islamic Constitution, Khomeini had just been given "supreme power for life" over Iran. The eyes of the world now were on the United States.

President Carter responded cautiously. Unwilling to risk the lives of the hostages, he took no military action. Instead, he halted oil imports from Iran, froze Iranian assets in the United States, and called on the United Nations for assistance. Khomeini decided to release women and blacks, leaving fifty-three Americans held captive. In January 1980 the UN Security Council, by a vote of 11 to 0, demanded the release of the hostages without delay. One of the four abstaining nations was the Soviet Union, which complained that the tone of the resolution was "too belligerent." The Soviet delegate failed to note that, while he spoke, Russian tanks were rolling into Afghanistan.

The geopolitical effects of the shah's demise were now becoming evident. The loss of Iran as a reliable Western ally had no doubt emboldened the Soviet Union when contemplating the possible costs of the invasion of Afghanistan. If the United States would not move to save a valuable friend, why should it move to save a neutral country? The conviction of the shah that the United States would not permit events in Iran to run out of control had been shared widely by friends and enemies alike. Now that this assumption had proved to be completely wrong, the Soviet Union drew the logical conclusion. It began to lean toward Iran in its test of wills with the United States. In short, it began to support nationalism—even Moslem fundamentalism—against the "imperi-alism" of the United States. When, in late January 1980, the United States asked for economic sanctions against Iran by the United Nation, the Soviet Union cast a veto, thus preventing any forceful action. The shah, before his fall, had predicted an "unholy alliance" between the mullahs and the communists.[47] It seemed that, by 1980, he was not altogether wrong.

The year 1980 was dominated by the hostage crisis. Hopes were in turn raised and dashed: UN Secretary-General Kurt Waldheim went to Teheran only to return empty-handed. "I do not trust this man," Khomeini had said about the secretary-general. Nor did the Ayatollah agree to see a UN commission of five men who had flown to Teheran. The United States brought its complaint against Iran to the International Court of Justice at The Hague. The court ordered the captors to release the hostages, but Iran ignored the ruling. Finally, in April 1980, President Carter ordered a helicopter rescue mission, which ended in a debacle in the Iranian desert. The Soviet Union, eager to exploit the United States' discomfort, accused the President of an "abortive provocation" that could have caused "mass bloodshed and the death of the hostages," lives the Soviets claimed "the president was willing to sacrifice for his election interests." Carter's misadventure not only lowered the United States' esteem throughout the world, it also shifted international attention away from the Soviet Union's invasion of Afghanistan.[48] Once again, the Soviet Union had exploited the struggle between Iran and the United States for its own purposes.

The shah's death in July 1980 had no effect upon the situation. One of the hostages had been released by Khomeini for reasons of health, leaving fifty-two captives. Economic sanctions had no impact nor did the war between Iraq and Iran that broke out in the fall. In October there seemed to be some progress. Khomeini announced four conditions for the release of the hostages, who, since the rescue attempt, had been dispersed throughout Iran: a US pledge not to interfere, "either directly or indirectly, politically or militarily, in the affairs of the Islamic Republic of Iran"; return of the fortune of "the cursed Shah"; unfreezing of Iranian assets in US banks; and cancellation of US legal and financial claims against Iran.

On November 4, 1980, Jimmy Carter lost the presidential election to Ronald Reagan. An Iranian offer, made shortly afterward via Algeria, to release the hostages for a payment of $24 billion did little to alleviate the situation. President Carter turned the offer down and Ronald Reagan, the President-elect, declared that "the United States would not pay ransom to barbarians."[49] Finally, after a frenzy of negotiations, a deal was struck: the Iranians were to receive their money, and the Americans were to get their people back. After $3 billion of Iran's assets were transferred to that nation's central bank, the fifty-two hostages made their flight to freedom on January 20, 1981, Ronald Reagan's inauguration day as President. Apparently, the Iranians did not wish to deal with a new American administration that might have taken a much tougher line than that of President Carter.

In retrospect, it became clear how deep the chasm of misunderstanding had been between the United States and Khomeini's Iran. The Americans, basing their claim on the sanctity of embassies and international law, had forgotten that these concepts had their origin in the Judeo-Christian tradition and that revolutionary Iran had not participated in their formulation. Moreover, the Americans had tended to negotiate with their Western-educated counterparts in Iran, overlooking the fact that the real power rested with the Islamic clergy. They had also underestimated the Iranians' fury when the United States admitted the deposed shah into the country. The Iranians, in turn, had failed to appreciate the United States' commitment to principles of Western diplomacy. Their leaders had little understanding of the way the US government worked. The prime minister, for example, believed that Jimmy Carter's power in the United States was as absolute as that of Khomeini in Iran. Finally, several months passed before the Iranians believed that the United States had not instigated the Iraqi invasion of Iran. Thus, misperception and ignorance of each other's cultures were the real villains in the tragedy of the encounter between Iran and the United States.

In 1980, the conflict between the United States and Iran was eclipsed by what was to become one of the most ferocious conflicts of the century: the war between Iran and Iraq.

Ever since the end of World War II, the Islamic world has been divided against itself. Despite efforts by leaders with pan-Arabic ambitions, such as President Gamal Abdel Nasser of Egypt, to unite the Arab world in a resurgence of past greatness, these initiatives have foundered on the rocks of nationalism and religious warfare. As a result, alliances in the Moslem world have shifted over the years in almost kaleidoscopic fashion. Not even the common hostility against the state of Israel was able to give substance to the ancient dream of Moslem unity. Perhaps the best example of this complex rivalry within the world of Islam was the war between Iraq and Iran.

In the fall of 1980 Iraqi infantry punched across 500 miles of desert front, and Iraqi pilots flying Soviet-built Migs bombed military targets and oil facilities. Caught by surprise at first, the Iranians soon responded with attacks of their own, and US-made Phantom F-11 fighter bombers streaked toward Iraqi cities and military installations. A nightmare had become reality. An area that was crucial to the Western world's oil supply was aflame. Moreover, there was the dire possibility that the Strait of Hormuz might be closed by the Iranians. Forty percent of the West's oil passed through this vital shipping lane, and, hence, the war quickly assumed global implications. The United States and the Soviet Union had contributed to the problem by heavily arming Iran and Iraq in the 1970s when Washington had close relations with the shah and Moscow had equal influence in Baghdad.

There were several reasons for the outbreak of this dangerous conflict. First, the war between Iraq and Iran had the earmarks of a religious conflict between two major sects of Islam. The Shi'ite Moslems, under the leadership of the Ayatollah Khomeini of Iran, believed that there were intermediaries between Allah and humankind. These deputies of God were ''ayatollahs,'' an Arabic term signifying ''reflection of Allah.'' The Sunni Moslems, who were dominant in the Iraqi leadership of President Saddam Hussein, believed that there should be no such intermediaries and that each man had a personal relationship with Allah. To some degree, the conflict was reminiscent of the religious wars in seventeenth-century Europe between Catholics, who believed in a papacy, and Protestants, who did not. It may be significant, in this connection, that when Christianity was torn apart by these internal struggles, it was fifteen hundred years old, which is the age of Islam today. So fierce was the religious nature of the struggle that the Iraqi president, in a national broadcast in November 1980, declared the conflict a jihad, a holy war to defend the ideals of the prophet Mohammed. Khomeini reciprocated by pronouncing the Iraqis enemies of God and Islam. Iraqis and Iranians alike believed that, if they died in battle, they would go directly to paradise. Death in a jihad assured the Moslem warrior of immortality.

Nationalism was at least as strong a force as religious fanaticism. Although more than half of Iraq's population was Shi'ite, the Iranians were unable to incite them against the Sunni leadership of Saddam Hussein. However, Iraq's appeals to fellow Arabs in Iran's embattled Khuzistan province provoked an uprising there against Persian rule. Territorial ambitions further fueled nationalism. The Iraqi war plan apparently hinged on seizing enough territory in an initial strike to use as a bargaining counter to regain sovereignty over the Shatt-al-Arab waterway, which Iraq had agreed to share with Iran in a 1975 agreement with the shah. Iran, however, rebounded from the Iraqi attack and, fighting with fanatical zeal, turned the war into a prolonged and bloody stalemate.

Personal ambitions also played a role. The Ayatollah Khomeini, the self-appointed prophet of Islam, had spent thirteen years in exile in Iraq, preparing for the uprising that eventually ousted his enemy, the shah. But in 1978 Iraq's government asked him to leave the country, thereby obliging him to spend the final months of his exile in France. The Ayatollah never forgave nor forgot that insult. Saddam Hussein, on the other hand, eager to replace Anwar Sadat of Egypt as the most powerful leader in the Arab world, was convinced that a blitzkrieg-type victory over Iran would vastly enhance his status and prestige. He was eulogized in the Iraqi press as "the awaited, the promised one" to destroy the Persian tyrant. His portrait was prominently displayed all over Iraq, from coffeehouses to supermarket checkout counters. Both leaders thus had exalted perceptions of themselves while entertaining devil images of one another.

The course of the war itself resembled that of World War I. In an era when military thinking was dominated by nuclear weapons or guerrilla warfare, the Iran-Iraq war was reminiscent of the French battles of an earlier age. The Iranians mounted costly human-wave assaults against Iraqi troops who were entrenched behind tanks and artillery. Iraq even resorted to the use of poison gas, banned by international conventions after World War I. And again, as in 1914, neither side could make a decisive breakthrough. After eight years of surges and confrontations up and down the winding 700-mile boundary between the two countries, the battle lines returned almost exactly to their original borders. Like Britain, France, and Germany in 1918, Iran and Iraq lost a generation of their best young men.

On the Iranian side, an obsession with martyrdom helped sustain the war's popularity despite enormous casualties. In the martyrs' cemetery outside Teheran, a fountain of blood reminded visitors of the fallen heroes. Though only colored water, it was chillingly realistic. The visitors stood among row upon row, acre after acre, of graves. People came in cars, on bicycles, or on foot, the women wrapped in black *chadors*. "My country, my country is like Karbala now," they chanted. Karbala, in the deserts of Iraq, was the place where the seventeenth-century religious leader Hussein, the son of Ali, the successor to the prophet Mohammed, met his death at the hands of a rival caliph. As new victims of the war were laid to rest in the martyrs' cemetery, young men in black shirts carried bundles of chains which they whipped across the backs of their shoulders. "Allah akbar," they chanted. God is great.

Later in the war, when the Iranian army began to run out of men, these same teenagers were recruited by the Shi'ite clergy to clear battlefields of mines and barbed wire. Their tickets to paradise were blood-red headbands reading "Warrior of God" and small metal keys signifying that the Ayatollah had given them special permission to enter heaven. In some battles, the Iranian reinforcements arrived proudly, carrying their own coffins.

In Iraq, too, the coffins of the dead were borne home, visually on the roofs of taxis. These victims, too, were called martyrs.

In 1986, Iranian troops captured the Fao peninsula and mounted an offensive against Basra, Iraq's second-largest city. It appeared, for the moment, that Iran might be victorious. But then, the fortunes of war began to tilt against the Ayatollah.

In 1987, the United States made the decision to commit its navy to patrol the Persian Gulf. This was done for three reasons: first, to ensure freedom of navigation for oil-carrying tankers since an interruption of such shipping would threaten the industrial democracies with a recurrence of the oil shock of the 1970s which had produced inflation, recession, and unemployment; second, to prevent Soviet domination of the area—after all, Iran shared a 1500-mile border with the Soviet Union; and finally, to protect the safety of friendly Arab states such as Kuwait and the oil-rich Arab Emirates from the Iranian threat. The United States even decided to reflag Kuwaiti tankers with the US flag, thus placing them under the direct protection of its navy.

This policy suffered from an element of inconsistency, to put it mildly, since at that very time, the Reagan administration was engaged in selling arms to Iran in the hope of freeing its hostages held captive in Lebanon. Not surprisingly, an accident was now merely waiting to happen. In May, an Iraqi aircraft accidentally hit a US warship, the *USS Stark,* with a missile, killing thirty-seven men. A year later, in July 1988, a second, even more tragic, mistake occurred. A US warship, the *Vincennes,* shot down a civilian Iranian airliner, killing all 290 passengers. Captain Will Rogers of the *Vincennes* had only a few seconds to decide whether the blip on his radar screen was a civilian aircraft or a hostile fighter plane. Remembering the fate of the *Stark,* he took no chances, precipitating yet another disaster.

In the meantime, in the land war, the Iranian offensive against Basra collapsed, and the Iraqis quickly recaptured the Fao peninsula and recrossed the Iranian border. Exhausted after eight years of war with Iraq and checkmated by the US navy in the Gulf, the Iranians finally had enough. In July 1988, the Ayatollah Khomeini personally endorsed a cease-fire, declaring that his decision was more painful than taking poison. UN Secretary-General Javier Perez de Cuellar dispatched missions to Teheran and Baghdad to make arrangements for a formal end to the war.

What can be said of this conflict in historical perspective? First, the war took over one million lives and may thus claim the dubious distinction of being one of the most vicious wars of this century. Second, like most theological conflicts, the war ended inconclusively, with each country's borders having changed little. And finally, the conflict devastated the resources of both combatants, leaving their economies destroyed and deeply in debt. Stated bluntly, the war accomplished absolutely nothing. The ambitions of two ruthless men had created a wasteland.

In larger historical perspective, perhaps the Thirty Years War within Christendom in the seventeenth century may serve as the best historical analogy. Neither Catholics nor Protestants came out as winners thirty years and several million casualties later. Both had to settle for compromise and coexistence. Similarly, it appears that neither Israelis nor Palestinians will be able to make each other disappear from the Middle Eastern map; both will ultimately have to find a way to live together without victory or defeat. Iraqis and Iranians, too, will have to learn this terrible and costly lesson from history. Today, wars over God and land are fought with more awesome weapons and under bleaker skies than hundreds of years ago. But in one sense, they remain the same: All they do is kill for nothing.

REFERENCES

1 John Neary, "The Bloody Dawn of Israel," *Life*, May 1973, p. 28.
2 Dan Kurzman, *Genesis 1948*. New York: Signet, 1972, p. 26.
3 *Ibid.*, p. 27.
4 David Horowitz, *State in the Making*. New York: Knopf, 1953, p. 140.
5 *Ibid.*, p. 141.
6 Larry Collins and Dominique Lapierre, *O Jerusalem*. New York: Simon & Schuster, 1972, p. 27.
7 Kurzman, *op. cit.*, p. 38.
8 Collins and Lapierre, *op. cit.*, p. 30.
9 *Ibid.*, p. 78.
10 *Ibid.*, p. 80.
11 *Ibid.*, p. 81.
12 Kurzman, *op. cit.*, p. 120.
13 *Ibid.*, p. 123.
14 *Ibid.*, p. 124.
15 *Ibid.*, p. 126.
16 Collins and Lapierre, *op. cit.*, p. 345.
17 *Ibid.*, p. 300.
18 Anthony Nutting, *Nasser*. New York: Dutton, 1972, p. 143.
19 Hugh Thomas, *Suez*. New York: Harper & Row, 1966, p. 163.

20 *Ibid.*
21 *Ibid.*
22 Nutting, *op. cit.,* p. 145.
23 Anthony Eden, *Full Circle,* quoted by Herbert Feis in *Foreign Affairs,* July 1960, p. 600.
24 Nutting, *op. cit.,* p. 163.
25 *Ibid.*
26 United Nations Document 5/3712, October 29, 1956.
27 Thomas, *op. cit.,* p. 164.
28 Keesing's Research Report, *The Arab-Israeli Conflict.* New York: Scribner's, 1968, p. 8.
29 Michael Howard and Robert Hunter, *Israel and the Arab World: The Crisis of 1967.* London: Institute for Strategic Studies, 1967, p. 17.
30 *Ibid.*
31 *Ibid.,* p. 20.
32 *Ibid.,* p. 22.
33 Cited in *Ibid.,* p. 24.
34 Keesing's Research Report, *op. cit.,* p. 25.
35 Howard and Hunter, *op. cit.,* p. 39.
36 *The New York Times,* October 14, 1973.
37 *The New York Times,* October 21, 1973.
38 *Time,* October 29, 1973, p. 44.
39 *Ibid.,* p. 45.
40 *Time,* October 31, 1983, p. 18.
41 Mohammed Reza Pahlevi, *Answer to History.* Briarcliff Manor, N.Y.: Stein and Day, 1980, p. 175.
42 *Ibid.,* p. 176.
43 *Ibid.,* p. 158.
44 *Ibid.*
45 *Time,* November 15, 1977.
46 *The New York Times,* January 1, 1978.
47 Pahlevi, *op. cit.,* pp. 145–174.
48 *Time,* May 5, 1980, p. 14.
49 *The New York Times,* December 29, 1980.

SELECTED BIBLIOGRAPHY

Cottam, Richard W. *Iran and the United States: A Cold War Case Study.* Pittsburgh: University of Pittsburgh Press, 1988. An excellent dispassionate assessment of the turbulent relations between Iran and the United States.

Evron, Yair. *War and Intervention in Lebanon.* Baltimore: Johns Hopkins, 1987. The author traces the gradual disintegration of Lebanon as a national state.

Harkabi, Yehoshafat. *Israel's Fateful Hour.* New York: Harper & Row, 1988. Israel's former chief of military intelligence proposes that Israel negotiate directly with the PLO over the establishment of a Palestinian state.

Khadduri, Majid. *The Gulf War: The Origins and Implications of the Iraq-Iran Conflict.* New York: Oxford, 1988. A good historical and political study of the causes of the Iran-Iraqi War. The author shows convincingly why the war was so difficult to stop and why it became a test of martyrdom on both sides.

Kurzman, Dan. *Genesis 1948*. New York: Signet, 1972. A fine analysis of the birth of Israel.

Morris, Benny. *The Birth of the Palestinian Refugee Problem*. New York: Cambridge University Press, 1988. This book is a rarity: a truly objective historical evaluation of this emotional issue.

Shepherd, Naomi. *Teddy Kollek: Mayor of Jerusalem*. New York: Harper & Row, 1988. The story of Jerusalem told through the accomplishments of the man who has been at the center of the city for over two decades.

Study Group. *Toward Arab-Israeli Peace*. Washington: Brookings Institution, 1988. A well-conceived set of recommendations by a group of experts intended for possible use by the Bush administration.

6

THE MILITARY STRUGGLE FOR POWER: WAR IN THE NUCLEAR AGE

Blood and destruction shall be so in use,
And dreadful objects so familiar,
That mothers shall but smile when they behold
Their infants quartered with the hands of war.

William Shakespeare, *Julius Caesar,* III, 2

Even today, with the disarmament process at long last underway, we still live in a world of about fifty thousand nuclear warheads—with a destructive power one million times that of the bomb dropped on Hiroshima in 1945. These weapons of mass destruction are divided roughly evenly between the United States and the Soviet Union.

For almost half a century, two military blocs of unprecedented power and destructive capacity have faced each other across a chasm of apparently unbridgeable political differences. Each claimed to be a purely defensive instrument against a war that neither wanted, and each was engaged in a gigantic arms race which was to deter the other from starting such a war. NATO, created under US leadership, included fifteen states of the Atlantic community, and the Warsaw Pact committed the Soviet Union to the defense of seven Eastern European nations.

During that time, a precarious "balance of terror" prevailed between the superpowers. This balance did not prevent some of the bloodiest wars in modern history, and, on one occasion, it almost broke down completely. Yet the conflicts that were fought remained nonnuclear, and in 1962 the world pulled back just in time from the brink of nuclear holocaust.

In this chapter, we shall analyze these major wars of the nuclear era: the Korean War, which was the first modern conflict that ended without victory or defeat; the Cuban missile crisis, which was our closest brush with nuclear death; and Vietnam, which became a tragic watershed in US history.

Although each of the last four decades saw a devastating conflict, somehow we have survived. Today, as we move toward the year 2000, we witness the first successful efforts at disarmament, and no major new war seems on the horizon. Perhaps, by studying these three conflicts of the recent past in depth, we can look into the darkness and try to understand. And perhaps, through understanding, we can strengthen the roots of a still far too fragile and imperfect peace.

THE KOREAN WAR: A GENERAL'S HUBRIS

At 4 A.M. on Sunday, June 25, 1950, more than 100,000 North Korean troops charged across the thirty-eighth parallel into South Korea. This event presented the United States with two classical challenges of a genuine crisis: danger and opportunity.

At the time of the North Korean attack, Harry S Truman was sixty-six years old and had served as President for more than five years. Truman had always admired ''strong liberal Presidents'' and had singled out for his particular affection Thomas Jefferson, Andrew Jackson, Abraham Lincoln, Theodore Roosevelt, and Franklin D. Roosevelt. He saw himself as the champion of the common person and was deeply committed to the liberal tradition in US politics.

Perhaps most significant for the Korean decision was Truman's belief in a strong chief executive. In his view, whenever a President weakly deferred to Congress, the public interest was the real loser. A decade of experience as senator had made Truman wary of the power of special interests in the passage of legislation. Certain decisions, particularly those pertaining to foreign policy, could be made only by the President in a strictly bipartisan manner. His readiness to accept full responsibility for crucial decisions was expressed by the motto inscribed on the triangular block that was always prominently displayed on his desk: ''The buck stops here.''

Harry Truman was blessed with the capacity to make extremely tough decisions without tormenting afterthoughts. As he wrote in a letter to his mother shortly after he assumed office: ''I have to take things as they come and make every decision on the basis of the facts as I have them and then go on from there; then forget that one and take the next.''[1] At the time he made the decision to drop the atomic bomb on Japan, he wrote to his sister: ''Nearly every crisis seems to be the worst one, but after it's over, it isn't so bad.''[2] Critics of President Truman have never asserted that his ''resolution [was] sicklied o'er with the pale cast of thought.'' His advisers admired his readiness to accept full responsibility, although historians for decades to come will undoubtedly regard most of the Truman foreign policy decisions as controversial. In addition, Truman was deeply committed to the United Nations: "As long as I am President," he declared on May 10, 1950, "we shall support the United Nations with every means at our command."[3]

Secretary of State Dean Acheson, fifty-seven years old at the time of the Korean crisis, had been in office for almost a year and a half. Acheson's relationship with Truman was excellent; Acheson thought of himself as "the senior member of the Cabinet" and was completely loyal to the President. Truman, in turn, had great confidence in Acheson's judgment and, in disagreements between the secretary of state and other members of the cabinet, almost always ruled in Acheson's favor.

The secretary of state, too, admired his President's ability to make difficult decisions. "The decisions are his," wrote Acheson, "the President is the pivotal point, the critical element in reaching decisions on foreign policy. No good comes from attempts to invade the authority and responsibility of the President."[4] A secretary of state, in Acheson's view, should be the "principal, unifying, and final source of recommendation" on foreign policy matters to the President. Acheson's admiration for Truman was rooted in his belief that the more difficulty a problem presented, the less likely that one decision was right. As he put it:

> The choice becomes one between courses all of which are hard and dangerous. The "right" one, if there is a right one, is quite apt to be the most immediately difficult one.... In these cases the mind tends to remain suspended between alternatives and to seek escape by postponing the issue.[5]

Acheson saw it as his duty to give the President the "real issues, honestly presented, with the extraneous matter stripped away."[6] But the decision was the President's: "Ultimately, he must decide."[7] Finally, like his chief, Acheson was committed to the United Nations. On June 22, 1950, only two days before the North Korean attack, he had declared before a Harvard commencement that the United States would give its "unfaltering support to the United Nations."[8]

At 11:20 P.M. on Saturday, June 24, Dean Acheson telephoned President Truman at his home in Independence, Missouri, where he was spending a quiet weekend with his wife and daughter. "Mr. President, I have very serious news," the secretary of state reported, "the North Koreans have invaded South Korea."[9] He explained that a few minutes earlier a cable had been received from John J. Muccio, the US ambassador to South Korea, advising that North Korean forces apparently had launched "an all-out offensive against the Republic of Korea."[10]

Acheson recommended an immediate emergency meeting of the UN Security Council. The President concurred and expressed his strong conviction to bring the issue of the invasion before the United Nations. A few minutes later, Assistant Secretary of State John D. Hickerson telephoned the home of Ernest A. Gross, the US deputy representative to the United

Nations and, failing to reach him, telephoned the secretary-general of the United Nations, Trygve Lie.

Trygve Lie, the first secretary-general, had been active in Norwegian labor politics for many years before his election to the UN post. He was known as a man of strong convictions who did not hesitate to take positions on explosive issues. Only a few months before the Korean crisis he had provoked the extreme displeasure of the US government by publicly supporting the application of the People's Republic of China for membership in the United Nations. By summer, his relations with the host country had deteriorated even further because of Senator Joseph McCarthy's probe for disloyal Americans in the UN Secretariat.[11] Now the other superpower was reproached. "My God," Lie exclaimed on learning the news, "that's a violation of the United Nations Charter!"[12] He immediately decided to cable a request for full information to the UN Commission on Korea, whose observers were actually on the scene. In the meantime, Acheson and a small group of State Department officials in Washington considered possible courses of action.

What is most striking about these early US responses is the unanimous agreement that the United States would have to respond to the North Korean challenge through the United Nations. As Ambassador Philip C. Jessup summarized these first reactions: "We've got to do something, and whatever we do, we've got to do it through the United Nations."[13] At 2 A.M. on Sunday, Secretary Acheson again telephoned the President and informed him that a group of officials in the State Department had drafted a resolution charging North Korea with a "breach of the peace" and an "act of aggression" and asking the UN Security Council to put an end to the fighting. President Truman approved the draft, and at 3 A.M. Ambassador Gross telephoned Secretary-General Lie requesting a meeting of the Security Council by early afternoon.

During the early hours of Sunday morning top officials at the US Mission to the United Nations, under the guidance of Ambassador Gross, planned the US strategy for the Security Council meeting. Gross, greatly worried about a possible Soviet veto that would paralyze the council, made contingency plans for initiating an emergency session of the General Assembly within twenty-four hours. The delicate problem of whether the operative paragraph of the resolution should take the form of an "order" or a "recommendation" to the Security Council was side-stepped when Gross suggested that the phrase "call upon" be employed. This language was diplomatically strong but kept the precise legal status of the resolution somewhat in doubt. Another problem was resolved by midmorning when a message from the UN Commission on Korea became available. The commission reported a "serious situation which [was] assuming the character of full-scale war." Since sole reliance on US sources might have created difficulties in the Security Council, this UN source provided a most welcome basis for factual information. By noon the Americans were ready for the meeting.

Shortly after 11 A.M. Dean Acheson arrived, coatless, at the State Department. This was unusual behavior for Acheson, who had been named "Best-

Dressed Man of the Year" in 1949. Reporters thus deduced that the situation was most serious. Indeed, Acheson had just learned from military intelligence sources at General Douglas MacArthur's headquarters in Tokyo that the North Korean attack seemed like an "all-out offensive" and that "the South Koreans seemed to be disintegrating."[14] At 2:45 P.M. he telephoned the President, who decided to return to Washington without delay. At the Kansas City airport, the President was described by reporters as "grim-faced," and one of his aides privately told a reporter: "The boss is going to hit those fellows hard."[15]

According to his *Memoirs,* Truman spent most of the journey to Washington alone in his compartment, reflecting on the "lessons of history." The North Korean attack, in his view, was only another link in the chain of aggressive acts by the German, Italian, and Japanese military adventurers that had led to World War II. There was no doubt in the President's mind that a Soviet probing action was behind the North Korean invasion. Unless Communist belligerency was deterred promptly and effectively, a third world war between Communist and non-Communist states was inevitable. In addition, the principles of the United Nations, ratified with such high hopes in 1945, would have to be affirmed through a collective response to aggression.[16] Thus Truman would act through the United Nations if possible, but without it if necessary. While still airborne, the President sent a message to his secretary of state instructing him to arrange a dinner conference at Blair House to which leading State and Defense Department officials were to be invited. At that very moment, the UN Security Council was beginning its emergency session. Present in the council chamber were the representatives of China, Cuba, Ecuador, Egypt, France, India, Norway, the United Kingdom, the United States, and Yugoslavia. The Soviet Union, conspicuous by its absence, was boycotting the Security Council to express its opposition to the presence of Nationalist China.

Secretary-General Lie informed the council that, judging from information submitted by the UN Commission on Korea, he believed that North Korea had violated the charter. He then went on to say that he considered it "the clear duty of the Security Council to take steps necessary to re-establish peace and security in that area."[17] Immediately after the secretary-general had made his statement, Ambassador Gross proceeded to read the US draft resolution to the assembled delegates. He "called upon" North Korea to cease hostilities and to withdraw to the thirty-eighth parallel; he also "called upon" all member states "to render every assistance to the United Nations in the execution of this resolution."[18] Though no mention was made of the Soviet Union, US officials were convinced that that country was behind the North Korean move. As Edward W. Barrett, assistant secretary of state for political affairs, put it, "the relationship between the Soviet Union and the North Koreans [was] the same as that between Walt Disney and Donald Duck."[19] At 5:30 P.M. the council was ready to vote on the US draft resolution. The final vote would have been unanimous save for a single abstention: Yugoslavia. Several delegates, believing that the United Nations was fighting for its very life, actually risked their political futures by deciding to vote in the absence of instructions from their governments.[20] Independent voting of this nature was most unusual.

In spite of strong UN support, neither President Truman nor his secretary of state had any illusions about the situation. Both men knew that the United States would have to take unilateral military initiatives if the North Korean attack was to be stemmed successfully.

President Truman landed in Washington "in a grim mood." "That's enough," he snapped at reporters who crowded around him to take pictures; "we've got a job to do!"[21] Before departing for Blair House, he stated that he was going to "hit them hard."[22] Thirteen of the nation's top diplomatic and military leaders, including the Joint Chiefs of Staff, awaited the President at Blair House, and by dinner time Truman and Acheson were in complete agreement on the main proposals to be presented at the meeting.

After dinner the President opened the discussion by calling on the secretary of state to advance suggestions for consideration by the conference. He encouraged all those present to voice their opinions freely. Acheson then proceeded to make four specific recommendations: (1) that General MacArthur be authorized to furnish South Korea with generous supplies of military equipment; (2) that the air force be authorized to cover and protect the evacuation of US civilians; (3) that consideration be given to strengthening the role of the UN Security Council; and (4) that the Seventh Fleet be interposed between Formosa and the Chinese mainland.[23]

There was complete agreement on Acheson's first recommendation. As General Omar Bradley put it: "This is the test of all the talk of the last five years of collective security."[24] In view of the sparseness of information from the battle area, however, no one recommended that US ground forces be committed at that moment. "No one could tell what the state of the Korean army was on that Sunday night," the President later noted in his *Memoirs.*[25] Accordingly, as an interim measure, General MacArthur was authorized to give the South Koreans whatever arms and equipment he could spare. There was no disagreement whatsoever over the second recommendation, which was Ambassador Muccio's main concern. As Defense Secretary Louis A. Johnson put it, the measure was more of an "assumption" than a "decision." So far as the role of the United Nations was concerned, the President emphasized that in this crisis the United States was "working for" the world organization. He added that he would wait for the Security Council resolution to be flouted before taking any additional measures, although he instructed the Chiefs of Staff to "prepare the necessary orders" to make US forces available should the United Nations request them.[26] Finally, there was full agreement that the Seventh Fleet be used to restrain the Chinese Communists as well as the Chinese Nationalists from military operations that might widen the theater of war. The conference closed with a strong sense of resolve that the United States was prepared, under the UN banner, to take whatever measures were required to repel the invasion.

By Monday morning the situation had hardened. Ambassador Gross reported from the United Nations that there seemed to be growing support among the delegates for sterner measures to enforce North Korean compliance with the Security Council Resolution of June 25. Meeting with reporters in Washington, President Truman pointed to Korea on a large globe in his office and said to an aide: "This is the Greece of the Far East. If we are tough enough now, there won't be any next step."[27] Members of the White House staff commented on the President's mood of grim resolution. By 2 P.M. the military situation in Korea had grown so desperate that President Syngman Rhee placed a personal telephone call to Washington to plead with President Truman to rescue his government from complete disaster. The President and secretary of state met in seclusion during the afternoon to plan the next steps. By evening they had agreed that the situation had become serious enough to warrant another full-scale conference at Blair House at 9 P.M.

"There was no doubt! The Republic of Korea needed help at once if it was not to be overrun," President Truman recalled in his *Memoirs* about the second conference.[28] Unless such help was immediately forthcoming, no further decisions regarding Korea would be necessary. Accordingly, the President proposed that the navy and air force be instructed to give the fullest possible support to the South Korean forces south of the thirty-eighth parallel. In addition, the President recommended stepped-up military aid to the Philippines and the French forces engaged in fighting Communist Vietminh troops in Indochina. No mention was made of ground troops in Korea, but it was clear that US sea and air cover were logical preludes to such a commitment. It was thought unlikely that strong naval and air support would give the South Koreans sufficient superiority to render a ground commitment unnecessary. Ambassador Gross believed that the Security Council resolution could be "stretched" to cover the President's recommendations. The problem of possible Soviet or Chinese countermoves was discussed, and the conclusion was reached that neither the Soviet Union nor China was likely to intervene directly in Korea. Once again, the conferees drew historical parallels, this time from the Greek crisis of 1947 and the Berlin crisis of 1948, when resolute US resistance had been successful. Support for the President's position was unanimous. As Defense Secretary Johnson was to recall later: "If we wanted to oppose it, then was our time to oppose it. Not a single one of us did. There were some pointing out the difficulties...and then the President made his decision which...I thought was the right decision."[29]

Ambassador Jessup recalled that he "felt proud of President Truman" and General Bradley explained that "we did it so we wouldn't have one appeasement lead to another and make war inevitable."[30] The President confided to Acheson that "everything I have done in the last five years has been to try to avoid making a decision such as I had to make tonight."[31] In his *Memoirs* he later recalled that "this was the toughest decision I had to make as President."[32]

By Tuesday, June 27, General MacArthur had been notified of the President's decision. He reacted with pleasant surprise, since he had not expected such forceful action. At noon the President and Acheson briefed a group of congressional leaders on the most recent developments. The responses in both the Senate and House were overwhelmingly favorable. Although a few representatives and senators questioned the President's authority to make these decisions without prior congressional approval, not a single legislator openly doubted the wisdom of the decision.

During the afternoon attention shifted from Washington to the United Nations. At 3 P.M. the Security Council met in one of the most dramatic sessions of its short history. There was considerable apprehension in the US Mission that Ambassador Yakov A. Malik of the Soviet Union would be present in order to cast a veto. A great deal of thought had been given to this possibility, and various contingency procedures that would mobilize the General Assembly were under active consideration. Just before the Security Council meeting Ambassadors Gross and Malik were lunching with Secretary-General Lie and other UN delegates. As the delegates rose from the table, Lie approached Malik and told him that the interests of the Soviet Union demanded his participation in the meeting. "No, I will not go there," the Soviet delegate replied. Outside the restaurant Ambassador Gross heaved a huge sigh of relief.[33]

The Soviet absence from the council on that fateful afternoon has been the subject of a great deal of speculation. Most likely, it was a blunder. The cumbersome Soviet processes for making decisions probably had left Malik without instructions on what to do in the Security Council. Hence his only option was to be absent from the council altogether.

Chief delegate Warren R. Austin read the text of the US resolution, which had been approved personally by President Truman. Its operative paragraph recommended "that Members of the United Nations furnish such assistance to the Republic of Korea as may be necessary to repel the armed attack and to restore international peace and security in the area."[34] The council had before it another report from the UN Commission on Korea that stated that the North Korean regime was carrying out a "well-planned, concerted, and full-scale invasion of South Korea."[35] The council postponed a vote twice because the delegates of India and Egypt were waiting for instructions. Finally, just before midnight, the Security Council passed the American-sponsored resolution, with the United Kingdom, France, China, Cuba, Ecuador, and Norway in support, Egypt and India abstaining, Yugoslavia in opposition, and the Soviet Union absent. The Security Council had recommended military measures be taken to stem the North Korean assault. At almost precisely the time of the voting, Seoul, the capital of South Korea, was taken by the North Korean army.

On the following morning President Truman chaired a meeting of the National Security Council in Washington. Before the council was a report from General MacArthur stating that "the United States would have to commit ground troops if the thirty-eighth parallel were to be restored."[36] The President signed a bill to extend the Selective Service Act but stopped short of ordering US ground forces into combat in Korea. That afternoon, with the loud acclaim of the press, General MacArthur flew to Korea to conduct a personal reconnaissance of the military situation. The New York Times commented editorially that: "Fate could not have chosen a man better qualified to command the unreserved confidence of the people of this country. Here is a superb strategist and an inspired leader; a man of infinite patience and quiet stability under adverse pressure; a man equally capable of bold and decisive action."[37] The President decided to wait for the general's report from the scene of battle before taking the crucial step of committing ground forces.

MacArthur, with a small group of advisers, surveyed "the dreadful backwash of a defeated and dispersed army" during a convoy ride toward Seoul. The roads were clogged with thousands of southbound refugees, who were probably unaware that MacArthur was passing through. The South Korean army seemed to be in a state of complete and disorganized rout.[38] During his flight back to Tokyo, the general drafted a report to the President in which he made his position absolutely clear:

> The only assurance for holding the present line and the ability to regain the lost ground is through the introduction of United States ground combat forces into the Korean battle area.... Unless provision is made for the full utilization of the Army-Navy-Air team in this shattered area, our mission will at best be needlessly costly in life, money and prestige. At worst, it might even be doomed to failure.[39]

Specifically, the general declared that if the President gave the authorization he could "hold Korea with two American divisions."[40]

At the same time that MacArthur was drafting his report the President held a press conference in Washington. One reporter wanted to know whether the United States was at war or not. "We are not at war," the President replied. When another reporter queried the President whether "it would be possible to call the American response a police action under the United Nations," Truman responded that this was exactly what it was. The action was being taken to help the United Nations repel a raid by a "bunch of bandits."[41] Later that evening, President Truman and Acheson considered President Chiang Kai-shek's offer to send 33,000 Chinese Nationalist troops to Korea. The President was not inclined to accept the offer but delayed making a final decision.

General MacArthur's urgent recommendation to commit US ground forces in Korea reached Washington at dawn on June 30. "Time is of the essence and a clear-cut decision without delay is essential," the general insisted. At 5 A.M. Secretary of the Army Frank Pace, Jr. communicated MacArthur's recommendation to the President. Without hesitation, Truman approved the commitment of one regimental combat team. During the morning he met with the secretary of state and top military officials. At that conference it was decided to decline politely the Chinese Nationalist troop offer and to give General MacArthur "full authority to use the troops under his command."[42]

On the afternoon of June 30 Ambassador Austin informed the UN Security Council of the latest US decision. He emphasized again that the US action was being taken under the United Nations banner. Other members, however, would have to contribute if the Korean police action was to be a genuine collective security measure. The United States had taken the lead in protecting the UN Charter; now it was up to the others to assume their share of the responsibility.

In response to the Security Council Resolution of June 27 Secretary-General Lie had sent a cable to all member states asking for information on the nature and amount of assistance each member state was prepared to give. Of the fifty-nine replies, he felt fifty-three were generally favorable.[43] In concrete and specific terms, however, actual military contributions were slow to arrive. Within two weeks of the request, naval and air units from the United Kingdom, Australia, and New Zealand were actively involved, and units from the Netherlands and Canada were on their way. By the middle of September Lie had reported that fourteen members other than the United States had contributed ground forces. From the beginning, the United States had borne the main brunt of the fighting, with the Republic of Korea in second place. By services, the US contribution was 50.32 percent of the ground forces, 85.89 percent of the naval forces, and 93.88 percent of the air forces. The respective contributions of South Korea were 40.10 percent, 7.45 percent, and 5.65 percent.[44] From these figures it is clear that the contributions of other UN members were small indeed. Though military contributions from member nations remained disproportionate throughout the Korean War, it must be noted that thirty governments did render supplementary assistance in the form of field hospitals, blood plasma, rice, and soap. Iceland, for example, made a contribution of cod-liver oil for the troops.

In view of the predominant role played by the United States, the Security Council decided on July 7 to establish a "Unified Command" under the leadership of the United States and authorized this command to use the UN flag. On the following day President Truman designated General MacArthur as supreme commander of the UN forces. However, the general also retained his title of Commander in Chief of US Forces in the Far East; MacArthur viewed his connection with the United Nations as nominal and continued to receive his instructions directly from the President. On August 1, when Yakov Malik, the Soviet delegate, returned to the Security Council and assumed the presidency of that body, the council went into eclipse. On September 6 the Soviet Union cast its first veto on the Korean problem and thus removed any further possibility of using the Security Council to direct the UN action in Korea.

When the UN General Assembly met in mid-September, it was confronted with a dramatic change in the military situation in Korea. On September 15, General MacArthur had executed a daring amphibious landing at Inchon that had taken the North Koreans by complete surprise. Two weeks later the North Koreans were in full retreat and the UN forces, in hot pursuit, had reached the thirty-eighth parallel. The question now facing the United States and the UN General Assembly was whether the UN forces should cross into North Korea. Suddenly a desperate crisis had been resolved and an attractive new opportunity had arisen: The invader was on the run and could now be taught a lesson.

This prospect, however, raised serious tactical as well as policy questions that had to be resolved quickly. The relationship between the United States and the United Nations needed to be clarified, especially the role of the supreme commander, General MacArthur. The possible responses of the two great Communist powers, China and the Soviet Union, to a UN crossing of the parallel had to be weighed. In short, the sudden successes of MacArthur's forces presented entirely new challenges. But only a few weeks later, these events were to precipitate a massive military intervention by China and—in General MacArthur's words—an "entirely new war."

Two explosive events brought the UN forces face to face with China on the battlefields of Korea: first, the crossing of the thirty-eighth parallel in October and, second, the drive toward the Chinese border at the Yalu River in November. Crucial to both events was the personality of General MacArthur, who was widely acclaimed as, and probably believed himself to be, the United States' greatest living soldier. The startling success of his Inchon landing had made the general's confidence in his own military genius unshakable. President Truman and Secretary of State Acheson had full confidence in this country's most honored soldier and believed the armed might of the United States to be invincible. Nevertheless, UN Unified Command was badly mauled in its first encounter with Chinese troops, and MacArthur suffered the worst defeat in his entire military career. An analysis of the outbreak of this "entirely new war" may help to explain this paradox.

As the UN forces approached the parallel, the problem of whether to cross it presented the Unified Command with an acute dilemma. On the one hand, it was impossible to achieve total defeat of the North Korean invaders if the United Nations forces were not allowed to cross the parallel. It could be argued that the North Korean attack could be seen as having destroyed the sanctity of the thirty-eighth parallel as a boundary and that the "hot pursuit" of the invader was therefore perfectly in order. On the other hand, if the mission of the Unified Command was merely to "repel the armed attack," then the case could be made that the UN forces should not be permitted to cross into territory that was not a recognized part of the Republic of Korea before the North Korean attack. Moreover, there was the important question: Who was to decide whether UN forces should cross the parallel and, if so, for what purpose and within what limits? Finally, there was on record an explicit warning that had been made by Indian Ambassador K.M. Panikkar in Peking. If UN forces crossed the parallel, China probably would enter the war.[45]

In view of these conflicting considerations, there was considerable initial confusion over the matter. President Truman's first response on September 22 was to let the United Nations make the decision.[46] Less than a week later, however, he apparently changed his mind and instructed Secretary Acheson to declare that the resolutions passed by the Security Council in June and July gave the Unified Command the necessary authority to cross the parallel. This was also the position taken by General MacArthur and the Joint Chiefs of Staff. MacArthur, in particular, was of the opinion that the resolution of June

27 extended ample authority to cross the parallel. He felt that he required broad and flexible powers and that any restrictions placed on him would be rendered ineffective by the needs to ensure the safety of his troops. This view evidently impressed the President and his top advisers. As it turned out, it was never seriously disputed by most of the other members states of the United Nations.

When the UN General Assembly met in late September, most delegations were quite willing to follow the leadership of the United States. In view of the fact that the United States had been the first to come to the assistance of South Korea and had now apparently reversed the scales of battle in favor of the UN forces, this willingness to accept the US lead was considered quite natural. Ambassador Austin set forth the US position in a major speech before the General Assembly on September 30. He argued the case for crossing the parallel in the strongest possible terms:

> The artificial barrier which has divided North and South Korea has no basis for existence either in law or in reason. Neither the United Nations, its Commission on Korea, nor the Republic of Korea recognized such a line. Now, the North Koreans, by armed attack upon the Republic of Korea, have denied the reality of any such line.[47]

The United States took the lead in drafting an eight-power resolution calling for the taking of appropriate steps "to insure conditions of stability through Korea" and "the establishment of a unified, independent and democratic Government in the sovereign State of Korea."[48] Apart from the Soviet bloc, there was little opposition, and the final vote on October 7 was forty-seven in favor, five opposed, and seven abstentions.[49] The UN General Assembly had now placed its seal of approval on the twin US objectives: to destroy the North Korean forces and unify the entire country under the flag of the UN command.

On October 8 General MacArthur, speaking as UN commander in chief, called on the North Korean army to surrender and "cooperate fully with the United Nations in establishing a unified, independent, democratic government of Korea."[50] He informed the North Korean authorities that, unless a favorable response was immediately forthcoming, he would "at once proceed to take such military action as may be necessary to enforce the decrees of the United Nations." The ultimatum was drafted personally by MacArthur, and the style and phraseology were unmistakably his own.

There is no evidence to suggest that President Truman's position on the question of crossing the thirty-eighth parallel differed from MacArthur's. The President and his top aides felt that by its aggression North Korea had forfeited any right that it might previously have had to prevent the execution of the United Nations' decree by force. Neither the fact that the UN General Assembly lacked the legal authority to legislate decrees nor that its recommendation of October 7 had been only partially accepted deterred the US leadership from declaring its own military objectives as identical with those of the

United Nations. And neither the presence of Soviet advisers with the North Korean army down to the battalion level nor the fact that China had issued a stern warning deterred General MacArthur from crossing the parallel and initiating a rapid advance toward the Chinese border at the Yalu River.

South Korean troops crossed the parallel into the North on October 1, and the first US forces, the US First Cavalry Division, followed suit on October 7. Ambassador Panikkar issued his warning on October 2, and on October 10 China's Foreign Minister Chou En-lai announced that "the Chinese people [would] not stand idly by in this war of invasion." These warnings received only passing attention in Washington and Tokyo. The tendency among US government officials was to dismiss them as Chinese bombast.

On October 15, however, President Truman and General MacArthur met on Wake Island. As a result of the increasing frequency of Chinese warnings, the President had become sufficiently concerned to ask the general for a professional assessment about the possibility of Chinese intervention. MacArthur considered this possibility remote:

> Had they interfered in the first or second month, it would have been decisive. We are no longer fearful of their intervention. We no longer stand hat in hand. The Chinese have 300,000 men in Manchuria. Of these, probably not more than 100 to 125,000 are distributed along the Yalu River. They have no Air Force. Now that we have bases for our Air Force in Korea, if the Chinese tried to get down to Pyongyang, there would be the greatest slaughter.[51]

Four days later, when MacArthur's forces entered Pyongyang, the State Department also came to the conclusion that Chinese intervention in Korea was "unlikely." In the opinion of one leading authority:

> This assessment was by no means confined to the department over which Acheson presided. It was shared alike by the President, the Joint Chiefs of Staff, members of the National Security Council, General Walter Bedell Smith, Director of Central Intelligence, prominent senators, congressmen, and political pundits of all hues. If questioned, that amorphous character "the man in the street" would have expressed the same opinion.[52]

Nevertheless, at the very time that the US leadership denied the possibility of Chinese intervention, the Chinese Fourth Field Army crossed the Yalu and penetrated the ragged mountain terrain of North Korea.

Truman and MacArthur were convinced that China neither would nor could intervene in Korea and believed that their frequent pronouncements of the United States' nonaggressive intentions would reassure the Chinese leaders. On November 16 the President declared that the United States had "never at any time entertained any intention to carry hostilities into China."[53] He added that "because of the long-standing American friendship for the people of China, the United States [would] take every honorable step to prevent any extension of the hostilities in the Far East."[54] Thus US policy makers chose to view the tension between the United States and China as a passing phenomenon and felt that assurances of good will toward China would suffice to insulate the Korean conflict from Chinese intervention. Operating on the assumption of longstanding Sino-American friendship, both Truman and MacArthur were deeply astonished at the rising tone of violence in Chinese statements during the month of October. They simply did not see the intervention coming. That the illusion of a firm Sino-American friendship underlying a Communist veneer persisted in the face of growing evidence to the contrary suggests that the United States was not yet prepared to take the new China seriously. Her statements were not as yet considered credible. So far as Ambassador Panikkar's warning was concerned, neither Truman nor MacArthur took it seriously. Truman viewed it as "a bold attempt to blackmail the United Nations" and later observed in his *Memoirs* that "Mr. Panikkar had in the past played the game of the Chinese Communists fairly regularly, so that his statement could not be taken as that of an impartial observer."[55]

On the other side of the Yalu, the Chinese leaders regarded the United States as the heir to Japan's imperialist ambitions in Asia. They became increasingly convinced that only a powerful intervention in Korea would prevent the United States from invading China. As one scholar of Chinese-American relations has noted:

> While Secretary Acheson was talking about the traditional friendship of America, the Chinese Communists were teaching their compatriots that from the early nineteenth century onward the United States had consistently followed an aggressive policy toward China which culminated in her support for Chiang Kai-shek in the civil war and her present actions in Korea and Taiwan. The Chinese people were told to treat the United States with scorn because she was a paper tiger and certainly could be defeated.[56]

Truman, MacArthur, and the State Department perceived a China that no longer existed. The conviction that China would not intervene represented an emotional rather than an intellectual conclusion, an ascription to the enemy intentions compatible with the desires of Washington and Tokyo.[57] This misperception laid the groundwork for a military disaster of major proportions.

If the Americans misperceived Chinese intentions by refusing to take them seriously, the Chinese erred in the opposite direction. The world, as viewed in Peking, was rife with implacable US hostility. Not only were US troops marching directly up to the Chinese border at the Yalu River, but the United States was protecting the hated Nationalist regime on Taiwan and was siding with the French against the revolutionaries in Indochina. In addition, the United States was rehabilitating and rearming Japan. With this outlook, the Chinese leaders not surprisingly regarded verbal protestations of good will on the part of the United States as a mockery.

Most basic to an understanding of MacArthur's drive to the Yalu was his peculiar misperception of China's power. Even though he characterized China as a nation lusting for expansion, MacArthur had a curious contempt for the Chinese soldier. He equated the thoroughly indoctrinated, well-disciplined Communist soldier of 1950 with the demoralized Nationalist soldier of 1948.

To be blunt, he did not respect his enemy; and this disrespect was to cost him dearly. Far from regarding the Chinese as military equals, MacArthur insisted that "the pattern of the Oriental psychology [was] to respect and follow aggressive, resolute, and dynamic leadership, to quickly turn on a leadership characterized by timidity or vacillation."[58] This paternalistic contempt for the military power of the new China led directly to disaster in October and November 1950. The story is worth examining in some detail.

On October 26, to the accompaniment of fierce bugle calls, shrill whistles, and blasts from shepherds' horns, the Chinese launched a surprise attack on South Korean and US forces some fifty miles south of the Chinese border. The results were devastating. Several UN regiments were virtually decimated. Nevertheless, Major General Charles A. Willoughby, MacArthur's main intelligence officer, voiced the opinion on the following day that "the auspicious time for Chinese intervention [had] long since passed" and that "there [was] no positive evidence that Chinese Communist units, as such [had] entered Korea."[59] On November 1, the Chinese initiated a massive attack against the US Third Battalion and virtually tore it apart. Then, after shattering the US Eighth Cavalry, the Chinese abruptly broke contact and withdrew.

MacArthur's reaction to these events demonstrates how difficult it is for an old, stubbornly entrenched, misperception to yield to reality. On the day of the Chinese disengagement, his estimate of total Chinese strength in Korea was between 40,000 and 60,000 men.[60] In fact, as of October 31, the Chinese had deployed, with utmost secrecy and within short distances of the American forces they were about to strike, almost 200,000 men.[61] Some of these had crossed the Yalu before the Wake Island meeting Truman had with MacArthur.

The Chinese troops had done what MacArthur had deemed impossible. They had moved by night in forced marches, employed local guides and porters, and used the barren and hostile terrain of the north North Korean hills to their advantage. They then launched their assault on MacArthur's unsuspecting army. When the Chinese temporarily withdrew, MacArthur immediately ascribed this turn of events to the heavy casualties the enemy had sustained. In MacArthur's view, the Chinese meeded to rest; and so, a golden opportunity was at hand for a second and victorious US drive to the Yalu.

In retrospect, it is clear that:

> The Chinese withdrawal in early November was designed to encourage the enemy's arrogance; to lure the UN forces deeper into North Korea, where their tenuous supply lines could be interdicted and where units separated from one another by the broken terrain could be isolated and annihilated. This was the nature of the deadly trap which P'eng, at his Shenyang headquarters, was setting for the over-confident general in the Dai Ichi Building in Tokyo.[62]

Thus, MacArthur, believing that he was faced with 40,000 instead of 200,000 Chinese soldiers whom he believed were badly in need of rest after their encounter with the US army, advanced northward again for the "final offensive.'' The Chinese watched for three weeks until finally, on November 27, they attacked in overwhelming force, turning the US advance into a bloody rout. Thus a peasant army put to flight a modern Western military force commanded by a world-famous American general. In one bound China had become a world power; and the image of the Chinese ward, almost half a century in the making, was finally shattered at the cost of tens of thousands of battle casualties on both sides. MacArthur, incredibly enough, did not learn much from the experience. In the words of his aide-de-camp, Major General Courtney Whitney, the general ''was greatly saddened as well as angered at this despicably surreptitious attack, a piece of treachery which he regarded as worse even than Pearl Harbor.''[63] The stark truth was that MacArthur had fallen blindly into the trap of his own misperceptions.

The paternalistic attitude of US leaders toward Communist China died hard. It remained extremely difficult for the United States to admit that the new China was growing in power and was fiercely hostile, and that this attitude was more than a passing phenomenon. Many rationalizations were invoked to explain this disturbing new presence on the world scene. Communism was viewed as somehow ''alien'' to the ''Chinese character.'' It would pass, leaving the ''traditional friendship'' between China and America to reassert itself—although the paternalism implicit in this traditional relationship was never admitted.[64] At other times, Chinese hostility to the United States was explained as the result of the evil influence of the Soviet Union:

> On November 27, immediately following Mr. Vyshinsky's statement of charges of aggression against the U.S., the United States representative in this Committee (one of the United Nations), Ambassador Dulles....with a feeling of sadness rather than anger, said one could only conclude that the Soviet Union was trying to destroy the long history of close friendship between China and the United States and to bring the Chinese people to hate and, if possible, to fight the United States.[65]

One of the more bizarre examples of this attempt to maintain old attitudes in the face of bewildering new facts was the brief flurry of articles in the press during December 1950 reporting the possibility of a UN military action in China—directed not against the Chinese people but against the Mao faction, which was presumed to be their oppressor. A headline in *The New York Herald Tribune* proclaimed ''Declaration of State of War Against Mao's Faction Urged''; the text of the article read: ''So far as can be determined now, the action of the UN will not be one of war against China or the Chinese people but against one faction in China, namely the Communists.''[66] How this distinction was to be put into effect on the battlefield was never made clear. The utterly unrealistic nature of the proposal led to its early death. Nevertheless, the distinction between the Chinese people and their Communist leaders persisted for some time. On December 29, 1950, in a statement for the Voice of America, Dean Rusk, then assistant secretary of State for Far Eastern affairs, accused the Chinese Communists of having plotted the North Korean assault. The press reported that ''As all American officials have done consistently, Mr.

Rusk drew a distinction between the Chinese people, for whom the United States has a long tradition of friendliness, and their Communist rulers."[67] By denying that the new government of China had a power base and a measure of popular support, the United States tried to maintain intact its old illusions about the historical relationship between the two nations. But it had been a relationship between predator and hunted, a fact that had never been admitted.

Indian Ambassador Panikkar detected this blind spot in the American picture of China. He noted that in the early days of the Korean war, the Western military attachés in Peking had been utterly confident that Chinese troops could not possibly stand up to the Americans. He noticed that the defeat in late November came as a profound shock to the Americans, and their attitude thenceforth was very different.[68] In a good summation of the problem, he stated: "China had become a Great Power and was insisting on being recognized as such. The adjustments which such a recognition requires are not easy, and the conflict in the Far East is the outcome of this contradiction."[69]

The Chinese intervention in the Korean War provides a good illustration of the practical, operational consequences of divergent perceptions in world affairs. These perceptions are, in effect, definitions of the situation at hand. Once the situation has been defined, certain alternatives are eliminated. One does not conciliate an opponent who is perceived as implacably hostile; hence, the Chinese Communists felt in the end that they had no resort but to intervene in Korea. One does not credit the threats of an opponent whose powers one perceives as negligible; hence, the United States viewed even specific Chinese warnings as bluff. One does not compromise with an opponent whose ideology is perceived as antithetical to one's own values; hence, the United States and China remained poised on the brink of potentially disastrous conflict, neither one accepting the other's perception of its world role as legitimate. This was the central significance of the "entirely new war" that was to ravage the peninsula for another eighteen months.

Conclusions

The outbreak of the Korean war may be divided into three separate and distinct phases; the decision to repel the North Korean attack, the decision to cross the thirty-eighth parallel, and MacArthur's drive to the Yalu River which provoked the Chinese intervention. In my judgment, the first decision was correct, the second dubious, and the third disastrous.

When President Truman made his decision to commit US ground forces in Korea, Stalin was still alive and the global Communist movement still intact. China and the Soviet Union had just concluded an alliance. Korea was a test of whether the Communist movement could, by direct invasion, impose itself on the territory of another political entity, or whether that attack could be stemmed through collective action led by the United States.

The president's early decisions were firm, yet graduated: a full week elapsed between his initial response and the infantry commitment. During that week his top advisers were fully heard on several occasions and their support remained virtually unanimous throughout. The North Koreans had ample opportunity to stop their invasion and thus avoid a full-scale collision with US power. Instead, they pressed the attack and escalated the ferocity of the initial encounter. Finally, even though the President "jumped the gun" on the United Nations by twenty-four hours, he genuinely perceived his action as legitimate, taken on behalf of the principle of collective security set forth in the UN Charter.

Temptation beckoned when the tide of battle turned decisively in favor of the Unified Command. Initially, neither President Truman nor General MacArthur contemplated the seizure of North Korea; but the success of the Inchon landing provided the opportunity to turn the tables and invade the invader. At this critical juncture, the general, now speaking as a "United Nations commander," insisted on forging ahead, and the President gave his permission. The United Nations was treated rather cavalierly, as little more than an instrument of American policy. Although the UN secretary–general and most member nations accepted their role rather meekly, they had serious inner doubts. A victory, had it occurred, would clearly have been a victor's peace.

Disaster struck at the Yalu, largely because of the hubris of General MacArthur. The UN commander lacked all respect for the new China and preferred instead to act out of hopes and fears rather than realities and facts. By provoking the Chinese intervention, McArthur probably prolonged the war by another eighteen months and turned it into one of the bloodiest conflicts in recent history. Aside from the 34,000 American dead, South Korea suffered over 800,000 casualties, and North Korea more than 500,000. The Chinese suffered appalling losses of 1.5 to 2 million men. The war ended indecisively in a draw, with the two Koreas remaining fully armed dictatorships, bitterly hostile to one another.

Yet, paradoxically, the violent clash between the United States and China at the Yalu River might in one sense have contributed to long-run improved relations between the two countries, for the effectiveness of China's intervention in Korea established her as a power to be reckoned with. It shattered once and for all the patronization that had previously characterized the US view of China. One cannot, of course, answer with certainty the question of whether China and the United States would have gone to war over Vietnam in the 1960s if they had not fought in Korea. But it is highly probably that the Korean war served as a powerful corrective and thus as a restraining memory.

In the Korean war the victim of aggression was tempted by aggression and succumbed to the temptation. The United Nations became a party to the war and remained identified with one side in the conflict to the end. Since its identity became fully merged with the US cause, it lost the power to be a truly neutral mediator in Korea. This is perhaps the clearest lesson of the outbreak of this war: As the United Nations was captured by one of the parties to the conflict and made into its instrument, all sides suffered in the long run, particularly the United Nations itself. No objective entity could now be serve as referee or buffer. Hence, the fighting stopped only through exhaustion, when both sides finally despaired of victory.

One afterthought: Kim Il Sung, the man who launched the North Korean attack in 1950, remains in charge four decades later. Still a second-rater when compared with other Communist leaders, Kim has periodically attempted to enhance his image by printing excerpts from his memoirs in the Western press. The question of whether he might be tempted to try another 1950 has made vigilance at the thirty-eighth parallel a continuing priority.

THE CUBAN MISSILE CRISIS OF 1962: THE NUCLEAR ABYSS

The Cuban missile crisis was the climax to the rising tensions between the superpowers during 1961. The Soviet Union's action in testing nuclear weapons of unprecedented explosive force had triggered off a major debate over fallout shelters in the United States; the erection of the Berlin Wall had made the tension almost palpable; and the memory of the abortive US-sponsored invasion of Cuba was still fresh. But as yet there had been no "eyeball-to-eyeball" confrontation. The Cuban missile crisis was such a confrontation.

In mid-October 1962 hard evidence that the Soviet Union was secretly building offensive missile bases in Cuba with headlong speed had been gathered by US intelligence services. High-altitude photographs had disclosed a medium-range ballistic missile site near San Cristobal and one near San Diego de los Baños. Tanker trucks, power and instrument installations, missile guidance stations, and erector launchers were clearly visible. And pictures of cylindrical shapes on incoming Soviet freighters confirmed the worst.

It is difficult to determine with certitude why the Soviet leadership made the decision to try to make Cuba an offensive missile base. First, it has been suggested that Premier Khrushchev intended to use the bases as a psychological lever to make more effective his demands for Berlin. Indeed, in the summer of 1962 Khrushchev had announced that he would postpone the Berlin issue until after the US elections. He may have hoped that President Kennedy would not dare to disclose a missile buildup during an election campaign and that he could therefore confront the United States over Berlin with the Cuban bases as a fait accompli. Second, the Soviet leader probably underestimated the will of the US President. The Berlin Wall, Laos, and especially the fiasco in the Bay of Pigs may have suggested to Khrushchev that Kennedy lacked resolve and would not take determined action. Third, successful installation of the weapons would give the Soviet Union an important temporary military advantage; rockets launched from Cuba could destroy US cities and knock out US missiles and bombers on the ground in a first-strike attack, since the warning time would be critically reduced. The US weapons lead over the Soviet Union would not be canceled but would be seriously weakened. Fourth, neo-Stalinist pressures on Khrushchev may have played a role, although this is unlikely, since Stalinism was very much on the defensive in Russia at the time, and the Soviet leadership was emphasizing its policy of "peaceful coexistence" against the harsher line of Communist China. Nor is it likely that Cuban Premier Fidel Castro had persuaded the Soviet leader to install the missiles in order to prevent a US invasion of Cuba. On balance, Khrushchev probably calculated that, at best, a frightened United States would go down on its knees, lose the confidence of its military allies in Europe, Asia, and Latin America, and thus give the Soviet Union a new opportunity to resume the offensive in the cold war. If the United States insisted on the removal of the bases, perhaps a barter deal could be worked out over bases in Greece and Turkey. And, even if the United States took a resolutely uncompromising stand, Khrushchev could gain favor in world public opinion by a policy of withdrawal. At the very worst, then, the status quo ante would be maintained, with Soviet control over Cuba intact.

The US leadership, which had hard evidence of the missile sites by October 15, now weighed its decision silently. For one week the President and his closest associates constituted themselves as an Executive Committee of the National Security Council and pondered the alternatives. The President continued his preparations for the forthcoming political campaign, and as late as October 18 met with Soviet Foreign Secretary Andrei Gromyko, who professed ignorance of the offensive nature of the missile sites in Cuba.

Inside the White House and Pentagon, the war council considered the alternatives along a kind of "escalation ladder." There developed seven possible responses in ascending order of severity: first, a sharp protest note to the Soviet government; second, a US appeal to the UN Security Council; third, some form of economic retaliation against the Soviet Union; fourth, a naval blockade of Cuba; fifth, a "surgical air-strike" to eliminate the bases; sixth, invasion of the island; and seventh, direct nuclear retaliation against the Soviet Union. The war council immediately eliminated the first three alternatives as ineffective and the last as unwarranted. The discussion centered around the alternatives in the middle range. The problem confronting the US planners was the classic one of deterrence strategy: so to combine the twin demands of capability and credibility that the Soviet leader would be checked by the actual and potential display of US power. Too little power could be interpreted as surrender, too much power as a bluff. Only controlled and flexible use of power at every step would make deterrence effective in the mind of the opponent.

An immediate invasion of Cuba was ruled out because that might have provoked the war which deterrence was designed to prevent. An air strike at the missile bases was also rejected since Russian personnel would have been killed at the sites, and such an action would have been difficult to justify by a nation that had made Pearl Harbor a symbol of infamy. A quarantine seemed to hold out the best hope for a solution. It would entail the requisite amount of strength by throwing a naval ring around Cuba, especially if it were coupled with a demand that the Soviet Union dismantle its bases there. Yet it offered the Soviet Union a way out: Khrushchev could avoid a direct confrontation by ordering his ships to change their course. Also, a quarantine would entail no violence, at least not immediately. Thus, on the evening of October 22, President Kennedy announced the US decision to impose a quarantine and added that "any nuclear missile launched from Cuba against any nation in the Western Hemisphere" would be regarded "as an attack by the Soviet Union on the United States requiring a full retaliatory response on the Soviet Union."[70] The issue was now squarely joined between the superpowers in the most dramatic military confrontation of the cold war. It was clear to participants and onlookers alike that Castro's Cuba was by now only a pawn. The United States had announced a check to the king, and the king was Premier Khrushchev.

The quarantine announcement was accompanied by an unprecedented peacetime mobilization of military power in the United States. The Polaris fleet was moved within striking range of the Soviet Union, and for the first time Strategic Air Command (SAC) bombers were dispersed to civilian airfields. Half of the SAC force was on airborne alert. If necessary, the United States was ready to deliver an equivalent of thirty billion tons of TNT upon the Soviet Union. An atmosphere of impending showdown also pervaded the Soviet Union, where all military leaves were canceled. The next seven days took the world to the brink of war.

On October 23, the Organization of American States supported the quarantine in a unanimous vote. The NATO allies came to the support of the United States, though with misgivings and not without reminding the United States of its behavior during the Suez crisis. The UN Security Council met in the afternoon. The United States demanded the immediate withdrawal, under international inspection, of the offensive weapons; the Soviet Union condemned the blockade as piracy and asked for its immediate termination. Neither resolution was voted on, and the Security Council presented a spectacle of complete helplessness. Toward evening the Russian tanker Bucharest approached the blockade zone and the US destroyer *USS Gearing* steamed to meet it. Since the Russian vessel carried no contraband, it was allowed to proceed. Khrushchev claimed that the ship had not stopped; the United States claimed that the captain had acknowledged inspection. Neither side had backed down. October 24, United Nations Day, took the world a step closer to the brink. Secretary-General U Thant advanced a plan for a two-week cooling-off period to explore the issues. Khrushchev accepted the proposal at once, but Kennedy rejected it on the ground that the issue of removing the missiles was not negotiable. An appeal by Premier Khrushchev to the British pacifist leader Bertrand Russell to use his influence to effect a general lowering of temperatures was also rejected as irrelevant by the United States. On October 25, Ambassador Stevenson challenged Soviet Ambassador Valerian Zorin to admit the existence of the missiles, stating that he was ready to wait for his answer "until hell freezes over."

On October 26 it was learned that several Soviet ships bound for Cuba were changing their course. But continued photo scrutiny of the missile bases indicated a speed-up in their construction since the announcement of the quarantine. The US offensive had to gather speed before the sites were ready and the missiles operational. President Kennedy spoke of possible "further measures" and did not rule out an air strike at the bases. He also pointed out the numerous possibilities for accidental war if the Soviet Union would not comply. That evening a telegram from Premier Khrushchev arrived which looked like a conditional surrender. In it the premier indicated his willingness to withdraw the missiles provided Cuba was guaranteed against invasion. This seemed like a fair offer.

On the morning of the following day, however, the White House received a second telegram from the Soviet leader which was much tougher in tone and more demanding in content. This time a deal was suggested: The United States was to dismantle her missile bases in Turkey and the Soviet Union would withdraw her missiles from Cuba.

The war council now had to make a crucial decision. Superficially the Soviet proposal seemed reasonable. It expressed a widespread feeling among neutralists that both sides should compromise and sacrifice something. It was generally approved in the United Nations, and several distinguished Western commentators such as Walter Lippmann supported it. Nevertheless, the war council turned down the proposal. In the first place, President Kennedy felt that the first Soviet telegram reflected more clearly than the second the Soviet leader's real feelings. And second, to bargain away NATO bases under pressure would be to undermine the entire alliance and engender a Munich psychology. Each time the Soviet Union would gain a strategic advantage in the cold war, it might offer to give it up in exchange for an existing NATO base until the alliance would be totally dismantled. Thus, by turning down the barter offer, the United States in effect presented the Soviet Union with an ultimatum: Remove the bases or "further measures" will be taken. The brink had been reached.

On Saturday morning, October 27, the Soviet Union "blinked," and the eyeball-to-eyeball confrontation came to an end. Kennedy's gamble on the first Soviet telegram had paid off. The Soviet leader reiterated his offer of withdrawing the missiles in return for an American "no-invasion" pledge. The US President accepted immediately and welcomed Khrushchev's "constructive contribution to peace." Other differences were settled in short order. Castro refused to admit on-site inspection by the United Nations to survey the dismantling of the bases, but the United States decided to forgo such inspection and continued to rely upon its own aerial surveillance. The missile sites were completely stripped within a few weeks, and outgoing Soviet ships laden with shrouded shapes that everyone took to be missiles brought the crisis to an end. The world had gone to the brink of nuclear hell and come back.

An analysis of the Cuban missile crisis reveals all the strengths and weaknesses of deterrence strategy. A strong case can be made for the US President's action on several grounds. Diplomatically, the action exhibited a combination of toughness and flexibility worthy of a great chess player. It never lost sight of the ultimate goal—the removal of the bases—yet it at all times offered the Soviet leader the possibility of a retreat with dignity. Militarily, it prevented a serious upset of the distribution of power by forcing the removal of medium-range ballistic missile bases ninety miles from US shores. And, historically, US action was based on the bitter lesson of Munich that appeasement under pressure is the road to war.

Yet there is a case to be made against deterrence. First, it is accident-prone. Many times during those crucial days in October 1962 the world could have been destroyed by accident. The sinking of a US or Soviet ship could have triggered off a naval war. Indeed, an accident almost did occur. An American U-2 plane on a routine mission over Alaska on October 26 lost its bearings and headed for Siberia. Khrushchev hesitated, but in the atmosphere of crisis he might have ordered a full retaliatory blow.[71] Second, the quarantine demonstrated that when power speaks, international law declines in importance. It is not difficult to see that a blockade, traditionally regarded as an act of war, does not advance the cause of world law in international relations. And finally, one should not lightly assume that deterrence will always work because it once did in a major showdown.

On balance, deterrence strategy was applied with consummate skill in the Cuban crisis. All things considered, the US President's determination was matched only by his prudence. He merely demanded the restoration of the status quo. Any additional demand, such as the withdrawal of Russian forces from Cuba, might have been intolerable to the Soviet Union and provoked a thermonuclear war. This feeling for nuance seems to be one of the integral requirements for a successful deterrence strategy. After all, the world's two most powerful politicians had to make decisions that no mortal before them ever had the power to make. Hence, they had to speak to each other in a language the grammar of which they had to learn in action. Advisers on both sides could clarify the choices, but the two leaders had to make them. This truth was well expressed by President Kennedy when he cited the following poem:

> Bullfight critics ranked in rows
> Crowd the enormous Plaza full;
> But only one is there who knows
> And he's the man who fights the bull.[72]

Even Premier Khrushchev paid a grudging compliment to his opponent when he admitted to a Western diplomat: "Had I been in the White House instead of the Kremlin, I would have acted like Kennedy."[73]

A good case may be made for the proposition that the successful application of deterrence strategy by the United States in 1962 ushered in a period of détente in East-West relations. The partial nuclear test-ban treaty concluded in 1963 was probably a result of it. And the installation of a "hot line" between the White House and the Kremlin reduced the chances of war through misunderstanding or accident. Thus, power, when prudently and judiciously applied, can give life to new elements of order, which in turn may soften the fierce edge of the power struggle among states.

In 1987, an interesting footnote was added to history. During a reunion marking the twenty-fifth anniversary of the missile crisis, the men of October

1962 were informed by an aging Dean Rusk that President Kennedy had instructed him to yield on the Turkish missiles if Khrushchev had rejected the US ultimatum. A reassuring postscript? Perhaps.

And yet, how close we had come! A few days after the resolution of the Cuban missile crisis, John F. Kennedy granted an interview to CBS. What were the chances of nuclear war, the interviewer wanted to know. ''Between one out of three and even,'' the President of the United States replied.

VIETNAM: AN AMERICAN TRAGEDY

The origins of the Vietnam conflict go back to the end of World War II. The Japanese surrender in August 1945 had left a vacuum that two different forces now attempted to fill. On one side stood Ho Chi Minh, a typical product of the cross-fertilization of Vietnamese nationalism and European communism, leader of the Vietminh forces, most of whom were Vietnamese nationalists with Communist leadership cadres. Ho quickly established control over much of Vietnam. There was little effective immediate competition, since the Japanese had driven out the French and the Americans had beaten the Japanese. France, however, was determined to regain its old colonial holding in Indochina. After a number of efforts at negotiations had failed, the mounting tension culminated in November 1946 when a French naval bombardment of Haiphong touched off major hostilities. For the next eight years, France fought a bitter war against the Vietminh. With its superior firepower, France was able to hold many of the cities, but the Vietminh gained more and more of the countryside. In 1949, the French installed a Vietnamese emperor, Bao Dai, but to no avail. France was simply unable to gain the confidence of the non-Communist Vietnamese nationalists, and Ho Chi Minh organized more and more determined opposition to France under his Vietminh leadership. Thus, the Communists used nationalism more effectively against the French than the French were able to use anticommunism against the nationalists. In short, although the war in its early phase was primarily a struggle between nationalism and colonialism, gradually it tended to take on overtones of an East-West conflict.

Between 1946 and 1949 the United States remained aloof from the war in Indochina. With the victory of communism on the Chinese mainland, however, and the massive US involvement in the Korean war during the following year, the US attitude toward Indochina underwent a significant change. On February 7, 1950, the United States recognized the Bao Dai government, and a few months later President Truman announced that the United States would supply substantial military assistance to the French forces. By late 1950 United States aid was flowing in support of the French war effort; by 1953, this aid had reached the $500 million mark. By 1954 the United States was deeply committed to the French cause in Indochina and was paying for 50 percent of the costs of the war.

Nevertheless, in the spring of 1954 the United States still decided against military intervention. On March 20, 1954, the French Chief of Staff, General

Paul Ely, informed President Eisenhower that only massive US military intervention could save the French at Dienbienphu. This prospect touched off a vigorous debate within the US government. Vice President Nixon and the chair of the Joint Chiefs of Staff, Admiral Radford, favored prompt US intervention. However, President Eisenhower's Army Chief of Staff, General Matthew B. Ridgway, and several members of the State Department's Policy Planning Staff, urged a policy of restraint. President Eisenhower finally decided not to intervene. He feared that the French had engendered too much popular antagonism to win the war and also felt that his administration would get little backing from the Congress and from Great Britain for even a limited intervention.

The Geneva Conference of mid-1954 and the formation, a few weeks later, of the Southeast Asia Treaty Organization signified the end of French military involvement and the beginning of a US military presence in Indochina. The Geneva Conference resulted in the signing of several agreements to cease hostilities in Indochina and to establish three independent sovereign states: Laos, Cambodia, and Vietnam. The agreement on Vietnam provided for a "provisional military demarcation line" at the seventeenth parallel. Vietminh forces were to regroup north of the line, and the forces of the French Union were to regroup to the south. The line was to have military significance only, and the political unification of Vietnam was to be brought about through a general election two years hence under the supervision of a neutral three-powered International Control Commission consisting of Canada, India, and Poland.

France had little choice, but its exit was made somewhat more graceful. Ho Chi Minh's Vietminh forces were dominant in more than three-quarters of Vietnam and were poised to overrun considerably more. To Ho, the terms of the agreement were acceptable, since he was convinced that the general election of 1956 would win him all of Vietnam. From his point of view, the certainty of a military victory was simply replaced by the certainty of a political victory. Both the Soviet Union and Communist China, reflecting their recently adopted line of "peaceful coexistence," applied pressure on Ho to accept the terms of the agreement, reassuring him that his victory at the polls was certain.

The United States never signed the Geneva Accords. However, in a unilateral declaration at the end of the Geneva Conference, the US government pledged to "refrain from the threat or the use of force to disturb" the settlement and added that it would view any violation of the Geneva Agreement with grave concern.

The general US position at the conference remained ambivalent, since, on the eve of a congressional election campaign, the maintenance of Eisenhower's domestic appeal as peacemaker in Asia was of great importance. Moreover, to block a peaceful settlement of the Indochina war would also have jeopardized French participation in European defense plans. These conflicting considerations led the Eisenhower administration to dissociate the United States from the Geneva Agreement and to seek another solution that would prevent any further territory in Asia from falling under Communist control. The answer was the creation of

SEATO. Secretary of State Dulles declared that now that the war had ended, the United States could make arrangements for collective defense against aggression and build up "the truly independent states of Cambodia, Laos, and South Vietnam." On the day the treaty was signed at Manila, by an additional protocol, its eight members designated the states of Cambodia and Laos and "the free territory under the jurisdiction of the state of Vietnam" to be under SEATO protection. The United States thus created SEATO to offset the results of Geneva. It also decided to consider South Vietnam as a separate state.

The Vietminh, however, regarded SEATO as a clear violation of the spirit of the Geneva Agreement. Ho Chi Minh saw the US position as an effort to deprive the Vietminh in the political arena of what it had gained militarily on the battlefield. Nevertheless, Ho withdrew his forces from the South, assuming that he would get enough votes there in 1956 so that he would emerge with a clear majority on a nationwide basis at election time. After all, his election in the North would be a certainty, and if only a minority would support the Vietminh in the South, his election would be assured. President Eisenhower, too, thought that elections, if held on the basis of the Geneva Agreement, would lead to a Communist victory. As he put it in 1954, "Had elections been held as of the time of the fighting, possibly 80 percent of the population would have voted for the Communist Ho Chi Minh as their leader rather than Chief of State Bao Dai."[74]

In the meantime, Ngo Dinh Diem, a US-backed Roman Catholic from a Mandarin family, began to challenge Emperor Bao Dai in the South. The United States strongly supported Diem in his bid for power, and in October 1955, Diem proclaimed the establishment of a Republic of Vietnam, with himself as president.

Hence, Geneva and the SEATO Treaty meant the end of French power in Indochina and the beginnings of the US effort to enter the struggle with military might. As yet there were no significant military encounters between Vietminh and US forces. But the issue was joined. The Vietminh now saw the Americans as following the path of French imperialism, and the Americans perceived Geneva as a well-laid Communist trap to engulf all of Vietnam. The end of a colonial war merely signified the beginnings of a war between Americans and Communists. Thus, once again the continuum pattern appeared: the East-West conflict simply grew out of the struggle between nationalism and colonialism.

As the East-West conflict superseded the colonial war, the pace of battle gradually intensified. A pattern of escalation emerged by which every diplomatic failure to achieve negotiations paved the way for yet another upward step on the scale of violence.

The first such discernible move after Geneva was the US effort between 1954 and 1956 to strengthen President Diem's military establishment and Ho Chi Minh's visit to Moscow and Peking in 1955 to negotiate aid and friendship treaties with the two Communist powers. Diem declared in July 1955 that, since South Vietnam had not signed the Geneva Agreements, he was not prepared to permit elections under the conditions specified by it. He also added that there was no freedom in the North to campaign for any opposition to Ho Chi Minh. The US government supported this view, and July 1956, the date scheduled for general elections in the Geneva Accords, passed without elections being held. Ho, in retaliation, began to train Communist cadres for guerrilla war in the South. He also became the recipient of aid from the Soviet Union and China for the purpose of shoring up the economic base of the North Vietnamese state.

On December 20, 1960, a National Liberation Front was created in South Vietnam. The Front announced a ten-point program calling for the overthrow of the incumbent Saigon government and the removal of US military advisers.

During the remaining years of the Eisenhower administration, the United States continued to support the increasingly unpopular President Diem with military advisers. The second rung of the escalation ladder was reached in January 1961 when Hanoi announced its endorsement of the National Liberation Front in South Vietnam.

The three years of the Kennedy administration were years of gradually deepening, though always limited, US involvement. By the time of President Kennedy's death, the United States had approximately 17,000 advisers in Vietnam, although there was no direct US participation in actual combat. A further complicating factor was the increasingly oppressive nature of Diem's regime, which was ultimately overthrown by a military coup in November 1963. Kennedy himself always tried to draw a distinction between US assistance to South Vietnam and Americanization of the war. "In the final analysis," he said, "it is their war. They are the ones who have to win it or lose it."[75] In the meantime, the growth of Communist insurgency in the South was rapid. The resurrected Vietminh, now called Vietcong by the Americans, infiltrated the South in increasing numbers. The National Liberation Front built a highly efficient network of political cadres which began a campaign of terror and assassination in South Vietnamese villages. By late 1963 both sides had raised the stakes, and the United States, though not yet directly involved in actual combat, began to establish the necessary logistical base for further action.

Another threshold was crossed in the summer of 1964. In July the new South Vietnamese prime minister, General Khan, delivered a major address, the keynote of which was "to the North." Two days later, Nguyen Cao Ky, the commander of the South Vietnamese Air Force, announced that he was prepared to bomb North Vietnam at any time. In early August North Vietnamese torpedo boats launched attacks on two US ships in the Gulf of Tonkin. President Johnson retaliated by bombing oil depots and other facilities in North Vietnam. On August 19 the President secured the passage of the Tonkin Gulf Resolution in Congress, which authorized him "to take all necessary measures to repel any armed attack against the forces of the United States and to prevent further aggression." The air war had gone north of the seventeenth parallel for the first time.

The next rung on the ladder was reached in February 1965. On February 7 the Vietcong staged a night raid against US barracks at Pleiku, killing 8 Americans and wounding 126. Twelve hours later, US jets attacked North Vietnam in what was to be the first of an almost uninterrupted series of daily air attacks against the North. In the South, marines were introduced into the ground war which was now rapidly Americanized. By 1966 US fighting units were frequently suffering higher casualty rates than their South Vietnamese allies. The Liberation Front responded to these events with its harsh five-point manifesto of March 1965 in which it refused to enter into negotiations until after US troops had been withdrawn. Three weeks later, however, Hanoi published its own "four-point program" in which it did not rule out the possibility of negotiations. In mid-May, the United States stopped its bombings of the North for five days, but no talks ensued; the air attacks were resumed.

In February 1966, President Johnson met with the South Vietnamese leader, Air Marshal Ky, at Honolulu, where the two men underlined their solidarity against "the aggression from the North." In mid-1966 President Johnson announced that guerrilla infiltration from the North had increased at an alarming rate and that further US retaliatory action might be necessary. In June the United States bombed the North Vietnamese capitol of Hanoi and its largest port, Haiphong. In the South, US forces had risen from 17,000 to 500,000 by 1968. There was no evidence, however, that this policy of "strategic persuasion" had deterred the Hanoi regime from sending more guerrillas to the South or the Liberation Front from attempting to infiltrate the countryside. The war had escalated in ever more violent bursts, but no decisive change had occurred in the balance of power among the main belligerents.

By this time, a deep division had occurred within the United States about the US commitment in Vietnam and the future course of US foreign policy in Southeast Asia. The administration defended its policy in Vietnam on the following main grounds: First, it defended the air attacks as "strategic persuasion" of the North to leave its neighbors to the South alone. Also, the bombing raids, in the view of the administration, "raised the costs of aggression" and made it more difficult to send guerrillas to the South via the "Ho Chi Minh trail." Second, a withdrawal would, in the eyes of the administration, signify a tremendous victory for the Chinese view on "wars of liberation," showing up the United States as a "paper tiger" and encouraging stepped-up aggressive moves by communism elsewhere in the world. Third, "aggression must be stopped at the source." In the view of the administration, Hanoi stood behind the National Liberation Front, and China stood behind Hanoi. Hence China must be contained on her periphery as the Soviet Union was successfully contained twenty years earlier. A withdrawal, on the other hand, would produce a "row of falling dominoes" and bring to an end the US presence in Southeast Asia altogether.

Critics of the administration pointed to the experience of 400,000 French troops in Indochina and wondered whether the United States could fare better in a counterinsurgency war in which a ten-to-one troop ratio in favor of the

United States might be necessary for victory over the Vietcong. Opponents of the war also accused the United States of destroying the social fabric of South Vietnam—the very nation it had set out to save from communism—through air bombardments and ground warfare. Third, the danger of Chinese or Soviet intervention on Hanoi's side took a prominent place in the view of most critics. Finally, opponents asserted that the United States still behaved as if communism were a monolithic force that had to elicit a US response whenever a Communist regime appeared. Actually, the argument continued, communism was now much more diffuse, and each such regime should be evaluated in a specific and pragmatic manner by the United States rather than seen automatically as an attempt to extend the design of world communism. Hence, the argument concluded, the US involvement in Vietnam would have made sense twenty years earlier, as did the formation of NATO in Europe, but in the 1960s a strategic US commitment in Southeast Asia was at best an anachronism and at worst a catastrophe. These differing perceptions of the nature of communism lay at the heart of the dialogue between "hawks" and "doves" in the United States.

By 1968, the impasse over negotiations between the NLF and North Vietnam on one side and the United States and South Vietnam on the other had crystallized into a single issue: the bombing of North Vietnam. Hanoi and the Front demanded the cessation of bombings as a precondition to talks; the United States and South Vietnam demanded an end to Communist infiltration into the South as a precondition to the cessation of air attacks on the North. On March 31, 1968, President Johnson decided to stop all bombings north of the nineteenth parallel. Shortly thereafter, peace talks began in Paris between the United States and North Vietnam. At these talks, the North Vietnamese negotiators insisted on a total halt to the bombings, but the United States in turn insisted on the simultaneous reduction of guerrilla infiltration into South Vietnam as an act of reciprocity. On October 31, President Johnson ordered the complete cessation of the bombings. The Paris peace talks were broadened to include South Vietnam and the National Liberation Front. But as in Korea, the peace talks were only a prologue to the difficult business of peace making.

The war continued during Richard M. Nixon's presidency. The objective of the new President was "Vietnamization," or the turning over of the ground war to the combat forces for South Vietnam. Under this policy, Nixon gradually withdrew US combat troops from South Vietnam. In March 1972, however, the North Vietnamese launched a major offense in the most impressive show of force since the Tet assault in 1968. The North Vietnamese leadership had decided to make an all-out effort to seize what it could in the South at a time when it was facing a new form of diplomatic isolation. The latest US overtures to China and the Soviet Union threatened to separate North Vietnam from its two major Communist allies. The offensive began shortly after President Nixon's visit to Peking in February but before his trip to Moscow, scheduled for May.

In April and May of 1972, Nixon took two gambles that escalated the war to new levels of violence. In April, B-52 bombers struck Hanoi and Haiphong in saturation bombings that by far exceeded the ferocity of the Johnson raids. And in May, the President took a step that his predecessor had always ruled out as too perilous: Nixon ordered the mining of North Vietnam's harbors to cut off the flow of tanks, artillery, and other offensive weapons supplied to Hanoi by the Soviet Union and other Communist nations. At the same time, however, he offered a total troop withdrawal from South Vietnam four months after an Indochina-wide cease-fire and the return of prisoners of war. The risk of Soviet-American confrontation at sea dominated world attention for several days, but only verbal denunciations emanated from Moscow and Peking. The Soviet Union by now placed a higher priority on the growing détente with the United States than on the interest of North Vietnam. The Soviet-American summit took place on schedule, and the President's gamble paid off. North Vietnam now realized that it had been virtually abandoned by its own allies. The United States suddenly found itself in the anomalous position of having reached détente with the two colossi of communism—China and the Soviet Union—while it continued to wage war against a small Communist peasant country which it accused of aggression.

In July the Paris peace talks resumed, and troop withdrawal continued. On October 26, in a dramatic announcement, Henry Kissinger predicted that "peace was at hand." This optimism proved to be premature. Early in December, Kissinger's "final talks" with the North Vietnamese were broken off, and he reported a stalemate.

On December 18, President Nixon ordered all-out bombing attacks on Hanoi and Haiphong. Millions of tons of explosives were dropped on the North. The fierce intensity and relentlessness of the attacks produced an outcry of protest against "terror bombings" from many parts of the world. The raids were halted on December 30, and the Paris peace talks once again resumed. On January 23, 1973, after almost three decades of war, a cease-fire was reached.

The Paris Accords provided for the withdrawal of all US troops and military advisers, an exchange of prisoners, consultations between South and North Vietnam on general elections, new supervisory machinery, and the withdrawal of all foreign troops from Laos and Cambodia.

In essence, what was achieved in Paris in 1973 was a reversion to the status of Vietnam at the time of the 1954 Geneva Accords. The United States had come full circle in Vietnam. The clock was turned back twenty years. There was an Orwellian irony to the situation. Progress was regress: 1954 by 1973.

The US hope, after the withdrawal of American troops, was that South Vietnam would be able to defend itself against the North with military and financial assistance from the United States. For two years that hope seemed justified, but then the dam broke. In the spring of 1975, the Communist insurgents in Cambodia, the Khmer Rouge, marched upon the capital, Phnom Penh, and forced Marshal Lon Nol, Cambodia's American-supported president, to flee the country. Thus, the US "incursion" of 1970 finally produced the opposite of what it had intended: a Communist instead of a neutralist Cambodia. At the same time, the South Vietnamese army lost its fighting spirit and collapsed entirely. In a matter of weeks, almost all of South Vietnam fell to the Communists. In the United States, a test of wills took place between the administration of President Gerald R. Ford, who favored continued military aid to Cambodia and to South Vietnam, and the Congress, which became increasingly reluctant to cooperate. Finally, the United States was left with the humanitarian responsibility of rescuing terror-stricken refugees who were fleeing from the advancing North Vietnamese armies. In April Saigon surrendered to the Communists and was renamed Ho Chi Minh City. Twenty years of American effort thus ended in failure. As Dean Rusk, one of the main architects of US Vietnam policy during the 1960s, put it in April 1975: "Personally, I made two mistakes: I underestimated the tenacity of the North Vietnamese and overestimated the patience of the American people."[76]

By the mid-1970s, both the supporters and the critics of the Vietnam war in the United States tended to regard the second Indochina war as one of the most terrible episodes in the history of US foreign policy. There was a general consensus that it would take a long time for the wounds to heal, both in Indochina and in the United States.

The US involvement in Indochina had begun imperceptibly, almost like a mild toothache. At the end, it ran through Vietnam and the United States like a pestilence. Each President based his policies on exaggerated fears and later on exaggerated hopes. Thus, each President left the problem to his successor in worse shape than he found it.

The United States dropped more than seven million tons of bombs on Indochina. This is eighty times the amount that was dropped on Britain during World War II and is equal to more than three hundred of the atomic bombs that fell on Japan in 1945. The bombs left twenty million craters. After the bombardments much of Vietnam looked like a moonscape. Nothing will grow there for generations.

The United States also was in anguish over the war. Its leadership lost respect in the eyes of an entire generation, universities were disrupted, careers were blighted, and the economy was bloated with war inflation. The metal caskets in which the remains of 56,000 Americans came back from Vietnam were to symbolize the war's ultimate and only meaning.

In historical perspective, the great unanswered question will probably be: Which would have been less costly, an earlier Communist victory or the agony of this war? One cannot help but wonder what might have happened if not one single US soldier had ever come to Indochina. History does not reveal its alternatives, and thus one cannot say with certitude where this road not taken would have led. Vietnam might indeed have gone Communist much earlier. It would, however, probably have been a form of communism of the Titoist variety—with a strong dose of nationalism and a fierce tradition of independence vis-à-vis Moscow and Peking. The United States could have lived with that, it seems. Certainly, its postponement was hardly worth the sacrifice of more than 56,000 American lives, hundreds of thousands of Vietnamese lives, and $150 billion.

As the war cost more and more in blood and treasure, it tended to resolve less and less. Finally it ended in the stunned exhaustion of defeat for two American-supported regimes. Ironically, despite Indochina, the United States had reached détente with the two major Communist powers. The hopes, rather than the fears, of five presidents were borne out by long-range international developments. A calmer world had begun to emerge, and the Vietnam conflict, first initiated to combat the spread of communism, had become a deadening anachronism. This, perhaps, is the bitterest lesson of this terrible war. It had begun in the world of the cold war and ended, a generation later, in a world of détente. Thus, the reasons for the war's outbreak had almost become irrelevant: History had simply passed it by. When considered in this perspective, the awesome logic about Vietnam is apparent: It was probably in vain that combatants and civilians had suffered, the land was devastated, and the dead had died.

WAR IN THE NUCLEAR AGE

"If you look deeply into the abyss," said Nietzsche, "the abyss will look into you." The face of war in our time is so awesome and so terrible that the first temptation is to recoil and turn away. Medusa-like, the face of war, with its relentless horror, threatens to destroy anyone who looks at it for long. Yet we must find the courage to confront the abyss. I deeply believe that war is a sickness, though it may be humankind's "sickness unto death." No murderous epidemic has ever been conquered without exposure, pain, and danger, or by ignoring the bacilli. But in the end, humanity's faculty of reason and courage have prevailed, and even the plague was overcome. The Black Death that ravaged our planet centuries ago is but a distant memory today.

It is true that the analogy between sickness and war may be open to attack. It has been fashionable to assert that war is not an illness but, like aggression, an ineradicable part of human nature. This is a dubious assumption. Although aggression may be inherent in us all, war is learned behavior and, as such, can be unlearned and, ultimately, selected out entirely. There have been other habits of humankind that seemed impossible to shed. In the Ice Age, when people lived in caves, incest was perfectly acceptable; often there were no people other than father, mother, sister, or brother around. Today, incest is virtually gone. Cannibalism provides an even more dramatic case. Thousands of years ago, human beings ate each other and drank each other's blood. That, too, was part of "human nature." Even a brief century ago, millions of Americans believed that God had ordained white people to be free and black people to be slaves. Why else would God have created them in different colors? Yet slavery, once a part of "human nature," was abolished because human beings showed a capacity for growth. The growth came slowly, after immense suffering, but it *did* come. "Human nature" had been changed. Like slavery and cannibalism, war too can be eliminated from humankind's arsenal of horrors.

It seems, however, that people abandon their bad habits only when catastrophe is close at hand. The intellect alone is not enough. Humans must be shaken, almost shattered, before changing. A grave illness must pass its crisis before we know whether the patient will live or die. Most appropriately, the ancient Chinese had two characters for the word *crisis*—one connoting danger and the other, opportunity. The danger of extinction is upon us, but so is the opportunity for a better life for all on this planet.

We must therefore make an effort to look Medusa in the face and to diagnose the sickness. Diagnosis is no cure, of course, but it is the first and the most necessary step. I shall attempt this diagnosis by suggesting certain common themes about war in this century.

The first general theme that compels attention is that no nation that began a major war in this century emerged a winner. Austria-Hungary and Germany, which precipitated World War I, went down to ignominious defeat; Hitler's Germany was crushed into unconditional surrender; the North Korean attack was thwarted by collective action and ended in a draw; in the Vietnamese war it is difficult if not impossible clearly to identify the aggressor; the Arabs who invaded the new Jewish state in 1948 lost territory to the Israelis in four successive wars; and Pakistan, which wished to punish India through pre-emptive war, found itself dismembered in the process. In all cases, those who began a war came out losers. The nature or the ideology of the government that started a war seems to have made little, if any, difference. Defeat came to aggressors whether they were capitalists or Communists, white or nonwhite, Western or non-Western, rich or poor.

In the nineteenth century, by contrast, most wars were won by the governments that started them. Only those like Napoleon, who aspired to the big prize, suffered ultimate defeat. War then was still a rational pursuit, fought for limited objectives. Twentieth-century aggressors, however, tended to be more demanding and more ruthless: They fought for total stakes and hence made war a question of survival. Those who were attacked had to fight for life itself. Courage born of desperation proved to be a formidable weapon. In the end, those who began the war were stemmed, turned back, and in some cases, crushed completely. In no case has any nation that began a war in our time achieved its ends.

In the atomic age, war between nuclear powers is suicidal; wars between small countries with big friends are likely to be inconclusive and interminable; hence, decisive war in our time has become the privilege of the impotent. It has become almost banal to say that the atomic age has fundamentally altered the nature of war. No nuclear power can tell another: "Do as I say or I shall kill you"; each is reduced to saying: "Do as I say or I shall kill us both," which is an entirely different matter. Thus, when everybody is somebody, nobody is anybody. But it is not only nuclear countries that cannot win wars against each other. A small country with a good tie to a big ally also can no longer be defeated. The wars in Korea, Vietnam, and the Middle East all il-lustrate this point. The North Koreans were unable to defeat South Korea so long as the United States was willing to support the South and to neutralize the North's successes. And the South Koreans could not defeat the North so long as China and the Soviet Union were willing to render assistance. Thus, in the end, the Korean war ended with the frontiers virtually unchanged. The main difference was the large number of dead Koreans on both sides. In Vietnam, the Soviet Union and China sent enough supplies to offset the results of US bombings. In 1980 the deserts of the Middle East became veritable proving grounds for the testing of new superpower weapons. Iraq bombed Iran with Soviet Migs, and Iran reciprocated by bombing Iraq with American-made Phantom jets. Thus, wars between small nations with big weapons will be in-terminable so long as the ally of the weaker side is willing to continue its sup-port. Neither side can win; only the casualties mount. In our time, decisive victories seem possible only for nations without big friends or for the impo-tent. Thus, Bangladesh was able to break away from Pakistan because none of the great powers considered the issue important enough to restore the status quo by force of arms. Nor did the genocidal violence perpetrated by the Tutsi tribe against the Hutu people in Central Africa stir the great powers into ac-tion. Thus, the paradox of war in the atomic age may be summarized as fol-lows: The power of big states vis-à-vis each other has been reduced if not al-together canceled out, but the power of small and friendless states vis-à-vis each other has been proportionately enhanced.

In our time, unless the vanquished is destroyed completely, a victor's peace is seldom lasting. Those peace settlements that are negotiated on a basis of equality are much more permanent and durable. In 1918, Germany was de-feated but not crushed. Versailles became the crucible for Hitler's Germany, which was then brought down only through unconditional surrender. The Korean truce of 1953 was negotiated between undefeated equals. Both sides were unhappy, but neither side was so unhappy that it wished to overturn the settlement and initiate yet another war. An uneasy armistice or truce was grad-ually recognized as a basis for a legitimate peace settlement. The relative in-security of each side thus became the guarantor of the relative security of both. Israel learned this lesson in October 1973. The victor's peace of 1967 had left the Arabs in a state of such frustration that they were compelled to try their hand once more at war. With their dignity restored in 1973, they found it psychologically possible a decade and a half later to confront the Israelis with a new and most effective challenge: the Palestinian uprising.

Turning to the problem of the outbreak of war, the record indicates the cru-cial importance of the personalities of leaders. One is less impressed by the role of abstract forces such as nationalism, militarism, or alliance systems that traditionally have been regarded as the causes of war. Nor does it seem that economic factors played a vital part in precipitating war. The personalities of leaders, however, have often been decisive. The outbreak of World War I il-lustrates this point quite clearly. Conventional wisdom has blamed the alliance system for the spread of the war. Specifically, the argument runs, Kaiser Wilhelm's alliance with Austria dragged Germany into the war against the Allied powers. This analysis, however, totally ignores the role of the Kaiser's personality during the gathering crisis. Supposing Wilhelm had had the fortitude to continue his role as mediator and to restrain Austria instead of engaging in paranoid delusions and accusing England of conspiring against Germany? The disaster might have been averted, and then the conventional wisdom would have praised the alliance system for saving the peace instead of blaming it for causing the war. In truth, the emotional balance or lack of balance of the German Kaiser turned out to be absolutely crucial. Similarly, the relentless mediocrity of the leading personalities on all sides no doubt contributed to the disaster. Look at the outbreak of World War II; there is no doubt that the victor's peace of Versailles and the galloping inflation of the 1920s brought about the rise of Nazi Germany. But once again, it was the personality of Hitler that was decisive. A more rational leader would have consolidated his gains and certainly would not have attacked the Soviet Union. And if Russia had to be attacked, then a rational man would have made contingency plans to meet the Russian winter instead of counting blindly on an early victory. In the Korean War, the hubris of General MacArthur probably prolonged the conflict by two years, and in Vietnam, the fragile egos of at least two US presidents who could not face the facts first escalated the war quite disproportionately and then postponed its ending quite unreasonably. In the Middle East, the volatile personality of Gamal Abdel Nasser was primarily responsible for the closing of the Gulf of Aqaba which precipitated the Six-Day War of 1967. In all these cases, a fatal flaw or ego weakness in a leader's personality turned out to be of crucial importance. It may, in fact, have spelled the difference between the outbreak of war and the maintenance of peace.

Perhaps the most important single precipitating factor in the outbreak of war is misperception. Such distortion may manifest itself in four different ways: in a leader's self-image; a leader's view of an adversary's character; a leader's view of an adversary's intentions toward the leader; and, finally, a leader's view of an adversary's capabilities and power. Each of these is of such importance that it merits separate and careful treatment.

There is a remarkable consistency in the self-images of most national leaders on the brink of war. Each confidently expects victory after a brief and triumphant campaign. Doubt about the outcome is the voice of the enemy and therefore incomprehensible. This recurring atmosphere of optimism is not to be dismissed lightly by the historian as an ironic example of human folly. It assumes a powerful emotional momentum of its own and thus itself becomes one of the causes of war. Anything that fuels such optimism about a quick and decisive victory makes war more likely and anything that dampens it becomes a cause of peace.

This common belief in a short, decisive war is usually the overflow from a reservoir of self-delusions held by the leadership about both itself and its nation. The Kaiser's appearance in shining armor in August 1914 and his promise to the German nation that its sons would be back home "before the leaves had fallen from the trees" was matched by similar scenes of overconfidence and military splendor in Austria, in Russia, and in the other nations on the brink of war. Hitler's confidence in an early German victory in Russia was so unshakable that no winter uniforms were issued to the soldiers and no preparations whatsoever made for the onset of the Russian winter. In November 1941, when the mud of autumn turned to ice and snow, the cold became the German soldier's bitterest enemy. Tormented by the arctic temperatures, men died, machines broke down, and the quest for warmth all but eclipsed the quest for victory. Hitler's hopes and delusions about the German superman were shattered in the frozen wastes of Russia. The fact that Hitler had fought in World War I and seen that optimism crumble in defeat did not prevent its reappearance. When North Korea invaded South Korea, her leadership expected victory within two months. The Anglo-French campaign at Suez in 1956 was spurred by the hope of a swift victory. In Pakistan, Yahya Khan hoped to teach Indira Gandhi a lesson modeled on the Six-Day War in Israel. And in Vietnam, every US escalation in the air or on the ground was an expression of the hope that a few more bombs, a few more troops, would bring decisive victory.

Thus, leaders on all sides typically engage in self-delusions on the eve of war. Only the war itself then provides the stinging ice of reality and ultimately helps restore a measure of perspective in the leadership. The price for this recapture of reality is high indeed. It is unlikely that there ever was a war that fulfilled the initial hopes and expectations of both sides.

Distorted views of the adversary's character also help to precipitate a conflict. As the pressure mounted in July 1914, the German Kaiser explosively admitted that he "hated the Slavs, even though one should not hate anyone." This hatred no doubt influenced his decision to end his role as mediator and to prepare for war. Similarly, his naive trust in the honesty of the Austrian leaders prompted him to extend to them the blank check guarantee that dragged him into war. In reality, the Austrians were more deceitful than he thought and the Russians more honest. Worst of all, the British leadership, which worked so desperately to avert a general war, was seen by Wilhelm as the center of a monstrous plot to encircle and destroy the German nation. Hitler, too, had no conception of what Russia really was like. He knew nothing of the history and depth of the Russian land and believed that it was populated by subhuman barbarians who could be crushed with one decisive stroke and then be made to serve as slaves for German supermen. This relentless hatred and contempt for Russia became a crucial factor in Hitler's ill-fated assault of 1941. Perhaps the most important reason for the US military intervention in Vietnam was the misperception on the part of US leadership about the nature of communism in Asia. President Lyndon Johnson committed more than half a million combat troops to an Asian land war because he perceived the Vietnam war in terms of purely Western categories: a colossal shootout between the forces of communism and those of anticommunism. The fact that Ho Chi Minh saw the

Americans as the successors of French imperialism whom he was determined to drive out was completely lost upon the President. Virtue, righteousness, and justice were fully on his side, he thought. The United States, the child of light, had to defeat the child of darkness in a twentieth-century crusade. Mutual contempt and hatred also hastened the coming of the wars between the Arab states and Israel and between India and Pakistan. In the former case, the Arab view of Israel as an alien and hostile presence was a precipitating cause of conflict. And, in the latter, the two religions of Hinduism and Islam led directly to the creation of two hostile states that clashed in bloody conflict three times in a single generation.

If leaders on the brink of war believes that their adversary will attack them, the chances of war are fairly high. If both leaders share this perception about each other's intent, war becomes a virtual certainty. The mechanism of the self-fulfilling prophecy is then set in motion. If leaders attribute evil designs to their adversaries, and if they nurture these beliefs for long enough, they will eventually be proved right. The mobilization measures that preceded the outbreak of World War I were essentially defensive measures triggered by the fear of the other side's intent. The Russian tsar mobilized because he feared an Austrian attack; the German kaiser mobilized because he feared the Russian "steamroller." The nightmare of each then became a terrible reality. Stalin, imprisoned by the Marxist dogma that capitalists would always lie, disbelieved Churchill's truthful warnings about Hitler's murderous intent: He was so blind to it that Russia almost lost the war. Eisenhower and Dulles were so convinced that the Chinese would move against the French in Indochina in the way they had against MacArthur's UN forces that they committed the first US military advisers to Vietnam. The Chinese never intervened, but the Americans had begun their march along the road to self-entrapment in the Vietnam quagmire. Arabs and Israelis and Indians and Pakistanis generally expected nothing but the worst from one another, and these expectations often led to war. The conviction held by Syria and Egypt after 1967 that Israel intended to hold on to the occupied territories forever was the immediate precipitating cause of the October War of 1973, in which the Arabs made a desperate attempt to reconquer their lost lands. And Yahya Khan's perception of India's intention to fight on the side of the secessionist movement in Bengal led directly to his abortive and suicidal air attack.

A leader's misperception of an adversary's power is perhaps the quintessential cause of war. It is vital to remember, however, that it is not the actual distribution of power that precipitates a war but rather how a leader thinks that power is distributed. A war itself then becomes a dispute over measurement. Reality is gradually restored as war itself cures war. And the war will end when the fighting nations perceive each other's strength more realistically.

Germany and Austria-Hungary in 1914 had nothing but contempt for Russia's power. This disrespect was to cost them dearly. Hitler repeated this mistake a generation later, and his misperception led straight to his destruction. One of the clearest examples of another misperception of this kind took place in the Korean War. MacArthur, during his advance through North Korea toward the Chinese border, stubbornly believed that the Chinese Communists did not have the capacity to intervene. When the Chinese did cross the Yalu River into North Korea, MacArthur clung to the belief that he was facing 40,000 men while in truth the figure was closer to 200,000. And when the Chinese forces temporarily withdrew to assess their impact on MacArthur's army, the US general assumed that the Chinese were badly in need of rest after their encounter with superior Western military might. And when the Chinese attacked again and drove MacArthur all the way back to South Korea, the leader of the UN forces perceived this action as a "piece of treachery worse even than Pearl Harbor." The most amazing aspect of this story is that the real facts were quite available to MacArthur from his own intelligence sources, if only the general had cared to look at them. But he knew better and thus prolonged the war by two years. Only at war's end did the Americans gain respect for China's power and take care not to provoke it again beyond the point of no return. Yet in the Vietnam War, the US leadership committed precisely the same error vis-à-vis North Vietnam. Five successive presidents believed that Ho Chi Minh would collapse if only a little more military pressure would be brought to bear on him either from the air or on the ground. The North Vietnamese leader proved them all mistaken, and only when the United States admitted that North Vietnam could not be beaten did the war come to an end. In both Korea and Vietnam the price of reality came high indeed. As these wars resolved less and less, they tended to cost more and more in blood and treasure. The number of dead on all sides bore mute testimony to the fact that the United States had to fight two of the most terrible and divisive wars in her entire history before she gained respect for the realities of power on the other side. In 1948, the Arabs believed that an invasion by five Arab armies would quickly put an end to Israel. They were mistaken. But in 1973, Israel, encouraged to the point of hubris after three successful wars, thought of Arab power only with contempt and of Israel's own as unassailable. That, too, was wrong, as Israel had to learn in the bitter war of October 1973. And in the 1980s the Iraqi leadership discovered that its attack on Iran, far from being a knock-out blow, only served to inflame the Iranians' fanatical fighting zeal. As a result the Iraq-Iran war became a terrible war of attrition that cost each side hundreds of thousands of casualties.

Thus, on the eve of each war at least one nation misperceives another's power. In that sense, the beginning of each war is a misperception or an accident. The war itself then slowly, and in agony, teaches people about reality. The most tragic aspect of this truth is that war has continued to remain the best teacher of reality and thus has been the most effective cure for war.

Despite the persistence of so much human tragedy and folly, it is nevertheless possible to conclude on a note of hope. There has been a slow dawning of compassion and of global consciousness over humanity's bleak skies in our generation. This has manifested itself both in a new awareness of and even resistance to the havoc that war wreaks upon the human spirit. It is no longer quite acceptable to our sense of logic that throwing a human being into a fire is an atrocity but throwing fire on many human beings may be designated as a military operation. We can no longer quite understand how one man who kills another is punished as a murderer while another man who murders thousands anonymously from the sky may be acclaimed as a patriot or hero. This new dawning has come through dreadful suffering, but it has come.

A US president and a Soviet chief of state had the foresight and the courage—at long last—to embark on a course of serious disarmament. For that achievement alone, Ronald Reagan and Mikhail Gorbachev have entered history.

It is this new, slow dawning of compassion and of global consciousness that is our greatest hope. From this new spirit that is stirring deep within us we shall forge the weapons against war. Humanity has built both cathedrals and concentration camps. We have descended to unprecedented depths in our time, but we also have soared to greater heights than ever before. Humanity is not burdened with original sin alone; we also have the gift of original innocence.

REFERENCES

1 Harry S Truman, *Memoirs, Vol. I: Year of Decisions*. Garden City, N.Y.: Doubleday, 1955, p. 293.
2 *Ibid.*, p. 433.
3 Raymond Dennett and Robert R. Turner, eds., *Documents on American Foreign Relations*. Princeton, N.J.: Princeton University Press, 1951, p. 4.
4 Dean G. Acheson, ''Responsibility for Decision in Foreign Policy,'' *Yale Review*, Autumn 1954, p. 12.
5 *Ibid.*, p. 7.
6 *Ibid.*
7 *Ibid.*
8 US Department of State, *Bulletin*, July 1950, No. 23, 574, p. 17.
9 Harry S Truman, *Memoirs, Vol. II: Years of Trial and Hope*. Garden City, N.Y.: Doubleday, 1952, p. 332.
10 US Department of State, *United States Policy in the Korean Crisis*, Far Eastern Series, No. 34, Washington, D.C.: Government Printing Office, 1950, p. 1.
11 For a full treatment of this subject, see John G. Stoessinger, *The United Nations and the Superpowers*, 3d ed. New York: Random House, 1973, Chap. 3.
12 Cited in Glenn D. Paige, *The Korean Decision*. New York: Free Press, 1968, p. 95.
13 *Ibid.*, p. 100.
14 *The New York Herald Tribune*, June 26, 1950.
15 *The New York Times*, July 2, 1950.
16 Truman, *Years of Trial*, pp. 332ff.
17 United Nations Security Council, Fifth Year, *Official Records*, No. 15, 473d Meeting, June 25, 1950, p. 3.
18 *The New York Times*, June 26, 1950.
19 *Ibid.*
20 Paige, *op. cit.*, p. 120.
21 *The Chicago Tribune*, June 26, 1950.
22 *Ibid.*

23 Paige, *op. cit.*, p. 127.

24 Truman, *Years of Trial*, p. 334.

25 *Ibid.*, p. 335.

26 *Ibid.*

27 Beverly Smith, "The White House Story: Why We Went to War in Korea," *Saturday Evening Post,* November 10, 1951, p. 80.

28 Truman, *Years of Trial*, p. 337.

29 Cited in Paige, *op. cit.*, p. 179.

30 *Ibid.*

31 Smith, *op. cit.*, p. 80.

32 Truman, *Years of Trial*, p. 463.

33 Paige, *op. cit.*, p. 203.

34 United Nations Document S/1508, June 26, 1950.

35 United Nations Document S/1507, June 26, 1950.

36 Roy E. Appleman, *South to the Naktong, North to the Yalu.* Washington, D.C.: Government Printing Office, 1960, p. 34.

37 *The New York Times,* June 29, 1950.

38 Courtney Whitney, *MacArthur: His Rendezvous with History.* New York: Knopf, 1956, p. 327.

39 *Ibid.*, pp. 332–333.

40 Marguerite Higgins, *War in Korea.* Garden City, N.Y.: Doubleday, 1951, p. 33.

41 Paige, *op. cit.*, p. 243.

42 Truman, *Years of Trial*, p. 343.

43 *United Nations Bulletin,* July 15, 1950, pp. 50–53, and August 1, 1950, pp. 95, 99.

44 Leland M. Goodrich, *Korea: A Study of U.S. Policy in the United Nations.* New York: Council on Foreign Relations, 1956, p. 117.

45 K. M. Panikkar, *In Two Chinas.* London: Allen and Unwin, 1955, p. 110.

46 *The New York Herald Tribune,* September 22, 1950.

47 UN General Assembly, *Official Records,* Fifth Session, First Committee (September 30, 1950), p. 39.

48 *Ibid.*

49 The negative votes were case by Byelorussia, Czechoslovakia, Poland, the Ukraine, and the USSR. Abstaining were Egypt, India, Lebanon, Saudi Arabia, Syria, Yemen, and Yugoslavia.

50 *The New York Times,* October 9, 1950.

51 US Senate, *Military Situation in the Far East, Hearings before the Committee on Armed Services and the Committee on Foreign Relations,* 82d Congress, 1st Session, 1951, p. 3483.

52 Samuel B. Griffith II, *The Chinese People's Liberation Army.* New York: McGraw-Hill, 1967, p. 124.

53 *The New York Times,* November 17, 1950.

54 *Ibid.*

55 Truman, *Years of Trial*, p. 362.

56 Tang Tsou, *America's Failure in China,* 1941–1950. Chicago: University of Chicago Press, 1963, p. 578.

57 Griffith, *op. cit.*, p. 124.

58 Douglas MacArthur, Message to Veterans of Foreign Wars, August 28, 1950.

59 US Senate, *Military Situation in the Far East,* p. 3427.

60 Griffith, *op. cit.*, p. 134.

61 *Ibid.*, p. 129.

62 *Ibid.*, p. 134.

63 Whitney, *op. cit.*, p. 394.

64 Allen S. Whiting, *China Crosses the Yalu.* Stanford: Stanford University Press, 1960, pp. 169–170.

65 United States Mission to the United Nations, Press Release No. 1129, February 2, 1951.

66 *The New York Herald Tribune,* December 6, 1950.

67 *The New York Herald Tribune,* December 30, 1950.

68 Panikkar, *op. cit.*, p. 117.

69 *Ibid.*, pp. 177–178.

70 US Department of State, *Bulletin,* Volume XLVII, No. 1220, November 12, 1962, pp. 715–720.

71 Cited in Henry M. Pachter, *Collision Course: The Cuban Missile Crisis and Coexistence.* New York: Praeger, 1963, p. 58.

72 *Ibid.*, p. 89.

73 *Ibid.*

74 Dwight D. Eisenhower, *Mandate for Change.* New York: Doubleday, 1963, p. 372.

75 US Department of State, *Bulletin,* Washington, September 30, 1973, pp. 498–499.

76 Interview on NBC Television, April 3, 1975.

SELECTED BIBLIOGRAPHY

Hastings, Max. *The Korean War.* New York: Simon & Schuster, 1987. In this thorough and well-written study, a British military historian concludes that the West had been ''utterly right to fight'' the Korean War, despite its frustrating and unsatisfactory conclusion.

Karnow, Stanley. *Vietnam.* New York: Penguin Books, 1984. Probably the definitive account of the Vietnam War.

Kearns, Doris. *Lyndon Johnson and the American Dream.* New York: Signet, 1977. A wrenching, intimate psychohistorical portrait of a haunted man. Compelling and immensely valuable.

Kennedy, Robert F. *Thirteen Days.* New York: Norton, 1969. An invaluable insight into crisis decision making at the highest level, by a major participant in the Cuban quarantine decision of 1962.

Kissinger, Henry. *White House Years.* Boston: Little, Brown, 1979. A colorful, detailed account of the author's tenure as Richard Nixon's national security adviser, with extended chapters on Vietnam and Cambodia.

Sheehan, Neil. *A Bright, Shining Lie: John Paul Vann and America in Vietnam.* New York: Random House, 1988. A memorable, vivid, searing account of the Vietnam War by a combat journalist.

Stoessinger, John G. *Why Nations Go To War.* 5th ed. New York: St. Martin's Press, 1990. How the major wars of this century erupted, with emphasis on personalities.

Walzer, Michael. *Just and Unjust Wars.* New York: Basic Books, 1977. An original and highly sophisticated analysis of a number of wars, with emphasis on the moral dilemmas involved.

CHAPTER 7

THE ECONOMIC STRUGGLE FOR POWER

My credit now stands on such slippery ground.

William Shakespeare, *Julius Caesar,* III, 1

As the twentieth century nears its end, the world has become the stage for a three-cornered economic power struggle: first, the fierce trade competition between Japan and the United States; second, the struggle between OPEC and the industrialized world over energy; and finally, the struggle of the world's poor against the rich for a place at the world's banquet table. These three struggles—deeply interwoven as they are—have profoundly changed the world's power constellation. In the space of a few decades, weak states have become powerful and strong states have become vulnerable. Seldom if ever before in history has weakness become strength so quickly, and strength, weakness. These upheavals will form the substance of Chapter 7.

JAPAN AND THE UNITED STATES: THE STRUGGLE OVER WHO IS NUMBER ONE

In the fall of 1945, shortly after the Japanese surrender at the end of World War II, I had the occasion to visit Tokyo. The city was a rubble heap with hardly a stone left on top of another. Forty-three years later, in 1988, I visited Tokyo again. This time, a taxi ride from the airport came to $150. A modest hotel room downtown cost $500 a night, and a mediocre dinner set me back $100. On my return flight to the United States, I stopped in Hawaii and discovered that numerous luxury hotels there had been bought up by Japanese investors. The same was true of choice real estate properties in California. It occurred to me that if anyone had made such a prediction to me in 1945, I probably would have dismissed it as a complete absurdity. And yet, the incredible had come about. In the relatively short span of less than half a century, the United States had skidded from being the world's richest country to the status of the world's largest debtor. Japan, on the other hand, had risen, Phoenixlike, from atomic ashes to being the world's leading creditor nation, with the United States deeply in its debt. How could this have happened? The story is an intriguing and dramatic one.

To begin, no two nations could be more different than China and Japan. China had been a centralized empire for 2,000 years, whereas Japan did not emerge into nationhood until around 1600. China had rarely, if ever, ventured beyond the Great Wall to conquer other peoples, whereas Japan, at least during the last 100 years, had been a fiercely expansionist nation. And finally, whereas China had always been reluctant to borrow from abroad, taking refuge instead in a sense of self-defined superiority, Japan had been willing and eager to borrow heavily, first from China, and then from the West, in particular the United States.

Although the assault on China in the nineteenth century was mounted by seven or eight Western nations, Japan's door was forced open by a single nation: the United States. In the middle of the nineteenth century, the United States was the last major Western country without overseas colonies or possessions, and Japan, aside from Thailand, was the only Asian nation not yet colonized. The opportunity was not lost upon US Commodore Matthew C. Perry, who, with the help of several battleships, forced open the Japanese door in 1854. The commodore, with the help of a resourceful consul-general, Townsend Harris, a lawyer from Newburyport, Massachusetts, tried his best to emulate the example of the western powers in China by subjecting Japan to a number of humiliating concessions including extraterritoriality. What worked in China, however, quickly came to naught in Japan. The Emperor of Japan at the time, known as the Meiji Emperor, was determined to prevent a Chinese-type fiasco. With extraordinary determination, this resourceful ruler dispatched tens of thousands of young Japanese to the United States, Britain, and Germany, to study not only science and technology but politics, economics, and philosophy as well. His purpose was to rid Japan as quickly as possible of the unwelcome foreign intruders. With amazing speed, the Japanese simply changed mentors. The Chinese, who had been dismembered by the West, were now regarded with a tinge of contempt. The Western countries had become the new model to emulate.

During the Meiji Emperor's reign more than a century ago, modern Japan's major problem was already becoming apparent. This was a small island nation with far too many people and far too few natural resources. Then, as now, it faced an existential imperative: expand or perish. The only choice was *how* to expand: militarily, through conquest, or economically, through trade.

The young Japanese who came to the United States in the nineteenth century were fascinated not only by baseball, which they promptly borrowed, but also by US elections and democratic institutions. Those who went to the United Kingdom not only borrowed the concept of the British Parliament, but were also impressed by the power of the British Navy. And those who visited Kaiser Wilhelm's Germany were even more impressed by the Prussian military staff which was not accountable to civilian authority. The German military quickly became the model for a formidable Japanese army and navy.

In the tug of war between those who wished to expand peacefully through trade and those who preferred military expansion through conquest, the latter gradually won the upper hand. In 1904, the Japanese navy humbled the Russian fleet by sinking most of its ships in a naval battle at Tsushima Straits. In 1910, the Japanese army occupied Korea almost effortlessly, and the peninsula remained a Japanese colony for the next 35 years. After these victories, however, the Japanese militarists began to overreach themselves. In 1931, they attacked China in Manchuria and fairly soon thereafter became bogged down in the vast expanses of the Chinese hinterland. The attack on Pearl Harbor in 1941 was designed not only to destroy the US navy but to conquer most of Asia and annex it to Japan, which would then become the center of a "South East Asia Co-Prosperity Sphere." This dream of the Japanese militarists came to an abrupt end when the United States dropped two atomic bombs on Hiroshima and Nagasaki in August 1945. A few days later Japan surrendered, and General Douglas MacArthur took over the task of rebuilding the shattered nation under US military occupation. By 1945, the military phase of Japanese expansion had definitely ended.

The US occupation of Japan was probably the most successful military occupation in modern history. The Americans were generous in victory and the Japanese compliant in defeat and eager to learn from the victors. The Emperor was stripped of his divinity, and General MacArthur became a kind of US proconsul with his headquarters in Tokyo. Thousands of Japanese would line the streets every morning to watch his limousine make its way to his office at the Dai Ichi Building. MacArthur relished his role and did an excellent job in laying the groundwork for what was to become one of the most remarkable economic recoveries in modern times. He brought to Japan the United States' leading business, technology, and reconstruction experts and taught the Japanese virtually everything they needed to know to rebuild their economy. In addition, the general personally drafted a new constitution for Japan which contained a clause that was to haunt the Americans several decades later: Japan was never again to possess an army or navy powerful enough to make war. When the United States signed a peace treaty with Japan in 1951, the defeated nation had been transformed into a democracy, with an elected prime minister and parliament. The Japanese government had become a unique fusion of US and British institutions. Yet, some of the conditions that had precipitated Japan's military adventures still prevailed: Japan was still a small island with far too many people and too few resources. Expansion, far from disappearing, was merely to change form.

The next four decades, from 1951 to the present, may justly be described as the period of the Japanese economic miracle. Through a combination of iron discipline, a relentless work ethic, and the waging of ruthless economic warfare, Japan, by the late 1980s, had become one of the world's wealthiest nations, with almost everyone else, including the United States, in her debt. The United States, however, once the world's richest power, had become by the late 1980s the world's leading debtor country, with the spending habits, however, of a creditor country. A gigantic role reversal had taken place. Japan and the United States were now tied together as allies, as it were, for richer or for poorer, but Japan was getting richer and the United States was getting poorer.

The explanation for this amazing turn of events may be found in the historical events that followed World War II and in the cultural differences between the two nations. The United States not only chose to maintain an expensive network of military alliances spanning most of the globe but also fought two bloody and costly wars in Korea and Vietnam. Yet, US spending habits did not decline. Quite on the contrary, the United States borrowed more and more from foreigners, and her savings rate went down to a pitiful 4 percent. The Japanese, however, had only modest military expenditures, since they were sheltered by the United States; under this protective umbrella, Japan mounted a fierce economic offensive against her former mentor. Gradually at first, and then in floods, high-quality Japanese automobiles, computer chips, and other high-technology products began to inundate the US market. The Americans bought these superior products eagerly, going yet more deeply into debt. In numerous instances, the Japanese adopted extremely unfair trade practices. For example, the Hitachi Corporation stole patents from IBM and, when caught red-handed, was forced to pay a heavy fine. Moreover, the Japanese were most reluctant to open their own markets to US imports, such as beef and citrus fruit. The Americans, for their part, were slow to learn. Instead of adapting their exports to the Japanese culture, they would persist in shipping cars with right-hand steering, oblivious of the fact that the Japanese drove on the left, or they would export refrigerators much too large for small Japanese apartments. As the Japanese businessman put it, "If we had approached the American market in the way the Americans have approached ours, we would still be selling paper fans."

By 1987, the United States had become dependent on Japan for regular purchases of treasury bonds, in other words, its debt instruments. Several times a year, when the US Treasury would auction bonds, the Japanese were the major buyers, since they still regarded the United States as a safe haven of political stability. By mid-1987, approximately one-quarter of the US standard of living was supported by credits from Japan. As a result, the US dollar by now was cut in half vis-à-vis the Japanese yen, and the United States had become a fire sale for wealthy Japanese eager to invest in US stocks, bonds, and real estate. But a reckoning was in the making: the stock market crash of October 1987.

I believe that the US market crashed because the United States had become overly dependent on Japanese investments. When the Japanese became afraid that the United States was no longer the safe haven that it had been, they began to pull their money out, thus drying up the huge liquidity that had fuelled the great bull market of 1987.

What persuaded the Japanese to pull out in the fall of 1987? First, a typical Japanese investor in US stocks tended to lose money even though the US markets were rising, since the dollar was losing ground rapidly against the yen. Hence, in yen terms, the Japanese took heavy losses in both the US stock and bond markets. Second, when several members of Congress took a hammer and smashed a Toshiba radio in full view of the media, demonstrating their indignation at illegal Toshiba sales of high-technology products to the Soviet Union, the Japanese became fearful of rising protectionist sentiment in the United States and pulled out even more of their money. And when, finally the US trade deficit climbed to ever higher levels during 1987, the Japanese began to regard the Americans as spendthrifts who were no longer a very good credit risk. In early October, the Japanese refused to purchase their usual large chunk of US Treasury bonds. As a result, US interest rates soared, and this provided the catalyst for the October stock market catastrophe.

On October 19, 1987, the US economy, metaphorically speaking, had a heart attack. When one suffers a heart attack, one is forced to change one's life-style, and observe strict diet and exercise rules, because the alternative is very unattractive indeed. Americans, however, did not change their life-styles very significantly. By the late 1980s, they still spent too much, although their trade deficit had begun to decline a little. The Japanese, on the other side of the Pacific, had to make a few concessions to appease a US Congress which had finally become aroused. The Japanese permitted US imports of beef and citrus, but they continued to flood the US markets with their manufactured goods, investing much of their profits in US real estate and business enterprises. But by now, many Americans were deeply angry. Japan's challenge now was plain: to cease waging economic warfare from behind its island walls and to join the rest of the world.

Perhaps in its simplest form, the essence of the Japanese-American economic power struggle is the following: The Americans have enormous creativity but lack discipline. After all, they did invent the computer and the airplane. But Americans became complacent in victory after World War II. By the 1980s, they were importing Japanese managers to teach them what MacArthur had taught the Japanese almost half a century before: discipline and productivity. Japan's strengths and weaknesses were exactly the reverse of those of the United States. They were a little short on creativity, often imitating the US technology, but they then improved it through hard work and relentless discipline.

That nation which combines creativity and discipline into a single economic engine is probably destined to conquer the enormous markets that are now virtually on the auction bloc between Japan and the United States: China, the Pacific Rim, much of the developing world in the Middle East, Africa, and Latin America, and possibly even some of the Communist countries.

Destiny has assumed a strange and somewhat paradoxical form in Japanese-American relations. Japan, the pupil, learned her lessons all too well from her teacher, the United States. The teacher, for her part, forgot some of her lessons and had to relearn them from her former pupil. The challenge for the 1990s is clear for both Japan and the United States: Military allies cannot conduct economic warfare and remain allies. They must learn to relate to one another as equals on a level playing field. In that sense, neither has to be a winner or a loser. Both can share the privilege of being industrial power number one.

THE WEST VERSUS OPEC

At the beginning of the 1970s, the United States and the industrialized world including Japan clearly controlled the international economy. For practical purposes, the global economy was the economy of the Western world. The West did not depend on the economic behavior of other nations in any significant way and largely controlled what it needed.

In 1973, all this changed dramatically. A relatively small group of oil-producing countries suddenly assumed tremendous power through cartel pricing of oil. In effect these countries levied a huge tax on the economies of the world's oil-importing countries.

During the 1970s the world's oil-producing countries took over complete control of the oil industry in their countries. They coordinated their policies through the Organization of Petroleum Exporting Countries (OPEC). This organization consists of six Middle Eastern countries with relatively sparse populations—Saudi Arabia, Kuwait, Iraq, Libya, Qatar, the United Arab Emirates—and seven countries with large populations and large development needs—Iran, Algeria, Ecuador, Gabon, Nigeria, Venezuela, and Indonesia. Between 1970 and 1974, the OPEC cartel achieved increases in oil prices that raised the income of the Middle East producing countries from $4 billion in 1970 to $60 billion in 1974. The oil revenues of all the OPEC countries reached $100 billion in 1974. Allowing for their own foreign exchange requirements, the OPEC producing countries enjoyed surplus revenues of $60 billion in 1974.[1]

The Arab oil embargo against the West, which was decided upon in late 1973, thus became a major threat to the industrialized but oil-poor nations of Western Europe and Japan, all of which imported most of their oil from the Middle East. Even the United States, which imported only 10 percent of its energy requirements from the Arab world, found the embargo irritating enough to modify its Middle Eastern policy from a pro-Israel to more "even-handed" posture. The control of the producing countries over the international oil companies had become so complete that US- and Dutch-owned oil companies had no choice in 1973 but to become the instruments for carrying out the embargo policy on oil shipments to their own home countries. Faced with a major "supply shock" in October 1973, the immediate reaction of practically every importing country was to engage in a competitive scramble for oil supplies,

coupled with offers to adapt its Middle East policy to Arab demands and promises of all kinds of inducements. Arab foreign petroleum ministers skillfully
manipulated individual importing countries through the device of handing out
oil rewards and punishments.

The oil embargo was followed by a quadrupling of oil prices. These price
rises were of such magnitude that practically every importing nation was suddenly confronted with major balance-of-trade problems of immediate and continuing effect. The cost of foreign oil supplies for all importing nations exceeded $100 billion in 1974, compared with $20 billion in 1972. For the
developing countries alone, foreign oil costs jumped from $5 billion in 1973 to
$15 billion in 1974. This $10 billion increase exceeded all the foreign aid that
these countries had received in 1973. Meanwhile, as noted above, during 1974
alone the OPEC countries accumulated surplus holdings of some $60 billion:
nearly two-thirds of the total US private foreign investments. Clearly, a massive transfer of wealth from oil-consuming to oil-producing nations had taken
place.

In 1979 the Iranian revolution dealt a second "oil supply shock" to the
Western world. Supplies from the nation that had been OPEC's second-largest
exporter next to Saudi Arabia plunged, and prices tripled once again, to over
$30 a barrel. In 1980 the war between Iraq and Iran reduced supplies even fur-
ther and drove the price of oil to over $40 a barrel in the spot market. When
one considers that, during the 1960s, the price of oil had held at $2 a barrel,
this twentyfold increase in a decade was nothing less than shattering.

The OPEC countries did not feel defensive about the sharp increase in the
price of their product. They maintained that, in the past, cheap oil had been a
major factor in the growth of the industrialized countries. In that sense, the
developed countries achieved their present status as a result of a parasitical
relationship to the oil-producing countries. Moreover, in the opinion of the
OPEC nations, oil prices simply caught up with the inflationary prices that the
industrialized countries demanded for their technology and commodity products. When considered in that light, oil prices had been depressed for far too
long. "Coca Cola cost a nickel not too long ago," a Saudi prince commented
recently. "Now it costs fifty cents, but I don't hear anyone complaining. Why
is everyone complaining about oil prices? Oil is all we've got to sell."[2]

By the 1970s a situation without historical precedent had arisen: A handful
of countries which had little but oil managed to hold hostage most of the military and political power wielders of the modern world. Countries with almost
none of the traditional elements that made up national power found themselves
able to influence the policies of nations with the most formidable military arsenals.

By the mid-1970s, the Western industrial democracies and Japan recognized
the gradual but relentless shift of wealth and industry to those parts of the
world that had once been their colonies. The most immediate manifestation of
that shift was the disastrous combination of inflation and economic stagnation
that began to gnaw at the economies of the Western nations. Growth slowed in

all these countries while unemployment rose. As late as 1977, most observers still believed that the Western world could blast itself back into the 1960s through the "locomotive recovery theory." The United States, Germany, and Japan, it was hoped, would pull the West out of its recession by expanding their economies more quickly. The plan, however, did not work. The oil price rises proved to be too much for even these powerful economies. "Stagflation" buried Western hopes for quick recovery. By 1980 Western leaders were gloomy in their forecasts. Chancellor Helmut Schmidt of West Germany warned that his nation's "economic miracle" was not invulnerable to the recessionary forces loose in the world. France's prime minister, Raymond Barre, predicted that the West would have to brace itself for yet another decade of sluggish growth and high unemployment while it adapted to the "new realities" of international economic life. And former British Chancellor of the Exchequer Denis Healey declared that "all the evidence indicate[d] that for the foreseeable future, the average growth of output in the free world [was] not going to recover to the level which we enjoyed during those golden days from 1951 to 1973."[3] Rising oil prices, unemployment, and inflation had robbed the Western economies of the resilience and dynamism that they exhibited in earlier years.

In the meantime, the OPEC countries discovered that they had found almost unimaginable wealth, but they could find no safe haven to invest it in. The Third World was too unstable, and the Western economies were ailing. Hence, OPEC surpluses were piling up on an increasingly shaky pyramid of credit that seemed more of a threat than an aid to global recovery. This had been foreseen by Juan Pablo Perez Alfonso, OPEC's founder. "A wave of money can destroy as well as create," the Venezuelan had warned in 1973. By 1980 this warning seemed prophetic.

Thus, three oil shocks—all triggered by geopolitical events in the Persian Gulf region—had created the most massive transfer of wealth in the history of the world. But then—yet again—the struggle between OPEC and the West changed complexion.

By the mid-1980s, oil prices had dropped below $30 a barrel, and it was OPEC's turn to be in difficulties. In the first place, a determined conservation campaign all over the Western world had begun to bear fruit. Small cars were popular, alternate fuel sources were being explored, and speed limits were lowered. Second, new oil and gas discoveries were made in non-OPEC countries, such as Britain and Mexico. Third, several OPEC countries, in particular Ecuador, Nigeria, Indonesia, and Venezuela, had spent themselves into debt and, in their eagerness to increase their share of the oil market, were shaving their prices. Fourth, oil production in the non-OPEC countries—the United States, Britain, the Soviet Union, Mexico, and Canada—exceeded that of OPEC. Finally, in 1984, the first cracks appeared in OPEC's price structure when Nigeria and Algeria lowered their prices for oil. Stated bluntly, OPEC had ceased to be an effective cartel, and even the expansion of the Iran-Iraq war into the shipping lanes of the Persian Gulf resulted in only a modest temporary rise in prices. It appeared that, although the 1970s had been the decade of OPEC, the West's relative determination and OPEC's internal disunity put an end to the cartel's dominance by the 1980s. Once again, the industrial economies assumed the lead.

By 1986, the shoe was clearly on the other foot. Persistent cheating on production quotas by virtually all OPEC members finally triggered a price war. The crisis came when Saudi Arabia suddenly abandoned her traditional role of swing producer and joined the scramble for market share. As everyone in OPEC turned the oil faucet full blast, shortages quickly turned into gluts, and the oil price plummeted to $10 a barrel. To the horror of the oil-producing countries and the delight of consumers, the price of oil was cut to one-quarter of its former value. It seemed that OPEC had virtually disappeared as an economic force to be reckoned with.

For the remainder of the decade, OPEC fought an uphill battle to regain control. In this effort, the cartel was only partially successful. A concerted effort to police cheating on production quotas and to peg the oil price at $18 a barrel worked for a few months, but in 1988 cheating resumed, and prices drifted downward once again toward the $15 mark. OPEC still existed, but only as a shadow of its former self. Hubris had been the instrument of its undoing. No tree grows into heaven, and what went up too far too fast was bound to come down hard. By decade's end, market forces had restored a rough equilibrium between OPEC and the West.

THE RICH-POOR ECONOMIC CONFRONTATION: FOOD, PEOPLE, AND MONEY

If the impact of oil prices on the Western world was dramatic, it was devastating on the poorer nations of the earth. In 1976, for example, when OPEC quadrupled oil prices, the increase in the oil bill for the developing countries more than canceled out the foreign aid they were receiving. It was estimated that at least $3 billion in extra concessional aid would have to be granted to these countries to avoid economic disaster. By 1981 it was estimated that the nations of the Third World had accumulated a total debt of $500 billion.[4] Since such sums could not be repaid, a "Fourth World" emerged from the Third. Its members were those that lacked resources or economic power. Bangladesh, for example, had neither food nor oil but did have a rapidly growing population. Such nations were more dependent and more desperate than any other large segment of the world's population in history. They faced not only an oil cartel but a food cartel as well, and they had no resources to pay for either. To them, hopeless poverty in a world that had the means to stop it had become intolerable.

Oil was not the only world product that was the object of a fierce power struggle during the 1970s. Food loomed equally large as an object of competition. Here the United States has been in a commanding position. The United States has controlled a larger share of the world's exportable food than the Arab countries' share of oil. The world of the 1970s and 1980s depended on US agriculture for its well-being. However, the surge in world food demand and huge Soviet grain purchases directly affected food prices in the United States. Drought in the United States and Canada and crop failures in the Soviet Union and India forced foreign buyers to compete directly with US bakers, cattle ranchers, and other food processors for increasingly more expensive products. The relationship of much of the world to the United States in food terms began to resemble the relationship of much of the world to the OPEC countries in energy terms.

The more than a hundred nations that gathered in Rome in November 1974 for the first World Food Conference in history tended to regard the global food situation not merely as an acute crisis but as the beginning of a chronic global condition that called for unprecedented cooperative measures. Famines in India, Bangladesh, and several sub-Saharan African countries had claimed hundreds of thousands of lives. World food reserves were the lowest in a twenty-year period that saw world population grow by one billion. The rampant inflation of food prices everywhere threatened the livelihood of millions of people who literally could no longer afford to eat. Economic disasters tended to have far-reaching political repercussions. The experience of flood in Pakistan in 1970, for example, had contributed directly to the secession of Bangladesh in 1971.

The United States recognized the long-term need to increase the world's food supply through helping to stimulate improved farming techniques in the poor countries and, in desperate short-term cases, to supply food relief on a humanitarian basis. The severe inflation in food prices in the United States itself, however, made it difficult to meet these needs. The peoples of the rich, industrialized countries became increasingly reluctant to make sacrifices for the benefit of starving Asians and Africans when their own high living standards were threatened by rapidly rising prices. Economic interdependence had not yet become enough of a "gut reality" for the rich countries to justify that kind of sacrifice.

Two points emerged with great clarity from the world food crisis of the mid-1970s: first, the need for a global food reserve bank to be drawn upon in bad years. This idea is as old as the biblical Joseph's granary, but there was considerable disagreement over whether such a world granary should be under national or international controls. Second, there was almost universal recognition of the need to increase the world's agricultural production. On the techniques and methods of achieving this goal, however, sharp differences continued to persist. The point had not yet been reached where famine, wherever it took place, was seen as the enemy of humanity. When asked when a man should eat, the Cynic Diogenes said 2,500 years ago: "A rich man when he will, a poor man when he can." In general, this melancholy answer is still valid in today's world.

The 1980s did not bring much improvement. The Western nations, plagued first by recession and later by droughts, became more penurious in their foreign aid policies. When a horrendous famine struck Ethiopia and tens of thousands of children died there like flies, the industrial world was slow to respond. Finally, a rock concert organized in London in 1985 raised $70 million for the starving Africans. Yet, by and large, the world's rich were still getting richer, and the poor were still getting poorer.

The rich-poor global economic confrontation became even more acute by a dramatic rise in world population. The tragedy has been that the resource-poor developing nations have been precisely those with the sharpest rises in their birth rates. The birth rate itself has become a fairly dependable way of distinguishing developing from developed countries. There are few exceptions to the rule of thumb that developing countries have birth rates above thirty per thousand while developed countries have birth rates well below thirty per thousand. It is estimated that the planet's population of 5 billion in the late 1980s will grow to more than 8 billion by the year 2000. The largest growths will take place in those countries least able to afford them.

In the light of the above projections, few responsible politicians would argue for unlimited population growth. Most agree that in the long run, the necessity for zero population growth will be seen as a truism rather than a slogan, since the alternative of unending population growth in a world of scarce and finite resources is patently absurd. Obviously, the combination of dwindling resources and rising populations presents a mortal danger to the planet.

There are sharp differences, however, over the process by which population growth will decline and eventually cease and the need for efforts directed specifically toward this end. The debate is essentially one of international politics, crosscut by ethical principles and religious and ideological doctrines. The main differences, however, fall fairly neatly across the great divide between the rich and the poor countries of the world.

In general, the rich industrialized countries incline toward the need for special population programs and policies. They maintain that unrestrained population growth is the principal cause of poverty, malnutrition, and environmental disruption. They also tend to believe that it is a fundamental human right for each person to determine the size of his or her family, including the right to contraception and abortion. Finally, the developed countries are inclined to believe that too rapid population growth seriously intensifies other social and economic problems and thus tends to disrupt society.

However, many of the poor countries regard the motives of rich countries which are pushing them to adopt aggressive population programs with suspicion. These rich countries went through a period of rapid population growth as a component of their own development processes, and their current efforts to restrain population growth in the developing countries are perceived as an attempt to maintain the status quo by retarding the development of these countries—in short, a form of racial imperialism. Many of the poorer countries also adopt a religious doctrinal position that population is not a serious problem. Be faithful and multiply, they say. God will provide. Moreover, the world has already shown that Malthus's predictions were incorrect as were the neo-Malthusian predictions and solutions.

Not all nations fit neatly into these two general categories, of course. China, for example, practices population control, and India, though poor, has embarked on a systematic population control program. On the whole, however, the general pattern that emerges is a melancholy one: The world's rich nations are approaching zero population growth while the poor are still multiplying with headlong speed.

A survey of food, people, and money in our time thus shows us a world torn between rich and poor, producers and consumers, a world of rising costs and dwindling supplies, of growing populations and declining production. The economic struggle for power may degenerate into global chaos unless a balance is struck among the three major types of states in today's world: the oil-producing states, which seek a high return for their diminishing resources; the developed nations, which find the industrial civilization they have built up over centuries in jeopardy; and the developing nations, which face the disintegration of their striving for development as a result of price policies over which they have no control.[5]

Perhaps the most widely publicized plan for bridging the gap between the world's rich and poor has been the project known as the New International Economic Order. In 1974 Algeria convened a special session of the UN General Assembly to explore various ways of transferring wealth from the rich to the poor. At first, the industrialized countries complained bitterly, but gradually, over the years, a North-South confrontation gave way to a North-South dialogue. Innumerable proposals were advanced by the Third World majority in the United Nations. Their essence was always the same: The world's poor wanted one-quarter of the world's goods and resources by the year 2000. By the 1980s the poor had turned the United Nations into a kind of collective bargaining agent through which they demanded their seat at the world's table. The New International Economic Order had become their vehicle.

By the 1980s the poor demanded three concessions from the rich: doubling the rate of foreign aid; legalizing cartels to push up the prices of raw materials produced by developing countries; and lowering trade barriers against finished products sold by the poorer nations. The rich, in turn, resisted the demand that the UN General Assembly—dominated by Third World countries—be authorized to deal with these critical matters. The developed nations insisted that Western-controlled bodies such as the International Monetary Fund (IMF) and the General Agreement on Tariffs and Trade (GATT) be entrusted with crucial decisions. The rich, in short, were fearful of being soaked by the poor. And the poor became bitter as they contemplated a world that was two-thirds hungry and one-third on reducing diets.

But remember that the poor are not entirely without economic power. Southern Africa, for example, by the 1980s, had become the "Persian Gulf of minerals." The region contained 52 percent of the world's reserves of manganese, 52 percent of cobalt, and 95 percent of chromium. Manganese is indispensable to steel production. A single mine in Zaire provides the bulk of the United States' and Western Europe's cobalt, a necessary element in jet aircraft production. And without chromium, available in Zimbabwe, Western industries could not make cars, computer components, airplanes, stainless steel, and hospital equipment. Hence, the Third World's grip on certain vital resources can be ignored by the West only at its own peril.

Solutions for these economic confrontations will not be easy to find. Logic and reason may founder on the rocks of selfishness and fear. It is both logical and reasonable that the "old rich" of the developed world should join hands with the "new rich" of the OPEC countries in order to grant concessional food and oil supplies to the poor nations of the Fourth World. It is quite another thing for "have" nations to act in such a manner toward "have-not" nations. It is one thing to talk about the need for a general restructuring of rich-poor economic relations for the purpose of creating a more just and workable global economic order. It is quite another to translate the rhetoric into a concrete act of policy through a "survival pact" between the world's rich and poor. Both producers and consumers have legitimate claims and will have to seek to reconcile them for the common good. But for real progress to be made, economic breakthroughs will not be enough. The poor will need patience and fortitude and the rich will have to make spiritual and moral breakthroughs in order to develop the compassion and the empathy that will move us closer to the family of humans.

THE DEBT BOMB

The confrontation between the world's rich and poor has reached its most explosive form in the so-called debt bomb. Never have so many nations owed so much money with so little promise of repayment. By the late 1980s, about thirty developing countries all over the Third World owed the colossal sum of $700 billion to a group of Western banks, governments, and international institutions. Half of this sum was owed by Latin American countries. Of these, Brazil and Mexico were in debt for more than $100 billion each, and Argentina owed $50 billion. A major default by one of the debtors could trigger a financial crisis of catastrophic proportions. The risks, according to former US Federal Reserve Chairman Paul Volcker, were "without precedent in the post-war world." The global economy was sitting on a debt bomb. How did this situation come about?

The origins of the debt crisis date back to the first OPEC "oil shock" in 1973. Suddenly, the oil-rich nations began to earn billions of dollars. However, poor nations that had no oil found themselves hard pressed to pay for much higher energy costs. The answer to the problem for both rich and poor lay in a magic new concept: recycling. The oil-rich nations deposited most of their excess wealth in the world's major banks; these, in turn, lent the "petrodollars" to the developing countries that needed to buy oil or were eager to modernize their economies. This new business became a bonanza for many banks. A bank arranging a loan deal normally received a service fee of one-eighth of 1 percent. On a $1 billion loan, this produced an instant profit of $1.25 million. Not surprisingly, the competition was keen, and between 1973 and 1982 more than sixty banks entered the international lending business each year. There was not much concern about repayment terms. The fact that Mexico sat on oceans of oil or Zaire on mountains of copper was thought to be collateral enough. And if one bank did not compete for the business, another would. Finally, life was glamorous. Meetings were held in beautiful resorts in exotic locations. It was an easier and far more exciting way to make money than to negotiate a loan with some coal concern in Pittsburgh.

Borrowing countries snapped up the petrodollar loans with enthusiasm. Most were assured that their economies would grow faster than oil prices. Besides, since international loans were mainly in dollars, and inflation in the United States was rising during the 1970s, borrowers believed that they could repay loans taken today with cheaper dollars tomorrow. Thus, going into debt seemed a painless alternative to prudence and belt-tightening. Yet, the day of reckoning was on the horizon.

During the first years of the Reagan administration, inflation declined and the dollar strengthened vis-à-vis other currencies. No longer could loans be paid off with less expensive dollars. Now the contrary was true. Even more important, rising oil prices had triggered a global recession that depressed commodity prices on which the borrowing countries depended. Sugar, cotton, coffee, and copper fell to new lows. Tanzania's President Julius Nyerere put it plainly: to buy a 7-ton truck in 1981, his country had to produce four times as much cotton, or three times as much coffee, or ten times as much tobacco as it took to purchase the same vehicle five years earlier.[6] Thus, the developing countries found themselves in a classic squeeze: Rising debt costs were eating up ever larger chunks of declining export earnings. In most borrowing countries, interest payments that did not even reduce the principal devoured more than half of export earnings. In some cases, particularly in Latin America, debt service payments exceeded all export revenues. A massive almost perverse redistribution of income from the poor to the rich was taking place. Obviously, a crunch was in the making.

The first SOS was sent out by Mexico in 1982. With oil prices declining, that nation requested a postponement of interest payments. Since banks regarded the payment of interest as the main criterion of a "performing loan," this request, in the words of J. P. Morgan Guaranty's chair, was "like an atom bomb dropped on the world financial system."[7] Thirteen leading US, Japanese, British, and West German bankers worked around the clock for two weeks in a kind of money-raising telethon to put together a rescue package. Why did the bankers work so desperately to help out Mexico? Because if Mexico defaulted, some of the lending banks might have gone broke. Thus, for the first time in history, international bankers had to face a cruel paradox: If they made a small loan to a borrower, they owned a piece of the borrower, but if they made a huge loan and the borrower threatened to default, it was the borrower who owned the bank. Hence, the banks, in desperation, had to violate Gresham's Law and throw good money after bad in order to prevent borrowers' defaults and, ultimately, their own.

Mexico's fate was soon shared by Brazil, Argentina, and a dozen other developing countries. The International Monetary Fund (IMF) soon had to participate in almost monthly rescue operations. The IMF was a currency pool supported by over 140 countries. Its purpose was to provide loans to countries in trouble. It was never, however, designed for the crises which it was now called upon to resolve. Besides, it followed fairly conservative fiscal practices and usually exacted strict austerity measures as a condition for its help. Among these were import restrictions and wage controls that did not endear it to the borrowing countries. IMF help usually presented the debtor country with a stark dilemma: If it chose to default, it would be ostracized by the world capital markets; if it accepted IMF terms and practiced austerity, the result might be depression and riots in the streets. As one observer put it: "If the IMF route might leave a Latin American dictator swinging from a tree branch, he may decide to go the default route."[8]

By the late 1980s, no easy solutions were in sight. Some of the creditor banks, with Citicorp in the lead, decided to write down a portion of their Latin American loans as bad debts. Others resorted to similar devices. Yet, huge amounts of indebtedness remained which might never be repaid. What seemed certain was that in the not too distant future the lending institutions would have to take a beating by either writing off some of the loans completely or sharply reducing interest rates or both. Many bankers looked to the US Federal Reserve for help in case of a default. Few bankers, however, understood that this "debt bomb" was much more than just another financial crisis. The Third World bought more than a third of US exports. Lost exports to Latin America alone cost some 340,000 US jobs.[9] Third World markets cannot revive unless their economies get some relief from crushing debt service burdens. Ultimately, what was at stake was the fate of millions of poor people in the Third World who, unless the rich practiced unprecedented wisdom and generosity, were faced with disaster or revolution.

As if to underline this interdependence between the world's rich and poor, two problems surfaced in the late 1980s that could be attacked only through a globally unified approach: the gradual depletion of the world's ozone layer and the growing threat of the contamination of the oceans through reckless disposal of hazardous wastes.

As usual, it took a crisis to focus people's attention. The drought and heat waves of the late 1980s in the United States and Canada attracted the attention of meteorologists, some of whom advanced the theory that the "greenhouse effect" was here at last: a gradual warming of the world's climate and depletion of its protective ozone layer. The villain was identified as decades of pollution heedlessly emitted into the atmosphere. In addition, reports surfaced in 1988 that coastal waters in many parts of the industrial world had become unsafe for swimming and fish unsafe for eating. Decades of mindless waste disposal had finally taken its toll on the sea. For far too long people had used the sea as a garbage dump. Now it was taking its revenge.

Perhaps today, the danger of death by atomic fire has receded. But now the destruction of our air and water looms on the horizon. This is the stuff of life itself.

THE FUTURE OF THE ECONOMIC POWER STRUGGLE

As we move into the final decade of the twentieth century, the nature of the economic power struggle will no doubt become more and more global. Interdependence is no longer an abstraction or a slogan but has become an economic reality. The crucial distinction will no longer be between capitalists or Communists, blacks or whites, rich or poor, but between those who perceive the world as an arena for competition among self-contained economic entities and those who perceive it as a "global village," as planet earth, which will survive as one or not at all. No nation can deal with survival alone. In that sense, we must defend Spaceship Earth as a whole, precious and indivisible. Perhaps it was no accident that the first astronauts, when they glimpsed the earth from outer space, floating through infinity, beautiful and vulnerable, read passages from Genesis. They suddenly remembered that national boundaries and sovereignties were put on earth by humans, not by the Creator.

One thoughtful student of the international economy conjured up a vision which he described as "The Ghost of the World Future." The vision is nightmarish, but could become the reality of the coming generations unless our growing global interdependence will lift up the nations of the world instead of dragging them down together:

> I awoke at about 2 A.M. this morning and saw a thin, emaciated-looking man standing in front of my bed. "Who are you?" I asked.
>
> "I am the ghost of the world future," he answered. And with that he grabbed me with a bony hand and took me on a voyage through time and space. We came somehow to a dwelling where two old people, a man and a woman, were sitting at a table.
>
> "Who are these people?" I asked.
>
> "They are your children," said the spirit.
>
> "But they are old and bent and their hair is gray," I said.
>
> "Of course. This is the year 2030," said the spirit.
>
> "Why are my children all alone?" I asked. "Didn't they marry, don't they have children?"
>
> "I'm sorry to tell you that your daughter's husband and your son's wife died in a terrorist raid on the city many years ago."
>
> "But surely their children had children—surely there must be grandchildren to comfort them in their old age?"
>
> "There are no grandchildren. When world population passed 12 billion in the year 2020, all but a relatively few privileged couples were sterilized."
>
> "Why are they nibbling those strange pills at the table?" I asked.
>
> "That's their dinner. You can't expect them to eat bread, now that it's selling for $300 a loaf." At that point an entire wall of the room suddenly lit up and the image of a man appeared about ten-feet high in living color.

"What's that?" I asked.

"It's time for the evening television news," the spirit answered. "You see, the one thing that people still have is television. It's bigger and better than ever, and it takes their minds off their problems."

"Spirit," I said, "I can stand no more. You must tell me something: Is this a vision of what must be, or is it only a vision of what might be if mankind doesn't change its ways?"[10]

This future must not be. In the second half of this book we shall examine humanity's efforts to avert such a future in its struggle toward international order.

REFERENCES

1 Walter J. Levy, "World Oil Cooperation or International Chaos," *Foreign Affairs,* July 1974, p. 696.
2 Conversation with the author at the United Nations, December 1980.
3 *The New York Times,* January 8, 1981.
4 Trilateral Commission, *A Turning Point in North-South Economic Relations.* New York, 1974, p. 9.
5 Address delivered by Secretary of State Henry A. Kissinger before the 29th UN General Assembly, September 23, 1974. Press Release USUN-118(74), September 23, 1974, pp. 8–9.
6 "The Debt Bomb," *Time,* January 10, 1983, p. 46.
7 *Ibid.,* p. 48.
8 Stuart Greenbaum, professor of banking and finance, Northwestern University, quoted in *ibid.,* p. 50.
9 *The New York Times,* December 22, 1988.
10 Richard N. Gardner, "The Ghost of the World Future," *The Inter Dependent,* October 1974, p. 6. Reprinted by permission of *The Inter Dependent,* ©1974, United Nations Association of the U.S.A.

SELECTED BIBLIOGRAPHY

Aho, Michael C. and Marc Levinson. *After Reagan: Confronting the Changed World Economy.* New York: Council on Foreign Relations, 1988. An excellent exposition of the main economic issues confronting the Bush administration: the deficits, trade, agriculture, and Third World debt.
Berliner, Joseph S. *Soviet Industry from Stalin to Gorbachev.* Ithaca, N.Y.: Cornell University Press, 1988. Illuminating on the intractable difficulties Gorbachev faces on his economic reform program.
Bhagwati, Jagdish. *Protectionism.* Cambridge: MIT Press, 1988. An authoritative statement in favor of reducing trade barriers throughout the Western world.
Frost, Ellen L. *For Richer, For Poorer.* New York: Council on Foreign Relations, 1987. An excellent analysis of why Japan is getting richer and the United States is getting poorer.
Kuczynski, Pedro-Pablo. *Latin American Debt.* Baltimore: Johns Hopkins, 1988. The author, a former official of the World Bank, offers an objective history of the debt problem as well as some thoughtful prescriptions for possible solutions. A first-rate book with insight and depth.

Reischauer, Edwin O. *The Japanese Today*. Cambridge: Harvard University Press, 1988. A new, expanded edition of the classic work by the former US ambassador to Japan.

Tyson, Laura, ed. *The Dynamics of Trade and Employment*. Cambridge: Ballinger, 1988. The authors offer useful case studies on automobiles, apparel, semiconductors, and telecommunications equipment. A well balanced work.

THREE

THE INTERNATIONAL STRUGGLE FOR ORDER

CHAPTER 8

DIPLOMACY AND POLITICAL ORDER

Diplomacy is the art of avoiding the appearance of victory.

Metternich

THE NATURE OF DIPLOMACY

Diplomacy may be defined as the conduct of international relations by negotiation. It is a process through which nations attempt to realize their national
interests. It is, of course, not always an instrument of political order. Its object
at times may be the intensification of a struggle between nations, or it may be
a neutral tool that regards order as irrelevant to the pursuit of the national interest. But more often than not, diplomacy is an important instrument of political order, for the very process of negotiation implies that nations settle their
differences through peaceful change within the framework of a given system
rather than by resorting to the overthrow of the system through violence.
When a nation has decided in favor of war, the instrument of diplomacy becomes superfluous. But so long as the national interest dictates the avoidance
of war, diplomacy works on behalf of peace. And since most nations feel most
of the time that their policies may be realized by means short of war, diplomacy has been, and remains, a major highway to political order.

Diplomacy antedates the nation-state system by almost two thousand years.
The city-states of ancient Greece had developed diplomatic intercourse to a
high level. On reading Thucydides' *Peloponnesian War,* one is struck by the
profound insights that the ancients had gained into the subtle arts of negotia-

tion. If the Greeks made a major contribution to the essence of diplomacy—the accommodation of conflicting interests—the Romans' contribution was the equally important one of investing the practice of diplomacy with legal authority. The reemergence of the city-state system in Italy during the Renaissance was once more accompanied by a great burgeoning in the arts of diplomacy. Machiavelli's *The Prince* was the most famous of many contemporary discourses on the subject. The coming of the nation-state system in the seventeenth century ushered in an age of even greater diplomatic activity. This era of the so-called old diplomacy dominated the scene until World War I. When we contemplate the quaint practices that prevailed during these three hundred years—boudoir intrigues, powdered wigs, and "waltzing congresses"—we are tempted to smile indulgently. But before we decide that this period is of only historical and archaeological interest, we would do well to remember that the "waltzing Congress of Vienna" of 1815 ushered in a century in which there occurred not a single major world war. The diplomatic dramas in which Metternich, Castlereagh, and Talleyrand were the major actors are well worth rereading.[1] Hence, before we turn to an analysis of the more modern techniques of negotiation, we shall evaluate the traditional methods of diplomacy.

Hans Morgenthau has defined the task of diplomacy as a fourfold one:

> Diplomacy must determine its objectives in the light of the power actually and potentially available for the pursuit of these objectives. Diplomacy must assess the objectives of other nations and the power actually and potentially available for the pursuit of these objectives. Diplomacy must determine to what extent these different objectives are compatible with each other. Diplomacy must employ the means suited to the pursuit of its objectives. Failure in any one of these tasks may jeopardize the success of foreign policy and with it the peace of the world.[2]

Eighteenth- and nineteenth-century diplomacy seems to have fulfilled these conditions rather well. Few nations set themselves goals that were not commensurate with their power. Only rarely did nations make gross errors in assessing the power or the objectives of others. Underrating or overrating the power of the antagonist was the exception, not the rule. Nations constantly compared their own goals with those of others and weighed their compatibility. Since the national substance of a nation was rarely if ever threatened, it was generally possible to compromise on most outstanding issues. Sometimes nations resorted to a threat of force. But most of the time, traditional diplomacy was characterized by a spirit of compromise. The hallmark of the old diplomacy was the rule of *quid pro quo*.

The greatest success of traditional diplomacy was, as we have mentioned, the Congress of Vienna of 1815. At Vienna, the diplomats of Austria, Prussia, Britain, Russia, and France managed to negotiate their differences and as a result ushered in one of the longest periods of peace in Western history. How was this feat accomplished? In the first place, the fundamental structure of the international system was accepted by the negotiating powers as "legitimate." No nation at Vienna threatened the existence of the others with aspirations to world conquest. Nor did the congress have to cope with the presence of any revolutionary power whose ideology dictated the absorption of the others. Each of the participants advanced limited objectives and expressed them in terms of limited territorial claims and counterclaims. This happy state of affairs provided the second condition of success, namely, that each nation found itself in a relationship of reasonable satisfaction and security vis-à-vis the others. This point has been well stated by Henry A. Kissinger in his analysis of the Vienna Congress:

> Since absolute security for one power means absolute insecurity for all others, it is obtainable only through conquest, never as part of a legitimate settlement. An international settlement which is accepted and not imposed will therefore always appear *somewhat* unjust to any one of its components. Paradoxically, the generality of this dissatisfaction is a condition of stability, because were any one power *totally* satisfied, all others would have to be *totally* dissatisfied and a revolutionary situation would ensue. The foundation of a stable order is a *relative* security—and therefore the *relative* insecurity—of its members. Its stability reflects, not the absence of unsatisfied claims, but the absence of a grievance of such magnitude that redress will be sought in overturning the settlement rather than through an adjustment within its framework.[3]

The conditions that contributed to the success of the Congress of Vienna do not prevail in the modern world. Yet if we study the Vienna Congress we find that there are important insights to be gained nevertheless. These do not, of course, derive from the *conditions* of the international order in 1815. They apply, rather, to the diplomatic *conduct* by which the diplomats at Vienna pursued their objectives.

All important negotiations at the Congress of Vienna took place in private. Only the ministers and their most trusted subordinates participated in the crucial discussions. Camouflaged by the glitter of nineteenth-century Vienna and the pomp of the Habsburg court, the diplomatic interchanges proceeded strictly behind closed doors. In our own time "secret diplomacy" has become a term of disapprobation. And to be sure, secrecy often led to extreme suspicion even among the diplomats of the earlier period. Thus, when Prince Metternich, the Austrian plenipotentiary, was told that the Russian ambassador in Vienna had died during the negotiations, he was reported to have asked: "Ah, is that true? What may have been his motive?" Yet despite its inevitable drawbacks, this method gave the statesmen of the time a priceless advantage that contemporary diplomats have largely been denied: it enabled them to conduct their negotiations in private, free from the pressures and inhibitions of constant publicity.

The old diplomacy fell into disrepute with the coming of the twentieth century. Liberal optimists who believed that power politics could be banished from the earth through the establishment of a universal League of Nations took a dim view of the old-fashioned secret diplomacy and considered it the symptom of a corrupt and bygone era. The new spirit was expressed most eloquently by Woodrow Wilson in his Fourteen Points: "Open covenants of peace, openly arrived at, after which there will be no private understanding of any kind, but diplomacy shall proceed frankly and in the public view.'' The advocates of the "new diplomacy" urged that not only the results of diplomacy should be made public, but that even the process of negotiation itself ought to be subject to the scrutiny of the people. The implication was that the business of diplomacy was too important to be entrusted to diplomats alone. The principles of democratic government demanded that in matters affecting the vital interests of the nation the public be kept informed and allowed to express itself at every stage of the proceedings. The reason for this, as Wilson and the proponents of open diplomacy saw it, was that the national interest was safer in the hands of the public than it would be if left in the hands of some elite group, no matter how well versed in the arts of negotiation the latter might be.

It is a curious irony that Wilson, the great advocate of open diplomacy, seldom practiced it. His efforts to realize his dream—the creation of the League of Nations—were conducted with considerable secrecy. When he returned from Versailles, he confronted the American people with a *fait accompli*. The Senate's refusal to ratify the treaty incorporating the League of Nations was in some measure attributable to the fact that the senators had not been taken into the President's confidence during the formulation of policy. Wilson wanted the "consent," but not the "advice" of the Senate and the people. In other words, the major architect of "open convenants openly arrived at" was one of the great practitioners of secret diplomacy. Nevertheless, the impact of the new Wilsonian conception was enormous. To a world grown deeply weary of war and the struggle for power, the prospect of a new system of international conduct that, in the words of one caustic observer, would no longer be governed by "men who were sent abroad to lie for their country,"[4] looked desirable indeed.

Yet it soon became evident that if the new diplomatic techniques dispelled some long-standing fears, they also raised some serious problems. There was little disagreement that the *results* of diplomatic negotiations should be disclosed to the people, but many observers began to question the wisdom of exposing the *negotiations* themselves to the searchlight of publicity. It was soon discovered that under such conditions an atmosphere was created that precluded genuine bargaining. It became increasingly difficult, if not impossible, for a diplomat to yield on a point, to give up a claim, or to admit that there was at least a modicum of justice on the other side when he knew that each such action would be condemned by his compatriots as an act of cowardice and as a retreat in the face of the enemy. Thus, more and more frequently, diplomacy fell victim to publicity. Diplomats came to the bargaining table with maximum demands which they defended "on principle." Positions grew brittle, compromise became the exception rather than the rule, and the negotiators tended to address the audience rather than each other. This transformation of diplomacy into an instrument of propaganda was accelerated by the rapid development of the media of communication. A diplomat who was not only exposed to the physical presence of an attentive public but had to cope with a network of television cameras as well was not likely to run the risk of looking like a fool or a knave before millions of people.

Secret diplomacy seldom involved more than a small number of negotiators. The new diplomacy, in contrast, has through the coming of the United Nations and the various regional organizations acquired an even further complicating dimension in that most negotiations must be conducted multilaterally. Once a dispute is brought before the United Nations, for example, it becomes the business of the entire General Assembly. Representatives from more than one hundred fifty nations express themselves on the matter while the entire world watches. Such a state of affairs is hardly conducive to effective bargaining. The issue generally is not resolved through negotiations but through attempts by the leading forces in the General Assembly to obtain a majority vote with which to defeat a recalcitrant minority. It need not be emphasized that this method frequently exacerbates differences among nations instead of composing them.

All these developments have radically changed the nature of both diplomacy and the diplomat. While a plenipotentiary attending the Congress of Vienna had large powers of discretion, the modern diplomat is frequently little more than a messenger who communicates the instructions of his government. Frequently heads of state even short-circuit their emissaries altogether by dealing with each other directly. During World War II, for example, Roosevelt, Churchill, and Stalin by no means relied solely on the talents of their diplomats. In fact, many of their most vital policy decisions were hammered out in telegrams and long transatlantic telephone conversations among themselves. In the 1970s and 1980s, this kind of "back channeling" was even more extensive. Key negotiations with the Soviet Union in the Nixon, Ford, Carter, and Reagan administrations were usually carried out by secretaries of state directly with long-time Soviet ambassador Anatoly Dobrynin. This procedure did not please Malcolm Toon, the United States ambassador to Moscow. And Joseph Sisco, who was twice offered the Moscow embassy by Richard Nixon, turned down the post. "So long as Nixon and Kissinger were around," Sisco said, "they were going to be the Soviet desk officers. And if I decided to go to Moscow, Nixon would have a personnel problem within six weeks." Clearly, a talented diplomat desires to be more than a messenger, travel agent, or innkeeper.

The modern phenomenon that combines both the strengths and weaknesses of the new diplomacy most dramatically is the "summit conference." Geneva in 1985, Reykjavik in 1986, Washington in 1987, and Moscow in 1988 became the capitals of the world while President Reagan and General-Secretary Gorbachev met there to air their differences. The participants found themselves cast in the role of political gladiators, with the rest of humanity as their audience. In Geneva, the two men took each other's measure; in Reykjavik, an audacious Gorbachev almost overwhelmed a poorly prepared Reagan; in Washington, both men walked away as winners with an historic disarmament treaty; and by the time they met for the fourth time in Moscow, they had developed a good working relationship.

The key to a successful summit no doubt is adequate preparation. American diplomats had not prepared President Reagan well for Reykjavik, but, learning from that failure, they had prepared their chief of state thoroughly for the Washington conference in 1987. Numerous working meetings between Secretary of State George Shultz and Soviet Foreign Minister Eduard Shevarnadze had taken place before Reagan and Gorbachev met personally to affix their signatures to the treaty. Hence, to complete our analysis, we must turn from our consideration of diplomacy in general to an examination of the nature of the diplomat.

The best portrait of the modern diplomat is probably that painted by Sir Harold Nicolson in his classic treatise, *Diplomacy*. First among the diplomat's virtues, according to Nicolson, must be truthfulness. By this he means "not merely abstention from conscious misstatements but a scrupulous care to avoid the suggestion of the false or the suppression of the true."[5] The modern diplomat must also possess the quality of intellectual integrity. Ideally, too, he should be good-tempered or, at least, able to keep his temper under complete control at all times. A display of anger, for example, is regarded as a betrayal of weakness. When Napoleon flung his hat upon the carpet in front of Prince Metternich in June 1813, the latter knew that the emperor's strength was ebbing. Next on the list is patience, which Nicolson considers an indispensable quality for the successful negotiator. Modesty is considered important since vanity may tempt the diplomat into imprudence. The negotiator should also bear a special loyalty to his country, a loyalty that will prompt him to tell his government what it ought to know rather than what it wants to hear. And finally, the author reminds us that he has not forgotten the qualities of intelligence, knowledge, discernment, prudence, hospitality, charm, industry, courage, and tact. He has simply taken them for granted.[6]

It is clear from the above that the combination of characteristics required of the diplomat is unusual indeed. Yet even if people who measure up to this high standard can be recruited, the measure of success they may achieve in the job of international order-building remains to the largest degree dependent upon the complex and trying conditions under which they must work.

For example, so long as even one of the negotiators dogmatically adheres to universal aspirations, diplomacy's perennial quest for compromise is bound to continue to be frustrated. When two combatants, each claiming to represent the one true secular religion, meet in the arena, there remains almost no room for accommodation at all. Both tend to invoke the authority of God or the historical process and forget that "they meet under an empty sky from which the gods have departed."[7] Proselytizing should have little room at the bargaining table. Only to the extent that the negotiator can free himself from the onesidedness and biases of his own particular ideology is he able to think and feel himself into the position of other diplomats. Such empathy can contribute a great deal to successful negotiation. For though it in no way implies a yielding of one's own position, it makes possible the placing of questions at issue in as broadly conceived and mutually respecting a framework as possible.

The modern statesman-diplomat in a democracy faces a unique dilemma of responsibility to his nation. From this he cannot escape, whether he engages in secret or in open negotiations. Should his goals simply reflect the will of the people whose servant he is supposed to be? Or does his greater knowledge of the international scene entitle him to lead the people in some new direction if he believes that the common man's judgment is in error? Moreover, how important is domestic support, politically speaking? The experience of Woodrow Wilson and the League of Nations demonstrated that the statesman-diplomat ignores his people at his own peril. But the generation that ratified the United Nations Charter hailed this same man, repudiated only a quarter century before, as a great visionary. The fate of Wilson therefore seems to indicate that the diplomat who would also be a statesman must lead more than follow. Yet since he cannot but act on incomplete knowledge, and so can never "prove" that his vision is correct, this task may be a trying and cruel one. As Henry A. Kissinger has pointed out in his analysis of the Congress of Vienna,

> The statesman is therefore like one of the heroes in classical drama who has had a vision of the future but who cannot transmit it directly to his fellowmen and who cannot validate its "truth." Nations learn only by experience; they "know" only when it is too late to act. But statesmen must act *as if* their intuition were already experience, as if their aspiration were truth. It is for this reason that statesmen often share the fate of prophets, that they are without honour in their own country, that they always have a difficult task in legitimizing their programmes domestically, and that their greatness is usually apparent only in retrospect when their intuition has become experience. The statesman must therefore be an educator; he must bridge the gap between a people's experience and his vision, between a nation's tradition and its future. In this task his possibilities are limited. A statesman who too far outruns the experience of his people will fail in achieving a domestic consensus, however wise his policies; witness Castlereagh. A statesman who limits his policy to the experience of his people will doom himself to sterility; witness Metternich.[8]

Two decades after he wrote *A World Restored*, Henry Kissinger became Secretary of State. In many ways, his unique form of diplomacy was rooted in the intellectual insights of his academic career and represented a remarkable fusion between scholarship and statesmanship. The impact of his diplomacy was so profound that it merits special attention.

Henry Kissinger differs from most American statesmen in the sense that his policies were based on doctrine and deliberate design rather than on the more pragmatic day-to-day approach that has been typical of American diplomacy. This doctrine, which rested on three main pillars, emerged very clearly in *A World Restored*. The reason Kissinger undertook this study was that he was interested in the manner in which the European statesmen of the early nineteenth century secured the peace of Europe for a hundred years. He found three answers to this question. First, to be secure, a peace must be based on a negotiated settlement, with all sides in equilibrium, rather than on a victor's peace. Everybody is a little bit unhappy, but no one is completely unhappy. Thus, no one will try to overthrow the settlement through yet another war, and the relative insecurity of each guarantees the relative security of all. Second, a victorious power, in order to have peace, will not attempt to annihilate the vanquished but will coopt it into the established order by giving it something of its own substance. Thus, the victor decontaminates the defeated of his revolutionary ardor and transforms him subtly from a "have not" into a "have" nation. Third, in the absence of a globally controlled system, the best guarantor of peace is balance and, hence, a balancer is essential. This balancer will seldom ask the question, "Who is right and who is wrong?" but rather, "Who is weak and who is strong?" He will throw his weight on the weaker side whenever an imbalance occurs and by so doing restore the equilibrium and maintain the peace. Hence, peace, to Henry Kissinger, is a bonus of a successful balance policy.

Kissinger's policy, in fact, was a transplantation process of these three concepts into the modern world. The first principle was adopted in the Middle East, where Kissinger's policy supported neither Israel nor the Arabs but was committed to the principles of balance and equilibrium that made possible the disengagement treaties separating Israel from Syria and Egypt. He hoped to achieve a modern peace of Westphalia without victory or defeat. The second principle was applied to the Soviet Union, which received gigantic credits from the United States, and unlike Mr. Khrushchev who in 1959 talked about "burying" capitalism, Mr. Brezhnev began to be engaged in "borrowing" from capitalism. Kissinger's hope was that, subtly and over time, a community of economic interests would be established between the capitalist and communist worlds. The third principle was illustrated by President Nixon's trip to China, which created a triangle between the Soviet Union, China, and America in which Kissinger attempted to place the United States into the role of balancer, where it would be wooed by both China and the Soviet Union.

The weaknesses of the Kissinger diplomacy flowed from the fact that the transplantation had perhaps been too literal. This was, after all, not the early nineteenth century, but the late twentieth, and the world's center of gravity no longer rested in Europe. Kissinger was often accused of paying more attention to the adversaries of the United States than to her friends, and of not being sufficiently sensitive to the aspirations of the small and poor nations of the Third World. More fundamentally, perhaps, he followed the famous dictum of the classical German poet Johann Wolfgang von Goethe, in his essay *Poetry and Truth:* "If I had to choose between justice and disorder, on the one hand, and injustice and order, on the other, I would always choose the latter." In short, he tended to make stability a goal in itself. This, at times, compelled him to sacrifice humanitarian considerations on the altar of a larger strategic vision. During the war between India and Pakistan in 1971, for example, Kissinger "tilted" toward Pakistan and China because these two allies were weaker than the alliance on the other side, India and the Soviet Union. But by choosing Pakistan, he gave that government the green light to persecute and chase into exile ten million Bengalis without arousing any criticism from the United States. Kissinger responded to this critique by stating that the alternative might have been a major Soviet incursion into the Indian subcontinent, which would have been a greater evil. Of the two evils, he thus chose the lesser in an inherently tragic world.

Unlike John Foster Dulles, who divided the world into "good" and "evil" states and tended to judge those in the middle as "immoral," Henry Kissinger perceived the international arena as infinitely more complex. In his view, the statesman could only seldom choose between right and wrong. Most of the time, he had to choose between one right and another right or one wrong and a greater wrong. And there was no escape from choice itself for, as Camus reminded us, "not to choose is also a choice." Nor could one wait until all the facts were in, because, by then, foreign policy had become history.

If the task of the diplomat is difficult, that of the statesman who instructs him is indeed formidable. For the latter, the greatest challenge of all concerns the role of ethics in a world of power. What is the relationship between "personal" and "political" morality? Does diplomacy leave room for morality at all? How should we judge a statesman—by his intentions or by the consequences of his actions? What should be the criterion of success for the statesman-diplomat? In short, what must concern us now is the problem of statesmanship and moral choice.

Diplomacy in the era of Woodrow Wilson looked confidently to the possibility of continuous progress in the relations among nations toward the goal of justice and brotherhood. Most contemporary observers of the new diplomacy were convinced that the inherent rationality and morality of man could not fail to assert themselves in diplomatic intercourse. The growth of democratic institutions would help immeasurably in this process. It was assumed, also, that statesmen would conduct diplomatic relations exclusively on a basis of goodwill and cooperation. In other words, this group of thinkers, whom we shall call the "idealists," deeply believed that it was only a question of time until a congruence would be achieved between personal and political morality. The cataclysm of World War II, however, cast serious doubts on these assumptions. It was no longer at all clear that historical progress toward cooperation among nations was inevitable. Nor was there sufficient evidence for the assertion that human nature was infinitely improvable. As a result, a second group of thinkers emerged who were no less concerned about peace and justice than were the idealists, but who felt that the very nature of the international struggle set unavoidable limits to the moral aspirations of man. These "realists" were convinced that international behavior was governed by its own objective laws, the most important of which was an immutable struggle for power. The idealist who attempted to deal with international relations in terms of morality did so at his own peril. Thus, at one end of the diplomatic spectrum, the Wilsonian idealists hoped to infuse international behavior with high moral standards. At the other end, the realists contended that international relations were neither moral nor immoral. The latter, indeed, defining the relations among nations as predominantly a matter of power, saw considerations of morality as irrelevant.

A careful analysis of the dilemmas of statesmanship indicates that the dichotomy between idealists and realists is too simple. The purely idealist statesman would be a saint, while a purely Machiavellian one would be a beast.[9] Few statesmen, however lofty their purposes, dare to ignore the reality of power, but equally few statesmen, however Machiavellian, venture to ignore the existence of morality. The crucial difference between interpersonal and international relations is not that the former permit moral behavior, whereas the latter do not. It resides, rather, in the fact that personal behavior is usually judged by an ethic of *intention* while that of the statesman is essentially one of *consequence*. Morgenthau cites an interesting example that illustrates this point:

> Neville Chamberlain's policies of appeasement were, as far as we can judge, inspired by good motives; he was probably less motivated by considerations of personal power than were many other British prime ministers, and he sought to preserve peace and to assure the happiness of all concerned. Yet his policies helped to make the Second World War inevitable, and to bring untold miseries to millions of men. Sir Winston Churchill's motives, on the other hand, have been much less universal in scope and much more narrowly directed toward personal and national power, yet the foreign policies that sprang from these inferior motives were certainly superior in moral and political quality to those pursued by his predecessor.[10]

Power and morality are, in fact, inseparable and must be so considered by the diplomat. Perhaps it is helpful to think of the two as two concentric circles, of which power is the larger. Morgenthau, for example, asserted repeatedly that what he regarded as a morally dubious policy of the United States in Vietnam had hurt the United States' power position in other parts of the world. Or to take a hypothetical example, let us suppose that the United States promises Portugal a large loan. It then decides to withdraw the offer, breaking its promise. As a result, Portugal leaves NATO and becomes nonaligned. If this actually occurred, it might be said that the United States lost some of its power because it acted unethically. In some cases, therefore, power may be said to include morality. Of course, Portugal would base its decision on a multiplicity of factors, only one of which would be the US breach of promise. Hence, this generalization, like all others on ethics and power, is subject to exceptions. At times, indeed, morality may be the larger of the two concentric circles.

More generally, the role of ethics in foreign policy has had a dual tradition in US diplomacy. On one side of the spectrum was the *Realpolitik* of a Henry Kissinger, who conceived of peace as the result of equilibrium rather than of justice and who never tired of pointing out that diplomacy, to be successful, had to be based on power and had to risk resort to war. On the other side were the globalism of a Woodrow Wilson, who wanted to make the world "safe for democracy"; the moral crusade of a John Foster Dulles, who divided the world into free and unfree states; and the missionary zeal of a Jimmy Carter, who declared that the abuse of human rights was no longer any single nation's exclusively domestic business.

South Africa provides another example. Jimmy Carter based his policy on ethics, claiming that apartheid was immoral; Ronald Reagan, aware of South Africa's gold, platinum, and uranium resources, thought more in terms of strategy and power. But as we have seen, these two principles have never been applied mutually exclusively in practice. Just as Kissinger and Reagan could not remain indifferent to problems of morality, Wilson and Carter were forced to recognize the reality of power. Neither a beast nor a saint would make an effective architect of a modern foreign policy.

The subtle interdependence between ethics and power compels the statesman to engage in a process of continual balancing. He is forever having to weigh alternatives. And in this enterprise it is very rare for the merits in favor of one course of action to be clearly greater than the arguments for another. As one careful student of diplomacy has pointed out:

> The merits in arguments for and against an acceptable line of action never occur in ratios of 100 to 0 or even of 80 to 20. They tend rather to occur in the order of 55 to 45 or even 51 to 49. Even at best, the arguments against a line of action in foreign policy tend to be almost as weighty as the considerations in favor. Yet these small margins of difference constitute the distinction between success and failure and are all-important.[11]

Almost never is the statesman called upon to decide between a clear-cut right and a clear-cut wrong. Here international relations resemble interpersonal behavior; most decisions must be taken along a continuum of varying shades of gray. But there does remain one crucial difference: the fact that the statesman's decision may affect the lives of millions of his fellow men. The diplomat must act with the tragic knowledge that he or she cannot choose between good and evil but only among varying stages of evil. Indeed, whatever decision is made, *some* evil consequences are bound to result from it. In such a situation, is it not easier to abstain from *any* decision? Yet such "abstention from evil does not at all affect the existence of evil in the world but only destroys the faculty of discriminating between different evils. The perfectionist thus becomes finally a source of greater evil."[12] This tragic condition has been painted in all its starkness by Morgenthau:

> We have no choice between power and the common good. To act successfully, that is according to the rules of the political art, is political wisdom. To know with despair that the political act is inevitably evil, and to act nevertheless, is moral courage. To choose among several expedient actions the least evil one is moral judgment. In the combination of political wisdom, moral courage and moral judgment, man reconciles his political nature with his moral destiny. That this conciliation is nothing more than a modus vivendi, uneasy, precarious, and even paradoxical, can disappoint only those who prefer to gloss over and to distort the tragic contradictions of human existence with the soothing logic of a specious concord.[13]

Morgenthau, in fact, maintains that statesmen, if they are political realists, should maintain the autonomy of the political sphere and merely ask themselves the question of power.[14] This would seem too one-dimensional a view, for as we have seen, most of the time power includes considerations of morality and law.

During the mid-1980s, an event occurred which illuminates all the dilemmas we have discussed so far: open versus secret diplomacy; morality versus *Realpolitik*, and above all, the dilemma of negotiating with terrorists. This event was the Iran-Contra affair, which constitutes the subject of our next case study.

THE IRAN-CONTRA AFFAIR

President Reagan's perception of the Soviet threat resembled that of Lyndon Johnson. When it came to Communism, both men had an "us versus them," "good versus evil" attitude. Joseph Stalin, in his grave since 1953, was a kind of Frankenstein monster ready to spring to life at any moment. World conquest was still the Soviet goal, in both men's view. Hence, while objectively there was only a superficial resemblance between Vietnam and Central America, Ronald Reagan perceived the challenge to the United States in similar terms: as a test of America's resolve to turn back the Communist tide.

By the mid-1980s, the United States had not only invaded Grenada; its warships were deployed off the coast of Central America. Fifteen thousand guerrillas covertly funded by the CIA and openly endorsed by the Reagan administration were trying to bring down the Marxist Sandinista regime in Nicaragua. In addition, the CIA was engaged in the mining of Nicaraguan ports, and the administration refused to recognize the jurisdiction of the World Court in the affair. In El Salvador the administration funded the training of officers and cadets in the government's war against Marxist guerrillas. In November 1983 Undersecretary of Defense Fred C. Iklé warned in a White House-approved speech that in El Salvador "we do not seek a military defeat for our friends; we do not seek a military stalemate; we seek victory for the forces of democracy." In his appraisal of the threat from Nicaragua, Iklé was even more forceful:

> We must prevent consolidation of the Sandinista regime in Nicaragua; if we cannot prevent that, we have to anticipate the partition of Central America. Such a development would then force us to man a new military front line of the East-West conflict, right here on our continent.

In 1984 a CIA handbook detailing the art of political assassination in Nicaragua became a source of considerable embarrassment for the Reagan administration.

In other words, in order to roll back Communism, the United States supported a government against guerrillas in El Salvador and guerrillas against a government in Nicaragua. Sandinistas and Salvadoran guerrillas perceived the conflict in terms of "Yankee imperialism" versus self-determination. The

Reagan administration, on the other hand, viewed it as a struggle between Communism and democracy.

By late 1983 neither the "contras" in Nicaragua nor the Salvadoran army had been particularly successful in containing, let alone rolling back, Marxist advances. On the contrary, the Salvadoran guerrillas were making major advances and the Sandinista regime seemed firmly entrenched in Nicaragua despite the mining of its harbors. The logic of the Reagan administration thus seemed open to serious question.

In January 1984 a National Bipartisan Commission on Central America, headed by former Secretary of State Henry Kissinger, presented its findings to the President. The essence of the Commission's report was that the exploitation of Central American unrest by the Soviet Union and Cuba threatened American security interests. The solution was to be found in offering pro-United States regimes military assistance to defeat externally supported insurgencies and economic assistance to overcome the poverty and misery that triggered such insurgencies. The amount of aid recommended was $8 billion over a five-year period. Failure would constitute a significant victory for the Soviet Union and a serious defeat for the United States. In short, Central America was to become an East-West military and economic battleground.

It was in the Commission's findings that a disturbing analogy to Vietnam became apparent. The United States strongly supported José Napoleon Duarte as its candidate for the presidency of El Salvador. Duarte duly won the election and thereby became America's "client." In the past, in China and Vietnam, such "clients" had lost popular support precisely because of their close association with the "imperialist" power. The title to the revolution was then captured by Mao Tse-tung and Ho Chi Minh because of their unrelenting hostility to Western imperialism. Could this be the reason why five thousand Marxist guerrillas could not be eliminated by the Duarte government in El Salvador and why fifteen thousand U.S.-supported contras could do little to weaken the Marxist regime in Nicaragua? Might the United States, in its frustration in Central America, assume a more direct military role as it did in Vietnam and try to do the job itself?

A warning voiced by four countries far more familiar with the Central American terrain than the twelve members of the Kissinger Commission went unheeded. Mexico, Venezuela, Colombia, and Panama, known as the "Contadora Group," did not see the Soviet threat as apocalyptically as the commission members who had spent only one day each in El Salvador, Nicaragua, Honduras, Guatamala, and Costa Rica. The Contadora Group urged that the problems of the region be resolved by diplomatic means rather than by military force.

President Reagan, however, remained deeply and unalterably committed to the cause of the Contras. "I am a Contra," he exclaimed on one occasion, a statement that was to haunt him not too long thereafter.

The connection between the Contras and Iran began to emerge in November 1986 when a Lebanese magazine disclosed that the United States had sold weapons to Iran after a secret visit to Teheran by Robert McFarlane, the former national security adviser. Reports then started to circulate that President Reagan, who had repeatedly declared that he would never negotiate with terrorists and who had condemned Iran as a member of a new international "Murder, Inc.," had in fact authorized clandestine shipments of weapons to Iran in an effort to gain the release of several US hostages who had been kidnapped by Islamic extremists in Lebanon. Two days before Thanksgiving, the President went on national television to announce that Vice Admiral John Poindexter, Reagan's national security advisor, had resigned and that Oliver North, Poindexter's deputy, had been relieved of his duties. Attorney General Edwin Meese then revealed that money from the sales of weapons to Iran had been diverted to the Nicaraguan rebels. But he insisted that the President knew nothing of the Iran-Contra diversion. Only Colonel North knew the entire story.

These sudden revelations were so staggering that two major congressional inquiries were authorized. The first took place under the chair of Texas Senator John Tower; the Tower commission issued its findings in February 1987. The second report was published by the entire Congress in November. The facts that were brought to light were shocking, to say the least. They showed how a secret foreign policy, not authorized by a single elected official of the United States, came together and then came unraveled. A summary of these facts is most illuminating.

During 1984 and 1985, seven Americans were kidnapped by Islamic extremists in Lebanon: William Buckley, the CIA station chief in Beirut; the Reverend Benjamin Weir; Peter Kilburn and Thomas M. Sutherland of the American University in Beirut; the Reverend Lawrence M. Jenco; Terry Anderson of the Associated Press; and David Jacobsen of the American University Hospital.

In February 1986, President Reagan signed an order authorizing arms shipments to Iran in an effort to improve relations with officials in Iran believed to be moderates and to bring about the release of the US hostages. A few days later, the United States sent 1,000 Tow missiles to Israel, from US stocks, for shipment to Iran. A year later, the Tower commission was to describe this transaction as clearly an "arms for hostages" deal.

In April 1986, Colonel North outlined his plan to have $12 million in profits from the Iran arms sales diverted to the Contras. The plan was prepared for Admiral Poindexter to relay to the President. Poindexter later testified that he never showed the memo to the President. Reagan, in his own testimony, denied any knowledge about the diversion of funds to the Contras until November 1986. In July, the terrorists freed Father Jenco but killed Kilburn and Buckley and then kidnapped two more Americans, Frank Reed and Joseph Cicippio. In October, they freed Jacobsen but kidnapped yet another victim, Edward Tracy. In November, *Al Shiraa,* a Lebanese magazine, revealed the US arms sales to Iran. Three weeks later, Poindexter and North were dismissed, and in December, a special prosecutor, Lawrence E. Walsh, was appointed to investigate the entire Iran-Contra affair. In January 1987,

Islamic terrorists kidnapped yet four more Americans—all teachers at Beirut University.

The findings of the congressional committee of inquiry published in November 1987 were devastating. Lee Hamilton, chairman of the panel, summed them up in the following words: "I am impressed that policy was driven by a series of lies: lies to our friends and allies, lies to the Congress, and lies to the American people." Colonel North admitted that he had indeed lied to the Congress and shredded potentially incriminating documents. However, he placed the blame squarely upon the Congress, accusing it of a policy of vacillation toward the Contras. "We live in a dangerous world," he proclaimed. Secrecy had become necessary because, without it, there would have been no military assistance to the Contras. And besides, in the colonel's words, making the Ayatollah pay for the Contras was "a neat idea." The President, although exonerated by the Congress of any criminal liability, was nonetheless accused of creating an environment in which such pervasive dishonesty and secrecy were allowed to flourish.

Nobody emerged very well from this affair. The President appeared as a man who had lost control of his own administration. In a way, not knowing what had gone on was almost as bad as knowing. Poindexter and North, his two subordinates, had set up a secret government within the executive branch to execute their plan to divert Iranian funds to the Contras. They justified their actions by the classic "end justifies the means" argument. The Contras were a worthy cause, and the Congress could no longer be trusted. Thus, they usurped the authority of their commander in chief who had declared earlier that he himself was a Contra. Hence, they were executing his policy, merely filling in details of a grand presidential design.

The Congress, for its part, accused Poindexter and North of deceit on a massive scale, of subverting US democracy by keeping all elected officials in the dark about an important initiative in US foreign policy. In the last analysis, however, it blamed the President for allowing a "cabal of zealots" to make foreign policy without the slightest input from the Congress of the United States. No end could possibly justify such means. "The idea of monarchy," the Congress concluded, "was rejected in the United States 200 years ago and since then the law—not any official or ideology—has been paramount."[15] In response to these congressional charges, the President admitted his "mistakes" and pledged his determination to change and grow from the experience. Unlike President Nixon, he survived. In its essence, the Iran-Contra affair was a classic conflict between means and ends, and between secret and open diplomacy.

Ironically enough, in historical perspective, both objectives of the Iran-Contra policy ultimately failed. In August 1987, President Oscar Arias of Costa Rica persuaded Nicaragua, El Salvador, Honduras, and Guatamala to sign a peace agreement for Central America. For this effort, he was awarded the Nobel Peace Prize. Even though friction and fighting between the Nicaraguan Sandinista regime and the Contras continued, the Sandinistas remained firmly in control. Oliver North's secret operations to overthrow them had come to nought. Nor did the arms sales to Iran achieve their intended purposes. When the arms negotiations began, seven American hostages were incarcerated in Lebanon. During the subsequent negotiations, two were killed, two were freed, and four more were kidnapped. Thus, the Iranians wound up with the US arms and with more hostages than before. The United States had been played for a sucker. The Iran-Contra affair had convulsed the country for nothing.

In the light of this melancholy episode, we must examine the problem of modern terrorism in greater detail.

TERRORISM AND THE TWILIGHT OF DIPLOMACY

By the mid-1980s, the world's diplomats were very much concerned. Since 1971, terrorists had waged hundreds of assaults on embassies and diplomatic missions. More than half of these had taken place during the 1980s. Twenty-five countries had been victimized, with the Americans held captive in Iran and Lebanon only the most widely publicized examples. A diplomat's job, formerly held sacrosanct, had become as dangerous as that of a police officer in an angry crowd. Seldom before in modern history had diplomacy been so dangerous a calling. Some career diplomats expressed the fear that terrorism had struck at the very heart of diplomacy itself. A survey of the most significant of these terrorist attacks makes melancholy reading.

On December 28, 1972, four Palestinian "Black September" terrorists seized the Israeli embassy in Bangkok, Thailand. After negotiations with the Thai government, they surrendered the hostages and fled to Egypt. On March 1, 1973, "Black September" terrorists seized the Saudi embassy in Khartoum, Sudan, and killed several American and Belgian diplomats. After three days, they surrendered to Sudanese authorities. On September 13, 1974, three Japanese Red Army terrorists seized the French embassy in The Hague, Netherlands. They demanded—and got—a ransom of $1 million, flew to Damascus on a French plane, and surrendered to the Palestine Liberation Organization. On April 24, 1975, terrorists seized the West German embassy in Stockholm, Sweden, and demanded the release of twenty-six Baader-Meinhof gang members being held in German prisons. Two diplomats were killed before the terrorists surrendered. On December 4, 1975, gunmen demanding independence for Molucca seized the Indonesian consulate in Amsterdam, Netherlands, and took thirty hostages, including sixteen children. The terrorists only gave up after a sixteen-day siege during which one hostage died and three were injured. On December 21, 1975, three people were killed and seven wounded when six pro-Palestinian terrorists seized eighty-one persons attending an OPEC conference in Vienna, Austria. The terrorists fled to Tripoli, Libya. On June 15, 1977, three members of a Croatian separatist movement shot their way into the Yugoslav mission to the United Nations in New York, seeking to take the ambassador hostage. After wounding a chauffeur, they surrendered to the police. On March 26, 1979, Palestinians stormed the Egyptian embassy in Kuwait to protest the conclusion of a peace treaty between Egypt and Israel. On May 4, 1979, guerrillas in San Salvador seized several ambassadors as hostages in the French and Costa Rican embassies. Some of the hostages were held for a month before they were released. Two months later, Colombian guerrillas seized twenty diplomats from eighteen countries, including the papal nuncio, the American envoy, and thirteen other ambassadors. Only after protracted negotiations lasting several months were the diplomats released. On July 13, 1979, Palestinian terrorists attacked the Egyptian embassy in Ankara, Turkey, killed two security guards, and took nineteen hostages. On January 13, 1980, peasants and students seized the Spanish embassy in Guatemala City to protest army repression. Two embassy staff members and two Guatemalan officials were killed. On March 2, 1981, Pakistani terrorists hijacked a Pakistani airliner and flew it to Damascus, demanding the freeing of fifty-five Pakistani political prisoners in exchange for more than one hundred passenger hostages. After twelve days of negotiations, the government of Pakistan bowed to the hijackers' demands. Terrorism had chalked up another victory in its assault on civilization. In May 1981 a Moslem terrorist shot and severely wounded Pope John Paul II in St. Peter's Square in Rome, and in 1983 terrorists destroyed the American Embassy in Beirut. In June 1985, forty American passengers on a TWA airliner were hijacked by Shi'ite terrorists and held as hostages in Beirut for two weeks.

Between 1985 and 1987, as we have seen above, a dozen Americans were kidnapped in Lebanon. Two of them were killed. In August 1988, President Zia of Pakistan and the US ambassador to that country were murdered when their plane exploded in midair. And in December 1988, a Pan Am jet was blown up over Scotland; over 200 casualties resulted.

The United States, as a major target of left-wing discontent, has been disproportionately victimized over the years, even aside from Teheran and Lebanon. From 1971 to 1988, the State Department listed more than 1,000 significant terrorist actions against US diplomatic installations or individuals. Five top officials were killed, including the ambassadors to Afghanistan and Pakistan as well as the president of the American University in Beirut. The terror on embassy row everywhere took its toll on the morale of career diplomats. Diplomacy had suddenly become a very dangerous profession.

Perhaps most frightening is the fact that some of the most devastating acts of terrorism in the 1980s were apparently initiated not by crazed individuals but by coldly calculating leaders of sovereign states. By the mid-1980s, for example, the would-be assassin of Pope John Paul II confessed that he had been in the pay of the Bulgarian KGB. Since the Bulgarian KGB was clearly a puppet of its Soviet master, strong circumstantial evidence pointed to Yuri Andropov, the deceased Soviet leader and ex-KGB boss, as the prime mover to eliminate the troublesome Polish Pope. The destruction of the Korean airliner in 1983 and the murder of 269 innocent people may also be cited as an example of state-initiated terrorism. And the three suicide missions that led to the death of hundreds of American and French soldiers in Beirut were apparently of Iranian or Libyan origin. A case could in fact be made that a car bomb triggered the American withdrawal from Lebanon.

Perhaps the most painful dilemma of modern diplomacy is whether one should negotiate with terrorists. There are no clear or simple answers. Virtually every Western country, including the United States, has declared that it will not negotiate and then, contrary to its public pronouncements, has in fact negotiated. If one says no, one may be right to stand on principle and to adhere to the ideals of moral courage. If one says yes, one, too, may be right by being compassionate and placing precious human lives above abstract principles. It is easy to stand on principle, of course, if one's loved ones are not at risk. But if one's husband, son, or father is held captive in a dungeon in Beirut, such a principled stand becomes a lot more difficult. Presidents Carter and Reagan became impaled on the horns of this dilemma. Not surprisingly, they vacillated and lost on both counts.

The Western democracies, by placing a high value on each individual human life, are particularly vulnerable to the modern terrorist who has contempt for life. Perhaps the most appropriate policy for the United States may be a public declaration that any of its private citizens who insist on living in countries such as Libya, Iran, or Lebanon do so at their own risk. And even then, there would have to be exceptions for embassy personnel or passengers of highjacked airliners. Civilized countries will have to continue to wrestle with this terrible dilemma of courage versus compassion.

It is clear from the above examples that, apart from state-initiated terrorism, most of this kind of violence has emanated from postcolonial Third World countries. Not only have most terrorists perceived themselves as "freedom fighters," but the new nations of the Third World have been less inclined than Western states to abide by the old rules of discourse among nations. Modern diplomacy was, after all, a Western invention developed by European diplomats. The "inviolability" of embassy grounds and diplomats, too, was a Western concept. In the aftermath of the Hungarian revolution in 1956, for example, Cardinal Jozsef Mindszenty sought asylum in the American embassy in Budapest. In 1984 in London, on the other hand, the Libyan embassy became a source of terrorism when gunmen sprayed the streets below with machine-gun fire, killing a policewoman. The British had to let the killers go since the Libyans threatened to take reprisals against the British embassy in Tripoli. It appeared that Libyan leader Muammar Qadaffi was in personal charge of the operation.

Thus, traditional principles of diplomacy are no longer accepted by many of the new nations, such as Khomeini's Iran or Qadaffi's Libya. In short, the West wanted to export its diplomatic way of life, and this simply did not work. A custom that had evolved over five hundred years of time had virtually broken down in a single decade. And, as a consequence, as we move toward the year 2000, diplomacy itself is now on trial.

REFERENCES

1 For a perceptive analysis of the Congress of Vienna, see Harold Nicolson, *The Congress of Vienna*. New York: Harcourt, Brace, 1946; or Henry A. Kissinger, *A World Restored*. Boston: Houghton Mifflin, 1957.

2 Hans Morgenthau, *Politics Among Nations*. 3d ed. New York: Knopf, 1960, pp. 539–540.

3 Henry A. Kissinger, "The Congress of Vienna," *World Politics*, January 1956, pp. 264–265.

4 This is a statement attributed to a British ambassador, Sir Henry Wotton, cited by Sir Harold Nicolson in *Diplomacy*. New York: Oxford University Press, 1955, p. 44.

5 Nicolson, *op. cit.*, p. 110.

6 *Ibid.*, p. 126.

7 Morgenthau, *op. cit.*, p. 259.

8 Kissinger, *op. cit.*, p. 329.

9 Morgenthau, *op. cit.*, p. 14.

10 *Ibid.*, p. 6.

11 Charles Burton Marshall, *The Limits of Foreign Policy*. New York: Henry Holt, 1954, p. 33.

12 Hans J. Morgenthau, *Scientific Man versus Power Politics*. Chicago: University of Chicago Press, 1952, p. 202.

13 *Ibid.*, p. 203.

14 Morgenthau, *Politics Among Nations*, pp. 11–12.

15 *The New York Times*, November 19, 1987.

SELECTED BIBLIOGRAPHY

Eban, Abba. *The New Diplomacy: International Affairs in the Modern Age*. New York: Random House, 1983. A leading Israeli politician-diplomat reflects on the dilemmas of modern diplomacy. A book full of wisdom.

Kennan, George F. *Memoirs: 1925–1950* and *Memoirs: 1950–1963*. Boston: Atlantic-Little, Brown, 1967 and 1972. A lifetime of reflections on US diplomacy by one of its most distinguished practitioners. Invaluable reading.

Kissinger, Henry. *A World Restored: Metternich, Castlereagh and the Problems of Peace 1812–1822*. Boston: Houghton-Mifflin, 1952. Henry Kissinger's doctoral dissertation and probably his most significant historical work. In examining the 1815 peace treaty, the author discovers valuable insights into the arts of diplomacy which he applied twenty years later as secretary of state.

Kissinger, Henry. *Years of Upheaval*. Boston: Little, Brown, 1982. The emphasis here is on diplomacy toward the Middle East and the Soviet Union. A rich, detailed, and colorful book with marvelous vignettes of world leaders, including one of Richard Nixon on the brink of Watergate.

Ledeen, Michael A. *Perilous Statecraft: An Insider's Account of the Iran-Contra Affair*. New York: Scribner's, 1988. The author, an early intermediary with Israeli and Iranian players in the drama, offers a fascinating though somewhat arrogant account. Bottom line: Poindexter and North made serious mistakes, but committed no crimes: the real villains were Congress and the investigating committees.

Sterling, Claire. *The Time of Assassins*. New York: Holt, Rinehart, and Winston, 1984. A diligent effort to show that terrorist organizations coordinate their efforts to bring down the Western democracies. A persuasive argument, but case remains not proven.

CHAPTER 9

INTERNATIONAL LAW AND POLITICAL ORDER

Inter armis silent leges. In the clash of arms the laws are silent. We may add that in the truce of arms the laws are heard.

Walter Lippmann, *The Public Philosophy*

INTERNATIONAL RELATIONS AND THE RULE OF LAW

Between the evolution of political order among nations and the development of world law—a body of rules and principles of action that are legally binding upon states in their relations with one another—there is undoubtedly a vital connection, yet there remains wide disagreement on the nature of this connection. Many observers of the international scene feel that political order building has to precede the establishment of a rule of law; that, in fact, a legal consensus can grow only in the soil of a community based on social and political harmony. Others are equally convinced that the establishment of a rule of law can help knit the bonds of social and political order, that the promulgation of legal documents such as covenants and treaties can weave the fabric of community. The former tend to favor a "political" approach to order-building and prefer to work through the processes of political accommodation and diplomacy; the latter are inclined toward a "legal" approach and look with greater hope to the role of international law. In the present chapter we shall be concerned with this legal approach to political order.

The modern law of nations has its origins in antiquity and in medieval times. It has four chief roots. A first important source is the work of classical writers. The most famous of these is Hugo Grotius, frequently described as the "father of international law." His fame rests mainly on a monumental work, *The Law of War and Peace,* published in 1625 as an impassioned protest against the carnage of the Thirty Years' War. It was this treatise that laid the groundwork for the modern laws of war. A key passage in its preface sounds amazingly modern:

> Throughout the Christian world I observed a lack of restraint in relation to war, such as even barbarous races should be ashamed of; I observed that men rush to arms for slight causes, or no cause at all, and that when arms have once been taken up there is no longer any respect for law, divine or human; it is as if, in accordance with a general decree, frenzy had openly been let loose, for the committing of all crimes.[1]

A second significant source of international law is custom. If certain customary practices among nations persist for a long period of time, and if no state expressly rejects them, they eventually may be absorbed into the body of international law. For example, it had long been the custom to exempt unarmed fishing vessels from war booty. Finally, in 1900, this custom came to be recognized as law.[2] This role of custom, however, illustrates a major problem of international law. Since only those practices become law that are not strongly opposed by any state, the rules that nations observe represent only a lowest common denominator. It is for this reason that international law is not only threatened by the ever-present danger of not being abided by, but it is also permanently plagued by low moral standards. The reason for this is, of course, that while international law is intended to control states, it is in effect controlled by them.

A third major source of international law derives from treaties. These have played an important role since the days of Greek antiquity. Thucydides' *History of the Peloponnesian War,* for example, speaks extensively about treaties among the city-states of the ancient Mediterranean world. The Congress of Vienna, the Versailles Settlement, the United Nations Charter, and NATO have all rested on treaties that have contributed importantly to international law. Yet, though more specific than custom and requiring the deliberate commitment of states through ratification, treaties also are often ambiguous and do not necessarily ensure just relationships among nations, for the treaty makers' first responsibility is attempting to strike a delicate balance between justice and peace. If they overemphasize the former, the peace may be lost—witness Versailles. The same is true if they lean too much toward the latter—witness Munich. The revision of a treaty is often an arduous and painful process. It took fourteen years of negotiations between Panama and the United States, for example, to renegotiate a 1903 treaty governing the Canal Zone, which had granted the United States control "in perpetuity" and to transfer sovereignty over the Zone to Panama by the year 2000.

The fourth important source of international law is the decisions of courts. The contribution of international tribunals in the establishment of international law is a recent development, largely a product of the twentieth century. The most important of the judicial bodies have been the Permanent Court of International Justice under the League of Nations and the International Court of Justice under the United Nations system.

Traditionally, only states have been subjects of international law. In the absence of a higher secular arbiter, each state has tended to recognize or refuse to recognize its fellow members of the world community. The practice of recognition has followed fairly arbitrary rules of co-option which each state has developed on its own. Since the advent of the United Nations, the practice of "collective recognition" has gained currency. In the case of the birth of new states, such as Israel and Ghana, admission to the United Nations has become a kind of imprimatur by the world community. This rise of "collective recognition" may be a hopeful sign for the development of more uniform legal standards. Our generation has also seen the extension of international law to subjects other than states: semigovernmental organizations such as the Jewish Agency; nongovernmental organizations like the International Red Cross; international organizations such as the United Nations and its specialized agencies; and, perhaps most important, individuals, who also now have rights and duties before international law. Even stateless people have come to enjoy at least a minimum of international protection. And for the first time in history the attempt was made at Nuremberg in 1945 to bring individuals before the bar of international law.*

The question of jurisdiction over individuals demonstrates that the problem of "progress" in international law is a highly complex one. It would be too one-dimensional to state that international law advances simply by the expansion of jurisdiction. The ambiguity of the problem was demonstrated during the Nuremberg War Crimes Trials in 1945.

The Nuremberg Tribunal was set up by the victorious powers—the United States, the Soviet Union, Britain, and France—to try the major leaders of the Nazi government. The indictment against them was threefold: (a) crimes against peace (i.e., planning, preparing, initiating, or waging aggressive war or taking part in a common plan to do so); (b) war crimes (i.e., violations of the rules of war); (c) crimes against humanity (crimes against civilians before or during the war). On the basis of one or more of these counts, a number of the leading Nazis were either executed or given prison sentences, while others were acquitted. However, several questions have been raised as to the legality of the Nuremberg trials. For example, since international law had never before applied to individuals, was not the Nuremberg judgment ex post facto? Some observers felt that the Nuremberg trials set a dangerous precedent. In a future war, would it not be possible—on the basis of the Nuremberg judgment—for the victor nation to bring to trial the statesmen of the defeated country? To take the point ad absurdum, if in a war between the United States and the So-

---

*While an attempt was made by the victorious powers after World War I to bring to trial certain German "war criminals," including Kaiser Wilhelm, these so-called Leipzig Trials were a failure.

viet Union the latter should be victorious, might not the victor try an American President as a "warmonger and imperialist aggressor"? Hence, it is difficult to assert with finality that the subjecthood of individuals under international law has necessarily served the cause of world order. And even if this were so beyond a doubt, it must be remembered that, before international law was able to hold individuals criminally liable, it first had to destroy the sovereignty of the nation of which they were members.

The dubiousness of the Nuremberg precedent prompted the General Assembly of the United Nations to direct its International Law Commission to formulate the principles of international law established at Nuremberg. The commission in its findings approved the principle of individual responsibility and denied the immunity of high government officials who committed crimes in the name of obedience to orders. But the commission was also convinced that the ad hoc character of the Nuremberg trials pointed up the necessity for a Criminal Chamber of the International Court of Justice. However, owing to disagreement among the major powers, an international criminal code does not yet exist. From the above example one may draw the possible conclusion that "progress" in international law is perhaps better served through the development of its "facilitative" rather than its "punitive" aspects.

If international law still applies largely to states, it is also primarily interpreted by states. Self-judgment as the logical adjunct of sovereignty still dominates the scene. Only minor incursions have been made into the principle of "domestic jurisdiction." The only international body with military enforcement power is the United Nations Security Council, and its power is severely curtailed through the veto of the Big Five. The rule of self-judgment also applies in questions of revision and repeal of international law. For example, the Western powers took the position that the Potsdam Agreement could be revised only with the unanimous consent of the signatories. They invoked the principle of *pacta sunt servanda*—"pacts must be observed." The Soviet Union, on the other hand, desirous of evicting the Western powers from Berlin, invoked the opposing principle of *rebus sic stantibus*—"matters have changed." Quite clearly, such an explosive political issue cannot be settled by judicial means, but can only yield to the processes of diplomacy.

In view of the tremendous obstacles in the path of international law, it is remarkable that in certain limited areas a respectable body of substantive law has in fact crystallized. International law has come to serve a useful function in the demarcation of boundaries among states; the acquisition of a "no man's land" and the regulation of minor territorial disputes fall in this category. Even in this area, however, great difficulties may arise. It has been impossible, for example, to agree upon a uniform definition of territorial waters. The law of the sea, too, has been the subject of numerous inconclusive global conferences. Similarly, each state still claims sovereignty over its airspace. International law also defines the privileges and immunities of ambassadors, of heads of state, and of their immediate entourage. Certain rules have developed on the basis of reciprocity under customary international law. Ambassadors, for example, may not be taxed and may be sued only with their own consent. High-ranking United Nations officials also enjoy "diplomatic immunity." Finally, the right of political asylum for refugees has long been sanctioned by customary international law.

The law of nations also facilitates normal and peaceful relations among nations. Numerous claims by one state against another have been settled through "good offices," mediation and arbitration tribunals, and judicial decisions. A useful body of law also exists for the purpose of regulating strained and hostile international relations. For example, under the Drago Doctrine of 1902, international law holds that the forcible collection of debts through blockade is illegal. An attempt has also been made to determine the rights and duties of neutrals in times of war. Of course, the fiercer and more "total" war has become, the more difficult it has been to define these rights and duties.

International law has also attempted to come to grips with war itself. Two approaches have dominated international legal thinking. The first has been a modern version of the assumption that first guided Hugo Grotius: that war cannot be eliminated by legal means, but that its worst horrors may be somewhat mitigated through the development of laws governing its conduct. An impressive body of laws aimed at this end today exists. To name but a few: the Geneva Protocol of 1925 on the Prohibition of Chemical and Bacteriological Warfare and Poison Gas; the Geneva Convention of 1929 on the Treatment of Sick and Wounded; the Washington Pact of 1935 for the Protection of Museums and Historic Sites; the London Protocol of 1936 regulating submarine warfare; the Hague Convention of 1938 outlawing inhuman weapons; the Geneva Convention of 1949 governing the protection of civilian populations; and the UN Genocide Convention of 1948. The observance of these laws of war has varied. International laws proved almost completely impotent during World War II, though even Hitler decided against the use of poison gas for fear of retaliation in kind. The laws of war have been observed far more scrupulously in the nuclear age. For example, owing to the fear of an atomic holocaust both sides decided to keep the Korean conflict limited and demonstrated a considerable respect for the laws of war.

The second attempt by international law to deal with war has been its legal prohibition. In 1928, in the Kellogg-Briand pact, most states of the world "renounced war as an instrument of national policy." But no sanctions were included in the pact against a possible aggressor. During the entire lifetime of the League of Nations, international lawyers grappled with the intricate problems of defining "aggression" and of deciding what constituted a "just," that is "defensive," war. It was impossible to reach agreement and in the end the League of Nations Covenant in fact left certain loopholes for legal resort to war. Similarly, the United Nations Charter, while expressly outlawing war, permits the creation of regional arrangements for the purpose of collective self-defense. The United Nations, however, after more than two decades of legal controversy, in 1974 finally emerged with a definition of aggression. Needless to say, the definition was so ambiguous that its application in a concrete case of war remains very dubious indeed.

The record demonstrates that of the two approaches to dealing with war, the more realistic is through the development of laws governing its conduct. The elimination of war is clearly not a legal problem, but the most brutal effects of modern warfare may perhaps be somewhat softened through the development of such a body of laws. Perhaps not surprisingly, as the horrors of war in our time have increased there has also occurred a revival of concern and respect for laws concerning the waging of war. Some of this concern was expressed quite belatedly in some cases. It took the United States forty years, for example, to ratify the Genocide Convention. It finally did so in 1988.

On the whole, we must admit that the contribution of international law to the building of political order has been modest. In the first place, most international disputes simply do not lend themselves to a judicial approach since they are much too deeply involved in questions of power and prestige. Hence international law, unlike domestic law, suffers from a paucity of cases and cannot easily grow into a codified system. A second obstacle is the stubborn fact that the very states that are to be governed by international law are the sovereign masters of that law, rather than its servants. In other words, international law suffers from the lack of a centralized enforcement agency. These truths have raised the question of whether there is such a thing as international law at all. The record shows that the answer is definitely in the affirmative, yet it also shows that the main usefulness of international law is in technical and fairly noncontroversial matters. In these areas, it has crystallized into a respectable body of international rules and regulations which are invaluable aids in the normal day-to-day conduct of international relations.

As a general rule, the "legal approach" to political order-building has been most effective among those nations that are held together by a sense of political community. But law has not been able to produce this community. Rather, its existence has seemed to depend on the prior existence of a cultural and political community. Where there is no such community—as in the relations between the two superpowers—the "political approach" of diplomacy is likely to yield more fruitful results than the judicial. Indeed, the true relation between diplomacy and international law has not been one in which the latter has displaced the former, but one in which more successful diplomacy has resulted in more ungrudging consent to better laws.

The most ambitious example of the legal approach to political order in our time is the International Court of Justice. We shall now explore the question of whether this institution accurately reflects the role of international law in general.

THE INTERNATIONAL COURT OF JUSTICE

The International Court of Justice, better known as the World Court, came into existence in 1945 as part of the United Nations system. Actually, the Court was a reincarnation rather than a birth. It was the successor to the Permanent Court of International Justice of the League of Nations. The old World

Court had been one of the more successful institutions of the League. In the eighteen years of its activity, the old World Court rendered thirty-two judgments and handed down twenty-seven advisory opinions. The new World Court broke the continuity as little as possible. It established itself at The Hague, and the statute governing its activities became virtually a carbon copy of its predecessor's.

The fifteen justices of the Court are elected for nine-year terms by a majority of votes in the General Assembly and the Security Council. The veto power of the Big Five does not apply. The statute of the Court provides that the justices be chosen "from among persons of high moral character who possess...recognized competence in international law." They should also represent "the main forms of civilization and the principal legal systems of the world." Hence, individuals rather than states are to be elected to the Court. This proviso, it was hoped, would increase the Court's impartiality. It was also assumed that the fifteen justices would represent a wide geographic distribution and that no two members of the Court would be of the same nationality. These clauses were inserted owing to the conviction of the founders that the impartiality of the Court would have to be safeguarded as much as possible. They realized that the judicial value of the Court as an international tribunal might be totally defeated if the justices were to be swayed by national loyalties or the political interests of particular states. On the other hand, the founders had to make their peace with the fact that judges, like other human beings, were nationals of a particular country, and that the Court might have to deal with explosive political issues on which national sentiment would run high and on which Olympian dispassionateness would be hard to achieve. One important concession was made in this direction in the statute. If a case were to come before the Court and there was no judge of the nationality of one of the parties among the permanent justices, that party would have the right to choose an additional ad hoc judge of its own or any other nationality. This right has been exercised invariably. The Court was thus an expression not only of the hope that the justices would rise above all national allegiance and serve only the law, but also of the realization that this level of detachment might not always actually prove possible.

The record of the World Court, while modest, indicates the nature of the relationship between political order-building and the rule of law. The Court has been involved in four different types of cases: it has dealt with both the East-West and the colonial-anticolonial conflicts; it has passed on disputes within the Western Hemisphere; and it has been called upon to interpret the legal competence of the United Nations. A closer look at some significant cases from each of these four areas will shed further light on the role of the Court.

The World Court's *cause célèbre* was the Corfu Channel case, involving two countries separated by the Iron Curtain—Albania and Great Britain. This was the only contentious East-West case ever to come before the Court. In October 1946 two British warships were sunk by mines as they passed through the Corfu Channel in the territorial waters of Albania. Forty-four British sailors were killed and the British government brought the matter before the Security Council, where a resolution that held Albania responsible for the tragedy was vetoed by the Soviet Union. Subsequently, the question of responsibility was referred by both parties to the International Court of Justice. Since there was no Albanian judge on the Court, a Czechoslovak justice—Judge Ecer—was appointed to the Court, which now comprised sixteen members. The British contention was that the Albanian government had laid the mines or must have known about them, that it was therefore guilty of criminal negligence, and that it should therefore be held responsible. Albania claimed that the British ships had violated its sovereignty and that its action was a justifiable act of self-defense. The Court, in an eleven to five opinion, held in favor of the British contention. As a result of this opinion, the British government requested that the Court also fix the amount of damages to be paid by Albania. Although the Albanians claimed that the Court had no jurisdiction over this part of the case, the Court held that the decision of the two parties to submit the dispute gave it the right to fix the damages as well. In a ten to six opinion, the Court held that the Albanian government must have known of the existence of the mines and should therefore pay compensation to Great Britain. The amount of the damages was fixed at $2.4 million. The six dissenting justices contended that it had not been proved that the Albanian government knew of the mines and that Albania could therefore not be held liable. The dissenting justices represented Egypt, Brazil, the Soviet Union, Poland, Yugoslavia, and Czechoslovakia. Albania refused to honor the decision of the Court, despite the fact that the majority opinion had been based on numerous reports by experts who had visited the localities adjacent to the scene of the incident. In thus declining to pay the amount awarded, Albania became the first state in history to "refuse in principle to comply with the decision of the Court in a contentious proceeding to which it was a party."[3] Neither the Court nor the British government has been able to enforce the decision.

A second problem involving the East-West struggle reached the Court in November 1947 when the General Assembly requested an advisory opinion on the controversial question of the admission of new members to the United Nations. The Court was asked to pass on the question of whether a member state could make its consenting vote subject "to the additional condition that other states be admitted." The General Assembly's request for an advisory opinion on this matter grew out of the Soviet Union's proposal of a membership "package deal." This was rejected by the United States, which held that each application should be considered on its individual merits. The Court, in a nine to six opinion, upheld the American view and declared that Article IV of the Charter, stating that admission was to be open to all "peace-loving" states, was to govern admissions procedure rather than extraneous political considerations. The minority, which included not only the Soviet, Polish, and Yugoslav justices, but also the French, British, and Canadian members of the Court, contended that the question of membership was essentially a political one and that political considerations were therefore admissible. Though the decision itself was superseded through a membership "package deal" in 1955, the fact that it witnessed three Western justices voting with the anti-Western minority has made it of more than passing interest. What was significant was not the "rightness" or "wrongness" of the opinion of these three Western justices but the simple fact that what they considered to be an objective appraisal of the case led them to an opinion that contravened that of their national governments at the time.

The only colonial issue to reach the Court to date has concerned the disposition of Southwest Africa, which had been a mandate under the League of Nations. The Court has been concerned with various aspects of this problem intermittently since 1950. In that year the General Assembly requested an advisory opinion on whether or not the former mandate could be administered as an integral part of South Africa. The issue aroused much interest because of South Africa's adamant refusal to place the territory under any form of international supervision. The Court, in a unanimous opinion, declared that "the United Nations [was] entitled to exercise supervisory functions over the administration of the mandate, and [that] the Union acting alone [was] not competent to modify the international status of the territory."[4] Specifically, the court stated that the Union government was under the obligation to submit periodic reports on the status of Southwest Africa to the United Nations. In a later case, in 1956, the Court upheld the legality of oral reports to the UN from the contested territory.

In the third round, in 1962, the Court took yet another step when, by a vote of eight to seven, it rejected South Africa's objections to its jurisdiction. On the basis of this opinion, the two plaintiffs, Ethiopia and Liberia, submitted lengthy substantive briefs. The Union of South Africa, too, submitted its defense. In July 1966, by the narrowest possible majority—a seven to seven tie being broken in favor of South Africa by the "casting vote" of the president, Sir Percy Spender of Australia—the Court dismissed the complaint against South Africa on the grounds of insufficiency of legal interest on the part of the complaining states. The Court, in short, decided not to decide. The reaction of the Afro-Asian group was violent. It expressed its disinclination to resort to the Court in the future and secured the passage of a resolution in the General Assembly withdrawing the right to administer Southwest Africa from South Africa and conferring this right upon the General Assembly. Defenders of the decision, on the other hand, asserted that it was better for the Court to dismiss the case than to make a decision against South Africa that would have been unenforceable. In 1971, at long last, the Court got off the fence and declared South Africa's occupation of Namibia to be illegal. This still did not change the *de facto* situation, since South Africa chose to ignore this latest ruling.

In 1972, in a dramatic move, the UN Security Council decided to meet in Addis Ababa, Ethiopia, in order to underline the importance of the problems besetting Africa. In one of its resolutions it strongly urged a United Nations role in "Namibia"—the new African term now used for the territory of Southwest Africa—and requested the Secretary-General to travel there in order to see to it that the resolution was implemented. Secretary-General Kurt Waldheim duly went to South Africa and tried his best to persuade the South African government but to no avail. For all practical purposes, South African control over Namibia remained intact, despite an African initiative in 1974 to expel South Africa from the United Nations that was blocked by American, British, and French vetoes in the Security Council, and despite a General Assembly decision, taken a few weeks later, to suspend South Africa's participation. Four major UN organs—the World Court, the General Assembly, the Security Council, and the Secretary-General—had come to grief on the unyielding rock of South African sovereignty. Only the diplomatic initiative of Secretary of State Henry Kissinger in 1976 finally managed to move Namibia closer to black majority rule and independence. And by the early 1980s, with Zimbabwe's emergence as a sovereign state, Namibia's freedom was only a matter of time. In 1988, after eight years of arduous negotiations orchestrated by US Assistant Secretary of State Chester Crocker, South Africa finally agreed to permit elections in Namibia under UN supervision, in exchange for Cuba's pledge to pull its 50,000 troops out of Angola. After four decades of legal and political maneuvering, Namibia was to be free.

While the Court's role in the settlement of disputes involving the two great political struggles obviously has been minimal, it has played a significant part in intraregional controversies, especially within the Western Hemisphere. Here the Court has made an important contribution to political order-building. Some of these cases have been fairly technical, as for example the question of fishing rights by Britain off the Icelandic coast, or a claim to the ruins of the ancient temple at Angkor which strained relations between Cambodia and Thailand. Others have had greater political import. One of the most typical of these cases to reach the Court was a boundary dispute between Honduras and Nicaragua. In November 1960 the Court ruled that Nicaragua was obligated to give effect to a 1906 arbitration award settling its boundary with Honduras. This award had been made by King Alfonso XIII of Spain, who had established a boundary line that would cause the transfer to Honduras of frontier regions claimed by Nicaragua. In 1912 Nicaragua had challenged the award, and repeated attempts to settle the issue had failed. Finally, in 1957, the Organization of American States brought about an agreement between the two countries to submit the case to the World Court. The Court supported the 1906 award by a vote of fourteen to one. The dissenting vote was cast by a Colombian justice who had been designated by Nicaragua as ad hoc judge for the case. The dissenting opinion held that the 1906 arbitration award was invalid because of errors made by the arbitrator. The permanent judges, however, ruled in favor of Honduras and declared that the king of Spain had been a proper arbitrator under the terms of an 1894 treaty between Nicaragua and Honduras and that Nicaragua had accepted the king's decision at the time. Nicaragua complied with the decision.

The broader significance of this case was the fact that justices from both sides of the Iron Curtain ruled in effect that once a valid arbitration award is made in an international dispute, it becomes effective and remains so despite any lapse of time in its implementation. The judgment displayed a broad support for the principle of arbitration and laid the groundwork for the future settlement of similar international disputes.

More recently, the Court has expanded its influence to Africa. In 1986, the Court delivered a decision in a border dispute between Burkina Faso (formerly Upper Volta) and the Republic of Mali. Both states accepted the opinion and have abided by the Court's decision.

Perhaps the most important contribution of the World Court to international order-building has been the strengthening of the United Nations as a juridical and political entity. When Count Folke Bernadotte, the United Nations mediator in Palestine, was assassinated by a Jewish terrorist group, the United Nations requested an advisory opinion on the question of whether the world organization was entitled to bring a claim against a state for damages caused to the United Nations by injuries suffered by one of its representatives while acting on its behalf. The Court, in an eleven to four opinion, held that the United Nations was entitled to claim such reparation. The majority, in a far-reaching opinion, stated that

> Fifty states, representing the vast majority of the members of the international community, had the power, in conformity with international law to bring into being an entity possessing objective international personality, not merely personality recognized by them alone, together with capacity to bring international claims.[5]

Thus, the United Nations was granted a "personality" by the Court, a kind of sovereignty all its own which the majority saw implied in the Charter:

> Under international law, the Organization must be deemed to have those powers which, though not expressly provided in the Charter, are conferred upon it by necessary implication as being essential to the performance of its duties.[6]

The four dissenting justices—Egyptian, Polish, Russian, and American—held that this "implied powers clause" was not inherent in the Charter. On the strength of this advisory opinion, the United Nations claimed reparations from Israel for the death of Count Bernadotte and injuries to other United Nations personnel in the pursuit of their duties. The government of Israel has honored these claims. Thus, the Court helped to endow the United Nations with an international legal personality entitled to protect its officials by bestowing upon them the legal status of world civil servants.

In July 1962 the Court once again interpreted the United Nations Charter in a very important advisory opinion. In response to a request by the General Assembly, the Court declared, by a vote of nine to five, that the expenses of the United Nations Emergency Force (UNEF) and the United Nations Congo Force (ONUC) constituted expenses of the United Nations within the meaning of Article 17, paragraph 2 of the Charter, which declares that "the expenses of the Organization shall be borne by the members as apportioned by the General Assembly."[7]

By this opinion, the Court confirmed the General Assembly's authority to impose legally binding assessments on the member states. In effect, a two-thirds majority could now bind the entire membership, including those states that voted in the negative. In that sense, the opinion signified a tentative step toward the principle of international taxation by the world community and lent support to the principle of majority rule in international relations. It also gave the Assembly and the Security Council free rein to establish peace forces of the UNEF or ONUC type and to provide for their financing, thus underwriting the late Secretary-General Dag Hammarskjöld's conception of the UN as a "dynamic instrument" capable of executive action, in contrast to the notion of the UN as a mere "static conference machinery."

Despite the far-reaching implications of the opinion, its practical effects on the UN treasury were not too significant. The two great powers that had refused for reasons of political opposition to pay for UNEF or ONUC—the Soviet Union and France—continued to withhold payment. But thirty-one smaller states that had been in arrears for reasons of alleged financial hardship decided to clear their accounts.[8]

Any analysis of the World Court must be tempered with caution, for the number of cases that have been brought before it have thus far been few— fewer, indeed, than the number earlier submitted to the League of Nations Court. Moreover, it is difficult to determine the Court's role as an impartial arbiter in political disputes. It is true that in both East-West cases, the justices from the Soviet bloc voted with the minority, but this fact alone is inconclusive evidence. It may be explained by political considerations but it may also be attributable to the fact that the justices have been trained in different legal systems and rooted in different political beliefs. On the other hand, the vote of the three Western justices in the membership case indicated a high degree of objectivity.

An obvious and irritating problem consistently plaguing the Court has been that of enforcement. The World Court has no police power by which it can actually implement its decisions against recalcitrant parties to a dispute. When Albania refused to abide by its decision and the Union of South Africa paid no attention to its advisory opinion, the Court was helpless. The Albanian fiasco even raised the question of whether it might not have been better for the Court to stay out of a dispute in which it would be unable to enforce a decision. Some observers have argued that in this instance the Court had "frozen" a quarrel rather than resolved it and that it might have been wiser to leave the matter to the political processes of diplomatic negotiations. Iran was another case in point. In September 1980, the World Court, in a unanimous ruling, ordered Iran to release the American hostages who had been held captive for almost a year. The United States' legal advisor to the Department of State called the ruling "splendid." Nonetheless, Iran not only ignored the opinion entirely but failed to appear before the Court. Nothing could be done to enforce the Court's decision.

In 1984 the Court suffered another setback, this time at the hands of the United States. In April of that year Nicaragua lodged a complaint against the United States, charging that the mining of its ports was an illegal intrusion in its domestic affairs. The United States announced that it was suspending its acceptance of World Court judgments on matters concerning Central America for a period of two years. Moreover, it asserted that Nicaragua had never filed its instruments of ratification and thus had no right to plead before the Court in the first place. The Nicaraguans declared that the United States was guilty of aggression and should be compelled to pay damages. "If the United States does not accept the Court's decision," the Nicaraguan representative announced, "it becomes an outlaw government."

On May 10, 1984, the World Court ruled unanimously that the United States should cease to blockade or mine the ports of Nicaragua. It also asserted by a vote of 14 to 1, with the American judge dissenting, that Nicaragua's political independence "should be fully respected and should not be jeopardized by any military action." In effect, the Court dismissed American procedural objections and found in favor of Nicaragua.

The United States, while rejecting the Court's jurisdiction, nonetheless ceased the mining activities in Nicaragua's harbors. The blockade, however, had been quite ineffectual anyway, and most of America's allies had voiced strong objections. France had even undertaken to remove some of the mines. Thus, the American decision had little to do with the World Court ruling. In the light of the United States' appearance before the Court as plaintiff four years earlier in the Iranian case, its disrespect when it was a defendant was, to say the least, inconsistent. The American judge on the Court apparently realized this inconsistency when he voted with the majority to order the United States to halt the mining. Had the United States not chosen to do so voluntarily and for reasons unrelated to the ruling, the Court could have done nothing to enforce its decision.

Next to enforcement, the Court's most serious problem has been how to encourage nations to avail themselves of its services. In Article 36 of the statute (the so-called optional clause) the Court has given states the opportunity to recognize "as compulsory, *ipso facto* and without special agreement, in relation to any other state accepting the same obligation, the jurisdiction of the Court in all legal disputes." Thirty-eight states have signed this optional clause, and it therefore seems that any legal disputes concerning any one of them would automatically fall under the Court's jurisdiction. This, however, has not been the case, because most states have found it necessary to qualify their adherence to the optional clause through numerous reservations. These reservations have done much to choke off the Court's jurisdiction, since in most cases states have tended to define almost everything as remaining "within their own domestic jurisdiction." To make matters worse, some states have reserved the right to decide unilaterally which matters were to be within their domestic jurisdiction. This was the legal basis on which Iran denied jurisdiction to the Court during the hostage crisis and the United States did the same in its dispute with Nicaragua. Many observers interested in strengthening the Court have pointed out that a beginning could be made if nations withdrew their reservations of unilateral competence to determine which matters were to fall within their domestic jurisdiction. As early as 1959, the Commission to Study the Organization of Peace made a sensible recommendation:

> There is a widespread recognition, reflected in President Eisenhower's 1959 State of the Union message, that the United States has set a bad example for other states in qualifying its ratification of the optional clause so severely as to make that ratification virtually meaningless. No amount of exhortation by American leaders in favor of promoting the rule of law in international affairs would be so effective as the simple act of transforming United States ratification of the optional clause into a genuine acceptance of the Court's compulsory jurisdiction in legal disputes. Such an act might stimulate widespread alteration of attitudes toward the International Court of Justice and pave the way for the full realization of the Court's potential as an instrument for the settlement of disputes and the clarification and development of international law. The Court has a limited but vitally important role to play in the evolution of world order, and it is essential that its opportunities for service through both decisions and advisory opinions be expanded.[9]

In 1989, exactly forty years after the Commission's recommendation, one of the superpowers took the lead in expanding the jurisdiction of the World Court. Paradoxically, this was done by the Soviet Union, not the United States. Under the leadership of Mikhail Gorbachev, the Soviet government permitted the Court jurisdiction over the interpretation of several treaties to which the USSR was a party. The United States, not wishing to be left behind, followed suit. Thus, with an assist from Soviet *glasnost*, the World Court managed to make a small dent in the shield of national sovereignty.

The plight of the International Court of Justice is a fairly accurate reflection of the plight of international law in general. The great issues of international relations—the East-West and the colonial-anticolonial struggles—have remained largely outside its purview. The reason for this is that matters of national prestige and power status have been so much involved that nations have been unwilling to submit such disputes to judicial settlement. Even if states were more inclined to submit disputes to the Court, the problem of enforcement in an anarchic world would still remain. Hitler could not be stopped by a court decision. On the other hand, the World Court has made a vital contribution to order-building in technical and fairly noncontroversial matters, and—in intraregional disputes—even in some important political questions. Perhaps most important, it has become the constitutional arbiter of the United Nations Charter.

REFERENCES

1 *De jure belli ac pacis libri tres*, in *Classics of International Law*, Francis Kelsey, trans., *Prolegomena*, p. 20.

2 U.S. Supreme Court, 1900, *Paquete Habana and the Lola*, 175 U.S. 677.

3 Oliver J. Lissitzyn, *The International Court of Justice*. Carnegie Endowment for International Peace. New York: St. Martin's Press, 1951, p. 80.

4 *Ibid.*, p. 94.

5 *Ibid.*, p. 59.

6 Advisory Opinion Concerning Reparation for Injuries Suffered in the Service of the United Nations, *International Organization,* August 1949, p. 575.
7 International Court of Justice, *Certain Expenses of the United Nations (Article 17, paragraph 2 of the Charter), Advisory Opinion of 20 July 1962:* I.C.J. Reports, 1962.
8 John G. Stoessinger et al., *Financing the United Nations System.* Washington, D.C.: Brookings Institution, 1964.
9 Report of the Commission to Study the Organization of Peace, *Organizing Peace in the Nuclear Age.* New York: New York University Press, 1959, p. 14.

SELECTED BIBLOIGRAPHY

Falk, Richard. *Reviving the World Court.* Charlottesville: University Press of Virginia, 1986. The author suggests that the World Court's justices are too much under the influence of traditional Western concepts of international law. He would like them to be more in tune with the pluralism of today's world.
Franck, Thomas M. *Judging the World Court.* New York: Priority Press Publications, 1986. The author makes a persuasive case for the United States to use the World Court more widely and to accept its jurisdiction more generously.
Hollick, Ann L. *U.S. Foreign Policy and the Law of the Sea.* Princeton: Princeton University Press, 1981 The author traces the tortuous road travelled by US policy makers in search of a viable international legal order for the world's oceans.
Kuper, Leo. *The Prevention of Genocide.* New Haven: Yale University Press, 1985. Now that the United States has, at long last, ratified the UN Genocide Convention of 1948, this full-scale study of genocide and its prevention is most welcome.
Murphy, John F. *Punishing International Terrorists: The Legal Framework for Policy Initiatives.* Totowa, NJ: Rownean & Allanheld, 1985. A useful exploration of specific provisions in international and national law applicable to terrorism. More of a guide to future action than a primer on current practice.
Smith, Bradley F. *The Road to Nuremberg.* New York: Basic Books, 1980. A useful, objective account of the Nuremberg trials.

CHAPTER 10

THE UNITED NATIONS
SYSTEM AND
POLITICAL ORDER

Out of this nettle, danger, we pluck this flower, safety.

Shakespeare, *Henry IV*, 1, 3

THE IDEA OF THE UNITED NATIONS

The United Nations is the most ambitious order-building experiment in history. In one very fundamental sense, its conception is rooted in the past. Its edifice was erected in times of war, during a period of concerted effort to defeat the Axis powers. The Organization was to be called into existence "to kill another Hitler in the shell ere he become too great." The nations were to be "united" against a criminal outlaw. In that sense, the United Nations was to prevent another World War II, just as the League of Nations before it had been created to prevent another World War I. Few of the United Nations' founders at San Francisco were aware of the titanic proportions of the coming East-West struggle. The rock on which the United Nations was to stand was to be the unity of the Great Powers, which would assume among them the major responsibility for peace and order. The United Nations was ill-equipped to deal with a world in which this unity would no longer exist and ill-prepared to answer the vital question: "Who will control the controllers if they should fight among each other?" In that sense, the thinking of the founders was oriented backward in time rather than forward. The future was mobilized once more to slay the dragons of the past.

But in another, equally fundamental sense, the conception of the United Nations was broad and forward-looking. The new world organization was to

261

be created "to save succeeding generations from the scourge of war." But how to accomplish this end when so little was known about the causes of war and the roads to peace? The answer, which found its expression in the structure of the United Nations, was at once simple and sophisticated. It was simple in its failure to anticipate some of the major causes of subsequent international conflict. But it was sophisticated in the various new trails it blazed in the pursuit of peace.

To enable it to work toward its goal, the United Nations was equipped with six major organs. The ambitious task of achieving collective security was assigned to the Security Council. Based on the assumption that peace was indivisible and that the Big Five—the United States, the Soviet Union, Britain, France, and China—could reach unanimity, the Security Council was to be the great international guardian of peace. If challenged by an aggression, it would confront the aggressor with an incontrovertible law based on the irresistible force of the world community.

If the Security Council was thus to find the road to peace through military security, a second major United Nations organ, the General Assembly, was to utilize the time-honored technique of talking things out. It was to function as the world's forum, a Parliament of Man in embryo, a meeting-place in which all member nations were to confer on the basis of sovereign equality. The General Assembly's underlying assumption was that the rational, and sometimes irrational, airing of disputes among nations could contribute importantly to the pacific settlement of those disputes as well as to peaceful changes in the system of international relations itself.

A third principal organ, the Economic and Social Council, was created in the belief that a great deal of international strife was rooted in poverty and misery and that, therefore, the United Nations should do its utmost to help raise standards of living and improve economic conditions throughout the world. Since the founders of the United Nations saw colonialism as another frequent source of war, they felt it necessary also to employ the new world organization to mitigate the anger of dependent peoples against their colonial masters. Hence, to devise a technique whereby independence could be gained with as little bloodshed as possible, they provided a fourth major organ, the Trusteeship Council. The theory behind this latter institution was that if the colonies could be viewed as responsibilities to be shouldered, rather than real estate to be owned and exploited, the colonial nations might prove more amenable to the liquidation of their empires, with the result that violent eruptions of the struggle over colonialism might be avoided. Yet another cause of war was believed by the founders of the United Nations to lie in the absence of common legal standards among nations. For this reason, they included within the United Nations framework the World Court, which we have analyzed earlier (see Chapter 9). The purpose of the World Court was to pass on justifiable disputes and, by building on precedent, to lead in the creation of a uniform international legal system. Finally, the founders of the United Nations were convinced that the maintenance of peace required a nucleus of men and women whose loyalty was first and foremost not to any particular nation but to the entire international community. To head such an international civil service, they established a sixth major organ of the United Nations, the Office of the Secretary-General.

The United Nations was thus designed to attack the problem of war on six principal fronts, each the responsibility of one of its major organs. In addition, the struggle for international peace and stability was also to be waged in a number of more peripheral ways. These became the province of the so-called specialized agencies. Like the United Nations' main organs, these specialized agencies were designed to serve their own particular tasks, and all of them shared the same theoretical assumption. They were based on the premise that sovereignty—the behavior of nations as though they were a law unto themselves—vastly increased the danger of war. Whereas the major organs, however, were to attempt to persuade the nations to give up portions of their sovereignty, the specialized agencies were intended to proceed more indirectly. Their purpose was to engage the nations in enterprises of common interest and thus to bring them actively together in spite of their sovereignty. The reasoning behind this method was that if the United Nations could induce nations to cooperate in economic, social, and cultural activities, giving up some of their sovereignty in these relatively noncontroversial areas, habits of collaboration and a fabric of cohesion would develop that gradually might be transferred to matters of more vital political significance. It was hoped that the nations would then yield some of their sovereignty because it had become superfluous. This indirect approach to peace of the specialized agencies, working toward international cooperation and compromise in regard to specific matters of common interest, was the technique of functionalism.[1]

The specialized agencies that were absorbed into the United Nations system can be divided roughly into two groups. The first group, whose major purpose was to broaden and facilitate communication among nations, included the Universal Postal Union (UPU), the International Telecommunication Union (ITU), the International Civil Aviation Organization (ICAO), the World Meteorological Organization (WMO), and the Inter-Governmental Maritime Consultative Organization (IMCO). Some of these, like UPU and ITU, antedated the creation of the United Nations by several decades. Others, like IMCO, did not come into existence until years after the ratification of the Charter. But all were made part of the United Nations system and all were based on the premise that good "housekeeping" and good communications among nations might decrease the dangers of war.

It is less easy to generalize about the specialized agencies in the second group. For lack of a better term they may be called the "welfare" agencies, in the sense that each was intended to improve world economic, social, and cultural conditions and thus build defenses for the peace. The oldest of these, the International Labor Organization (ILO), was to better conditions of labor throughout the world on the assumption that the equalization of labor standards was a necessary condition of peace. The Food and Agriculture Organization (FAO) hoped to raise nutritional levels and improve agricultural technology. The International Refugee Organization (IRO), conceived as a temporary agency, was to find resettlement opportunities for the uprooted and homeless of the world. It was based on the assumption that nations could make a common effort to salvage refugees from intolerance and thus learn to yield part of their sovereignty in this common enterprise. The World Health Organization (WHO) was based on the premise that ill health and epidemics might be precursors of war. Hence, the objective of this agency was to be the attainment by all peoples of the highest possible level of health. The United Nations Educational, Scientific and Cultural Organization (UNESCO) was established by the framers of the United Nations because they believed that nations' ignorance of one another's ways and lives was a common cause of distrust leading to war. Hence UNESCO was to advance understanding among nations through research and the exchange of scholars and scientists. The International Bank for Reconstruction and Development (IBRD), or World Bank, was to bind up the wounds of war through loans for the reconstruction of devastated areas and to better the chances of peace by granting loans for the development of resources in lesser-developed countries. The International Development Association (IDA), an affiliate of the World Bank, was formed to provide long-term loans at low interest rates to underdeveloped countries that could not obtain World Bank loans. The International Finance Corporation (IFC), another affiliate of the bank, was to promote the growth of productive private enterprise in the developing countries. The International Monetary Fund (IMF) was to aid peace through the promotion of exchange stability and the use of a fund to support weak currencies. Finally, and more recently, the International Atomic Energy Agency (IAEA) was to consecrate the energy of the atom to the cause of peace, and the United Nations Industrial Development Organization (UNIDO) was to encourage the industrial growth of developing countries.

The idea of the United Nations was thus a multidimensional one. But though it was much more ambitious in its conception than the comparable post-World War I project of the League of Nations, it did not attempt the impossible. The UN founders were quite aware that the members of the world organization about to be born were not ready for anything like a world government. They knew that as yet, at least, the only world government that could hold together the heterogeneous population of the earth would have to be one based on force. And this would hardly be an improvement over what already was.

In not attempting the impossible, the founders of the UN were realists. But in seeking to go to the very limits of the possible, they were also visionaries. And necessarily so, for the idea of the United Nations had to take into account the full import of the cruel paradox that, in the nuclear age, the national sovereignty of nations would have to be controlled by an international order, but that this international order would have to be created and even controlled by sovereign nations. The plan therefore had to combine the dictates of national power with those of international order. We shall now see how the United Nations as a working reality has measured up to the original conception.

THE UNITED NATIONS: A BALANCE SHEET

The Security Council and Collective Security

The complexity of the United Nations system makes analysis a formidable task. It makes little sense to evaluate the world organization as a whole. Each organ has its distinctive goals and tools and has established its own unique record. In order to do justice to the United Nations family, each of its members must be considered separately. We shall begin with the organ that the framers of the Charter conceived as the hub of the organization—the Security Council.

The Security Council was given extensive powers to keep the peace. It was to consist of eleven members, of which five—the United States, the Soviet Union, Great Britain, France, and China—were to be permanent. Six nonpermanent members were to be elected by the General Assembly for two-year terms. The Charter empowered the Security Council to recommend means of peaceful settlement of disputes; if a nation committed an act of aggression, the Council would have the power to apply sanctions against the aggressor. These might range from the severance of diplomatic relations to the taking of collective military measures. With a view to the latter, there was also contemplated a Military Staff which would be permanently available to the Security Council.

It thus seemed that the principle of collective security, embodied in the Security Council, had at last acquired teeth. Since the Big Five were to dominate the Council, no aggressor would be able to challenge such an overwhelming agglomeration of power. Yet the Big Five, fully conscious of their preponderant power and their primary responsibility in keeping the peace, demanded proportionate privileges. They not only insisted on their permanent status on the Council, but also demanded that if a Council decision concerned a matter of substance and not a mere question of procedure, the majority would have to include all five of the permanent members. This was the origin of the much discussed "veto power," by which each of the five Great Powers could prevent the Security Council from taking action. This veto power deserves careful analysis.

The exact original wording of Article 27 of the Charter, which gives the right of veto, is as follows:

1 Each member of the Security Council shall have one vote.

2 Decisions of the Security Council on procedural matters shall be made by an affirmative vote of seven members.

3 Decisions of the Security Council on all other matters shall be made by an affirmative vote of seven members including the concurring votes of the permanent members; provided that in decisions under Chapter VI, and under paragraph 3 of Article 52, a party to a dispute shall abstain from voting.

The principal questions to which the veto power was to apply were the admission of new members to the United Nations, enforcement actions to meet a threat to the peace, proposals for the peaceful settlement of disputes, amendments to the Charter, and the election of a Secretary-General.

Three of the Great Powers at San Francisco—the United States, the Soviet Union, and Great Britain—insisted on the right of veto. None of them would have acceded to the United Nations without that right. China and France at first took a more flexible position, but the rigid stand of the Big Three soon resulted in their equally firm insistence on the veto rule. As a further safeguard of their sovereignty, moreover, the Great Powers insisted that the decision as to whether a vote was to be substantive or procedural was itself a substantive question and hence subject to the veto. This meant that in theory at least, anything was vetoable that a Great Power might choose to veto. Needless to say, this possibility of the use of the veto being expanded to apply to any matter at all did not augur well for the effective functioning of the Security Council. It thus seemed that from the very beginning the Great Powers' uncompromising insistence on their sovereignty, combined with the intensification of the East-West struggle, might well turn the Security Council into a moribund agency.

It has almost become a cliché to assert that the Security Council was paralyzed through the Soviet Union's abuse of the veto power. While there is some validity to this charge, the truth is far more complex. It is true that the Soviet Union has been responsible for more than 80 percent of the total number of vetoes cast. By the late 1980s it had cast well over one hundred vetoes. But the figures themselves do not sufficiently explain the picture. In the first place, the Soviet Union has not had a monopoly of negative votes. The negative votes of the other Great Powers were usually not classed as vetoes because others of the Big Five—as well as some nonpermanent members—voted the same way. As Normal J. Padelford has pointed out:

> It is clear from the record that when the Soviet Union finds its vital interests at stake there are now no other great powers generally inclined to stand with it. Therefore the negative vote of the Soviet delegate usually becomes a sole veto, accompanied ordinarily only by the vote of whatever satellite holds a non-permanent seat on the Council. When other great powers, particularly the United States and Great Britain, find their national interests at issue they can usually persuade other permanent members to go along with them either in casting a multiple negative vote sufficient to stop a proposal without the stigma of exercising a sole veto (or near-sole veto), or to join in introducing and passing a resolution more suitable to their desires.[2]

Second, the Western powers on the Security Council were able to make the Soviet Union appear even more obstructionist by forcing votes on issues that they knew would elicit a Soviet veto. Thus over half of the Soviet vetoes were cast against the admission of Western and Western-oriented nations to the United Nations. Italy's application, for example, was vetoed six times before that nation was finally admitted as part of a "package deal" in December 1955, as a result of which sixteen new members were permitted to join the United Nations. Finally, the Soviet Union has declared that it has been forced to use the veto extensively because of the composition of the Security Council. In the words of Premier Khrushchev in 1958:

> It is common knowledge that the majority in the Security Council is composed of the votes of countries dependent, in one way or another, primarily economically, on the U.S.A. Thus, the Security Council in its present composition cannot be regarded as an impartial arbiter, and that is why it has of late ceased to play the important role in the maintenance of international peace and security which devolved upon it by virtue of the United Nations Charter.[3]

It is true that when Khrushchev made the above statement, there was no member of the Security Council upon whose support the Soviet Union could count. The Soviet Union was the only Communist state with a vote in the Security Council. Eight votes were controlled by military allies of the United States in NATO and SEATO. Two members—Iraq and Sweden—were neutralists in the East-West struggle. In the following year, Sweden was replaced by Italy, a member of NATO, and Iraq by Tunisia. Thus, in 1959, the composition of the Security Council began to resemble that of a Western military alliance. A good illustration of a typical case is provided by the U-2 plane episode in 1960. In May of that year, the Soviet Union brought the case before the Security Council and introduced a resolution branding the flights by American planes over Soviet territory as "acts of aggression." Two states—the USSR and Poland—voted in favor of the Soviet motion; seven states—Argentina, China, Ecuador, France, Italy, the United Kingdom, and the United States—voted against. The latter were all members of the Western alliance system. Two non-aligned states—Ceylon and Tunisia—abstained.

This pattern began to change somewhat in 1966, when four nonpermanent members were added to the Security Council. The passage of a resolution now required nine affirmative votes instead of seven. Since the enlargement of the Council was undertaken primarily for the benefit of the new nations, most of which were nonaligned on East-West issues, it now became more difficult for the United States to control the Council. In 1966, for example, when the United States attempted to have the Vietnam question inscribed on the Council's agenda, it found itself dependent upon the vote of Jordan. The move succeeded, but just barely. The days of an automatic American majority or of a "hidden veto" achieved by mobilizing this majority against a Soviet-sponsored resolution were over. United States influence was still very great, but now had to depend on bargaining and persuasion rather than reliance on an absolute majority.

On the whole, the Security Council tended to narrow rather than expand the scope of the veto power. It established that the abstention of a Great Power was not tantamount to veto, and, in the Korean police action decision of 1950, went even further by declaring that the absence of a Great Power should merely be regarded as abstention but not as a veto *in absentia*. Perhaps most important, the potential threat inherent in the "double-veto" has not materialized. It has been used relatively sparingly.

The tendency to blame the veto power—especially its excessive use by the Soviet Union—for the decline of the Security Council is to confuse the symptoms with the causes. The membership of the Security Council reflects the two great political struggles of our time. The Great Power veto has simply been a constant reminder that, in an international system of sovereign nation-states, no important action may be taken against a major power without its consent. In fact, it may be argued that abolition of the veto might increase the danger of war, since the majority might then be tempted into precipitous action against the recalcitrant superpower. The unanimity principle has also taught the lesson that, in the nuclear age, the technique of arriving at decisions by counting votes has not been the most fortunate one for the solution of international problems. The principle of voting by majority does make sense in a homogeneous political context, but in a world of profound schisms, negotiating with the opponent rather than out-voting him or her may be a wiser method of intercourse. All this is not to say that the veto has been a blessing. But certainly, it has not been the unmitigated evil that some observers have made it seem to be. Indeed, many Soviet vetoes have been circumvented through action in the General Assembly or through other means.

The 1970s witnessed significant changes in the power balance of the Security Council. As the United States lost its automatic majority, it too resorted to the use of the veto power. American virginity was lost in March 1970 when the United States cast its first veto to prevent the use of force against the regime of Southern Rhodesia. Subsequently, the United States used its veto to defeat hostile majorities on issues primarily concerning Middle Eastern and African affairs. By the late 1980s, thirty American vetoes had been cast. Most of these were cast against Middle Eastern resolutions that the United States considered unbalanced and against the use of force to bring down the two white minority regimes in Southern Africa. In 1977, for example, the United States approved an arms embargo against South Africa but joined Britain and France in vetoing a resolution that would have imposed full economic sanctions against the Pretoria government. Another typical American veto was one cast in 1983 against a resolution that would have condemned Israel for settling the West Bank. Yet another was cast in 1985, once again to prevent mandatory economic sanctions against the government of South Africa, which had just proclaimed a state of national emergency.

The composition of the Council changed dramatically with the seating of the People's Republic of China in 1971. The old bipolar tug of war between the Soviet Union and the United States gave way to a new and different constellation. This became clear during the Indo-Pakistan war of 1971 when the Soviet Union backed India and China supported Pakistan. The Security Council was paralyzed not by the familiar United States-Soviet deadlock, but by a Chinese-Soviet confrontation during which the latter cast three consecutive vetoes. In 1972 China cast its first veto in order to block the admission of Bangladesh to the United Nations. It now seemed as if effective Council action would be possible only through consensus of the Big Three, no longer just the Big Two. Despite this new and complicating element, the Security Council did not break down. Every six months it managed to extend the mandate of the peace force in Cyprus (UNFICYP), which it had established in 1964. The mandate continued even during the hostilities that erupted on the island in 1974. In 1973 and 1974, in the wake of the October War in the Middle East, the Security Council even managed to create two new peace forces: a United Nations Emergency Force (UNEF II), which was to supervise the disengagement agreement between Israel and Egypt, and a United Nations Disengagement Observer Force (UNDOF), which had similar responsibilities in the wake of the Syria-Israeli agreement. (See Chapter 12.)

In 1978, the Council established a United Nations Interim Force in Lebanon (UNIFIL). Although bypassed by Israeli troops during their 1982 invasion, UNIFIL has remained in Lebanon to prevent a Beirut-type chaos in the southern part of that tragic country.

In 1988, the Security Council experienced a new resurgence, partially as a result of the flexibility of the new Soviet leader, Mikhail Gorbachev, and partially due to the resourcefulness of UN Secretary-General Javier Perez de Cuellar. For five years, the Secretary-General had been trying to mediate the eight-year-old conflict between the Soviet Union and Afghanistan. When, at long last, Gorbachev decided to end the war and to pull out Soviet troops, the Secretary-General's efforts came to fruition. The Security Council authorized a small UN observer group for Afghanistan consisting of fifty soldiers to monitor the terms of the Soviet withdrawal (see Chapter 12). Equally important, the Secretary-General had engaged in tireless efforts to bring the Iran-Iraq war to a close. Finally, after eight years of bloody conflict and one million casualties, the combatants agreed to a unanimous Security Council resolution demanding a cease fire. The Council also authorized the establishment of a 300-person UN observer group from thirty countries, to be deployed on the Iran-Iraqi border to monitor the cease fire (see Chapter 12), as well as a 70-person force to observe the withdrawal of Cuban troops from Angola. After a decade of inertia, the Security Council was once more coming into its own. It could not stop wars, but it could help warring states who had had enough of war to bring it to an end.

The General Assembly

The General Assembly was conceived as a world forum, a talking-shop in which the world's nations were to be given the broad mandate "to discuss any questions or any matters within the scope of the Charter." It was to be the largest although not the most important organ of the United Nations. Each nation, large or small, was to have one vote. The Assembly was to have no enforcement powers but merely the authority to recommend courses of action.

Like a national legislature, it was organized into committees. A survey of its seven standing committees gives a bird's eye view of the Assembly's responsibilities: two Committees on Political and Security Questions; an Economic and Financial Committee; a Social, Humanitarian, and Cultural Committee; a Trusteeship Committee; an Administrative and Budgetary Committee; and a Legal Committee. Thus the Assembly was given the power to discuss almost anything within the purview of the Charter: the maintenance of peace and security; the financial contributions of member states, the raising of economic, social, education, and health standards; the disposition of former colonies; the promotion of human rights; and the development of international law. Much United Nations activity was to be initiated in the Assembly and also was to be approved by it. The Assembly was to be the world's town meeting, but its bailiwick was to be a highly heterogeneous society of nation-states. It was to have no power of compulsion; enforcement was to be the exclusive domain of the Security Council.

When, quite early in the life of the UN, it became apparent that the Security Council—paralyzed by the unanimity rule—was falling victim to the East-West struggle, the Assembly was given certain "implied powers" through a liberal interpretation of the Charter. In 1947 the Assembly voted to create an Interim Committee, or Little Assembly, which was to meet whenever circumstances might require during intervals between sessions of the Assembly. More important was the so-called Uniting for Peace Resolution adopted by the Assembly in November 1950. This resolution grew out of the American conviction that the Security Council action to meet aggression in Korea had been made possible only through a fortuitous circumstance—the absence of the Soviet delegation. Hence, the United States proposed that the Assembly exercise a residual responsibility in any threat to the peace in case the Security Council was hamstrung by the veto. The resolution contained five major provisions of far-reaching import:

1 It authorized the General Assembly to meet on short notice in an emergency in which the Security Council was prevented from acting, and to recommend appropriate collective measures, including the use of armed force when necessary.

2 It established a fourteen-nation Peace Observation Commission to observe and report on dangerous situations in any part of the world.

3 It asked all members to maintain in their armed forces special elements which could be made available for United Nations service on call of the Security Council or the General Assembly.

4 It established a fourteen-nation Collective Measures Committee to study and report on these and other methods for maintaining and strengthening international peace and security.

5 It urged all UN members to renew their fidelity to the United Nations, honor its decisions, and promote respect for human rights and achievement of economic stability and social progress.

The resolution became the subject of heated controversy. The Soviet Union, holding to a narrow interpretation of the Charter, declared that most of its provisions were illegal. The United States, on the other hand, construing the Charter more broadly, declared that the provisions were in accordance with its spirit and that they clearly served the need of strengthening international peace and security. The resolution was adopted by a vote of 52 to 5, with 2 abstentions. It greatly broadened the scope of the General Assembly which, as a result of its new mandate, was able to deal with several matters of security: the Chinese military intervention in Korea, the Suez crisis of 1956, Soviet intervention in Hungary, the Lebanese crisis of 1958, and the Congo crisis of 1960. Thus, the Assembly became a backstop of the Security Council. The Charter, like a constitution, had shown itself to be amenable to interpretation in order to keep pace with changing events.

Since its inception, the United Nations has rapidly been approaching the ideal of universal membership. It started out with fifty-one original members, and for years the East-West struggle resulted in a policy of competitive exclusion of new applicants. "Package deals" in the mid-1950s resulted in the admission of over a score of new members, and by the 1980s—following the birth of many newly sovereign states in the Third World—membership in the Assembly was approaching the 160 mark.

The most significant consequence of the Assembly's growing comprehensiveness has been the emergence of blocs and the development of bloc voting. The Assembly has thus tended to become one of the arenas in which the two major political struggles of our time are being waged. In fact, the Assembly has begun to take on the complexion of a multiparty system. The uneven degree of discipline within each bloc or party has made the picture somewhat analogous to the French Parliament under the Fourth Republic. Roughly speaking, six blocs have emerged in the Assembly: the Afro-Asian bloc (the largest but least cohesive) has at times commanded over seventy votes; the Latin American bloc has been able to muster twenty votes, the Atlantic Community eighteen, the British Commonwealth twenty, and the Arab bloc ten. The most highly disciplined group has been the Communist bloc which, not including Yugoslavia, has controlled nine votes.

The vast majority of votes taken in the General Assembly have involved one or both of the two great political struggles. According to the voting rules of the General Assembly, important questions are to be decided by a two-thirds vote, and "other matters" by simple majority. In view of this fact it is clear that, under certain conditions, some blocs—singly or in combination with others—may exercise what amounts to a collective veto over decisions of the General Assembly. Theoretically, for instance, the Afro-Asian bloc, if united, could effectively block any important decision. In practice, however, this has not tended to occur. The Afro-Asian bloc has often been deeply divided. Also, party discipline has been loose and, in many instances, "crossing the floor" has become a frequent phenomenon. In this connection, it is useful to point out that in the General Assembly—unlike a national legislature—there are not two but three sides to a controversial question. Abstentions are freely re-corded and frequently their high number has demonstrated that many nations have refused to stand up and be counted in the East-West or the colonial-anticolonial struggle.

A good case can be made that by the mid-1970s the radical wing of the new Afro-Arab-Asian nationalism had captured control of the General Assembly. Var-ious "national liberation" groups demanded and received legitimacy. The most prominent case in point was the decision of the General Assembly in 1974 by overwhelming vote to invite Yasir Arafat, the leader of the Palestinian Liberation Organization, to address the world body. When Arafat appeared, he was ac-corded all the ceremonial honors usually reserved for heads of state. Only 4 states out of the 138 that then made up the Assembly's membership had opposed the invitation, the United States among them. When during the Palestine debate As-sembly president Abdelaziz Bouteflika in effect curbed Israel's right to speak by limiting the debate to one speech from each country, this ruling was vainly op-posed by the United States. And when the Assembly, in late November 1974, by a vote of 89 to 8, with 37 abstentions, affirmed the right of the Palestinian people to be free and sovereign and, in a companion vote of 95 to 17, with 19 abstentions, awarded permanent observer status to the Palestine Liberation Organization, the United States again was on the side of the opposition. The trend spilled over from the General Assembly into one of the United Nations' "nonpolitical" specialized agencies. The General Conference of UNESCO adopted several highly contro-versial resolutions unfavorable to Israel including one that rejected Israel's re-quest to participate in UNESCO's European regional grouping. On December 6, 1974, the United States delegate, John A. Scali, warned the General Assembly that when the majority rule becomes "the tyranny of the majority, the minority will cease to respect or obey it."

The rise of the Afro-Asian-Arab bloc brought the one nation-one vote rule under heavy fire. It became increasingly difficult for the Great Powers, espe-cially the United States, to accept the fact that Chad's or Iraq's vote should have the same weight as that of a major power. The question has been raised whether it was reasonable to expect the United States or the Soviet Union to accept decisions reached by a body in which a nation with a small and largely illiterate population and an underdeveloped economy should have the same voice as a superpower, or whether the United States, which has contributed one fourth of the budget, should have the same voting power as a nation with an assessment of less than 0.1 percent. These considerations have led to many informal "weighted voting" proposals designed to bring voting power into line with the realities of political power and influence in the Assembly. These pro-posals have all foundered on the question of what would constitute an objec-tive criterion for weighting. Should it be population, military strength, literacy, wealth, or other more intangible factors? Moreover, since the distribution of power among nations is in constant flux, whatever weighting was decided upon would require constant revision. For these reasons, the Assembly's sys-tem of equality has been retained despite its obvious inequities.

During the years of cold-war political confrontation between East and West, the United States had a relatively easy time in the General Assembly. Of the original fifty-one members of the United Nations in 1945, at least thirty-five were closely associated with the United States, only five with the Soviet Union, and only ten were nonaligned. In those early years, the United States delegation could easily muster majority votes and even two-thirds votes when required.

The United States did not hesitate in those years to use its "automatic majority" in its own national interest. Former Ambassador Scali would have done well to concede, in his comments on the "tyranny of the majority," that the United States was once able to keep Communist China out of the United Nations, to persuade the United Nations to intervene in Korea, and to shift peace-keeping from the Security Council, in case of veto, to the General Assembly under the Uniting for Peace Resolution of 1950.

Today, the shoe is on the other foot. Because of the liquidation of the colonial empires, the more than one hundred developing countries, usually backed by the Communist countries, can easily muster a two-thirds vote in the General Assembly. Perhaps the most dramatic and controversial event that shook the General Assembly during the 1970s was a vote taken on November 10, 1975, defining Zionism as "a form of racism and racial discrimination." The vote was 72 in favor, 35 against, with 32 abstentions and 3 delegations absent.

The majority, consisting of all the Communist states save Rumania and most Third World countries, charged Israel with white settler and military expansion policies reminiscent of the imperialist powers of a bygone era. Those states in opposition, led by the United States and the Western European powers, deplored the resolution as infamous and harmful to the United Nations' cause.

It was indeed ironic that, thirty years after the death of Hitler, the victims of the worst excesses of racism in modern history should now be accused of a similar transgression. There was little doubt that the anti-Zionist resolution was a triumph for the forces of radicalism among the Third World, and that these forces, armed with centuries of anticolonial fury and modern petrodollars, had now come close to making the UN General Assembly into their vehicle. But a closer scrutiny of the vote does not suggest that the General Assembly had succumbed to a wave of anti-Semitism of the Hitler variety. The reasons for the anti-Zionist vote were much more complex.

In the first place, a number of Third World votes were simply bought with petrodollars. Second, several African states supported the resolution for reasons of Third World solidarity without much substantive knowledge about either Israel or Zionism. As the delegate of Mauritius put it, "Many people voted without knowing what Zionism is. I am confused." Third, many delegates supported the anti-Zionism drive because they were against what the Palestinians told them Israel was: a white imperialist military state reminiscent of the Western colonial regimes. Fourth, Israel was perceived by many of the nations of the Third World as the protégé of the United States, which in turn was perceived by them as the military leader of all the former colonial powers in NATO. Fifth, Israel, it was pointed out, was settled largely by whites, and its early leaders were Europeans from Russia. Finally, many states voted for the resolution because of fear of Arab oil retaliation or abstained for similar reasons, as in the case of Japan.

Thus, the anti-Zionism vote of 1975 signified the confluence of a number of factors. The most prominent were the petrodollar, opportunism, and ignorance, as well as pride and prejudice. One final observation about the resolution is worthy of mention: those nations that voted in favor were largely dictatorships, both of the left and of the right, while those in opposition were largely, though by no means exclusively, the Western democracies. In the General Assembly of the 1970s, the democracies numbered less than two dozen states and appeared almost like an endangered species.

Similar resolutions were passed in other UN bodies, and even some specialized agencies, such as UNESCO and ILO, became arenas of political contention. The American response was one of anger and withdrawal. In 1976, Secretary Kissinger announced that the United States would reduce economic assistance to countries that had voted against the United States in the United Nations. He also declared his intention to take the United States out of the International Labor Organization, which had passed a number of Third World-sponsored anti-Western resolutions. He was supported in this move by George Meany, head of the American Federation of Labor and Congress of Industrial Organizations (AFL-CIO), which represented American workers in the ILO. Meany also objected to the presence of Soviet officials in the governing body of the ILO. In 1977, the United States made good on its threat and withdrew from ILO membership, thus depriving that specialized agency of 25 percent of its budget. The move was symptomatic of the American dissatisfaction with having become a minority party in the United Nations. Money was used as a tangible weapon to express that growing discontent.

Under the Reagan administration, the United States became increasingly disillusioned with the General Assembly. Its preoccupation with East-West issues made the United States impatient with the Assembly's North-South perception of most of the world's conflicts. On one occasion in 1984, a member of the United States delegation declared in a moment of pique that, if the United Nations should choose to leave New York, the Americans would gladly wave goodbye as the delegates sailed into the sunset. The President, while not endorsing this comment, did suggest that it might make sense for the United Nations to divide its working year between New York and Moscow. In addition, the State Department announced that the United States would withdraw from UNESCO within two years unless that specialized agency's anti-Western bias and wasteful financial practices were promptly corrected. Clearly, the United States had put much distance between itself and the world body since the days of John F. Kennedy, who had described the United Nations as "the cornerstone of American foreign policy."

The United States' displeasure with the General Assembly came to a head on yet another issue in 1987. Late that year, the Congress had mandated the closing of the PLO mission to the United Nations on the grounds that the PLO was a terrorist organization. In March 1988, the General Assembly, by overwhelming vote, challenged the US position, maintaining that it breached its treaty obligations to the United Nations. In addition, the Assembly asked the World Court to render an advisory opinion on the matter. In the meantime, in June 1988, a US federal judge upheld the PLO's right to maintain an observer mission at UN headquarters. To deny it that right, the judge opined, would be a violation of the UN Headquarters Agreement with the United States. Five months later, the US Department of State denied a visa to Yasir Arafat, who wanted to address the General Assembly in New York. Finally, in December 1988, in Geneva, the Assembly, in an overwhelming vote, with only the United States and Israel in opposition, heard Arafat and recommended the creation of a state of Palestine and the placing of Gaza and the West Bank under UN supervision.

This protracted confrontation between the US Congress and the UN General Assembly did not help the UN's treasury. American displeasure was now translated by the Congress into financial penny-pinching. Congress refused to pay its full contributions to the various UN budgets and fell more and more into arrears. During the 1960s and 1970s, the Soviet Union had been the UN's "deadbeat," and the United States was prodding it to pay its debts. By the late 1980s, Mikhail Gorbachev had cleared the Soviet Union's accounts, and the United States had become the deadbeat. It was the Soviet Union's turn now to appreciate the UN's role as face-saver in Afghanistan, Africa, and other areas of conflict. And it was the United States' turn, apparently, to sulk. Only in 1988 did the Reagan administration decide to pay a portion of its arrears.

It will take patience and understanding for the United States to adjust itself to a United Nations shaped and dominated by Third World nations, most of which were born since the end of the Second World War. It must be remembered, however, that the General Assembly reflects the interests and objectives of politically motivated governments and thus reflects the politics of a world that itself has changed profoundly since the years of the cold war. In every debate, there are grounds for differences on the merits of both sides of every argument. It is the essence of statesmanship to reconcile these competing interests and differing points of view for the common good, through negotiation and compromise. Just as very few decisions of the American Congress satisfy all its members, very few decisions of the United Nations will satisfy all its members. The Congress may make mistakes in the eyes of some citizens, but these mistakes do not justify scrapping the Constitution. Similarly, if the General Assembly makes mistakes in the eyes of the United States, this perception does not justify scrapping the Charter. In the long run, the success of the United Nations system will not depend upon the votes on some specific issues in a particular session of the General Assembly, but rather, in the words of the Charter, upon "harmonizing the actions of nations in the attainment of these common ends."

The Economic and Social Council

The framers of the United Nations Charter were profoundly impressed by the functional theory of international order-building. This conviction found its most ambitious institutional expression in the Economic and Social Council (ECOSOC). This organ was to be an instrument for coordinating an entire galaxy of functional activities, ranging from aid to needy children to technical assistance to lesser-developed areas. The common denominator of all these activities was the functional premise that the bonds of international political order could be forged more readily by first concentrating on specific common problems in the politically less formidable spheres of economic, social, and cultural affairs. It was hoped that such activities could be kept out of the arena of political controversy and that the habits of collaboration thus developed might little by little reach over into the strife-torn areas of political and even military security. In order to emphasize and facilitate this work, the Economic and Social Council became one of the principal United Nations organs.

ECOSOC was made up originally of eighteen members, elected for three years by the General Assembly. In 1966, the membership was enlarged to twenty-seven, and in 1988 it stood at fifty-eight. Although the Charter contains no specific membership provisions, in practice the permanent members of the Security Council have had permanent seats on ECOSOC as well. The rest of the membership has tended to reflect the power alignments of the General Assembly, although there has been a slight imbalance in favor of the more advanced industrial states. ECOSOC is responsible to the Assembly and, in effect, has frequently served as a committee of the Assembly on functional matters. Since ECOSOC itself is not an operational organ, most of its energies have been absorbed in coordinating the numerous commissions which are under its control. There are eight such functional commissions in all. They deal with a wide variety of subject matter: transport, statistics, population, social matters, human rights and protection of minorities, status of women, commodity trade, and narcotic drugs. In addition, ECOSOC has set up a number of regional commissions: the Economic Commission for Europe (ECE) and parallel bodies for Asia and the Far East, Latin America, and Africa. There are also four special voluntary programs which depend for their support exclusively upon donations from governments and private sources: the United Nations Children's Fund (UNICEF); the United Nations Development Program (UNDP), consisting before the merger of 1966 of two separate bodies known as the Expanded Program for Technical Assistance (EPTA) and the Special Fund; the United Nations High Commissioner for Refugees (UNHCR); and the United Nations Relief and Works Agency for Palestine Refugees in the Near East (UNRWA). Finally, ECOSOC receives reports from all the specialized agencies. The difficulties in coordinating this vast array of functional bodies have therefore been enormous. In general, the job has been somewhat easier in economic than in social fields, and less trying in regional than in global matters. But ECOSOCS's role as a clearing-house for the UN's functional activities has been complicated even further through the participation in its affairs of various citizens' organizations. Among these, and enjoying consultative status in ECOSOC, have been such nongovernmental organizations as the YMCA, the YWCA, and the US Chamber of Commerce.

So great has been the proliferation of functional activities under UN auspices that they virtually defy systematic analysis. Ironically, among the organs coordinated by ECOSOC there have even developed certain empire-building tendencies. In areas of overlapping activity, some agencies have claimed "sovereignty" over responsibilities to which other agencies have at the same time stoutly laid claim. And inevitably, the problem of deciding priorities is a difficult one at best. Given the inescapable realities of a limited budget, who, for example, is to determine which will be more conducive to the building of international order: the exchange of scientists or advancement in the status of women?

The General Assembly, at its sixteenth session in 1961, proclaimed a Development Decade to mobilize support for the poorer nations of the earth. A second Development Decade was announced in 1971 and a third in 1981. The UN Development Program and the specialized agencies were seen as the chief instruments of this bold plan.

In December 1964, the General Assembly, prodded by the developing nations in ECOSOC, passed a resolution creating a new United Nations organ, the UN Conference on Trade and Development (UNCTAD). The main purpose of the Conference, as seen by the "Group of 77" developing nations, is to help the poor nations of the world rectify the imbalances in their international trade and thus to achieve industrialization and economic self-sufficiency. Toward that end, the conference, which includes the entire UN membership, meets at least once every four years and its permanent organ, the Trade and Development Board, once every six months. An UNCTAD secretariat, headed by a secretary-general, has its headquarters in Geneva, where the first conference convened in 1964.

UNCTAD is now a regular United Nations body in which the poor regularly confront the rich and demand better terms for their economies. It has become the principal forum for negotiating commodity agreements, for example. The conference has not remained insulated from political controversy, however. At first, the Soviet Union and the United States engaged in a kind of "aid race" for the allegiance of the poor nations, but by the 1970s the richer nations developed a tougher attitude and the aid race was gradually replaced by a silent United States–Soviet agreement not to accede to unreasonable demands. Thus, UNCTAD has highlighted the political patterns that link the East-West struggle with that of the world's poor for their place in the sun.

There is a measure of competition between ECOSOC and the General Assembly. The former is constituted on a regional basis and consists of only fifty-four members, while the latter comprises the entire UN membership. Hence, the rich industrialized nations have more influence in ECOSOC than in the General Assembly, where the developed countries are outnumbered. When the World Food Conference in 1974 decided to establish a World Food Council, for example, the United States and the Soviet Union wanted to make the new organ responsible to ECOSOC, while the Third World nations preferred that the General Assembly serve as the coordinating umbrella. A compromise solution was finally worked out with the Food Council reporting to the Assembly through the Economic and Social Council. In 1978, the General Assembly, in an effort to coordinate all these activities, empowered the Secretary-General to appoint a Director-General for Economic and Social Operations.

ECOSOC continues to be one of the six principal organs of the United Nations and continues to serve as an important clearing house for functional programs. But recently it has become more of a technical organ than a political decision-making body. As the divisions between rich and poor, consumers and producers, have assumed increasing importance in the United Nations, ECOSOC's political role has been eclipsed to a considerable extent by the General Assembly. During the Twenty-ninth session in 1974, for example, the General Assembly adopted a Charter of Economic Rights and Duties of States which was highly favorable to the developing countries. The vote was 120 in favor, 6 against, including the United States, with 10 abstentions. The adoption of this new document was one of the events that brought about former Ambassador Scali's warning about the "tyranny of the majority." Since then, the Assembly, rather than ECOSOC, has been the leading forum for resolutions related to the advancement of the New International Economic Order.

Throughout most of the 1980s, the Economic and Social Council was plagued by the UN's financial crisis precipitated by the United States' decision to cut back its voluntary contributions and to withhold its assessed share of the UN budget. One shining moment, however, brightened up that melancholy decade. In December 1988, the United Nations celebrated the fortieth anniversary of the Universal Declaration of Human Rights. Perhaps it was not lost upon the US Congress, still penny-wise and pound-foolish in its attitude toward the United Nations, that the author of that historic Declaration in 1948 had been Eleanor Roosevelt.

The Trusteeship Council

The concept of trusteeship was devised by the United Nation's founders primarily as a weapon against the struggle they anticipated over the liquidation of colonialism. If only the United Nations could turn the colonies from lucrative benefits into "sacred trusts," the quest for dependencies might die from lack of incentive. Colonial powers might develop greater inhibitions in their quest for colonies, and anticolonial powers greater patience in their struggle for independence. If, indeed, colonialism was a cause of war, then the United Nations should make as international as possible the administration of dependent areas and the process by which their colonial status finally came to be terminated. This, in general terms, was the thinking that underlay the concept of trusteeship.

In setting up the Trusteeship Council, the UN founders were able to build on the precedent of the mandate system of the League of Nations. While the League's mandate system had in essence been a thinly disguised technique of annexation, with its Permanent Mandates Commission controlled exclusively by colonial powers, it nevertheless represented a first tentative attempt at internationalization. The United Nations' framers were determined to expand this experiment considerably. Their first step was to dispose of the mandates that had been held by the now-defunct League system. For the most part, these were immediately turned into trusteeships of the United Nations. Exempted from this transfer, however, were the former Middle Eastern mandates—Syria, Lebanon, Jordan, and Israel—which were soon to achieve national independence; Southwest Africa, which was lost to the United Nations because of the stubborn refusal of the Union of South Africa to permit it to be placed under trusteeship; Japan's Pacific holdings, which were taken over as a so-called Strategic Trust Territory by the United States; and Somaliland, which had not been a League mandate and which was entrusted to Italy. Beyond these changes, the trusteeship system continued very much in the footsteps of the League. Britain was to administer Tanganyika and parts of Togoland and the Cameroons; the remainder of Togoland and the Cameroons remained under France; Ruanda-Urundi continued as a Belgian trust; to Australia were entrusted Nauru and New Guinea; and New Zealand was to administer Western Samoa. In all, the Trusteeship Council was thus to supervise eleven trust territories, seven of them in Africa, and a total population of fifteen million people.

The most radical departure from the League precedent was the widespread conviction among UN members that administration not only of trust territories but of *all* colonial possessions should be internationalized. This principle became the subject of heated controversy. The colonial powers insisted that the colonial possessions were to be under their jurisdiction exclusively, whereas the anticolonial bloc saw no further justification for the continuation of colonialism at all. The outcome of this struggle was Chapter XI of the Charter, The Declaration Regarding Non-Self-Governing Territories, which represented a modest triumph for the forces of anticolonialism. For one thing, the United Nations was no longer to use the term "colony." In its place was to be substituted the more innocuous phrase "Non-Self-Governing Territory." In addition, the colonial powers committed themselves to transmit information on economic, educational, and social conditions in their respective dependencies. The new nations pressed for the submission of political information as well, but the colonial powers insisted that this matter be left to their own discretion. Thus, when the new trusteeship system was launched, it was not only responsible for the administration of eleven trust territories but also, for the first time in history, possessed the power of imposing a minimum of international control over all colonies.

In composition, the Trusteeship Council was originally a fourteen-nation body, with its membership divided equally between colonial and anticolonial powers, or in United Nations terminology, "administering" and "nonadministering" powers. Australia, Belgium, France, Italy, Great Britain, New Zealand, and the United States represented the first group. The Soviet Union and China plus five other nonadministering powers made up the anticolonial bloc. As a result of the liquidation of two thirds of the trust territories, the size of the Trusteeship Council has diminished considerably. By 1980 it consisted of only five states: the permanent members of the Security Council. The transition from trusteeship status to independence has, on the whole, been orderly. The exodus began in 1960 with the granting of independence to Cameroon, Togo, and Somalia. Tanganyika was next, receiving independence in 1961. On January 1, 1962, Western Samoa became the first independent Polynesian state and on the same day the Belgian trust, Ruanda-Urundi, was transformed into two independent countries, Rwanda and Burundi. By 1980 only the Pacific Islands remained under the authority of the Trusteeship Council.

Each of the trust territories was administered under a Trusteeship Agreement. These agreements were concluded between the administering powers and the United Nations, but in most cases the former were able to determine the nature of the agreement. The United States, for example, insisted that the Pacific Islands be made into a Strategic Trust Territory under the Security Council, and therefore subject to American veto. The terms of the agreements were approved by the General Assembly, to which the Trusteeship Council has been responsible on all important matters. Like ECOSOC, the council has, in effect, become a committee of the Assembly. Owing to the stronger representation of the colonial powers on the Trusteeship Council, its recommendations—especially those dealing with advancement toward self-government in the trust territories—have at times been criticized by the General Assembly as lacking in vigor. Responsibility for the supervision of Non-Self-Governing Territories, under Chapter XI of the Charter, has not been exercised by the Trusteeship Council itself but by a separate body, the Committee on Information from Non-Self-Governing Territories. The membership of that committee has been patterned after that of the council.

Where the Trusteeship Council was directly involved in its dealings with the trust territories, its responsibilities were threefold: preparation of annual reports, examinations of petitions, and dispatch of visiting missions. Annual reports were based on lengthy written questionnaires, to be completed by the administering powers. If the replies seemed incomplete or unsatisfactory, the Trusteeship Council had the right to proceed to written and oral cross-examination. On the basis of these reports, the council then formulated its own recommendations for the General Assembly. These recommendations were far-reaching and related to economic development, health services, educational facilities, labor conditions, and the participation of the indigenous population in the affairs of government. The Trusteeship Council also permitted the inhabitants of trust territories to submit petitions on specific grievances. This procedure was a radical departure from the League precedent, since it by-passed the colonial power and established direct contact between the trust and the United Nations. At first this opportunity was utilized infrequently, but during and since the 1950s the number of petitions grew considerably. A typical petition brought before the Trusteeship Council concerned the fate of the Ewe tribe in West Africa, which claimed that the boundary line between French and British Togoland divided its people. The following excerpt will convey its flavor:

> About 2 years ago both french and british government promised to have constituted a conventional zone for the amendment of the frontiers regulations, amidst the Ewe people. This problem is very hard to be solved, because it is impossible for two persons to wear one trousers. Only their guilty conscience forced them to make this promise, but in reality they are unfit to complete this task just like two persons suggesting of wearing one trousers.
>
> Therefore we beg to have explained the things to the general assembly of the UNO properly; in order to have considered or rescue from this cruelty in due time.[4]

On the whole, the Trusteeship Council took such petitions very seriously. The council's most effective device was the visiting mission. Every three years the council dispatched missions to each of its territories. These ventures were not only of great symbolic value but had the great advantage of actual contact with the populations of the territories. At times there was friction between the visiting missions and the administering powers over the tempo of advancement toward self-government. This was not surprising, since the visiting missions were generally most interested in how quickly the administering powers were eliminating themselves, whereas the latter tended to regard the trusts as quasi-colonies. But most of these tensions were fruitful and yielded worthwhile results.

While the Trusteeship Council has been a notable success, as its overall record indicates, it has not always been able to remove the trust territories from the colonial power struggle. Libya, for example, became the subject of a heated political controversy among the several powers eager to administer it as a trust. Since no solution satisfactory to all seemed possible, Libya was granted its independence. This was a case in which the necessity for trusteeship was clearly apparent but in which, owing to the disagreement of the powers concerned, it could not be worked out in practice. Of the consequences of this fact for Libya itself, Inis L. Claude, Jr., has written that "...in terms of the objective of the rational and orderly liquidation of colonialism, the excessive prolongation of dependence [was] hardly more unfortunate than the premature conferment of independence."[5]

In a general analysis of the United Nations trusteeship systems, several factors emerge. For one thing, while the system has had little effect on the rate at which colonies have been liquidated, it has contributed considerably to making their liquidation more *responsible*. Moreover, in view of the fact that all but one of the trust territories have already received independence, the Trusteeship Council may soon find itself without a function. Of course, a liberal interpretation of the Charter would open the possibility of bringing new trusts under the council's responsibility. There are still a few colonies that might be possible candidates, although the political atmosphere in the General Assembly strongly favors immediate independence without an intermediate stage.

A word should be said here about the Trusteeship Council's final client, the Pacific Islands, also known as Micronesia. This vast area of 2,100 islands has 170,000 inhabitants, divided into four districts: Palau, the Marshall Islands, the Federated States of Micronesia, and the Northern Marianas. The first three chose a "compact of free association" with the United States, and the Marianas opted for commonwealth status. In 1986, President Reagan signed a proclamation implementing these arrangements. Yet, the decision to sever the final link between the United Nations and Micronesia—the only "strategic trust" ever created—belongs to the Security Council.

Perhaps the most significant feature of the trusteeship system has been its prophylactic quality. It has belied the facile assumption that the United Nations has been ineffective because of its inability to enforce decisions. Trusteeship has proved that effectiveness without sanctions is possible. As Claude has pointed out, it has attempted to deal with a situation *before* rather than *after* it reached the crisis stage.[6] In the Congo the United Nations was compelled to create a kind of trusteeship after the crisis had become acute.

In the general struggle over the liquidation of colonialism, the trusteeship system has played a significant, but not decisive, role. More recently, with the influx of new African and Asian members into the United Nations, the Trusteeship Council has dealt more with the problems of Southern Africa than with the problem of the single remaining trust territory. The original concept of the trusteeship system—to prepare the territories for independence with all deliberate speed—has been expanded by the General Assembly to apply to *all* colonial possessions via the Declaration Regarding Non-Self-Governing Territories. On the whole, the United Nations institutions set up to deal with problems of colonialism have been successfully used by the anticolonial majority of the General Assembly in its relentless drive toward full self-determination for all dependent peoples.

The Secretary-General and the Secretariat

One of the greatest fears of the founders of the United Nations was that the new world organization would be no more than the sum of its parts—a group of delegates each loyal to his own nation and perceiving the world through the particular lenses of his own nationality. The men and women at San Francisco were deeply convinced that one important road to international order could be constructed by providing the United Nations with a nucleus of people who, for the duration of their tenure as world civil servants, would place loyalty to the world community on an equal level with their other, more parochial commitments. It was this notion of international loyalty-building that provided the basis for the Office of the Secretary-General and of his staff, the United Nations Secretariat.

The Office of the Secretary-General of the United Nations is not without precedent. The League of Nations had also made provision for such a post. Its first incumbent, Sir Eric Drummond, a British civil servant, was primarily an administrator who made it his policy to remain aloof from the political disputes that were sapping the life-blood of the League. Albert Thomas, on the other hand, the Director-General of the League's International Labor Organization, set quite another precedent. Not content with anonymous administrative responsibilities, he ventured into the uncharted land of international statesmanship and did not shrink from taking a stand on controversial policy issues. Weighing these two precedents and tending to prefer the latter, the UN architects endowed the Office of the United Nations Secretary-General with political as well as administrative powers. The Secretary-General was not only to be the chief administrative officer of the United Nations, but, in the words of the Preparatory Commission in 1945, his Office was to represent

> A quite special right which goes beyond any power previously accorded to the head of an international organization. The Secretary-General more than anyone else will stand for the United Nations as a whole. In the eyes of the world, no less than in the eyes of his own staff, he must embody the ideals and principles of the Charter.[7]

This conception of the Office led to the inclusion in the Charter of Article 99, which set forth the Secretary-General's significant political powers: "The Secretary-General may bring to the attention of the Security Council any matter which in his opinion may threaten the maintenance of international peace and security." The founders of the UN thus clearly intended the Secretary-General to be an international statesman, a kind of conscience of the world. In order to equip him adequately for this role, they gave him what, in some respects at least, amounted almost to the power of acting as a twelfth member of the Security Council.

The first incumbent of the Office was Trygve Lie of Norway. Lie used his political powers abundantly and frequently took positions in the conflicts among the major powers. In the early years he tended to stay aloof from the most inflammable issues of the East-West struggle but defended the interest of the world community as he conceived it by taking stands on minor political disputes. He supported the European Recovery Program and opted in favor of the partition of Palestine. Soon thereafter, however, he became embroiled in political controversies of the first magnitude. Early in 1950 Mr. Lie advocated the seating of the Chinese Communist delegation in the United Nations and provoked the extreme displeasure of the United States. Several weeks later he strongly supported the American initiative in the "police action" to repel aggression by North Korea, and went so far as to label the North Koreans as the aggressors. While this action reconciled the United States, it provoked the implacable hostility of the Soviet Union. When, in late 1950, the question of Lie's reappointment came up, the United States threatened to veto the appointment of any other candidate, while the Soviet Union declared with equal conviction that it would not tolerate him. The United States prevailed upon the General

Assembly to extend his term, but the value of Trygve Lie as a peacemaker between East and West was irretrievably impaired. In November 1952, after two years of fruitless bickering, Lie resigned from the post of Secretary-General.

The experience of Trygve Lie pointed up the great dilemma, if not the inherent contradiction, of international statesmanship. The Secretary-General, to be an effective spokesman for the interests of the world community, must at times take a stand on major current political issues. But he also has to retain the confidence of all the actors in the drama. The utmost diplomatic skill and political sensitivity are needed for this task. Lie, for example, never violated the Charter. He took positions on both sides of the East-West struggle and became the object of severe criticism by both antagonists. But whereas one was willing to forgive, the other thought he had gone too far. Hence his effectiveness as a possible bridge-builder was ended.

These lessons were not lost on Trygve Lie's successor, Dag Hammarskjöld of Sweden. Hammarskjöld had been an economist and chairman of the Swedish National Bank as well as Deputy Minister for Foreign Affairs. He had never been a member of a political party and was known to have a "passion for anonymity." By background he was a civil servant, not a politician. Not surprisingly, therefore, the new Secretary-General approached his Office with somewhat greater restraint than had his predecessor. Unlike Lie, Hammarskjöld at first chose not to take overt political initiative. Public diplomacy was replaced by quiet diplomacy. This is not to say that the increasing ferocity of the two great international political struggles left the new Secretary-General untouched. But Mr. Hammarskjöld's approach to political disputes differed in two important respects from that of his predecessor. First, he always attempted to gain authority for his actions from the Security Council or the General Assembly. Second, most of his diplomatic maneuvers were carried on behind the scenes, away from the searchlight of publicity. The former habit gained him the confidence of the major powers, while the latter made possible agreements without serious loss of face for any nation. A survey of Mr. Hammarskjöld's major activities in this respect is quite revealing.

In 1954 the Secretary-General flew to Peking to negotiate the release of eleven American airmen who were interned there as United Nations personnel. Virtually no publicity was released about the trip, but a year later the airmen were released. In 1956, during the Suez crisis, the Secretary-General was confronted with an international problem of the first magnitude. Two permanent members of the Security Council were accused of military aggression and a third, the Soviet Union, threatened them with rocket bombardment. In addition, the Arab states and Israel seemed locked in mortal combat. Mr. Hammarskjöld, under the authority of the General Assembly, equipped the United Nations with an unprecedented military instrument, the United Nations Emergency Force (UNEF), which helped to restore order to the troubled area. (For a more detailed analysis of UNEF, see Chapter 12.) By taking this action, the Secretary-General became deeply involved in the political drama being acted out in the Middle East. But as always, his decisiveness was tempered with circumspection. Mr. Hammarskjöld's declaration before the Security Council, when that body met to consider the Middle Eastern crisis, is worth quoting:

> The Principles of the Charter are, by far, greater than the Organization in which they are embodied, and the aims which they are to safeguard are holier than the policies of any single nation or people. As a servant of the Organization, the Secretary-General has the duty to maintain his usefulness by avoiding public stands on conflicts between Member Nations unless and until such an action might help to resolve the conflict. However, the discretion and impartiality thus imposed on the Secretary-General by the charter of his immediate task may not degenerate into a policy of expediency. He must also be a servant of the principles of the Charter, and its aims must ultimately determine what for him is right and wrong. For that he must stand. A Secretary-General cannot serve on any other assumption than that—all Member Nations honour their pledge to observe all Articles of the Charter. He should also be able to assume that those organs which are charged with the task of upholding the Charter will be in the position to fulfill the task.
>
> The bearing of what I have just said must be obvious to all without any elaboration from my side. Were the Members to consider that another view of the duties of the Secretary-General than the one here stated would better serve the interests of the Organization it is their obvious right to act accordingly.[8]

This declaration, expressing Mr. Hammarskjöld's conception of his office, not only won him the Council's confidence during the Suez crisis but also resulted in his unanimous election to a second five-year term of office. This second term, moreover, was marked by a growing tendency in both the General Assembly and the Security Council to grant the Secretary-General broad powers for the exercise of his quiet diplomacy. The Assembly requested Mr. Hammarskjöld to facilitate the withdrawal of foreign troops during the Lebanese crisis in 1958. In 1960, when racial violence in the Union of South Africa convened the Security Council in an emergency session, a strong resolution against the Union government would have produced a British or French veto whereas a weak resolution might have provoked a Soviet veto. But East and West and colonial and anticolonial governments alike were able to agree on a mild resolution requesting the Secretary-General to use his good offices with the Union government in order to ameliorate racial tensions.

In mid-1960, when the Belgian withdrawal from the Congo left the new republic strife-torn and threatened by Great Power intervention on the model of the Spanish Civil War, the talents of the Secretary-General were called upon once more. Acting under the authority of the Security Council, he organized a United Nations Force, excluding the Great Powers, which was to restore peace and order in the Congo until responsible self-government could be established. When the Congo was threatened by civil war through the secession of the province of Katanga, Mr. Hammarskjöld—again after securing Security Council authorization—entered Katanga at the head of the United Nations Force to prevent a major conflagration. By this time, the Secretary-General had won the respect of most observers and had established the unique political value and significance of his Office. As James Reston put it in August 1960:

> In the present state of diplomatic relations between East and West, it is unlikely that agreement could have been reached between Washington and Moscow on what should be done [in the Congo]. But in the all-night debate both the United States and the Soviet Union were able to agree, as they have had to do in several crises in the past, to trust in the intervention of the U.N. Secretary-General, Dag Hammarskjöld.
>
> This remarkable man is proving to be one of the great natural resources in the world today, and it is difficult to think of another in the field of world diplomacy who could do the job as well.
>
> He is tireless. He is infinitely patient. He is sensitive to the slightest troublesome breeze in the world. He knows exactly what his job will let him do and forbid him from doing. And he knows when to be ambiguous; he also knows when to be precise.
>
> When he said that the Congo was "a question of peace or war," the Security Council paid attention, because he does not use three-letter words often or carelessly.
>
> That he has exercised these powers with such skill as to win the respect, if not the affection, of the contending states is one reason why the U.N. is now a refuge for common sense in a satanic world.[9]

As the Congo crisis developed further, however, Hammarskjöld began to run into major difficulties. Though ordered to do so by Patrice Lumumba, the deposed premier of the fledgling republic, he refused to withdraw the United Nations Peace Force. He maintained that Lumumba did not speak for the Congo and that it was necessary for the force to remain until peace and order were restored. This action resulted in a vehement attack on the Secretary-General by the Soviet Union, which had supported Lumumba in the Congolese power struggle. Disappointed by its setback in the Congo, the Soviet Union now accused the Secretary-General of having exceeded his authority. At the Fifteenth General Assembly, Premier Khrushchev violently attacked Mr. Hammarskjöld, demanded that his Office be abolished, and proposed that in his place there ought to be a three-man committee representing the Communist bloc, the Western bloc, and the uncommitted countries. The Secretary-General refused to resign and stated that he was no longer deferring primarily to the Great Powers—a radical shift from his position during the Suez crisis. His position was firm and clear: "I would rather see that Office [the Secretary-Generalship] break on strict adherence to the principle of independence, impartiality and objectivity than drift on the basis of compromise."[10]

The Assembly affirmed his stand by a resounding vote of confidence of 70 to 0 with the nine Soviet bloc countries, the Union of South Africa, and France abstaining. While it thus seemed clear that the Soviet triumvirate proposal would not be adopted, two other suggestions were made, both with a view to curtailing the Secretary-General's powers. Premier Nkrumah of Ghana offered a plan to equip the Secretary-General with three deputies, chosen from the East, West, and Third World blocs, each with "clearly defined authority" in

United Nations affairs. And Prime Minister Nehru of India proposed an advisory committee from different geographical areas, a sort of inner cabinet whose views and perhaps even approval would have to be sought on any important matters.

The tragic death of Dag Hammarskjöld on the eve of the opening of the Sixteenth General Assembly caused great anxiety, since the Soviet Union had a veto over the election of a successor. Actually, the Soviet leadership was quite aware that it could not get the "troika" plan through the Assembly, but hopeful that it would be able to effect a drastic cutback in the power of the Office. The United States attempted to rally the General Assembly behind its view that the Secretary-General's authority must not be compromised and that a single person be named in an acting capacity until a new Secretary-General could be elected. President Kennedy expressed this view forcefully before the Assembly:

> However difficult it may be to fill Mr. Hammarskjöld's place, it can better be filled by one man rather than by three. Even the three horses of the troika did not have three drivers, all going in different directions. They had only one, and so must the United Nations executive. To install a triumvirate, or any rotating authority, in the United Nations administrative offices would replace order with anarchy, action with paralysis, and confidence with confusion.[11]

A number of Soviet attempts to get support for a troika at the undersecretary level were unsuccessful and, on November 3, 1961, the General Assembly upon recommendation of the Security Council unanimously named U Thant of Burma Acting Secretary-General for the remainder of Dag Hammarskjöld's term.

This decision postponed the troika issue until April 10, 1963, when Hammarskjöld's term of office was to expire. But Soviet reservations about U Thant were apparently dispelled by his conciliatory mediation during the Cuban crisis of 1962, and he was elected to a full term, retroactive, according to his own wish, to his designation as Acting Secretary-General. The Office itself had now moved eastward from Trygve Lie of Norway, a NATO country, and Hammarskjöld of neutral Sweden, to a citizen of a neutralist country in Asia.

U Thant, though very different in background and training from his predecessor, nevertheless introduced no sharp changes in policy. Most of his energies at first were taken up with the continuing crisis in the Congo and the looming threat of bankruptcy which the United Nations faced as a result of having mounted two major peace-keeping operations. Still as Acting Secretary-General he played a major role in the establishment of the UN Temporary Executive Authority (UNTEA), which supervised the transfer of West New Guinea from the Netherlands to Indonesia. And in 1964 he met a major challenge when called upon to put together a UN peace force to keep apart the warring factions on Cyprus and to prepare the way for a more fundamental solution for the problems of that tormented island.

In 1966, U Thant was elected unanimously to another five-year term. He accepted reluctantly, and only after great pressure had been put on him by many member states, both large and small. The continuing escalation of the war in Vietnam and his own inability to bring the combatants to the negotiating table gnawed at him. Moreover, he had been unable to improve substantially the finances of the Organization. In 1967, acceding to the demand of Egypt's President Nasser, he decided to withdraw the UN Emergency Force from the Middle East, where it had been stationed for more than a decade. Though political controversies continued to surround him, he nevertheless continued to enjoy the support of most of the membership. Whatever opposition there was remained fairly passive and never reached the vehemence of the attacks that had been made upon his two predecessors. In 1971, after two full terms in office, U Thant retired from his post, the first Secretary-General to do so with the blessing of most members, whether large or small. His successor was an Austrian, Kurt Waldheim.

The election of the fourth Secretary-General was particularly significant because it coincided almost exactly with the seating of the People's Republic of China in the United Nations. Despite Cassandra-like predictions emanating from many quarters that the Chinese would make difficulties, none occurred. Mr. Waldheim received the support of the five permanent members, which made his election unanimous. During his first term in office, the new Secretary-General offered the UN's good offices in the settlement of the Vietnam conflict, traveled to numerous countries on a variety of missions, and worked hard to put the UN's financial house in order. In 1972, after Palestinian guerrillas murdered eleven Israeli athletes at the Munich Olympics, he took the initiative in asking the General Assembly to discuss the problem of terrorism on an international scale. In 1974, he visited fourteen famine-stricken countries in the Sahelian region of Africa in order to draw the world's attention to their plight. In the wake of the October War in the Middle East, he set up two new peace forces in the area, separating the Israelis from Egypt and from Syria. And when hostilities erupted on Cyprus, he maneuvered adroitly in order to maximize the effectiveness of the small United Nations peace force on that troubled island. On the whole, he tried his best to be an activist Secretary-General, but to do so without antagonizing any of the major powers. This was not an easy task since Mr. Waldheim's constituency was both larger and more complicated than that of each of his three predecessors. In 1976, the membership rewarded Mr. Waldheim by electing him for a second five-year term.

Shortly after the expiration of his second term in 1981, Mr. Waldheim ran for the presidency of his native country, Austria. During the election campaign it was alleged not only that he had served as a lieutenant in the German army during World War II but also that he had participated in the deportation of Jews and partisans in the Balkans. These charges were particularly sensational because none of these alleged activities by the former Secretary-General had been discussed in his autobiography, *In the Eye of the Storm,* published shortly after his retirement from the United Nations. In fact, in his book, Mr. Waldheim had asserted that he had been wounded on the Russian front in 1942 and had subsequently returned to his law studies. This effort to "sanitize" his autobiography made it appear that the author did indeed have something to hide. Be that as it may, the negative publicity did little to mend the reputation of an organization already far too often accused of being an irrelevant haven for mediocrities or worse. Fortunately, however, the office of the Secretary-General survived the crisis more or less intact, largely because of the qualities of Mr. Waldheim's successor.

The fifth Secretary-General, Javier Perez de Cuellar, was a professional diplomat from Peru. His tenure, which began in 1982, was at first one of considerable frustration. Though an extremely tactful and even self-effacing man, de Cuellar was not able to involve the United Nations in the Great Power conflicts in a truly meaningful sense. The Lebanese tragedy ran its melancholy course without the United Nations, and not even Britain and Argentina permitted a role for the world body during the Falklands crisis. Perhaps de Cuellar's earliest achievement was his decision, in 1983, in an unusually blunt and straightforward report, to draw the world's attention to the rapidly declining role of the United Nations. In none of the major world conflicts, the Secretary-General asserted, had the United Nations been allowed to inject itself into the peace-making process. Even multinational peace-keeping forces in the Middle East, which in earlier years used to be provided by the United Nations, were now being carried on by NATO powers. Unless this negative trend was reversed, the Secretary-General warned, the UN's future looked bleak indeed.

Perez de Cuellar's second term, however, was to be a great deal more successful.

The ascendancy of Mikhail Gorbachev to power in the Soviet Union gave the United Nations a new lease on life. Not only did the Soviet Union pay its financial obligations to the United Nations, including its arrears, but it even permitted—in fact encouraged—mediation efforts by the Secretary-General to bring festering military conflicts to an end. Gorbachev himself opened the door in 1987 by inviting the United Nations to supervise the withdrawal of Soviet troops from Afghanistan. By 1988, de Cuellar was deeply involved in conducting face-to-face peace negotiations between Iran and Iraq as well as between Turks and Greeks in Cyprus. In addition, his services as mediator were welcomed in the disputes between Cambodia and Vietnam, Morocco and the Polisario resistance movement, and even in the seemingly endless struggle between South Africa and Namibia over the latter's independence. Enjoying the confidence and support of the superpowers as well as of most of the UN membership, Perez de Cuellar had made the Secretary-Generalship once again an object of respect and admiration.

In a general evaluation of the Secretary-Generalship, it is probably fair to say, as did Trygve Lie upon looking backward on his experience, that the office is "in many ways...far ahead of our times."[12] And always, it remains beset by an unavoidable dilemma. If, in the fulfillment of his duties, the

Secretary-General speaks out too loudly, he will incur the wrath of one or more of the Great Powers and thus doom himself to inefficacy. Yet if he refuses to speak out at all, he dooms himself to sterility. To live under the strains of this dilemma and play the most forceful possible part in the work of the United Nations in spite of it requires a most gifted and unusual person.

If the Secretary-General is the world's chief civil servant, the United Nations Secretariat is its international civil service. This international staff has not limited its activities solely to United Nations Headquarters in New York City. Each of the autonomous specialized agencies in the United Nations family has its own director-general and secretariat. The functions of the various levels of the Secretariat have been largely of a "housekeeping" nature. The Secretariat's responsibilities have been legion and have included the planning of conferences, the gathering of information, interpreting, and the publication of a yearbook. In all these activities the international civil servant must demonstrate scrupulous objectivity in order not to antagonize any member government. Employment policy for members of the Secretariat was laid down in Article 101 of the Charter:

> The paramount consideration in the employment of the staff and in the determination of the conditions of service shall be the necessity of securing the highest standards of efficiency, competence, and integrity. Due regard shall be paid to the importance of recruiting the staff on as wide a geographical basis as possible.

It was hoped to combine the principles of merit and geography. While competence should be the main criterion, a truly international service could not be indifferent to considerations of nationality. But once a national of a member state had joined the Secretariat he was expected to take an oath of allegiance to the United Nations and not to accept instructions from any government. In other words, during the time of his tenure the world civil servant—like his chief, the Secretary-General—was expected to contribute to international order-building by developing a loyalty to the world community.

The potential and at times actual conflict between the demands of a national and a world outlook have frequently placed a great strain on members of the Secretariat and on the Secretary-General. A principal source of that strain was the United States government which, in the early 1950s, subjected American members of the Secretariat to intensive loyalty investigations. Although not a single member was convicted, large sections of the American public began to regard the Secretariat as a sanctuary for American Communists and saboteurs. The United States government exerted great pressure on Trygve Lie to dismiss those American members of his staff who had been accused of disloyalty to the United States. The Secretary-General faced a formidable dilemma: if he acceded to the American demands, he would impugn the integrity of the international civil service; if he refused, he ran the risk of alienating a government without whose support the United Nations could hardly continue to exist. In his plight, he asked the opinion of a special committee of legal advisers. This group suggested that membership in the Secretariat in no way abrogated the loyalty a person owed to the state of which he was a citizen, and that, there-fore, Lie was justified in dismissing "disloyal" Americans. Accordingly, nine American members of the Secretariat with permanent contracts who had re-fused to answer questions of investigating committees or had invoked the Con-stitutional privilege of silence were dismissed from active service. One year later, however, an Administrative Tribunal of the United Nations ruled that the dismissed employees were entitled to compensation. The General Assem-bly—over American opposition—voted to make amends after having re-quested an advisory opinion of the World Court, which supported the view of the Administrative Tribunal. Nevertheless, the U.S. Congress, in a concurrent resolution, declared that no American funds paid to the UN could be used to pay compensation to the dismissed UN officials.[13]

This episode demonstrated that in a conflict between national and world loyalty in the Secretariat, the national probably remains paramount. This is further borne out by the fact that in early 1961, the Soviet Union extended its critique of the Secretary-General to the Secretariat and demanded that the en-tire staff be reorganized on the basis of equal representation for "the three main groups of states—socialist, neutralist, and Western." Thus, until the in-ternational civil service can ask for and find in its members unreserved world loyalty, the Secretariat member must continue to reconcile his national and in-ternational allegiances as best he can. However, by the time the United Na-tions celebrated its fortieth birthday in 1985, both superpowers had come a great deal closer to accepting the concept of a truly international civil service.

That a fruitful synthesis between national and world loyalty is indeed pos-sible has been demonstrated in a classic statement by C. Wilfred Jenks, one of the early pioneers of a global civil service:

> A lack of attachment to any one country does not constitute an international out-look. A superior indifference to the emotions and prejudices of those whose world is bounded by the frontiers of a single state does not constitute an international out-look. A blurred indistinctness of attitude toward all questions, proceeding from a freedom of prejudice born of lack of vitality, does not constitute an international outlook. The international outlook required of the international civil servant is an awareness made instinctive by habit of the needs, emotions, and prejudices of the peoples of differently-circumstanced countries, as they are felt and expressed by the peoples concerned, accompanied by a capacity for weighing these frequently impon-derable elements in a judicial manner before reaching any decision to which they are relevant.[14]

It could justly be said of the United Nations civil service that seldom has so much been done for so many by so few. In New York, Rome, Paris, Geneva, and Vienna, there have emerged small but compact nuclei of a nascent world loyalty. They have often been threatened with disintegration but have always managed somehow to survive. By the late 1980s, the number of international civil servants dispersed throughout the world approached the 15,000 mark.[15]

"It may be true," said Dag Hammarskjöld shortly before he died, "that in a very deep human sense there is no neutral individual, because everyone, if he is worth anything, has to have his ideas and ideals....But what I do claim is that even a man who is in that sense not neutral can very well undertake and carry through neutral actions because that is an act of integrity.''[16] This statement, which was made in response to Premier Khrushchev's blunt assertion that no man could be neutral, probably best expresses the philosophical conception of the international civil service.

The United Nations and Planetary Management

The 1970s and 1980s witnessed an integrated approach by the United Nations to some of the world's most critical problems. A series of global conferences was organized under UN auspices to address the main challenges to an endangered Planet Earth. The first of these was the World Conference on the Human Environment held in Stockholm in 1972. The year 1974 saw a whole bevy of global conferences: the Sixth Special Session of the General Assembly on raw materials and development; a Conference on the Law of the Sea, held in Caracas; a World Population Conference, held in Bucharest; and a World Food Conference, held in Rome. All these conferences emphasized the need to respond to planetary challenges with planetary initiatives. What became painfully clear during the debates in Stockholm, New York, Caracas, Bucharest, and Rome was that interdependence was no longer a slogan or an abstraction but had become a gut reality. Planetary crisis demanded planetary management.

The Sixth Special Session of the General Assembly on raw materials and development met in New York in April 1974 in order to search for a more just and viable basis for international economic cooperation. A package of proposals was adopted including a Declaration and Program of Action on the Establishment of a New International Economic Order. The poor countries demanded the establishment of a special emergency fund and rejected as insufficient an American proposal for a $4 billion assistance program for the most seriously affected. The oil-rich Arab nations pressed the point that the industrialized countries should shoulder the main burden of aiding the world's poor. The Western nations rejected this point of view and the session ended with few concrete achievements. The plight of the poor was clear to all but no consensus was reached as yet on how to share the responsibility of helping them.

The United Nations Conference on the Law of the Sea was held in Caracas in the summer of 1974 after six years of preparation. It continued into the 1980s with numerous conferences held in other world capitals. The major problem areas before the conference were the establishment of the limits of national jurisdiction over territorial waters presently ranging from three to two hundred miles; fisheries questions; preservation of the marine environment; the establishment of international machinery to regulate activities on the high seas such as the dumping of waste into the oceans; passage through international straits; the exploitation of the mineral resources of the seabed; and the conduct of scientific research. Negotiations were arduous, but the conferences represented tentative first steps in the direction of a new international regime governing the world's oceans. The participating nations all agreed that the need for new laws was urgent and that the process of forging them should be continuous.

By the late 1980s, reckless dumping of hazardous wastes had produced dangerous levels of coastal water pollution in the United States, lending a new sense of urgency to the question of jurisdiction over territorial waters. Disease was not about to respect national boundaries.

The World Population Conference that was held in Bucharest in August 1974 placed the problem of population squarely onto the front pages of the world's agenda. Since population was related to the issues of economic development, diplomacy, human rights, and institutional change, it was analytically impossible to insulate it from the crosscurrents of international politics. Despite wide divergencies among the participating countries, a consensus was reached on a World Population Plan of Action which looked toward a target of reducing world fertility from 38 per 1,000 to 30 per 1,000 by 1985. In addition, there was general agreement on certain key principles of population planning and individual human rights. For example, all countries agreed to respect and ensure the right of persons to determine, in a free, informed, and responsible manner, the number and spacing of their children, and to encourage the participation of women in educational, social, economic, and political life on an equal basis with men. On the whole, the Bucharest Conference symbolized the evolution of the international population movement from a preoccupation of scholars and students to a global need and a major political force. As in the Conference on the Law of the Sea, the delegates realized that only a beginning had been made, and that the problem required the continuous and vigilant attention of the United Nations and its member states. And, indeed, in 1987, the world's population reached the five billion mark after remaining below one billion for most of human existence. To address this problem, an International Conference on Population and the Urban Future was convened in Barcelona, Spain. July 11, 1987, the "Day of the Five Billion," symbolized both a triumph and a new challenge in the story of humanity.

In November 1974, most of the world's nations gathered in Rome on the occasion of the first World Food Conference in history, sponsored by one of the United Nations' specialized agencies, the Food and Agriculture Organization. The delegates met under the specter of famine in Africa and on the Indian subcontinent and amid reports that the world's food reserves had reached levels that were dangerously low. Flood, drought, and fertilizer shortages had created grain shortages that were estimated at 20 million tons. The United States, Canada, and Australia agreed to make emergency food supplies available on a short-term basis. The most concrete long-term achievement of the Rome Conference was the establishment of a World Food Council, which was to serve as an umbrella organization to funnel food and money to needy nations. Donor nations consisting of the "old rich" of the industrialized West and the "new rich" of the oil-producing areas agreed to provide both food and money to ensure that 10 million tons of food would be shipped annually to the needy nations. The conference also accepted a proposal by Secretary of State Kissinger for a system of nationally held but internationally coordinated grain banks for emergency needs in natural disasters. The conference also adopted a declaration accepting the removal of the scourge of hunger and malnutrition as the objective of the international community as a whole. All things considered, the Rome meeting signified the beginning of a global survival pact between the rich and the poor nations of the world.

By the late 1980s, the World Food Council had become a generally accepted institution. Under its aegis, biennial pledges of more than $1 billion were made by wealthy donor countries to needy nations in Africa and Asia. In addition, donor nations made annual contributions of more than 10 million tons of food to an International Emergency Food Reserve. The world's rich had begun to assume a measure of responsibility for the world's hungry.

Finally, the United Nations has begun to deal with the human threat to the global environment. In 1972, 1,200 delegates from 114 nations met in Stockholm, Sweden, to produce a framework for international action to halt the deterioration of the environment and to conserve the earth's dwindling resources. The UN Conference had been four years in the making and was initiated by a 1968 resolution of the General Assembly, originally proposed by the government of Sweden. The conference was to be humanity's first global attack on the deepening environmental crisis, mounted under the aegis of the United Nations.

Humans have always lived in two worlds: the "biosphere," which is the world of natural things from which we draw our physical existence, and the "technosphere," the world of tools and artifacts, of social and political institutions that we forge for ourselves. For centuries, the planet's fields and forests, its reserves of fertile soil and minerals, its oceans and rivers could carry without strain the entire freight of human technological inventions and desires. In the last few decades, however, and with explosively increasing force in the last few years, the balance between the planet's biosphere and the technosphere has been critically affected. People no longer live almost overwhelmed by the scale of their environment. Instead, the environment is beginning to be overwhelmed by humanity. At stake is nothing less than the quality of life on this planet.

Under the leadership of Maurice F. Strong, the secretary-general of the conference, the delegates debated multiple aspects of a single theme: How should humans control their growth to save the planet?

At one end of the spectrum were the advocates of a "zero-growth" world, in which the current progressive deterioration of the environment, degrading the quality of the world's air, land, and water, would be virtually halted. Such a world would see population stabilized and the consumption of raw materials held to a level not substantially greater than the production of such materials. Energy use would be compatible with the planet's long-term reserves of nuclear and fossil fuels. Zero-growth supporters believed that social chaos and major wars would erupt over access to the world's depleting resources unless the industrialized countries decided to arrest their heedless growth.

At the other extreme were those—largely the developing countries—who saw no need in the foreseeable future to alter the emphasis on growth. They contended that a zero-growth world would lead to the destruction of the world's economies, which must expand to prosper.

In this tug-of-war between "environmentalists" and "developmentalists," Secretary-General Strong took a middle course. "No growth is not a viable policy for any society today," he said. "Indeed, people must have access to more, not fewer, opportunities to express their creative drives. But these can only be provided within a total system in which man's activities are in dynamic harmony with the natural order." "To achieve this," he added, "we must re-think our concepts of the basic purposes of growth. Surely we must see it in terms of enriching the lives and enlarging the opportunities of all mankind. And if this is so, it follows that it is the more wealthy societies—the privileged minority of mankind—which will have to make the most profound, even rev-olutionary, changes in attitudes and values."[17]

Mr. Strong's carefully charted middle course between the advocates of de-velopment and the defenders of the environment avoided a confrontation be-tween the have and the have-not nations at the conference. The latter feared that the advanced countries might set high environmental standards for their imports that would seriously damage the export capabilities of poorer nations. Brazil, for example, asked to be compensated for building environmental pro-tection devices into its new automobile plants. Lurking in the background was the suspicion of Third World nations that the industrial countries might set lim-its on international pollution that would inhibit the poor nations' uphill fight toward industrialization.

In the end, the conference was able to point to some very notable accom-plishments. In the first place, the conference ratified a Declaration on the Hu-man Environment. The first draft of this document was a delicately balanced compromise between the rich and the poor that had been hammered out in dozens of diplomatic sessions before the Stockholm meeting. Like its prede-cessor, the Universal Declaration of Human Rights, the Declaration on the Human Environment was binding to no one. But the diplomats hoped that the declaration would set a standard of environmental behavior that would be ob-served voluntarily by most of the UN membership.

The second concrete achievement of the conference was a set of "action plans." At the core of these was to be "Earthwatch"—the systematic moni-toring and assessment of global conditions as a basis for national measures to curb environmental abuses. Typical examples of such action plans included an appeal to all nations to minimize the release of toxic metals and chemicals into the environment; a global early-warning system designed to monitor changes in the world's climate and levels of air pollution; and action to save certain species, such as the whale, from complete extinction.

Finally, the conference established a new United Nations Environment Program (UNEP), to be based in Nairobi, Kenya. The permanent new organ, consisting of a fifty-eight member governing council, a small secretariat, and an executive director—set up under the aegis of the Economic and Social Council—was to follow up on the world community's continuing concern with the environmental crisis beyond the immediate issues raised at the Stockholm Conference.

By the late 1980s, UNEP's Governing Council had begun work on a report entitled "Environmental Perspective to the Year 2000 and Beyond." In 1987, it convened a "Convention for the Protection of the Ozone Layer" in Montreal and another for the "Environmentally Sound Management of Hazardous Wastes."

Environmental breakdown does not respect national or ideological boundaries. It threatens capitalists and communists, the rich and the poor alike. The environmental challenge may yet prove to be the great leveler of international relations. Environmental concern might even become a catalyst toward a saner world order, since such concern may compel nations to cooperate on basic problems common to all. More than one hundred nations did find it possible to face a crisis before it had reached the point of no return and did take action on a global basis to arrest it. Most of the delegates to UNEP sensed that the planet would survive the ecological crisis as a whole or not at all. Hence, they turned to the United Nations as a logical vehicle for action.

The global conferences held under the United Nation's aegis were an impressive beginning. Primarily diagnostic, the conferences tried to focus attention on the most dangerous illnesses of the planet. What emerged with clarity and force, however, was the new insight that the real divisions in the world of the 1980s were no longer between capitalists and communists, or white or nonwhite, young and old, or even rich and poor, but between those who could see only the interests of a limited group and those who could see the interests of humanity. The 1980s saw the beginnings, through the United Nations, of a world environment policy, a world food policy, and a world population policy, to bring humans and nature into balance.

Although skeptics have tended to dismiss these conferences as little more than global debating sessions, their assessment seems too bleak. Whatever the achievements or failures of this form of "planetary management," these global "town meetings" represent the first evolutionary pooling of the world of its intellectual and financial resources in the battle against dangers that are common to all. These conferences are the first gropings by the passengers of Spaceship Earth toward a common survival policy.

FINANCING THE UNITED NATIONS SYSTEM

Before attempting a general evaluation of the UN system, a word must be said about financing, especially because this issue threw the organization into a major crisis in the 1960s, again in the 1970s, and yet again in the 1980s. Always,

Cassandras have predicted that the United Nations would end with a bang. However, several times during the United Nation's lifetime, a real possibility existed that the organization might end with a whimper. The first such crisis developed in the early 1960s and threatened the United Nations' very life. The heart of the crisis lay squarely in two operations that the United Nations had mounted to keep the peace: the United Nations Emergency Force in the Middle East (UNEF) in 1956 and the United Nations Congo Force (ONUC) in 1960.

Altogether, the UN system spends a little over $2 billion annually—or a fraction of what it takes to run the New York City government for a year. First, there is the regular assessed budget for the normal day-to-day expenses of the Organization, amounting to about $500 million a year. Second, there are the assessed budgets of the specialized agencies, which come to roughly twice that sum. Third, there are the special voluntary programs such as the Children's Fund, which subsist solely on the generosity of governments' and private citizens' voluntary contributions, amounting to approximately another $500 million a year for four programs.

Finally there are the expenses for peace-keeping operations. The UN Operation in the Congo (ONUC) cost the United Nations roughly $120 million a year and the expenses of the UN Emergency Force (UNEF) which patrolled parts of the Arab-Israeli border between 1956 and 1967 came to approximately $20 million a year. Since these two major UN peace forces had been responsible for the Organization's first fiscal crisis, their financing deserves special analysis.

Never have so many people argued so much about so little money, the reason being that the financial problem of the peace-keeping operations was, in reality, a political problem. The financial crisis was first and foremost a political crisis over the proper role that the UN was to play in the national policies of its member states. And only secondarily was it a crisis over the financial burdens of UN membership.

When the General Assembly authorized the establishment of UNEF in 1956, Dag Hammarskjöld urged that a special account be set up to finance the force as a collective responsibility of the entire membership. Most of the Western members supported the Secretary-General in this view, but the Soviet bloc asserted that the "aggressors" should pay, namely Britain, France, and Israel. Between these two opposing views, yet a third emerged: most of the new nations claimed that everyone should pay something, but that the Great Powers, which had special privileges under the Charter, should also shoulder special responsibilities and pick up the major portion of the bill. This "rebate formula" won the day: the costs of UNEF were assessed upon the membership, but the underdeveloped nations were given rebates of 50 percent and the wealthier nations were invited to make up the deficits through voluntary contributions.

During the next few years, however, deficits gradually developed. The Soviet Union, for example, opposed the force on political grounds and hence was unwilling to pay. And many of the smaller nations, though approving of the force, claimed that they were unable to pay even their reduced assessments. By 1960, when the Congo Force was created, the problem of arrears had all the earmarks of a major crisis.

The problem of paying for the $120 million ONUC budget brought the United Nations to the brink of bankruptcy. The Secretary-General once again supported the principle of collective responsibility. This time the Western nations broke ranks. France was unwilling to pay and joined the Soviet Union in its political opposition. The majority of the membership agreed to another rebate formula, but this time the reductions granted the poorer states reached 80 percent.

The deficits now began to mount sharply. Two permanent members were unwilling to pay, and over half the membership claimed incapacity to pay. By late 1961 the UN debt approached the $100 million mark, and the General Assembly was forced to take emergency action. First, it authorized a $200 million bond issue and invited governments to subscribe, hoping to tide the peace forces over until a more permanent solution could be found. And second, it requested an Advisory Opinion of the World Court as to the legal status of the peace force assessments.

The response to the bond issue was fairly generous. By 1963 sixty governments had purchased approximately three fourths of the total subscription, with the United States buying half of the total amount. This made it possible to meet the costs of the two forces until early 1963 without having to assess the membership during that period. The Court Opinion did not persuade the Soviet Union and France to clear their accounts, but did elicit payments from numerous smaller nations, totaling over $6 million.

In keeping with its increasingly conservative mood, the General Assembly gradually retreated from the principle of collective responsibility for the funding of peace-keeping operations. Thus, in 1962 the costs of the UN Temporary Executive Authority in West New Guinea (UNTEA) were divided evenly between the two direct beneficiaries, the Netherlands and Indonesia, and in 1963 the costs of a UN Observer Group sent to Yemen were split between Egypt and Saudi Arabia. And in 1964, the costs of the UN Peace Force dispatched to Cyprus had to be raised through voluntary contributions.

Finally, in 1964, the United States and the Soviet Union had a major showdown over the payments for UNEF and ONUC. The United States insisted that every member state that was in arrears for more than two years would have no vote in the General Assembly under Article 19 of the Charter. The Soviet Union rejected this view and was supported by France in the case of ONUC. The United States, despite strenuous efforts, was unable to muster enough support in the General Assembly for its strict interpretation of Article 19. An impasse resulted that produced the famous ''voteless'' Nineteenth Session. Finally, in August 1965, Ambassador Arthur J. Goldberg abandoned this position, but declared that the United States, too, would henceforth reserve its right not to pay for peace-keeping operations of which it disapproved. Thus, the assessment principle, the financial bedrock of collective responsibility in peace-keeping, was, temporarily at least, defeated.

At the heart of the financial crisis was, of course, the fact that no power, least of all a great power, would adopt or easily pay for a policy that it considered inimical to its national interest. Thus, the United States supported the peace forces essentially because it found them compatible with its own national goals. And the Soviet Union opposed them because UNEF challenged the formation of a Soviet bridgehead in the Middle East and ONUC forced the liquidation of a Soviet bridgehead in the Congo. To sum up, the positions of the major powers had relatively little to do with finances per se. In the case of the middle and smaller powers, money per se played a far larger and, in some instances, a decisive role. Hence, while the financial crisis of UNEF and ONUC was caused primarily by the political attitude of the few, it was deepened considerably by the real or alleged financial limitations of the many.

After the seating of the People's Republic of China in the United Nations, it was the turn of the United States to regard UN finances with a more penurious eye. In the wake of a popular wave of anti-UN feeling in 1972, the House Appropriations Committee, without consulting any of the organs of the United Nations, moved to reduce the American contribution to the regular budget from 31 percent to 25 percent. In view of the fact that under the UN Charter only the General Assembly had the right to determine the assessments for the regular budget, this unilateral action was widely interpreted as illegal. On sober second thought, the United States brought the question of its contribution before the General Assembly in the fall of 1972. Reluctantly, the world body approved the reduction of the American contribution to 25 percent. The impact of the American move on the UN treasury was serious but not catastrophic since the admission of the two Germanys to the United Nations in 1973 more than made up the difference. China, too, in an unprecedented move, offered to raise its contribution to the regular budget from 3 to 7 percent over a period of several years.

By the late 1970s, the financing of the three peace-keeping operations was determined exclusively by the Security Council. The Cyprus Force continued to subsist solely on the basis of voluntary contributions, but the assessment principle was applied once again to the two new peace forces in the Middle East. The Soviet Union made a contribution for the first time to UNEF II and to UNDOF in 1973 and 1974 respectively. China expressed its ambivalence toward the United Nations' role in the Middle East by refusing to pay for the two forces. In 1979, UNEF II was terminated because the peace treaty between Israel and Egypt had rendered it unnecessary. Thus, by 1980, the finances of the United Nations were not in the desperate straits in which they found themselves during the 1960s. A shortage of funds continued to plague the Organization as virtually a chronic affliction.

By 1985, however, this chronic shortage of funds turned into another full-blown crisis, this time precipitated not by the Soviet Union but by the United States. Late that year the United States informed the United Nations that the

US government would withhold a large portion of its contribution to the regular budget. The cuts would only be restored, officials announced, if sweeping reforms were instituted. These reforms would have to include major budget cuts and economies as well as a weighted voting system on budgetary matters to give a greater say to the largest contributors, the industrialized nations.

The Secretary-General moved swiftly to cut UN spending, improving economies in travel, documentation, and meetings. In late 1986, the General Assembly approved a modified budget process which met most of the US objections. By now, however, the matter of the US contribution to the United Nations had become mired down in the general budgetary crisis confronting the US Congress. In its desperate quest to look for economies, the Congress found a most likely candidate in the United Nations. Thus, although Vernon Walters, the US ambassador to the United Nations, praised the Secretary-General for the UN reforms, the Congress kept dragging its feet. Ironically, however, help came from a most unlikely source: the Soviet Union. Under the new leadership of Mikhail Gorbachev, the Soviet government paid up all its arrears, including even those for past peace-keeping operations. China quickly followed suit. By 1988, the United States had become the United Nations' largest debtor, with $467 million in arrears. This crisis came at the precise moment when the United Nations experienced a resurgence and was able to inject itself into the peace-making process in many parts of the world. Unfortunately, the fate of UN funding in the United States seemed to depend not so much on the progress of UN reforms as on US fiscal considerations. "If we had no budget constraints, the US might pay its arrears as well as the assessment," commented John Shank, minority clerk of the Senate Subcommittee on Appropriations, with disarming candor. "But in recent years, US policy has followed the budget and not the other way around. If the administration is unwilling to cut other programs or to raise revenues, then we will get nowhere fast."[18] "The United States is in favor of peace," Vernon Walters announced rather lamely in 1988. "Peace has its price," the Secretary-General retorted. Thus, during the 1960s and 1970s, the Soviet Union had crippled the United Nations. In the 1980s, it was the turn of the United States.

At long last, in September 1988, President Reagan announced that the United States would pay its dues as well as its arrears. The White House gave the United Nations a check for $15.2 million and promised to pay the remaining 1988 and 1989 dues if Congress agreed. In addition, the President asked the State Department to plan a schedule of payments for the $500 million in arrearages. Evidently, the United States was satisfied with the extent of the United Nations' personnel and budgetary reforms. And in December 1988, the General Assembly unanimously approved a $1.76 billion budget for 1990 and 1991, a $22 million cut from the 1988–1989 allocation.

Thus, by 1988, for the first time since its founding, the United Nations enjoyed the financial support of both superpowers. As a result of Mikhail Gorbachev's "new thinking," the Soviet Union, for the first time, tried to make the United Nations work, and the United States, unwilling to be left out in the cold, had a change of heart. And thus, the new détente of 1988 gave the United Nations a fresh lease on life.

THE UNITED NATIONS IN PERSPECTIVE

We are now ready to attempt a somewhat more general analysis of the United Nations family. A look at the record of each of the principal organs shows clearly that in no case have the hopes of the United Nations' founders been realized completely. Each organ has developed a life of its own, often quite different from the original conception, and has made its own unique contribution.

The record of the Security Council is uneven. It has not attained the goal of collective security, but the Great Powers have often been able to agree on investing the Secretary-General with significant responsibilities for keeping the peace. The General Assembly has certainly not become the world's parliament, but has shown a capacity for improvisation far greater than any of the United Nations' founders would have dared to predict. It has also shown a remarkable talent for international law-making, and it continues to be the last remaining global forum in which the two great political struggles are waged in an atmosphere of parliamentarianism. By the 1980s, however, the Third World majority had become so commanding that the Western nations felt outnumbered. While a generation earlier small nations had found it difficult to prevent great powers from making wars, by the 1980s the great powers had discovered the need to restrain small powers from starting wars that might engulf the superpowers. The war between Iraq and Iran was a case in point. Neither ECOSOC nor the specialized agencies have realized the original functionalist hope, since most economic, social, and cultural work has been too permeated with political significance. But the proliferation of functional activities under the aegis of ECOSOC has yielded a multitude of global "good works" of unprecedented magnitude and unquestioned value. While colonial dependencies never became "sacred trusts of civilization," the trusteeship system has doubtless contributed to the peaceful liquidation of Western colonialism. But unless new trusts are added, the Trusteeship Council may disappear from the United Nations family. The World Court's role has been modest. It has not been able to contribute much to global order-building but has managed to consolidate the gains of international law in the Western world. Of all the UN organs, the Office of the Secretary-General has come closest to approximating the conception of the framers of the Charter.

During the late 1980s, the Secretary-General was welcomed as a mediator to bring some of the bloodiest conflicts of the decade to a close. The UN Secretary-General had indeed become the repository of an invaluable new treasure—international diplomacy.

In 1956, the United Nations had invented the concept of a peace force. Since than more than 500,000 soldiers have seen service as "soldiers without enemies" in five UN peace forces: three in the Middle East, one in Cyprus, and one in Africa. In addition, in the late 1980s, small UN observer groups were dispatched to monitor the Soviet withdrawal from Afghanistan, to patrol the cease-fire line along the Iran-Iraq border, and to facilitate the accords agreed on by South Africa, Cuba, and Angola. Although none of these small peace forces could ever stop a war, the forces have nonetheless served as valuable buffers between contending armies. In 1988, these UN peace-keeping forces were awarded the Nobel Peace Prize, a fitting testimony to the men and women from many countries who had risked their lives in the cause of peace.[19]

Too often, the United Nations receives harsh criticism from many quarters. The United Nations' alleged impotence in dealing with political crises is also often identified. This criticism overlooks that many disputes are brought to the United Nations only when the crisis has become acute and violence has already erupted. Nations all too frequently "dump" quarrels into the lap of the United Nations when the nations literally no longer know what else to do. Thus, they make of the United Nations a kind of "receiver in bankruptcy" and then proceed to blame the organization for that sad state of affairs. In that sense, there is nothing wrong with the United Nations except its membership.

Given such adverse conditions, the United Nations has actually done quite well. But its task as crisis manager would be a great deal easier if nations submitted disputes *before* they went critical. It is wiser to deal with crises when they are still manageable than to engage in brilliant rescue operations at the brink of disaster. In that sense, the planetary conferences on population, food, resources and development, environment, and the laws of the sea held under the United Nations' aegis during the 1970s and 1980s were responses made in time by the world community to crises that endangered humanity.

In the final analysis, the most striking characteristics of the United Nations have been its *elasticity* and *adaptability*. The League of Nations, which did not subscribe to as eclectic an approach to peace as the United Nations, crumbled after the first onslaughts. The United Nations, however, has developed multiple lines of defense against war. In its short life it has been tested at least as severely as was the League of Nations. It has managed to respond to a multitude of challenges with amazing resiliency, an unmatched gift for innovation and improvisation, and a realistic sense of the politically possible. And most recently, as a result of renewed détente between the superpowers, the United Nations is experiencing a new political renaissance.

The fact that the United Nations has survived intact for almost half a century is in itself a political miracle. What has not killed it has made it stronger.

REFERENCES

1 For a full development of the functional approach to peace, see David Mitrany, *A Working Peace System*. London: Royal Institute of International Affairs, 1946.
2 Norman J. Padelford, "The Use of the Veto," *International Organization,* June 1948, pp. 231–232.
3 Quoted by Arthur N. Holcombe, "The Role of Politics in the Organization of Peace," *Organizing Peace in the Nuclear Age*. New York: New York University Press, 1959, p. 97.

4 Petition by E. M. Attiogbe, spokesman for the Ewe tribe, cited by John MacLaurin, *The United Nations and Power Politics*. London: Allen and Unwin, 1951, pp. 354–355.

5 Inis L. Claude, Jr., *Swords into Plowshares*. 2d ed. New York: Random House, 1959, p. 369.

6 *Ibid.*, pp. 370–372.

7 Cited by H. G. Nicholas, *The United Nations as a Political Institution*. New York: Oxford University Press, 1959, p. 153.

8 United Nations Security Council, *Official Records,* Eleventh Year, 751st Meeting, October 31, 1956, pp. 1–2.

9 *The New York Times,* August 10, 1960.

10 *New York Herald Tribune,* September 27, 1960.

11 Address by President Kennedy to the General Assembly, September 25, 1961, in *Documents on American Foreign Relations 1961*, pp. 473–484.

12 Trygve Lie, *In the Cause of Peace*. New York: Macmillan, 1954, p. 80.

13 House Congressional Resolution 262, 83d Congress, August 20, 1954.

14 Cited by Claude, *op. cit.*, p. 204.

15 Bernard D. Nossiler, "Parkinson's Law at the UN," *New York Times Magazine,* November 23, 1980, p. 60.

16 Cited in Wilder Foote, ed., *Dag Hammarskjöld: Servant of Peace, A Selection of His Speeches and Statements*. New York: Harper & Row, 1962, p. 351.

17 *The New York Times,* June 11, 1972.

18 "Issues before the 42nd General Assembly of the United Nations," *United Nations Association of the United States of America*. Lexington, MA: Lexington Books, 1988, p. 164.

19 For a more complete treatment of the UN peace forces, see Chapter 12.

SELECTED BIBLIOGRAPHY

Claude, Inis, Jr. *Swords into Plowshares*. 4th ed. New York: Random House, 1971. This book, though somewhat out of date on factual developments, is probably the finest conceptual treatise on the United Nations in existence today.

Finkelstein, Lawrence S., ed. *Politics in the United Nations System*. Durham, NC: Duke University Press, 1988. This excellent, well-balanced symposium by highly qualified experts places the United Nations squarely into the context of today's world politics.

Peterson, M. J. *The General Assembly in World Politics*. Winchester, MA: Allen & Unwin, 1986. A most useful, detailed analysis of the possibilities and limitations of the United Nations' plenary body.

Roberts, Adam and Kingsbury, Benedict, eds. *United Nations, Divided World*. New York: Clarendon Press, Oxford, 1988. Lectures by leading UN experts, delivered at Oxford University in 1986, during the low ebb of the United Nations' fortunes.

Singh, Nihal S. *The Rise and Fall of UNESCO*. Riverdale, MD: Riverdale Company, 1988. A distinguished Indian newspaper editor offers a realistic assessment of UNESCO's role in today's world.

Stoessinger, John G. *The United Nations and the Superpowers*. 4th ed. New York: Random House, 1977. Ten case studies of superpower interaction at the United Nations.

Stoessinger, John G. and Associates. *Financing the United Nations System*. Washington, DC: Brookings, 1964. The authors offer a detailed history of the troubled finances of the United Nations as well as some imaginative ideas about possible sources of future revenue.

11

REGIONALISM AND POLITICAL ORDER

Ours is essentially a tragic age, so we refuse to take it tragically. The cataclysm has happened, we are among the ruins, we start to build up new little habitats, to have new little hopes. It is rather hard work: there is now no smooth road into the future: but we go round, or scramble over the obstacles. We've got to live, no matter how many skies have fallen.

D. H. Lawrence, *Lady Chatterley's Lover*

THE IDEA OF REGIONALISM

Regionalism may be defined as a grouping of three or more states whose goal is the formation of a distinct political entity. A regional arrangement is a voluntary association of sovereign states that have developed fairly elaborate organizational tools to forge among them such bonds of unity. A purely military alliance among nations that do not pursue the goal of political order-building is not a regional arrangement. The Triple Entente was a purely military pact, but NATO, though primarily devised for defensive purposes, may be considered a regional arrangement since it has developed purposes other than military.

We have seen the role of regional arrangements as instruments of the international struggle for power. We shall now analyze their role as contributors to international order. Before we proceed to representative case studies, however, we must examine the concept of regionalism as a form of order-building.

Regionalism is based on the assumption that universalism is today still premature and too ambitious. Those who feel that the time is not yet ripe for order-building on a global scale want to use regionalism as an essential stepping-stone. They envisage the development of political unity within delimited geographic areas, which could then be used as building blocks in the construction of a future, world-wide political order. The classic statement of this idea was that of Clarence K. Streit, who, in his *Union Now,* proposed the unification of democratic countries in order to form the nucleus for a future world government. Streit conceived of regionalism as a vital intermediate stage in an organic evolution toward the more ambitious goal of globalism. Other proponents of regionalism, however, have felt that in view of the continuing heterogeneity of the world, it as yet makes little sense to speak of a world-wide political order at all. First, they insist, a universal framework of values and a global sense of community must be developed.

Regionalist thinkers have differed not only on goals but also on methods. Some have preferred the federal approach to order-building. This approach has emphasized the necessity for participating states to yield parts of their sovereignty to a "supranational" body. The latter would then, in effect, have some of the powers of a new state and its decisions would be binding on the member governments. The federal approach has tended to concentrate especially on the legal instruments of order-building, such as constitutions. Still other regionalists have advocated the functional method, and have pointed out the necessity for economic, social, and cultural cooperation as a prerequisite to political integration. The functionalists have tended to shy away from the formation of "supranational" organs and, instead, have encouraged the development of as many forms of intergovernmental collaboration as possible.

We have seen earlier how little we know about the nature and the causes of war. This is, of course, simply another way of admitting how little we know about the process of political order-building. Little empirical work has been done to examine the claims of the regionalists in relation to world order, or the approach of the federalists as opposed to that of the functionalists. Most of the arguments advanced have been based on the dubious foundations of historical analogy, popular belief, and dogmatic preference. There is ample descriptive and analytical literature about the regional and global arrangements that already exist, but relatively little material on the *process* whereby regional orders are actually built. One of the most illuminating studies of this kind was prepared by a group of scholars at Princeton University.[1] This study made a careful analysis of ten cases in which regional order-building had attained the level of "security-communities," a condition in which warfare among the members had become so highly improbable as to be practically out of the question. The authors distinguished between two types of security-community: one that had resulted from a formal merger of previously independent units into a single larger unit—like the United States; and a second, of a more pluralistic nature, which retained the legal independence of separate governments. This pioneering study in the formation of security-communities affords some penetrating insights into the dynamics of regionalism.

The Princeton study cast serious doubt on the validity of several popular beliefs that have long served as premises for regionalist thinking. The study exploded the notion of an organic, almost automatic evolution of the world into larger units; in fact, the authors pointed out that the closer they got historically to modern conditions and to our own time, the more difficult it was to find the successful formation of security-communities. Nor did the widely held belief that the establishment of one successful "security-community" would have a bandwagon effect stand up under scrutiny. Even more important, the authors placed in question the popular notion that a principal motive for the regional integration of states had been the fear of anarchy or of warfare among themselves. These important negative findings were matched by equally significant positive insights into the nature of the integrative process.

The authors isolated several conditions that they considered essential for the establishment of regional security-communities. In all successful cases they found a compatibility of values and expectations among the participating units. These common values were most helpful when they were incorporated in similar types of political institutions, thus creating a common political way of life. The authors further discovered that the competition between the federalist and the functionalist approaches to political order-building was largely irrelevant to the dynamics of regional integration. While they did find that the establishment of pluralistic security-communities through functionalism was somewhat easier than the creation of amalgamated security-communities through federalism, the difference was not considered crucial. What did seem decisive for the outcome was whether the integrative process was accompanied by widespread expectations and experiences of joint rewards for the participating states. In this regard, the functional technique seemed somewhat more successful, since it usually implied strong economic ties that, in the cases where regionalism proved successful, in turn led to economic rewards for the member states. Another essential condition was seen in a marked increase in political and administrative capabilities of the participating states, as well as in the presence of superior economic growth within the region. Other preconditions for the establishment of security-communities appeared to be the presence of a multiplicity of unbroken links of social communication and considerable mobility of people among the states concerned. Finally, a degree of mutual predictability of behavior was considered an essential prerequisite.

In addition to these general conditions, the authors developed the concept of "take-off," which they used to describe the conditions most favorable to the *beginning* of regional integration. The study pointed out that nations have been more likely to begin the process when they have felt strong rather than when they have seen themselves as weak. The authors also discovered that a military alliance usually turned out to be a relatively poor pathway toward building a security-community, since "the presence of excessive military commitments—excessive in the sense that they were felt at the time to bring considerably more burdens than rewards—had a disintegrative effect."[2] Finally, the study pointed out that not all security-communities were "final," but that, indeed, it was possible to cross, recross, or even stand poised upon a broad threshold of integration.

A great deal of research has taken place in the fields of international organization and regional integration since the Princeton study appeared. One particularly fine study was *Power and Interdependence* by Robert O. Keohane and Joseph S. Nye.[3] In it the authors explored the costs and benefits of mutual dependence in international relationships. They wisely pointed out that rising interdependence was not creating a brave new world of cooperation to replace the bad old world of international conflict. "As every parent of small children knows," the authors noted, "baking a larger pie does not stop disputes over the size of the slices."[4] Interdependence has conferred some benefits upon states, but it has also made them more vulnerable. The energy dependency of oil-consuming states on OPEC is only one example of such new vulnerability. Interdependence is, therefore, not an unmixed blessing.

These pioneering studies have forced us to reexamine a number of widely held beliefs about both the relationship of regionalism to world order and the dynamics of the regional order-building process in general. None of the ten cases selected for the Princeton study went beyond World War II. We shall therefore attempt to apply a similar empirical analysis to some of the representative regional political groupings of our current period. We must remember, of course, that the process of regional integration does not proceed only on a political level. Most of the existing regional entities have followed a whole range of pathways to unity. But each has tended to emphasize one approach more than others. NATO, for example, has stressed military bonds of unity; the European Coal and Steel Community and the Common Market have operated largely in the realm of economics; and the Council of Europe has stressed the principles of political association. The regional arrangements that are based primarily upon economic and military premises are discussed elsewhere in this volume. The present analysis will concern itself with those regional instruments of orderbuilding that are *primarily* political in character.

POLITICAL ORDER-BUILDING IN EUROPE

The Council of Europe

The ideal of a politically united Europe has its roots in antiquity. It makes its appearance in the political and philosophical literature of each major epoch in European civilization. But at no time prior to our own era had the movement for European unity been a popular one, capturing strong and widespread support. Indeed, the European idea had remained largely an abstraction, the preserve of philosophers and visionaries. Only after World War I did it enter into the thinking of statesmen and diplomats as a concrete possibility and, perhaps, even as a necessity. The Balkanization of Europe in the wake of World War I made many thoughtful observers fearful of the danger of a new struggle and so led them to look and work toward the gradual acceptance by the sovereign states of Europe of a common political mechanism. Foremost among the advocates of a united Europe was a count of the Holy Roman Empire, Richard Coudenhove-Kalergi.[5] He first expressed his thoughts in a book, *Pan Europa*, published in 1923, and he organized the first Pan-European congress, in Vienna, which mobilized public opinion for his ideas. The promotional efforts of the count and his followers succeeded, in the inter-war period, in winning over several prominent European statesmen. Aristide Briand of France, one of the great European figures in the League of Nations, and Gustav Stresemann of Germany made European unity a cornerstone of their national policies. But these early efforts were doomed to failure. The death of Stresemann, the lengthening shadow of Hitler over Europe, and the incapacity of the League of Nations drove the ideal of European union into temporary eclipse. Yet even during the darkest days of World War II, statements by the most prominent European leader of the Allied powers gave indication that the ideal would emerge with increased vitality once Europe was again at peace. As early as October 1942, Winston Churchill expressed the hope that

> Hard as it is to say now, I trust that the European family may act unitedly as one under a Council of Europe. I look forward to a United States of Europe in which the barriers between the nations will be greatly minimized and unrestricted travel will be possible. We must try to make this Council of Europe into a really effective League, with all the strongest forces woven into its texture, with a High Court to adjust disputes, and with armed forces, national or international or both, held ready to enforce these decisions and to prevent renewed aggression and the preparation of future wars. This Council when created, must eventually embrace the whole of Europe, and all the main branches of the European family must someday be partners in it.[6]

It had taken a Hitler to compel Europe to take union really seriously. At war's end, Sir Winston and Count Coudenhove found massive support among the statesmen of Europe. In May 1948 an attempt was made to organize the first truly continental demonstration of unity—the Congress of Europe. This congress, held at The Hague, was the birthplace of the Council of Europe.

It is noteworthy that each of the major European countries produced statesmen deeply committed to the European Movement. All of them came from the border lands of their respective countries and all of them shared a cosmopolitan world view. The list of these European-minded political leaders is impressive indeed: Konrad Adenauer of Germany, staunch fighter against the tyranny of Hitler and devoted disciple of Stresemann's European policy; Leon Blum and Robert Schuman of France, who carried on the tradition of Briand; Alcide de Gasperi of Italy, who saw in unity the fulfillment of a Christian ideal; Paul-Henri Spaak of Belgium; Sir Winston Churchill, one of the grand architects of the idea but one who remained ambivalent about the role of Britain in such a venture; and finally, Count Coudenhove, the pioneer who had indefatigably prepared the way.

In January 1949 the foreign ministers of the major European powers convened and drafted the Statute of the Council of Europe. The council's primary goal, as set forth in Article I, was to be the achievement of "a greater unity between its Members for the purpose of safeguarding and realizing the ideals and principles which are their common heritage." Progress toward unity was to proceed on several fronts. The statute listed an extensive range of subjects that were to be within the competence of the council. Among them were legal matters, human rights, and cultural and social questions. While no specific reference was made to political questions in the statute, it was clearly implied that the council was to function as essentially a political body. It was to consist of a Committee of Ministers whose members were to be the foreign ministers of the member states and of a Consultative Assembly whose membership was to be drawn from the legislatures of the participating countries. The original membership of the council comprised ten states: Belgium, Denmark, France, Ireland, Italy, Luxembourg, Holland, Norway, Sweden, and Great Britain. Since then, seven more have been added: Austria, West Germany, Greece, Iceland, Cyprus, Turkey, and Switzerland. The council's membership policy was conceived as open-ended and it was hoped that it might serve as a first step toward a United States of Europe.

It is an ancient truth that organizational realities tend to be far more modest than the ideas that underlie them. In view of its broad membership base, it is not surprising that both of the council's main organs have witnessed a continuing struggle between two quite differing conceptions of what European unity should be and how it might best be achieved. On the one hand have been the "federalists," favoring a "supranational" organ with real powers; on the other have been the "functionalists," who have advocated the more traditional "transnational" path to unification. The former have consistently urged that the member states yield more of their sovereignty to the council, whereas the latter have jealously sought to preserve their sovereign rights. The preferability of the supranational approach has been defended by France, West Germany, Italy, and the Benelux countries, which together have come to be known as The Six. More conservative, the transnationalists have been led by Great Britain, which has continued to see itself not only as a European power but, at the same time, as the leader of the Commonwealth. This British ambivalence toward Europe has been aptly expressed in a classic statement of Sir Winston Churchill: "We have our own dreams and our own tasks. We are linked but not comprised. We are with Europe, but not of it. We are interested and associated but not absorbed."[7]

The council's organizational structure reflects a clear-cut victory for the more conservative approach. Neither the Committee of Ministers nor the Consultative Assembly has supranational powers. Both are intergovernmental arrangements in which sovereignty has been entirely preserved. Any resolutions are merely recommendations and must be ratified by the participating member states before they become binding. The Committee of Ministers is the executive organ, consisting of one representative from each member state. In principle, these should be the respective foreign ministers; in practice, they have frequently been alternates. All important decisions are made unanimously, "in the belief that this procedure serves the interests of European unity better than the imposition of the will of the majority on a reluctant minority."[8] Once decisions are reached, the ministers are to take the initiative for their adoption in their respective national governments.

The council's deliberative organ has been the Consultative Assembly. Its membership has comprised 132 delegates, with representation ranging from three in the case of Iceland and Luxembourg to eighteen for France, Great Britain, and West Germany. The assembly has borne only a superficial resemblance to a national parliament. Although there have developed various party groupings, the assembly has, in effect, been an assembly of individuals rather than a body of legislators representing constituencies.

One is tempted, in the light of the above, to conclude that the council has been little more than a debating society of European parliamentarians on vacation in Strasbourg and speaking for no one but themselves. Indeed, such a judgment could be supported by some of the facts. For one thing, the mandate of the council has been so broad that it has frequently led to vagueness. The tendency to make unity a goal in itself has led to an absence of specific programming. Moreover, while the delegates have frequently been enthusiastic about proposals in Strasbourg, they have suffered from inertia when it came to taking up the same matters in their own parliaments. The main weakness of the Council of Europe has thus not been its lack of supranational authority but its lack of a clearly defined program. The capacity to deal with everything in breadth has led to few accomplishments in depth. Nevertheless, the organization's record is not without its significant positive achievements. For example, there has developed in the council an interesting tendency toward transnational party caucusing. The leaders of the Italian Center Party, for instance, have gotten along better with their political counterparts in the German and French delegations than with their respective opposition parties at home. Though the contribution of this phenomenon to regional order-building cannot yet be accurately assessed, other achievements of the council have been more concrete. Its most significant accomplishment has been in the field of human rights. Intensive debates in both organs of the council led to a deep concern with this subject in the parliaments of the member staffs. In effect, the Council of Europe thus provided a springboard for the adoption of the European Convention of Human Rights. This became a legally binding document signed and ratified by all members of the council. The following human rights were to be guaranteed:

> Security of persons; exemption from slavery and servitude; freedom from arbitrary arrest, detention or exile; freedom from arbitrary interference in private and family life, home and correspondence; freedom of thought, conscience and religion; freedom of opinion and expression; freedom of assembly; freedom of association; freedom to unite in trade unions; the right to marry and found a family.[9]

Implementing the provisions of the convention, a European Commission on Human Rights was created, the first international body established by governments and competent to receive and act on individual petitions concerning violations of the rights set forth in the convention. Moreover, there was set up a European Court on Human Rights, whose function was to be the adjudication of infringements of the convention. These institutions have gone far beyond the purely hortatory Universal Declaration of Human Rights passed by the United Nations General Assembly. This is due mainly to the regional character of the experiment but also, in some degree, to the impetus provided by the Council of Europe. The recognition of obligations in the matter of these rights and freedoms has become the principal condition of membership in the council.

Despite its vagueness and lack of authority, the Council of Europe has served one vital function: it has remained the only European forum that has included countries neutral in the East-West struggle and in which, therefore, it has been possible to discuss the problems of Europe as a whole. This is exactly what happened in 1989 when Mikhail Gorbachev addressed the Council in Strasbourg, shortly after a free election had taken place in Poland. He declared that the member states should be free to determine their own destinies and clearly implied that the Brezhnev Doctrine which had justified Soviet intervention in Eastern Europe was now obsolete. A few weeks later, President Geroge Bush, echoing that sentiment, declared that Europe should be whole and free, with its citizens entitled to move from room to room in their European home. American and Soviet perceptions of Europe's future suddenly seemed quite compatible. At long last, forty years after the birth of the Council of Europe, the vision of its founders no longer seemed unattainable.

NATO

NATO is not only the West's major military instrument in the East-West struggle. It has been, at the same time, intended as a major means for the advancement of European unity. In fact, it was quite clear to the founders of NATO that without strong political bonds the Treaty's effectiveness as a military alliance would be minimal. This was the reason for the inclusion in the NATO Charter of its Article II:

> The Parties will contribute toward the further development of peaceful and friendly international relations by strengthening their free institutions, by bringing about a better understanding of the principles upon which these institutions are founded, and by promoting conditions of stability and well-being.

NATO includes two organs that are to contribute to political integration in the North Atlantic Community. One is the North Atlantic Council, composed of the foreign ministers of the member countries and concerned chiefly with military matters. Yet since the exchange of military intelligence necessary for joint planning has made it almost impossible for members of NATO to go to war against one another, the council's work has profound political implications as well. The other politically significant NATO organ is its unofficial Parliamentarians' Conference. This conference draws its membership from all fifteen NATO countries and acts as a consultation forum for the coordination of national policies among member states.

The main weakness of NATO's nonmilitary work has been that statesmen have tended to "inform other member countries about decisions of national policy that have already been taken unilaterally, instead of consulting them fully before making decisions.''[10] Clearance in NATO has at times been noticeably absent during the formulation stage of policy. This became tragically clear during the Suez crisis of 1956, when Britain and France failed to consult with the United States. The divergence between American and Anglo-French policies seriously weakened the bonds of NATO and resulted in the adoption by the North Atlantic Council in 1956 of a proposal to establish a Committee of Three to study possibilities for the improvement of consultation procedures among the NATO powers. This committee, consisting of the foreign ministers of Norway, Italy, and Canada, expressed the opinion that NATO had been concerned too much with problems of military strategy and too little with progress toward political unity. The withdrawal of French forces from the NATO integrated command in 1966 further weakened the alliance. As NATO Headquarters were moved from Paris to Brussels, the prospects for strengthening political bonds in the Atlantic Community seemed to recede further into the distance. And when, in 1974, hostilities erupted on Cyprus and strained relations between Greece and Turkey to the breaking point, virtually severing Greece's ties with NATO, political integration in the alliance suffered yet another setback.

In overall perspective, however, the political cohesion of NATO has nevertheless been quite remarkable. It is frequently forgotten that under the NATO Charter, member states are merely obligated to do what they ''deem necessary'' in case of an outside attack. Moreover, all policy decisions must be reached by unanimous vote. In purely structural terms, national sovereignty looms larger in NATO than in the United Nations Charter, where majority decisions are possible. Hence, as Claude has pointed out, ''the flight of security-minded statesmen from the veto-bound Security Council of the United Nations to NATO was not an escape from a primitive to a more advanced form of international organization so far as voting procedures are concerned, for the North Atlantic Treaty permits a much more thoroughgoing application of the veto principle than the Charter provisions concerning the Security Council.''[11] The explanation may be found in the fact that political cohesion in NATO, despite all the tensions and all the setbacks, is relatively high.

During the 1970s and 1980s, NATO as a military alliance came under increasing scrutiny. The withdrawal of US missiles from Western Europe in the face of overwhelming Soviet superiority in conventional arms caused considerable anxiety in NATO during the late 1980s. Mikhail Gorbachev's offer, made in 1988, to cut troops and conventional weapons in Europe helped to allay these suspicions to some extent. George Bush's proposal, advanced in Brussels in 1989, designed to bring NATO and Warsaw Pact troops into numerical parity, was a further positive step. It appeared that NATO, on its fortieth birthday, could justly call itself a success. It had served its original purpose: the deterrence of the Soviet Union. But henceforth, its members might have to rally around a new cause: the building of a common political community.

Western European Union

A third major European regional arrangement that has promoted political order-building is the Western European Union (WEU). The European statesmen resuscitated a treaty that had been superseded by NATO. This was the Brussels Treaty of 1948, which had created a joint command for British, French, and Benelux forces. The Brussels Powers agreed that this structure might be expanded to admit Germany and Italy. The latter proposal proved generally acceptable and quickly crystallized into the Western European Union, which came into force in May 1955 after parliamentary ratification by the seven member states.

In terms of supranationality, WEU falls short of military union. There is no fusion of armies nor is there a central organ with decision-making powers in matters of common defense. Each member state continues to have a national army and exercises a veto power over its disposition. WEU's central policy-making organ is its council, composed of the foreign ministers of the seven member states. The more important defense questions, such as the size of the armed forces to be contributed by each member state, must be approved unanimously. But decisions on types of conventional weapons to be used are taken by majority vote in the council. In addition to the council, a deliberative body, the assembly, coordinates the military policies of the seven states. This assembly has a purely advisory status and its members have usually been the same parliamentarians who also attend the meetings of the Consultative Assembly of the Council of Europe.

In sum, WEU has been a useful order-building device. It is a "little NATO" within NATO. Yet, by having succeeded in attracting Britain to its purposes and activities WEU, several years before Britain joined the Common Market in 1971, made a major contribution to the European political order-building process.

If we apply to the Council of Europe, NATO, and WEU the criteria formulated in the Princeton study of the building of security-communities, we see that all three rate rather high. For one thing, all three of these European regional arrangements involve nations with a fairly high compatibility of values, expectations, and political forms. In NATO and WEU, which are held together by the need for common security, the expectation of joint rewards is great. In the Council of Europe, which is concerned more with the goal of unity than with the achievement of tangible returns, it is almost entirely absent. Save for Portugal, moreover, all the nations concerned enjoy relatively high levels of economic development. Mobility of persons is also very considerable, being highest among the nations of WEU and lowest in NATO—owing to the rather restrictive immigration policies of the United States and Canada. On the whole, political integration is fairly high in WEU and NATO, but quite low in the Council of Europe. The crucial factor seems to be the expectation of joint rewards from the integrative process. This is present in the two military alliances but not in the Council of Europe. Yet the authors of the Princeton study have warned that though an outside military threat may provide the original impetus toward political order-building, more permanent unions derive their main support from other factors.[12] This would seem to indicate that the high degree of political integration in NATO and WEU may be transitory unless it is buttressed through specific programs that hold out to the member nations the promise of substantial and sustained rewards of a nonmilitary kind as well. NATO officials seem to have recognized this fact. On the occasion of the fortieth birthday of the alliance in 1989, all member states stressed the need to forge political, economic, and social bonds in addition to those imposed by the dictates of collective self-defense.

OTHER EXPERIMENTS IN REGIONAL ORDER-BUILDING

The Organization of American States

One of the earliest post-World War II regional arrangements to be established was the Organization of American States (OAS). The treaty, which formalized the solidarity of the Western Hemisphere against both external and internal threats to the peace, was the culmination of a long and arduous road to inter-American political order. The highlights of this history of hemispheric relations are well worth reviewing.

The famous Monroe Doctrine of 1823 declared that the United States reserved to itself the right to act as the protector of Latin America in case of outside aggression:

> We owe it, therefore, to candor, and to the amicable relations existing between the United States and those [European] powers, to declare that we should consider any attempt on their part to extend their system to any portion of this hemisphere as dangerous to our peace and safety.

In 1904 President Theodore Roosevelt interpreted the doctrine to mean that in cases of intra-hemispheric disputes the United States could also exercise the right of "an international police power." This controversial Roosevelt Corollary gave rise to several instances of United States intervention in the Caribbean. In all of these interventions—in Cuba, Haiti, the Dominican Republic, Nicaragua, and Panama—the United States attempted to restore political and economic stability. However, the novel interpretation that the Monroe Doctrine not only forbade intervention from Europe but permitted United States intervention in order to forestall any *possible* European incursion led to widespread resentment in Latin America. At the turn of the century, the Latin American nations began to exert pressure upon the United States to renounce its claims to intervene. Gradually, these efforts met with success. The Roosevelt Corollary was officially discarded in 1926, and the Good Neighbor Policy initiated by Franklin D. Roosevelt in 1933 put an end to the practice of unilateral intervention. The Axis threat to the Western Hemisphere during World War II consolidated inter-American solidarity even further. And when the Americas emerged victorious, the time was ripe for the conclusion of a regional arrangement dedicated both to the maintenance of reciprocal security and to a common effort toward political order-building.

Accordingly, delegates from the twenty Latin American nations and from the United States met in Rio de Janeiro and drafted the famous Rio Treaty—an Inter-American Treaty of Reciprocal Assistance. Article III, the heart of the treaty, provided that "an armed attack by any state against an American state shall be considered as an attack against all American states." This provision was in essence a recognition of the fact that the Monroe Doctrine had become multilateralized. It also furnished a pattern for the NATO Charter that would be concluded two years later. The drafters of the Rio Pact, unlike the framers of NATO, were not solely concerned with protection against external aggression. Most of the members were equally eager to guard against the possibility of internal schism. The immediate reason for their apprehension was the government of Argentina, which had sided with the Axis during World War II. Argentina was the only member state which wanted a treaty only against aggression by non-American states, but its position was voted down. The Rio Treaty as first constituted in 1947 was primarily an instrument of military security against internal and external attack. A year later, at a conference in Bogotá, Colombia, the pact was further elaborated by the inclusion of provisions for political order-building. This new and sophisticated system, in the words of the then American Secretary of State, George C. Marshall, was to be "the very heart of hemispheric organization." It was named the Organization of American States (OAS).

The structure of the OAS provides for an eclectic approach to political order-building. An annual Assembly of Foreign Ministers constitutes the organization's main organ. The foreign ministers consider all urgent problems of internal and external security. Conference procedure for the settlement of intra-hemispheric disputes differs from that which governs cases of outside attack. The procedure adopted for the former is as follows: First, the foreign ministers may issue a call to the parties to cease hostilities; next, they may recommend various techniques of conciliation and mediation; they may then impose diplomatic and economic sanctions; and finally, if all the foregoing measures fail, they may recommend the use of armed force to restore order. It is significant that the first three of these provisions may be initiated by a two-thirds vote, which thereby becomes binding on all members. There is no veto. However, in the case of military enforcement measures, no state may be compelled to contribute armed forces without its consent. In the eventuality of an external threat, the arrangement is somewhat looser. The member states are obligated merely to consult with one another in order to arrive at a common policy, but each state may do what it "deems necessary" to help the victim— or not to help it.

In addition to its central organ, the OAS also works through several subsidiary bodies. There is, first, the OAS Council, which is the organization's central administration and coordinating organ. Second, there is an Inter-American Economic and Social Council, but, unlike its United Nations counterpart, this is not a major organ and does not have a very extensive program. Third, an Inter-American Cultural Council, designed for the promotion of friendly relations and cultural understanding among the American peoples, is patterned after UNESCO. The OAS also enjoys the services of a very active Inter-American Council of Jurists, which roughly parallels the International Law Commission of the United Nations. Finally, OAS, like the United Nations, has its international secretariat, the Pan-American Union. This is headed by a secretary-general who is chosen by the Inter-American Conference for a ten-year term, not subject to reelection.

A survey of the OAS structure indicates that the attention of the organization is about equally divided between the negative function of resolving disputes and the positive task of political integration. The achievements of OAS in the former category have been considerable. In December 1948 Costa Rica complained to the council that Nicaragua was trying to overthrow its government through revolution. The council blamed Costa Rica for negligence and Nicaragua for not preventing the revolutionary activity. A Committee of Five was appointed to mediate between the disputants. The effort was successful and the two parties signed a Treaty of Friendship in 1949. In 1950 Haiti accused the Dominican Republic of fostering subversion aimed at the overthrow of the Haitian government. The OAS Council found the Dominican Republic responsible and called upon it to desist from further subversive activities in the Western Hemisphere. In June 1954 a more complicated issue arose. The pro-Communist government of Guatemala charged Honduras and Nicaragua with U.S.-inspired aggression. The matter was discussed first in the United Nations Security Council, but it was decided that that body would not pursue the matter further until OAS had completed its investigation. This investigation never took place because the Guatemalan government was overthrown and replaced by a new, anti-Communist government. As a result, the matter was dropped by all concerned. In 1955 Costa Rica charged Nicaragua with fomenting a revolt. The OAS Council was successful in settling the matter through an investigating committee which made a series of recommendations accepted by both parties.

Four serious intra-hemispheric crises occupied the OAS in the 1960s. The first concerned the policy of subversion that had been pursued by the Dominican Republic in 1960 against Venezuela, including a plot to assassinate the Venezuelan president. The organization decided to take a strong stand against the Dominican Republic not only in the light of this specific provocation but because it was determined to end the thirty-year dictatorship of Generalissimo Trujillo. For the first time, the OAS decided to apply sanctions against one of its members for actions against another. The punishment consisted of a collective break in diplomatic relations and of "partial sanctions," including the suspension of arms shipments. The assassination of Trujillo in 1961 radically changed the Dominican picture and in 1962 the OAS voted to end the sanctions.

The second crisis grew out of the Cuban revolution and the apparent desire of Premier Fidel Castro to turn his revolution into an export commodity. The fact that the Soviet Union had gained a firm foothold in Cuba was especially distasteful to the United States and introduced further complications. The United States wanted desperately to prevent the spread of communism in the Western Hemisphere but was now forced to pursue this aim within the context of a multilateral conference, rather than by a unilateral wielding of the Monroe Doctrine. The other delegates were not as openly fearful of the Cuban revolution, but expressed varying degrees of ambivalence. Nevertheless in 1962, by a two-thirds vote, the foreign ministers at Punta del Este declared the Marxist-Leninist foundations of Castro's Cuba incompatible with membership in the Organization of American States. Cuba was also explicitly excluded from the Inter-American Defense Board and had an arms embargo imposed upon it. In October 1962, during the missile crisis, the OAS unanimously endorsed the American naval quarantine and Argentina and Venezuela actually sent ships to help United States naval forces. The response of the OAS to the missile crisis marked the first time that any military action was taken by the organization against a country in the Western Hemisphere. It took a dozen years for the first signs of a thaw to appear. In 1974 two American senators visited Cuba to explore the possibility of rapprochement; but despite this move, the OAS failed to remove the quarantine against Cuba. In 1975, at a meeting in Costa Rica, the OAS finally lifted the sanctions against Cuba that had been imposed in 1964.

Another precedent was set in January 1964 when the OAS took up a dispute involving the United States. Panama charged the United States with aggression after American troops had fired on Panamanian demonstrators in the Canal Zone. A more basic cause of the dispute, however, was the Panamanian demand to renegotiate the 1903 treaty giving the United States sovereign rights in the Canal Zone "in perpetuity." The OAS found itself in a dilemma. On the one hand, it wanted to help a small sister republic, but on the other, it was loath to place the United States in the role of the accused. Thus, it constituted itself as an "organ of consultation" to look into the charges and to help the two parties in reaching an amicable settlement. The peace-keeping mechanism of the organization was adapted to the situation in a flexible and imaginative manner. Finally, in 1978, Panama and the United States managed to renegotiate the 1903 treaty bilaterally and to transfer sovereignty over the Canal Zone to Panama by the year 2000.

A highly controversial situation arose in April 1965 when the United States decided to intervene in the Dominican Republic and sent in marines in order to stave off an alleged Communist coup. Proponents of the move defended it by pointing out that the United States could not afford another Castro, but critics deplored the unilateral intervention and feared the imminent end of the Good Neighbor Policy. In order to give the intervention a semblance of multilateralism, the United States in May 1965 requested an inter-American military force for the restoration of order in the Dominican Republic. The OAS foreign ministers, in a vote of fourteen to five, which was barely the required two-thirds majority, authorized the force. The five states opposing its creation resented what they felt to be an OAS ratification of American unilateralism. Nevertheless, the first inter-American military force entered Santo Domingo in May 1965, and thus established yet another precedent in the evolution of the OAS as an intra-hemisphere peace-keeping organ. In late 1966, after a little over a year of successful peace-keeping, the force was withdrawn from Santo Domingo.

The order-building task of the OAS has been made rather difficult because the Latin American countries and the United States have had different reasons for supporting the organization. For Latin America, OAS implied the legal sanctification of American nonintervention in the affairs of the hemisphere. It was also seen as a device for countering the supremacy of the "Colossus of the North." And most important, the Latin American countries looked forward to economic and technical assistance from the United States. The motives of the United States were somewhat different. From the American viewpoint, the OAS was to be a vital regional alliance in the East-West struggle. In 1961 the United States, in an effort to reconcile these different perspectives, launched a massive economic development program within the context of the OAS—the Alliance for Progress.

The Alliance for Progress got off to a fairly slow start. Tensions between the United States and the Latin American members of the alliance over American trade and aid policies retarded progress. In particular, the Latin Americans resented the requirement that American goods and services would have to be purchased with American aid funds. The United States, during the early years of the alliance, also continued to give bilateral aid to Latin American countries. This disappointed those who preferred greater emphasis on a multilateral program of hemispheric development. Finally, in 1966, at a major conference at Punta del Este, President Johnson and eighteen other heads of state, in a "Declaration of the Presidents of America," outlined plans for a Latin American common market to be in operation twenty years hence. The foundation for this emerging common market would be laid through multinational projects, the modernization of agriculture, the development of science and technology, and the advancement of education.

The continued presence of dictatorships—notably in Cuba, Haiti, and Nicaragua—has had a retarding effect on order building. Some members have advocated the encouragement of democracy in the Western Hemisphere, but others have declared that such a policy would negate the principle of nonintervention. The United Nations has not been able to pursue both goals simultaneously. In addition, many Latin American countries have lacked internal stability. Coups d'état are not infrequent. In 1961 a coup ended a thirty-year dictatorship in the Dominican Republic, and in 1964 another coup stemmed the drift toward anarchy in Brazil. During the 1980s unrest was rampant in Nicaragua and El Salvador. The United States was profoundly at odds with many members of the OAS over the US "contra" policy in Nicaragua. Venezuela and Mexico, for example, totally disagreed with US policy in these two Central American countries.

In the light of these divergent patterns and interests, unity and solidarity have been expressed primarily in general statements, but more concrete steps in order building have proved very difficult. Despite these shortcomings, OAS remains one of the most advanced regional arrangements in the world. It alone has provisions for internal security and has acquitted itself well in this respect. However, its progress toward political integration has been far more hesitant. During the late 1980s, for example, OAS faced serious financial problems because of US cutbacks in contributions. If we apply the criteria of the Princeton study, we notice that OAS is not blessed with a system of common values, which the authors considered one of the essentials for the building of a security-community. However, OAS meets another key condition admirably. All its members have high expectations of concrete rewards. Although these expectations differ—being primarily military in the eyes of the United States and economic in the view of Latin America—they are nonetheless effective. At present, therefore, OAS may be considered what the Princeton group would call a "pluralistic security-community" at a low level. Further political integration would seem to depend on continuing and expanded expectations of joint rewards and on the improvement and enlargement of communications that will enhance mutual responsiveness among the members.

The Arab League

The most prominent regional arrangement in the Middle East has been the Arab League. It was organized on the eve of the San Francisco Conference in 1945 and comprised seven states: Egypt, Syria, Lebanon, Jordan, Iraq, Saudi Arabia, and Yemen. The purpose of the league as set forth in its Charter was

> ...to strengthen the ties between the participating states, to coordinate their political programs in such a way as to effect real collaboration between them, to preserve their independence and sovereignty, and to consider in general the affairs and interests of the Arab countries.

In practice, "strengthening the ties" between the members of the Arab League was a subordinate goal. There were two overriding causes for the creation of the league: first, to present a united front against the return to the Middle East of French and British colonialism; and second, to prevent the creation of a Jewish state in Palestine.

The most powerful organ of the league has been the Majlis, a council comprising the prime ministers of the member states. All important decisions, including any kind of collective action, have required unanimity. Majority decisions have been binding only on those states that have voted for a particular resolution. On intraleague disputes, the council may act by majority vote, provided the "independence, sovereignty or territorial integrity of a member are not involved." As a result of this reservation, all but very minor questions have in practice required unanimous decision. In 1950 the structure of the Arab League was developed further by the adoption of a Treaty of Joint Defense and Economic Cooperation modeled after the NATO Pact. Like NATO, this treaty stipulated the peaceful settlement of all disputes among the members; stated that an attack upon one was to be regarded as an attack upon all; and included a statement that armed attack from the outside would be met by collective military measures. In addition, for the purpose of coordinating the economies of the Arab countries, it created an Economic Council consisting of the member states' ministers of economic affairs. Finally, the office of a secretary-general was added whose incumbent was to be appointed by a two-thirds vote of the Council.

The formal structure of the Arab League has had relatively little to do with the actual policy-making process. In the opinion of one expert student of the Arab League:

> The real activities of the League are carried on in private and secret talks and through conversations held outside regular meetings. The careful elaboration of agreements, with each stage consigned to writing—so customary in the West—is utterly unfamiliar. When the prestige of man comes into conflict with the prestige of the written word, the former prevails. Furthermore, the activities of the League are unknown and misunderstood abroad, and even in the Arab world, because the organization has been reluctant to secure publicity for its activities.[13]

The league's official purpose and its formal structure thus provide few clues to its actual goals and operations.

In its first aim, the liberation of Egypt, Lebanon, Syria, and Libya from colonial rule, the Arab League was clearly successful. When France attempted to resume control of Lebanon and Syria in 1945, the league pressed for submission of the dispute to the United Nations Security Council. When in 1946 the Security Council took up the problem, the league presented a united front and succeeded in preventing the French from returning to Lebanon and Syria. Similarly the league supported the complete evacuation of British troops from Egypt. When Egypt emerged as an independent state after seventy-two years of British rule, this victory was attributable in no small measure to the efforts of the Arab League.

Finally, the Arab League played a decisive role in securing the independence of Libya by acting as the spokesman for that new state in the United Nations. Actually, the intervention on behalf of Libya probably owed its success more to the inability of the Big Four to agree on a new status for Libya than to the inherent strength of the league itself. When neither the Big Four nor the United Nations was able to decide what to do with the former Italian territory, the Arab League's insistent pressure for independence weighed heavily in the balance. Libya became independent in 1951 and was admitted as the eighth member of the Arab League in 1953. The Sudan received its independence and joined the league in 1956, and two years later Morocco and Tunisia were admitted. Kuwait became a member in 1961 and in the following year Syria resumed its separate seat, which it had relinquished by joining the United Arab Republic. Finally, in 1962 Algeria became the thirteenth member of the Arab League. By the early 1960s it was clear that the first major political goal of the league—the emancipation of the Arab states from Western colonialism—had been achieved.

In its second major objective, the prevention of the Jewish state in Palestine, the Arab League has failed. In 1946 the league developed a common policy toward Palestine: Jewish immigration and land purchases were to be stopped; Jewish products were to be boycotted; and Palestine was to be admitted to the league as an independent Arab nation. An attempt was made to create a common front against the creation of the state of Israel by threatening a general war for the liberation of the area if the new state were to come into being. When on May 15, 1948, Israel achieved its independence, the secretary-general of the Arab League informed the United Nations Security Council that the league was forced to intervene "to achieve peace and order and to restore the territory to the Arabs of Palestine."[14] In its war against Israel, however, the latent internecine schisms within the league quickly came to the surface. It found itself unable to coordinate the armies of its members. Since each state claimed the honor for itself, the League Council was not even able to agree on a commander-in-chief. "Iraq refused to accept an Egyptian commander. Egypt rejected an Iraqi general. And the commander-in-chief of the Jordan army was of British origin and therefore out of the question. The result was that each Arab army that entered Palestine fought on its own."[15] When in May 1949 Israel was admitted to the United Nations, the league faced complete defeat. The state that the league had vowed to destroy was not only in existence but was now recognized as an official member of the world community. The league defeat was made even more bitter when one of its members, Jordan, declared itself ready to accept the establishment of Israel and seemed intent on annexing the remaining portions of Palestine. Under the impact of total defeat the league began to disintegrate completely. Iraq and Jordan developed an increasing suspicion of Egyptian domination in the league and accused the secretary-general, Azzam Pasha, of pro-Egyptian leanings. As a result, an innocuous former civil servant, Abdel Khalek Hassouna, was appointed to the post. Nevertheless, Iraq refused to pay its membership contribution to the league and began to look around for new allies. To the consternation of the entire league, Iraq became the keystone of the Baghdad Pact, linking it to Britain, Turkey, Iran, and Pakistan. Only a revolution in 1958 brought it back into the fold. Jordan narrowly escaped expulsion because of its flirtation with Israel. The Arab League as a regional arrangement seemed to have turned into a complete debacle.

The pattern of internal conflict among the Arab states continued. In 1961 the United Arab Republic disintegrated and Syria seceded. Later that year, a bitter feud erupted between Egypt and Saudi Arabia over Yemen. In 1962 Syria lodged a formal complaint with the Arab League, charging that President Nasser was trying to effect a reunion of Syria with Egypt by forcible means. In 1963 Iraq's Premier Kassem was assassinated by pro-Nasser revolutionaries. In Syria the nationalistic Baath party took control. During the same year actual warfare broke out between Algeria and Morocco over the ill-definedSahara border. After a league call for a cease-fire, a shaky truce was established.

In 1967 almost all of the above conflicts were temporarily obscured when war erupted between Israel and three members of the Arab League, Egypt, Syria, and Jordan. Again, however, there was little effective coordination among the Arab armies, although King Hussein of Jordan placed his armed forces under Egyptian command. Shortly after the war, the members of the league met at Khartoum, in the Sudan, to discuss future policies toward Israel but, once again, many of the stubborn intra-Arab rivalries came to the surface and made any concerted policy difficult.

In late 1973, in the wake of the October War, the Arab League experienced a dramatic resurgence. The key to its new-found power, of course, was oil, or rather the ability to agree for the first time on a common oil price policy vis-à-vis the consuming countries. While only a few of the Arab League states—Saudi Arabia, Kuwait, Algeria, and the United Arab Emirates—were major oil producers, all league members benefited from the new policy. The ability to affect the Middle East postures of powerful industrialized states such as the United States and Japan gave the Arab League a new sense of heady confidence and power. Traditional rivalries were submerged and at a summit meeting in Rabat, Morocco, in 1974, the Palestine Liberation Organization was given the status of a government in exile. The league's anti-Israel policy, doomed to failure for over a quarter of a century, was suddenly infused with fresh hope in the mid-1970s. The league's new-found ability to act in unison led to significant policy successes that, in turn, endowed it with an internal cohesion and vigor that it had not exhibited since its inception. But then again, President Sadat's dramatic visit to Jerusalem in 1977 divided the league into a moderate group led by Egypt and a more radical alignment led by Syria.

By 1980 the Arab League was virtually a shambles. It was difficult to find two Arab countries that enjoyed friendly relations with one another. The immediate cause of this disarray was the Iraqi-Iranian war. Libya and Syria leaned toward Iran while Jordan and Saudi Arabia supported Iraq. Syria and Jordan had come close to war and Iraq was trying to replace Egypt as the "gendarme" of the Persian Gulf. The PLO, locked in a power struggle with Israel, was still trying to establish a Palestinian state. When the Arab League met in Amman, Jordan, in November 1980, Syria, Libya, Algeria, Southern Yemen, Lebanon, and the PLO refused to attend. Clearly, the unity of the Arab League had reached a new nadir.

The Arab League as a regional arrangement has not invested much energy in forging concrete political instruments of internal political order. One such peace-keeping operation was a joint Egyptian-Saudi Arabian military force dispatched to Kuwait in 1961 to replace British troops which had entered the newly independent country to protect it against the irredentist claims of Premier Kassem of Iraq. In addition, beginning in 1972, the league, under the leadership of its new secretary-general, Mahmoud Riad, took on the responsibility of mediating between Palestinian guerrillas and several Arab governments, such as Lebanon, that had large numbers of guerrillas on their soil. In 1979 a Syrian "peace-keeping" force entered war-torn Lebanon. Other non-political order-building efforts have included the passage by the League Council of legislation for inter-Arab private international law, the dissemination throughout the Arab world of the language of the Koran, and the organization of several cultural, scientific, and educational conferences.

If we analyze the Arab League in terms of the criteria of the Princeton study, we encounter the strange paradox of a regional arrangement that fulfills almost none of the essential conditions of a security-community. The absence of common values and mutual responsiveness among the members of the league is all too evident. The hostility between pan-Arabism and pan-Islam, the traditional authoritarianism of the monarchies and the rampant nationalism of the new republics, the fratricidal strife within the camp of the new nationalism—all these have made a mockery of unity in the Arab League. And yet there were times when it has held together. It held together because it was able to offer its members the expectation of two great rewards: the liquidation of Western colonialism and the destruction of Israel. It made a vital contribution to the achievement of the first objective and this success has solidified its bonds. Its total failure in the latter over more than thirty years almost brought about the league's disintegration, but in the mid-1970s the oil weapon infused the Arab League with new hope and strength. Then, by the 1980s, the league almost succumbed to fratricidal slaughter. Ironically, however, since opposition to Israel is the one thing that *all* league members save possibly Egypt have in common, the league's very existence appears to depend on the continued existence of the entity that it seeks to destroy. In the late 1980s, the Palestinian uprising in Gaza and the West Bank and the Algiers declaration of Palestinian independence infused some new life into the league. Because of its primarily negative goals, however, the league has done little to advance political order in the Middle East. And, as the authors of the Princeton study have pointed out, a unity that is based chiefly on common hostility against an outside force is bound to be transitory, since it imposes too many burdens and realizes too few rewards. Hence, it seems safe to say that unless the Arab League develops more positive methods of integration, it may face complete disintegration.

The Organization of African Unity

The Organization of African Unity (OAU) was created at the Conference of African Nations meeting in Addis Ababa, Ethiopia, in May 1963 with thirty-one independent African nations attending.

There was some disagreement among the delegates over the best method of furthering the cause of African unity. President Nkrumah of Ghana urged the creation of a unitary African state with a strong central government, but the conference was more impressed with the more moderate proposals of Emperor

Haile Selassie of Ethiopia, who quickly became the major spokesman of the majority view.

The conference decided upon a basic charter which listed the goals of the new organization: freedom, dignity, and equality for all Africans; continuation of the struggle against colonialism; preservation and consolidation of the territorial integrity of the members; and the establishment of common institutions. These aims were to be pursued in harmony with the United Nations Charter.

The conference was also able to agree on institutions for the OAU. It established, as the supreme authority of the OAU, an Assembly composed of the heads of the member states which would meet at least once every year; a Council of Ministers to meet at least twice a year, with each country having one vote and decisions to be made by simple majority; and a Secretary-General and Secretariat. In addition, a special Commission for Mediation and Arbitration of Inter-African disputes was set up. The costs of the new organization were to be met by assessing the members, using the United Nations scale as a model.

Since its inception in 1963, most of the energies of the OAU have gone into the struggle to eliminate the vestiges of Western colonialism in Africa. The heads of the member states have met at least once a year and much of their planning has centered on speeding the decolonization process. In 1964, for example, they decided to deny OAU ports and airfields to ships and planes that served South Africa. In 1965 the delegates unanimously urged Britain to use force against Rhodesia if the latter would seize independence from Britain. In 1966 the members urged the UN Security Council to adopt mandatory sanctions against the Smith regime in Rhodesia. During the late 1960s and the 1970s two-thirds of the OAU's budget was set aside to help guerrilla activity in the "white redoubt" countries of Southern Africa. When, in April 1980, Zimbabwe emerged as the fifty-first sovereign black African state, the OAU had only two targets left for liberation: Namibia and apartheid's last fortress, South Africa. During the 1980s, the dismantling of apartheid in South Africa has been the OAU's main preoccupation.

The OAU, however, has also been increasingly concerned about peace-keeping among its own members. In 1964, for example, it established a permanent commission to arbitrate border disputes. In 1965, it arranged for liaison with the UN General Assembly. In 1966, at the OAU Council of Ministers' meeting in Addis Ababa, the members were sharply divided over the seating of the Ghanaian delegation in the wake of Nkrumah's ouster. In 1967 the OAU sent a six-man mission to Lagos in search of Nigerian-Biafran peace and Zambia agreed to serve as moderator in the border dispute smoldering between Kenya and Somalia. At the same conference, UN Secretary-General U Thant urged the OAU to pay more attention to internal peace-keeping. While in 1968, the war between Nigeria and its breakaway province of Biafra assumed the proportions of a major human tragedy, Somalia agreed to resolve its boundary dispute with Kenya. In 1972 the OAU's prestige was further enhanced when the UN Security Council held a series of meetings in Addis Ababa for the express purpose of underlining the urgency of the problems that were besetting the African continent. In 1981 an OAU peace-keeping force consisting of troops from Nigeria, Senegal, and Zaire arrived in Chad in an effort to replace Libyan forces. And in 1988, the OAU helped in the mediation effort that brought about a ceasefire in the war between Morocco and the Polisario resistance over the Western Sahara.

While much of the momentum of the OAU is still derived from its original anticolonial raison d'être, it is beginning to exhibit some of the earmarks of a pluralistic security-community at a low level in its increasing role as internal peace-keeper. As colonialism recedes more and more into the past, it seems safe to predict that this latter function of the OAU will assume greater prominence in the future.

The British Commonwealth

Another case study in political order-building deals with the British Commonwealth. This is a unique international phenomenon and defies easy definition. As one observer has put it, "If it did not exist you could not invent it."[16] The Commonwealth's uniqueness as a regional arrangement lies in the first instance in the fact that it originated not as a congeries of independent states, but as an empire. The other regional arrangements we have analyzed have attempted to build unity by forging bonds where none have existed before. The Commonwealth, in essence, represents an effort to create political unity through the dissolution of existing political bonds that have become too onerous. For this reason the roots of the Commonwealth are radically different from those of other regional arrangements.

The present membership of the Commonwealth comprises thirty-one states, consisting of almost one billion people. The thirty-one members are: Australia, Barbados, Botswana, Canada, Ceylon, Cyprus, Fiji, Gambia, Ghana, Guyana, India, Jamaica, Kenya, Lesotho, Malawi, Malaysia, Malta, Mauritius, New Zealand, Nigeria, Pakistan, Sierra Leone, Singapore, Swaziland, United Republic of Tanzania, Tonga, Trinidad and Tobago, Uganda, the United Kingdom of Great Britain and Northern Ireland, Western Samoa, and Zambia. The Union of South Africa withdrew from the Commonwealth in 1961 and became the Republic of South Africa. In addition to the sovereign states listed above, the Commonwealth also includes a number of dependencies that are in the process of transition toward sovereign status.

It is difficult to discern what common purpose holds together this highly diversified group of states known as the Commonwealth. Very generally, however, the Commonwealth can be said to be dedicated to at least two objectives: common defense against external threats and common policies for economic betterment. The organizational structure of the Commonwealth is extremely loose. It has neither charter nor treaty and membership in it confers no legal rights and imposes no legal obligations. In terms of formal machinery, the

Commonwealth is the least developed of all regional arrangements. The most important of the Commonwealth institutions is a symbolic one—the Crown. Even India and Pakistan, although republics, have accepted the Crown as a symbol of their free association in the Commonwealth. The wearer of the Crown dedicates herself equally to many different peoples and many different faiths. Yet the Crown is considered indivisible. In L. S. Amery's telling metaphor, "it is a jewel of many facets, not a string of disconnected pearls."[17] The informality of Commonwealth relations is reflected in the main political organ, the Conference of Prime Ministers. This conference is simply an annual or biennial forum with no executive authority. Resolutions that may be passed by the conference merely have the status of recommendations until ratified by the individual members. This procedure is analogous to that in the Committee of Ministers of the Council of Europe. The conference is primarily a means of consultation rather than an organ for reaching decisions. But the techniques of consultation and the exchange of information among the Commonwealth countries have reached a high level of sophistication. Each member sends to each of the others a High Commissioner whose relationship to the host country is far less formal than that of the ordinary ambassador. In addition, massive exchanges of personnel in fields of mutual interest at the administrative level have helped to solidify the bonds of the Commonwealth. Common defense problems are discussed and functional matters like shipping and communications receive close attention. There also exists a Commonwealth Secretariat.

The complete absence in the Commonwealth of any pretensions to supranationality has not prevented large areas of friction among the members. Ireland preferred to leave the Commonwealth rather than discuss its differences with Great Britain. Burma decided to leave it when granted independence. The membership of India introduced serious disputes with other members: the struggles with Pakistan over Kashmir and Bangladesh and the perennial friction with the Union of South Africa over the question of apartheid.

The Commonwealth has not been able to evolve any common parliamentary or executive institutions. All such efforts have come to nought, owing to the stubborn insistence of each member on its complete sovereignty. Among the many paradoxes of the Commonwealth is the fact that whatever unity it has achieved as a regional arrangement has been attained without the development of institutional limitations on the sovereignty of its members.

Measured in terms of its own purposes, the record of the Commonwealth has been a mixed one. One of its most notable achievements has been its ability to attract into what once was an empire countries that only recently and after long and bitter struggles succeeded in emancipating themselves from colonial tutelage. All the former colonial countries that joined the Commonwealth after receiving independence did so by their own free will. In an age of colonial liquidation and widespread anticolonial emotionalism this has been a remarkable accomplishment indeed. In 1979, at Lusaka, the members of the Commonwealth even hastened the emergence of Southern Rhodesia as independent Zimbabwe. The goal of common defense, on the other hand, has been achieved only partially. At the time of Britain's gravest crisis, during World War II, the members of the Commonwealth fought freely on its side—though some, like India, exacted a heavy price. In the post-World War II world, however, the stategic interests of many of the member countries turned elsewhere. Canada solidified its ties with the United States. Because of its racial policies, the Union of South Africa became the *bête noire* of the Commonwealth and incurred the special animosity of such formerly colonial lands as Ghana and India. Australia and New Zealand, joined in the ANZUS Treaty, looked for protection more and more to the United States than to Great Britain. And India, attempting to follow its own independent course between East and West, more and more subordinated its commitment to the Commonwealth to the dictates of its own evolving strategy of "nonalignment."

How far this dissolution of strategic ties within the Commonwealth has progressed may be seen from the voting behavior of the Commonwealth countries in the United Nations. Of all the blocks in the General Assembly, the Commonwealth block has been the least cohesive. In fact, owing to wide divergencies on matters of foreign policy, its members have tended to vote almost completely independently. On the crucial issue of the Anglo-French invasion of Suez, only Australia and New Zealand supported the position of the United Kingdom. Ceylon, India, and Pakistan voted against Britain, and Canada and South Africa abstained. This lack of foreign-policy consensus has been fairly typical of the so-called Commonwealth bloc. Indeed, on any matter about which the members of the Commonwealth have strong convictions, each state can usually be expected to act strictly as it sees fit.

In its second purpose, that of improving economic relations, the Commonwealth has been more successful, although the devaluation of the British currency in 1967 sent shock waves throughout the Commonwealth. All parts of the Commonwealth, with the exception of Canada, share a "sterling area" in which trade and investment are greatly facilitated. Economic aid and technical assistance are administered under Commonwealth auspices through the Colombo Plan. This plan has been one of the most concrete incentives for Commonwealth membership in the lesser developed areas of the world. Its projects are undertaken as a joint enterprise on the basis of local development plans and mutual consultation.

Finally, the mobility of people among the member states has been fairly high. It would be too ambitious to speak of a "Commonwealth citizenship." But in many instances, Commonwealth status facilitates the right to enter or leave member states or to qualify for naturalization. By the late 1980s, most of the Commonwealth countries afforded privileges to other members not generally accorded to citizens of foreign countries.

In terms of the Princeton study, the Commonwealth can hardly be considered a security-community. The unity in political and security matters that once characterized the British Empire has been greatly weakened by powerful new centrifugal tendencies. The common commitment to parliamentarianism is threatened by the political instability of the new members in Africa. It would, moreover, be difficult to speak of the existence of common values throughout the Commonwealth. On the other hand, expectation of joint rewards has been fairly high. Membership in the Commonwealth has brought with it concrete economic benefits through joint projects like the Colombo Plan and the unhampered flow of trade. Informal order-building has been continuous without infringements of the members' sovereignty. Perhaps the most important factor of all in explaining the Commonwealth's continuing resiliency has been the fact that rewards and the expectation of rewards have always greatly exceeded burdens and responsibilities.

The Association of Southeast Asian Nations (ASEAN)

Our final case study will focus on Asia. In 1967, fearful of being drawn into the Indochina conflict, five Southeast Asian countries proclaimed themselves as "a zone of peace and neutrality." Thus was born the Association of Southeast Asian Nations (ASEAN), consisting of Indonesia, Malaysia, Thailand, the Philippines, and Singapore.

During its first ten years ASEAN resembled a debating society rather than a solid organization. But by the 1980s, largely because of the powerful economies of the five participating states, ASEAN had become a force to be reckoned with. Although it had no supranational powers, ASEAN had become an extremely useful instrument of regional communication. It had enabled the leaders of the region to become better acquainted with one another and to understand each other's perspectives. On numerous occasions ASEAN has spoken with a collective voice to the United States, China, Japan, and the Soviet Union.

Perhaps the major weakness of ASEAN has been that leadership in its five member countries has remained heavily dependent upon a few individuals: Corazon Aquino in the Philippines, Kriangsak in Thailand, Lee Kwan Yew in Singapore, Suharto in Indonesia, and Hussein Onn in Malaysia. Thus, the bonds of regionalism had to develop without the benefit of parliamentary democracy. In addition, each member state has had its own particular problems with a neighboring great power.

In the Philippines, the United States was critized when Ferdinand Marcos, the ousted leader, was granted asylum in Hawaii. Yet, by the late 1980s, Corazon Aquino, his successor, seemed to have consolidated her power. Thailand has been desperately concerned about the conflicts that have been raging on its borders. Not only have refugees from the Indochina conflict flooded into Thailand, but also the fighting between pro-Soviet Vietnam and pro-Chinese Kampuchea has threatened to spill over the borders into Thailand. The question of whether Thailand might become another domino also worried Malaysia and virtually defenseless Singapore. Indonesia, too, was torn between its continuing concern over the long-range problem of China and the more immediate problem of Vietnam. Yet, despite their differences, the five members of ASEAN were able to agree on one fundamental goal: to keep the region free from great power intervention.

Aware of the growing economic dynamism of the region, the superpowers have begun to pay attention. Walter Mondale toured the area in 1978 and President Carter played host to a conference of ASEAN ministers in Washington a few months later. China's Vice Premier Deng Hsiao-ping also visited the five countries and even went to the extraordinary length of genuflecting before the Crown Prince of Thailand. The Soviet Union, too, has wooed ASEAN, but has had a relatively cool reception because of its alliance with Vietnam.

The ASEAN community has attained the level of a low-level pluralistic security community even though its members are far from being parliamentary democracies. They have achieved this status because they all agree on one overriding objective: to maintain the neutrality of the area from outside disputes. So far, they have not only achieved this goal, but their strong economies have made them objects of courtship by big powers aiming to expand their markets. Far from threatening them militarily, the United States, China, and Japan have begun to look to ASEAN as a large potential market. Hence, it is very likely that ASEAN's bonds will tighten further as its members continue to coordinate their economic policies vis-à-vis the outside world. Originally, the five members of ASEAN were fearful of intrusion. By the late 1980s that danger had decreased significantly. Economic power had begun to shift away from Europe and America. The ASEAN countries have all been beneficiaries of this shift.

REGIONALISM AND THE UNITED NATIONS

The relation between regional arrangements and the United Nations has been a subject of heated controversy. Attitudes on the subject have fallen along a wide spectrum. At one extreme have been those who have defended the necessity of regional arrangements as building blocks toward globalism. Those who have advanced this view have held that regionalism is not only compatible with the United Nations but, in fact, is an essential stepping-stone to the world organization's successful functioning and further development. Winston Churchill expressed this position most forcefully when he stated before the opening of the San Francisco Conference that "there should be several regional councils, august but subordinate, and these should form the massive pillars upon which the world organization would be founded in majesty and calm."[18] At the other extreme in the controversy have been those who have tended to regard regional arrangements as little more than poorly camouflaged power alliances, evil creations of an anarchic world that are wholly incompatible with the principle of collective security.

At the San Francisco Conference, the problem of regional versus global organization was one of the thorniest issues. Many prospective members of the world organization were deeply committed to regional arrangements that antedated the United Nations Charter. The Inter-American system, the Arab

League, and the British Commonwealth commanded the loyalty of more than a score of the nations which assembled at San Francisco. The American republics wished to safeguard the hemispheric system, the Arab states were jealous of the rights of the Arab League, Britain had an eye on the Commonwealth, the Soviet Union wished to exempt its mutual assistance pacts from Security Council control, and most of the small states were suspicious of the Security Council because of the veto power. On the other hand, some members of the conference were deeply committed to universalism and tended to regard regional arrangements as a menace to peace and order. The interplay among these forces produced a compromise solution that was reflected in the Charter in a grudging acceptance of the fact that regionalism was here to stay and that its existence had to be reconciled with the principle of world organization. At first, there was an attempt to make regional organizations like the OAS into operating arms of the United Nations. Very soon, however, it had to be admitted that the very raison d'être of the regional organs was the preservation of their autonomous status vis-à-vis the United Nations. This autonomy was expressed as the right of "collective self-defense," recognized in Article 51 of the Charter. Under this provision NATO, OAS, and the Arab League were in practice exempted from external control by the United Nations. Soviet regional arrangements found a similar escape clause in Article 53 of the Charter, permitting "collective self-defense" against "enemy states" in World War II. Thus the Charter was compelled to recognize the coexistence of regionalism and universalism.

The problem for regionalists and universalists alike has, therefore, become the quest for a viable and productive division of labor between the two forms of political organization in order to maximize progress in order-building. If we compare the order-building record of the various regional organizations with that of the United Nations, the "building-block theory" advocated by the regionalists does not hold up. The Commonwealth, which prides itself on its sophisticated consultative machinery, has on several occasions been compelled to request the help of the General Assembly. It did not succeed in solving the stubborn conflicts between India and Pakistan over Kashmir and Bangladesh. Similarly, NATO was impotent in the three-cornered struggle involving three of its members over Cyprus, and the problem was handed over to the United Nations. The vital disagreements between the United States and Britain and France over the Suez question could not be composed within the framework of NATO. Only the OAS, with its highly developed order-building institutions, has made a creditable showing and has effectively dealt with serious disputes among its members. On the whole, NATO, the Commonwealth, and the Arab League have had to ask far more from the order-building capacities of the United Nations than they have been able to contribute to the resolution of international conflicts themselves.

If the record of the regional arrangements as independent instruments of order-building is thus not impressive, the reason would seem to lie chiefly in the fact that many of their energies have been absorbed in the two great struggles of our time. As major strategic instruments in these struggles, they have, in fact, been designed and operated so as to preserve the greatest possible degree of autonomy vis-à-vis the United Nations. This situation has, in turn, been reflected in a tendency to discuss more and more of the great international issues outside the world organization's framework. In the words of one scholar of regionalism, "The United Nations has been placed in a position of inferiority so that now the links between the regional arrangements and the world organization exist at the practical pleasure of the former."[19] This increasing habit of bypassing the United Nations on vital issues of high politics and security also troubled the late Secretary-General, Mr. Hammarskjöld, who urged a reversal of the trend:

> In recent years, the main attention has been concentrated on measures designed to give a measure of security on a regional basis, in the absence of a more universal system of security. If there is now to be a serious and sustained exploration of the possibilities for cooperation on a wider basis, the world organization must necessarily gain a new dimension.[20]

The problem of achieving a balance between regionalism and globalism cannot be solved in the theoretical realm. Each situation must be examined on its own merits and requires its own particular division of labor. In order to demonstrate the complexity of the problem, let us take the example of the peaceful uses of atomic energy. Should atoms-for-peace be given to needy nations through the universal channel of the United Nations International Atomic Energy Agency (IAEA)? Or should such a program be administered through regional organs like the European Atomic Energy Community (Euratom) in Western Europe? This case study shows that each problem requires its own unique solution.

It is generally agreed that the developmental aspects of atomic energy for peaceful purposes can and should be shared among organizations at the regional as well as the global level. It would indeed be difficult to make a case for totally shifting to the International Atomic Energy Agency all of the many atomic development activities that are at present being carried out through the various regional arrangements. Yet in view of the fact that the different atomic powers maintain different safeguard criteria and insist upon different standards of inspection, the entire matter poses a most difficult dilemma: how to share atomic development activities on different levels and, at the same time, work out the responsibility for adequate and generally acceptable control.

To the donor, the regional approach to atomic development may often seem preferable to working through United Nations channels. The donor's freedom to choose the recipient and to define precisely the conditions for cooperation may even result in more extensive assistance. In the case of United Nations assistance, in contrast, the donor's influence on the recipient must proceed through the machinery of the IAEA Board of Governors and the General Conference. For this reason, United Nations assistance cannot be identified with any one country and tends to assume a more apolitical character than its regional counterpart. This explains why United Nations assistance is at times preferred by the underdeveloped countries and why regional arrangements are frequently favored by donors. Finally, as recipients like to point out, an international organization like IAEA may be better suited for atomic development by virtue of the fact that its membership includes both the advanced and the underdeveloped areas—which means that it can fulfill the function of an intermediary more satisfactorily than can a regional organization.

For certain types of atomic development and research, cooperation through regional arrangements may often be more effective than through IAEA. The Western European and the Latin American countries, for example, form regions that are reasonably homogeneous both geographically and technologically. These factors inevitably favor a regional approach to the development of atomic energy. Moreover, regionalism may also in many cases be better suited to furthering atomic research. The European Organization for Nuclear Research (CERN), founded in 1956, is composed of twelve Western European countries at comparable stages of atomic research development. Its Eastern counterpart, the Joint Institute for Nuclear Research, also founded in 1956, consists of eleven countries from the Soviet bloc. Both these organizations are based on the common experiences and goals of the countries comprising their respective regions and, undoubtedly, derive considerable scientific and technological benefits from this fact.

Agencies engaged in nuclear development will probably continue to proliferate. It is not possible to make a case for exclusively regional or exclusively global nuclear development. In the absence of a general principle, the IAEA will have to adapt itself to constantly changing patterns of development.

In the area of control, however, uniform safeguards must be imposed to avert disaster. In 1974, for example, India announced a nuclear explosion and became the sixth member of the "nuclear club" as a direct result of having been party to a bilateral agreement with Canada. The donor nation had assumed that its assistance would be used exclusively for peaceful purposes. The IAEA is in a logical position to play the coordinating role in this task. Yet it is prevented from doing so because some regional and bilateral controls are less stringent than those demanded by the United Nations. Euratom, for example, does not require certain controls that are insisted upon in the IAEA Statute. However, since the member states of Euratom are also signatories to the IAEA Statute, this obstacle is by no means insurmountable. Moreover, periodic reports of the "disappearance" of fissionable materials and the growing threat of "nuclear theft" by terrorist groups makes the need for global inspection and control more urgent than ever before.

There are three possible ways in which regional development and control functions might be brought under the IAEA. First, the nuclear powers might arrange for IAEA to take over regional programs in their entirety. This is the hope of the IAEA's Director-General but is unlikely to materialize. Second, regional arrangements might continue, with the parties requesting the IAEA to assume responsibility for the administration of safeguards. The IAEA Statute permits this, and its realization is possible. The United States has already taken the initiative in bringing some of its bilateral agreements under IAEA control. Third, the regional arrangements might cover the same broad fields of development and control as are covered by IAEA. This is the most likely development. IAEA can therefore be expected to discharge a function of piecemeal coordination, dealing with limited and specific situations as they arise from day to day. The size of reactors, division of labor in isotope research, and concrete inspection provisions are likely to be some of the typical problems of coordination that IAEA will face. The reconciliation of regionalism with globalism in atomic energy will thus become primarily a process to be managed, rather than a problem to be solved.

The case of atomic energy demonstrates the extreme complexity of the relationship between regionalism and globalism. In this particular case, the regional approach seems quite appropriate for the developmental aspects, whereas in the matter of control a world approach seems required. Each problem, however, demands its own careful study and its own particular solution. Excessive theorizing and generalizing are likely to contribute very little.

The record supports neither the building-block theory of regionalism nor the opposite contention that regional arrangements are necessarily antithetical to the principles of the United Nations Charter. Rather, the evidence shows that frequently the United Nations has been a second line of defense for regionalism and that sometimes regional arrangements have served as backstops for the world organization. Certainly there is ample room for both types of political order-building on the international scene.

REFERENCES

1 Karl W. Deutsch et al., *Political Community and the North Atlantic Area.* Princeton, N.J.: Princeton University Press, 1957.
2 *Ibid.*, pp. 190–191.
3 Robert O. Keohane and Joseph S. Nye, *Power and Interdependence.* Boston: Little, Brown, 1977.
4 *Ibid.*, p. 10.
5 Richard Coudenhove-Kalergi, *An Idea Conquers the World.* London: Putnam, 1953, p. ix.
6 Cited by A. H. Robinson, *The Council of Europe.* New York: Praeger, 1956, pp. 1–2.
7 Cited by Arnold J. Zurcher, *The Struggle to United Europe.* New York: New York University Press, 1958, p. 6.
8 Political and Economic Planning (PEP), *European Organisations.* London: Allen and Unwin, 1959, p. 132.
9 Oscar Svarlien, *An Introduction to the Law of Nations.* New York: McGraw-Hill, 1955, p. 443.
10 PEP, *op. cit.*, p. 206.
11 Inis L. Claude, Jr., *Swords into Plowshares.* 2d ed. New York: Random House, 1959, p. 199.
12 Deutsch et al., *op. cit.*, p. 156.

13 B. Y. Boutros-Ghali, "The Arab League," *International Conciliation*, May 1954, p. 394.

14 United Nations Doc. S/745, May 16, 1948.

15 Boutros-Ghali, *op. cit.*, pp. 411–412.

16 K. C. Wheare, "The Nature and Structure of the Commonwealth," *American Political Science Review*, December 1953, p. 1016.

17 L. S. Amery, *Thoughts on the Constitution*. New York: Oxford University Press, 1953, p. 169.

18 Cited by Claude, *op. cit.*, p. 120.

19 Edgar S. Furniss, Jr., "A Re-examination of Regional Arrangements," *Journal of International Affairs*, IX (1955), 84.

20 Cited by Norman D. Palmer and Howard C. Perkins, *International Relations*. Boston: Houghton Mifflin, 1957, p. 641.

SELECTED BIBLIOGRAPHY

Andemicael, Berhanykum. *The OAU and the UN*. New York: Africana, 1976. A good historical assessment of the OAU's ceaseless struggle in the UN to dismantle apartheid in South Africa.

Butler, Sir Michael. *Europe: More Than a Continent*. London: Heinemann, 1988. Britain's former permanent representative to the European Economic Community offers a moderately optimistic assessment of its future prospects.

McDonald, Robert W. *The League of Arab States*. Princeton: Princeton University Press, 1965. A fine scholarly work on the history, structure, and objectives of the Arab League.

Palmer, Ronald D. and Thomas J. Rickford. *Building ASEAN: Twenty Years of Southwest Asian Cooperation*. New York: Praeger, 1987. An excellent introduction to the political, security, and economic issues facing ASEAN. The author's assessment is very positive, suggesting that ASEAN may be a model for successful regional organizations.

Sanger, Clyde and Arnold Smith. *Stitches in Time: The Commonwealth in World Politics*. New York: Beaufort Books, 1983. The authors demonstrate how Great Britain was able to transform the Empire into the Commonwealth without major upheavals or dislocations. A fascinating study.

Slater, Jerome. *The OAS and United States Foreign Policy*. Columbus: Ohio State University Press, 1967. A well-conceived study which shows that the United States was always more interested in using the OAS to stop communism in the Western Hemisphere than in forging the bonds of regional integration.

12

THE MILITARY STRUGGLE
FOR ORDER

To take arms against a sea of troubles.

Shakespeare, *Hamlet,* III, 1

DILEMMAS OF DISARMAMENT

The following is a description of Hiroshima shortly after the city was destroyed by an atomic bomb in August 1945:

> People are still dying, mysteriously and horribly—people who were uninjured in the cataclysm—from an unknown something which I can only describe as the atomic plague.
>
> Hiroshima does not look like a bombed city....I write these facts as dispassionately as I can, in the hope that they will act as a warning to the world. In this first testing ground of the atomic bomb...it gives you an empty feeling in the stomach to see such man-made devastation....I could see about three miles of reddish rubble. That is all the atomic bomb left....The Police Chief of Hiroshima...took me to hospitals where the victims of the bomb are still being treated. In these hospitals I found people who, when the bomb fell, suffered absolutely no injuries, but now are dying from the uncanny after-effects. For no apparent reason their health began to fail. They lost appetite. Their hair fell out. Bluish spots appeared on their bodies. And then bleeding began from the ears, nose and mouth.
>
> At first, the doctors told me, they thought these were the symptoms of general debility. They gave their patients Vitamin A injections. The results were horrible. The flesh started rotting away from the hole caused by the injection of the needle. And in every case the victim died.

A peculiar odour...given off by the poisonous gas still issues from the earth soaked with radioactivity; against this the inhabitants all wear gauze masks over their mouths and noses; many thousands of people have simply vanished—the atomic heat was so great that they burned instantly to ashes—except that there were no ashes—they were vaporised.[1]

The bomb here mentioned, it should be noted, is now considered obsolete. Its capacity for destruction has been dwarfed by an even more total weapon—the hydrogen bomb. That this development has engendered a more intensive quest for disarmament than ever before in history is by no means surprising. Indeed, the price of failure in this quest is not likely to be merely the kind of devastation that was loosed on Hiroshima and Nagasaki. It may well be the extinction of man as the dominant form of life on this planet.

Since 1945 the issue of disarmament has assumed paramount importance and has unceasingly occupied the thinking of diplomats and technical experts everywhere. The UN General Assembly has dealt with it during every session. The two major antagonists in the East-West struggle both agreed that disarmament was the most important problem facing the world.[2] Yet, not until 1987, more than forty years after the dawn of the nuclear age, did the two superpowers agree on their first disarmament treaty at a summit meeting in Washington. Why this agonizingly long delay? To answer this question we must analyze the disarmament dilemma in all its complexity.

If the objective of the political order-builders is a world without major disputes, the hope of those who would build order through disarmament is a world without weapons. In the view of the latter, arms races cause wars. If, as they see it, arms are permitted to accumulate, they will sooner or later be used. An arms race therefore becomes a relentless and self-propelling march to war. Both sides strain furiously to maintain or reclaim the lead. Finally, the tension reaches such a pitch that war is almost welcomed as a liberating explosion. If, on the other hand, nations are deprived of the means to fight, the proponents of disarmament maintain, wars will either cease to exist or, at worst, become relatively harmless. In the telling phrase of Maxim Litvinov: "the way to disarm is to disarm."

Here we encounter the first crucial problem. Is it true, as the advocates of disarmament hold, that arms races cause the political tensions that drive nations to war? Or are the political order-builders correct in asserting that though arms races may precipitate war, the real source of international conflict must be sought in the political tensions between nations that lead to arms races in the first place? The former tend to regard the arms race as a basic cause of war, the latter merely as a symptom of political pathology. Both groups are prepared to admit that the problem is really a circular one: that arms races breed political tensions; that these in turn lead to the development and acquisition of more destructive weapons; and that this situation raises temperatures even further—until the violent climax is reached. But the two groups differ as to the most effective point at which to intervene in the vicious circle. Those who see arms races as a basic cause of war assert the primacy of international order-building through disarmament. They maintain that halting the arms race will lead to a reduction in political tensions, which will likely result in an even further scrapping of weapons. On the other hand, a growing number of observers are defending the view that disarmament efforts are bound to fail unless they are preceded by more fundamental political accommodation. The way to disarm, according to this latter view, is not to begin by disarming but to concentrate instead on the settlement of political differences.

One of the most articulate spokesmen for the primacy of disarmament was the British Nobel Prize winner Philip Noel-Baker. This scholar attacks the thesis that disarmament can only be a consequence, never a cause, of improvement in international relations. In support of this view, Noel-Baker cites the Rush-Bagot Agreement of 1817 between Britain and the United States, which disarmed the Canadian frontier. In his view, this agreement was a great contribution to the establishment of friendly relations between Canada and the United States. He also points to the 1922 Washington Naval Disarmament Convention, which reduced the navies of Britain, the United States, and Japan, as producing a remarkable improvement in international relations. He suggests that the convention nipped in the bud an impending struggle for supremacy of the seas and played a major part in creating cordial relations between Britain and the United States. From these examples, the author concludes that the ending of the East-West nuclear arms race by a disarmament treaty would improve international relations, reduce tensions, and facilitate the settlement of outstanding political disputes.[3]

The opposing view was most eloquently defended by Hans J. Morgenthau. He attacks the view of the military order-builder as unrealistic. "Men do not fight because they have arms, but they have arms because they deem it necessary to fight." If deprived of weapons, nations will employ all their resources for the development of new ones. In fact, Morgenthau continued, the threat of all-out nuclear war may have been the most important single factor that has prevented the outbreak of general war in the nuclear age. The removal of that threat through disarmament might indeed increase the dangers of war. Disarmament might do away with weapons but not with the will and the technical knowledge to produce these weapons. In support of his argument, Morgenthau cited the Treaty of Versailles which, in his view, was a blessing in disguise for German militarism. Disarmament compelled Germany to project its military thinking in the future, to look at problems of strategy and technology *de novo*. Far from removing German ambitions of conquest, disarmament merely equipped it to fight World War II while France was ready merely for a repetition of World War I.[4] Hence, Morgenthau concluded, the first step toward order-building must always be political rather than military. Disarmament *in vacuo* is bound to be a failure.

In view of the sharp disagreement on the nature and significance of disarmament, it is necessary to subject the modern record of disarmament negotiations to careful scrutiny. Why did most of them fail? What was the secret of success of the few that did not? Does the record provide any clues for the crucial disarmament negotiations of our own time?

Before embarking on a survey of the disarmament record, it is useful to bear in mind a definition and three important distinctions. Central to the concept of disarmament is the term *reduction*. An actual reduction of weapons must take place before we can describe an act as *dis*armament. The first of the three distinctions is between *general* disarmament, which refers to efforts involving all nations, and *local* disarmament, which includes only a limited number of countries. The second is between *quantitative* disarmament, which concerns the reduction of all types of weapons, and *qualitative* disarmament, which concentrates upon a specific category of weapons. It is also useful to remember that the reduction of nonatomic weapons is referred to as "conventional disarmament," while "nuclear disarmament" refers to the reduction of atomic stockpiles.

In the entire history of the nation-state system up to World War II, there are on record only two disarmament conferences that proved successful. Both were local and quantitative. The first was the Rush-Bagot Agreement, concluded in 1817, limiting the naval forces of Canada and the United States to three vessels each on the Great Lakes. The agreement resulted in the demilitarization of the United States-Canadian frontier. With certain revisions that were added during World War II, the agreement has remained in force.

The more significant of the two successful ventures in disarmament was the Washington Treaty of 1922 for the Limitation of Naval Armaments. The aim of the treaty was to determine ratios for the allocation of capital ships among the major naval powers. The United States and Britain were to have the largest navies, while Japan, France, and Italy were given smaller allocations. A ratio of 5:5:3:1.67:1.67 was finally established for the capital ships of the United States, Britain, Japan, France, and Italy, in that order. As a result, the three leading countries scrapped approximately two-fifths of their capital ships. In regard to cruisers, destroyers, and submarines, however, the Washington Treaty failed to reach agreement. The London Naval Conference of 1930 attempted to complete the work begun at Washington by limiting the tonnage of naval craft other than capital ships. Parity for cruisers, destroyers, and submarines was agreed upon between the United States and Britain, while Japan was limited to two-thirds of American or British strength. Neither France nor Italy was a signatory to the London Treaty. Italy demanded parity with France, as in the Washington Agreement. This parity France was now unwilling to grant.

The agreements hammered out so painstakingly in Washington and London were not destined to endure. In 1934 Japan demanded parity with Britain and the United States in all naval craft. When this demand was rejected, Japan abrogated the treaty and embarked on an ambitious naval rearmament program. Hence, of the two successes on record, only the Rush-Bagot Agreement may be considered permanent. The Washington Treaty was moribund after a decade.

Unhappily, the list of failures is far longer. The pattern was set at the First Hague Peace Conference in 1899, when twenty-eight nations expressed themselves on the desirability of a reduction in armaments but were unable to agree on a specific formula. The failure was repeated by forty-four nations meeting at the Second Hague Peace Conference in 1907. As the Russian delegate put it at the time: "The question was not ripe in 1899, it is not any more so in 1907. It has not been possible to do anything on these lines, and the Conference to-day finds itself as little prepared to enter upon them as in 1899."[5] The next effort took place at Versailles in 1919, when disarmament was imposed upon Germany. As that nation became increasingly restive under the terms of the "Versailles Diktat" during the 1920s, the League of Nations sought desperately to keep German armaments at a minimum. Finally, a World Disarmament Conference was convened at Geneva in 1932. But that conference met under the shadow of Hitler, who was to come to power several months later. When Germany embarked on a relentless arms program in 1933, the World Disarmament Conference had to concede defeat.

Six years of world war, culminating in the ghastly spectacle of atomic destruction, convinced the founders of the United Nations that disarmament should be a permanent item on the agenda of the new world organization. Accordingly, in January 1946 the General Assembly created the Atomic Energy Commission for the specific purpose of eliminating atomic weapons from the nations' military arsenals. In addition, a Commission for Conventional Armaments was established by the Security Council in February 1947. When neither of these two organs made any progress, the General Assembly, in 1952, amalgamated them into one Disarmament Commission. This body originally consisted of the members of the Security Council plus Canada. However, each time the commission failed to achieve a consensus, the General Assembly attempted to remedy the matter by enlarging its membership. Finally, the General Assembly itself became a forum for disarmament proposals that were thinly camouflaged propaganda maneuvers in the East-West struggle rather than serious overtures to negotiation. Premier Khrushchev's proposal for general and complete disarmament, which he made in the General Assembly in 1959, was a case in point. Since 1954, indeed, Geneva, Vienna, Washington, and Moscow, rather than the United Nations, have become the meeting places for serious negotiations. The conferences that have been held there have usually included an equal number of representatives from East and West.

Thus, since the end of World War II, disarmament negotiations have been a permanent phenomenon. Yet until 1987 none of the conferences that were held—whether inside or outside of the United Nations—accomplished the elimination of a single atomic or conventional weapon. Even the Moscow Summit of 1972 was no exception. It achieved a limitation on the building of additional arms, not a reduction of existing arms. For forty years, most intensive disarmament efforts in Western history were a virtual failure. The only successes on record antedate World War II, and one of these was of too brief duration to be termed an unqualified success. We shall now look into the causes of this discouraging record.

One important reason for these many failures is the inherently *static* nature of all disarmament. It is a fact of international life that many nations are constantly engaged in attempts to manipulate the existing distribution of power in their favor. An increase in armaments is an obvious means to accomplish this end. The goal of disarmament, on the other hand, is in essence the freezing of a certain distribution of power which will be acceptable to some, but never to all the powers concerned. Most nations conceive of themselves as dynamic actors on the international scene, hoping to move from strength to strength. Such states will have little patience with policies that would deprive them of an important means whereby they can grow in power and stature. Indeed, one of the greatest obstacles to disarmament is the fact that nations are less concerned with what they are than with what they would like to be.

The technical counterpart of this political truth has been the enormous difficulty of *measurement*. Each disarmament conference has to grapple with this stubborn problem. Once the delegates get down to specifics, they constantly find themselves compelled to "compare apples with oranges." Which is more valuable to a military arsenal—a destroyer or a tank? How does the striking force of the American Strategic Air Command compare to the Soviet land army? How many Polaris missiles should be scrapped for each Soviet intercontinental ballistic missile? How do four million men in reserve compare to one million in active service? Precision is almost impossible to attain. Each side in the East-West struggle has advanced proposals that would leave its superiority intact or reduce that of the other side. Since both the United States and the Soviet Union conceive of themselves as dynamic contestants for supremacy, neither has been willing to accept an arms reduction that would freeze it at a level of inferiority. Salvador de Madariaga has illustrated the point admirably through the analogy of an imaginary conference of animals at which "the lion wanted to eliminate all weapons but claws and jaws, the eagle all but talons and beaks and the bear all but an embracing hug."[6]

The crucial cause of the failure of most disarmament negotiations was, of course, the absence of mutual trust. In technical terms this meant that each side attempted to impose rigorous requirements of *inspection* and *control* on the other in order to ensure that an agreement, once reached, would not be violated. Control and inspection were to be the technical substitute for mutual trust. But this condition invited a circular problem: each side required control because it did not trust the other; yet, the acceptance of a control system itself demanded a high degree of mutual trust. In short, whenever nations took the position that there could be no disarmament without security, they had to realize that foolproof security was equally impossible. A degree of mutual confidence was necessary for both disarmament and security. For four decades, the major powers were unable to escape from this predicament.

The control problem proved to be an insurmountable obstacle at the very beginning of the nuclear disarmament negotiations in the United Nations Atomic Energy Commission in 1946. At that time, when the United States still had an atomic monopoly, it proposed a far-reaching control plan known as the Acheson-Lilienthal Report, or Baruch Plan. The purpose of the plan was to ensure that atomic energy would be used exclusively for peaceful purposes. To accomplish this end, the United States proposed the internationalization of all facilities producing atomic power. All atomic plants would be owned and operated by an Atomic Development Authority that would have the powers of inspection, accounting, and licensing. The American hope was to place atomic energy firmly under international control before the Soviet Union would end the American monopoly and engage in an atomic arms race with the United States. The plan was widely heralded as a generous offer which would place the power of the atom under the authority of a limited world government. The Soviet Union's response, however, was negative. It insisted upon the continuance of national ownership and operation of atomic plants and advanced a plan of its own, which proposed the destruction of all existing stocks of nuclear weapons and a legal prohibition of their future manufacture. Only after existing stockpiles had been destroyed and a treaty outlawing nuclear weapons concluded would the Soviet Union be ready to proceed to international inspection. Most immediately, then, the impasse revolved around the problem of priorities. The United States insisted on the priority of international inspection before it was willing to undertake the destruction of its nuclear stockpiles. Control would have to come first and disarmament would follow. The Soviet Union, on the other hand, insisted on the prior destruction of American stockpiles before it was willing to allow international inspection. It reversed the sequence: disarmament must come first and control would follow.

It would seem from the above that the United States' offer was a generous one, whereas the Soviet Union's rejection was an unreasonable act of caprice. After all, the United States made its offer at a time when it had an atomic monopoly. It would therefore appear that the Soviet Union, which had not yet developed its own atomic bomb, could only gain from the internationalization of atomic power. Actually, however, the picture is considerably more complex. It is true that the American offer was an enlightened act of statesmanship. But it is equally true that, given the state of mistrust between the two superpowers, there were valid reasons from the Soviet point of view for rejecting the Baruch Plan. First and most important, the plan would have perpetuated the American monopoly of atomic weapons. And beyond that, the Soviet Union feared that the proposed Atomic Development Authority would be dominated by the Western powers with the Eastern bloc in a permanent minority without the right of veto. In the words of Andrei Gromyko, the Soviet delegate:

> The Soviet Union is aware that there will be a majority in the control organ which may take one-sided decisions, a majority on whose benevolent attitude toward the Soviet Union the Soviet people cannot count. Therefore, the Soviet Union, and probably not only the Soviet Union, cannot allow that the fate of its national economy be handed over to this organ.[7]

Most basically, Soviet suspicions grew out of the realization that only the United States would be in a position to cheat, i.e., withhold weapons from the authority, while the Soviet Union would be compelled to accept a permanent position of inferiority. All this is not to say that the United States' offer was not farsighted. What does seem clear, however, is that its chances of acceptance would have been considerably greater if it had permitted the continuation of national atomic research in the Soviet Union.

The struggle over priorities that began in 1946 continued without letup until the Moscow Summit of 1972. The United States and the Soviet Union both agreed that a viable disarmament treaty would have to include provisions for the prohibition of nuclear weapons as well as acceptable arrangements for control. The Soviet Union consistently defended the priority of prohibition in numerous ''ban the bomb'' proposals. These proposals were unacceptable to the United States, which feared that the Soviet Union would not accede to control once prohibition was accepted. The United States' insistence on the priority of control, on the other hand, was unacceptable to the Soviet Union because the latter consistently tended to regard all international inspection as a form of espionage. Hence the paradoxical situation that though both powers accepted the principle of simultaneous disarmament and control, they were unable to translate it into practice. Each side continued to postpone what for it would be the greater sacrifice and, instead, encouraged the opponent to take the first step. To try to expedite matters, the French in 1958 introduced the ingenious formula: ''Neither control without disarmament, nor disarmament without control but, progressively, all the disarmament that can at present be controlled.''[8] Though this proposal met the problem in principle, it, too, could not be applied in practice.

Fundamentally, the impasse stemmed from the fact that American proposals assumed a good deal of Soviet confidence in the United States, while the Soviet counterproposals assumed an equal amount of American faith in Soviet intentions. When the two rivals realized that this premise of mutual trust did not exist, they sought substitutes in various technical requirements for inspection and control. Yet they soon concluded that even such technical devices could never be completely foolproof; cheating would continue to be possible regardless of how intricate the safeguards. Indeed, there clearly seemed no other alternative: good faith was a necessary premise for *all* disarmament negotiations and arrangements.

A further reason for the failure of disarmament negotiations may be found paradoxically enough, in the very interest that the subject has continued to evoke in world public opinion. In the words of India's late Prime Minister Nehru:

> The arms race affects us nations and peoples everywhere, whether we are involved in wars or power blocs or not....There can be little doubt about the deep and widespread concern in the world, particularly among peoples, about these weapons and their dreadful consequences.[9]

The testing of hydrogen weapons on both sides of the Iron Curtain and the resulting problem of atomic radiation intensified public indignation the world over. Disarmament became the most emotional issue before the United Nations General Assembly. Not surprisingly, the rise of this passionate popular interest and involvement led both sides in the conflict to engage in open diplomacy. Vying for the allegiance of the uncommitted countries where disarmament was a burning issue, the two superpowers themselves turned the disarmament negotiations into a weapon in the East-West struggle. Open diplomacy in the sensitive and frequently technical field of disarmament inevitably culminated in propaganda battles in which both East and West felt compelled to appeal to the audiences rather than to each other.

Each side faced a similar dilemma in the conduct of these public negotiations. The demands of security forbade the advancement of proposals that the other side found genuinely acceptable. But the power of publicity demanded that the proposals appear as reasonable as possible in order to avoid the onus of sabotaging the negotiations. Hence, a curious pattern developed that one observer aptly called the "gamesmanship of disarmament."[10] This "game" was played according to certain tacit but well-defined rules:

> Every plan offered by either side has contained a set of proposals calculated to have wide popular appeal. Every such set has included at least one feature that the other side could not possibly accept, thus forcing a rejection. Then the proposing side has been able to claim that the rejector is opposed to the idea of disarmament *in toto*. The objectionable feature may be thought of as the "joker" in every series of proposals.[11]

As a result of this game, the illusion was sometimes created that the two sides had narrowed their differences. Actually, what had happened was that each side had expanded its range of acceptable proposals to ensure popular appeal, but had made equally sure that a "joker" would force rejection of the entire package. The Baruch Plan contained such a joker: the insistence that there be no veto on the question of sanctions against violators of the control agreement. Acceptance of this joker would have placed the Soviet Union in a position of permanent military inferiority. Soviet proposals made similar use of the joker technique. A typical case was a Soviet proposal, made on May 10, 1955, in which the USSR agreed to reduce its land armies to a maximum figure desired by the three Western powers. For five years the Western negotiators had proposed a reduction of Chinese, Soviet, and American forces to one million men each, with 650,000 each for France and the United Kingdom. But as public pressure mounted and the July 1955 Summit Conference drew nearer, the French delegate to the conference, Jules Moch, stated that "The whole thing look[ed] too good to be true." The spokesman for the United States, on the other hand, made the following, more optimistic statement:

> We have been gratified to find that the concepts which we have put forward over a considerable length of time, and which we have repeated many times during these past two months, have been accepted in a large measure by the Soviet Union.[12]

As it turned out, Moch's suspicions were fully justified. The proposal was indeed too good to be true. The Soviet concession was made conditional upon agreement that "states possessing military, naval and air bases in the territories of other states shall undertake to liquidate such bases."[13] In other words, the Soviet joker was a demand for the dissolution of the Western alliance system—a condition, of course, that was completely unacceptable without prior settlement of the major political differences between East and West. It is significant, nevertheless, that despite the obviousness of this joker, the onus for the collapse of the manpower reduction talks was placed by most observers at the Summit Conference squarely upon the United States. The public, eager for results, was hypnotized by what appeared to be a generous proposal and did not notice the jokers. Even as astute an observer as Philip Noel-Baker failed to perceive the deceptiveness of the Soviet bid. In his book, *The Arms Race,* he refers to May 10, 1955, the day of the Soviet manpower reduction proposal, as "the moment of hope," and attributes its failure directly to what he feels to have been the dogmatic unwillingness of the American State Department to disarm at all.[14]

Perhaps the really classic example of gamesmanship was Premier Khrushchev's dramatic proposal for "general and complete disarmament," made before the General Assembly in September 1959. In his speech, the Soviet premier suggested that "over a period of four years, all states should carry out complete disarmament and should divest themselves of the means of waging war."[15] The premier envisaged the dissolution of all armies, navies, air forces, general staffs, war ministries, and military schools as well as the destruction of all atomic weapons and missiles. Especially in the uncommitted countries, the publicity value of the Russian leader's speech was quite high, even though, by the late 1950s, the effectiveness of disarmament propaganda had begun to reach a point of diminishing returns. Yet as always, there was a joker. And this time it was the vagueness of the new proposal's references to the matter of control provisions. Indeed, the most to which the Soviet premier would commit himself was the establishment of "an international control body in which all states would participate."[16] Yet Mr. Khrushchev presumably knew full well that as far as the West was concerned, no disarmament proposal would be acceptable unless it at the same time provided for a rigorous and full-scale inspection system.

Another obstacle to disarmament was that one of the two main negotiators was a totalitarian power and, as such, a closed society. Yet, the unwillingness to accept international inspection has not always been a Soviet monopoly. As Claude points out, the United States expressed similar suspicions of foreign inspection in 1919 and again in 1927.[17] But in the United States and most other Western countries, this attitude appears now to have been largely transcended. In 1958, for example, the American Institute of Public Opinion conducted an extensive poll in six nations—the United States, Britain, France, West Germany, India, and Japan—to determine the climate of opinion in regard to international inspection of disarmament.[18] The following three questions were asked.

1 Would you favor or oppose setting up a world-wide organization which would make sure—by regular inspections—that no nation, including Russia and the United States, makes atom bombs, hydrogen bombs, and missiles?

2 If this inspection organization were set up, would you favor or oppose making it each person's *duty* to report any attempt to secretly make atom bombs, hydrogen bombs, and missiles?

3 If you, yourself, knew that someone in [name of country] was attempting to secretly make forbidden weapons, would you report this to the office of the world-wide inspection organization in this country?

The first question simply referred to a general disarmament proposal; the second, however, raised a potential conflict of values between national and international loyalty; and the third posed the problem of conflicting loyalties in its starkest form. Hence it was expected that favorable responses would be highest to question one and lowest to question three. Actually, the overall results of the six-nation poll were striking: an overwhelmingly positive response to all three questions in all six countries. Japan ranked highest, with West Germany, India, France, the United States, and Britain following, in that order. From these results the authors concluded that "Inspection by the People was not as visionary a proposal as one might have thought."[19] This conclusion is perhaps overly optimistic, since the authors did not take into account the probable differences between people's reactions to a set of hypothetical questions and their possible reactions when confronted with an actual situation. Yet the study did permit the conclusion that a cross section of the citizens of six democratic nations was definitely in favor of some form of international inspection of disarmament. The very fact, on the other hand, that the Soviet Union did not permit such a poll was itself indicative. Like all closed societies, it was obsessed with the importance of national sovereignty. And, of course, national sovereignty reaches its most absolute form in matters of military security. In view of this difference in the underlying political logic of East and West, differences between the two sides on such technical matters as to whether inspection or prohibition should have priority, or as to the allocation of specific ratios, are, in the last analysis, merely surface manifestations. The really fundamental difference, rather, had to be sought in the basically different characters of the two types of societies: the Western system, more "open" than that of the East, was able to absorb at least a minimum of international authority; the Soviet Union, largely a "closed" society, regarded all forms of foreign control as a menace and, hence, anathema.

We are now left with the crucial substantive question of whether the record indicates that order-building through disarmament is a valid approach. The evidence suggests that for four decades, it was not. Disarmament seemed to be not so much a means for the attainment of political order as a product of its achievement. We have seen that, as a rule, nations were concerned with disarmament only when they were engaged in a power struggle; yet it was precisely this condition that made the attainment of disarmament so difficult. Even the Washington Treaty of 1922 cannot be cited as an argument in favor of the effectiveness of disarmament. Most of the capital ships that were discarded under the terms of the treaty were obsolete and would have been scrapped anyway. The vessels considered most important in a future war were cruisers, destroyers, and submarines. And significantly, it was in these three categories that the five signatory powers failed to reach agreement. In fact, it might be said that all the treaty accomplished was a "naval holiday" in the building of capital ships that freed the energies of the five nations to engage in an arms race in the production of other naval craft that were considered more vital to the needs of modern warfare. Even if one rejects this uncharitable interpretation of the Washington Treaty, it would be difficult to regard it as a significant instrument of international order-building in view of the fact that Japan repudiated it the moment its new policy of imperialism dictated such a course. Disarmament as a direct approach to order seems feasible only when nations are interested in the enhancement rather than in the reduction of one another's strength. It is probably an exaggeration to claim, as does one authority, that because of the many technical obstacles involved, "even such inveterate friends as the United States and Britain probably could not agree on a formula of mutual arms limitation."[20] After all, the Rush-Bagot agreement of 1817 between the United States and Canada was just such a case. Yet the irony of this agreement lies in the fact that it was probably unnecessary since it was concluded between two neighbors, both of whom by then considered war between them most unlikely.

The discouraging record of disarmament in the modern world supports the proposition that order is fundamentally not a military problem. Disarmament negotiations per se will not reduce the tensions between the major powers unless such efforts are preceded by at least a minimum of success in the settlement of outstanding political differences. This is really another way of saying that the problem of disarmament is not disarmament at all, but is in essence the problem of forging the bonds of political community among nations. We have seen earlier that we know little about the causes of war. Similarly, we do not know enough about the process of community-building. Why should a pilot under orders drop a lethal weapon on a defenseless city in "enemy" country, but refuse to drop it on his own? At first glance, this question may seem naive. But when one considers its human implications, it is not. For if we could answer it, the issue of disarmament would have become largely irrelevant. As an order-building strategy, disarmament is chiefly concerned with symptoms. The real causes of the disease must be sought at a deeper level.

The frustrations over disarmament led some thinkers to approach the problem in a somewhat different way: arms *control* rather than disarmament. Whereas the disarmer is primarily concerned with the actual scrapping of existing weapons, the arms controller is more interested in stabilizing the climate in which these weapons exist and in the prevention of additional arms build-ups. The emphasis here is less on hardware and more on psychology. The hope is that progress can be made on issues related to disarmament, which might act as confidence-builders and ultimately lead to actual disarmament agreements. In December 1959, for example, a treaty was signed among twelve nations with claims in Antarctica demilitarizing that continent. The signatories pledged themselves neither to establish military fortifications nor to carry out military maneuvers in the Antarctic. In 1963, in the wake of the Cuban missile crisis, the Soviet Union and the United States established direct communications—a "hot line" between the White House and the Kremlin— and reached agreement on the peaceful uses of outer space. In 1964 the United States offered one of its large nuclear reactors to international inspection by a United Nations agency, and in the same year the two superpowers agreed on cutbacks in their stockpiles of fissionable materials—the raw materials for atomic weapons—thus retarding the growth of "overkill" capacity on both sides.

In 1967 the two superpowers, after lengthy negotiations, agreed to work in earnest on a formula for a treaty banning the proliferation of nuclear weapons. In January 1968 they presented a joint draft treaty on nonproliferation to the seventeen-member Disarmament Conference in Geneva. The draft treaty was designed to freeze the "nuclear club" at its membership of five: the United States, the Soviet Union, the United Kingdom, France, and Communist China. Several hurdles confronted the negotiators. First, neither France nor China was expected to sign. Second, certain "threshold" countries such as India and Israel were reluctant to sign, the former for fear of China and Pakistan and the latter because of Egypt. Finally, the matter of inspection posed formidable obstacles. Would the treaty be policed through self-inspection, regional bodies such as Euratom, or a United Nations organ, such as the International Atomic Energy Agency? These and other knotty problems defied easy solution and made progress on the treaty slow and arduous. Nevertheless, the very fact of superpower cooperation on such a sensitive issue as nonproliferation provided grounds for optimism. In June 1968 another forward step was taken when the UN General Assembly, in a vote of 95 in favor, 4 against, and 21 abstentions, gave its blessing to the draft treaty. Three nuclear and forty nonnuclear ratifications were now needed to make the document into a binding treaty. In March 1970, the nuclear nonproliferation treaty officially entered into force without the adherence of China and France. It has worked relatively well since then, although in 1974 India became the sixth member of the world's exclusive nuclear club. In 1981, however, Israel took unilateral measures by destroying an Iraqi nuclear installation in a preemptive strike. This event indicated the possibility that, in the future, states would depend more upon themselves than upon treaties to prevent the spread of nuclear weapons.

Several other arms control treaties are deserving of mention: In 1967 the two superpowers agreed on a treaty in which each pledged itself not to militarize outer space. The treaty was approved by the UN General Assembly in 1967 and entered into force that same year. In 1971 a similar treaty was signed in relation to the seabed and the ocean floors. In 1976 the Soviet Union and the United States agreed on a ban against environmental warfare and in 1978 they approved a similar ban against chemical warfare. It is important to note that none of these efforts achieved an actual reduction of existing weapons, but each went a long way in preventing their further dissemination and in preventing the construction of new weapons.

These arms control achievements were not insignificant. Without them, the world would be an even more dangerous place. Nuclear testing would poison the air and water; the superpowers might try to annex the moon and other planets; nuclear weapons would be emplaced on the bottom of the sea; tidal waves might be loosed and earthquakes triggered; and there might be a dozen nuclear powers instead of six. If, indeed, the nuclear nonproliferation treaty should break down, nuclear terrorism might become the biggest threat facing humanity. There are already some disturbing signs that point in this direction.

In July 1975, the mayor of New York City received the following unsigned note:

> We have successfully designed and built an atomic bomb. It is somewhere on Manhattan Island. We refer you to the accompanying drawing in ⅛ scale. We have plutonium and explosives for the bomb to function. This device will be used at 6 P.M. July 10 unless our demands are met. Do not notify the public. This will result in hysteria and the use of the bomb.[21]

The extortioners demanded $30 million in small unmarked bills. The FBI deposited the money at a designated drop site, but no one claimed it. The extortioners made no further contact.

Suppose that the bomb had gone off, or that some future nuclear terrorist might be more successful. The contemplation of such nightmares makes one realize that arms control, despite its imperfections, is useful nonetheless. It is *not* disarmament. But it is a great deal better than nothing.

Three case studies will be presented in this chapter. The first case is the partial nuclear test ban signed in Moscow in 1963, which was the first specific symptom of the new United States–Soviet détente; the second case describes the most significant fruits of that détente reached a decade later—the Strategic Arms Limitation Treaties; and, finally, we shall examine the most significant breakthrough on disarmament in recent history—the Intermediate Nuclear Forces (INF) Treaty, signed in Washington in 1987.

THE CESSATION OF NUCLEAR TESTING IN 1963

The goal of nuclear test cessation was always more modest than that of disarmament since it implied no reduction of stockpiles nor any fundamental change in the arsenals of the negotiating powers. A nuclear test ban would accomplish two things: it would limit the further development of nuclear weapons already stocked in great quantities in the Soviet Union, the United States, Britain, and France; and it would halt further contamination of the world's atmosphere through radioactive fallout.

If disarmament has been the most important general problem before the General Assembly, the cessation of nuclear weapons testing was the most crucial specific issue related to disarmament. The pressures on the nuclear powers, especially by the atomic have-not nations, were enormous. In 1959, for example, the General Assembly passed by overwhelming majorities four resolutions urging a moratorium on nuclear tests. These resolutions were primarily a reflection of a worldwide concern with the damage to human health if tests were to continue.

Scientists have differed widely on the amount of damage that radioactive fallout inflicts on the human system. But all agree that there are at least four areas in which *some* harm is certain to result. For one thing, it has been established that exposure to radiation shortens the human life span. In the opinion of Dr. H. J. Muller, a leading American geneticist, the shortening of the life span is "by far the most serious of the long term effects on the exposed person himself."[22] The second danger derives from strontium 90, a radioactive substance produced by nuclear explosions but unknown in nature. This byproduct of atomic tests causes cancer of the bone. Opinions differ on the extent of the damage but there is wide agreement that each test results in bone cancer being incurred by a number of people. Most scientists also agree that children are more susceptible to the poison than adults.[23] Leukemia, a fatal disease of the white blood cells, has also been related to strontium 90.[24] Finally, the most far-reaching effects of fallout seem to be genetic mutations in future generations. Again, estimates vary but there is wide agreement among geneticists that nuclear tests will be responsible for a considerable number of stillbirths, embryonic deaths, and defective mutations.[25]

As a result of constant prodding by the General Assembly, the Soviet Union, in May 1955, took the initiative in seeking a test ban. During the following year the Soviet Union pressed the United States for the conclusion of a bilateral agreement. The Soviet position was that the question of a test ban could be separated from the general problem of disarmament and that controls to detect violations were unnecessary. As Premier Bulganin wrote to President Eisenhower in 1956:

> It is a known fact that the discontinuation of such tests does not in itself require any international control agreements, for the present state of science and engineering makes it possible to detect any explosion of an atomic or hydrogen bomb, wherever it may be set off. In our opinion this situation makes it possible to separate the problem of ending tests of atomic and hydrogen weapons from the general problem of disarmament and to solve it independently even now, without tying an agreement on this subject to agreements on other disarmament problems.[26]

The Western powers agreed to discuss a test ban as a separate issue but flatly rejected the Soviet assertion that controls were unnecessary. In a counterproposal, the United States, Great Britain, and France suggested test cessation under an international control system. The Soviet Union declared itself willing to negotiate the vexatious matter of inspection. The next difficulty arose when the United States insisted on the need to continue testing until a cut-off agreement and a control plan had actually been negotiated. At this point, great pressure was exerted on the American government by a large majority in the General Assembly to agree to an informal test ban pending the conclusion of a formal treaty. Opinion among leading American scientists was deeply divided on this issue. On the one hand, Dr. Linus Pauling, an American Nobel Prize winner, represented a considerable body of opinion when he demanded that tests be halted immediately:

> Each added amount of radiation causes damage to the health of human beings all over the world and causes damage to the pool of human germ plasm such as to lead to an increase in the number of seriously defective children that will be born in future generations. An international agreement to stop all testing of nuclear weapons now could serve as a first step towards a more general disarmament, and the effective abolition of nuclear weapons, averting the possibility of a nuclear war that would be a catastrophe to all humanity.[27]

The case for continuing tests was largely defended by scientists in the United States Atomic Energy Commission. In the opinion of Dr. Edward Teller, a leading scientist, testing had to continue because

> further tests will put us into a position to fight our opponent's war machine while sparing the innocent bystanders. One development of the greatest importance is the progressive reduction of radioactive fallout. Clean weapons of this kind will reduce unnecessary casualties in a future war.[28]

Dr. Teller's colleague in the AEC, Dr. Willard F. Libby, also justified atomic tests on grounds of national defense:

> It is not contended that there is no risk to human health. Are we willing to take this very small and rigidly controlled risk, or would we prefer to run the risk of annihilation which might result, if we surrendered the weapons which are so essential to our freedom and actual survival?[29]

While the United States was engaged in weighing the alternatives of a provisional test ban, the Soviet Union, in March 1958, announced a unilateral cessation of nuclear tests. Once again on the defensive, the United States proposed a meeting of technical experts to study the feasibility of a control system to detect violations of a test ban. This conference, attended by an equal number of scientists from East and West, took place in July 1958 and submitted a positive report, calling for three steps by which a detection system might be implemented:

1 A network of control posts around the globe. About 170 would be land-based. Of these, 10 would be in the United States, 14 in the USSR, and 8 in Communist China. The remaining land-based posts would be distributed on the continents and on large and small oceanic islands. Ten additional posts would be on ships.

2 Creation of an "international control organ," which would run the global system, pick the staff, select the detection devices, study reports, and generally see to it that no nation violated the test suspension agreement.

3 Use of weather reconnaissance aircraft to sample the air for radioactivity. They would rush to a suspicious area to see if a bomb had been set off or whether the tremor was due to other causes.[30]

The scientists' report, while welcomed by the negotiators, raised important new problems. What would be the composition of the "international control organ"? What would be the voting procedure? Would there be a veto? What would be the authority of the inspectors? Serious bargaining took place on all of these questions at Geneva. The West suggested a veto-free control commission to be headed by a neutral administrator. The Soviet Union, however, insisted on a three-man directorate and the right of veto. The negotiators also disagreed on the number and role of the inspectors in the field. The West demanded international and mobile inspection teams with freedom of access to any area where an illegal atomic test was suspected. The Soviet Union emphasized the primacy of self-inspection but accepted the admission in principle of "foreign specialists" from the West. Another technical problem presented itself when the United States announced that it had underestimated the difficulty of detecting underground nuclear explosions. The United States position was that such explosions would be almost indistinguishable seismographically from natural shocks such as earthquakes. Hence, the American government demanded that the number of control stations be raised from 180 to 600.

More threatening than the technical problems of an atomic test ban was the sword of Damocles of the "*n*th nation." The main negotiators were three nuclear powers—the United States, the Soviet Union, and Britain. But France, of course, was already developing its own nuclear arsenal, and it was estimated that in the not too distant future several new nations would join the nuclear club: Belgium, Canada, China, Czechoslovakia, East Germany, West Germany, India, Israel, Italy, Japan, Sweden, and Switzerland.[31] Would the new atomic powers agree to be bound by a treaty to which they were not a party? France, for example, insisted on the completion of a series of tests while the Big Three were engaged in negotiations in Geneva. Far more serious, even, was the problem of Communist China. The 1958 Geneva report of the technical experts recommended that 8 of the 180 control stations be placed on mainland China. If the international control organ were placed under United Nations authority, would it be reasonable to expect Communist China to admit United Nations control posts on its territory while it was not a member of the world organization? Even if the control organ were set up outside the United Nations framework, would Communist China consider itself bound by a treaty with nations that continued to refuse to recognize it as a legal government?

Despite the numerous difficulties, a remarkable lessening of differences occurred during 1959 and 1960, but in late 1961 the Soviet Union broke the informal moratorium and tested weapons of unprecedented explosive force. By the time of the Cuban missile crisis a test ban agreement seemed more remote than ever. Yet the resolution of that crisis seemed to convince the Soviet leadership that more could be gained from a détente with the West than from a policy of intransigence. At any rate, in July 1963 Paul-Henri Spaak of Belgium reported that Premier Khrushchev seemed genuinely interested in a test ban. A few days later, American and British negotiators, led by Averell Harriman and Lord Hailsham respectively, arrived in Moscow to explore the seriousness of Soviet intentions. After five days of negotiations, tentative agreement was reached and a copy of the draft treaty was publicized on July 24. All nuclear tests in the atmosphere, under water, and in space were to cease, but underground tests were to be permitted. On August 5, Soviet Foreign Minister Andrei Gromyko, United States Secretary of State Dean Rusk, and British Foreign Secretary Lord Home put their signatures to the document. After a protracted debate, the United States Senate, on September 24, ratified the treaty by a vote of 80 to 19. A large majority of the world's nations quickly followed suit and deposited their instruments of ratification. A decade of arduous negotiations had finally produced concrete results.

On the negative side, France and China made a common front against the treaty. The former was bent on its own independent nuclear force and the latter attacked the treaty as a fraud and saw it as further proof of Soviet duplicity. Also, the test ban was only partial and underground tests continue to take place in many parts of the world to this day. Nevertheless, most observers agreed with President Kennedy's assessment of the treaty as a step toward reason and away from war. In specific and immediate terms, it solved a major problem of public health by halting the further contamination of the atmosphere by radioactive fallout. More broadly, it was the first East-West agreement in the tensely guarded realm of military security.

THE STRATEGIC ARMS LIMITATION TREATIES

On May 26, 1972, President Richard M. Nixon and Soviet Party Chairman Leonid Brezhnev signed in Moscow two historic arms control documents which represented the culmination of almost three years of arduous strategic arms limitation talks (SALT) in Helsinki and in Vienna.

The first document was an Anti-Ballistic Missiles Treaty of unlimited duration which placed limits on the growth of Soviet and American strategic nuclear arsenals. The treaty established a ceiling of two hundred launchers for each side's defensive missile system and committed both sides not to build nationwide anti-missile defenses. Each country was limited to two ABM sites, one for the national capital and the other to protect one field of ICBMs. Each site would consist of one hundred ABMs.

The United States already had a protected ICBM field in North Dakota and thus, under the terms of the treaty, could add an ABM site around Washington. The Soviet Union already had an ABM site for the defense of Moscow and thus was permitted to add an ABM site to protect an ICBM field. At the time of the agreement, the Soviet Union had a total of 2,328 missiles, 1,618 ICBMs and 710 on nuclear submarines, compared with 1,710 for the United States—1,054 ICBMs and 656 on submarines.

The second concrete arms control achievement of the Moscow Summit was an Interim Agreement limiting ICBMs to those under construction or deployed at the time of the signing of the agreement. This meant the retention of 1,618 ICBMs for the Soviet Union, including 300 large SS-98, and 1,054 for the

United States, including 1,000 Minutemen and 54 Titans. The agreement also froze the construction of submarine-launched ballistic missiles on all nuclear submarines at existing levels—656 for the United States and 710 for the Soviet Union. However, each side could build additional submarine missiles if an equal number of older land-based ICBMs or older submarine missile launchers were dismantled. The agreement was to be in force for five years and both sides pledged themselves to "follow-up negotiations" in order to achieve a full-fledged treaty.

Neither arms control instrument signed at Moscow placed limitations on the qualitative improvement of offensive or defensive missiles, nor were ceilings imposed on the number of warheads that could be carried by offensive missiles or on strategic bombers permitted each side. Modernization of missiles, including the emplacement of new missiles in new silos, was permitted. Both sides pledged "not to interfere with the national technical means of verification of the other party," and each side retained the right to withdraw from either agreement if it felt that its supreme national interest was in jeopardy.

The two agreements managed to freeze a rough balance into the nuclear arsenals of the two superpowers. There remained "missile-gaps," of course, in specific weapons. The United States, for example, retained the lead in the technology of "multiple independently targeted reentry vehicles" (MIRVs) while the Soviet Union possessed a larger quantity of missile launchers. Nevertheless, the overall effect was one of achieving a rough equilibrium.

The process of achieving this equilibrium went through eight stages lasting almost three years. SALT 1 was held in Helsinki in late 1969 and was exploratory without any formal proposals submitted by either side. SALT 2, held in Vienna from April to August 1970, got down to specific proposals. The two superpowers agreed in principle on the terms of a defensive missile treaty that would have limited each side to one hundred missiles each around Moscow and Washington. But several months later, the American delegation, fearful of Congress, backed away and advanced a new proposal which would have given the United States a four-to-one advantage. This was angrily rejected by the USSR, and it took a few more months before the original two-site 200-missile compromise was reaffirmed. SALT 3, held in late 1970, broke up in disagreement over offensive arms. SALT 4 took place in Vienna from March to May 1971 and during this period President Nixon and Chairman Brezhnev began to engage in top-secret correspondence. The result was a Soviet initiative proposing an ICBM freeze as well as an ABM treaty. SALT 5, held from July to September 1971 in Helsinki, saw further progress on the proposed ICBM freeze. SALT 6, in late 1971 and early 1972, produced the outlines of the ABM treaty, and SALT 7, the last round before the Moscow Summit, led to the inclusion of submarine-based missiles in the accord. The final accords were thus the result of protracted and painstaking bargaining and negotiations.

Several conclusions are worthy of note in connection with the two Moscow agreements. In the first place, the observation made earlier with regard to disarmament, namely that a measure of political accommodation must precede agreement on a technical formula, seems to apply with equal logic to arms control. It must be remembered that Soviet-American relations had improved significantly by the early 1970s, partly due to the common determination to resolve long-standing differences in Europe and partly due to the Soviet fear of China. At any rate, the political climate had thawed considerably since the days of the cold war. Second, the SALT agreements did not depend primarily on verification to be effective. Each side knew that, if it cheated and ''surprised'' the other with a devastating nuclear attack, the other side, though mortally wounded, could still inflict a retaliatory blow that would be ''unacceptable'' to the offender. Hence, the agreements were not based primarily on mutual trust, but on the mutual capacity to absorb a first strike. Besides, each side continued to spend gigantic sums on antisubmarine warfare (ASW). Since, in the mid-1970s, the stability of the nuclear deterrent was based mainly on the invulnerability of nuclear submarines and their missiles, a significant breakthrough in ASW by either side could destabilize the balance in a more serious way than an ABM system. Finally, however, there is no doubt that even if the two agreements did not qualify as disarmament, they nevertheless signified a momentous breakthrough in superpower relations and a modest step toward a saner world.

In November 1974 another advance was made. At their first meeting, in Vladivostok, President Ford and Soviet Party Chairman Brezhnev agreed to an overall ceiling of about 2,400 nuclear missiles and bombers on each side, with about half of these being missiles with multiple nuclear warheads (MIRVs). The advance was modest since these ceilings were high and, furthermore, were only quantitative. No restrictions were set on the development of qualitative improvements such as missile flight tests to increase accuracy or the development of land-mobile and air-mobile intercontinental ballistic missiles (ICBMs). Nor was the development of cruise missiles launched from submarines restricted under the terms of the accord.

Secretary Kissinger expressed the hope that SALT II would ''put a cap on the arms race'' for ten years ''between 1975 and 1985.'' This ''cap,'' however, did not signify a reduction of existing stockpiles of weapons, but merely a quantitative limitation on the development of further weapons. In that sense, the Vladivostok accord was a modest achievement.

The verification issue began to haunt Kissinger in 1975 and placed in serious question further progress toward SALT II. Admiral Elmo R. Zumwalt, retired chief of naval operations, declared in December 1975 that the Soviet Union had committed ''gross violations'' of the SALT I accord of 1972 and that Kissinger had not properly informed President Ford. He charged that the Soviets were constructing launch silos for additional missiles and thus were surreptitiously upgrading their ABM defensive potential. He also accused the Soviets of converting ''light'' ABM missiles into ''heavy'' ones and thus violating the spirit of SALT I. Kissinger heatedly denied the charges and was supported in his defense by the CIA. By this time, however, the ire of the Soviets was aroused. *Pravda* not only denied any violations of the 1972 accord, but in turn voiced serious doubts about American compliance. It now blamed the United

States for the delay in reaching a final SALT II agreement, which, Brezhnev had hoped, would be sealed by the time the Twenty-Fifth Communist Party Congress was to convene, in February 1976.

Progress toward SALT II was also stalled over two new weapons which the United States and the Soviet Union wanted to add to their respective arsenals. The Pentagon had developed a "cruise missile," which was a long-range, jet-propelled, extremely accurate guided nuclear bomb that could be launched from a bomber, a ship, or a submarine. Pentagon spokesmen declared that, since the cruise missile travelled through the atmosphere, it should not be included in the SALT II ceiling of 2,400 ICBMs, which traveled through space. The Soviet Union insisted that the "cruise missile" be included in the ceiling. At the same time, the Soviets had developed a new "Backfire" bomber, which, they declared, should be excluded from SALT II because of its limited range. The Pentagon, insisting that air-to-air refueling could enable it to reach the United States and return, demanded its inclusion in the ceiling. Thus, by early 1976, the future of SALT II was very much in doubt. The allegations of cheating by the Soviet Union, the dispute over the inclusion of newly developed weapons in the overall ceiling, and a deepening suspicion of Soviet behavior in Angola and in the Middle East made Kissinger's position on SALT II extremely vulnerable. It seemed that despite the breakthrough of SALT I, the safety of the superpowers still depended, first and foremost, on their capacity for mutually assured destruction. SALT had made a dent in the balance of terror, but it was little more than a beginning.

President Carter continued to pursue SALT II. During the first year of his presidency, negotiations were stalled because the new American initiatives on human rights and the encouragement Carter extended to Russian dissidents angered the Soviet leadership. By 1978, however, another breakthrough was in sight. Each superpower was prepared to place a ceiling of 2,250 on its total of land- and sea-based missiles and long-range bombers, almost a 10 percent reduction from the Vladivostok limits. In addition, three separate ceilings were placed on weapons armed with multiple warheads: 1,320 for land- and sea-based missiles and for bombers equipped with cruise missiles; 1,200 for land- and sea-based missiles alone; and 800 for land-based missiles alone. Finally, in June 1979, SALT II was signed by President Carter and Soviet Party Chairman Brezhev. It set an overall ceiling of 2,250 on each side's strategic arsenal of missiles and bombers and provided "subceilings" on weapons such as land-based American missiles equipped with multiple warheads and Soviet "heavy missiles." Congressional approval of the treaty would open the way for final ratification.

But then in early 1980, the Soviet Union invaded Afghanistan. SALT II was the major casualty of that decision. A new militancy rose throughout the United States and President Carter decided not to submit the treaty to the Congress. President Ronald Reagan's top priority was not arms control, but a massive armaments program. Once again, the two superpowers resumed their march toward Armageddon.

By the early 1980s the arms race had once more become a terribly expensive fact of life. Even though arms control negotiations between the superpowers resumed in 1985, the money devoted each year to military expenditures amounted to more than the total income of all the peoples of Africa and South and Southeast Asia. It was nearly three times what all the world's governments spent on health, nearly twice what they spent on education, and nearly thirty times what industrialized countries gave in aid to developing countries. These massive military expenditures rose over the years despite the modest arms control agreements that were now in effect. Arms control thus managed to slow down the mad momentum toward nuclear death, but not to arrest it.

THE FIRST DISARMAMENT TREATY SINCE WORLD WAR II: THE INTERMEDIATE NUCLEAR FORCES TREATY OF 1987

When Ronald Reagan and Mikhail Gorbachev signed the INF Treaty in Washington in December 1987, they set two historic precedents: Never before in the thorny relations between the two superpowers had its leaders been able to agree on the actual elimination of nuclear weapons, and never before had such a scrapping of weapons been monitored by mutual on-site inspections. This dramatic achievement deserves careful analysis.

One thoughtful journalist boiled down the essence of the treaty in a catchy paragraph:

> Once upon a time the man in the White House said to the man in the Kremlin, "Hey, you've got a whole category of weapons we don't like. We've got a whole category of weapons you don't like. Why don't we just wipe clean the slate?" After 72 months of contentious, suspenseful, stop-and-go negotiations, the man in the Kremlin said, "OK, it's a deal."[32]

The process began with Ronald Reagan's proposal, made in November 1981, that came to be known as the "zero option." That year, Leonid Brezhnev had arrayed against Western Europe a new class of nuclear missiles that could be fired over a distance of 3,000 miles. West Germany, Britain, and France could easily be reduced to heaps of rubble. The Pentagon was planning to offset these Soviet SS-20 missiles by deploying its own "Euromissiles"—cruises and Pershings—while making a good-faith effort to negotiate a compromise that might scale back the missiles on both sides.

Secretary of State Alexander Haig suggested a compromise that would reduce missiles in Europe but not eliminate them entirely. President Reagan, however, was interested in a proposal "that could be expressed in a single sentence and that sounded like real disarmament."[33]

Richard Perle, assistant secretary of Defense, gave the President what he was looking for: an all-or-nothing package—zero US missiles in Europe in exchange for zero SS-20s. That plan was at the heart of the President's November 1981 speech: "The United States is prepared to cancel its deployment of Pershing 2 and ground-launched cruise missiles if the Soviets will dismantle their SS-20, SS-4, and SS-5 missiles."

During the next four years, this zero option proposal lingered like an orphan looking for adoptive parents. Leonid Brezhnev, Yuri Andropov, and Konstantin Chernenko all angrily denounced the zero option as patently one-sided. The United States, the Soviet leaders asserted, was asking the Soviets to give up real weapons, already deployed at great expense, in return for the United States tearing up a piece of paper. The Americans, losing patience, began to deploy their "Euromissiles" on schedule in 1983. The Soviets, as a result, walked out of the arms control talks in Geneva and did not return for 1½ years. The subsequent downing of a Korean airliner by Soviet rockets took the Soviet-American relationship to a new nadir. Ronald Reagan now referred to the Soviet Union as an "evil empire" and passionately advocated his "Strategic Defense Initiative," to be deployed in space as a protective shield against Soviet attack. The Soviet press returned the compliment by comparing the US president to Adolf Hitler. Even a productive "walk in the woods in 1982" by two negotiators—Yuli Kvitsinsky, a bright young Soviet diplomat, and Paul Nitze, a grand old man of US nuclear strategy—leading to a tentative arms reduction deal was repudiated by both men's home offices. Amidst all this hostility, the zero option lapsed temporarily into a coma. But then—in 1985—everything changed.

The new Soviet General Secretary, Mikhail Gorbachev, began to assert himself, subtly at first, and then spectacularly. Slowly, and then with amazing speed, the glacial ice of Soviet policy toward the zero option began to melt. The Soviet leader developed a new order of priorities. First and foremost, he was intent on modernizing the Russian economy. If toward that end, some missiles would have to be sacrificed, so be it; second, he saw some intrinsic merit in the zero option: it would leave the United States without any ground-based missiles in Europe capable of hitting Soviet territory. Accordingly, Soviet policy under Gorbachev now became a great deal more flexible. A game of defensive chess suddenly changed to an offensive game with a dash of daring poker.

In May 1985, Gorbachev asserted that the Soviet Union would be willing to freeze its SS-20 forces east of the Ural Mountains. In October, he made a more far-reaching concession by allowing that an INF agreement might be possible "outside of direct connection with the problem of space and strategic arms." In plain English, the Soviet leader decided not to make an INF treaty contingent on a US decision to abandon "Star Wars."

Slowly, but steadily, the initiative on arms negotiations now shifted to the Soviet side. More and more, the United States found itself on the defensive, being bombarded with ever bolder and more comprehensive Gorbachev proposals. In 1986, for example, the Soviet leader proposed a three-stage, fifteen-year plan for total nuclear disarmament. The first stage called for cancellation of Star Wars, a 50 percent reduction in strategic weaponry, and "complete liquidation" of Soviet and US INF missiles "in the European zone." By now, the superpowers had traded places. The Soviet Union was making disarmament proposals, and the United States was rejecting them.

The Soviet proposal produced an outbreak of guerrilla warfare within the Reagan administration. Various interim and compromise proposals were drafted by the Pentagon, the State Department, and the Arms Control and Disarmament Agency. The Europeans, at first rather friendly to the zero option, had become increasingly ambivalent, since the removal of US missiles would expose their countries to a vastly superior Soviet conventional force. Yet, the Reagan administration was reluctant to back away from the zero option altogether. After all, it had been the President's own proposal to begin with.

Finally, early in 1987, Gorbachev made a final concession which tilted the negotiations toward acceptance of the zero option. He decoupled once and for all the INF treaty from the issue of "Star Wars." He was willing, in short, to accept a separate agreement along the lines of President Reagan's original zero option proposal made six years earlier.

And thus, in December 1987, the two leaders met in Washington and signed the first real disarmament accord in the postwar world. Just before the ceremony, the President led Mikhail Gorbachev to a little study next to the Oval Office and produced a baseball that Joe DiMaggio had hoped to have autographed by the Soviet leader. Reagan was not just fulfilling the old Yankee slugger's request. He had a metaphor in mind. Are we, he asked, going to play ball? Yes, Gorbachev firmly agreed. The two men signed the documents, exchanged pens, smiled warmly and shook hands, obviously moved by the occasion. When it was all over, Gorbachev called the three-day Washington summit a "main event in world politics," and Reagan declared that the meeting had "lit the sky with hope for all people of goodwill."

In the cooler light of political analysis, what did the INF treaty in fact achieve? On the credit side of the ledger, it eliminated an entire class of nuclear weapons, the "Euromissiles." The Soviets agreed to scuttle about 1,500 warheads on its medium-range SS-20 and SS-4 missiles, and the United States agreed to give up about 350 warheads on its Pershing 2 and ground-launched cruise missiles. An elaborate monitoring system was decided upon under which US and Soviet inspectors were stationed outside missile factories in each country to make sure no banned missiles were illegally produced. Inspectors were also permitted to visit missile bases and installations. After the missiles had been removed from bases by each side, special close-out inspections were arranged to make sure that the missiles were really gone. And finally, the actual physical destruction of the missiles was subject to rigorous supervision and inspection as well.

On the debit side, it might be said that the total number of missiles destined for the scrap-heap amounted to a mere 4 percent of the entire superpower arsenals. Moreover, Star Wars remained untouched by the treaty as did the strategic weapons that could incinerate each superpower from across the Atlantic, although both countries continued negotiations to attain deep cuts in these weapons. And, of course, the huge conventional arsenals of both superpowers remained untouched as well.

Having said all this, however, the net result was still historic. Each side got something that it wanted badly. The United States removed a major threat to its European NATO allies, and the Soviet Union removed a major threat to its own territory. Political circumstances and the timing were excellent as well. Mikhail Gorbachev's first priority was the Soviet economy, not superfluous "overkill" missiles. Rubles could now be spent on making the Soviet Union an economic superpower as well. Ronald Reagan assured himself the legacy of being the first US president to sign a genuine disarmament treaty with the Soviets and to have it ratified by the Senate. Nor did he had to abandon his fondest dream of Star Wars.

In larger historical perspective, the final truth perhaps is this: The problem of disarmament is not disarmament at all. Disarmament is the by-product of decisions by national leaders to reduce political tensions between their countries. Once such decisions are made, disarmament becomes a possibility and ultimately a reality. No amount of technical formulas can substitute for such leadership and courage. Gorbachev and Reagan found that kind of courage. For forty years, the doomsday clock had ticked away relentlessly toward Armageddon. On Christmas Day of 1987, at long last, humanity was granted a reprieve.

INTERNATIONAL PEACE FORCES AND COLLECTIVE SECURITY

The framers of the United Nations Charter foresaw that the elimination or even the substantial reduction of armaments would be an extremely difficult task. They had considerably greater faith in the possibility of fashioning a world in which arms would be redistributed and organized in such a way that lawbreakers could be confronted by preponderant military power. As the postwar world developed, however, the growing fury of the East-West struggle made it almost impossible for the UN Security Council really to function as the planned-for instrument of collective security. Consequently, the standing United Nations Armed Force that was envisaged by the UN founders in Article 43 was never permitted to come to life. It seemed, indeed, as though the East-West struggle would permanently prevent the creation of the one international instrument that could be the most valuable of all for military order building: a permanent and powerful international police force. What had happened, of course, was that the would-be international policemen had fallen out among themselves.

Yet if we survey the record, the East-West struggle has nevertheless not prevented the United Nations from engaging in military action to defend collective security. On several occasions the United Nations has managed effectively to meet serious threats to the peace. The first military action under the United Nations flag was fought in Korea from 1950 to 1953. In 1956 a United Nations Emergency Force was set up to restore order in the Middle East. In 1960 a United Nations Force was given prime responsibility for insulating the newly independent Congo from the East-West struggle. In 1964 a UN force was dispatched to Cyprus to prevent civil war between the island's Greek and Turkish communities. In 1973, 1974, and 1978 three UN buffer forces were dispatched to the Middle East to supervise disengagement agreements. And in 1988, the Security Council authorized one small UN observer group to monitor the Soviet withdrawal from Afghanistan, another to patrol the volatile border between Iran and Iraq, and a third to supervise the withdrawal of Cuban troops from Angola.

Each of these experiences had been unique in its highly improvised character; each has involved the UN in a most explosive situation and so has had a high quality of drama; and while all of them have fallen short of the original concept of collective security, each has made an important contribution to military order.

The Korean "Police Action"

We have seen earlier that in Korea the mobilization of an international police force was made possible only through the absence of the Soviet delegate from the Security Council in June 1950. But once the Council was freed from the paralyzing veto—albeit only temporarily—it was able to organize military action swiftly and effectively. This first modern effort of international policing therefore deserves careful analysis.

On June 27, two days after the North Korean attack, the Security Council called upon all members to "furnish such assistance to the Republic of Korea as may be necessary to repel the armed attack and to restore international peace and security in the area."[34] On July 7 the Council recommended that such forces and other assistance be placed under a Unified Command under United States operational control. It also authorized the Unified Command to use the United Nations flag. The response of the member nations to this first modern experiment in collective security was encouraging. Fifteen members other than the United States and the Republic of Korea offered to contribute troops: Australia, Belgium, Canada, Colombia, Ethiopia, France, Greece, Luxembourg, the Netherlands, New Zealand, the Philippines, Thailand, Turkey, the Union of South Africa, and the United Kingdom. In addition, thirty-seven other members offered to contribute a wide range of supplies and services, including food, clothing, medical supplies, and transportation.

Since almost 90 percent of the non-Korean forces fighting under the United Nations flag were United States forces, and since it had been the United States that had taken the initiative in this UN action, it was only logical that the Unified Command should be primarily an American operation. Accordingly, General Douglas MacArthur was placed in charge of the United Nations Command and, for all practical purposes, the United Nations Police Force became identical with the Far East Command of the United States. South Korean troops were integrated into American companies and joint actions with other UN allies were conducted through liaison officers. Moreover, since the United

States was bearing by far the largest share of the load, this preponderant American military role was accepted by all concerned as perfectly fair and proper.

While questions of military coordination in Korea were thus largely solved through the commanding position of the United States, the problem of providing the United Nations Force with political guidance presented almost insuperable obstacles. So long as the United Nations Forces were south of the 38th parallel, the problem was not acute. But by August 1, 1950, the day the Soviet delegate returned to the Security Council, the United Nations Forces were fast approaching the 38th parallel. A decision had to be made whether to stop at that point or to carry UN operations beyond it. In view of the Soviet Union's return to the Security Council and the consequent certainty of its veto in the matter, the decision had to be made by the General Assembly. Under American pressure, but with considerable misgivings, the General Assembly voted to authorize the entrance of United Nations Forces into North Korea. Yet in effect, this and subsequent decisions were made by the United States rather than by the General Assembly itself. In November 1950, after the Chinese intervention, there was formed a Committee of Sixteen for interallied consultation, but in practice the United States almost always prevailed. American domination of the international police force became most evident in the controversy involving the commander, General MacArthur. Most of the allies, and many Americans, viewed MacArthur's intentions to bomb military bases in Manchuria as a serious provocation to the Chinese. The removal of the general from the United Nations Command did not, however, take place in deference to the wishes of the allies, but was fundamentally the result of the general's challenge to the authority of his Commander-in-Chief, the President of the United States.

This first experiment in blocking aggression through an international police force was neither an unqualified success nor a complete failure. On the negative side, it owed its activation to a fortuitous circumstance—the Soviet Union's temporary absence from the Security Council; it fell far short of a genuine collective security action; though initiated as a "police action," it developed into a limited war; instead of crushing the aggressor, it resulted in the signing of an armistice with him on the basis of equality; it was in effect chiefly an American enterprise and, aside from the forces of the Republic of Korea, involved the participation of only thirty-six thousand combatants from the other United Nations countries; and its political direction was dominated chiefly by the United States. In fact, if it had not been for American initiative, the international police force in Korea would not have come into existence at all.

On the other hand, the Korean experience broke precedent in several important ways. It saw sixteen nations fighting as a United Nations army, under the United Nations flag, and led by a United Nations commander. Moreover, despite the disproportionate role played by the United States, its image as a United Nations action has remained largely intact. Most important, the United

Nations Force succeeded in halting aggression and restoring what was in effect the *status quo ante bellum*. Even when comparing this achievement with the League of Nations' dismal failure in Manchuria in 1931, it would be an exaggeration to characterize it as a complete success. Yet the fact remains that the United Nations Force in Korea took a big step along the road to collective security.

The greatest weakness of the Korean action was the lack of planning for the transition from military enforcement to the tasks of consolidating the peace. Though the aggressor had been thrown back, Korea remained as politically divided as before—and, ironically, along a line only a short distance from the 38th parallel where the fighting had begun. At best, therefore, the United Nations action provided a breathing spell during which political differences could once more be subjected to negotiation. This in itself was a great service. Yet the final lesson of Korea is nonetheless clear: that the pursuit of order through purely military techniques is bound to fail unless it is shored up by equally determined efforts to reach a political settlement.

Historically, the Korean experience has by no means been an unmixed blessing. In the United Nations of the 1980s, the Korean "police action" of the 1950s was widely regarded as an historical anomaly. Moreover, since it had placed the United Nations at war with China, the People's Republic harbored a great deal of resentment. And perhaps most important, the history of the Korean War had made it difficult, if not impossible, for North Vietnam to regard the United Nations as an impartial mediator in its war with the United States during the 1960s and 1970s.

The Four United Nations Peace Forces in the Middle East

United Nations military action in the Middle East was considerably less dramatic than the Korean campaign. The first UN Emergency Force that was dispatched to the troubled area never exceeded six thousand men. Moreover, UNEF was never meant to be a fighting army. Its purpose, rather, was to serve as a symbol of the United Nations' involvement which, it was hoped, would succeed in bringing about the neutralization of the disputed areas. Its unique achievement, in which it went importantly beyond the Korean action, was that it constituted for the first time a genuine international police force that was not dominated by any single power. In fact, all of the Great Powers were specifically excluded from it. For this reason the significance of UNEF greatly transcends its modest physical dimensions.

The father of the United Nations Emergency Force was Lester B. Pearson of Canada. When on November 2, 1956, the General Assembly was locked in acrimonious debate over British-French-Israeli action in Suez, Pearson proposed that peace and security be restored through a United Nations Force. United States and Afro-Asian approval encouraged the Canadian diplomat to draft a resolution requesting the Secretary-General to draw up a plan for the creation of an international military force to be submitted to the General Assembly within forty-eight hours. The Canadian resolution passed without a negative vote at a time when Britain and France were still bombing Egyptian territory. Secretary-General Hammarskjöld and Mr. Pearson immediately set about to improvise the force. They decided to appoint Major General E. L. M. Burns, chief of staff of the United Nations Truce Supervison Organization in Palestine, as head of the new United Nations Command. The next vital decision concerned the composition of troops to be sent. The Secretary-General thought it wise to exclude the Great Powers from the force. It would have been ill-advised to deputize Britain and France as United Nations policemen, since Egypt would never have agreed to admit them. If the United States were included, the Soviet Union would demand a role, and hence it was best to keep the two superpowers out altogether.

To the delight of leading United Nations officials, twenty-four members agreed to make troops available for the enterprise, with offers ranging from 1,180 from Canada to 250 from Finland. However, this delight began to give way to embarrassment when, in order not to jeopardize relations with Egypt, it became necessary to reject some of the offers. For example, the Canadian contingent, especially a battalion of the "Queen's Own Rifles," resembled the British too much in appearance. Pearson tactfully decided to use them as maintenance and administrative personnel in roles where they would be least conspicuous. New Zealand troops were politely rejected because New Zealand had voted with Britain and France in the General Assembly on the Suez affair. Pakistan was considered unsuitable because it was a member of the Baghdad Pact and an irritant to India. Troops from the Soviet bloc—Czechoslovakia and Rumania—were not "rejected" but simply not "activated."[35] Finally a contingent of six thousand troops from ten countries—Brazil, Canada, Colombia, Denmark, Finland, India, Indonesia, Norway, Sweden, and Yugoslavia—was ready for action.

The composition of the force was very important since its admission to the contested area depended upon the permission of Egypt. Though this condition was distasteful to many members of the Assembly, it was, according to the Secretary-General, the "very basis and starting point" of the entire operation. In effect, Egypt therefore had a veto over the national makeup of the force and could, as well, determine the length of its stay in the Suez area. On November 12 Egypt granted UNEF permission to enter. Shortly thereafter, Britain, France, and Israel were persuaded to withdraw from Egyptian territory and UNEF proceeded to neutralize the contested boundary zones. Its function became essentially that of a "buffer" between Israel and Egypt.

In May 1967 President Nasser abruptly demanded that UNEF be withdrawn from the borders which it had patrolled for over a decade. Secretary-General U Than complied with the Egyptian demand, though with serious misgivings, and the force was promptly removed.

U Thant's decision was a very controversial one. The Secretary-General was widely criticized for giving in too hastily to Egyptian pressure. Critics pointed out that while it was true that UNEF's presence on the Egyptian border depended on the consent of the Egyptian government, the Secretary-General could have stalled by requesting an emergency session of the Security Council or of the General Assembly and thus gained time. The Israeli delegate to the United Nation, Abba Eban, stated caustically that "the umbrella was removed at the precise moment when it began to rain." The Secretary-General defended his action by pointing out that there would have been no legal basis for maintaining the force on Egyptian soil without that nation's consent. Moreover, the force had never been permitted to patrol on the Israeli side of the border, and when the Israeli government was asked whether it would invite the UNEF troops to its side after leaving Egypt, Israel had refused to do so. Both governments were within their legal rights, the Secretary-General asserted.

A further complication in the picture was the fact that two nations that had given contingents to UNEF—India and Yugoslavia—were removing their forces even before the Secretary-General had given the order to withdraw. Moreover, several UNEF soldiers were killed by Egyptian troops who threatened that unless UNEF were promptly withdrawn, it would be regarded as an "army of occupation." Finally, the Secretary-General reasoned that if he did not comply with the request of a sovereign government, it might be infinitely more difficult to obtain consent for the admission of a peace-keeping force in a future crisis. Given all these conflicting considerations, the Secretary-General made his difficult and fateful choice.

An overall analysis of the UNEF experience points up a striking dilemma for any international peace force. In order to be an effective instrument of collective security and a respectable military force, it must include one or more of the Great Powers. But if it does, it is likely to find itself dominated by a Great Power, as was the case in Korea, and to suffer a proportionate loss of its international character. Hence, since in order to steer clear of the East-West struggle it must exclude the Great Powers, a truly international force can hardly be more than a buffer. The Korean Force, organized and operated as an instrument of enforcement, came closer to the ideal of collective security in terms of its *action*. The Middle East Force, though compelled to limit itself to the task of neutralization, more closely approached the collective security ideal in terms of its *composition*. While its dependence on the sufferance of Egypt made it a fragile instrument of peace-keeping, it nevertheless helped to restore peace in the Middle East in 1956 and to maintain an uneasy truce on the Israeli-Egyptian border for over a decade.

The second UN Emergency Force (UNEF II) was established immediately after the conclusion of the Yom Kippur war, in late October 1973. The force was deployed by the Security Council for an initial six-month period, subject to renewal, along the disengagement line that had been negotiated between Israel and Egypt by Secretary Kissinger. UNEF II differed from its predecessor in three important respects. First, it was placed under the exclusive mandate of the Security Council. This meant that it could not be terminated *during* each six-month period except with the unanimous consent of the permanent members. Every six months, however, each of the Big Five had the power to prevent its prolongation when the Security Council voted on the renewal of the mandate. Thus, UNEF I could be killed at any time by the host country, but UNEF II could be killed only on a regular six-month interval by the veto of a permanent member. Second, while the troop composition of UNEF II consisted primarily of small neutral countries, Poland became a part of the force in addition to Austria, Sweden, Finland, Ireland, Ghana, Senegal, Kenya, Nepal, Panama, Peru, Canada, and Indonesia. Thus, a Warsaw Pact nation for the first time became a member of a UN peace force. And finally, another precedent was set when the Soviet Union agreed to share in the $30 million assessed budget, which was authorized by the Security Council for the first six-month period, as well as in several subsequent appropriations of similar amounts. China, however, decided not to participate in the votes either authorizing or extending the peace force nor did it choose to share in the costs, even though these were defined as regular "expenses" in accordance with Article 17 of the Charter.

UNEF II operated at a level of approximately seven thousand men under the direction of a Finnish commander, Major-General Siilasvuo. The Security Council maintained tight political control, and despite some minor areas of friction, the force operated very effectively. When violence erupted in Ireland, however, the Irish contingent was withdrawn. UNEF II, like its predecessor, still consisted of borrowed troops who could be recalled at will by their national governments. In 1979, in the wake of the peace treaty between Israel and Egypt, UNEF II was terminated. There was a consensus that, during the five years of its existence, it had acquitted itself well.

In May 1974, in the wake of the disengagement arrangement that had been worked out by Secretary Kissinger between Israel and Syria, the Security Council established a small UN Disengagement Observer Force (UNDOF). The new force was to draw its contingents from UNEF. Five hundred Austrians, 350 Peruvians, 100 Canadians, and 100 Poles were transferred for patrol duty to the Golan Heights. Once again, the Security Council authorized an initial six-month period and once again China did not vote. UNDOF's expenses were subsumed under the UNEF budget. A formula was worked out under which those nations that contributed troops to UNEF or UNDOF received reimbursements so that they did not have to shoulder a double burden of both manpower and money. UNDOF performed creditably under the leadership of Brigadier-General Gonzalo Briceño Zevallos of Peru, who exercised his command under the watchful eye of the Security Council. In the late 1980s UNDOF was still patrolling the Israeli-Syrian border, keeping incidents there to a minimum.

In late November 1974, after a trip by Secretary-General Waldheim to the Middle East, Syria acquiesced to a six-month extension of UNDOF's mandate to patrol the Golan Heights, and the Security Council approved the prolongation. Thereafter, regular six-month renewals were granted by the Security Council to both UNEF II and UNDOF. Thus, by the early 1980s, UN peace-keeping operations had clearly become the exclusive province of the Security Council.

In 1978 the Security Council authorized a United Nations Interim Force in Lebanon (UNIFIL), which was to supervise the withdrawal of Israeli forces from southern Lebanon. UNIFIL was brought to a strength of about six thousand men, most of whom were drawn from small neutral states. However, the force also included a thousand French paratroopers. The job of UNIFIL was particularly difficult since fighting was still in progress and the numerous warring factions made it almost impossible to define UNIFIL's mandate clearly. The little force was to prevent not only clashes between Israeli forces and PLO guerrillas, but also clashes between Lebanese Christians and Moslems. Ultimately, it was hoped, authority over Lebanon would revert to the Lebanese government. It was a credit to UNIFIL that by the late 1980s the force was still operating in Lebanon despite the fact that, in 1989, Moslem extremists murdered one of its officers, Colonel William Higgins of the United States. Perhaps the more neutral composition of the UNIFIL explained its greater longevity. Soldiers from Fiji, Ghana, Ireland, Nepal, the Netherlands, Norway, Senegal, and Sweden probably did not constitute as much of a threat to the Lebanese Moslems as did the troops from former colonial countries.

The United Nations Congo Force (ONUC)

Perhaps the most complex military challenge to confront the United Nations was the one that occurred in the Congo between 1960 and 1964. Historians may differ with Mr. Hammarskjöld's view that the United Nations' task in the Congo was the most important responsibility that the world organization had to shoulder in the first fifteen years of its lifetime, but most will agree that the Congo problem required every diplomatic and military resource that the United Nations could possibly muster.

We have seen earlier that the United Nations was first called into the infant African republic in order to take the place of Belgian troops whose sudden withdrawal had left the Congo in a state of political unrest verging on anarchy and civil war. The Secretary-General's problems in putting together a United Nations Force for the Congo resembled those that had been faced in the Middle East. Once again, the Great Powers had to be kept out of the conflict. Furthermore, it was deemed advisable to employ mostly African troops for the United Nations Force. The Secretary-General, together with UN Under-Secretary Ralph J. Bunche, appealed to the new African nations for support. The response again was encouraging: almost all the African nations offered contributions. In addition, troops were accepted from Ireland, Sweden, Indonesia, Malaya, the United Arab Republic, and India. At its high point, the Congo Force comprised over 20,000 men from twenty-nine different countries. The task of the force became vastly more complex, however, when tribal warfare broke out between the central government in Leopoldville under Premier

Lumumba and secessionist movements in the two provinces of Katanga and Kasai. The United Nations Force faced an almost insoluble dilemma: how to restore order while avoiding the charge of intervention in a civil war. As in the Middle East, the presence of the force had to be approved by a sovereign government. But whereas in the case of Egypt, President Nasser had retained control, the Congolese government was in a state of disintegration. The premier and the president of the central government were locked in a power struggle. Moreover, the Soviet Union gave material help to the Lumumba government in direct contravention of the wishes of the United Nations Command and refused to pay its share of the cost of the Peace Force. Racial tension entered the picture when ex-Premier Lumumba accused the non-African contingents of the force of being pro-Belgian. Several member states withdrew their contingents from the force in protest against "neocolonialism."

Financial crises constantly threatened the life of the force. Even after the General Assembly recognized President Kasavubu as the legitimate spokesman for the Congo, United Nations personnel were beaten up by Congolese and frequently had to shoot in self-defense. The UN troops were authorized to use force "only in the last resort." Some were killed. All these factors conspired to make the operation a most difficult and delicate one. While the tribal fighting was going on, the United Nations Force could do little more than protect civilians. It served as a sort of fire brigade: Though unable to prevent the outbreak of civil war, it managed to keep it within bounds. Most important, the United Nations Force prepared the ground for the more difficult and complex task of restoring political stability in the Congo.

The Congo experience was a repeat performance of UNEF, with all of UNEF's difficulties vastly magnified. Again, the force had to be improvised at a moment's notice. It, too, was dependent on the good will of a sovereign state, this time a fledgling state on the verge of collapse. Once again, the Secretary-General had to race against time in order to forestall Great Power intervention. The force itself, once established, again was little more than a buffer, but this time its task was not limited to patrol duty in the desert. It had to keep brutal tribal warfare in the jungle to a minimum and even to assume some of the administrative functions of government. Finally, like UNEF, the Congo Force accomplished its primary mission before it was disbanded in 1964: it succeeded in preventing the Congo from becoming a seedbed of a general war.

The United Nations Cyprus Force (UNFICYP)

In March 1964 yet another peace-keeping experiment was launched, this time in Cyprus. When the Greek and Turkish communities on that island found themselves unable to resolve their differences and civil war became an increasingly ominous threat, the Security Council met in emergency session and authorized a peace force. Once again, the force was tailored to the situation. Three thousand British troops already on the island were deputized as UN policemen, and in addition Canada, Sweden, Ireland, and Finland contributed troops, bringing the total up to seven thousand men. The new force also differed from previous ones in its financing arrangements. Since the mood was definitely set against another assessment, the $6 million required for six months was raised through voluntary contributions, with $2 million supplied by the United States, $1 million by the United Kingdom, and the remainder by Greece, Turkey, Italy, Australia, and the Netherlands. The Cyprus Force also set a new precedent in that the Secretary-General appointed a high-level diplomat as mediator to help bring about a political settlement between the two hostile communities. By 1968 the Cyprus Force was the only major UN peace-keeping operation still in the field. It was still on active duty in the early 1970s, though its strength had been reduced to three thousand men. China's accession to the Security Council did not lead to the termination of the force. When the Council considered the extension of the force in 1972, fourteen members voted in favor. China, not wishing to disrupt the consensus, chose to abstain rather than to veto. Despite its voluntary financial base, the Cyprus Force had become an important military order-builder in the Mediterranean.

In late 1973, when UNEF II was being organized, its first contingents were drawn from the force on Cyprus which, as a consequence, was reduced to a level of two thousand men. But when hostilities erupted on the island, UNFICYP had to be brought up to its original strength of over four thousand men. Costs were kept low, because Britain provided the logistical support base for the force, and never exceeded $12 million a year. During the hostilities on Cyprus, the Secretary-General had to maneuver deftly in order to maintain the strictly neutral character of the force and not to incur the wrath of the Security Council. A number of peace soldiers were killed in the crossfire between Greek and Turkish Cypriots. On the whole, UNFICYP acquitted itself remarkably well under heavy pressure. By the late 1980s, the Security Council had renewed its mandate more than forty times. Given the political struggles that divided the Security Council, this was an extraordinary achievement.

THE FUTURE OF UN PEACE-KEEPING

Since 1956, the United Nations has fielded a permanent procession of temporary peace-keeping operations. Not unreasonably, the question has frequently arisen whether the organization should not be equipped with a permanent force, a kind of standing army of peace.

The years 1988 and 1989 gave additional impetus to that initiative. During these two years, once again, four observer forces were created. The first, consisting of 50 observers, was set up to monitor the Soviet troop withdrawal from Afghanistan. The second, made up of 350 observers from two dozen countries, was to supervise the cease-fire that was announced between Iraq and Iran in August of that year. The third, consisting of 70 observers, was sent to Angola to oversee the withdrawal of Cuban troops. Finally, in 1989, a 4500-member peace force was dispatched to Namibia in order to monitor elections that would pave that territory's way to independence.

When, in September 1988, the United Nations' peace-keeping forces were awarded the Nobel Peace Prize, the Soviet Union, to the surprise of most Western observers, did not scoff at the award but suggested that countries should routinely earmark some of their armed forces for UN peace-keeping duty, thus effectively giving the organization a modest army of its own. Although the idea itself was not new, its Soviet sponsorship was nothing short of sensational. Mikhail Gorbachev's "new thinking" now clearly included the United Nations. Hence, the concept deserves serious analysis.

The United Nations experiences in peace-keeping discussed above were all successful in at least one sense: They restored military order and thus bought time. In the past three decades, more than 500,000 "soldiers without enemies" have served in this capacity. Whether the peace forces prevented general conflagrations is an open question, and clearly the forces did not provide genuine collective security, but that their limited success provided renewed opportunity for political order-building is indisputable. This is a major accomplishment, especially since all these ventures started out as complete improvisations.

The fact that peace-keeping seems to have become an integral UN responsibility has convinced many observers today than an even more effective performance would be possible if a permanent international peace force were established under UN authority. Article 43 of the UN charter, which contemplated such a force, was never implemented because of the intensity of the East-West struggle. Yet, the new détente between the superpowers in the late 1980s seems to extend to the United Nations. Hence, a modest force with permanent status might now be a possibility.

It is immediately apparent that such a force would differ from that contemplated under Article 43. The framers had assumed that concerted military action by the great powers would nip any conflict in the bud. Ironically, however, in the crises we have analyzed, the peace depended not on how quickly the great powers could be brought to the scene but on how successfully they could be kept at arm's length. Hence, the great powers would probably have to be excluded from a permanent force, at least at the beginning.

In composition, such a force might consist of long-term volunteers recruited individually by the United Nations, with quotas for different nations. The commanding officer and other high-ranking personnel might be chosen from nationals of middle and smaller states. The force would not be furnished with heavy arms or atomic weapons but might have its own permanent bases and training depots. Its commander in chief would be the Secretary-General.

Proposals along these lines have been considered in UN circles and have received a mixed reaction, including several serious reservations. First, such a permanent force would have to be very large and expensive to be able to meet different kinds of emergencies. Korea, for example, necessitated a fighting force to repel an armed attack; UNEF I and II as well as UNDOF and the

Iran-Iraq Observer Group were patrol forces in the desert; ONUC had to help save a new country from anarchy and civil war; and the Cyprus force was needed to prevent two hostile communities on an island from sparking off an international crisis. Thus, the argument runs, the unique character of each experience suggests an ad hoc approach. Second, few nations would be willing to commit troops to the United Nations for unspecified future operations and to give the Secretary-General the authority of commander in chief over these forces. Third, in view of the melancholy financial histories of UNEF and ONUC, it is most doubtful whether the membership would be willing to underwrite the costs of a standing UN Force.

The above difficulties suggest a more modest approach. The consensus is growing that the next step should not be an existent UN Force but a flexible call-up system under which members would be asked to earmark contingents for UN duty on a standby basis. By the late 1980s, Denmark, Norway, Sweden, Finland, Canada, Italy, and the Netherlands had already offered to earmark units for UN use under such an arrangement. Most of them volunteered to send observers to Afghanistan and to the Iran-Iraq border. And, as already mentioned, the Soviet Union has now followed suit. Nevertheless, the knotty problem of political control of these units remains, and unless the nations earmarking the troops also "pay their own beat," the fiscal obstacles may prove difficult indeed.

If such a standby UN Force could be established as a first step toward a permanent force, the results would be most beneficial. Such a force would be a most useful instrument in the struggle for military order. But its function in the general quest for order would still be a *transitional* one. As the record of disarmament and arms control negotiations has clearly demonstrated, military instruments per se cannot create political order. But a standby or permanent UN Peace Force might at least make a limited contribution by preparing the ground. It might thus embody the best that military order-building has to offer in our time.

REFERENCES

1 Peter Burchett, reporting for the *London Daily Express,* September 5, 1945; cited by Philip Noel-Baker, *The Arms Race.* New York: Oceana, 1958, pp. 119–120.
2 A joint statement by President Eisenhower and Premier Khrushchev made at Camp David in 1959.
3 Noel-Baker, *op. cit.,* p. 86.
4 Hans J. Morgenthau, *Politics Among Nations.* 3d ed. New York: Knopf, 1960, pp. 410–411.
5 James Brown Scott, *The Proceedings of the Hague Peace Conference of 1907,* Vol. I. New York: Oxford University Press, 1920, pp. 89–90.
6 Cited by Inis L. Claude, Jr., *Swords into Plowshares.* 2d ed. New York: Random House, 1959, p. 308.
7 Security Council Official Records, March 5, 1947, p. 453.

8 Yves Collart, *Disarmament: A Study Guide and Bibliography on the Efforts of the United Nations*. The Hague: Nijhoff, 1958, p. 55.

9 Cited by Joseph Nogee, "The Diplomacy of Disarmament," *International Conciliation*, January 1960, p. 280.

10 *Ibid.*, p. 282.

11 *Ibid.*

12 Noel-Baker, *op. cit.*, p. 22.

13 Nogree, *op. cit.*, p. 286.

14 Noel-Baker, *op. cit.*, pp. 12–30.

15 General Assembly Official Records, Fourteenth Session, September 18, 1959.

16 *Ibid.*

17 Claude, *op. cit.*, p. 314.

18 William M. Evan, "An International Public Opinion Poll on Disarmament and 'Inspection by the People': A Study of Attitudes Toward Supranationalism," *Inspection for Disarmament*, Seymour Melman, ed. New York: Columbia University Press, 1958, pp. 231–250.

19 *Ibid.*, p. 234.

20 Claude, *op. cit.*, p. 308.

21 Larry Collins, "Combating Nuclear Terrorism," *The New York Times Magazine*, December 14, 1980, p. 37.

22 "Race Poisoning by Radiation," *Saturday Review*, June 9, 1956.

23 "The Biological Effects of Bomb Tests," *New Statesman and Nation*, June 8, 1957.

24 *The New Scientist*, May 16, 1957.

25 Noel-Baker, *op. cit.*, p. 255.

26 Cited by Nogee, *op. cit.*, p. 263.

27 *The New York Times*, January 14, 1958.

28 Cited by Noel-Baker, *op. cit.*, p. 261.

29 *The New York Times*, June 8, 1957.

30 *New York Herald Tribune*, September 1, 1958.

31 Nogee, *op. cit.*, p. 298.

32 Strobe Talbot, "The Road to Zero," *Time*, December 14, 1987.

33 *Ibid.*

34 United Nations Doc. S/1511, June 27, 1950.

35 William R. Frye, *A United Nations Peace Force*. New York: Oceana, 1957, p. 23.

SELECTED BIBLIOGRAPHY

Davis, Lynn E. "Lessons of the INF Treaty," *Foreign Affairs*, Spring 1988. A sober realistic assessment. In the author's view, the security of Western Europe is the United States' next priority.

Dyson, Freeman. *Weapons and Hope*. New York: Harper & Row, 1984. The great merit of this sensitive book is the author's conscientious search for a common language and common ground between what he calls the "victims" and the "warriors" of the nuclear age.

Nerlich, Uwe, and James A. Thompson, eds. *Conventional Arms Control and the Security of Europe*. Boulder, Colo: Westview Press, 1988. In the light of Mikhail Gorbachev's offer to cut troops and tanks in Europe, this book, written by experienced analysts and officials, is an excellent primer on the subject.

Newhouse, John. *Cold Dawn: The Story of SALT*. New York: Holt, Rinehart and Winston, 1973. The definitive account of the tortuous negotiations leading to the Strategic Arms Limitation Treaty of 1972.

Nye, Joseph S., Graham T. Allison, Jr., and Albert Carnesale. *Fateful Visions: Avoiding Nuclear Catastrophe*. Cambridge: Ballinger, 1988. In a carefully crafted, admirably modest analysis, the authors place their faith in "lengthening the fuse" of nuclear weapons in a further evolution of United States–Soviet relations. So far, so good.

Reiss, Mitchell. *Without the Bomb: The Politics of Nuclear Proliferation*. New York: Columbia University Press, 1988. A valuable study of six nations *with* the technological capability who decided *not* to go nuclear.

Seaborg, Glenn T. *Kennedy, Khrushchev, and the Test Ban*. Berkeley: University of California Press, 1981. The definitive account of the 1963 partial nuclear test ban treaty.

Wiseman, Henry, ed. *Peacekeeping: Appraisals and Proposals*. Elmsford, NY: Pergamon Press, 1983. A very useful survey of UN peace-keeping operations over a quarter of a century.

13

THE ECONOMIC STRUGGLE FOR ORDER

It is not from the benevolence of the butcher, the brewer, or the baker that we expect our dinner, but from their regard to their self-interest. We address ourselves, not to their humanity, but to their self-love, and never talk to them of our necessities, but of their advantages.

Adam Smith, *The Wealth of Nations*

The world since 1945 has been one gigantic experimental station in economic order-building. But while a generation ago the central problem was to create new institutions where none existed, today it is to get a whole bevy of global and regional economic agencies to work together effectively. The "house of economic order" in today's world looks like a great "booming, buzzing confusion," to use William James' famous description of reality. There is little doubt that it will have to be built from the bottom up rather than from the top down. For the sake of organization and clarity, we have divided the economic order-building institutions into two major categories: global and regional. In the former group there are a number of institutions affiliated with the United Nations, such as the World Bank and the International Monetary Fund, as well as the global conferences on food, population, and environment which have been discussed in Chapter 10. Outside the UN framework, the General Agreement on Tariffs and Trade (GATT) is probably the most significant. In addition, the recent growth of so-called multinational enterprises is deserving of analysis. The most important experiment in regional economic order-building is probably taking place in Western Europe. The second part of this chapter will deal with the evolution of the European Economic Community (EEC), which has managed, in some degree, to transcend the traditional bonds of the nation-state system. Both the global and the regional agencies share the common functionalist premise that the economic path to order may pave the way for the order-builders in the political and military realms. Beyond this, each has been unique, attuned to its own particular objectives and accumulating its own special experiences.

ECONOMIC ORDER-BUILDING AT THE GLOBAL LEVEL

Four horsemen of the Apocalypse are galloping across the world of the 1980s: food shortage, debt crisis, inflation, and population explosion. It is essential to remember that the order-building institutions that make up the contents of the present chapter all live in the shadow of these recent apocalyptic developments and have been profoundly affected by them. Their task of building a more stable economic order has, as a result, been made a great deal more difficult, especially on the global level.

The International Bank for Reconstruction and Development (IBRD), or World Bank, and its two affiliates, the International Development Association (IDA) and the International Finance Corporation (IFC), are all members of the United Nations family and are committed to the industrial development of the economically underdeveloped countries. The World Bank is controlled primarily by the rich industrialized countries, but its former president, Robert S. McNamara, underscored the need to bridge the widening gulf between the rich and the poor and used the bank's resources toward that objective. Similarly, the International Monetary Fund (IMF), which also is a nominal member of the UN system, has tended to function primarily as a Western-controlled short-term currency loan operation. Recently, however, pressures have built up to negotiate a reform of the international monetary system, aimed at developing a new system of reserves and settlements to replace the dollar standard and at improving the balance-of-payments adjustment process. The achievement of these objectives would give the fund the power to create international reserves and to influence national decisions on exchange rates and on domestic monetary and fiscal policies. Developments in both the bank and the fund have reflected a steady increase in recent years in the resources of multilateral development and assistance agencies in contrast to static or declining bilateral efforts. The growing economic interdependence of the world has, of course, been the major reason for the faster growth of the multilateral approach. The membership of both the bank and the fund has increased considerably in recent years. Even China joined both institutions in 1980.

The UN conferences on environment, food, and population have been discussed extensively in Chapter 10. Suffice it to say in the present context that perhaps the most impressive feature that these conferences had in common was their truly planetary character. Representatives of all mankind gathered in

Stockholm, Rome, and Bucharest in order to forge common action plans against scourges that were common to all. The fact that action plans emerged at all from these town meetings of the world came as a surprise to the skeptics. The UN Environment Program established in Nairobi and the World Food Council established at the Rome Conference were concrete testimonies to the fact that the "New International Economic Order" was not just an empty slogan. A real beginning had been made in the slow and painful evolution toward global consciousness.

The General Agreement on Tariffs and Trade (GATT) today comprises over eighty nations. It was formed originally in 1947 by twenty-three Western nations which were interested in lowering tariff and trade barriers among themselves. A generation later, in the 1980s, the dollar and the British pound sterling had been devalued, Western Europe was struggling on the road to economic unification, and debt crisis had begun to plague the world economy. Tariffs, in short, were no longer the most significant hindrance to world trade. Nontariff barriers loomed as far more important. The energy and food crises stimulated a new concern about access to raw materials and a clear need for new ground rules on export controls. It is very likely that GATT will become one of the instruments in such a fundamental revision of the entire world trade system.

Finally, the 1980s have witnessed the rapid growth and proliferation of a unique phenomenon in the global economy: the multilateral enterprise. Observers of these powerful economic entities are sharply divided. Some perceive them as greedy, disruptive colossi, motivated solely by profit; others see them as forces that transcend the iron bonds of the nation-state system and as forerunners of a saner economic order. While both extreme views are exaggerated, it seems that, on balance, the order-building potential of the multinational corporations exceeds their disruptive potential. Hence, they are discussed in the context of the present chapter.

During 1973 a "Group of Eminent Persons" met under the auspices of the UN Economic and Social Council to study the role of multinational corporations in international relations and the process of development.[1] There are currently some two hundred large multinational enterprises which operate simultaneously in twenty or more different nations and are joined together by common ownership and management strategy. The $3 billion of value added annually by each of the top ten multinationals is already greater than the gross national product of some eighty member states of the United Nations, and some observers are predicting that by the end of the century three hundred giant corporations will account for the large majority of world industrial production.[2] Yet, even weak states can and sometimes have nationalized the local affiliate of a multinational corporation. For the foreseeable future, the two kinds of entities will continue to coexist, in uneasy tension.

The relationship of the multinationals to the developing countries is highly complex. At present 95 percent of the world's multinationals are domiciled in highly developed countries, such as the United States, Britain, Germany,

France, Japan, Sweden, Holland, and Switzerland. The developing countries need the jobs the multinationals have to offer, but at times political or economic considerations may dictate nationalization. Thus, the multinationals exert massive economic power, but the developing nations retain political power by exercising their prerogatives as sovereign entities.

In rare cases a multinational corporation can influence the foreign policy of a country directly. The impact of the International Telephone and Telegraph Company (ITT) on Chile was a case in point and stimulated the creation of the special UN group. Such examples of private foreign policy are relatively rare. More commonly, the existence of corporations with decision domains crossing several national boundaries has provided an additional instrument that governments may attempt to use in their relations with each other. Manipulation of transnational corporations, however, is an instrument available to the host as well as the home government. The most dramatic example was the 1973 oil embargo. While the companies exerted some independence in diverting non-Arab oil to the Netherlands and the United States, the Arab countries were able to obtain almost total company compliance in regard to Arab oil. Thus, control has worked as a two-way street.

Perhaps the most important order-building function of the multinational corporation is its capacity to tie the global economy together in a more meaningful way. It tends to shift industrial production toward the poorer parts of the globe. It transfers technology and managerial resources from advanced to less-developed countries. It promotes both regional and global economic integration. It may also help to erode the great ideological cleavage between East and West. Already there are more than a thousand agreements between Western corporations and Communist countries.

There is, of course, the danger that the diminution of the role of the nation-state might signal a new feudalism rather than healthy progress. Kings and corporate barons might engage in conflicts and coalitions and the serfs would suffer. If that were to happen, the real global divisions would not be among nations, but between a world city knit together by transnational elites and the diverse but intense parochialisms of the world countryside.

On balance, it seems clear that the role of the multinational corporation in international politics is already very substantial. Its impact is not only economic but political as well. Its challenge is so powerful that it is beginning to elicit concerted responses in the world community. Since these responses are being made manifest at a fairly early stage in the evolution of the multinational corporation, there is hope that its enormous potential will not further exacerbate the struggle for power, but will help pave the way toward a saner international economic order.

ECONOMIC ORDER-BUILDING IN WESTERN EUROPE

It has been at the regional level, and especially in Western Europe, that functional collaboration has been really tested. We shall now examine the various regional arrangements aimed at Western European economic integration. These arrangements include chiefly the Organization for Economic Cooperation and Development (OECD); the European Coal and Steel Community (ECSC); the European Atomic Energy Community (Euratom); and the European Economic Community, or Common Market (EEC). Behind the façade of these prosaic-sounding names, real pioneer work has been accomplished in the forging of economic order.

The nations which signed the Organization for European Economic Cooperation (OEEC) Convention in April 1948 were all members of the Atlantic Community: Austria, Belgium, Denmark, France, Greece, Iceland, Ireland, Italy, Luxembourg, the Netherlands, Norway, Portugal, Sweden, Switzerland, Turkey, and the United Kingdom. Canada and the United States became associate members while the Federal Republic of Germany and Spain joined soon afterward as full members. Yugoslavia took part as an observer. The machinery of OEEC included a Council composed of all the member governments, an Executive Committee, several Technical Committees, and a Secretariat. Thus equipped, the organization embarked on its two main responsibilities: the apportioning of American aid and the liberalization of trade restrictions in the Western European economy.

The structure of OEEC was the subject of some disagreement. The French wanted a strong executive organ with some supranational characteristics. This was opposed by Britain, which insisted that the new organization remain under the direct control of the participating governments with no abrogation of sovereignty whatsoever. The British view prevailed both in form and in practice and OEEC was constituted as a purely transnational body, a conference of sovereign states in permanent session. The power of decision rested in the council, which was bound by the rule of unanimity. It would be false to assume, however, that the unanimity rule was a hindrance to the work of OEEC. The rule resulted in a practice of careful deliberating at all levels of policy making. In fact, when one or more states threatened to veto a decision, it was not uncommon for them to be "shamed" into agreement. A carefully prescribed procedure, including hearings and cross-examinations, made it almost impossible for a state to claim that it had been left out of the policy-making process. The veto was used only as a last resort. If a state used it too often, it found itself isolated and even ostracized. Diplomatic pressure was usually sufficient to persuade a reluctant member. On the other hand, the veto was a constant reminder to the large states that the smaller ones could not simply be out-voted but had to be persuaded. At times, the strict application of the unanimity rule even enabled the small states to exert a disproportionate amount of influence, as for example, when "a struggle over regulations concerning dried fruit among some of the smaller powers once held up far more important business."[3] But on the whole, the veto rule did not lead to paralysis; rather, it opened new avenues of improvisation and innovation. Of these, perhaps the most important was what OEEC officials came to call the "confrontation technique." The continuous process of intergovernmental consultation that went on at all levels of the organization encouraged a "European way of thinking" and an "OEEC point of view" in the permanent national delegations accredited to OEEC.[4] In making this view known to their national governments and in pressing for its acceptance, these officials imposed a moral obligation upon their governments that could not be lightly ignored. Indeed, the members of OEEC learned always to bear in mind the international consequences of national decisions. To be sure, there existed no legal obligation to do so, but long years of conditioning created a high degree of sensitivity to the interests of Europe as a whole. It may be said of most OEEC officials that this dual loyalty to their own country and to Europe seldom caused any serious difficulties. In most instances it proved possible for them to find a workable balance.

OEEC began as a "crisis organization" primarily concerned with the distribution of American aid. But as European recovery progressed, its second major responsibility, the liberalization of trade, assumed increasing importance. In this respect also, OEEC was very successful. It brought about a great increase in intra-European trade as well as in European production. The OEEC Code of Trade Liberalization resulted in the modification and withdrawal of numerous quota restrictions among the member states. A European Productivity Agency under the aegis of OEEC brought about major improvements in European industrial and agricultural productivity. Yet in the area of tariff reduction, OEEC also suffered a number of failures. Most notable among these were the major rifts that developed on the question of tariff reduction between The Six—France, Italy, West Germany, and the Benelux countries—and the rest of the OEEC membership. The increasing impatience of the Inner Six members of OEEC with the more conservative policies of the Outer Seven placed the organization under strain.

When OEEC went out of existence in 1960, it had demonstrated that a functional organization need not be supranational to be moderately successful. The OEEC had managed to improvise a number of successful techniques of economic cooperation despite its council's unanimity rule. The decisive factor in the organization's success, however, was not structural. It was the fact that OEEC had served two real and tangible purposes—the distribution of Marshall Plan aid and the liberalization of intra-European trade. It was these well-defined purposes that saved it from the fate of the Council of Europe, in whose case cooperation was defined much less concretely and sharply.

In 1961 OEEC was replaced by the Organization for Economic Cooperation and Development (OECD). The new body included the eighteen OEEC members plus the United States and Canada. Its goals were described as close cooperation on economic and business cycle policy, expanded aid to underdeveloped countries, and further progress in trade liberalization. During the 1970s and 1980s, the OECD countries' major challenge was to combat inflation and recession. The OPEC oil cartel had inflicted heavy damage on the industrial oil-importing nations of the OECD. In fact, it may not be incorrect to say that OPEC had become OECD's main preoccupation.

Neither OEEC nor its successor had any supranational features. Quite early in the life of the OEEC, this absence of supranationality gave rise to disagreements and eventually prompted six member nations to launch a far more ambitious project in economic collaboration. In May 1950 French Foreign Minister Robert Schuman made a dramatic announcement. He proposed to pool the resources of the French and German coal and steel industries under a common supranational authority that was to be open to other European countries. The motives underlying this far-reaching proposal were both economic and political. A rational distribution of European coal and steel throughout Western Europe would be highly desirable. But far more important was Schuman's desire to end Franco-German enmity. By the pooling of two raw materials vital for war, military conflict between Germany and France would become next to impossible. The bold conception of the Schuman Plan thus combined both realism and vision.

A month after the initial proposal, negotiations began among six European countries—France, West Germany, Italy, and the Benelux states. The moving spirit behind the negotiations was Jean Monnet, another major architect of the European idea. Monnet's hope was that economic union among the participating states would ultimately lead to political union. He envisaged a supranational authority with well-defined but real powers over coal and steel. Subsequently, other sectors of the economy might be added, leading logically to the goal of political fusion. The treaty negotiations proceeded fairly smoothly, since all participating states saw great advantages in the proposal. The French feared that an uncontrolled revival of the German Ruhr industries might once again herald the start of German aggression. Hence France was willing to give up a degree of control over its own industries in exchange for some control over those in Western Germany. The Germans hoped that the Schuman Plan would greatly improve their coal and steel production, expand markets, and create new outlets for foreign investment. Italy looked forward to new capital and the possibility of relieving its population problem through emigration. The Benelux countries hoped for increased exports and a greater volume of transit trade.

The great disappointment encountered by the negotiators was the attitude of Great Britain. The Six had invited the Labour government to participate but had been turned down. The main objection on the other side of the Channel was to the proposed supranational character of the organization. The British, in consideration of their unique international position and their ties to the Commonwealth, were simply unwilling to allow control of coal and steel to pass to a supranational authority. Prime Minister Attlee rejected the Schuman Plan in the strongest terms:

> We on this side are not prepared to accept the principle that the most vital economic forces of this country should be handed over to an authority that is utterly undemocratic and is responsible to nobody.[5]

Similarly, the Scandinavian countries, Austria, and Switzerland rejected the supranational features of the proposed treaty. Thus, negotiations remained limited to The Six. The entire process took a little over two years. Italy was the last of the members to ratify, in June 1952. In September of that year the new European Coal and Steel Community, creating a single market for coal and steel for the 160 million people of the six participating states, became a reality.

The structure of ECSC before the fusion of its executive with those of the other European communities in 1967 deserves close analysis. At least one of the community's institutions—the High Authority—possessed powers previously exercised only by national governments and some powers that even those governments did not possess. Hence, a real curtailment of national sovereignty by The Six was involved. The core and executive institution of ECSC, the High Authority, made all important decisions. This body consisted of nine members who held office for six-year terms. Eight of these were chosen by agreement among the six member governments and the ninth was co-opted by the other eight. The High Authority never included more than two members of the same nationality. In practice, ECSC's main organ was composed of two members from France, two from Germany, and one each from Belgium, Italy, Luxembourg, and the Netherlands. The ninth member always came from a country providing only one official. The members of the High Authority did not regard themselves as political spokesmen for their respective governments but as international civil servants of an independent European institution. Decisions of the High Authority were made by majority vote but, so far as the outside world was concerned, the principle of collective responsibility was observed.

The main supranational features of the High Authority were threefold: first, its legal right to bypass the six national governments and to deal with the coal and steel industries of the community directly; second, to make binding decisions in its area of competence; and third, to impose sanctions against violators. In carrying out its functions, the High Authority took the following types of action: first, it could direct the industries through decisions which were legally binding in every respect; second, it could act through recommendations; and finally, it could express opinions. Recommendations and opinions usually carried great weight but engendered no legal compulsion. Sanctions against violators of binding decisions took the form of monetary fines. Over twenty industrial enterprises in the community were thus fined, principally for such infractions as exceeding the price ceiling, breaking price equalization schemes, and forming cartels without approval. The fines were usually light but increased in severity if violations continued. The first president of the High Authority was Jean Monnet. During his tenure, Monnet always emphasized that the federal aspects of ECSC were superior in actual power to those of the member governments. "In a sense, Monnet considered the High Authority as the repository of the European General Will, with the evil governments merely the spokesmen for the selfish particular wills."[6] In brief, the High Authority seemed to be the embodiment of "the European point of view."

It would be erroneous, however, to regard the High Authority as a kind of Platonic Nocturnal Council. There were important checks on its power. The most important of these was the Community's Court of Justice, established under the terms of the ECSC Treaty. This court assumed its functions in January 1955. It was composed of seven judges elected for six years and served as an appellate body of redress against the High Authority when that body was accused of exceeding its jurisdiction. Both private firms and member states could appeal to the court, which in fact became the constitutional arbiter of the Schuman Treaty. As such, the court had the power to annul the High Authority's decisions. The record of the court has been marked by a high degree of objectivity and independence. A large number of appeals came before it. On some occasions the court upheld the High Authority against member governments and private enterprises. In 1955, for example, the court rejected an appeal by the government of the Netherlands against the Authority's decision to maintain ceiling prices for coal and steel. On the other hand, the court upheld appeals by the French and Italian governments and reversed High Authority decisions on the sale of scrap iron.

A second important check on the High Authority's power was exercised by the Council of Ministers, which was composed of the Ministers for Economic Affairs from the six member countries. The council was introduced as a result of pressure by the Benelux governments, which were fearful that the Schuman Community's coercive authority might be too great. The council's task was to harmonize the actions of the High Authority with those of the participating governments. In practice, the council advised the High Authority and made sure that the interests and policies of the member countries were given due weight. It constantly confronted the High Authority with "national" points of view, thus serving as a vital link between national policy and the "European policy" of the Authority.

The High Authority also depended for advice upon a Consultative Committee consisting of producers, workmen, distributors, and consumers from the six member states. Before coming to any important decision, the Authority reviewed any proposed action with the committee. The final institution in the ECSC structure was the Assembly. Since 1958, the Assembly has also served Euratom and the Common Market and is now known as the European Parliament. The 142 members of this body were chosen either by the respective parliaments of the six states or by popular election. The delegates were all parliamentarians and in most cases also attended the sessions of the Assembly of the Council of Europe. At least once a year the Assembly reviewed the action of the High Authority, acting very much like a stockholders' meeting. Unlike a national parliament, it had no legislative power and could not initiate policy. Its one great power was a negative one: it could remove the High Authority by a two-thirds vote of censure. This never actually occurred. In practice, the Assembly attempted to influence the shaping of policies. The most interesting development in this respect was the development of supranational political parties.[7] It was not uncommon for the Socialist members from the six participating states to form a common front against the Assembly's conservatives, including even their own countrymen.

In sum, the High Authority was a supranational organ with considerable power over the coal and steel industries of The Six. It must be remembered, however, that this power applied only to these two sectors of the member countries' economies and that an effective system of checks and balances was written into the treaty. If the High Authority was the motor of ECSC, the Council of Ministers, the Consultative Committee, the Assembly, and the Court of Justice were its brakes. The total structure of ECSC was thus a unique phenomenon, falling somewhere along the continuum between a purely transnational organization and a federal government. Its High Authority certainly had far more power than the central agency of a conventional international organization, though less than is generally yielded to a federal government.

We must now assess the accomplishments of this unique functional organization. Some friends of ECSC feared that the community would atrophy and that its supranational features would not long endure. These fears proved unwarranted. The proposed common market for coal, iron ore, steel, and scrap went into effect in 1953. Apparently unconcerned about its isolation, the High Authority launched a massive program. A timetable was laid down by which all tariffs, quotas, currency restrictions, and discriminations among the coal and steel industries were to be eliminated. The High Authority tried its utmost to ensure fair conditions of competition and to eliminate monopolistic buying and selling practices. The Authority's most difficult task was ''trust-busting''—implementing the anti-cartel provisions of the treaty. Success on this front was limited because of resistance in all the six member states. French and German industrial interests especially complained that the Authority moved too quickly. Actually, on the cartel question, the High Authority's approach was quite cautious. By and large, the High Authority showed itself to be understanding of special problems and to be dedicated to making the most constructive contribution possible to the industries concerned. Investment in the coal and steel industries of The Six was encouraged. The Authority endeavored to raise loans for the purpose. And it even ventured into the social realm through research into occupational diseases, safety problems, and the harmonization of wage levels and fringe benefits.

There was some friction among the five institutions of ECSC but, on the whole, these tensions were useful rather than damaging. The system of checks and balances built into the treaty worked very well. The four ''brakes'' attached to the High Authority effectively prevented the latter from assuming the proportions of a Frankenstein monster. Indeed, ECSC became a unique showcase of functional cooperation.

There was, however, one serious weakness from which ECSC suffered: the absence of Great Britain from its membership. Not that the participating powers did not make a determined effort to secure Britain's membership in the organization. They realized from the beginning that the absence of Britain would constitute a very serious obstacle to the building of a European economic order. And they feared that it might eventually even compel The Six to erect protective barriers against Britain and the other nations closely associated with it in economic matters. Yet both Labour and Conservative governments in Britain firmly rejected participation in any supranational body that would entail a formal surrender of sovereignty. In view of their wider commitments to the Commonwealth, the British considered it ill-advised to wed themselves irrevocably to the European continent through ECSC. The net result of this policy, however, was that during the first decade of ECSC's life, Britain and the Scandinavian countries increasingly became economic "outsiders" to the European Six. At first, Britain did not take ECSC seriously, but by 1960 it found itself left out of something of key economic importance. Hence, to try to remedy the situation, in 1960 Great Britain decided to launch a rival economic order-building scheme of its own, the European Free Trade Association. We shall examine this scheme in its proper context below.

On balance, ECSC demonstrated that the delegation of limited sovereign powers to a supranational body could work in practice. When in 1954 the community was left on its own through the demise of the European Defense Community, it was given a short life expectancy. Yet it not only survived, but encouraged The Six to engage in further supranational experimentation among themselves. If it was possible to internationalize coal and steel, could not the same thing be accomplished in other sectors of the economy? Atomic energy, a new source of power with as yet few vested interests, might lend itself to a similar approach. This idea was to provide the seed for the new European Atomic Energy Community (Euratom). By the late 1950s it seemed to many observers that the "sector" approach to economic integration was the most effective road to international order-building that had yet been devised. The basis for this optimism was the impressive record of the European Coal and Steel Community.

The European Atomic Energy Community was born at a meeting of the foreign ministers of "little Europe" in June 1955. What Jean Monnet of France did for ECSC, Paul-Henri Spaak of Belgium accomplished for Euratom. Determined to "relaunch Europe," Spaak guided the draft treaty through a maze of technical committees during the summer of 1955. From this process there emerged the Spaak Report, which became the basis for the Euratom Treaty. After protracted negotiations, the treaty was signed in Rome in March 1957, and after ratification by the six member states went into effect on January 1, 1958. Therewith another sector of the economies of The Six, atomic energy, was absorbed into a supranational community.

The essential purpose of Euratom was the pooling of the atomic energy resources of The Six for peaceful purposes. The treaty steered clear of the military implications of atomic power. This limitation was inserted at the insistence of France, which wanted its defense program to remain outside of Euratom's control. Hence, Euratom's main responsibilities included the development of nuclear research and the dissemination of technical knowledge; the development of uniform health and safety standards; the construction of nuclear reactors for peaceful purposes; and the development of control and inspection measures to prevent the member states from diverting Euratom-supplied nuclear materials to military purposes. The working capital of Euratom was supplied by the United States, which sold 30,000 kilograms of fissionable materials to the community in 1958. Under the terms of the agreement, Euratom was given property rights over these materials. At the insistence of Euratom officials, the community was also given the right of self-inspection by the United States government.

The structure of Euratom was made similar to that of ECSC. "Supranational" authority was vested in a Euratom Commission, which was composed of five members from different nationalities chosen on the basis of their competence. The commission's powers with respect to atomic energy were even greater than those of the ECSC High Authority in matters of coal and steel. This difference may be attributed to three factors: first, the Euratom Treaty was highly technical, which meant that only nuclear specialists could discuss its implications in a meaningful sense; second, the treaty was narrower in scope than ECSC and did not arouse as much resistance; and, most important, atomic energy was a relatively new field in which neither vested interests nor national habits were deeply rooted. Thus it proved relatively easy to endow the new commission with very considerable powers.

Euratom, like ECSC, was a structure with checks and balances. It was decided to make the ECSC Assembly also the parliamentary body of Euratom. Even more significant, the ECSC Court of Justice also became the "conscience" of the Euratom Commission. The court was given the power to remove the members of the commission from office "for cause." In addition, the court became the constitutional arbiter of the Euratom Treaty and was given the right to pass on the legality of commission decisions if these were challenged by the member states.

Euratom has encountered relatively few serious obstacles. Atomic energy was still so new that the benefits to be derived from common action were greater and more apparent than in the conventional industries of coal and steel. Besides, matters of health and safety could be dealt with more efficiently through a community approach. Second. the establishment of Euratom marked the beginning of the injection of order into the confusing array of functional organizations in Western Europe. The Court of Justice and the Assembly began to serve both ECSC and Euratom. By 1958 the "Community" of The Six had come to represent not only form but ever-growing substance. It was quite clear, indeed, that the ultimate objective of The Six was a United States of Europe via the road of economic order.

The second offspring of the ECSC was the European Economic Community (EEC) or Common Market. This is the most ambitious functionalist scheme of our time. The idea for EEC was contained in the Spaak Report of 1956, which forcefully outlined the advantages of further steps toward economic union among The Six. The draft treaty proposed a twelve- to fifteen-year transitional period during which tariffs and quantitative restrictions for all commodities, including agricultural products, were to be eliminated among the six participating states. A single tariff schedule to be applied to outside countries was to be developed; freedom of movement for workers was also envisaged; exchange policies were to be coordinated; a common transportation policy was to be hammered out; and common provisions for social benefits were contemplated. In brief, EEC was to become an arrangement that went much further than the abolition of tariffs and quotas among The Six, and was to be a halfway house toward complete political union.

Once again, Paul-Henri Spaak guided the project through the delicate formative stages. As in the ECSC, each of the prospective member states saw definite advantages. Only France had serious reservations and wanted to bring its overseas territories into the community. France had great bargaining power because the other members feared its volatile parliament. France was especially afraid of competition in the agricultural field and received numerous concessions in that area. France knew well that its participation was indispensable and used its advantage with consummate political skill. West Germany was eager to join since it perceived an opportunity for increasing markets and investment. Moreover, Chancellor Adenauer was deeply committed to supranationality among The Six, even as an ideal. Italy was most impressed by the goal of freedom of movement for workers which, it hoped, would contribute to the solution of its population and unemployment problems. The Benelux countries hoped for increased exports and transit trade. In spite of this favorable climate, negotiations at various times appeared on the point of breaking down. Finally, the EEC Treaty was signed in March 1957 in Rome and, together with the Euratom Treaty, went into effect on January 1, 1958.

The institutional structure of the Common Market was again patterned on the example of ECSC. A commission composed of nine members chosen on the basis of "general competence" played the role of the High Authority. It was to perform its duties "in the general interest of the Community with complete independence." Its supranational authority largely flowed from the power to fix and amend the timetables for freeing the various "sectors" from trade restrictions. The Assembly of the ECSC also served the Common Market and was given the power to remove members of the EEC Commission through a vote of censure. The ECSC Court of Justice was also made into a court of appeal in the framework of EEC. Thus the three "Communities" of The Six had a common Assembly and a common Court of Justice. In addition, EEC had a Council of Ministers which served as the link between the community and the national governments. An Economic and Social Committee similar in function to the Consultative Committee of the ECSC completed the institutional picture in the early 1960s.

A dramatic structural step toward union was taken in 1967 when the three executive bodies of ECSC, Euratom, and the EEC were fused into a single fourteen-member European Commission. France, West Germany, and Italy supplied three commissioners each, Belgium and the Netherlands two each, and Luxembourg one. With this event, the pattern of a rudimentary federal structure clearly emerged among The Six.

The policy of Britain has gone through a full circle. As we have seen, Britain was unwilling to join any of the three supranational experiments because of its reluctance to give up any of its sovereign power. In 1950 Britain was courted by The Six. But a decade later the wheel had turned full circle. In 1959, fearful of being left behind and outside, Britain began to woo The Six, but now it was the turn of The Six to be reluctant. France had consolidated relations with West Germany and no longer needed Britain to balance German power in the community. President de Gaulle, eager for French grandeur, saw Britain rather than Germany as his chief rival in the race for nuclear greatness; and it was Britain, not Germany, that had delivered arms to Tunisia—a fact that the new French government, which viewed EEC as as much "Eurafrican" as European, could not easily overlook. Nor did the other members of the Common Market show great eagerness to admit Britain to the community.

In self-defense, Britain therefore assumed the leadership of a rival scheme of her own, the European Free Trade Association. Those European countries that were interested in freer trade but also had reservations about supranationality followed the British lead. In December 1959 Britain, Austria, Denmark, Norway, Portugal, Sweden, and Switzerland signed the Convention setting up the new association. Britain, rejected by the Inner Six, took the initiative in forming the Outer Seven. The seven member states contemplated the abolition of tariffs in annual installments by 1970. This was the main goal. Unlike EEC, the European Free Trade Association did not include planning for agricultural products, transport, and labor movements. It was a far more modest venture to be approached through the traditional transnational channels patterned after the OEEC model.

It soon became apparent, however, that EFTA, with its market of 90 million people, was no match for the 170 million inhabitants of The Six. In August 1961 the British government finally decided to apply for membership in the EEC. Negotiations proved difficult because of Britain's Commonwealth and EFTA commitments, special agricultural problems, and the issue of supranationality. While the British application was pending, EEC in January 1962 moved into its second stage of integration, which involved majority voting on numerous important issues. Even while compromises making it possible for Britain to join were weighed, President de Gaulle, to the dismay of the other EEC members, not to mention Britain itself, vetoed British membership in January 1963. The French president, eager to construct a Western Europe in which France would play a leading role, was intent on excluding what he described as the "Anglo-Saxon presence" from the continent. In 1967 yet another British effort to enter the Common Market came to grief on the rock of French resistance.

The turning point for Britain came in 1969. That year, President de Gaulle was defeated in a referendum on a domestic question and was succeeded by Georges Pompidou. In 1970 Edward Heath led the British Conservatives to a resounding victory over the Labour party. Mr. Heath took Britain's case for entry into the Common Market directly to President Pompidou and found the new French president much more receptive than his predecessor. Protracted negotiations ensued between Britain's Geoffrey Rippon and France's foreign minister, Maurice Schumann. Finally, in early 1972, a new chapter in European history was opened when Britain was formally admitted to the Common Market.

With Britain's accession to EEC, EFTA went into eclipse. Ireland, Denmark, and Norway were invited together with Britain, but Norway refused to join. The welcome extended to Britain was generally warm since the French especially perceived Britain as a counterweight to West Germany, whose economic power was of some concern to France and to the Benelux countries. In June 1975, in a national referendum on membership in the Common Market, the British people by a solid majority vote gave their approval to continued membership. Thus, by the mid-1970s the Common Market was a power to be reckoned with, a group of nine nations comprising more than a quarter of a billion people well on their way toward economic union. In 1981 a tenth nation—Greece—was admitted to membership in the Common Market.

In 1984 the Common Market faced a serious crisis. Huge agricultural subsidies had brought the Community to the brink of bankruptcy. Moreover, Britain demanded a $1.5 billion rebate on its contribution to the Community's budget, which the continental members were unwilling to grant. Once again, customs officials harassed truckers at borders and petty squabbles over relatively insignificant amounts obscured the larger vision of European unity. Nonetheless, in 1985, Spain and Portugal were admitted to the EEC, raising the Community's membership to twelve. Pessimists still complained about "squalid squabbles over money," but optimists continued to adhere to the ultimate vision of a United States of Europe.

The European Community had a watershed year in 1988. Fearful of being left behind in economic development by the United States and Japan, the Europeans set themselves an ambitious deadline: the lifting of all economic barriers by 1992, in short, a Europe without frontiers. "The uniting of Europe will come," Willy de Clerq, the Community's commissioner of External Relations, announced in July 1988, "it is written in the stars."[8]

Even if one discounts the commissioner's hyperbole, the practical achievements of the twelve EEC nations have been impressive. Many economic obstacles have been removed since 1988. As a step toward permitting the free flow of people, for example, the twelve members approved a plan for the mutual recognition of university degrees so that a doctor trained in Portugal could now work in Denmark. The Community also agreed to end restrictions on the movement of capital and made rapid progress on the removal of border posts so that people could drive from Munich to Malaga, for example, without stopping at customs.

Needless to say, much ambivalence remains about the creation of a "Europe without frontiers." German unions, for example, worry about losing jobs to countries such as Spain and Portugal where wages are lower. Environmentalists everywhere worry that the drive to harmonize conflicting national standards may result in watered-down pollution rules. Hence, progress toward economic union takes place in fits and starts.

On balance, however, the drive toward the economic unity of Europe apparently will continue for both profound and trivial reasons. In the profound category, most Europeans want to be seen as equals by the superpowers and by Japan. Such equality may be difficult to achieve by twelve squabbling economic entities, but a United Europe of 320 million people might be a different story. In the trivial category, the lack of a single European currency has meant, for example, that a traveler who started with $100 and changed it in each country of the Community would end up with a mere $47 because of money-changers' fees.

Even if economic unity is in fact achieved by 1992, the twelve members of the EEC will are not likely to make a quantum leap from economic to political integration. A United States of Europe, in short, is not likely to emerge in this century. Margaret Thatcher, for example, has steadfastly opposed such a plan. "They say, let's have a European Union," she exclaimed in 1988. "I say, I can't see any of you dissolving your own countries into a United States of Europe. When I go to Europe, I am answerable to my own Parliament and therefore to my own people. They are proud of being British and so am I."⁹ In other words, Britain is not in Europe. One travels *to* Europe *from* Britain. It is not likely that this sort of national pride will permit an early merger of the twelve into a single European superpower.

Yet, a considerable number of "Eurocrats" still believe that Europe will emulate the United States and ultimately move from an economic to a larger "more perfect" union. One must remember, of course, that the Americans had an easier task: They shared a common past and a common language. Yet even with these advantages, union was difficult to achieve, as the Civil War so painfully demonstrated. In Europe, different languages and different national traditions will surely remain. But, the rights to live, work, and travel freely across Europe will probably prevail before the end of the century. Perhaps even a common currency may emerge by then. Given the wars that Europeans have fought among themselves during the past few centuries, it is amazing how much they have achieved since the Treaty of Rome was signed less than half a century ago. In historical perspective, no doubt, Europe's progress toward unity has been a most significant accomplishment.

Despite the serious, growing pains described above, the Western European economic integration movement has already had profound effects upon the rest of the world. The reaction in the United States has been ambivalent. On the one hand, the United States welcomes a strong and united Europe as a more dependable ally in the struggle against communism; but on the other, the United States confronts real economic power on the other side of the Atlantic, which can no longer be dealt with lightly and which may force major reevaluations of economic policy. The Soviet Union has not been able to ignore the Common Market either. Its answer to the Common Market has been COMECON, an effort to forge a common economic policy for the Eastern bloc countries. COMECON, however, has proved to be no match for the Common Market's economic power. Most Eastern European countries, as well as the Soviet Union itself, are already trading with the EEC. China, perceiving the Common Market as an irritant to the Soviet Union, has expressed its approval. And even the more remote countries in the developing parts of the world have had to pay attention to this bold new experiment now taking place in Western Europe.

A word should be said here about another experiment in integration: that between Canada and the United States. In November 1988, the Canadian electorate approved a free-trade agreement with the United States under which the two nations would pursue a goal of gradual integration of their economies. Given the enormous economic power of the two partners, it would not be surprising if the US-Canadian agreement might not have even more far-reaching ultimate consequences than its Western European counterpart.

We are now ready for a more general evaluation of functionalism as a technique for the building of economic order. On a global scale, as we have seen, the functional approach is still in its infancy. But the efforts undertaken by the World Bank and its affiliates to bridge the gulf between the world's rich and poor have been commendable. Similarly, the UN's global approach to food, resources, environment, and population has demonstrated a nascent consciousness of the world's economic interdependence. And the evidence suggests that the order-building potential of most of the world's proliferating multinational enterprises may outweigh their potential for conflict and disruption.

Our Western European case study in functional order-building on a regional basis affords some interesting insights. For one thing, supranationality per se is not necessarily a precondition for an organization's success. The Organization for European Economic Cooperation was a singularly successful venture although it did not embody any supranational features. What seems to determine an organization's operational effectiveness is whether it has a concrete and tangible job to do. If it does, institutional gadgetry becomes more or less irrelevant. A vague desire for cooperation without clearly defined goals will lead to atrophy; the Council of Europe is a case in point. What distinguishes all the regional economic organizations of Europe, whether supranational or not, is the fact that they have clearly defined operational programs. This was true especially of the three "Communities" of The Six and certainly continues to be true of the Common Market of twelve since the accession of Britain. The integration process is also furthered by the fact that all participants have expectations of concrete economic rewards. The nature of these expectations differs from state to state, but all members hope to derive considerable benefits in one form or another.

The increasing complexity of the European organizational picture cries out for a measure of coordination. It is unlikely that an overall scheme or Grand Design will be acceptable to all the states of Western Europe in the immediate future. The ultimate objective of some Western European states is nothing less than a United States of Europe. This aim is not yet shared by others, especially Britain and France. Coordination will probably have to proceed within each of the two camps. Some progress has been made. Already, the European Community prides itself on having a common Assembly, a common Court of Justice, and a common Executive. These may be the forerunners of a European federal system.

Perhaps the most encouraging by-product of functional experimentation in Western Europe has been the development of a "European outlook." The constant process of consultation and the complexity of international machinery have persuaded most Western European statesmen to consider national policy decisions in the broadest possible context. In 1979, for example, the members of the Common Market permitted the creation of a European Parliament through direct elections. By the 1980s they pursued coordinated agricultural policies and common external economic relations. Despite occasional setbacks such as Prime Minister Margaret Thatcher's demand in 1984 that Britain's contribution to the funding of EEC should be reduced, the Common Market has become an established fact of European economic life.

In the 1960s the Common Market had six members. In the 1970s it had nine; in 1981 the admission of Greece brought the membership to ten; the admission of Spain and Portugal in 1985 doubled the Community's original membership. And in 1988, Turkey was knocking at the door and applying for inclusion.

Size, of course, creates new tensions. The Nine had a harder time agreeing than The Six. Twelve nations make consensus even harder to achieve. But the Common Market has, over a bumpy road, overcome far more serious strains. The European communities may well be the early forerunners of the first political system transcending the sovereign nation-state since Machiavelli wrote *The Prince* almost 500 years ago.

THE WORLD ENERGY FUTURE

The entire world today stands at the edge of an awesome watershed: the coming energy transition. For decades the rich industrial countries depended on cheap oil as their major energy resource. Most poor developing countries, until recently, eagerly looked forward to their own entry into the petroleum era. But the Arab oil embargo of 1973–1974, the Iranian revolution, and the war between Iraq and Iran rudely reminded the industrial countries of their dependency and the poor countries of their poverty. The price of oil rose from $2 a barrel in 1960 to $40 in 1980. Even though oil prices declined substantially by the late 1980s, the long-term outlook is still disturbing. The generation of my students may be the last of the petroleum era. What will their children and grandchildren use as *their* major energy resource? How will they prepare for the transition? Or will they say, with the last of the French monarchs, "Après nous, le déluge"? That is the real challenge of the energy future.

Let us look at the inventory. The United States produces approximately 10 percent of the world's petroleum. Regrettably, America's oil is now almost certainly half gone. Most experts agree that the rate of extraction will decline sharply after 1990, with total depletion a real prospect by around 2020. The Middle East has roughly 30 percent of the world's oil, of which one-tenth has been consumed. The Soviet Union has 25 percent, of which one-tenth has been used up. Africa has about 10 percent, most of which is still in the ground. Latin America is believed to have 10 percent, of which one-fifth has been consumed, and Western Europe produces less than 5 percent. The remaining 10 percent is distributed throughout other parts of the world. The trilateral nations—the United States, Western Europe, and Japan—are always in danger of an oil squeeze. Most other areas still have ample oil to meet their immediate requirements. But the oil-short nations encompass most of the world's industrial base and all import huge amounts of oil from the oil-rich regions. Even if one assumes a relatively peaceful Middle East—a dubious assumption at best in the light of events in Iran and Iraq—the prospects are bleak. It is highly probable that the world will have reached the end of its oil supplies sometime before the year 2050. What, then, are the alternatives as we enter the twilight of an era?

Coal has been the world's most plentiful fossil fuel and has been used for at least two thousand years. There is no shortage of coal, yet it is not likely that coal will ever replace petroleum. At best, it will be a transitional source of energy. There are several compelling reasons for this. In the first place, coal is very unevenly distributed geographically. The Soviet Union, the United States, and China—in that order—have 90 percent of the world's coal resources, with the Soviet Union having nearly twice those of the United States and the United States having about three times those of China. This uneven distribution may be politically significant. The Soviet Union, for example, has a much higher percentage of the world's coal than the Middle East has of the world's oil. Second, even though world coal resources seem adequate for at least two hundred years, only a portion of these resources is "recoverable." In an average mine, only about half of the coal is actually mined, with the rest being left standing as "pillars." Third, as everyone knows, coal mining is an unpleasant, unhealthy, and often dangerous occupation. And finally, a conversion to coal as a major energy resource would create formidable environmental problems. Specifically, it would release huge amounts of carbon dioxide into the atmosphere, which might raise the earth's temperature to a dangerous level. Recent droughts and other climatic changes all over the world have already served as serious warnings. Moreover, some scientists have warned that soot might blanket the Northern Hemisphere, shield the sun, and thus usher in a new ice age. Either way, the consequences of a new coal era might prove catastrophic. Coal will never replace petroleum.

Many countries have long nurtured the hope that nuclear power would reduce their dependence on oil and perhaps even replace it altogether. As early as 1960, for example, the U.S. Air Force invested over $1 billion in an attempt to build a nuclear-powered airplane. Some critics pointed out that the plane would be too heavy and cumbersome to be militarily useful. Others feared that radioactive debris would be scattered all over the countryside if the plane should crash. In 1962 President Kennedy finally ordered the project scrapped. This episode foreshadowed some of the dilemmas posed by nuclear power.

The dream of replacing oil with atomic energy seems to be fading fast. In the first place, nuclear power is not cheap. Research and development as well as capital construction costs are formidable. The hope for "electricity too cheap to meter" has proved to be unfounded. Second, the dangers of converting to a nuclear-powered world are legion. Problems of radiation, radioactive waste, and reactor safety loom large. Even worse, it is very difficult to divorce the peaceful from the warlike atom, as the history of the International Atomic Energy Agency has amply shown. India's explosion of a "peaceful bomb" in 1974 is another compelling example of this danger. The nuclear nonproliferation treaty does not cope adequately with these perils. Moreover, in a nuclear world, terrorists and criminals would have far more ready access to nuclear bombs, with potentially disastrous consequences for society. Perhaps the only way to deal with these dangers would be to centralize far more authority in the hands of governments. Such a course of action, obviously, would not be very desirable. Optimists have always regarded a nuclear world as a forward step. But if humanity today stands at the edge of an abyss, a step forward is not necessarily progress.

More recently, some energy experts have turned to the sun for new hope. One scholar, for example, maintains that, by the year 2000, the sun's inexhaustible energy could provide 40 percent of the global energy budget, by furnishing heat and electricity.[10] Wind and water could also be tapped more efficiently. Solar energy, this advocate declares, would be clean, cheap, safe, and self-sustaining.

While the prospect of a solar-powered world is seductively attractive, it is not likely to be translated into reality in the near future. The sun, despite its enormous heat, is not very efficient as an energy provider. Solar power involves using a source which has a temperature of 6,000 degrees centigrade to heat water to less than 100 degrees. The almost boundless potential of the sun, while theoretically available to us, simply still eludes us in practical commercial terms. Solar energy is indeed a hope, but it is a rather distant hope.

A more hopeful prospect may be natural gas. Huge supplies of natural gas are available for industrial use in the United States and Canada. Some of the excess could be stored as a reserve in nonproductive wells. There are industries that now burn oil that could convert to gas without much difficulty. The search for new synthetic fuels, while expensive, must also not be abandoned. It may take an imaginative combination of the old and of the new.

Perhaps our best chance to get through the transition period without major turbulence may lie in conservation. A barrel of oil saved may be as useful as a barrel produced—perhaps even better in some respects. In view of the fact that the waste of energy throughout the industrialized world is enormous, conservation has vast possibilities. More than half of the current U.S. energy budget is waste. For the next quarter of a century, the United States could meet all its new energy needs simply by improving the efficiency of existing uses. One must bear in mind here a crucial distinction between curtailment and conservation. Curtailment means a cold, dark house; conservation means a well-insulated house with an efficient heating system. Gas-guzzling cars might have to give way for good to less conspicuous, more energy-efficient models. Small may truly have to be beautiful. A vigorous conservation program might see the world through the coming energy transition without becoming hooked on hazardous technologies or unreliable sources of supply.

The search for new sources of energy will be painful and competitive. But there is a strangely positive side to it as well. We shall have to struggle for our survival. Hence, there is bound to be a great deal of international cooperation. The long-term demands for energy are so gigantic and the economic and political linkages among nations are so strong that, as a practical matter, competition may very well give way to cooperation in conservation, research, development, and discovery. The energy transition will not respect national boundaries or sovereignties. Any contribution to the global energy supply is bound to be of general benefit. For essentially selfish reasons, nation-states will be obliged to wish each other well. The quest for clear air and clean water will only emphasize this truth.

In 1492 Imperial Spain financed the explorations of Christopher Columbus in the New World. During the next one hundred years, the flow of precious metals from the New World made Spain one of the dominant states of Europe. When Philip III assumed the throne in 1598, he was convinced that the glory of Spain would last forever. What he did not know, however, was that the flow of gold and silver had already peaked. During the next century, it declined precipitously. This unanticipated decline brought the Spanish Empire to its knees. Spain had had its golden moment in the sun.

The Spanish experience may hold a special meaning for our modern world. The industrial nations were shaped by the availability of cheap oil at least as much as Spain was by the flow of gold and silver.[11] But unlike Spain, we can see the end ahead, and can choose to begin a meaningful transition. Unless we do so, we may share the fate of Spain. Once again, as so often in the past, the challenge is plain: we shall have to learn to change *before* we are shaken and shattered into doing so. Hopefully, we shall not have to learn again through trauma and catastrophe.

THE COMING ENVIRONMENTAL CRISIS

The paramount international challenge of the 1990s may well be the need once again to save the planet from our own heedlessness. But this time the threat may not stem from nuclear holocaust but from the total breakdown of our natural environment, an environment we have for far too long taken for granted.

Consider the events of 1988 alone. During that summer, a lot of things went wrong. An unnerving global heat wave made scientists take the planet's temperature. Quite a few concluded that it was running a fever and heating up dangerously. On beaches in the United States, syringes replaced seashells. The massive destruction of forests in India and Nepal caused massive flooding in

Bangladesh. Firefighters in Yellowstone Park stood by helplessly as they watched the worst forest fire in a century. Fish in US coastal waters were diagnosed as riddled with cancerous tumors caused by the dumping of toxic wastes. The Soviet Union did not do much better. There, sturgeon were infected by toxic wastes, threatening the caviar supply. Stated bluntly, people have made their habitat into a garbage dump for decades. At long last, the earth is striking back.

The most immediate and pressing of these problems probably is the greenhouse effect. The industrial age has been fueled by the burning of coal, wood, and oil, which spew wastes—most notably carbon dioxide—into the sky. This thickens the layer of atmospheric gases that traps heat from the sun and keeps the earth warm. This greenhouse effect is expected to bring about more changes more quickly than any other climatic event in the earth's history. Scientists warn that the changes cannot be stopped, only slowed. But the time is short. According to Robert Dickinson, a senior scientist at the National Center for Atmospheric Research: "We don't have 100 years; we have ten or twenty at most."[12]

If the warming is not slowed, scientists predict, the greenhouse effect will melt enough of the polar ice caps to threaten the water supply of New York City and the very existence of New Orleans within two to three decades. And areas that are now productive farmlands will become parched and arid dustbowls.

The second major environmental crisis involved the earth's thinning ozone layer, caused mainly by the production of chlorofluorocarbons, chemical carbons that can be found in styrofoam cups and fast-food containers and in the freon used in air conditioners. These chemicals float up into the stratosphere and break down the layer of ozone gas which serves as a shield against the sun's harmful ultraviolet radiation. The disruption of the ozone layer could have devastating effects on plant growth and photosynthesis. This, in turn, could upset the very foundations of the food chain. After all, plants and trees, as producers of oxygen, are the very lungs of the planet.

Finally, there are the polluted oceans. Not only were syringes with infected blood found on beaches, but it is virtually impossible today to sail the seas without encountering floating reminders of human recklessness: empty six-packs, plastic containers of every shape and form, and refuse beyond description. Fish die or choke to death from ingesting this refuse, plant life is impaired, and the ocean's ecological balance is disrupted. The "shining sea" has become an anachronism, because we have made the sea a garbage dump.

These terrible and imminent dangers also present the glimmer of a great opportunity: The planet's problems could become so critical that they might make military needs and budget deficits seem almost trivial. In short, the environmental crisis might force a new spirit of global cooperation that could strengthen the fabric of international order. Clearly no nation can tackle these problems alone. Only a truly global effort will get the job done.

The industrial nations will have to burn less coal and oil. Industrializing nations such as China will have to be discouraged from burning fossil fuels. Alternatives including nuclear and solar energy will have to be taken seriously. The production of chlorofluorocarbons will have to be stopped altogether. Consciousness about the need to preserve the ozone layer will have to be raised everywhere. President Reagan's remark made in 1980—that trees were responsible for most pollution—betrayed an abysmal ignorance of the facts and pointed to the need for more vigorous environmental education in most nations' schools. Deforestation must be stopped. Perhaps a plan might be encouraged whereby the debts of some Third World countries might be swapped for their agreement to grow tropical forests. Reforestation will have to be encouraged elsewhere as well to help cleanse the atmosphere of carbon dioxide. Ocean and beach pollution must be stopped as well and must be considered as a serious crime everywhere. Plastics will have to be replaced with "biodegradable" substances as soon as possible. Otherwise, waste will float in the oceans forever.

The global community has barely begun to take up the challenge. In October 1987, under the auspices of the UN Environment Program, a treaty to restrict chemicals that damage the earth's ozone layer was signed in Montreal by thirty-three nations including the United States and the Soviet Union. Under this "Montreal Protocol," the signatories agreed to reduce the production of chlorofluorocarbons by 20 percent by 1993, and by an additional 30 percent by 1998. Unfortunately, this time schedule seemed far too slow when a group of scientists called together by the U.S. National Aeronautics and Space Administration (NASA) concluded in 1988 that ozone depletion was progressing at a rate three times their original estimates. The group sounded an ominous warning:

> If current estimates of the ozone threat are confirmed, the next step should be a new international agreement to tighten the CFC production target. An 85 percent reduction is needed simply to prevent the ozone hole from getting any worse; a 95 percent reduction would let it heal over decades. The Montreal Treaty is a fine first step if a second will follow quickly.[13]

The UN Environment Program has also sounded the alarm bell about the greenhouse effect and ocean pollution. Most scientists now agree that the "outer limits" have been reached and that any additional stress on climate or oceans would cause permanent damage to occur. In the words of Michael Oppenheimer, of the Environmental Defense Fund, "If we don't move fast there will be so much climate warming that our policy options will be narrowed in the future."[14] Yet, no concrete steps have as yet been taken on these issues by the United Nations or other international agencies. Once again, it may take an acute crisis to trigger concerted action.

The challenge is plain enough. Our generation has taken air and water for granted and squandered these priceless resources recklessly. The next generation will not have that luxury and will have to engage in a determined effort to save its habitat and, hence, the future. And that effort will have to be worldwide, for humanity will survive as one or not at all.

REFERENCES

1 United Nations Economic and Social Council, *The Impact of Multinational Corporations on Development and on International Relations,* E/5500/Rev. 1, 1974.
2 Joseph S. Nye, Jr., "Multinational Corporations in World Politics," *Foreign Affairs,* October 1974, p. 153.
3 *Ibid.,* p. 58.
4 *Ibid.,* p. 53.
5 *Hansard,* June 27, 1950.
6 Ernst B. Haas, *The Uniting of Europe.* Stanford, Calif.: Stanford University Press, 1959, p. 456.
7 *Ibid.,* Chap. 11.
8 *The New York Times,* July 31, 1988.
9 *Ibid.*
10 Denis Hayes, *Rays of Hope.* New York: Norton, 1977, p. 155.
11 *Ibid.,* p. 47.
12 *Time Magazine,* September 19, 1988.
13 *The New York Times,* March 24, 1988.
14 United Nations Association of the United States. *Issues before the 43rd General Assembly of the United Nations.* Lexington, Mass: Lexington Books, 1989, p. 120.

SELECTED BIBLIOGRAPHY

DeVries, Barend A. *Remaking the World Bank.* Cabin John, Md: Seven Locks Press, 1987. A longtime member of the World Bank's staff offers a most informative analysis of the Bank's practices as well as a series of thoughtful practical recommendations for the future.

Dell, Edmund. *The Politics of Economic Interdependence.* New York: St. Martin's 1987. A witty and lively critique of free trade by a distinguished British parliamentarian.

Funabashi, Yoichi. *Managing the Dollar: From the Plaza to the Louvre.* Washington, DC: Institute for International Economics, 1988. A Japanese journalist shows how the leading Western governments manipulated the dollar's value between 1985 and 1987. A first-rate account.

Gardner, Richard N. "Practical Internationalism," *Foreign Affairs,* Spring 1988. A cogent argument for promoting the national interests of the United States through multilateral diplomacy and international organizations.

Kolko, Joyce. *Restructuring the World Economy.* New York: Pantheon, 1988. A Marxist interpretation of the world economy's ills.

Panic, M. *National Management of the International Economy.* New York: St. Martin's, 1988. "Growing global interdependence turns national problems into international problems—yet each country is left to deal with them in isolation, as best it can." The author, a British economist of Yugoslav origin, explores this paradox in an excellent, clearly written book.

Taylor, Paul. *The Limits of European Integration.* New York: Columbia University, 1983. The sober assessment which anyone interested in the "Europe 1992" project would be well advised to ponder.

PART FOUR

TOWARD A THEORY OF INTERNATIONAL RELATIONS

PERCEPTION AND REALITY IN WORLD POLITICS

Behold! human beings living in a sort of underground den, which has a mouth open toward the light and reaching all across the den; they have been here from their childhood, and have their legs and necks chained so that they cannot move, and can only see before them; for the chains are arranged in such a manner as to prevent them from turning round their heads. At a distance above and behind them the light of a fire is blazing, and between the fire and the prisoners there is a raised way; and you will see, if you look, a low wall built along the way, like the screen which marionette players have before them, over which they show the puppets.

I see, he said.

And do you see, I said, men passing along the wall carrying vessels, which appear over the wall; also figures of men and animals, made of wood and stone and various materials; and some of the prisoners, as you would expect, are talking, and some of them are silent?

This is a strange image, he said, and they are strange prisoners. Like ourselves, I replied; and they only see their shadows, or the shadows of one another, which the fire throws on the opposite wall of the cave?

True, he said: how could they see anything but the shadows if they were never allowed to move their heads?

And of the objects which are being carried in like manner they would see only the shadows?

Yes, he said.

And if they were able to talk with one another, would they not suppose that they were naming what was actually before them?

Very true.

And suppose further that the prison had an echo which came from the other side, would they not be sure to fancy when one of the passers-by spoke that the voice which they heard came from the passing shadow?

No question, he replied.
To them, I said, the truth would be literally nothing but the shadows of the images.
That is certain.

Plato, "Allegory of the Cave," *Republic,* VII

This book has attempted to present an analysis of international relations in our time. In so doing, we have dealt with a wide range of phenomena. For the purpose of ordering this body of material, we have employed two key concepts. First, and very broadly, we have analyzed world politics in terms of the ever-present tension between the struggle for power and the struggle for order among nations. We have seen that these two struggles are at many points closely interwoven. Indeed, the very soil which produces struggles for power also provides the nourishment for new institutions of order. Thus, World War I brought forth the League of Nations and World War II the United Nations. The Suez crisis of 1956 and the Congo crisis of 1960 led to the creation of unprecedented UN peace forces. The Cuban missile crisis of 1962 ushered in a bevy of arms control agreements. And the excesses of nationalism in Germany and Italy led to the dawn of European unity. Similarly, every struggle for order among nations also involves some kind of power struggle. Witness the United Nations, the most imaginative instrument for order-building thus far devised, yet at the same time the arena for some of the most stubborn vying for power in history. The evidence suggests that self-styled realists and idealists are both wrong: power alone is no reliable guide through the landscape of international politics, nor is the quest for order. The relationship between power and order in world politics is inherently dialectical in nature. Fundamentally, therefore, these two pervasive struggles must be recognized as two sides of a single coin.

Within this broad and general conceptual framework, we have introduced a specific substantive theme as our second key concept: the linkage between the triangular East-West struggle involving China, Russia, and the United States, and the struggle between North and South, the rich and the poor. The pattern of interdependence between these two great conflicts of our time is woven into the entire fabric of contemporary international relations. The struggle for power and order may be seen as the essence of international relations everywhere and always. The East-West struggle and the struggle between the rich and the poor provide their particular form of expression here and now.

To these two organizing concepts which deal with the substance of world politics we may now add a third, which concerns a further vital dimension of international relations: *the frequent and highly significant differences between the way nations perceive one another and the way they really are.* For the titanic struggles among the nations of our time are not only waged on the basis of objective realities. They are also fought out in the realm of imagery and illusion. It is the thesis of this concluding chapter that there are often great gaps between *perception* and *reality* in world politics and that these integrally affect all aspects of international relations, deeply exacerbating the international struggle for power and seriously slowing down the international struggle for order.

The assumption underlying this thesis is that to some degree, at least, international relations are what people think they are; or, to put it in other words, that, under certain conditions, people respond not to realities but to fiction that they have themselves created. To say that there are no objective problems in world politics would be gross exaggeration. But the stage of world politics lends itself all too easily to the development of wide gaps between what that reality is and the way it is perceived. And because of this fact, perception probably plays as important a role in international relations as does objective reality itself.

Before we can analyze the significance of perception in international relations, we must define it and search out its origins. Perception in international relations may be defined as the total cognitive view a nation holds of itself and of others in the world. As such, it is a most complex phenomenon and includes both reality and distortion. There is little doubt that many nations much of the time see themselves and others the way they really are; but it is equally certain that many nations much of the time see themselves and others in stereotyped one-dimensional ways. Nationalism and ideology contribute much to seeing other nations as "bad" and one's own as spotless. Stereotyped images on one side elicit similar ones on another, often compounding the distortion. Even worse, if one believes a stereotype long enough it may become reality by setting in motion the mechanism of the self-fulfilling prophecy. Thus, if a nation believes that another is its implacable enemy and reiterates this often enough, making it the guideline of its national policy, it will eventually be right.

Our first task, then, is to isolate those factors in a nation's overall perception that are distorted; to extrapolate from the composite picture of reality and illusion the elements of illusion. Here we encounter a major difficulty. Throughout this book, we have referred to nations as if they were cohesive entities speaking with a single voice on the world scene: "The United States agreed," "the Soviet Union feared," "India proposed." Such statements, while unavoidable in an analysis of international relations, tell only part of the story. The next crucial question we must ask ourselves is *who* in the United States agreed, *who* in the Soviet Union feared, and *who* in India proposed. Put differently, *who* is it that speaks for nations in world politics? To answer this question, we must analyze the nature of public opinion and its impact on a nation's decision-making process in international relations. Then, we must attempt to differentiate between those decision makers and "influencers" who tend to perceive the outside world in terms of preconceived images and stereotypes and those who evaluate their environment more in accordance with objective reality.

It would, of course, be folly to attempt a generalized answer that would be true for all nations. Fortunately, excellent studies have been made of the impact of public opinion and of stereotypes on the foreign policy-making process of three different types of nations. Walter Lippmann's study, *Public Opinion,* and Gabriel Almond's *The American People and Foreign Policy* are both classics dealing with the American scene.[1] Alex Inkeles' *Public Opinion in Soviet Russia* gives us a revealing picture of that aspect of the Soviet Union.[2] And Gabriel Almond and James S. Coleman have edited and contributed to a study on *Politics of the Developing Areas* which provides many valuable insights into the public opinion and decision-making process of the emergent nations.[3] A comparative analysis of these studies yields much valuable information on the role of distorted perception in world politics.

It was Walter Lippmann who first subjected perception in American politics to a scrupulous analysis. In his trailblazing study, he pointed out that, for most people, "the world they have to deal with politically is out of reach, out of sight, out of mind."[4] Hence, the only reaction they can have to an event that they can neither reach, see, nor care about is one conditioned by their mental predisposition toward that event. Almond further refined this theme and applied it more specifically to Americans' reactions to matters of foreign policy. He discovered that only a small segment of the American public—the elite—is able to grasp the complex realities of international relations. This group consists largely of interest groups, professional organizations, and government officials. A second layer of American public opinion he identified as the "attentive public," those people who, while not themselves experts, continuously expose themselves to information on matters of world politics. The vast majority of Americans, however, Almond discovered, respond to matters of foreign policy largely on the basis of mood. They tend to exhaust their emotional and intellectual energies in private pursuits and thus approach problems of world politics with a perfunctory attitude. Moreover, they feel that "they cannot affect foreign policy anyway," and that, therefore, a serious investment of time and energy is not worthwhile. As a result, this "mass public" tends to respond to the complex reality of world politics with simplified and frequently distorted images. It has replaced the real environment with a "pseudo-environment" largely compounded of prejudices and stereotypes.

As a result of these observations, it follows that the mass public is to some extent responsible for distorted American perceptions of world politics. Most scholars feel that this mass public exerts a great deal of influence through its electoral powers. Lippmann argues, however, that such control, to be beneficial, must emanate from a broadly educated public. If the mass public continues to perceive public policy in terms of "pictures in their heads," Lippmann sees the coming of a functional derangement between the mass of the people and the government in which "the people will have acquired power which they are incapable of exercising, and the governments they elect will have lost power which they must recover if they are to govern."[5] Carl J. Friedrich, on the other hand, has greater faith than Lippmann in the good political sense of the common man.[6] Be that as it may, it is clear that as a result of mass public influence, *some* degree of distortion enters the American perception of world politics, and that when "the United States speaks" in world affairs, its position is therefore to *some* degree colored by images which depart from reality.

It is subject to serious doubt, however, whether Lippmann and Almond are justified in locating the source of distortion primarily in the mass public. The record of American foreign policy suggests the possibility that distortions may also originate in the elite. The relationship between the mass public and the elite seems to be a highly complex one. At times the interaction between the two may further compound distortions. At other times, the elite may serve as a corrective and educate the mass public. But on some occasions, and this is no less important, the mass public may have a sounder perception than the elite. It was the policy elite surrounding the US President in 1961, for example, not the mass public, that misperceived the situation in Cuba that in turn led to the fiasco of the Bay of Pigs. Nor did the "best and the brightest" in the US foreign policy establishment of the 1960s and 1970s have a monopoly of wisdom in Vietnam. Many students with far less formal education perceived the situation much more clearly and fought hard to avert a national disaster. The same observation may be made about US foreign policy toward Iran and Nicaragua during the 1980s. At any rate, the gaps between perception and reality that exist in the US view of world politics are not readily attributable to any one segment of the US people.

Studies of public opinion in Soviet Russia also suggest great distortions in the Soviet perception of world politics, although Mikhail Gorbachev's commitment to *glasnost* has no doubt served as a remarkable correction recently. As we have seen in an earlier chapter, Communist ideology to some degree colors the lenses through which the Soviet regime perceives the world. These lenses are distributed to the mass public in the Soviet Union through cadres of party members who do their best to ensure that people will perceive world politics through the reddish prism of Communist ideology. Ideology thus provides a kind of built-in distortion. As Inkeles points out in a striking analogy, this effort is only partially successful:

> The figure most apt for describing the state of Soviet public opinion is that of a forest fire. On the broad peripheral front the blaze rages in full intensity. Here is found a thin line of convinced and confirmed Communists. But behind this line comes a much larger area, which has already been swept by the flames and which now boasts only glowing embers. This is the line of the half-believers, which includes some party members as well as the nonparty supporters of the regime. And beyond that there lies a still broader sweep of the burned-over timber, in which here and there a spark still glows but which is predominantly cold, ashen, and gray. The work of mass persuasion is the wind which fans this blaze. But like the wind in the forest fire, it not only spreads the flames but hastens the burning, and behind the line of flames and embers it can only stir up little swirls and eddies of ash.[7]

Thus the Soviet Union, too, is bound to perceive world politics to some extent in terms of distorted images and stereotypes. Since these are rooted primarily in Communist ideology, the width of the gap between perception and reality in Soviet foreign policy is determined by the degree to which the Soviet leaders themselves uncritically accept the doctrine with which they have so relentlessly proselytized the rest of the world. With the advent of the Gorbachev era, however, at long last, ideology may take a backseat to reality. The more honest attitude toward the horrors of the Stalin era recently prevailing in the Soviet Union is an encouraging case in point. The sunlight of truth is no longer excluded.

It is an open question to what extent personal contact between national leaders and peoples reduces the power of distorted imagery. It is difficult to say whether Nikita Khrushchev's visit to America in 1959 confirmed or reduced whatever false perceptions he might have had of the United States. The visit was probably too brief to make a deep impression either way. Similarly, one cannot say with certitude whether President Nixon's visits to China and to the Soviet Union in 1972 displaced clichés about communism that he might have believed with more realistic perceptions of Chinese and Soviet life. Probably the visits helped to decontaminate the minds of American, Soviet, and Chinese leaders of shopworn slogans at least to some extent since they were all vitally interested in establishing new relationships with one another, and thus were more responsive to reality. It seems clear, however, that Mikhail Gorbachev's visit to Washington in 1987 and Ronald Reagan's trip to Moscow in 1988 had beneficial effects. The two men related to one another less in terms of stereotypes and more as human beings. The result was the first genuine disarmament treaty since World War II.

The Third World nations present yet a third pattern of the impact of public opinion on the foreign policy-making process. As several expert students of the developing nations have pointed out, there is a minimum of contact between the government elite and the mass public in most of the new nations:

> There exists a wide gap between the traditional mass and the essentially modern subsociety of the Westernized elite. The latter controls the central structures of government and essays to speak and act for the society as a whole. This elite subsociety is the main locus of political activity and of change in the society at large.[8]

There are exceptions to this pattern, of course. India, for example, is a democracy in which there exists an intimate connection between public opinion and the government elite. But in most cases, the new nations have evolved authoritarian forms of government in which a high degree of alienation between the mass public and the government is typical. Hence, the pattern differs from that of the United States, since, in the developing nations, the mass public is, politically speaking, relatively powerless. It also differs from the Soviet and Chinese models since the leadership, as a general rule, does not make a concerted attempt to indoctrinate the population with an ideology. Iran under the Ayatollah Khomeini was a striking exception to this rule.

The attitudes of most Third World leaders are deeply colored by their colonial past. In their case, the memory of colonialism persists much longer than the fact. Once again, therefore, some distortion does result. To put it as precisely as possible, the degree of divergence between perception and reality in the new nations' view of world politics is determined by the degree to which the memory of colonialism outlives the reality. In Iran, for example, the bitter memories of the late pro-American Shah prevented an accurate perception of the United States, and, in the Arab Middle East, Israel is widely perceived as the modern successor to Western colonial rule.

Now that we have at least a tentative insight into the nature of public opinion and its effect on a nation's perception of world politics, we may proceed to an analysis of some of the major gaps between perception and reality in present-day world politics.

The two main political power struggles of our time are being fought on the dual plane of perception and reality. First, if we consider the East-West struggle, it is obvious, as we have seen earlier, that a great number of objective differences exist which defy easy solution. But to a considerable degree, the conflict also takes place in the realm of distorted imagery. On the Soviet side, the main cause of this distortion, until recently, has been Communist ideology. Quite early in the Soviet Union's life, the ideological factor generated a distorted self-image of historically ordained invincibility. It was also responsible for a perception of other nations that did not tally with reality. Thus, the Soviet Union tended to view the West through Marxist-Leninist lenses as being engaged in an effort to impose ''capitalist encirclement'' on the Soviet Union. Indeed, the Soviet leadership began to believe that it understood the West better than the West understood itself and as a result struggled not so much with the West as with its image of the West.

The West, in turn, became seriously affected by Soviet imagery and, despite a number of striking blunders committed by the Comintern during its first thirty years of operation, tended to perceive the Soviet Union as a kind of chess master on the world scene. The West's self-image, in turn, approached a collective inferiority complex. This ''superman'' view of communism and the inferiority complex that followed made the West more fearful of the image of the Soviet Union than of the Soviet Union itself. Indeed, the hypnotic spell that the Soviet Union was able to cast over the West became one of that nation's greatest assets in the struggle. In sum, the net result has been a twofold distortion. The two superpowers have struggled not only with each other, but also with their perceptions of each other. This divergence between perception and reality exacerbated the conflict enormously.

Only when the cold war abated during the 1960s, and the desire for détente grew on both sides of the Iron Curtain, did the old stereotypes give way to more realistic perceptions. By the 1970s, the Soviet Union and the United States had entered a relationship that included elements of *both* conflict and cooperation. As cooperation grew, so did the willingness and the capacity on both sides to perceive complex realities rather than to remain wedded to simple-minded and one-dimensional clichés. Policies began to be shaped less by shadows and fears and more by facts. By the early 1980s, however, an American President once again perceived the Soviet Union as ''the focus of evil in the world.'' And since that President was a masterful ''communicator,'' that perception no doubt came to be shared by a large segment of the American population. Thus, by 1983, the atmosphere prevailing between the two superpowers was a great deal more conducive to distortion than that which had prevailed a decade earlier. Only by 1985, with the resumption of arms control negotiations and the ascendancy to power in Russia of Mikhail Gorbachev, a younger and more pragmatic leader, did the reality principle once again begin to assert itself. By the late 1980s, the reality principle had gained considerable momentum.

The struggle between North and South also bears the stamp of distortion. Although the record demonstrates that Western colonialism is largely a phenomenon of the past, the new nationalism acts as if it were very much alive. Indeed, as we have seen, in the life of the new nations the past often lives on with a fierce intensity. Khomeini's hatred for the late Shah of Iran is a case in point. And his perception of the United States as "the great Satan" because of its previous friendship with the Iranian monarch no doubt helped precipitate the hostage crisis and the agony that followed. Although our case studies of interaction between nationalism and colonialism (Chapter 4) demonstrated that the colonial experiment was a very diversified experience, ranging from outright exploitation to the bestowal of generous benefits, the new nationalism always regarded, and still regards, the entire colonial record as an unmitigated evil and fails to differentiate among the many varying shades of the spectrum. Our case studies also failed to support the conception held by most leaders of the Third World that their movement was antithetical to imperialism. Indeed, we have seen that the new nationalism may readily become a seedbed for new conflicts. This is what happened in the relations between Jewish and Arab nationalism in the Middle East. To hear Arabs and Israelis describe each other at times seemed like listening to two sets of fantasies with little relation to the realities in the countries concerned, and even less to the images each country had of itself. Similarly, the devil images held by Iran and Iraq about each other during their war in the 1980s bore only a small resemblance to reality. These vast gulfs between perception and reality were at the heart of the conflicts in the Middle East and the Persian Gulf. Hence, not only the struggle over colonialism but also the struggle between divergent forms of nationalism is intensified by gaps between perception and reality.

No less affected by this type of distortion has been the relationship between the two political struggles for power. Engagement in one of the two major conflicts has tended to obscure an accurate perception of the other. The United States has perceived the world primarily in terms of East and West; Zimbabwe, on the other hand, has seen the great divide between black and white. The United States has often been uncommitted in the struggle between nationalism and colonialism and has frequently been accused of nonalignment by the new nationalist powers. But the new nations have been equally uncommitted in the East-West struggle in which the two superpowers have perceived *them* as nonaligned. In short, the perceptions of the major protagonists have largely remained limited to only one of the two great political struggles. However, each protagonist has been sufficiently aware of the struggle in which he has not seen himself directly involved to exploit it for his more conscious purposes. Thus both the Soviet Union and the United States, though primarily concerned with the East-West struggle, have consistently striven to gain support for themselves by seeking to play the most advantageous possible role in the North-South struggle.

The divergencies between perception and reality in the political power struggle of our time thus boil down to this: though both titanic conflicts are inseparably connected and are being waged simultaneously, those involved in the East-West struggle see the world chiefly in terms of this dichotomy, and those engaged in the North-South struggle see that conflict as all-important. Moreover, similar distortions characterize the views of each other held by the protagonists in each of the two struggles separately. And in every case, the imagery tends to depict the "enemy" as a more deadly threat than the objective record would seem to justify. As a result, the political struggle is greatly intensified in all its aspects.

The gap between fact and fiction has been even more dangerous in the military realm. Until the Cuban missile crisis of 1962, the United States and the Soviet Union had held the most extreme images of one another. The United States was convinced that "conquering the world for communism" was the sole motivation of the Soviet alliance system. On the basis of this view, it sought to arm itself with an irresistible destructive capacity through the policy of massive retaliation. When this posture was criticized as too exclusively nuclear-minded, the United States began to experiment with the more flexible policy of graduated deterrence. The Soviet Union, for its part, developed an image of the West of "imperialist aggression and encirclement" bent upon the destruction of communism. Logically enough, the view each side held of its own camp was one of defense against the other.

The great danger in the military struggle between the United States and the Soviet Union during the 1950s and 1960s lay in the possibility that the extreme image that each side held of the other might have become reality, and that the circle of suspicion and countersuspicion might have precipitated a "preventive" war. If each side had continued to believe that the other was its mortal enemy, this view might have influenced behavior to such a point of rigidity and compulsiveness that the "inevitable conflict" could have been a self-fulfilling prophecy. The missile crisis cleared the air between the superpowers, at least to some extent, and introduced a larger measure of reality into their relations. After the invasion of Afghanistan in 1980, however, with a massive arms build-up gathering momentum on both sides, these dangerous cold war images began to dominate superpower relations once again.

Distortion was massive in the early relations between the China of Mao Tse-tung and the United States. The Korean War and the conflict in Vietnam accelerated this process, and by the late 1960s a vicious spiral had been set in motion. Both China and America began with the a priori assumption of the other's implacable hostility; the power of this conviction caused all the adversary's actions to be interpreted as confirming the validity of the original assumption; hence, the adversary was found hostile a posteriori as well, since his actions had "proved" that the original assumption was correct. The very actions that the Chinese perceived as an American plot to encircle them were perceived by the Americans as necessary measures to forestall Chinese aggression. Confronted by a series of American policies that appeared to them to prove American enmity toward them, the Chinese embarked upon an increasingly virulent "Hate America" campaign that the United States in turn took as proof of their implacable hostility toward America. What seemed patently provocative to one appeared obviously defensive to the other. In this tragic spiral of reciprocally negative reinforcement, the borderline between real and imagined threats tended to blur and finally disappear altogether.

It is easy to see why political accommodation would be well nigh impossible under such conditions. On a deeper psychological level, such devil mirror images are the stuff that holy wars are made of. For to each side in the conflict, the enemy is not quite human and it becomes difficult, if not impossible, to identify with any part of him. Hence, each adversary is left with fears and terrors which are in no way allayed by their failure to materialize. Such fears, however, can call forth a reality as terrible as the most anguished nightmare. This was the peril of the encounter between China and America during the 1950s and the 1960s. With the visit of President Nixon to China in 1972 and the extrication of the United States from the Vietnam war in 1975, the danger began to diminish. And by the 1980s, when Vice Premier Deng Hsiao-ping embarked on rapprochement with the United States, the old devil images had almost disappeared. Within a single generation, the Soviet Union had replaced the United States as China's major adversary.

One cannot help but wonder, when one contemplates the spectacle of American businesspeople and tourists streaming into China during the 1980s, how transient was the cause that had sent American soldiers to die in Korea and Vietnam. In those not-so-distant days, the Chinese were perceived as monstrous architects of evil; not much later, they were seen as possible business partners in a common enterprise and then, in 1989, when contested elections took place in the Soviet Union at the very moment when China's leaders crushed the student uprising in Beijing, American perceptions of Russia and China changed places once again. Is it not frightening to see how quickly perceptions can change about the same people? And that these perceptions may sway men toward life or toward death?

The United States and the Soviet Union are still engaged in an economic struggle with each other. Each covets the distinction of being the world's leading industrial power. This economic competition has led to a curious paradox: in the imagery of each superpower, the economic system of the antagonist is alien; in reality, however, the exigencies of competition have led to a high degree of mutual emulation which, in turn, has made the economies of the Soviet Union and the United States increasingly alike. The hostile images dictate further competition but this competition will probably increase the objective similarities between the two economies still further. It is therefore possible that the common dictates of industrial production may divest the East-West struggle of some of its messianic ideological character. Once global ideology atrophies, the fierceness of the struggle may abate. Hence the gap between perception and reality in the economic realm is a danger chiefly in the short run. In the long run—assuming that the two great antagonists settle for coexistence without victory or defeat—it may actually prove a force making for order.

Yet both superpowers are aware that at least in the economic realm a decisive victory is still possible in the East-West struggle. They have become convinced that such a victory can be won by gaining the allegiance of the world's uncommitted countries. Both sides have therefore waged the economic struggle with the weapon of foreign aid. In this competition, too, images have greatly diverged from realities. Both superpowers, aware of the sensitivities of the new nations, have attempted to project an image of selflessness and generosity. The secret of success in the economic struggle seems indeed to lie in the realm of imagery. Not only must each of the superpowers learn to see itself as the new nations see it, but it must learn how the new nations perceive the other "enemy" superpower. It is difficult enough for a nation to see itself as others see it; it is far more difficult to see a second nation as a third sees it. Yet this ability is turning out to be of the utmost importance in the economic competition for the new nations. The Soviet Union has been able to project itself into the thinking of the uncommitted nations somewhat more successfully than the United States. It has frequently been able to exploit the anticolonial images of the new nationalism to its own advantage. In its reaction to the "blindness" of the nonaligned leaders in accepting Communist aid, the United States has failed to comprehend a most basic fact: that to most of the new nations, communism is not an unmitigated evil, but merely an alternative to democracy—an alternative, in fact, that, as they see it, may quite possibly produce the desired results faster. Moreover, the West has tended to define democracy primarily in terms of political liberty. In countries without a tradition of democracy, this has often seemed like a luxury commodity. The Soviet Union, on the other hand, has tended to emphasize economic security, a more meaningful concept in countries where this is the overriding concern.

Aware of their strategic position in the East-West struggle, most of the new nations have developed an often rather inflated self-image. This has led to curious psychological inversions—almost an upside-down world. At times, the new nations have "rewarded" one of the superpowers by accepting its gifts or loans. Because of the peculiar constellation of world politics, and the linkage of the two great political struggles, the power of the new nations has vastly increased. So long as the two superpowers continue to believe that the uncommitted countries may vitally affect the distribution of power, this strange divergence between perception and reality is likely to persist.

In addition, the debt crisis, food shortages, financial dislocations, and the population explosion have widened the gulfs between the world's rich and poor. The severity and suddenness of these developments have led to serious perceptual distortions that have exacerbated the objective conflicts even further. There is little if any empathy for another point of view. The poor nations of the Third World see only their own misery, and in their anger and desperation perceive the rich nations as greedy Shylocks. And the industrialized nations of the West, fearing for their standard of living and their technological achievements, have little patience and little sympathy for the world's poor who outnumber and therefore threaten them.

In sum, then, an analysis of the political, military, and economic aspects of the international struggle for power reveals that, on the whole, great divergencies exist between perception and reality. In the political realm, these divergencies have intensified the fierceness of both the East-West struggle and the struggle between rich and poor. This has been true in the military arena until the catalyst of Mikhail Gorbachev defused the situation, at least to some extent.

The relationship between perception and reality has also affected the international struggle for order. In the political realm, the United Nations is a case in point. Public opinion studies show that, in the United States, for example, the mass public and even the attentive public tend to evaluate the United Nations fairly indiscriminately. There is little awareness of differences among the major organs of the world organization. It is either praised or condemned as a whole. Images swing all the way from cynical disillusionment through apathy to an exaggerated "panacea" view. Yet the record of the United Nations demonstrates that it is quite impossible to generalize about the world organization in its entirety. The performance of each of its major organs and specialized agencies has been different. In other words, in the imagery of the United States there is little or no awareness of the United Nations' most important characteristics: its elasticity, and the fact that it is working on many fronts and with varying degrees of effectiveness at one time. The unfortunate result of this one-dimensional image is to encourage all-too-quick disillusionment. The failure of a single UN organ, such as the Security Council, or the adoption of the anti-Zionist resolution by the General Assembly, seem like failures of the organization as a whole. Hence, American support of the United Nations has tended to be based on the very unstable factor of popular oversimplification. This gap between perception and reality thus slowed the development of a firm and dependable basis of political and financial support for the United Nations.

Such distortion also extends to specific institutions of the United Nations. The veto power of the Big Five in the Security Council affords an interesting example. In the Soviet view, this power saves the USSR from being continuously outvoted in an organization consisting largely of non-Communist nations. The United States, while equally adamant on maintaining the veto power, holds the view that the Soviet Union has used it excessively and thus crippled the organization. Neither of these views tallies with the record. The truth is that only a few of the many Soviet vetoes cast in the Security Council have been final. Many of them have been circumvented through action taken in the General Assembly under the Uniting for Peace Resolution or otherwise.[9] Besides, during the 1970s and 1980s, the United States cast far more vetoes than the Soviet Union. Thus, the view that the veto can paralyze the world organization as a whole—a view held by the Soviet Union, the United States, and most of the new nations—does not square with the facts.

For the first thirty-five years of the United Nations' life, it was crippled by Soviet hostility and financial penury. Then it was the United States' turn to withdraw its political and financial support. Only in the late 1980s, when *both* superpowers perceived the United Nations more realistically as a useful vehicle of their foreign policies, did the world organization experience a new resurgence.

The tug-of-war between regionalists and globalists also has relevance to our thesis. Typically, regionalist thinkers conceive of globalism as either premature or altogether unworkable. Internationalists, on the other hand, have developed an image of regional arrangements as harmful roadblocks on the path to world order. Neither perception leaves room for what the record demonstrates: that frequently globalism has served as a second line of defense for regionalism and that regional arrangements have served as backstops for the world organization. Certainly, there is ample room for both types of political order-building on the world scene. In this case, the gap between perception and reality has sometimes led to unnecessary friction between the two approaches and thus slowed down the advance toward political order.

A serious divergence has existed, until quite recently, in the military realm of political order-building. The widespread view that arms races cause wars led to passionate popular demands for disarmament virtually everywhere. This, in turn, led to propagandistic flourishes of diplomacy in disarmament negotiations because diplomats were compelled to address a world audience instead of engaging in the exacting business of searching for compromises. It appears that the prolonged arms race during the postwar era was merely the symptom of a deeper pathological condition. The search for a technical disarmament formula was bound to fail unless it was preceded by a more fundamental political accommodation. Such an accommodation finally emerged in the late 1980s when Ronald Reagan modified his image of the Soviet Union as an "evil empire" and Mikhail Gorbachev embraced *glasnost* and *perestroika*. The consequence was modest but real disarmament. Indeed, the history of disarmament supports the proposition that order is fundamentally a political, not a military, problem. This gap between the simple popular image of disarmament and the complex reality has caused a great deal of unnecessary disillusionment.

The economic field alone has escaped serious distortions. The functionalist hope has largely been vindicated by the record on the regional level, and even on the global level promising beginnings have been made. Within the framework of Western Europe, two basic conceptions of economic order-building have developed, both of which have enjoyed a measure of success. Supranational and more traditional intergovernmental organizations alike have mushroomed. Wherever a concrete task had to be accomplished, the record has been good, regardless of the formal structure of the organization. Since a well-defined task has existed in most instances, serious gaps between perception and reality have been avoided. One interesting development is worthy of mention: the widely prevalent conception that a clear line of demarcation may be drawn between national governments and international organizations no longer seems to be valid. Recent developments, chiefly in Western Europe, indicate that the two are beginning to blend into one another. Indeed, some regional organizations, like the European Communities, may some day exercise powers previously enjoyed only by national governments. Whether these groupings will justify the fear of the globalists and develop into a kind of regional nationalism remains to be seen. For the present, accomplishments have not fallen too far short of expectations. Hence, an unusual congruence exists between perception and reality in economic order-building in Western Europe.

In conclusion, then, the gaps between perception and reality have exacerbated the fierceness of the international struggle for power and also have done much to slow down the advance toward international order. In view of this fact, it seems vital for students of international relations to expose themselves to the work of scholars in the area of human perception—sociologists, social psychologists, and even depth psychologists. This is not to say that the objective realities of world affairs should be neglected. Yet since these are so vast and complex, the least we can hope for is that they not be rendered even more inaccessible to reason by our unsubstantiated preconceptions. The perils of our age demand our every effort to see and deal with the world as it really is. Once again humanity must escape from Plato's Cave, in which it perceives only shadows instead of realities. Only when our reason thus acquires passion will we remove the Sword of Damocles which has been suspended for far too long over our tormented world.

REFERENCES

1 Walter Lippmann, *Public Opinion*. New York: Macmillan, 1922; Gabriel Almond, *The American People and Foreign Policy*. New York: Harcourt, Brace, 1950.
2 Alex Inkeles, *Public Opinion in Soviet Russia*. Cambridge, Mass.: Harvard University Press, 1950.
3 Gabriel Almond and James S. Coleman, *The Politics of the Developing Areas*. Princeton, N.J.: Princeton University Press, 1960.
4 Lippmann, *op. cit.*, p. 29.
5 Walter Lippmann, *The Public Philosophy*. Boston: Little, Brown, 1955, p. 14.
6 Carl J. Friedrich, *The New Image of the Common Man*. Boston: Beacon Press, 1950, *passim*.
7 Inkeles, *op. cit.*, p. 323.
8 Almond and Coleman, *op. cit.*, p. 535.
9 For a complete analysis of this point, see John G. Stoessinger, *The United Nations and the Superpowers*. 4th ed. New York: Random House, 1977, pp. 3–25.

SELECTED BIBLIOGRAPHY

Almond, Gabriel A. *The American People and Foreign Policy*. New York: Praeger, 1960. The classic analysis of the role of elites and of the "common man" in the formulation and control of US foreign policy.

Cottam, Richard W. *Foreign Policy Motivation*. Pittsburgh: University of Pittsburgh Press, 1977. The author navigates the treacherous waters of motivation in foreign policy most skillfully.

Isaak, Robert A. *Individuals and World Politics*. North Scituate, Mass: Duxbury Press, 1975. A trailblazing study of the impact of eight national leaders on their countries and the world.

Jervis, Robert. *Perception and Misperception in International Relations*. Princeton: Princeton University Press, 1976. A first-class analysis for the sophisticated reader.

Lifton, Robert J. and Eric Olson. *Explorations in Psychohistory*. New York: Simon & Schuster, 1975. The best general introduction to the subject.

Morgenthau, Hans J. and Kenneth W. Thompson. *Politics among Nations*. 6th ed. New York: Knopf, 1985. A new revision of the classic work of the "realist" school in international relations. Shows little patience with "moralism" and "legalism" in the conduct of foreign policy.

Index